THE SPORT AMERICANA ®

BASEBALL
COLLECTIBLES

PRICE GUIDE

By
DR. JAMES BECKETT

ISBN 0-937424-31-5

ABOUT THE AUTHOR

Jim Beckett, the leading authority on sport card values in the United States, maintains a wide range of activities in the world of sports. He possesses one of the finest collections of sports cards and autographs in the world, has made numerous appearances on radio and television, and has been frequently cited in many national publications. Dr. Beckett has been the recipient of the first Special Achievement Award for Contribution to the Hobby from the National Sports Collectors Convention in 1980 and the Jock-Jasperson Award for Hobby Dedication in 1983. He is the author of The Sport Americana Football, Hockey, Basketball and Boxing Price Guide, The Official Price Guide to Football Cards, The Sport Americana Baseball Card Price Guide, The Official Price Guide to Baseball Cards, The Sport Americana Baseball Memorabilia and Autograph Price Guide, and The Sport Americana Alphabetical Baseball Card Checklist. In addition, he is the founder, author, and editor of Beckett Baseball Card Monthly, a magazine dedicated to the card collecting hobby.

Jim Beckett received his Ph.D. in Statistics from Southern Methodist University in 1975. He resides in Dallas with his wife Patti and their daughters, Christina and Rebecca, while actively pursuing his writing and consultancy services.

ACKNOWLEDGEMENTS

A great deal of hard work went into this volume, and it could not have been done without a considerable amount of help from many people. Our thanks are extended to each and every one of you.

First, we owe a special acknowledgement to Dennis W. Eckes, Mr. Sport Americana, who had the vision to see where the hobby was going and the perseverance and drive to help it get there. The success of the Beckett Price Guides has been the result of a team effort. Although Denny has chosen no longer to be a co-author on the sport card price guides -- in order to devote more time to his business, Den's Collector's Den -- he is still on board as a special consultant.

Those who have worked closely with us on this and many other books, have again proven themselves invaluable in every aspect of producing this book -- Jim Bordonaro, Cartophilium (Andrew Pywowarczuk), Mike Cramer (Pacific Trading Cards), Dick DeCourcy (Georgia Music and Sports), Bill and Diane Dodge, Gervise Ford, Larry and Jeff Fritsch, Tony Galovich, Mike and Howard Gordon, John Greenwald, Wayne Grove, Bill Haber, Don Hazelwood, Danny Hitt, Stewart Jones, Steve Leone, Lew Lipset, Bill Mastro, Dr. Joe Michalowicz, Brian Morris, Ralph Nozaki, Jack Pollard, Tom Reid, Gavin Riley, Alan Rosen (Mr. Mint), John Rumierz, San Diego Sports Collectibles (Bill Goepner and Nacho Arredondo), John Spalding (special thanks for his definitive work on Wheaties issues), and Kit Young.

Special thanks are extended to the Donruss Company, The Fleer Corporation, and the Topps Chewing Gum Company, who have consistently provided checklists and visual materials in order that this Price Guide could be complete.

Many other individuals have provided price input, illustrative material, checklist verifications, errata, and/or background information. At the risk of inadvertantly overlooking or omitting these many contributors, we should like to personally thank Ab.D Cards (Dale Wesolewski and Denny Demm), Jerry Adamic, Bob Alexander, Dennis Anderson, Sam Armao, Neil Armstrong (World Series Cards), Mike Aronstein (TCMA), Frank and Vivian Barning (Baseball Hobby News), Ed Barry (Ed's Collectibles), Bob Bartosz (Baseball Card Shop), Dennis Baumgardner, Bay State Cards (Lenny DeAngelico), Chris Benjamin, Beulah Sports, Big Andy's, Blue Chip (Howie Levy), Mark Borckardt, Joe Borte, Bill Bossert (Mid- Atlantic Coin Exchange), Ron Buller, Michael Burns, James Byrnes, Larry Calder, Murray Calder, California Card Co., Ira Cetron, Dwight Chapin, Chriss Christiansen, Barry Colla, Collectibles Unlimited, Collection de Sport AZ, Terry Constable, Kevin Cormier, Taylor Crane, James Critzer, Raymond Curiale, Alan Custer, Elaine Daku, Dave Dame, Dixie Dugout, Dick Dobbins, Richard Dolloff, John Douglas, Mike Drahovsky, James Eastman, Jack Eisenstein, John Esch, Doak Ewing, David and Mark Federman, David Festberg, Frank Fox (The Card Shop), Steve Freedman, Dan Gantt, Bob Gilbert, Dick Goddard, Ron Gold, Steve Gold (AU Sports), Jeff Goldstein, Michael Grady (Collectors Heaven), Grand Slam Sports Collectibles, Mary Gregory, Julie Grove, David Hadeler, Dean Haley, Hall's Nostalgia, Joe Hammann, Ernie Hammond, Hershell Hanks, Pepper Hastings, Rich Hawksley, Don Hazelwood, Joel Hellman (JJ's Budget Baseball Cards), Bill

Henderson, Ryan Hurba, Robert Jacobson, Henry Janoski, James Johnston, Rosie Jones, Dave Jurgensmeier, Chuck Kalan, Marvin Kaufman, Alan Kaye (Baseball Card News), Jim Kelley, Jeff Kepley, Rick Keplinger, Tom Kiecker, Mike Klauser, Ray Klotkowski, Jim Knowler, Ernie Kohlstruk, Terry Kors, Thomas Kunnecke, Michael Lamone, Dan Lavin, Morley Leeking, Don Lepore, Irv Lerner, Rod Lethbridge, Robert Lifson, LNW Sports, Chris Lockwood, Mike London, Anne Lowe, Jim Macie, Paul Marchant, Raymond May, Dr. William McAvoy, Mike McDonald (Sports Page), Tony McLaughlin, Mendal Mearkle (Chariots, Inc.), John Mehlin, Martin Mettee, Blake Meyer (Lone Star Sportscards), Dick Miller, Wayne Miller, Dick Millerd, Ashby Milstead, Dick Mueller, and Ray Murphy.

Also, thanks to Frank Nagy, Edward Nazzaro (The Collector), Chip Nelson, Murry Nelson, North Conway Baseball Card Shop, Mike O'Brien, Michael Olenick, Carl Olsen (Baseball Card Express), Don Olson, Dwayne Painter, Vincent Pape, Jeff Parlow, Clay Pasternack, Joe Pasternack, Nancy Paterson, Matt Pederson, Bill Pekarik (Pastime Hobbies), Michael Perrotta, Gerald Perry, Mansco Perry, Tom Pfirrmann, Pinocchio Discounts, Radford Press, Rick Rapa (Atlanta Sports Cards), Bill Reed, Gordon Reid, Ralph Reitsma, Owen Ricker, Dave Ring, Jim Rose, Clifton Rouse, Jack Rudley, Mitch Rudoff, Wes Ruhrig, Terry Sack, Jennifer Salems, John Salsido, Ang Savelli, Robert Scagnelli, Don Schlaff, Bob Schmierer, Peter Selan, Larry Shane, David Shannon, Gerry Shebib, Larry Shipley, Chris Shore, Art Smith, Howard "Smitty" Smith, Sports Collector's Digest (Bob Lemke), Don Steinbach, Leonard Stock, Strikeout Sports Cards, Richard Strobino, Barrie Sullivan, Ian Taylor, Lyle Telfer, Lee Temanson, 20th Century Collectibles, Ernest Unrath, Rich Unruh, Kurt Utley, John Vanden Beek, John Vangen, Bill Wesslund, Richard West, Bob Wilke (The Shoe Box), Jeff Williams, Wayne Wiskow, Ted Zanidakis, Greg Zayatz.

Finally, writing this book would have been a very unpleasant experience without the understanding and cooperation of my wife, Patti, and daughters, Christina and Rebecca. I thank them and promise them that I will pay them back for all those hours. While on the subject of family, my sister, Claire Beckett, who is my full-time assistant on Beckett Monthly, put in extensive overtime herself carrying the administrative load on the magazine single-handedly during the time that I was working on this book; those of you who subscribe to the Monthly already know what a super job Claire is doing. Thank you, everyone.

The Sport Americana
Baseball Collectibles
Price Guide
Table Of Contents

INTRODUCTION

Baseball "collectibles" is a general classification for many items related to the game of baseball from its inception up to the present time. This volume lists collectibles of various types from various time periods. You will find herein stickers, stamps, coins, pins, exhibits, lids, and many others ... oh yes, there are a few cards included too. In fact this edition provides the first comprehensive checklist and price guide of the popular Canadian O-Pee-Chee baseball sets all the way back to 1965. We regret that we can not be as comprehensive with everything. Nevertheless, if your favorite collectible is not included in this book, let us know as so that we can plan for the next edition. Subsequent editions will, of course, include more material.

This Baseball Collectibles Price Guide is an outgrowth of the successful Sport Americana Baseball Card Price Guide, now in its eighth edition. One of the shortcomings of the baseball card price guide is that it covers but one portion, albeit by far the largest portion, of the sports collectibles hobby. We hope with this book to at least partially fill the information need of collectors of items other than the most popular baseball cards. The format of the baseball card price guide has been maintained whenever possible for those items that lend themselves to it.

Beckett Guides have been successful where other attempts have failed because they are complete, current, and valid. This Price Guide contains not just one, but three, prices, by condition, for all the baseball items in the issues listed. The prices were added just prior to printing and reflect not the author's opinions or desires but the going retail prices for each item, based on the marketplace (sports memorabilia conventions and shows, hobby papers, current mail order catalogs, local club meetings, auction results, and other first hand reportings of actual realized prices.)

To facilitate your use of this book, read the complete introductory section in the pages following before going to the pricing pages. Every collectible field has its own terminology; we've tried to capture most of these terms and definitions in our glossary. Please read carefully the section on grading and condition as you will not be able to determine which price column is appropriate without first knowing its condition.

Welcome to the world of baseball collectibles.

Sincerely,

Dr. James Beckett

HOW TO COLLECT

There are no set rules on how to collect. Collecting is a hobby, a leisure pastime. What you collect, how much you collect and how much time and money you spend collecting are entirely up to you; the funds you have available for collecting, and your own personal taste should determine how you collect. The information and ideas presented here are intended to help you get the most enjoyment from this hobby.

It is impossible to collect everything ever produced. Therefore, beginners as well as intermediate and advanced collectors usually specialize their collecting in some way. One of the reasons this hobby is popular is that individual collectors can define and tailor their collecting methods to match their own tastes.

OBTAINING COLLECTIBLES

Several avenues are open to collectors. Recent items such as stickers can be purchased in the traditional way at the local candy, grocery, or drug store. Many collectors will begin by subscribing to at least one of the monthly hobby publications, all with good up-to-date information; in fact, subscription offers can be found in the advertising section of this book. Most serious collectors obtain old (and new) items from one or more of the following three sources: (1) trading or buying from other collectors or dealers; (2) responding to sale or auction ads in the monthly hobby papers; and/or (3) attending sports collectibles shows or conventions. We advise that you try all three methods as each has its own distinct advantages: (1) trading is a great way to make some new friends; (2) monthly hobby papers help you keep up with what's going on in the hobby (and tell you when and where the conventions are happening); and (3) shows provide enjoyment and the opportunity to see millions of collectibles under one roof, along with hundreds or even thousands of other collectors attending who all share a common interest.

REGIONAL VARIATION

Although prices may vary from the East to the West, or from the Southwest to the Midwest, the prices in this guide are none the less presented as a consensus of all sections of this large and diverse country. Likewise, the prices for a particular player's memorabilia may well show a higher price in his home team's area. Sometimes even common players command a higher price to hometown collectors than in other parts of the country.

Two types of price variations exist among the sections of the country where collectibles are bought or sold. The first is the general price variation on all collectibles bought and sold in one geographical area as compared to another. Prices are slightly higher on the East and West coasts, and slightly lower in the middle of the country. The second is the specific price variation for a player found in a certain geographical area and not found in another. For example, an Al Kaline would be valued higher in Detroit than in Cincinnati because Kaline played in Detroit; therefore, the demand for Al Kaline is higher in Detroit than it is in Cincinnati. On the other hand, a Johnny Bench would be priced higher in Cincinnati than in Detroit for similar reasons.

NOMENCLATURE

Each hobby has its own nomenclature to describe the collectibles of that particular hobby. The nomenclature traditionally used for trading cards is derived from the American Card Catalog, published in 1960 by Nostalgia Press. This catalog, written by Jefferson Burdick (who is called the Father of Card Collecting for his pioneering work), uses letter and number descriptions for each separate set of cards.

The letter used in the ACC number refers to the generic type of card. While both sport and non-sport issues are classified in the ACC, we shall confine ourselves in this description to the sport issues. The following list defines the letters and their meanings as used by the American Card Catalog.

(none) or N - 19th Century U.S. Tobacco
B - Blankets
D - Bakery Inserts Including Bread
E - Early Candy and Gum
F - Food Inserts
H - Advertising
M - Periodicals
PC - Postcards
R - Candy and Gum Cards 1930 to Present
T - 20th Century U.S. Tobacco
UO - Gas and Oil Inserts
V - Canadian Candy
W - Exhibits, Strip Cards, Team Issues

Following the letter designation and an optional hyphen are one, two, or three digit numerical descriptors which typically represent the company or entity issuing the cards, i.e., numbers 1-999. In several cases, the ACC number is further extended by an additional hyphen and an additional one or two digit numerical descriptor. For example, the 1957 Topps regular series baseball card issue carries an ACC designation of R414-11. The "R" indicates a Candy or Gum Card produced after 1929. The "414" is the ACC designation for Topps Chewing Gum baseball card issues. And, the "11" is the ACC designation for the 1957 regular issue (Topps eleventh baseball set).

Like other traditional methods of identification, this system provides order to the process of cataloguing cards; however, most serious collectors learn the ACC designation of the popular sets by repetitive use and familiarity, rather than by attempting to "figure out" what they might or should be.

From 1948 forward, all sets are normally referred to by their year, maker, type of issue, or any other distinguishing characteristic. An example of such a characteristic could be an unusual issue or one of several regular issues put out by a specific maker in a single year. Regional issues are usually referred to by year, maker, and sometimes by title or theme of the set.

GLOSSARY/LEGEND

Our glossary defines common terms frequently used in the card collecting hobby. Many of the terms are also common to other types of sports memorabilia collecting. There are exceptions to some of the definitions presented; however, listing all the exceptions would confuse the reader and detract from the usefulness of the glossary.

AAS - Action All Stars, a postcard sized set issued by the Donruss Company.

ACC - acronym for American Card Catalog.

AD CARD - See Display Card.

AL - abbreviation for American League or American Leaguer.

ALL STAR CARD - A card portraying an All Star Player of the previous year that says "All Star" on its face.

ALPH - Alphabetical.

AS - abbreviation for All-Star (card).

ATG - All Time Great card.

AUTOGRAPHED CARD - A card that has been signed (usually on the front of the card) by the player portrayed on the card with a fountain pen, felt tip, magic marker, or ball-point pen. This term does not include stamped or facsimile autographed cards.

BLANKET - A felt square (normally 5" to 6") portraying a baseball player.

BOX - Card issued on a box or a card depicting a Boxer.

BRICK - A group of cards, usually 50 or more and having some common characteristics, that is intended to be bought, sold or traded as a unit.

C - abbreviation for Catcher.

CABINETS - Very popular and highly valuable cards on thick card stock produced in the 19th and early 20th century.

CF - abbreviation for Centerfielder.

CHECKLIST - A list of the cards contained in a particular set. The list is always in numerical order if the cards are numbered. Some unnumbered sets are artificially numbered in alphabetical order, or by team and alphabetical within the team for convenience.

CHECKLIST CARD - A card which lists in order the cards and players in the set or series. Older checklist cards in Mint condition which have not been checked off are very desirable.

CL - abbreviation for Checklist.

COA - abbreviation for Coach.

COIN - A small disc of metal or plastic portraying a player in its center.

COLLECTOR - A person who engages in the hobby of collecting cards primarily for his own enjoyment, with any profit motive being secondary.

COLLECTOR ISSUE - A set produced for the sake of the card itself, with no product or service sponsor. It derives its name from the fact that most of these sets are produced by collector/dealers.

COMBINATION CARD - A single card depicting two or more players (but not a team card).

COMMON CARD - The typical card of any set; it has no premium value accruing from subject matter, numerical scarcity, popular demand, or anomaly.

COMP - Card issued by the (Post Cereal) Company through their mail in offer.

CONVENTION - A large weekend gathering at one location of dealers and collectors for the purpose of buying, selling and sometimes trading of sports memorabilia items. Conventions are open to the public and sometimes feature celebrities, door prizes, films, contests, etc.

CONVENTION ISSUE - A set produced in conjunction with a sports collectibles convention to commemorate or promote the show.

COR - Correct or corrected card.

COUPON - See Tab.

CREASE - A wrinkle on the card, usually caused by bending the card. Creases are a common defect in cards usually caused by careless collectors.

CY - Cy Young Award.

DEALER - A person who engages in buying, selling, and trading sports collectibles or supplies. A dealer may also be a collector, but as a dealer, he anticipates a profit.

DH - Double Header (1955 Topps) or Designated Hitter.

DIE-CUT - A card which of which the stock is partially cut, allowing one or more parts to be folded or removed. After removal or appropriate folding, the remaining part of the card can frequently be made to stand up.

DISC - A circular shaped card.

DISPLAY CARD - A sheet, usually containing three to nine cards, that is printed and used by the manufacturer to advertise and/or display the packages containing his products and cards. The backs of display cards are blank or contain advertisements.

DK - Diamond King (artwork produced by Perez-Steele for Donruss).

DP - Double Print (a card which was printed in double the quantity compared to the other cards in the same series.

E CARD - A candy or gum card produced and issued prior to 1930.

ERA - Earned Run Average.

ERR - Error card (see also COR).

ERROR CARD - A card with erroneous information, spelling or depiction on either side of the card. Note that not all errors are corrected by the producing card company.

EXHIBIT - The generic name given to thick stock, postcard sized cards with single color obverse pictures. The name is derived from the Exhibit Supply Co. of Chicago, the principal manufacturer of this type of card. These are also known as Arcade cards as they were found in many arcades.

FULL SHEET - (Also called an uncut sheet) A complete sheet of cards that has not been cut up into individual cards by the manufacturer.

HALL OF FAMER - (HOF'er) A card which portrays a player who has been inducted into the Hall of Fame.

HIGH NUMBER - The cards in the last series of numbers in a year in which these higher numbered cards were printed or distributed in significantly lesser amounts than the lower numbered cards. The high number designation refers to a scarcity of the high numbered cards. Not all years have high numbers in terms of this definition.

HL - Highlight card.

HOC - House of Collectibles.

HOF - Acronym for Hall of Fame.

HOR - Horizontal pose on card as opposed to the more standard vertical orientation found on most cards.

HR - Abbreviation for Home Run.

IA - In Action (type of card).

INF - Abbreviation for Infielder.

INSERT - A card of a different type, e.g., a poster, or any other sports collectible contained and sold in the same package along with a card or cards of a major set.

ISSUE - Synonymous with set, but usually used in conjunction with a manufacturer, e.g. a Topps issue.

KP - Kid Picture (a sub-series issued in the Topps Baseball sets of 1972 and 1973).

LAYERING - The separation or peeling of one or more layers of the card stock, usually at the corner of the card.

LEGITIMATE ISSUE - A set produced to promote or boost sales of a product or service, e.g. bubble gum, cereal, cigarettes, etc. Most collector issues are not legitimate issues in this sense.

LHP - Left hand Pitcher.

LID - A circular (possibly with tab) shaped card that forms the top of the container for the product being promoted.

LL - Living Legends (Donruss 1984) or large letters.

MAJOR SET - A set produced by a national manufacturer of cards containing a large number of cards. Usually 100 or more different cards are in the set.

MGR - Abbreviation for Manager.

MINI - A small card; specifically, a Topps baseball card of identical design but smaller dimensions than the regular Topps issue of 1975.

MISCUT - A card that has been cut particularly unevenly at the manufacturer's cutting stage.

ML - Major League.

MVP - Most Valuable Player.

N CARD - A tobacco card produced and issue during the 19th Century.

NL - National League.

NNOF - No Name on Front (see 1949 Bowman).

NOF - Name on Front (see 1949 Bowman).

NON-SPORT CARD - A card from a set whose major theme is a subject other than a sports subject. A card of a sports figure or event that is part of a non-sport set is still a non-sport card, e.g. while the Look 'N' See non-sport card set contains a card of Babe Ruth, a sports figure, the card is a non-sport card.

NOTCHING - The grooving of the edge of a card, usually caused by the fingernail, rubber bands, or bumping the edge against another object.

NY - New York.

OBVERSE - The front, face, or pictured side of the card.

OF - Outfielder.

OLY - Olympics (see 1985 Topps Baseball; the members of the 1984 U.S. Olympic Baseball team were a featured sub-series).

OPT - Option.

P - Pitcher or Pitching pose.

P1 - First Printing.

P2 - Second Printing.

P3 - Third Printing.

PANEL - An extended card that is composed of two or more individual cards. Often the panel forms the back part of the container for the product being promoted, e.g., a Hostess panel, a Bazooka panel, an Esskay Meat panel.

PCL - Pacific Coast League.

PG - Price Guide.

PLASTIC SHEET - A clear vinyl plastic page which is punched for insertion into a binder with standard 3-ring spacing) containing pockets for insertion of cards. Many different styles of sheets exist with pockets of varying sizes to hold the many different sizes of cards.

PREMIUM - A card, sometimes on photographic stock, that is purchased or obtained in conjunction with or redemption for another card or product. The premium is not packaged in the same unit as the primary item.

PUZZLE CARD - A card whose back contains a part of a picture which, when joined correctly with other puzzle cards, forms the complete picture.

PUZZLE PIECE - An actual die-cut piece designed to interlock with similar pieces.

R CARD - A candy or gum card produced and issued after 1930.

RARE - A card or series of cards of very limited availability. Unfortunately, rare is a subjective term sometimes used indiscriminantly. Rare cards are harder to obtain than scarce cards.

RB - Record Breaker card.

RBI - Abbreviation for Runs Batted In.

REGIONAL - A card issued and distributed only in a limited area of the country. The producer is not a major, national producer of trading cards.

REPRINT - A reproduction of an original card, usually produced by a maker other than the original manufacturer from a source other than the original artwork or negative.

REVERSE - The back or narrative side of the card.

RHP - Right hand Pitcher.

ROOKIE CARD - The first regular card of a particular player or a card which portrays one or more players with the notation on the card that these players are Rookies.

ROY - Acronym for Rookie of the Year.

RR - Rated Rookies (a subset featured in the Donruss Baseball sets.

SA - Super Action or Sport Americana.

SASE - Self Addressed Stamped Envelope.

SB - Stolen Bases.

SCARCE - A card or series of cards of limited availability. This subjective term is sometimes used indiscriminantly to promote or hype value. Scarce cards are not as difficult to obtain as rare cards.

SCR - Script name on Back (see 1949 Bowman Baseball).

SEMI-HIGH - A card from the next to last series of a sequentially issued set. It has more value than an average card and generally has less value than a high number. A card is not called a semi-high unless the next to last series in which it exists has an additional premium attached to it.

SERIES - The entire set of cards issued by a particular producer in a particular year, e.g., the 1971 Topps series. Also, within a particular set, series can be referring to a group of (consecutively numbered) cards printed at the same time, e.g., the first series of the 1957 Topps issue (numbers 1 through 88).

SET - One each of the entire run of cards of the same type produced by a particular manufacturer during a single year. In other words, if you have a (complete) set of 1976 Topps then you have every card from number 1 up through number 660, i.e., all the different cards that were produced.

SF - San Francisco.

SKIP-NUMBERED - A set that has many card numbers not issued between the lowest number in the set and the highest number in the set, e.g., the 1948 Leaf baseball set contains 98 cards skip- numbered from number 1 to number 168. A major set in which a few numbers were not printed is not considered to be skip-numbered.

SO - Strikeouts.

SP - Single or Short Print (a card which was printed in lesserquantity compared to the other cards in the same series; see also DP and TP).

SPECIAL CARD - A card that portrays something other than a single player or team, for example, a card that portrays the previous year's statistical leaders or the results from the previous year's post season action.

SS - Abbreviation for Shortstop.

STAMP - Adhesive backed papers depicting a player. The stamp may be individual or in a sheet of many stamps. Moisture must be applied to the adhesive in order for the stamp to be attached to another surface.

STAR CARD - A card that portrays a player of some repute, usually determined by his ability; however, sometimes referring to sheer popularity.

STICKER - A card with a removable layer that can be adhered to (stuck onto) another surface.

STOCK - The cardboard or paper on which the card is printed.

STRIP CARDS - A sheet or strip of cards, particularly popular in the 1920's and 1930's, with the individual cards usually separated by a broken or dotted line.

SUPERSTAR CARD - A card that portrays a superstar, e.g., a Hall of Fame member or a certain future Hall of Fame member.

SV - Super Veteran.

T CARD - A tobacco card produced and issued during the 20th Century.

TAB - A part of a card set off from the rest of the card, usually with perforations, that may be removed without damaging the central character or event depicted by the card.

TBC - Turn Back the Clock cards.

TEAM CARD - A card which depicts an entire team.

TEST SET - A set, usually containing a small number of cards, issued by a national card producer and distributed in a limited section or sections of the country. Presumably, the purpose of a test set is to test market appeal for this particular type of card.

TL - Team leader card.

TP - Triple Print (a card which was printed in triple the quantity compared to the other cards in the same series.

TR - Trade or Traded.

TRIMMED - A card cut down from its original size. Trimmed cards are undesirable to most collectors.

UMP - Umpire (see 1955 Bowman Baseball last series).

VARIATION - One of two or more cards from the same series with the same number (or player with identical pose if the series is unnumbered) differing from one another by some aspect, the different feature stemming from the printing or stock of the card, not from an alteration. This can be caused when the manufacturer of the cards notices an error in one (or more) of the cards, makes the changes, and then resumes the print run. In this case there will be two versions or variations of the same card. Sometimes one of the variations is relatively scarce.

VERT - Vertical pose on card.

W CARD - A card grouped within a general miscellaneous category by the ACC. Included in this category are exhibits, strip cards, team issues, and those issues which do not conveniently fall into other established categories.

WASH - Washington.

WL - White Letters (see 1969 Topps Baseball).

WS - World Series card.

YL - Yellow Letters (see 1958 Topps Baseball).

YT - Yellow Team (see 1958 Topps Baseball).

1B - First Base or First Baseman.

2B - Second Base or Second Baseman.

3B - Third Base or Third Baseman.

ADDITIONAL READING

Other literature on the collecting hobby can be divided into two categories: books and periodicals. We have furnished a listing for both books and periodicals that we feel would further your knowledge and enjoyment.

BOOKS AVAILABLE

The Sport Americana Baseball Card Price Guide, Author: Dr. James Beckett, Eighth Edition, $11.95, released 1986, Published by Edgewater Book Company -- The Sport Americana Baseball Card Price Guide is the most comprehensive price guide/checklist ever issued on baseball cards. No serious hobbyist should be without it.

The Official Price Guide to Baseball Cards, Author: Dr. James Beckett, Sixth Edition, $4.95, released 1986, Published by House of Collectibles, Inc. -- The Official Price Guide is an abridgement of the Sport Americana Price Guide immediately above in a convenient and economical pocket size format providing Dr. Beckett's pricing of the major baseball sets since 1948.

The Sport Americana Football, Hockey, Basketball and Boxing Card Price Guide, Author: Dr. James Beckett, Fourth Edition, $11.95, released 1985, Published by Edgewater Book Company -- The Sport Americana Football Card Price Guide is the most comprehensive price guide/checklist ever issued on football cards. No serious hobbyist should be without it.

The Official Price Guide to Football Cards, Author: Dr. James Beckett, Third Edition, $4.95, released 1985, Published by House of Collectibles, Inc. -- The Official Price Guide is an abridgement of the Sport Americana Price Guide immediately above in a convenient and economical pocket size format providing Dr. Beckett's pricing of the major football sets since 1948.

The Sport Americana Baseball Memorabilia and Autograph Price Guide, Authors: Dr. James Beckett and Dennis W. Eckes, First Edition, Co-published by Den's Collectors Den and Edgewater Book Company -- This book is the most definitive book ever produced on baseball memorabilia other than baseball cards. Over one year in the making, this book attempts to present in an illustrated, logical fashion information on baseball memorabilia and autographs which had been heretofore not available to the collector.

The Sport Americana Alphabetical Baseball Card Checklist, Authors: Dr. James Beckett and Dennis W. Eckes, Second Edition, Co-published by Den's Collectors Den and Edgewater Book Company -- An illustrated, alphabetical listing, by the last name of the player portrayed on the card, of virtually all baseball cards produced up to 1983.

The Sport Americana Price Guide to the Non-Sports Cards, Authors: Christopher Benjamin and Dennis W. Eckes, Second Edition, released 1983, Co-published by Den's Collector's Den and Edgewater Book Company -- This second edition is the definitive guide on all popular non-sports American tobacco and bubble gum cards. In addition to cards, illustrations and prices for wrappers are also included.

The Sport Americana Baseball Address List, Authors: Jack Smalling and Dennis W. Eckes, Fourth Edition, released 1986, Co- published by Den's Collector's Den and Edgewater Book Company -- This third edition is the definitive guide for autograph hunters giving addresses and deceased information for virtually all major league baseball players past and present.

The Sport Americana Baseball Card Team Checklist; Authors: Jeff Fritsch and Dennis W. Eckes, Second Edition, released 1985, Co- published by Den's Collectors Den and Edgwater Book Company -- Includes all Topps, Bowman, Fleer, Play Ball, Goudey, and Donruss cards, with the players portrayed on the cards listed with the teams for whom they played. The book is invaluable to the collector who specializes in an individual team as it is the most complete baseball card team checklist available.

Hockey Card Checklist and Price Guide, Fifth Edition, Author and Publisher: Cartophilium (Andrew Pywowarczuk) -- This book contains the most complete list of hockey card checklists ever assembled including a listing of Bee Hive photos.

The Encyclopedia of Baseball Cards, Volume I: 19th Century Cards, released 1983, Author and Publisher: Lew Lipset -- Everything you ever wanted to know about 19th century cards.

The Encyclopedia of Baseball Cards, Volume II: Early Gum and Candy Cards, released 1984, Author and Publisher: Lew Lipset -- Everything you ever wanted to know about Early Candy and Gum cards.

PERIODICALS AVAILABLE

There are several magazines and periodicals about the card collecting hobby which are published monthly, bi-weekly, quarterly, etc. One (or more) of those listed below should be just right for you.

Beckett Baseball Card Monthly, author and editor: Dr. James Beckett -- Contains the most extensive and accepted monthly price guide, large color photos, feature articles, who's hot and who's not section, convention calendar, numerous letters to and from the editor. It is the hobby's fastest growing magazine.

Baseball Hobby News, published by Frank and Vivian Barning -- Monthly tabloid newspaper format with good mix of news, editorials, features, and ads.

Sports Collectors Digest, published by Krause Publications -- Bi-weekly tabloid issues loaded with ads.

Baseball Card News, published by Krause Publications -- Monthly tabloid format with good mix of editorials, features, and ads.

Baseball Cards, published by Krause Publications -- Sharp- looking quarterly magazine with interior color and mix of features and ads.

GRADING

Each hobby has its own grading terminology -- stamps, coins, comic books, beer cans, right down the line. The collectors of sports memorabilia are no exception. The one absolute criterion for determining the value of an item is its condition: the better the condition, the more valuable. However, condition grading is very subjective. Individual dealers and collectors differ in the strictness of their grading. The stated condition should be determined without regard to whether the item in question is being bought or sold.

The physical defects which lower the condition of a card or other item are usually quite apparent, but each individual places his own value (negative value in this case) on the defects. We present the condition guide for use in determining values listed in this price guide.

The defects listed in the condition guide below are those either placed in the card or other item at the time of printing -- uneven borders, focus -- or those defects that occur under normal handling -- corner sharpness, gloss, edge wear -- and finally, environmental conditions -- browning. Other defects are inflicted by human carelessness and in all cases should be noted separately and in addition to the condition grade. Among the more common alterations are tape, tape stains, rubber band marks, water damage, smoke damage, trimming, paste, tears, writing, pin or tack holes, any back damage, and missing parts (tabs, tops, coupons, backgrounds).

Rather than confuse the issue further let us present the Condition Guide used for values in this Price Guide.

CONDITION GUIDE

MINT (M OR MT) - A card with no defects. The card has sharp corners, even borders, original gloss or shine on the surface, sharp focus of the picture, smooth edges, no signs of wear, and white borders. There is no allowance made for the age of the card.

EXCELLENT (EX OR E) - A card with very minor defects. Any of the following qualities would be sufficient to lower the grade of a card from mint to the excellent category: very slight rounding or layering at some of the corners, a very small amount of the original gloss lost, minor wear on the edges, slight unevenness of the borders, slight wear visible only on close inspection; slight off-whiteness of the borders.

VERY GOOD (VG) - A card that has been handled but not abused. Some rounding at all corners, slight layering or scuffing at one or two corners, slight notching on edges, gloss lost from the surface but not scuffed, borders might be somewhat uneven but some white is visible on all borders, noticeable yellowing or browning of borders, pictures may be slightly off focus.

GOOD (G) - A well handled card, rounding and some layering at the corners, scuffing at the corners and minor scuffing on the face, borders noticeably uneven and browning, loss of gloss on the face, notching on the edges.

FAIR (F) - Round and layering corners, brown and dirty borders, frayed edges, noticeable scuffing on the face, white not visible on one or more borders, cloudy focus.

POOR (P) - An abused card, the lowest grade of card, frequently some major physical alteration has been performed on the card, collectible only as a fill-in until a better condition replacement can be obtained.

Categories between these major condition grades are frequently used, such as, very good to excellent (VG-E), fair to good (F-G), etc. The grades indicate a card with all qualities at least in the lower of the two categories, but with several qualities in the higher of the two categories.

The most common physical defect in a trading card is the crease or wrinkle. The crease may vary from a slight crease barely noticeable at one corner of the card to a major crease across the entire card. Therefore, the degree that a crease lowers the value of the card depends on the type and number of creases. On giving the condition of a card, creases should be noted separately. If the crease is noticeable only upon close inspection under bright light, an otherwise mint card could be called excellent; whereas noticeable but light creases would lower most otherwise mint cards into the VG category. A heavily creased card could be classified fair at best.

PRICES IN THIS GUIDE

Prices found in this guide reflect current retail rates just prior to the printing of this book. They do not reflect the FOR SALE prices of the author, the publisher, the distributors, the advertisers or any dealers associated with this Guide. No one is any way obligated to buy, sell or trade based on these prices. The price listings were compiled by the author from actual buy/sell transactions at sports conventions, buy/sell advertisements in the hobby papers, for sale prices from dealer catalogs and price lists, and discussions with leading hobbyists in the U.S. and Canada. All prices are U.S. prices in U.S. dollars.

INTERESTING NOTES

Sports collectibles have no intrinsic value. The value of a card, as the value of other collectibles, can only be assessed by you and your enjoyment in viewing and possessing it.

Remember, you the buyer ultimately determine the price. You are the determining price factor in that you have ability to say "No" to the price by not exchanging your hard-earned money for a given item. When the cost exceeds the enjoyment or utility you will receive from it, your answer should be "No." We assess and report the prices. You set them!

We are always interested in receiving price input from collectors and dealers from around the country; we happily credit major contributions. We welcome your opinions; your contributions assist us in ensuring a better guide each year. If you would like to join our survey list for the next edition of this book, and others authored by Dr. Beckett, please send your name and address to Dr. James Beckett, 3410 MidCourt, 110, Carrollton, Texas 75006.

ADVERTISING

Within this Price Guide you will find advertisements for sports memorabilia material, mail order and retail sports collectibles establishments. All advertisements were accepted in good faith based on the reputation of the advertiser; however, neither the author, the publisher, the distributors, nor the other advertisers in the Price Guide accept any responsibility for any particular advertiser not complying with the terms of his or her ad.

Should you come into contact with any of the advertisers in this Guide as a result of their advertisement herein, please mention to them this source as your contact.

ERRATA

There are thousands of names and prices in this book. There are going to be a few typographical errors, a few mispellings (sic), and possibly, a number or two out of order. If you catch a blooper, drop me a note directly or in care of the publisher, and we will fix it up in the next year's issue.

1961-62 Cloverleaf Dairy

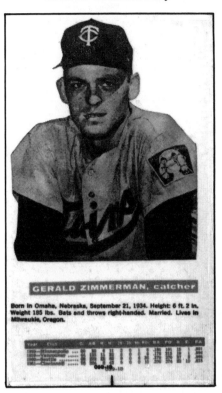

		MINT	VG-E	F-G
□ 23	Rich Rollins (62)	18.00	8.50	1.80
□ 24	Theodore Sadowski (62) ...	18.00	8.50	1.80
□ 25	Albert Stange (62)	18.00	8.50	1.80
□ 26	Dick Stigman (62)	18.00	8.50	1.80
□ 27	Chuck Stobbs (61)	21.00	9.50	2.10
□ 28	Bill Tuttle BOTH	15.00	7.00	1.50
□ 29	Jose Valdivielso (61)	20.00	9.00	2.00
□ 30	Zoilo Versalles BOTH	16.00	7.50	1.60
□ 31	Gerald Zimmerman (62) ...	18.00	8.50	1.80

1985 Donruss HOF Sluggers

This eight card set of Hall of Fame players features the artwork of resident Donruss artist Dick Perez. These oversized (3 1/2" by 6 1/2"), blank backed cards actually form part of a box of gum distributed by the Donruss Company through supermarket type outlets. These cards are reminiscent of the Bazooka issues. The players in the set were ostensibly chosen based on their career slugging percentage, which is listed below each player. The cards themselves are numbered by (slugging percentage) rank. The boxes are also numbered on one of the white side tabs of the complete box; this completely different numbering system is not used.

These large (3 3/4" by 7 3/4") cards are unnumbered; they made up the side of a Cloverleaf Dairy milk carton. Cards still on the carton are valued double the listed price below. The year of issue for each player is given in parentheses. However those players appearing both (BOTH) years are indistinguishable (as to which year they were produced) when cut from the carton. There were 16 cards produced in 1961 and 24 cards produced in 1962. The catalog designation for this set is F103.

	MINT	VG-E	F-G
COMPLETE SET	500.00	225.00	50.00
COMMON PLAYER	15.00	7.00	1.50

		MINT	VG-E	F-G
□	1 Bernie Allen (62)	18.00	8.50	1.80
□	2 George Banks (62)	18.00	8.50	1.80
□	3 Earl Battey BOTH	16.00	7.50	1.60
□	4 Joe Bonikowski (62)	18.00	8.50	1.80
□	5 Billy Gardner (61)	21.00	9.50	2.10
□	6 Paul Giel (61)	21.00	9.50	2.10
□	7 John Goryl (62)	18.00	8.50	1.80
□	8 Lenny Green BOTH	15.00	7.00	1.50
□	9 Jim Kaat BOTH	30.00	14.00	3.00
□	10 Harmon Killebrew (61)	75.00	35.00	7.50
□	11 Jack Kralick BOTH	15.00	7.00	1.50
□	12 Don Lee (61)	20.00	9.00	2.00
□	13 Jim Lemon BOTH	16.00	7.50	1.60
□	14 Manager/Coaches (62)	16.00	7.50	1.60
□	15 Georges Maranda (62)	18.00	8.50	1.80
□	16 Orlando Martinez (62)	18.00	8.50	1.80
□	17 Don Mincher BOTH	16.00	7.50	1.60
□	18 Ray Moore (62)	18.00	8.50	1.80
□	19 Hal Naragon (62)	18.00	8.50	1.80
□	20 Camilo Pascual BOTH	18.00	8.50	1.80
□	21 Vic Power (62)	18.00	8.50	1.80
□	22 Pedro Ramos (61)	21.00	9.50	2.10

	MINT	VG-E	F-G
COMPLETE SET	4.00	1.85	.40
COMMON PLAYER	.50	.22	.05

	MINT	VG-E	F-G
□1 Babe Ruth	1.00	.45	.10
Slugging % .690			
□2 Ted Williams	.70	.32	.07
Slugging % .634			
□3 Lou Gehrig	.75	.35	.07
Slugging % .632			
□4 Johnny Mize	.50	.22	.05
Slugging % .562			
□5 Stan Musial	.60	.28	.06
Slugging % .559			
□6 Mickey Mantle	1.00	.45	.10
Slugging % .557			
□7 Hank Aaron	.60	.28	.06
Slugging % .555			
□8 Frank Robinson	.50	.22	.05
Slugging % .537			

1971 Milk Duds

The cards in this 69 card set measure 1 13/16" by 2 5/8". The 1971 Milk Duds set contains 32 American League cards and 37 National League cards. The cards are sepia toned on a tan background and were issued on the backs of five-cent boxes of Milk Duds candy. The prices listed in the checklist are for complete boxes. Cards cut from boxes are approximately one-half of the listed price.

	MINT	VG-E	F-G
COMPLETE SET	500.00	225.00	50.00
COMMON PLAYER (1-69)	3.50	1.65	.35

AMERICAN LEAGUE

		MINT	VG-E	F-G
☐ 1	Luis Aparicio	10.00	4.75	1.00
☐ 2	Stan Bahnsen	3.50	1.65	.35
☐ 3	Danny Cater	3.50	1.65	.35
☐ 4	Ray Culp	3.50	1.65	.35
☐ 5	Ray Fosse	3.50	1.65	.35
☐ 6	Bill Freehan	4.00	1.85	.40
☐ 7	Jim Fregosi	4.00	1.85	.40
☐ 8	Tommy Harper	3.50	1.65	.35
☐ 9	Frank Howard	5.00	2.35	.50
☐10	Jim Hunter	7.50	3.50	.75
☐11	Tommy John	7.50	3.50	.75
☐12	Alex Johnson	3.50	1.65	.35
☐13	Dave Johnson	4.00	1.85	.40
☐14	Harmon Killebrew	12.50	5.75	1.25
☐15	Sam McDowell	4.00	1.85	.40
☐16	Dave McNally	4.00	1.85	.40
☐17	Bill Melton	3.50	1.65	.35
☐18	Andy Messersmith	4.00	1.85	.40
☐19	Thurman Munson	12.50	5.75	1.25
☐20	Tony Oliva	6.00	2.80	.60
☐21	Jim Palmer	10.00	4.75	1.00
☐22	Jim Perry	4.00	1.85	.40
☐23	Fritz Peterson	3.50	1.65	.35
☐24	Rico Petrocelli	3.50	1.65	.35
☐25	Boog Powell	4.00	1.85	.40
☐26	Brooks Robinson	15.00	7.00	1.50
☐27	Frank Robinson	12.50	5.75	1.25
☐28	George Scott	4.00	1.85	.40
☐29	Reggie Smith	4.00	1.85	.40
☐30	Mel Stottlemyer	4.00	1.85	.40
	(sic, Stottlemyre)			
☐31	Cesar Tovar	3.50	1.65	.35
☐32	Roy White	3.50	1.65	.35

NATIONAL LEAGUE

		MINT	VG-E	F-G
☐33	Hank Aaron	25.00	11.00	2.50
☐34	Ernie Banks	15.00	7.00	1.50
☐35	Glen Beckert	3.50	1.65	.35
	(sic, Glenn)			
☐36	Johnny Bench	20.00	9.00	2.00
☐37	Lou Brock	15.00	7.00	1.50
☐38	Rico Carty	4.00	1.85	.40
☐39	Orlando Cepeda	5.00	2.35	.50
☐40	Roberto Clemente	20.00	9.00	2.00
☐41	Willie Davis	4.00	1.85	.40
☐42	Dick Dietz	3.50	1.65	.35
☐43	Bob Gibson	10.00	4.75	1.00
☐44	Bil Grabarkewitz	3.50	1.65	.35
☐45	Bud Harrelson	3.50	1.65	.35
☐46	Jim Hickman	3.50	1.65	.35
☐47	Ken Holtzman	3.50	1.65	.35
☐48	Randy Hundley	3.50	1.65	.35
☐49	Fergie Jenkins	5.00	2.35	.50
☐50	Don Kessinger	4.00	1.85	.40
☐51	Willie Mays	25.00	11.00	2.50
☐52	Willie McCovey	15.00	7.00	1.50
☐53	Dennis Menke	3.50	1.65	.35
☐54	Jim Merritt	3.50	1.65	.35
☐55	Felix Millan	3.50	1.65	.35
☐56	Claud Osteen	3.50	1.65	.35
	(sic, Claude)			
☐57	Milt Pappas	3.50	1.65	.35
☐58	Tony Perez	6.00	2.80	.60
☐59	Gaylord Perry	10.00	4.75	1.00
☐60	Pete Rose	50.00	22.00	5.00
☐61	Manny Sanguillen	3.50	1.65	.35
☐62	Ron Santo	4.00	1.85	.40
☐63	Tom Seaver	15.00	7.00	1.50
☐64	Wayne Simpson	3.50	1.65	.35
☐65	Rusty Staub	5.00	2.35	.50
☐66	Bobby Tolan	3.50	1.65	.35
☐67	Joe Torre	5.00	2.35	.50
☐68	Luke Walker	3.50	1.65	.35

☐69 Billy Williams	6.00	2.80	.60

1983 Nalley's Mariners

The cards in this 6 card set measure 8 11/16" by 10 11/16". This set of Seattle Mariners is reminiscent of the 1960 Post Cereal issue. An extremely attractive photo card which covers the entire back panel of the Nalley's Potato Chip box, these cards were issued in the Washington State area. The side panels of the box contain a very extensive player biography and statistical record on one side and a Seattle Mariner schedule with a bonus coupon enabling the remitter to save two dollars on a Seattle Mariners ticket on the other. The prices below are for complete boxes. The Rick Sweet card is reportedly more difficult to obtain than others in this set.

	MINT	VG-E	F-G
COMPLETE SET	25.00	11.00	2.50
COMMON PLAYER	3.00	1.40	.30

☐1	Gaylord Perry	8.00	3.75	.80
☐2	Al Cowens	4.00	1.85	.40
☐3	Richie Zisk	4.00	1.85	.40
☐4	Todd Cruz	3.00	1.40	.30
☐5	Bill Caudill	4.00	1.85	.40
☐6	Rick Sweet	5.00	2.35	.50

1961 Peter's Meats

The cards in this 26 card set measure 3 1/2" by 4 5/8". The 1961 Peter's Meats set of full color, numbered cards depicts Minnesota Twins players only. The individual cards served as partial packaging for various meat products and are blank-backed and heavily waxed. Complete boxes are sometimes available and are valued approximately 50% more than single cards. The catalog designation is F173.

	MINT	VG-E	F-G
COMPLETE SET	250.00	110.00	25.00
COMMON PLAYER (1-26)	7.50	3.50	.75

		MINT	VG-E	F-G
☐ 1	Zoilo Versalles	9.00	4.25	.90
☐ 2	Ed Lopat	12.00	5.50	1.20
☐ 3	Pedro Ramos	7.50	3.50	.75
☐ 4	Chuck Stobbs	7.50	3.50	.75
☐ 5	Don Mincher	9.00	4.25	.90
☐ 6	Jack Kralick	7.50	3.50	.75
☐ 7	Jim Kaat	25.00	11.00	2.50
☐ 8	Hal Naragon	7.50	3.50	.75
☐ 9	Don Lee	7.50	3.50	.75
☐10	Cookie Lavagetto	9.00	4.25	.90
☐11	Pete Whisenant	7.50	3.50	.75
☐12	Elmer Valo	7.50	3.50	.75
☐13	Ray Moore	7.50	3.50	.75
☐14	Billy Gardner	9.00	4.25	.90
☐15	Lenny Green	7.50	3.50	.75
☐16	Sam Mele	7.50	3.50	.75
☐17	Jim Lemon	9.00	4.25	.90
☐18	Harmon Killebrew	75.00	35.00	7.50
☐19	Paul Giel	9.00	4.25	.90
☐20	Reno Bertoia	7.50	3.50	.75
☐21	Clyde McCulloch	7.50	3.50	.75
☐22	Earl Battey	9.00	4.25	.90
☐23	Camilo Pascual	9.00	4.25	.90
☐24	Dan Dobbek	7.50	3.50	.75
☐25	Jose Valdivielso	7.50	3.50	.75
☐26	Billy Consolo	7.50	3.50	.75

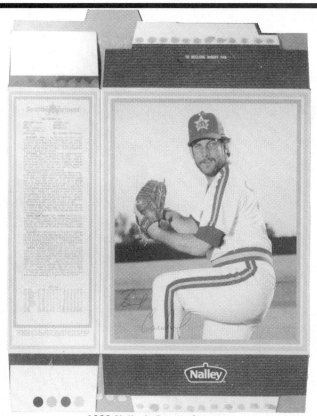

1983 Nalley's Potato Chip Box

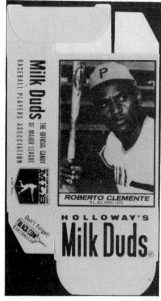

1971 Milk Duds Box

"the Original"
PORKETTES

"MINNESOTA TWINS
Baseball Pictures
on Bottom"!

KEEP UNDER REFRIGERATION
PRE-COOKED

1. Place in skillet with 1/2 in. of cold water. Place over burner with medium flame and brown evenly. When heated turn off and serve. 2. Place on rack in pan. Add small amount of water. Steam until heated through.
INGREDIENTS: Pork, beef, water, nonfat dried milk solids, salt, sugar, flavoring, spices, sodium brylturbom, sodium nitrate, sodium nitrite
PETERS MEAT PROD. INC., ST. PAUL, MINN., EAU CLAIRE, WIS.

#13 (COLLECT ALL 26) MINN. TWINS
RAY MOORE

Age 34 — Height 6'1" — Weight 205.

NET WT. 12 OZS.

O. A. 53.4

NET WEIGHT
ONE POUND

"MINNESOTA TWINS
Baseball Pictures
On Bottom"!

INGREDIENTS: Beef, pork, veal, water, nonfat dried milk solids, salt, dried corn syrup solids, flavoring, sodium erythorbate, sodium nitrate, sodium nitrite

PETERS MEAT PROD. INC., ST. PAUL, MINN., EAU CLAIRE, WIS.

KEEP UNDER REFRIGERATION

COOKING INSTRUCTIONS

THOROUGHLY COOKED • NEED ONLY BE HEATED

TO HEAT: Place Wieners in a pan of boiling water. Turn off heat at once. Allow to stand 10 minutes to heat through. Do not boil.

THE TWINS PLAYERS PICTURES CAN ALSO BE FOUND ON THE BACKS OF ALL Peters PORKETTE PACKAGES

#19 (COLLECT ALL 26) MINN. TWINS
PAUL GIEL

The only major leaguer to be all American in two sports, baseball and football. Signed for a $60,000 bonus by the New York Giants. Has been on the verge of making it big but couldn't quite get over the hump. This may be the year. Playing in front of fans who regard him as one of the University of Minnesota greatest stars. May make the difference. Paul is a fierce competitor who goes all out. Has played with Pittsburgh as well as the Giants. Pitched fine ball for Pirates early last year before going to Salt Lake. Has strong arm and desire. Could be sleeper of the year. Bats right, throws right.
Age 27 — Height 5'11" — Weight 185

SKINLESS
WIENERS

O. A. 64.3

1961 Peters Meats Boxes

1949-51 Royal Desserts

This set of 24 black and white, numbered cards has a red band across the top which calls the set "Royal Stars of Baseball". Each card when cut off the back of the box measures 2 1/2" by 3 1/2". These cards were issued on the backs of Royal Pudding packages in 1949 and 1951. The two years are best distinguished by biographical changes. Card numbers 6, 7, 8, 14, 19 and 21 all appear with team changes. The ACC designation is F219-1.

		MINT	VG-E	F-G
COMPLETE SET		500.00	225.00	50.00
COMMON PLAYER		15.00	7.00	1.50
☐ 1	Stan Musial	75.00	35.00	7.50
☐ 2	Pee Wee Reese	30.00	14.00	3.00
☐ 3	George Kell	21.00	9.50	2.10
☐ 4	Dom DiMaggio	18.00	8.50	1.80
☐ 5	Warren Spahn	30.00	14.00	3.00
☐ 6	Andy Pafko	15.00	7.00	1.50
☐ 7	Andy Seminick	15.00	7.00	1.50
☐ 8	Lou Brissie	15.00	7.00	1.50
☐ 9	Ewell Blackwell	16.00	7.50	1.60
☐ 10	Bobby Thomson	18.00	8.50	1.80
☐ 11	Phil Rizzuto	30.00	14.00	3.00
☐ 12	Tommy Henrich	18.00	8.50	1.80
☐ 13	Joe Gordon	18.00	8.50	1.80
☐ 14	Ray Scarborough	15.00	7.00	1.50
☐ 15	Stan Rojek	15.00	7.00	1.50
☐ 16	Luke Appling	21.00	9.50	2.10
☐ 17	Willard Marshall	15.00	7.00	1.50
☐ 18	Alvin Dark	16.00	7.50	1.60
☐ 19	Dick Sisler	15.00	7.00	1.50
☐ 20	Johnny Ostrowski	15.00	7.00	1.50
☐ 21	Virgil Trucks	15.00	7.00	1.50
☐ 22	Eddie Robinson	15.00	7.00	1.50
☐ 23	Nanny Fernandez	15.00	7.00	1.50
☐ 24	Ferris Fain	16.00	7.50	1.60

1952 Royal Premiums

The 1952 Royal Desserts (premium) set features 16 black and white, unnumbered large (5" by 7") cards with facsimile autograph portraits. The designation "To a Royal Fan" appears on the cards. The ACC designation is F-219-6.

		MINT	VG-E	F-G
COMPLETE SET		250.00	110.00	25.00
COMMON PLAYER		10.00	4.75	1.00
☐ 1	Ewell Blackwell	11.00	5.25	1.10
☐ 2	Leland Brissie Jr.	10.00	4.75	1.00
☐ 3	Alvin Dark	12.00	5.50	1.20
☐ 4	Dom DiMaggio	16.00	7.50	1.60
☐ 5	Ferris Fain	11.00	5.25	1.10
☐ 6	George Kell	20.00	9.00	2.00
☐ 7	Stan Musial	60.00	27.00	6.00
☐ 8	Andy Pafko	10.00	4.75	1.00
☐ 9	Pee Wee Reese	30.00	14.00	3.00
☐ 10	Phil Rizzuto	30.00	14.00	3.00
☐ 11	Eddie Robinson	11.00	5.25	1.10
☐ 12	Ray Scarborough	10.00	4.75	1.00
☐ 13	Andy Seminick	10.00	4.75	1.00
☐ 14	Dick Sisler	10.00	4.75	1.00
☐ 15	Warren Spahn	30.00	14.00	3.00
☐ 16	Bobby Thomson	15.00	7.00	1.50

1935 Wheaties BB1

This set is referred to as "Fancy Frame with Script Signature". These cards (which made up the back of the Wheaties cereal box) measure 6" by 6 1/4" with the frame and about 5" by 5 1/2" if the frame is trimmed off. The player photo appears in blue on a blue-tinted field with a solid orange background behind the player. The player's facsimile autograph is displayed at the bottom of the card.

		MINT	VG-E	F-G
COMPLETE SET		600.00	275.00	60.00
COMMON CARD		15.00	7.00	1.50
☐ 1	Jack Armstrong (batting pose) (fictitious character)	15.00	7.00	1.50
☐ 2	Jack Armstrong (throwing) ("your friend") (fictitious character)	15.00	7.00	1.50
☐ 3	Wally Berger (batting follow through) ("Sincerely Yours")	15.00	7.00	1.50
☐ 4	Tommy Bridges (pitching)	15.00	7.00	1.50
☐ 5A	Mickey Cochrane (squatting, wearing black hat and uniform with stripes)	25.00	11.00	2.50
☐ 5B	Mickey Cochrane (squatting, wearing white hat and uniform with no stripes)	100.00	45.00	10.00
☐ 6	James "Rip" Collins (jumping)	15.00	7.00	1.50
☐ 7	Dizzy Dean (pitching follow through)	50.00	22.00	5.00
☐ 8	Dizzy Dean and Paul Dean (squatting)	35.00	16.50	3.50
☐ 9	Paul Dean (pitching)	15.00	7.00	1.50
☐ 10	William Delancey (catching)	15.00	7.00	1.50
☐ 11	"Jimmie" Foxx (facing camera, knee up)	35.00	16.50	3.50
☐ 12	Frank Frisch (stooping to field)	25.00	11.00	2.50
☐ 13	Lou Gehrig (batting follow through)	100.00	45.00	10.00
☐ 14	Goose Goslin (batting)	20.00	9.00	2.00

1952 Royal Premiums

ROYAL STARS OF BASEBALL No. 2

"PEE WEE" REESE

Harold (also "Little Colonel") Reese has been a Brooklyn Dodger since 1940, excepting 3 years in the Navy. Born in Ekron, Ky., July 23, 1919, Pee Wee is 5' 10", weighs 168, hits and throws right-handed.

Pee Wee's 1949 fielding averaged .977, tops for National League short-stops. He scored 132 runs to lead the league. Reese has played in 3 World's Series and on 4 All-Star teams.

Send for a Plastic Album to Hold Your Royal Stars Collection!

Eight clear envelopes, bound with colorful cover; displays 16 photo-graphs. Mail 15¢ and 3 Royal Desserts package fronts to Royal, Box 89, New York 46, N. Y.

This *FREE* Card Starts _Your_ ROYAL STARS Collection!

Look on the other side of this card for a signed photo and short life story of "Pee Wee" Reese. You will find other photos and histories of many more famous Movie and Baseball Stars on the package backs of Royal Puddings and Royal Gelatin Desserts. Use this card to start your exciting collection of ROYAL STARS of Baseball and Movies!

P-4075   10/51 PRINTED IN U.S.A.

1949-51 Royal Desserts

ROYAL STARS OF BASEBALL No. 11

PHIL RIZZUTO

One of the Majors' smallest men, Phil is 5' 6", weighs 160. The right-hander was born in New York City, Sept. 25, 1918.

The New York Yankees' shortstop is an exceptional bunter and an out-standing fielder. Excepting a 3-year service hitch, Phil has been with the Yanks since 1937. He tied the major league record for short-stops by taking part in 5 double plays in one 1942 game.

Send for a Plastic Album to Hold Your Royal Stars Collection!

Eight clear envelopes, bound with colorful cover; displays 16 photo-graphs. Mail 15¢ and 3 Royal Desserts package fronts to Royal, Box 89, New York 46, N. Y.

			MINT	VG-E	F-G
☐ 15	Lefty Grove .... (holding trophy)		30.00	14.00	3.00
☐ 16	Carl Hubbell .... (pitching)		25.00	11.00	2.50
☐ 17	Travis C. Jackson .... (stooping to field)		20.00	9.00	2.00
☐ 18	"Chuck" Klein .... (with four bats)		20.00	9.00	2.00
☐ 19	Gus Mancuso .... (catching)		15.00	7.00	1.50
☐ 20A	Johnny"Pepper" Martin .. (batting)		15.00	7.00	1.50
☐ 20B	Pepper Martin .... (portrait) ("Sincerely Yours")		15.00	7.00	1.50
☐ 21	Joe Medwick .... (batting follow through)		25.00	11.00	2.50
☐ 22	Melvin Ott .... (batting follow through)		30.00	14.00	3.00
☐ 23	Harold Schumacher .... (pitching)		15.00	7.00	1.50
☐ 24	Al Simmons .... (batting follow through) ("Sincerely Yours")		25.00	11.00	2.50
☐ 25	"Jo Jo" White .... (batting follow through)		15.00	7.00	1.50

			MINT	VG-E	F-G
	"Manager, World Champion Detroit"				
☐ 3	Jimmy Foxx .... (batting) "All Around Star"		35.00	16.50	3.50
☐ 4	Lou Gehrig .... (stooping to field) "Iron Man"		100.00	45.00	10.00
☐ 5	Hank Greenberg .... (jumping) "Home Run Champion"		35.00	16.50	3.50
☐ 6	"Gabby" Hartnett .... (squatting) "Catcher Voted Most Valuable"		25.00	11.00	2.50
☐ 7	Carl Hubbell .... (ready to throw) "Star Pitcher"		25.00	11.00	2.50
☐ 8	"Pepper" Martin .... (jumping) "Heavy Hitter"		15.00	7.00	1.50
☐ 9	Van L. Mungo .... (pitching) "Star Pitcher"		15.00	7.00	1.50
☐ 10	"Buck" Newsom .... (pitching) "Star Pitcher"		15.00	7.00	1.50
☐ 11	"Arky" Vaughan .... (batting) "Batting Champion"		20.00	9.00	2.00
☐ 12	Jimmy Wilson .... (squatting) "Manager and Star Catcher"		15.00	7.00	1.50

1936 Wheaties BB3

This set is referred to as "Fancy Frame with Printed Name and Data." These cards (which made up the back of the Wheaties cereal box) measure 6" by 6 1/4" with the frame and about 5" by 5 1/2" if the frame is trimmed off. This set is distinguished from BB1 (above) in that this set also shows the player's name and some fact about him. The player's facsimile autograph is displayed at the bottom of the card. In the checklist below, the first few words of the printed data found on the card is also provided.

			MINT	VG-E	F-G
COMPLETE SET		....	300.00	130.00	30.00
COMMON CARD		....	15.00	7.00	1.50
☐ 1	Earl Averill .... (batting) "Star Outfielder"		21.00	9.50	2.10
☐ 2	Mickey Cochrane .... (catching)		30.00	14.00	3.00

1936 Wheaties BB4

This set is referred to as "Thin Orange Border / Figures in Border." These unnumbered cards (which made up the back of the Wheaties cereal box) measure 6" by 8 1/2". This set is the first at this larger size. The figures in the border include drawings of men and women competing in baseball, football, hockey, track, golf, tennis, skiing, and swimming. A train and an airplane also appear. The rectangular photo of the player appears in a 4" by 6 1/2" box above an endorsement for Wheaties. The player's name is in script below the endorsement, but his printed name, team, and some other information about him is near the top in the solid orange background.

		MINT	VG-E	F-G
COMPLETE SET		300.00	130.00	30.00
COMMON CARD		15.00	7.00	1.50
☐ 1 Curt Davis .... Philadelphia Phillies		15.00	7.00	1.50
☐ 2 Lou Gehrig .... New York Yankees		100.00	45.00	10.00
☐ 3 Charley Gehringer .... Detroit Tigers		30.00	14.00	3.00
☐ 4 Lefty Grove .... Boston Red Sox		30.00	14.00	3.00
☐ 5 Rollie Hemsley .... St. Louis Browns		15.00	7.00	1.50
☐ 6 Billy Herman .... Chicago Cubs		20.00	9.00	2.00
☐ 7 Joe Medwick .... St. Louis Cardinals		25.00	11.00	2.50
☐ 8 Mel Ott .... New York Giants		35.00	16.50	3.50
☐ 9 Schoolboy Rowe .... Detroit Tigers		15.00	7.00	1.50
☐ 10 Arky Vaughn .... Detroit Tigers		20.00	9.00	2.00
☐ 11 Joe Vosmik .... Cleveland Indians		15.00	7.00	1.50
☐ 12 Lon Warneke .... Chicago Cubs		15.00	7.00	1.50

1936 Wheaties BB5

This set is referred to as "How to Play Winning Baseball." These cards, which made up the back of the Wheaties cereal box, measure 6" by 8 1/2". These panels combine a photo of the player with a series of blue and white drawings illustrating playing instructions. All of the players are shown in full length poses, except Earl Averill, who is pictured to the thighs. The players appear against a solid orange background. In addition to the numbers 1 through 12, these panels are also found with a small number 28 combined with capital letters "A" through "L". However, panels are known without these letter-number combinations. This set is sometimes referred to as the "28 Series."

		MINT	VG-E	F-G
COMPLETE SET		300.00	130.00	30.00
COMMON CARD		15.00	7.00	1.50
☐ 1	Lefty Gomez (28E) "Pitching, How to Throw the Fast Ball"	25.00	11.00	2.50
☐ 2	Billy Herman (28D) "How to Run The Bases"	20.00	9.00	2.00
☐ 3	Luke Appling (28C) "Shortstop, Putting 'Em Out at Second"	25.00	11.00	2.50
☐ 4	Jimmie Foxx (28A) "Tells How to Play First Base ..."	35.00	16.50	3.50
☐ 5	Joe Medwick (28K) "Tells How to Play Outfield ..."	25.00	11.00	2.50
☐ 6	Charles Gehringer (28G) "Tells How to Play Second Base ..."	25.00	11.00	2.50
☐ 7A	Mel Ott "Bunting, Put 'Em Where They Count" (large figure, tips in vertical sequence)	35.00	16.50	3.50
☐ 7B	Mel Ott (28H) "Bunting, Put 'Em Where They Count" (small figure, tips in two horiz. rows)	35.00	16.50	3.50
☐ 8	Odell Hale (28B) "Third Base -- Fine Play at the Hot Corner"	15.00	7.00	1.50
☐ 9	Bill Dickey (28I) "Catching Pointers Behind the Plate"	35.00	16.50	3.50
☐ 10	"Lefty" Grove (28J) "Tells You About Pitching ..."	30.00	14.00	3.00
☐ 11	Carl Hubbell (28F) "Pitching the Slow Ball"	25.00	11.00	2.50
☐ 12	Earl Averill (28L) "Batting -- Get Those Extra Bases"	21.00	9.50	2.10

1937 Wheaties BB6

This set is referred to as "How to Star in Baseball." These numbered cards, which made up the back of the Wheaties cereal box, measure 6" by 8 1/4". This series is very similar to BB5. Both are instructional series and the text and drawings used to illustrate the tips are similar and in some cases identical. Each panel is a full-length photo. The player's name, team, and a script signature also appears. The tips are illustrated in a variety of drawings which appear in stars and boxes.

		MINT	VG-E	F-G
COMPLETE SET		300.00	130.00	30.00
COMMON CARD		15.00	7.00	1.50
☐ 1	Bill Dickey "How to Catch"	30.00	14.00	3.00
☐ 2	Red Ruffing "Pitching the Fast Ball"	25.00	11.00	2.50
☐ 3	Zeke Bonura "First Base -- Make More Outs"	15.00	7.00	1.50
☐ 4	Charlie Gehringer "Second Base as the Stars Play It"	25.00	11.00	2.50
☐ 5	"Arky" Vaughn "Shortstop, Play It Right"	20.00	9.00	2.00
☐ 6	Carl Hubbell "Pitching the Slow Ball"	25.00	11.00	2.50
☐ 7	John Lewis "Third Base, Field Those Hot Ones"	15.00	7.00	1.50
☐ 8	Heinie Manush "Fielding for Extra Outs"	21.00	9.50	2.10
☐ 9	"Lefty" Grove "Pitching the Outdrop Ball"	30.00	14.00	3.00
☐ 10	Billy Herman "How to Score" (baserunning)	21.00	9.50	2.10
☐ 11	Joe DiMaggio "Bat Like a Home Run King"	125.00	57.00	12.50
☐ 12	Joe Medwick "Batting for Extra Bases"	25.00	11.00	2.50

1937 Wheaties BB7

This set is referred to as the "29 Series." These numbered cards, which made up the back of the Wheaties cereal box, measure 6" by 8 1/4". The player's name, position, team, and some information about him are printed near the top. His signature appears on the lower part of the panel near a printed endorsement for the cereal. This set contains several different card designs. One design shows the player outlined against an orange (nearly red) background. A two or three line endorsement is at the bottom in white. DiMaggio, Bonura, and Bridges appear in this form. Another design shows the player against an all white background, but the panel is rimmed by a red, white, and blue border. Players shown in this fashion are Moore, Radcliff, and Martin. A third style offers a panel with an orange border and a large orange circle behind the player. The rest of the background is white. Lombardi, Travis, and Mungo appear in this design. The final style is a tilted, orange background picture of the player with white and blue framing the photo. Trosky, Demaree, and Vaughan show up in this design. This set also has three known Pacific Coast League players. One number, 29N, which could be a PCL player, is unknown.

		MINT	VG-E	F-G
COMPLETE SET		500.00	225.00	50.00
COMMON CARD		15.00	7.00	1.50
☐ 29A	"Zeke" Bonura (batting)	15.00	7.00	1.50
☐ 29B	Cecil Travis (reaching left)	15.00	7.00	1.50

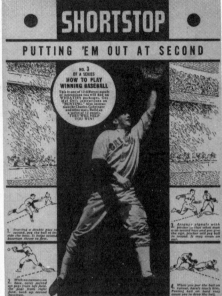

1936 Wheaties BB4   **1936 Wheaties BB5**

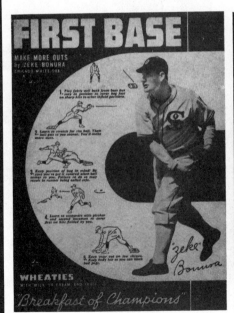

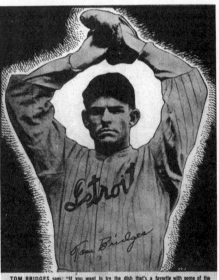

1937 Wheaties BB6   **1937 Wheaties BB7**

		MINT	VG-E	F-G
☐ 29C	Frank Demaree (batting)	15.00	7.00	1.50
☐ 29D	Joe Moore (batting)	15.00	7.00	1.50
☐ 29E	Ernie Lombardi (crouch)	21.00	9.50	2.10
☐ 29F	John L. "Pepper" Martin (reaching)	15.00	7.00	1.50
☐ 29G	Harold Trosky (batting)	15.00	7.00	1.50
☐ 29H	Raymond Radcliff (batting)	15.00	7.00	1.50
☐ 29I	Joe DiMaggio (batting)	125.00	57.00	12.50
☐ 29J	Tom Bridges (hands over head)	15.00	7.00	1.50
☐ 29K	Van L. Mungo (pitching)	15.00	7.00	1.50
☐ 29L	"Arky" Vaughn (batting)	21.00	9.50	2.10
☐ 29M	Arnold Statz (PCL)	75.00	35.00	7.50
☐ 29O	Fred Muller (PCL)	75.00	35.00	7.50
☐ 29P	Gene Lillard (PCL)	75.00	35.00	7.50

1937 Wheaties BB8

This set is referred to as the "Speckled Orange, White, and Blue Series." These unnumbered cards, which made up the back of the Wheaties cereal box, measure 6" by 8 1/2". This set also contains several different card designs. One design (DiMaggio and Feller) shows the player surrounded by orange speckles on a white background with a group of four blue and white drawings of players in action along the panel's right side. Another design shows the panel divided into four rectangles -- white at upper right and lower left and orangfe on the other two -- with the players (Appling and Averill) leaping to catch the ball. Blue circles surrounded by orange and white speckles appear on the pictures of Hubbell and Grove. Medwick and Gehringer appear on white panels with a cloud of orange speckles behind them. The player's name in script style appears along with printed data about his 1936 season and a brief endorsement of the cereal. Wheaties appears in large block letters along with slogans elsewhere on the lower part of the panel. The color orange is very dark and appears red to some collectors.

		MINT	VG-E	F-G
COMPLETE SET		250.00	110.00	25.00
COMMON CARD		15.00	7.00	1.50
☐ 1	Luke Appling (reaching)	21.00	9.50	2.10
☐ 2	Earl Averill (reaching)	21.00	9.50	2.10
☐ 3	Joe DiMaggio (batting)	125.00	57.00	12.50
☐ 4	Robert Feller (throwing)	50.00	22.00	5.00
☐ 5	Chas. Gehringer (batting)	25.00	11.00	2.50
☐ 6	Lefty Grove (throwing)	30.00	14.00	3.00
☐ 7	Carl Hubbell (throwing)	25.00	11.00	2.50
☐ 8	Joe Medwick (fielding)	25.00	11.00	2.50

ATTEND a sports collectibles convention in your area this year. Improve your collection by buying or trading, meet new (and old) friends, have a great time.

1937 Wheaties BB9

This set is referred to as the "Color Series." These unnumbered cards, which made up the back of the Wheaties cereal box, measure 6" by 8 1/2". Photos of the players appear in circles, "V" shapes, rectangles,and stars among others. A player from every Major League team is included. The player's name is in script with the team name printed below. The name, endorsement, and 1936 season highlights are printed near the bottom. John Moore and Harland Clift have been reported on paper stock. The back of the paper is buff brown and blank. Whether these were advertisements used in stores or if they were cut from some larger display sheet is unknown.

		MINT	VG-E	F-G
COMPLETE SET		400.00	180.00	40.00
COMMON CARD		15.00	7.00	1.50
☐ 1	Zeke Bonura Chicago White Sox (fielding, crossed bats, glove, ball at upper left)	15.00	7.00	1.50
☐ 2	Tom Bridges Detroit Tigers (pitching, figure in large orange circle)	15.00	7.00	1.50
☐ 3	Harland Clift St. Louis Browns (batting, large baseball behind him)	15.00	7.00	1.50
☐ 4	Kiki Cuyler Cincinnati Reds (batting on green background)	21.00	9.50	2.10
☐ 5	Joe DiMaggio New York Yankees (leaping, green and white circle behind)	125.00	57.00	12.50
☐ 6	Robert Feller Cleveland Indians (pitching, blue circle on left knee)	50.00	22.00	5.00
☐ 7	Lefty Grove Boston Red Sox (pitching, red orange home plate)	30.00	14.00	3.00
☐ 8	Billy Herman Chicago Cubs (throwing, yellow star behind him)	21.00	9.50	2.10
☐ 9	Carl Hubbell New York Giants (pitching, orange, yellow V's behind)	25.00	11.00	2.50
☐ 10	Buck Jordan Boston Bees (batting, dark orange rectangle, blue sides)	15.00	7.00	1.50
☐ 11	"Pepper" Martin St. Louis Cardinals (reaching, orange rectangle)	15.00	7.00	1.50
☐ 12	John Moore Philadelphia Phillies (batting, blue background, stands on green)	15.00	7.00	1.50
☐ 13	Wally Moses Philadelphia A's (leaping, dark orange background, yellow and blue)	15.00	7.00	1.50
☐ 14	Van L. Mungo Brooklyn Dodgers (pitching, green background, orange and blue)	15.00	7.00	1.50
☐ 15	Cecil Travis Washington Senators (batting, orange lightning)	15.00	7.00	1.50
☐ 16	Arky Vaughan	21.00	9.50	2.10

1937 Wheaties BB8

1937 Wheaties BB9

1938 Wheaties BB10

1938 Wheaties BB11

Pittsburgh Pirates
(batting, blue
diamond, green frame)

1937 Wheaties BB14

This set is referred to as the "Small Panels with Orange Background Series." These numbered (and unnumbered) cards, which made up the back of the Wheaties individual serving cereal box, measure about 2 5/8" by 3 7/8". These small panels have orange backgrounds and some, but not all, use poses that appear in some of the regular sized panels. Joe DiMaggio, for example, is the same pose as in the large Wheaties BB7 set and the Mel Ott is similar to the BB5 pose, but cropped a little differently. Some panels have been seen with and without the number 29 in combination with a letter, so apparently there were several printings. The player's name is in all capitals with his position and team in smaller caps. A printed block of data about him is on the main part of the card with a Wheaties endorsement in a white strip at the bottom.

	MINT	VG-E	F-G
COMPLETE SET	650.00	300.00	60.00
COMMON CARD	35.00	15.00	3.00
☐ 1 "Zeke" Bonura (29A) "Led all A.L. First Basemen (BB7 pose)	35.00	15.00	3.00
☐ 2 Tom Bridges (29J) "Struck Out Most Batters, 173 ..." (not BB7 pose)	35.00	15.00	3.00
☐ 3 Dolph Camilli "Most Put Outs, 1446 ..." (unnumbered)	35.00	15.00	3.00
☐ 4 Frank Demaree (29C)	35.00	15.00	3.00
☐ 5 Joe DiMaggio (29I) "Outstanding Rookie, 1936 ..." (BB7 pose)	150.00	70.00	15.00
☐ 6 Billy Herman "Lifetime .300 Hitter ..." (unnumbered)	45.00	20.00	4.00

☐ 7 Carl Hubbell "Won Most Games, 26 ..." (unnumbered)	60.00	25.00	5.00
☐ 8 Ernie Lombardi (29E) (leading Cincinnati hitter)	45.00	20.00	4.00
☐ 9 "Pepper" Martin (29F)	35.00	15.00	3.00
☐ 10 Joe Moore (29D) (not BB7 pose)	35.00	15.00	3.00
☐ 11 Van Mungo (29K)	35.00	15.00	3.00
☐ 12 Mel Ott (cropped BB5 pose) (unnumbered)	60.00	25.00	5.00
☐ 13 Raymond Radcliff (29H) (most one-base hits) (BB7 pose)	35.00	15.00	3.00
☐ 14 Cecil Travis (29B) "One of the Leading Bats in ..." (BB7 pose)	35.00	15.00	3.00
☐ 15 Harold Trosky (29G)	35.00	15.00	3.00
☐ 16A "Arky" Vaughan (unnumbered)	45.00	20.00	4.00
☐ 16B "Arky" Vaughan (29L) "Lifetime .300 Hitter who ..." (BB7 pose)	45.00	20.00	4.00

1938 Wheaties BB10

This set is referred to as the "Biggest Thrills in Baseball." These numbered cards, which made up the back of the Wheaties cereal box, measure 6" by 8 1/2". A player from every Major League team is included. Each panel describes the player's greatest thrill playing the game. The thrill is announced in large banner headline type and described in a block of copy over the player's script signature. His team and position are printed below the name. All sixteen are are known on paper stock as well as on the heavy cardboard package backs.

	MINT	VG-E	F-G
COMPLETE SET	300.00	130.00	30.00
COMMON CARD	15.00	7.00	1.50
☐ 1 Bob Feller Cleveland Indians (Two Hits in One Inning for Feller)	50.00	22.00	5.00
☐ 2 Cecil Travis Washington Nationals (Clicks in First Big League Games)	15.00	7.00	1.50
☐ 3 Joe Medwick St. Louis Cardinals (Goes on Batting Spree Twice)	25.00	11.00	2.50
☐ 4 Gerald Walker Chicago White Sox (World Series Game, 1934, Gives ...)	15.00	7.00	1.50
☐ 5 Carl Hubbell New York Giants (Strikes Out Murderer's Row)	25.00	11.00	2.50
☐ 6 Bob Johnson Philadelphia A's (Setting New A.L. Record)	15.00	7.00	1.50
☐ 7 Beau Bell St. Louis Browns (Smacks First Major League Homer)	15.00	7.00	1.50
☐ 8 Ernie Lombardi Cincinnati Reds (Sold to Majors)	21.00	9.50	2.10
☐ 9 Lefty Grove Boston Red Sox (Fans Babe Ruth)	30.00	14.00	3.00
☐ 10 Lou Fette Boston Bees	15.00	7.00	1.50

(Wins 20 Games)
- ☐ 11 Joe DiMaggio 125.00 55.00 12.00
  New York Yankees
  (Home Run King Gets
  Biggest Thrill ...)
- ☐ 12 Pinky Whitney 15.00 7.00 1.50
  Philadelphia Phillies
  (Hits Three in a Row)
- ☐ 13 Dizzy Dean 40.00 18.00 4.00
  Chicago Cubs
  (11-0 Victory
  Clinches World Series)
- ☐ 14 Charley Gehringer 30.00 14.00 3.00
  Detroit Tigers
  (Homers Off
  Dizzy Dean)
- ☐ 15 Paul Waner 21.00 9.50 2.10
  Pittsburgh Pirates
  (Four Perfect Sixes)
- ☐ 16 Dolf Camilli 15.00 7.00 1.50
  Brooklyn Dodgers
  (First Hit a Homer)

1938 Wheaties BB11

This set is referred to as the "Dress Clothes or Civies Series." These unnumbered cards, which made up the back of the Wheaties cereal box, measure 6" by 8 1/4". The panels feature the players and their friends in blue photos. The rest of the panel uses the orange, blue, and white Wheaties colors.

	MINT	VG-E	F-G
COMPLETE SET	150.00	70.00	15.00
COMMON CARD	15.00	7.00	1.50

- ☐ 1 Lou Fette 15.00 7.00 1.50
  (pouring milk
  over his Wheaties)
- ☐ 2 Jimmie Foxx 30.00 14.00 3.00
  (slices banana for
  his son's Wheaties)
- ☐ 3 Charlie Gehringer 25.00 11.00 2.50
  (and his young fan)
- ☐ 4 Lefty Grove 25.00 11.00 2.50
  (watches waitress
  pour Wheaties)
- ☐ 5 Hank Greenberg 25.00 11.00 2.50
  and Roxie Lawson
  (eat breakfast)
- ☐ 6 Ernie Lombardi 21.00 9.50 2.10
  and Lee Grissom
  (prepare to eat)
- ☐ 7 Joe Medwick 25.00 11.00 2.50
  (pours milk
  over cereal)
- ☐ 8 Lon Warneke 15.00 7.00 1.50
  (smiles in anticip-
  ation of Wheaties)

1938 Wheaties BB15

This set is referred to as the "Small Panels with Orange, Blue, and White Background Series." These numbered (and unnumbered) cards, which made up the back of the Wheaties individual serving cereal box, measure about 2 5/8" by 3 7/8". These small panels have orange, blue, and white backgrounds and some, but not all, use poses that appear in some of the regular larger sized panels. Greenberg and Lewis are featured with a horizontal (HOR) pose.

	MINT	VG-E	F-G
COMPLETE SET	500.00	225.00	50.00
COMMON CARD	35.00	15.00	3.00

- ☐ 1 "Zeke Bonura 35.00 15.00 3.00
- ☐ 2 Joe DiMaggio 150.00 70.00 15.00
  (46 home runs)
- ☐ 3A Chas. Gehringer 60.00 25.00 5.00
  (leaping, MVP,
  American League)
- ☐ 3B Charles Gehringer 60.00 25.00 5.00
  (batting, 1937
  batting king)
- ☐ 4 Hank Greenberg HOR 60.00 25.00 5.00
  (second in home runs)
- ☐ 5 Lefty Grove 60.00 25.00 5.00
  (17-9 won-lost record)
- ☐ 6 Carl Hubbell 50.00 22.00 4.00
  (star pitcher,
  1937 Giants)
- ☐ 7 John (Buddy) Lewis HOR .. 35.00 15.00 3.00
  (batted .314)
- ☐ 8 Heinie Manush 45.00 20.00 4.00
  (batted .332)
- ☐ 9 Joe Medwick 45.00 20.00 4.00
- ☐ 10 Arky Vaughan 45.00 20.00 4.00

1939 Wheaties BB12

This set is referred to as the "Personal Pointers Series." These numbered cards, which made up the back of the Wheaties cereal box, measure 6" by 8 1/4". The panels feature an instructional format similar to both the BB5 and BB6 Wheaties sets. Drawings again illustrate the tips on batting and pitching. The colors are orange, blue, and white and the players appear in photographs.

	MINT	VG-E	F-G
COMPLETE SET	200.00	90.00	20.00
COMMON CARD	15.00	7.00	1.50

- ☐ 1 Ernie Lombardi 21.00 9.50 2.10
  "How to Place Hits
  For Scores"
- ☐ 2 Johnny Allen 15.00 7.00 1.50
  "It's Windup That
  Counts"
- ☐ 3 Lefty Gomez 25.00 11.00 2.50
  "Delivery That
  Keeps 'Em Guessing"
- ☐ 4 Bill Lee 15.00 7.00 1.50
  "Follow Through
  For Stops"

☐ 5	Jimmie Foxx "Stance Helps Sluggers"	35.00	16.50	3.50
☐ 6	Joe Medwick "Power-Drive Grip"	25.00	11.00	2.50
☐ 7	Hank Greenberg "Smooth Swing"	30.00	14.00	3.00
☐ 8	Mel Ott "Study That Pitcher"	35.00	16.50	3.50
☐ 9	Arky Vaughn "Beat 'Em With Bunts"	21.00	9.50	2.10

1939 Wheaties BB13

This set is referred to as the "100 Years of Baseball or Baseball Centennial Series." These numbered cards, which made up the back of the Wheaties cereal box, measure 6" by 6 3/4". Each panel has a drawing depicting various aspects and events of baseball in the orange, blue, and white Wheaties colors.

	MINT	VG-E	F-G
COMPLETE SET	120.00	55.00	12.00
COMMON CARD	15.00	7.00	1.50

☐ 1	Design of First Diamond with Picture of Abner Doubleday - 1938	15.00	7.00	1.50
☐ 2	Lincoln Gets News of Nomination on Base- ball Field - 1860	15.00	7.00	1.50
☐ 3	Crowd Boos First Baseball Glove (pictures of gloves) - 1869	15.00	7.00	1.50
☐ 4	Curve Ball Just an Illusion Say Scientists - 1877	15.00	7.00	1.50
☐ 5	Fencer's Mask is Pattern for First Catcher's 'Cage' - 1877	15.00	7.00	1.50
☐ 6	Baseball Gets "All Dressed Up" (pictures of uniforms) - 1890	15.00	7.00	1.50
☐ 7	Modern Bludgeon Enters Game (pictures of bats) - 1895	15.00	7.00	1.50
☐ 8	"Casey at the Bat" (eight verses of famous Mudville poem)	15.00	7.00	1.50

1940 Wheaties M4

This set is referred to as the "Champs of the U.S.A." These numbered cards made up the back of the Wheaties box; the whole panel measures about 6" by 8 1/4" but the drawing portion (inside the dotted lines) is approximately 6" by 6". Baseball players are on each card, joined by football players and coaches, race car drivers, airline pilots, a circus clown, ice skater, hockey star, and golfers. Each athlete appears in what looks like a stamp with a serrated edge. The stamps appear one above the other with a brief block of copy describing his or her achievements. There appear to have been three printings, resulting in some variation panels. The full panels tell the cereal buyer to look for either 27, 39, or 63 Champ stamps. The first nine panels apparently were printed more than once, since all

the known variations occur within those numbers.

	MINT	VG-E	F-G
COMPLETE SET	400.00	180.00	40.00
COMMON CARD	15.00	7.00	1.50

☐ 1A	Charles "Red" Ruffing Lynn Patrick Bob Feller (27 stamp series)	35.00	16.50	3.50
☐ 1B	Charles "Red" Ruffing Lynn Patrick Leo Durocher (39 stamp series)	30.00	14.00	3.00
☐ 2A	Joe DiMaggio Hank Greenberg Don Duge (27 stamp series)	75.00	35.00	7.50
☐ 2B	Joe DiMaggio Mel Ott Ellsworth Vines (39 stamp series)	75.00	35.00	7.50
☐ 3	Jimmie Foxx Bernie Bierman Bill Dickey	30.00	14.00	3.00
☐ 4	Morris Arnovich Earl "Dutch" Clark Capt R.L. Baker	15.00	7.00	1.50
☐ 5	Joe Medwick Madison (Matty) Bell Ab Jenkins	15.00	7.00	1.50
☐ 6A	John Mize Davey O'Brien Ralph Guldahl (27 stamp series)	15.00	7.00	1.50
☐ 6B	John Mize Bob Feller Rudy York (39 stamp series)	30.00	14.00	3.00
☐ 6C	Gabby Hartnett Davey O'Brien Ralph Guldahl (unknown series)	15.00	7.00	1.50
☐ 7A	Joe Cronin Cecil Isbell Byron Nelson (27 stamp series)	15.00	7.00	1.50
☐ 7B	Joe Cronin Hank Greenberg Byron Nelson (unknown series)	25.00	11.00	2.50
☐ 7C	Paul Derringer Cecil Isbell Byron Nelson (unknown series)	15.00	7.00	1.50
☐ 8A	Jack Manders Ernie Lombardi George I. Myers (27 stamp series)	15.00	7.00	1.50
☐ 8B	Paul Derringer Ernie Lombardi George I. Myers (39 stamp series)	15.00	7.00	1.50
☐ 9	Bob Bartlett Terrell Jacobs Captain R.C. Hanson	15.00	7.00	1.50
☐ 10	Adele Inge Lowell "Red" Dawson Billy Herman	15.00	7.00	1.50
☐ 11	Dolph Camilli Antoinette Concello Wallace Wade	15.00	7.00	1.50
☐ 12	Hugh McManus Luke Appling Stanley Hack	15.00	7.00	1.50
☐ 13	Felix Adler Hal Trosky Mabel Vinson	15.00	7.00	1.50

1941 Wheaties M5

This set is also referred to as the "Champs of the U.S.A." These numbered cards made up the back of the Wheaties box; the whole panel measures about 6" by 8 1/4" but the drawing portion (inside the

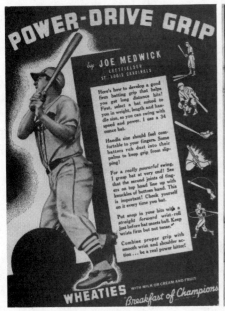

1939 Wheaties BB12

1939 Wheaties BB13

1940 Wheaties M4

1941 Wheaties M5

dotted lines) is approximately 6" by 6". Each athlete appears in what looks like a stamp with a serrated edge. The stamps appear one above the other with a brief block of copy describing his or her achievements. The format is the same as the previous M4 set -- even the numbering system continues where the M4 set stops.

	MINT	VG-E	F-G
COMPLETE SET	300.00	130.00	30.00
COMMON CARD	15.00	7.00	1.50

	MINT	VG-E	F-G
☐ 14 Jimmie Foxx Felix Adler Capt. R.G. Hanson	30.00	14.00	3.00
☐ 15 Bernie Bierman Bob Feller Jessie McLeod	30.00	14.00	3.00
☐ 16 Hank Greenberg Lowell "Red" Dawson J.W. Stoker	20.00	9.00	2.00
☐ 17 Joe DiMaggio Byron Nelson Antoniette Concello	75.00	35.00	7.50
☐ 18 Harold "Pee Wee" Reese Capt. R.L. Baker Frank "Buck" McCormick	30.00	14.00	3.00
☐ 19 William W. Robbins Gerald "Gee" Walker Gene Sarazen	15.00	7.00	1.50
☐ 20 Harry Danning Bucky Walters Barney McCosky	15.00	7.00	1.50
☐ 21 Joe "Flash" Gordon George I. Myers Stan Hack	15.00	7.00	1.50

1951-52 Fischer Baking Labels

One of the popular "Bread for Energy" end-labels sets, these labels are found with blue, red and yellow backgrounds. Each bread label measures 2 3/4" by 2 3/4". They were distributed mainly in the northeast section of the country and there may be an album associated with the set. The ACC designation is D290-3.

	MINT	VG-E	F-G
COMPLETE SET	1400.00	600.00	125.00
COMMON PLAYER (1-32)	40.00	18.00	4.00

	MINT	VG-E	F-G
☐ 1 Vern Bickford Boston Braves	40.00	18.00	4.00
☐ 2 Ralph Branca Brooklyn Dodgers	40.00	18.00	4.00
☐ 3 Harry Brecheen St. Louis Cardinals	40.00	18.00	4.00
☐ 4 Chico Carrasquel Chicago White Sox	40.00	18.00	4.00
☐ 5 Cliff Chambers Pittsburgh Pirates	40.00	18.00	4.00
☐ 6 Hoot Evers Detroit Tigers	40.00	18.00	4.00

	MINT	VG-E	F-G
☐ 7 Ned Garver St. Louis Browns	40.00	18.00	4.00
☐ 8 Billy Goodman Boston Red Sox	40.00	18.00	4.00
☐ 9 Gil Hodges Brooklyn Dodgers	70.00	32.00	7.00
☐ 10 Larry Jansen New York Giants	40.00	18.00	4.00
☐ 11 Willie Jones Philadelphia Phillies	40.00	18.00	4.00
☐ 12 Eddie Joost Philadelphia A's	40.00	18.00	4.00
☐ 13 George Kell Detroit Tigers	60.00	27.00	6.00
☐ 14 Alex Kellner Philadelphia A's	40.00	18.00	4.00
☐ 15 Ted Kluszewski Cincinnati Reds	50.00	22.00	5.00
☐ 16 Jim Konstanty Philadelphia Phillies	40.00	18.00	4.00
☐ 17 Bob Lemon Cleveland Indians	60.00	27.00	6.00
☐ 18 Cass Michaels Washington Senators	40.00	18.00	4.00
☐ 19 Johnny Mize New York Yankees	60.00	27.00	6.00
☐ 20 Irv Noren Washington Senators	40.00	18.00	4.00
☐ 21 Joe Page New York Yankees	40.00	18.00	4.00
☐ 22 Andy Pafko Chicago Cubs	40.00	18.00	4.00
☐ 23 Mel Parnell Boston Red Sox	40.00	18.00	4.00
☐ 24 Johnny Sain Boston Braves	50.00	22.00	5.00
☐ 25 Red Schoendienst St. Louis Cardinals	50.00	22.00	5.00
☐ 26 Roy Sievers St. Louis Browns	40.00	18.00	4.00
☐ 27 Roy Smalley Chicago Cubs	40.00	18.00	4.00
☐ 28 Herm Wehmeier Cincinnati Reds	40.00	18.00	4.00
☐ 29 Bill Werle Pittsburgh Pirates	40.00	18.00	4.00
☐ 30 Wes Westrum New York Giants	40.00	18.00	4.00
☐ 31 Early Wynn Cleveland Indians	60.00	27.00	6.00
☐ 32 Gus Zernial Chicago White Sox	40.00	18.00	4.00

1952 National Tea Labels

The bread labels in this set are often called "Red Borders" because of their distinctive trim. Each label measures 2 3/4" by 2 11/16". Issued with the bakery products of the National Tea Company, there are thought to be 48 different labels in the set. The six missing labels are thought to consist of two Yankees, two Indians, and two Red Sox -- so that there would be exactly three representatives from each of the 16 teams. The labels are also known as the "Bread For Health" set and may have included an album. This set is the toughest of the bread label sets listed. The ACC designation is D290-2.

		MINT	VG-E	F-G
	COMPLETE SET	3500.00	1500.00	300.00
	COMMON PLAYER	80.00	37.00	8.00
☐ 1	Gene Bearden Washington Senators	80.00	37.00	8.00
☐ 2	Yogi Berra New York Yankees	200.00	90.00	20.00
☐ 3	Lou Brissie Philadelphia A's	80.00	37.00	8.00
☐ 4	Sam Chapman Philadelphia A's	80.00	37.00	8.00
☐ 5	Chuck Diering St. Louis Cardinals	80.00	37.00	8.00
☐ 6	Dom DiMaggio Boston Red Sox	100.00	45.00	10.00
☐ 7	Hank Edwards Brooklyn Dodgers	80.00	37.00	8.00
☐ 8	Del Ennis Philadelphia Phillies	80.00	37.00	8.00
☐ 9	Ferris Fain Philadelphia A's	80.00	37.00	8.00
☐ 10	Howie Fox Cincinnati Reds	80.00	37.00	8.00
☐ 11	Sid Gordon Boston Braves	80.00	37.00	8.00
☐ 12	Johnny Groth Detroit Tigers	80.00	37.00	8.00
☐ 13	Granny Hamner Philadelphia Phillies	80.00	37.00	8.00
☐ 14	Sam Jones New York Giants	80.00	37.00	8.00
☐ 15	Howie Judson Chicago White Sox	80.00	37.00	8.00
☐ 16	Sherm Lollar St. Louis Browns	80.00	37.00	8.00
☐ 17	Clarence Marshall St. Louis Browns	80.00	37.00	8.00
☐ 18	Don Mueller New York Giants	80.00	37.00	8.00
☐ 19	Danny Murtaugh Pittsburgh Pirates	80.00	37.00	8.00
☐ 20	Dave Philley Chicago White Sox	80.00	37.00	8.00
☐ 21	Jerry Priddy Detroit Tigers	80.00	37.00	8.00
☐ 22	Bill Rigney New York Giants	80.00	37.00	8.00
☐ 23	Robin Roberts Philadelphia Phillies	125.00	57.00	12.50
☐ 24	Eddie Robinson Chicago White Sox	80.00	37.00	8.00
☐ 25	Preacher Roe Brooklyn Dodgers	100.00	45.00	10.00
☐ 26	Stan Rojek Pittsburgh Pirates	80.00	37.00	8.00
☐ 27	Al Rosen Cleveland Indians	100.00	45.00	10.00
☐ 28	Bob Rush Chicago Cubs	80.00	37.00	8.00
☐ 29	Hank Sauer Chicago Cubs	80.00	37.00	8.00
☐ 30	Johnny Schmitz Chicago Cubs	80.00	37.00	8.00
☐ 31	Enos Slaughter St. Louis Cardinals	125.00	57.00	12.50
☐ 32	Duke Snider Brooklyn Dodgers	250.00	110.00	25.00
☐ 33	Warren Spahn Boston Braves	150.00	70.00	15.00
☐ 34	Gerry Staley St. Louis Cardinals	80.00	37.00	8.00
☐ 35	Virgil Stallcup Cincinnati Reds	80.00	37.00	8.00
☐ 36	George Stirnweiss St. Louis Browns	80.00	37.00	8.00
☐ 37	Earl Torgeson Boston Braves	80.00	37.00	8.00
☐ 38	Dizzy Trout Detroit Tigers	80.00	37.00	8.00
☐ 39	Mickey Vernon Washington Senators	80.00	37.00	8.00
☐ 40	Wally Westlake Pittsburgh Pirates	80.00	37.00	8.00
☐ 41	Johnny Wyrostek Cincinnati Reds	80.00	37.00	8.00
☐ 42	Eddie Yost Washington Senators	80.00	37.00	8.00

1953 Northland Bread

This 32 label set features two players from each major league team and is one of the popular "Bread For Energy" sets. Each bread label measures 2 11/16" by 2 11/16". Although the labels are printed in black and white, the 1953 Northland Bread set includes a "Baseball Stars" album which provides additional information concerning "Baseball Immortals" and "Baseball Tips." The amended catalog designation is D290-3A.

		MINT	VG-E	F-G
	COMPLETE SET	1400.00	600.00	125.00
	COMMON PLAYER (1-32)	40.00	18.00	4.00
☐ 1	Cal Abrams Pittsburgh Pirates	40.00	18.00	4.00
☐ 2	Richie Ashburn Philadelphia Phillies	50.00	22.00	5.00
☐ 3	Gus Bell Cincinnati Redlegs	40.00	18.00	4.00
☐ 4	Jim Busby Washington Nationals	40.00	18.00	4.00
☐ 5	Clint Courtney St. Louis Browns	40.00	18.00	4.00
☐ 6	Billy Cox Brooklyn Dodgers	40.00	18.00	4.00
☐ 7	Jim Dyck St. Louis Browns	40.00	18.00	4.00
☐ 8	Nellie Fox Chicago White Sox	50.00	22.00	5.00
☐ 9	Sid Gordon Milwaukee Braves	40.00	18.00	4.00
☐ 10	Warren Hacker Chicago Cubs	40.00	18.00	4.00
☐ 11	Jim Hearn New York Giants	40.00	18.00	4.00
☐ 12	Fred Hutchinson Detroit Tigers	40.00	18.00	4.00
☐ 13	Monte Irvin New York Giants	60.00	27.00	6.00
☐ 14	Jackie Jensen Washington Nationals	50.00	22.00	5.00
☐ 15	Ted Kluszewski Cincinnati Reds	50.00	22.00	5.00
☐ 16	Bob Lemon Cleveland Indians	60.00	27.00	6.00
☐ 17	Mickey McDermott Boston Red Sox	40.00	18.00	4.00
☐ 18	Minnie Minoso Chicago White Sox	50.00	22.00	5.00
☐ 19	Johnny Mize New York Yankees	60.00	27.00	6.00
☐ 20	Mel Parnell Boston Red Sox	40.00	18.00	4.00
☐ 21	Howie Pollet Pittsburgh Pirates	40.00	18.00	4.00
☐ 22	Jerry Priddy Detroit Tigers	40.00	18.00	4.00
☐ 23	Allie Reynolds New York Yankees	50.00	22.00	5.00
☐ 24	Preacher Roe Brooklyn Dodgers	50.00	22.00	5.00
☐ 25	Al Rosen Cleveland Indians	50.00	22.00	5.00
☐ 26	Connie Ryan	40.00	18.00	4.00

Philadelphia Phillies
☐ 27 Hank Sauer 40.00 18.00 4.00
Chicago Cubs
☐ 28 Red Schoendienst 50.00 22.00 5.00
St. Louis Cardinals
☐ 29 Bobby Shantz 40.00 18.00 4.00
Philadelphia A's
☐ 30 Enos Slaughter 60.00 27.00 6.00
St. Louis Cardinals
☐ 31 Warren Spahn 80.00 37.00 8.00
Milwaukee Braves
☐ 32 Gus Zernial 40.00 18.00 4.00
Philadelphia A's

1952 Tip Top Labels

This set of 48 bread end-labels was issued by Tip Top in 1952. The labels measure 2 3/4" by 2 1/2". An album distributed with the labels names 47 ball players and has one blank slot with advertising. A second pose of Rizzuto -- which appears "cropped" from the first photo -- suggests either a last minute substitution for another player, or simply his popularity in the market area. The ACC designation is D290-1.

		MINT	VG-E	F-G
COMPLETE SET		2800.00	1250.00	250.00
COMMON PLAYER (1-48)		40.00	18.00	4.00
☐ 1	Hank Bauer	50.00	22.00	5.00
	New York Yankees			
☐ 2	Yogi Berra	100.00	45.00	10.00
	New York Yankees			
☐ 3	Ralph Branca	40.00	18.00	4.00
	Brooklyn Dodgers			
☐ 4	Lou Brissie	40.00	18.00	4.00
	Cleveland Indians			
☐ 5	Roy Campanella	125.00	57.00	12.50
	Brooklyn Dodgers			
☐ 6	Phil Cavarretta	40.00	18.00	4.00
	Chicago Cubs			
☐ 7	Murray Dickson	40.00	18.00	4.00
	Pittsburgh Pirates			
☐ 8	Ferris Fain	40.00	18.00	4.00
	Philadelphia A's			
☐ 9	Carl Furillo	50.00	22.00	5.00
	Brooklyn Dodgers			
☐ 10	Ned Garver	40.00	18.00	4.00
	St. Louis Browns			
☐ 11	Sid Gordon	40.00	18.00	4.00
	Boston Braves			
☐ 12	Johnny Groth	40.00	18.00	4.00
	Detroit Tigers			
☐ 13	Granny Hamner	40.00	18.00	4.00
	Philadelphia Phillies			
☐ 14	Jim Hearn	40.00	18.00	4.00
	New York Giants			
☐ 15	Gene Hermanski	40.00	18.00	4.00
	Chicago Cubs			
☐ 16	Gil Hodges	70.00	32.00	7.00
	Brooklyn Dodgers			
☐ 17	Larry Jansen	40.00	18.00	4.00
	New York Giants			
☐ 18	Eddie Joost	40.00	18.00	4.00

	Philadelphia A's			
☐ 19	George Kell	60.00	27.00	6.00
	Detroit Tigers			
☐ 20	Dutch Leonard	40.00	18.00	4.00
	Chicago Cubs			
☐ 21	Whitey Lockman	40.00	18.00	4.00
	New York Giants			
☐ 22	Eddie Lopat	50.00	22.00	5.00
	New York Yankees			
☐ 23	Sal Maglie	50.00	22.00	5.00
	New York Giants			
☐ 24	Mickey Mantle	800.00	360.00	80.00
	New York Yankees			
☐ 25	Gil McDougald	50.00	22.00	5.00
	New York Yankees			
☐ 26	Dale Mitchell	40.00	18.00	4.00
	Cleveland Indians			
☐ 27	Don Mueller	40.00	18.00	4.00
	New York Giants			
☐ 28	Andy Pafko	40.00	18.00	4.00
	Brooklyn Dodgers			
☐ 29	Bob Porterfield	40.00	18.00	4.00
	Washington Senators			
☐ 30	Ken Raffensberger	40.00	18.00	4.00
	Cincinnati Reds			
☐ 31	Allie Reynolds	50.00	22.00	5.00
	New York Yankees			
☐ 32	Phil Rizzuto (large)	60.00	27.00	6.00
	New York Yankees			
☐ 33	Phil Rizzuto (small)	60.00	27.00	6.00
	New York Yankees			
☐ 34	Robin Roberts	60.00	27.00	6.00
	Philadelphia Phillies			
☐ 35	Saul Rogovin	40.00	18.00	4.00
	Chicago White Sox			
☐ 36	Ray Scarborough	40.00	18.00	4.00
	Boston Red Sox			
☐ 37	Red Schoendienst	50.00	22.00	5.00
	St. Louis Cardinals			
☐ 38	Dick Sisler	40.00	18.00	4.00
	Cincinnati Reds			
☐ 39	Enos Slaughter	60.00	27.00	6.00
	St. Louis Cardinals			
☐ 40	Duke Snider	100.00	45.00	10.00
	Brooklyn Dodgers			
☐ 41	Warren Spahn	80.00	37.00	8.00
	Boston Braves			
☐ 42	Vern Stephens	40.00	18.00	4.00
	Boston Red Sox			
☐ 43	Earl Torgeson	40.00	18.00	4.00
	Boston Braves			
☐ 44	Mickey Vernon	40.00	18.00	4.00
	Washington Senators			
☐ 45	Eddie Waitkus	40.00	18.00	4.00
	Philadelphia Phillies			
☐ 46	Wes Westrum	40.00	18.00	4.00
	New York Giants			
☐ 47	Eddie Yost	40.00	18.00	4.00
	Washington Senators			
☐ 48	Al Zarilla	40.00	18.00	4.00
	Chicago White Sox			

1985 Leaf/Donruss Canadian

The cards in this 264 card set measure 2 1/2" by 3 1/2". In an effort to establish a Canadian baseball card market much as Topps' affiliate O-Pee-Chee has done the Donruss Company in conjunction with its new parent Leaf Company issued this set to the Canadian market. The set was later released in the United States through hobby dealer channels. The cards were issued in wax packs. Aside from card number differences the cards are essentially the same as the Donruss U.S. regular issue of the cards of the same players; however the backs are in both French and English. Two cards Dick Perez artwork of Tim Raines and Dave Stieb, are called Canadian Greats (CG) and are not contained in the Donruss U.S. set. As in most Canadian sets, the players featured are heavily biased towards Canadian teams

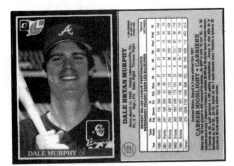

and those American teams who are closest to the Canadian border. The checklist cards (listed at the end of the list below) are numbered one, two and three (but are not given a traditional card number); the Diamond Kings checklist card is unnumbered; and the Lou Gehrig puzzle card is mistakenly numbered 635.

		MINT	VG-E	F-G
COMPLETE SET		18.00	8.50	1.80
COMMON PLAYER		.03	.01	.00

DIAMOND KINGS (1-26)

			MINT	VG-E	F-G
☐	1	Ryne Sandberg DK	.50	.15	.03
☐	2	Doug DeCinces DK	.11	.05	.01
☐	3	Richard Dotson DK	.07	.03	.01
☐	4	Bert Blyleven DK	.11	.05	.01
☐	5	Lou Whitaker DK	.20	.09	.02
☐	6	Dan Quisenberry DK	.20	.09	.02
☐	7	Don Mattingly DK	.80	.40	.08
☐	8	Carney Lansford DK	.11	.05	.01
☐	9	Frank Tanana DK	.07	.03	.01
☐	10	Willie Upshaw DK	.11	.05	.01
☐	11	Claudell Washington DK	.09	.04	.01
☐	12	Mike Marshall DK	.15	.06	.01
☐	13	Joaquin Andujar DK	.08	.03	.01
☐	14	Cal Ripken DK	.45	.20	.04
☐	15	Jim Rice DK	.30	.12	.03
☐	16	Don Sutton DK	.18	.08	.01
☐	17	Frank Viola DK	.10	.04	.01
☐	18	Alvin Davis DK	.30	.12	.03
☐	19	Mario Soto DK	.09	.04	.01
☐	20	Jose Cruz DK	.10	.04	.01
☐	21	Charlie Lea DK	.08	.03	.01
☐	22	Jesse Orosco DK	.08	.03	.01
☐	23	Juan Samuel DK	.20	.09	.02
☐	24	Tony Pena DK	.12	.05	.01
☐	25	Tony Gwynn DK	.35	.15	.03
☐	26	Bob Brenly DK	.08	.03	.01
☐	27	Steve Kiefer RR	.12	.05	.01
☐	28	Joe Morgan	.15	.06	.01
☐	29	Luis Leal	.03	.01	.00
☐	30	Dan Gladden	.20	.09	.02
☐	31	Shane Rawley	.07	.03	.01
☐	32	Mark Clear	.03	.01	.00
☐	33	Terry Kennedy	.07	.03	.01
☐	34	Hal McRae	.05	.02	.00
☐	35	Mickey Rivers	.05	.02	.00
☐	36	Tom Brunansky	.18	.08	.01
☐	37	LaMarr Hoyt	.10	.04	.01
☐	38	Orel Hershiser	1.25	.60	.12
☐	39	Chris Bando	.03	.01	.00
☐	40	Lee Lacy	.05	.02	.00
☐	41	Lance Parrish	.20	.09	.02
☐	42	George Foster	.15	.06	.01
☐	43	Kevin McReynolds	.12	.05	.01
☐	44	Robin Yount	.25	.10	.02
☐	45	Craig McMurtry	.03	.01	.00
☐	46	Mike Witt	.10	.04	.01
☐	47	Gary Redus	.07	.03	.01
☐	48	Dennis Rasmussen	.08	.03	.01
☐	49	Gary Woods	.03	.01	.00
☐	50	Phil Bradley	.80	.40	.08
☐	51	Steve Bedrosian	.05	.02	.00
☐	52	Duane Walker	.03	.01	.00
☐	53	Geoff Zahn	.03	.01	.00
☐	54	Dave Stieb	.20	.09	.02
☐	55	Pascual Perez	.05	.02	.00
☐	56	Mark Langston	.25	.10	.02

			MINT	VG-E	F-G
☐	57	Bob Dernier	.05	.02	.00
☐	58	Joe Cowley	.03	.01	.00
☐	59	Dan Schatzeder	.03	.01	.00
☐	60	Ozzie Smith	.12	.05	.01
☐	61	Bob Knepper	.08	.03	.01
☐	62	Keith Hernandez	.25	.10	.02
☐	63	Rick Rhoden	.06	.02	.00
☐	64	Alejandro Pena	.06	.02	.00
☐	65	Damaso Garcia	.09	.04	.01
☐	66	Chili Davis	.12	.05	.01
☐	67	Al Oliver	.10	.04	.01
☐	68	Alan Wiggins	.10	.04	.01
☐	69	Darryl Motley	.05	.02	.00
☐	70	Gary Ward	.05	.02	.00
☐	71	John Butcher	.03	.01	.00
☐	72	Scott McGregor	.06	.02	.00
☐	73	Bruce Hurst	.05	.02	.00
☐	74	Dwayne Murphy	.06	.02	.00
☐	75	Greg Luzinski	.09	.04	.01
☐	76	Pat Tabler	.05	.02	.00
☐	77	Chet Lemon	.05	.02	.00
☐	78	Jim Sundberg	.05	.02	.00
☐	79	Wally Backman	.07	.03	.01
☐	80	Terry Puhl	.05	.02	.00
☐	81	Storm Davis	.08	.03	.01
☐	82	Jim Wohlford	.03	.01	.00
☐	83	Willie Randolph	.06	.02	.00
☐	84	Ron Cey	.10	.04	.01
☐	85	Jim Beattie	.03	.01	.00
☐	86	Rafael Ramirez	.03	.01	.00
☐	87	Cesar Cedeno	.06	.02	.00
☐	88	Bobby Grich	.07	.03	.01
☐	89	Jason Thompson	.05	.02	.00
☐	90	Steve Sax	.12	.05	.01
☐	91	Tony Fernandez	.12	.05	.01
☐	92	Jeff Leonard	.10	.04	.01
☐	93	Von Hayes	.11	.05	.01
☐	94	Steve Garvey	.35	.15	.03
☐	95	Steve Balboni	.06	.02	.00
☐	96	Larry Parrish	.06	.02	.00
☐	97	Tim Teufel	.10	.04	.01
☐	98	Sammy Stewart	.03	.01	.00
☐	99	Roger Clemens	2.50	1.15	.25
☐	100	Steve Kemp	.08	.03	.01
☐	101	Tom Seaver	.50	.22	.05
☐	102	Andre Thornton	.08	.03	.01
☐	103	Kirk Gibson	.25	.10	.02
☐	104	Ted Simmons	.10	.04	.01
☐	105	David Palmer	.05	.02	.00
☐	106	Roy Lee Jackson	.03	.01	.00
☐	107	Kirby Puckett	1.25	.60	.12
☐	108	Charlie Hough	.05	.02	.00
☐	109	Mike Boddicker	.09	.04	.01
☐	110	Willie Wilson	.15	.06	.01
☐	111	Tim Lollar	.03	.01	.00
☐	112	Tony Armas	.10	.04	.01
☐	113	Steve Carlton	.25	.10	.02
☐	114	Gary Lavelle	.03	.01	.00
☐	115	Cliff Johnson	.03	.01	.00
☐	116	Ray Burris	.03	.01	.00
☐	117	Rudy Law	.03	.01	.00
☐	118	Mike Scioscia	.03	.01	.00
☐	119	Kent Tekulve	.05	.02	.00
☐	120	George Vukovich	.03	.01	.00
☐	121	Barbaro Garbey	.05	.02	.00
☐	122	Mookie Wilson	.06	.02	.00
☐	123	Ben Oglivie	.06	.02	.00
☐	124	Jerry Mumphrey	.03	.01	.00
☐	125	Willie McGee	.25	.10	.02
☐	126	Jeff Reardon	.08	.03	.01
☐	127	Dave Winfield	.30	.12	.03
☐	128	Lee Smith	.08	.03	.01
☐	129	Ken Phelps	.09	.04	.01
☐	130	Rick Camp	.03	.01	.00
☐	131	Dave Concepcion	.08	.03	.01
☐	132	Rod Carew	.30	.12	.03
☐	133	Andre Dawson	.20	.09	.02
☐	134	Doyle Alexander	.06	.02	.00
☐	135	Miguel Dilone	.03	.01	.00
☐	136	Jim Gott	.03	.01	.00
☐	137	Eric Show	.05	.02	.00
☐	138	Phil Niekro	.15	.06	.01
☐	139	Rick Sutcliffe	.12	.05	.01
☐	140	Winfield/Mattingly Two For The Title	.80	.40	.08
☐	141	Ken Oberkfell	.03	.01	.00
☐	142	Jack Morris	.16	.07	.01
☐	143	Lloyd Moseby	.12	.05	.01
☐	144	Pete Rose	.90	.40	.09
☐	145	Gary Gaetti	.07	.03	.01
☐	146	Don Baylor	.12	.05	.01
☐	147	Bobby Meacham	.05	.02	.00
☐	148	Frank White	.07	.03	.01

☐ 149	Mark Thurmond	.05	.02	.00
☐ 150	Dwight Evans	.11	.05	.01
☐ 151	Al Holland	.05	.02	.00
☐ 152	Joel Youngblood	.03	.01	.00
☐ 153	Rance Mulliniks	.03	.01	.00
☐ 154	Bill Caudill	.05	.02	.00
☐ 155	Carlton Fisk	.15	.06	.01
☐ 156	Rick Honeycutt	.05	.02	.00
☐ 157	John Candelaria	.06	.02	.00
☐ 158	Alan Trammell	.15	.06	.01
☐ 159	Darryl Strawberry	.60	.28	.06
☐ 160	Aurelio Lopez	.03	.01	.00
☐ 161	Enos Cabell	.03	.01	.00
☐ 162	Dion James	.05	.02	.00
☐ 163	Bruce Sutter	.15	.06	.01
☐ 164	Razor Shines	.10	.04	.01
☐ 165	Butch Wynegar	.05	.02	.00
☐ 166	Rich Bordi	.03	.01	.00
☐ 167	Spike Owen	.07	.03	.01
☐ 168	Chris Chambliss	.05	.02	.00
☐ 169	Dave Parker	.16	.07	.01
☐ 170	Reggie Jackson	.40	.18	.04
☐ 171	Bryn Smith	.06	.02	.00
☐ 172	Dave Collins	.06	.02	.00
☐ 173	Dave Engle	.05	.02	.00
☐ 174	Buddy Bell	.10	.04	.01
☐ 175	Mike Flanagan	.07	.03	.01
☐ 176	George Brett	.45	.20	.04
☐ 177	Graig Nettles	.12	.05	.01
☐ 178	Jerry Koosman	.07	.03	.01
☐ 179	Wade Boggs	.75	.35	.07
☐ 180	Jody Davis	.10	.04	.01
☐ 181	Ernie Whitt	.03	.01	.00
☐ 182	Dave Kingman	.09	.04	.01
☐ 183	Vance Law	.03	.01	.00
☐ 184	Fernando Valenzuela	.25	.10	.02
☐ 185	Bill Madlock	.10	.04	.01
☐ 186	Brett Butler	.10	.04	.01
☐ 187	Doug Sisk	.05	.02	.00
☐ 188	Dan Petry	.12	.05	.01
☐ 189	Joe Niekro	.08	.03	.01
☐ 190	Rollie Fingers	.15	.06	.01
☐ 191	David Green	.05	.02	.00
☐ 192	Steve Rogers	.07	.03	.01
☐ 193	Ken Griffey	.06	.02	.00
☐ 194	Scott Sanderson	.03	.01	.00
☐ 195	Barry Bonnell	.03	.01	.00
☐ 196	Bruce Benedict	.03	.01	.00
☐ 197	Keith Moreland	.05	.02	.00
☐ 198	Fred Lynn	.15	.06	.01
☐ 199	Tim Wallach	.11	.05	.01
☐ 200	Kent Hrbek	.25	.10	.02
☐ 201	Pete O'Brien	.12	.05	.01
☐ 202	Bud Black	.05	.02	.00
☐ 203	Eddie Murray	.40	.18	.04
☐ 204	Goose Gossage	.15	.06	.01
☐ 205	Mike Schmidt	.35	.15	.03
☐ 206	Mike Easler	.05	.02	.00
☐ 207	Jack Clark	.12	.05	.01
☐ 208	Rickey Henderson	.40	.18	.04
☐ 209	Jesse Barfield	.15	.06	.01
☐ 210	Ron Kittle	.12	.05	.01
☐ 211	Pedro Guerrero	.20	.09	.02
☐ 212	Johnny Ray	.10	.04	.01
☐ 213	Julio Franco	.10	.04	.01
☐ 214	Hubie Brooks	.12	.05	.01
☐ 215	Darrell Evans	.10	.04	.01
☐ 216	Nolan Ryan	.30	.12	.03
☐ 217	Jim Gantner	.05	.02	.00
☐ 218	Tim Raines	.30	.12	.03
☐ 219	Dave Righetti	.12	.05	.01
☐ 220	Gary Matthews	.07	.03	.01
☐ 221	Jack Perconte	.03	.01	.00
☐ 222	Dale Murphy	.45	.20	.04
☐ 223	Brian Downing	.03	.01	.00
☐ 224	Mickey Hatcher	.03	.01	.00
☐ 225	Lonnie Smith	.06	.02	.00
☐ 226	Jorge Orta	.03	.01	.00
☐ 227	Milt Wilcox	.03	.01	.00
☐ 228	John Denny	.06	.02	.00
☐ 229	Marty Barrett	.07	.03	.01
☐ 230	Alfredo Griffin	.05	.02	.00
☐ 231	Harold Baines	.16	.07	.01
☐ 232	Bill Russell	.05	.02	.00
☐ 233	Marvel Wynne	.05	.02	.00
☐ 234	Dwight Gooden	7.00	3.25	.70
☐ 235	Willie Hernandez	.12	.05	.01
☐ 236	Bill Gullickson	.05	.02	.00
☐ 237	Ron Guidry	.15	.06	.01
☐ 238	Leon Durham	.12	.05	.01
☐ 239	Al Cowens	.05	.02	.00
☐ 240	Bob Horner	.16	.07	.01
☐ 241	Gary Carter	.30	.12	.03

☐ 242	Glenn Hubbard	.03	.01	.00
☐ 243	Steve Trout	.03	.01	.00
☐ 244	Jay Howell	.05	.02	.00
☐ 245	Terry Francona	.06	.02	.00
☐ 246	Cecil Cooper	.12	.05	.01
☐ 247	Larry McWilliams	.05	.02	.00
☐ 248	George Bell	.15	.06	.01
☐ 249	Larry Herndon	.03	.01	.00
☐ 250	Ozzie Virgil	.05	.02	.00
CANADIAN GREATS (251-252)				
☐ 251	Dave Stieb CG	.40	.18	.04
☐ 252	Tim Raines CG	.40	.18	.04
☐ 253	Ricky Horton	.09	.04	.01
☐ 254	Bill Buckner	.08	.03	.01
☐ 255	Dan Driessen	.05	.02	.00
☐ 256	Ron Darling	.35	.15	.03
☐ 257	Doug Flynn	.03	.01	.00
☐ 258	Darrell Porter	.05	.02	.00
☐ 259	George Hendrick	.06	.02	.00
UNNUMBERED CHECKLISTS				
☐ 260	CL: DK (unnumbered)	.08	.01	.00
☐ 261	CL: 1 (unnumbered)	.07	.01	.00
☐ 262	CL: 2 (unnumbered)	.07	.01	.00
☐ 263	CL: 3 (unnumbered)	.07	.01	.00
☐ 635	Lou Gehrig Puzzle Card	.09	.04	.01

1986 Leaf/Donruss Canadian

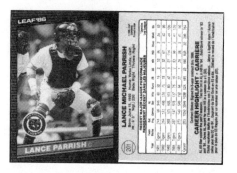

The cards in this 264 card set measure 2 1/2" by 3 1/2". Aside from card number differences the cards are essentially the same as the Donruss U.S. regular issue of the cards of the same players; however the backs are in both French and English. Two cards, Dick Perez artwork of Jesse Barfield and Jeff Reardonb, are called Canadian Greats (CG) and are not contained in the Donruss U.S. set. As in most Canadian sets, the players featured are heavily biased toward Canadian teams and those American teams closest to the Canadian border. The checklist cards (listed at the end of the list below) are numbered one, two and three (but are not given a traditional card number); the Diamond Kings checklist card is unnumbered.

	MINT	VG-E	F-G
COMPLETE SET	12.50	5.75	1.25
COMMON PLAYER	.03	.01	.00

DIAMOND KINGS (1-26)

☐ 1	Kirk Gibson DK	.25	.07	.01
☐ 2	Goose Gossage DK	.15	.06	.01
☐ 3	Willie McGee DK	.15	.06	.01
☐ 4	George Bell DK	.10	.04	.01
☐ 5	Tony Armas DK	.09	.04	.01
☐ 6	Chili Davis DK	.09	.04	.01
☐ 7	Cecil Cooper DK	.09	.04	.01
☐ 8	Mike Boddicker DK	.09	.04	.01
☐ 9	Davey Lopes DK	.08	.03	.01
☐ 10	Bill Doran DK	.08	.03	.01
☐ 11	Bret Saberhagen DK	.25	.10	.02
☐ 12	Brett Butler DK	.09	.04	.01

☐ 13	Harold Baines DK	.12	.05	.01
☐ 14	Mike Davis DK	.08	.03	.01
☐ 15	Tony Perez DK	.10	.04	.01
☐ 16	Willie Randolph DK	.08	.03	.01
☐ 17	Bob Boone DK	.08	.03	.01
☐ 18	Orel Hershiser DK	.20	.09	.02
☐ 19	Johnny Ray DK	.09	.04	.01
☐ 20	Gary Ward DK	.08	.03	.01
☐ 21	Rick Mahler DK	.08	.03	.01
☐ 22	Phil Bradley DK	.15	.06	.01
☐ 23	Jerry Koosman DK	.08	.03	.01
☐ 24	Tom Brunansky DK	.10	.04	.01
☐ 25	Andre Dawson DK	.15	.06	.01
☐ 26	Dwight Gooden DK	.75	.35	.07
☐ 27	Andres Galarraga RR	.35	.15	.03
☐ 28	Fred McGriff RR	.10	.04	.01
☐ 29	Dave Shipanoff RR	.10	.04	.01
☐ 30	Danny Jackson	.07	.03	.01
☐ 31	Robin Yount	.25	.10	.02
☐ 32	Mike Fitzgerald	.05	.02	.00
☐ 33	Lou Whitaker	.15	.06	.01
☐ 34	Alfredo Griffin	.06	.02	.00
☐ 35	"Oil Can" Boyd	.08	.03	.01
☐ 36	Ron Guidry	.15	.06	.01
☐ 37	Rickey Henderson	.30	.12	.03
☐ 38	Jack Morris	.15	.06	.01
☐ 39	Brian Downing	.03	.01	.00
☐ 40	Mike Marshall	.12	.05	.01
☐ 41	Tony Gwynn	.20	.09	.02
☐ 42	George Brett	.30	.12	.03
☐ 43	Jim Gantner	.05	.02	.00
☐ 44	Hubie Brooks	.12	.05	.01
☐ 45	Tony Fernandez	.12	.05	.01
☐ 46	Oddibe McDowell	.20	.09	.02
☐ 47	Ozzie Smith	.10	.04	.01
☐ 48	Ken Griffey	.07	.03	.01
☐ 49	Jose Cruz	.07	.03	.01
☐ 50	Mariano Duncan	.25	.10	.02
☐ 51	Mike Schmidt	.30	.12	.03
☐ 52	Pat Tabler	.05	.02	.00
☐ 53	Pete Rose	.50	.22	.05
☐ 54	Frank White	.06	.02	.00
☐ 55	Carney Lansford	.07	.03	.01
☐ 56	Steve Garvey	.30	.12	.03
☐ 57	Vance Law	.03	.01	.00
☐ 58	Tony Pena	.09	.04	.01
☐ 59	Wayne Tolleson	.03	.01	.00
☐ 60	Dale Murphy	.40	.18	.04
☐ 61	LaMarr Hoyt	.08	.03	.01
☐ 62	Ryne Sandberg	.25	.10	.02
☐ 63	Gary Carter	.25	.10	.02
☐ 64	Lee Smith	.06	.02	.00
☐ 65	Alvin Davis	.12	.05	.01
☐ 66	Edwin Nunez	.06	.02	.00
☐ 67	Kent Hrbek	.15	.06	.01
☐ 68	Dave Stieb	.15	.06	.01
☐ 69	Kirby Puckett	.25	.10	.02
☐ 70	Paul Molitor	.10	.04	.01
☐ 71	Glenn Hubbard	.03	.01	.00
☐ 72	Lloyd Moseby	.10	.04	.01
☐ 73	Mike Smithson	.03	.01	.00
☐ 74	Jeff Leonard	.06	.02	.00
☐ 75	Danny Darwin	.03	.01	.00
☐ 76	Kevin McReynolds	.07	.03	.01
☐ 77	Bill Buckner	.08	.03	.01
☐ 78	Ron Oester	.05	.02	.00
☐ 79	Tommy Herr	.08	.03	.01
☐ 80	Mike Pagliarulo	.25	.10	.02
☐ 81	Ron Romanick	.05	.02	.00
☐ 82	Brook Jacoby	.09	.04	.01
☐ 83	Eddie Murray	.30	.12	.03
☐ 84	Gary Pettis	.06	.02	.00
☐ 85	Chet Lemon	.05	.02	.00
☐ 86	Toby Harrah	.05	.02	.00
☐ 87	Mike Scioscia	.05	.02	.00
☐ 88	Bert Blyleven	.09	.04	.01
☐ 89	Dave Righetti	.12	.05	.01
☐ 90	Bob Knepper	.08	.03	.01
☐ 91	Fernando Valenzuela	.20	.09	.02
☐ 92	Dave Dravecky	.06	.02	.00
☐ 93	Julio Franco	.09	.04	.01
☐ 94	Keith Moreland	.05	.02	.00
☐ 95	Darryl Motley	.03	.01	.00
☐ 96	Jack Clark	.12	.05	.01
☐ 97	Tim Wallach	.09	.04	.01
☐ 98	Steve Balboni	.06	.02	.00
☐ 99	Storm Davis	.05	.02	.00
☐ 100	Jay Howell	.05	.02	.00
☐ 101	Alan Trammell	.16	.07	.01
☐ 102	Willie Hernandez	.12	.05	.01
☐ 103	Don Mattingly	.60	.28	.06
☐ 104	Lee Lacy	.05	.02	.00
☐ 105	Pedro Guerrero	.20	.09	.02
☐ 106	Willie Wilson	.12	.05	.01
☐ 107	Craig Reynolds	.03	.01	.00
☐ 108	Tim Raines	.20	.09	.02
☐ 109	Shane Rawley	.06	.02	.00
☐ 110	Larry Parrish	.06	.02	.00
☐ 111	Eric Show	.05	.02	.00
☐ 112	Mike Witt	.10	.04	.01
☐ 113	Dennis Eckersley	.05	.02	.00
☐ 114	Mike Moore	.05	.02	.00
☐ 115	Vince Coleman	1.00	.45	.10
☐ 116	Damaso Garcia	.07	.03	.01
☐ 117	Steve Carlton	.25	.10	.02
☐ 118	Floyd Bannister	.05	.02	.00
☐ 119	Mario Soto	.06	.02	.00
☐ 120	Fred Lynn	.15	.06	.01
☐ 121	Bob Horner	.15	.06	.01
☐ 122	Rick Sutcliffe	.12	.05	.01
☐ 123	Walt Terrell	.06	.02	.00
☐ 124	Keith Hernandez	.20	.09	.02
☐ 125	Dave Winfield	.25	.10	.02
☐ 126	Frank Viola	.06	.02	.00
☐ 127	Dwight Evans	.09	.04	.01
☐ 128	Willie Upshaw	.07	.03	.01
☐ 129	Andre Thornton	.07	.03	.01
☐ 130	Donnie Moore	.05	.02	.00
☐ 131	Darryl Strawberry	.35	.15	.03
☐ 132	Nolan Ryan	.25	.10	.02
☐ 133	Garry Templeton	.05	.02	.00
☐ 134	John Tudor	.08	.03	.01
☐ 135	Dave Parker	.15	.06	.01
☐ 136	Larry McWilliams	.03	.01	.00
☐ 137	Terry Pendleton	.07	.03	.01
☐ 138	Terry Puhl	.05	.02	.00
☐ 139	Bob Dernier	.05	.02	.00
☐ 140	Ozzie Guillen	.25	.10	.02
☐ 141	Jim Clancy	.05	.02	.00
☐ 142	Cal Ripken Jr.	.35	.15	.03
☐ 143	Mickey Hatcher	.03	.01	.00
☐ 144	Dan Petry	.10	.04	.01
☐ 145	Rich Gedman	.08	.03	.01
☐ 146	Jim Rice	.20	.09	.02
☐ 147	Butch Wynegar	.05	.02	.00
☐ 148	Donnie Hill	.03	.01	.00
☐ 149	Jim Sundberg	.05	.02	.00
☐ 150	Joe Hesketh	.05	.02	.00
☐ 151	Chris Codiroli	.03	.01	.00
☐ 152	Charlie Hough	.05	.02	.00
☐ 153	Herman Winningham	.05	.02	.00
☐ 154	Dave Rozema	.03	.01	.00
☐ 155	Don Slaught	.05	.02	.00
☐ 156	Juan Beniquez	.05	.02	.00
☐ 157	Ted Higuera	.50	.22	.05
☐ 158	Andy Hawkins	.05	.02	.00
☐ 159	Don Robinson	.05	.02	.00
☐ 160	Glenn Wilson	.08	.03	.01
☐ 161	Ernie Riles	.20	.09	.02
☐ 162	Nick Esasky	.15	.06	.01
☐ 163	Carlton Fisk	.15	.06	.01
☐ 164	Claudell Washington	.06	.02	.00
☐ 165	Scott McGregor	.06	.02	.00
☐ 166	Nate Snell	.10	.04	.01
☐ 167	Ted Simmons	.09	.04	.01
☐ 168	Wade Boggs	.60	.28	.06
☐ 169	Marty Barrett	.06	.02	.00
☐ 170	Bud Black	.05	.02	.00
☐ 171	Charlie Leibrandt	.07	.03	.01
☐ 172	Charlie Lea	.05	.02	.00
☐ 173	Reggie Jackson	.30	.12	.03
☐ 174	Bryn Smith	.05	.02	.00
☐ 175	Glenn Davis	.35	.15	.03
☐ 176	Von Hayes	.09	.04	.01
☐ 177	Danny Cox	.05	.02	.00
☐ 178	Sammy Khalifa	.09	.04	.01
☐ 179	Tom Browning	.12	.05	.01
☐ 180	Scott Garrelts	.07	.03	.01
☐ 181	Shawon Dunston	.08	.03	.01
☐ 182	Doyle Alexander	.05	.02	.00
☐ 183	Jim Presley	.20	.09	.02
☐ 184	Al Cowens	.05	.02	.00
☐ 185	Mark Salas	.15	.06	.01
☐ 186	Tom Niedenfuer	.06	.02	.00
☐ 187	Dave Henderson	.05	.02	.00
☐ 188	Lonnie Smith	.05	.02	.00
☐ 189	Bruce Bochte	.03	.01	.00
☐ 190	Leon Durham	.09	.04	.01
☐ 191	Terry Francona	.05	.02	.00
☐ 192	Bruce Sutter	.12	.05	.01
☐ 193	Steve Crawford	.03	.01	.00
☐ 194	Bob Brenly	.05	.02	.00
☐ 195	Dan Pasqua	.25	.10	.02
☐ 196	Juan Samuel	.12	.05	.01
☐ 197	Floyd Rayford	.03	.01	.00
☐ 198	Tim Burke	.20	.09	.02

☐ 199	Ben Oglivie	.06	.02	.00
☐ 200	Don Carman	.20	.09	.02
☐ 201	Lance Parrish	.16	.07	.01
☐ 202	Terry Forster	.06	.02	.00
☐ 203	Neal Heaton	.03	.01	.00
☐ 204	Ivan Calderon	.20	.09	.02
☐ 205	Jorge Orta	.03	.01	.00
☐ 206	Tom Henke	.06	.02	.00
☐ 207	Rick Reuschel	.05	.02	.00
☐ 208	Dan Quisenberry	.12	.05	.01
☐ 209	Pete (Rose) Does It	.25	.10	.02
☐ 210	Floyd Youmans	.50	.22	.05
☐ 211	Tom Filer	.05	.02	.00
☐ 212	R.J. Reynolds	.06	.02	.00
☐ 213	Gorman Thomas	.09	.04	.01
☐ 214	Jeff Reardon	.08	.03	.01
☐ 215	Chris Brown	.75	.35	.07
☐ 216	Rick Aguilera	.15	.06	.01
☐ 217	Ernie Whitt	.03	.01	.00
☐ 218	Joe Orsulak	.15	.06	.01
☐ 219	Jimmy Key	.08	.03	.01
☐ 220	Atlee Hammaker	.03	.01	.00
☐ 221	Ron Darling	.20	.09	.02
☐ 222	Zane Smith	.15	.06	.01
☐ 223	Bob Welch	.05	.02	.00
☐ 224	Reid Nichols	.03	.01	.00
☐ 225	Fleet Feet	.20	.09	.02
	Vince Coleman			
	Willie McGee			
☐ 226	Mark Gubicza	.15	.06	.01
☐ 227	Tim Birtsas	.15	.06	.01
☐ 228	Mike Hargrove	.05	.02	.00
☐ 229	Randy St. Claire	.03	.01	.00
☐ 230	Larry Herndon	.03	.01	.00
☐ 231	Dusty Baker	.06	.02	.00
☐ 232	Mookie Wilson	.05	.02	.00
☐ 233	Jeff Lahti	.03	.01	.00
☐ 234	Tom Seaver	.20	.09	.02
☐ 235	Mike Scott	.08	.03	.01
☐ 236	Don Sutton	.15	.06	.01
☐ 237	Roy Smalley	.05	.02	.00
☐ 238	Bill Madlock	.09	.04	.01
☐ 239	Charlie Hudson	.03	.01	.00
☐ 240	John Franco	.06	.02	.00
☐ 241	Frank Tanana	.05	.02	.00
☐ 242	Sid Fernandez	.20	.09	.02
☐ 243	Knuckle Bros.	.10	.04	.01
	Phil Niekro			
	Joe Niekro			
☐ 244	Dennis Lamp	.03	.01	.00
☐ 245	Gene Nelson	.03	.01	.00
☐ 246	Terry Harper	.03	.01	.00
☐ 247	Vida Blue	.08	.03	.01
☐ 248	Roger McDowell	.35	.15	.03
☐ 249	Tony Bernazard	.05	.02	.00
☐ 250	Cliff Johnson	.03	.01	.00
☐ 251	Hal McRae	.06	.02	.00
☐ 252	Garth Iorg	.03	.01	.00
☐ 253	Mitch Webster	.35	.15	.03
☐ 254	Jesse Barfield	.25	.10	.02
☐ 255	Dan Driessen	.05	.02	.00
☐ 256	Mike Brown	.03	.01	.00
☐ 257	Ron Kittle	.09	.04	.01
☐ 258	Bo Diaz	.03	.01	.00
☐ 259	Aaron Puzzle Card	.08	.03	.01
☐ 260	King Of Kings	.60	.28	.06
	Pete Rose			
	UNNUMBERED CHECKLISTS			
☐ 261	CL: DK (unnumbered)	.08	.01	.00
☐ 262	CL: 1 (unnumbered)	.07	.01	.00
☐ 263	CL: 2 (unnumbered)	.07	.01	.00
☐ 264	CL: 3 (unnumbered)	.07	.01	.00

1965 O-Pee-Chee

The cards in this 283 card set measure 2 1/2" by 3 1/2". The cards comprising the 1965 O-Pee-Chee set have team names located within a distinctive pennant design below the picture. The cards have blue borders on the reverse, but on a gray card stock. These cards are very similar to the 1965 Topps regular set except that they say "Printed in Canada" on the bottom of the reverse. Remember

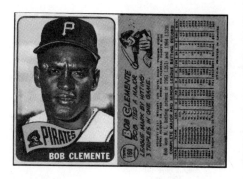

BOB CLEMENTE

the prices below apply only to the O-Pee-Chee cards -- NOT to the 1965 Topps cards which are much more plentiful.

		MINT	VG-E	F-G
COMPLETE SET (283)		625.00	300.00	60.00
COMMON PLAYER (1-283)		1.50	.70	.15
☐ 1	AL Batting Leaders	3.00	1.00	.20
	Tony Oliva			
	Elston Howard			
	Brooks Robinson			
☐ 2	NL Batting Leaders	2.50	1.15	.25
	Bob Clemente			
	Hank Aaron			
	Rico Carty			
☐ 3	AL Home Run Leaders	2.50	1.15	.25
	Harmon Killebrew			
	Mickey Mantle			
	Boog Powell			
☐ 4	NL Home Run Leaders	2.50	1.15	.25
	Willie Mays			
	Billy Williams			
	Jim Ray Hart			
	Orlando Cepeda			
	Johnny Callison			
☐ 5	AL RBI Leaders	2.50	1.15	.25
	Brooks Robinson			
	Harmon Killebrew			
	Mickey Mantle			
	Dick Stuart			
☐ 6	NL RBI Leaders	2.00	.90	.20
	Ken Boyer			
	Willie Mays			
	Ron Santo			
☐ 7	AL ERA Leaders	1.75	.85	.17
	Dean Chance			
	Joel Horlen			
☐ 8	NL ERA Leaders	2.50	1.15	.25
	Sandy Koufax			
	Don Drysdale			
☐ 9	AL Pitching Leaders	1.75	.85	.17
	Dean Chance			
	Gary Peters			
	Dave Wickersham			
	Juan Pizarro			
	Wally Bunker			
☐ 10	NL Pitching Leaders	1.75	.85	.17
	Larry Jackson			
	Ray Sadecki			
	Juan Marichal			
☐ 11	AL Strikeout Leaders	1.75	.85	.17
	Al Downing			
	Dean Chance			
	Camilo Pascual			
☐ 12	NL Strikeout Leaders	2.00	.90	.20
	Bob Veale			
	Don Drysdale			
	Bob Gibson			
☐ 13	Pedro Ramos	1.50	.70	.15
☐ 14	Len Gabrielson	1.50	.70	.15
☐ 15	Robin Roberts	4.00	1.85	.40
☐ 16	Houston Rookies:	15.00	7.00	1.50
	Joe Morgan			
	Sonny Jackson			
☐ 17	John Romano	1.50	.70	.15
☐ 18	Bill McCool	1.50	.70	.15
☐ 19	Gates Brown	1.50	.70	.15
☐ 20	Jim Bunning	3.00	1.40	.30
☐ 21	Don Blasingame	1.50	.70	.15

☐	22	Charlie Smith	1.50	.70	.15
☐	23	Bob Tiefenauer	1.50	.70	.15
☐	24	Twins Team	1.75	.85	.17
☐	25	Al McBean	1.50	.70	.15
☐	26	Bob Knoop	1.50	.70	.15
☐	27	Dick Bertell	1.50	.70	.15
☐	28	Barney Schultz	1.50	.70	.15
☐	29	Felix Mantilla	1.50	.70	.15
☐	30	Jim Bouton	2.00	.90	.20
☐	31	Mike White	1.50	.70	.15
☐	32	Herman Franks MGR	1.50	.70	.15
☐	33	Jackie Brandt	1.50	.70	.15
☐	34	Cal Koonce	1.50	.70	.15
☐	35	Ed Charles	1.50	.70	.15
☐	36	Bob Wine	1.50	.70	.15
☐	37	Fred Gladding	1.50	.70	.15
☐	38	Jim King	1.50	.70	.15
☐	39	Gerry Arrigo	1.50	.70	.15
☐	40	Frank Howard	2.00	.90	.20
☐	41	White Sox Rookies: Bruce Howard Marv Staehle	1.50	.70	.15
☐	42	Earl Wilson	1.50	.70	.15
☐	43	Mike Shannon	1.75	.85	.17
☐	44	Wade Blasingame	1.50	.70	.15
☐	45	Roy McMillan	1.50	.70	.15
☐	46	Bob Lee	1.50	.70	.15
☐	47	Tom Harper	1.50	.70	.15
☐	48	Claude Raymond	1.50	.70	.15
☐	49	Orioles Rookies: Curt Blefary John Miller	2.00	.90	.20
☐	50	Juan Marichal	4.00	1.85	.40
☐	51	Bill Bryan	1.50	.70	.15
☐	52	Ed Roebuck	1.50	.70	.15
☐	53	Dick McAuliffe	1.50	.70	.15
☐	54	Joe Gibbon	1.50	.70	.15
☐	55	Tony Conigliaro	2.00	.90	.20
☐	56	Ron Kline	1.50	.70	.15
☐	57	Cardinals Team	1.75	.85	.17
☐	58	Fred Talbot	1.50	.70	.15
☐	59	Nate Oliver	1.50	.70	.15
☐	60	Jim O'Toole	1.50	.70	.15
☐	61	Chris Cannizzaro	1.50	.70	.15
☐	62	Jim Katt (sic, Kaat)	3.00	1.40	.30
☐	63	Ty Cline	1.50	.70	.15
☐	64	Lou Burdette	1.75	.85	.17
☐	65	Tony Kubek	2.00	.90	.20
☐	66	Bill Rigney MGR	1.50	.70	.15
☐	67	Harvey Haddix	1.50	.70	.15
☐	68	Del Crandall	1.50	.70	.15
☐	69	Bill Virdon	1.75	.85	.17
☐	70	Bill Skowron	1.75	.85	.17
☐	71	John O'Donoghue	1.50	.70	.15
☐	72	Tony Gonzalez	1.50	.70	.15
☐	73	Dennis Ribant	1.50	.70	.15
☐	74	Red Sox Rookies: Rico Petrocelli Jerry Stephenson	2.00	.90	.20
☐	75	Deron Johnson	1.50	.70	.15
☐	76	Sam McDowell	1.75	.85	.17
☐	77	Doug Camilli	1.50	.70	.15
☐	78	Dal Maxvill	1.50	.70	.15
☐	79	1st Series Checklist	2.50	.40	.05
☐	80	Turk Farrell	1.50	.70	.15
☐	81	Don Buford	1.50	.70	.15
☐	82	Braves Rookies: Santos Alomar John Braun	1.50	.70	.15
☐	83	George Thomas	1.50	.70	.15
☐	84	Ron Herbel	1.50	.70	.15
☐	85	Willie Smith	1.50	.70	.15
☐	86	Les Narum	1.50	.70	.15
☐	87	Nelson Mathews	1.50	.70	.15
☐	88	Jack Lamabe	1.50	.70	.15
☐	89	Mike Hershberger	1.50	.70	.15
☐	90	Rich Rollins	1.50	.70	.15
☐	91	Cubs Team	1.75	.85	.17
☐	92	Dick Howser	2.00	.90	.20
☐	93	Jack Fisher	1.50	.70	.15
☐	94	Charlie Lau	1.50	.70	.15
☐	95	Bill Mazeroski	2.00	.90	.20
☐	96	Sonny Siebert	1.50	.70	.15
☐	97	Pedro Gonzalez	1.50	.70	.15
☐	98	Bob Miller	1.50	.70	.15
☐	99	Gil Hodges	3.50	1.65	.35
☐	100	Ken Boyer	2.00	.90	.20
☐	101	Fred Newman	1.50	.70	.15
☐	102	Steve Boros	1.50	.70	.15
☐	103	Harvey Kuenn	1.75	.85	.17
☐	104	2nd Series Checklist	2.50	.40	.05
☐	105	Chico Salmon	1.50	.70	.15
☐	106	Gene Oliver	1.50	.70	.15
☐	107	Phillies Rookies: Pat Corrales Costen Shockley	2.00	.90	.20
☐	108	Don Mincher	1.50	.70	.15
☐	109	Walt Bond	1.50	.70	.15
☐	110	Ron Santo	1.75	.85	.17
☐	111	Lee Thomas	1.50	.70	.15
☐	112	Derrell Griffith	1.50	.70	.15
☐	113	Steve Barber	1.50	.70	.15
☐	114	Jim Hickman	1.50	.70	.15
☐	115	Bob Richardson	2.00	.90	.20
☐	116	Cardinals Rookies: Dave Dowling Bob Tolan	1.75	.85	.17
☐	117	Wes Stock	1.50	.70	.15
☐	118	Hal Lanier	2.00	.90	.20
☐	119	John Kennedy	1.50	.70	.15
☐	120	Frank Robinson	6.50	3.00	.60
☐	121	Gene Alley	1.50	.70	.15
☐	122	Bill Pleis	1.50	.70	.15
☐	123	Frank Thomas	1.50	.70	.15
☐	124	Tom Satriano	1.50	.70	.15
☐	125	Juan Pizarro	1.50	.70	.15
☐	126	Dodgers Team	2.00	.90	.20
☐	127	Frank Lary	1.50	.70	.15
☐	128	Vic Davalillo	1.50	.70	.15
☐	129	Bennie Daniels	1.50	.70	.15
☐	130	Al Kaline	7.50	3.50	.65
☐	131	John Keane MGR	1.50	.70	.15
		WORLD SERIES (132-139)			
☐	132	World Series Game 1 Cards take opener	2.00	.90	.20
☐	133	World Series Game 2 Stottlemyre wins	2.00	.90	.20
☐	134	World Series Game 3 Mantle's clutch homer	7.00	3.00	.60
☐	135	World Series Game 4 Boyer's grand-slam	2.00	.90	.20
☐	136	World Series Game 5 10th inning triumph	2.00	.90	.20
☐	137	World Series Game 6 Bouton wins again	2.00	.90	.20
☐	138	World Series Game 7 Gibson wins finale	3.00	1.40	.30
☐	139	World Series Summary Cards celebrate	2.00	.90	.20
☐	140	Dean Chance	1.50	.70	.15
☐	141	Charlie James	1.50	.70	.15
☐	142	Bill Monbouquette	1.50	.70	.15
☐	143	Pirates Rookies: John Gelnar Jerry May	1.50	.70	.15
☐	144	Ed Kranepool	1.50	.70	.15
☐	145	Luis Tiant	3.00	1.40	.30
☐	146	Ron Hansen	1.50	.70	.15
☐	147	Dennis Bennett	1.50	.70	.15
☐	148	Willie Kirkland	1.50	.70	.15
☐	149	Wayne Schurr	1.50	.70	.15
☐	150	Brooks Robinson	7.50	3.50	.70
☐	151	Athletics Team	1.75	.85	.17
☐	152	Phil Ortega	1.50	.70	.15
☐	153	Norm Cash	1.75	.85	.17
☐	154	Bob Humphreys	1.50	.70	.15
☐	155	Roger Maris	6.50	3.00	.60
☐	156	Bob Sadowski	1.50	.70	.15
☐	157	Zoilo Versalles	1.75	.85	.17
☐	158	Dick Sisler	1.50	.70	.15
☐	159	Jim Duffalo	1.50	.70	.15
☐	160	Bob Clemente	16.00	7.00	1.50
☐	161	Frank Baumann	1.50	.70	.15
☐	162	Russ Nixon	1.50	.70	.15
☐	163	John Briggs	1.50	.70	.15
☐	164	Al Spangler	1.50	.70	.15
☐	165	Dick Ellsworth	1.50	.70	.15
☐	166	Indians Rookies: George Culver Tommie Agee	1.50	.70	.15
☐	167	Bill Wakefield	1.50	.70	.15
☐	168	Dick Green	1.50	.70	.15
☐	169	Dave Vineyard	1.50	.70	.15
☐	170	Hank Aaron	25.00	11.00	2.50
☐	171	Jim Roland	1.50	.70	.15
☐	172	Jim Piersall	1.75	.85	.17
☐	173	Tigers Team	1.75	.85	.17
☐	174	Joe Jay	1.50	.70	.15
☐	175	Bob Aspromonte	1.50	.70	.15
☐	176	Willie McCovey	6.50	3.00	.60
☐	177	Pete Mikkelsen	1.50	.70	.15
☐	178	Dalton Jones	1.50	.70	.15
☐	179	Hal Woodeschick	1.50	.70	.15
☐	180	Bob Allison	1.50	.70	.15
☐	181	Senators Rookies: Don Loun	1.50	.70	.15

Joe McCabe

☐ 182	Mike De La Hoz	1.50	.70	.15
☐ 183	Dave Nicholson	1.50	.70	.15
☐ 184	John Boozer	1.50	.70	.15
☐ 185	Max Alvis	1.50	.70	.15
☐ 186	Bill Cowan	1.50	.70	.15
☐ 187	Casey Stengel	4.00	1.85	.40
☐ 188	Sam Bowens	1.50	.70	.15
☐ 189	3rd Series Checklist	2.50	.40	.05
☐ 190	Bill White	1.50	.70	.15
☐ 191	Phil Regan	1.50	.70	.15
☐ 192	Jim Coker	1.50	.70	.15
☐ 193	Gaylord Perry	4.00	1.85	.40
☐ 194	Rookie Stars:	1.50	.70	.15
	Bill Kelso			
	Rick Reichardt			
☐ 195	Bob Veale	1.50	.70	.15
☐ 196	Ron Fairly	1.50	.70	.15
☐ 197	Diego Segui	1.50	.70	.15
☐ 198	Smoky Burgess	1.50	.70	.15
☐ 199	Bob Heffner	1.50	.70	.15
☐ 200	Joe Torre	2.00	.90	.20
☐ 201	Twins Rookies	1.50	.70	.15
	Sandy Valdespino			
	Cesar Tovar			
☐ 202	Leo Burke	1.50	.70	.15
☐ 203	Dallas Green	1.75	.85	.17
☐ 204	Russ Snyder	1.50	.70	.15
☐ 205	Warren Spahn	5.00	2.35	.50
☐ 206	Willie Horton	1.75	.85	.17
☐ 207	Pete Rose	125.00	50.00	12.00
☐ 208	Tommy John	3.00	1.40	.30
☐ 209	Pirates Team	1.75	.85	.17
☐ 210	Jim Fregosi	1.75	.85	.17
☐ 211	Steve Ridzik	1.50	.70	.15
☐ 212	Ron Brand	1.50	.70	.15
☐ 213	Jim Davenport	1.50	.70	.15
☐ 214	Bob Purkey	1.50	.70	.15
☐ 215	Pete Ward	1.50	.70	.15
☐ 216	Al Worthington	1.50	.70	.15
☐ 217	Walt Alston MGR	2.00	.90	.20
☐ 218	Dick Schofield	1.50	.70	.15
☐ 219	Bob Meyer	1.50	.70	.15
☐ 220	Bill Williams	3.00	1.40	.30
☐ 221	John Tsitouris	1.50	.70	.15
☐ 222	Bob Tillman	1.50	.70	.15
☐ 223	Dan Osinski	1.50	.70	.15
☐ 224	Bob Chance	1.50	.70	.15
☐ 225	Bo Belinsky	1.50	.70	.15
☐ 226	Yankees Rookies	1.50	.70	.15
	Elvio Jimenez			
	Jake Gibbs			
☐ 227	Bob Klaus	1.50	.70	.15
☐ 228	Jack Sanford	1.50	.70	.15
☐ 229	Lou Clinton	1.50	.70	.15
☐ 230	Ray Sadecki	1.50	.70	.15
☐ 231	Jerry Adair	1.50	.70	.15
☐ 232	Steve Blass	1.75	.85	.17
☐ 233	Don Zimmer	1.75	.85	.17
☐ 234	White Sox Team	1.75	.85	.17
☐ 235	Chuck Hinton	1.50	.70	.15
☐ 236	Dennis McLain	2.50	1.15	.25
☐ 237	Bernie Allen	1.50	.70	.15
☐ 238	Joe Moeller	1.50	.70	.15
☐ 239	Doc Edwards	1.50	.70	.15
☐ 240	Bob Bruce	1.50	.70	.15
☐ 241	Mack Jones	1.50	.70	.15
☐ 242	George Brunet	1.50	.70	.15
☐ 243	Reds Rookies	1.50	.70	.15
	Ted Davidson			
	Tommy Helms			
☐ 244	Lindy McDaniel	1.50	.70	.15
☐ 245	Joe Pepitone	1.75	.85	.17
☐ 246	Tom Butters	1.50	.70	.15
☐ 247	Wally Moon	1.50	.70	.15
☐ 248	Gus Triandos	1.50	.70	.15
☐ 249	Dave McNally	1.75	.85	.17
☐ 250	Willie Mays	25.00	11.00	2.50
☐ 251	Billy Herman MGR	2.00	.90	.20
☐ 252	Pete Richert	1.50	.70	.15
☐ 253	Danny Cater	1.50	.70	.15
☐ 254	Roland Sheldon	1.50	.70	.15
☐ 255	Camilo Pascual	1.50	.70	.15
☐ 256	Tito Francona	1.50	.70	.15
☐ 257	Jim Wynn	1.75	.85	.17
☐ 258	Larry Bearnarth	1.50	.70	.15
☐ 259	Tigers Rookies	1.75	.85	.17
	Jim Northrup			
	Ray Oyler			
☐ 260	Don Drysdale	4.50	2.10	.45
☐ 261	Duke Carmel	1.50	.70	.15
☐ 262	Bud Daley	1.50	.70	.15
☐ 263	Marty Keough	1.50	.70	.15

☐ 264	Bob Buhl	1.50	.70	.15
☐ 265	Jim Pagliaroni	1.50	.70	.15
☐ 266	Bert Campaneris	2.00	.90	.20
☐ 267	Senators Team	1.75	.85	.17
☐ 268	Ken McBride	1.50	.70	.15
☐ 269	Frank Bolling	1.50	.70	.15
☐ 270	Milt Pappas	1.50	.70	.15
☐ 271	Don Wert	1.50	.70	.15
☐ 272	Chuck Schilling	1.50	.70	.15
☐ 273	4th Series Checklist	3.00	.50	.05
☐ 274	Lum Harris MGR	1.50	.70	.15
☐ 275	Dick Groat	1.75	.85	.17
☐ 276	Hoyt Wilhelm	3.00	1.40	.30
☐ 277	John Lewis	1.50	.70	.15
☐ 278	Ken Retzer	1.50	.70	.15
☐ 279	Dick Tracewski	1.50	.70	.15
☐ 280	Dick Stuart	1.50	.70	.15
☐ 281	Bill Stafford	1.50	.70	.15
☐ 282	Giants Rookies	1.75	.85	.17
	Dick Estelle			
	Masanori Murakami			
☐ 283	Fred Whitfield	1.50	.70	.15

1966 O-Pee-Chee

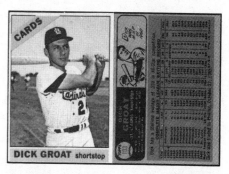

DICK GROAT shortstop

The cards in this 196 card set measure 2 1/2" by 3 1/2". The 1966 O-Pee-Chee set is very similar to the 1966 Topps set; the backs are colored slightly different and the bottom of the reverse says "Ptd. in Canada." Remember the prices below apply only to the O- Pee-Chee cards -- NOT to the 1966 Topps cards which are much more plentiful.

		MINT	VG-E	F-G
COMPLETE SET (196)		450.00	200.00	45.00
COMMON PLAYER (1-196)		1.50	.70	.15
☐ 1	Willie Mays	40.00	15.00	3.00
☐ 2	Ted Abernathy	1.50	.70	.15
☐ 3	Sam Mele	1.50	.70	.15
☐ 4	Ray Culp	1.50	.70	.15
☐ 5	Jim Fregosi	1.75	.85	.17
☐ 6	Chuck Schilling	1.50	.70	.15
☐ 7	Tracy Stallard	1.50	.70	.15
☐ 8	Floyd Robinson	1.50	.70	.15
☐ 9	Clete Boyer	1.75	.85	.17
☐ 10	Tony Cloninger	1.50	.70	.15
☐ 11	Senators Rookies	1.50	.70	.15
	Brant Alyea			
	Pete Craig			
☐ 12	John Tsitouris	1.50	.70	.15
☐ 13	Lou Johnson	1.50	.70	.15
☐ 14	Norm Siebern	1.50	.70	.15
☐ 15	Vern Law	1.50	.70	.15
☐ 16	Larry Brown	1.50	.70	.15
☐ 17	John Stephenson	1.50	.70	.15
☐ 18	Roland Sheldon	1.50	.70	.15
☐ 19	Giants Team	1.75	.85	.17
☐ 20	Willie Horton	1.75	.85	.17
☐ 21	Don Nottebart	1.50	.70	.15
☐ 22	Joe Nossek	1.50	.70	.15
☐ 23	Jack Sanford	1.50	.70	.15
☐ 24	Don Kessinger	1.75	.85	.17

□	#	Player			
□	25	Pete Ward	1.50	.70	.15
□	26	Ray Sadecki	1.50	.70	.15
□	27	Orioles Rookies	1.50	.70	.15
		Darold Knowles			
		Andy Etchebarren			
□	28	Phil Niekro	5.00	2.35	.50
□	29	Mike Brumley	1.50	.70	.15
□	30	Pete Rose	60.00	25.00	5.00
□	31	Jack Cullen	1.50	.70	.15
□	32	Adolfo Phillips	1.50	.70	.15
□	33	Jim Pagliaroni	1.50	.70	.15
□	34	1st Series Checklist	2.50	.40	.05
□	35	Ron Swoboda	1.50	.70	.15
□	36	Jim Hunter	4.00	1.85	.40
□	37	Billy Herman MGR	1.75	.85	.17
□	38	Ron Nischwitz	1.50	.70	.15
□	39	Ken Henderson	1.50	.70	.15
□	40	Jim Grant	1.50	.70	.15
□	41	Don LeJohn	1.50	.70	.15
□	42	Aubrey Gatewood	1.50	.70	.15
□	43	Don Landrum	1.50	.70	.15
□	44	Indians Rookies	1.50	.70	.15
		Bill Davis			
		Tom Kelley			
□	45	Jim Gentile	1.75	.85	.17
□	46	Howie Koplitz	1.50	.70	.15
□	47	J.C. Martin	1.50	.70	.15
□	48	Paul Blair	1.75	.85	.17
□	49	Woody Woodward	1.50	.70	.15
□	50	Mickey Mantle	60.00	25.00	5.00
□	51	Gordon Richardson	1.50	.70	.15
□	52	Power Plus	1.50	.70	.15
		Wes Covington			
		Johnny Callison			
□	53	Bob Duliba	1.50	.70	.15
□	54	Jose Pagan	1.50	.70	.15
□	55	Ken Harrelson	2.00	.90	.20
□	56	Sandy Valdespino	1.50	.70	.15
□	57	Jim Lefebvre	1.50	.70	.15
□	58	Dave Wickersham	1.50	.70	.15
□	59	Reds Team	1.75	.85	.17
□	60	Curt Flood	1.75	.85	.17
□	61	Bob Bolin	1.50	.70	.15
□	62	Merritt Ranew	1.50	.70	.15
		(with sold line)			
□	63	Jim Stewart	1.50	.70	.15
□	64	Bob Bruce	1.50	.70	.15
□	65	Leon Wagner	1.50	.70	.15
□	66	Al Weis	1.50	.70	.15
□	67	Mets Rookies	1.50	.70	.15
		Cleon Jones			
		Dick Selma			
□	68	Hal Reniff	1.50	.70	.15
□	69	Ken Hamlin	1.50	.70	.15
□	70	Carl Yastrzemski	35.00	15.00	3.00
□	71	Frank Carpin	1.50	.70	.15
□	72	Tony Perez	3.00	1.40	.30
□	73	Jerry Zimmerman	1.50	.70	.15
□	74	Don Mossi	1.50	.70	.15
□	75	Tommy Davis	1.75	.85	.17
□	76	Red Schoendienst	1.75	.85	.17
□	77	Johnny Orsino	1.50	.70	.15
□	78	Frank Linzy	1.50	.70	.15
□	79	Joe Pepitone	1.75	.85	.17
□	80	Richie Allen	2.00	.90	.20
□	81	Ray Oyler	1.50	.70	.15
□	82	Bob Hendley	1.50	.70	.15
□	83	Albie Pearson	1.50	.70	.15
□	84	Braves Rookies	1.50	.70	.15
		Jim Beauchamp			
		Dick Kelley			
□	85	Eddie Fisher	1.50	.70	.15
□	86	John Bateman	1.50	.70	.15
□	87	Dan Napoleon	1.50	.70	.15
□	88	Fred Whitfield	1.50	.70	.15
□	89	Ted Davidson	1.50	.70	.15
□	90	Luis Aparicio	3.50	1.65	.35
□	91	Bob Uecker	3.50	1.65	.35
		(with traded line)			
□	92	Yankees Team	2.00	.90	.20
□	93	Jim Lonborg	1.75	.85	.17
□	94	Matty Alou	1.75	.85	.17
□	95	Pete Richert	1.50	.70	.15
□	96	Felipe Alou	1.75	.85	.17
□	97	Jim Merritt	1.50	.70	.15
□	98	Don Demeter	1.50	.70	.15
□	99	Buc Belters	2.00	.90	.20
		Willie Stargell			
		Donn Clendenon			
□	100	Sandy Koufax	20.00	9.00	2.00
□	101	Checklist 2	2.50	.40	.05
□	102	Ed Kirkpatrick	1.50	.70	.15
□	103	Dick Groat	2.00	.90	.20
		(with traded line)			
□	104	Alex Johnson	2.00	.90	.20
		(with traded line)			
□	105	Milt Pappas	1.75	.85	.17
□	106	Rusty Staub	2.00	.90	.20
□	107	A's Rookies	1.50	.70	.15
		Larry Stahl			
		Ron Tompkins			
□	108	Bobby Klaus	1.50	.70	.15
□	109	Ralph Terry	1.50	.70	.15
□	110	Ernie Banks	6.00	2.80	.60
□	111	Gary Peters	1.50	.70	.15
□	112	Manny Mota	1.75	.85	.17
□	113	Hank Aguirre	1.50	.70	.15
□	114	Jim Gosger	1.50	.70	.15
□	115	Bill Henry	1.50	.70	.15
□	116	Walt Alston MGR	2.00	.90	.20
□	117	Jake Gibbs	1.50	.70	.15
□	118	Mike McCormick	1.50	.70	.15
□	119	Art Shamsky	1.50	.70	.15
□	120	Harmon Killebrew	5.00	2.35	.50
□	121	Ray Herbert	1.50	.70	.15
□	122	Joe Gaines	1.50	.70	.15
□	123	Pirates Rookies	1.50	.70	.15
		Frank Bork			
		Jerry May			
□	124	Tug McGraw	1.75	.85	.17
□	125	Lou Brock	7.00	3.25	.70
□	126	Jim Palmer	30.00	14.00	3.00
□	127	Ken Berry	1.50	.70	.15
□	128	Jim Landis	1.50	.70	.15
□	129	Jack Kralick	1.50	.70	.15
□	130	Joe Torre	2.00	.90	.20
□	131	Angels Team	1.75	.85	.17
□	132	Orlando Cepeda	2.00	.90	.20
□	133	Don McMahon	1.50	.70	.15
□	134	Wes Parker	1.75	.85	.17
□	135	Dave Morehead	1.50	.70	.15
□	136	Woody Held	1.50	.70	.15
□	137	Pat Corrales	1.75	.85	.17
□	138	Roger Repoz	1.50	.70	.15
□	139	Cubs Rookies	1.50	.70	.15
		Byron Browne			
		Don Young			
□	140	Jim Maloney	1.75	.85	.17
□	141	Tom McCraw	1.50	.70	.15
□	142	Don Dennis	1.50	.70	.15
□	143	Jose Tartabull	1.50	.70	.15
□	144	Don Schwall	1.50	.70	.15
□	145	Bill Freehan	2.00	.90	.20
□	146	George Altman	1.50	.70	.15
□	147	Lum Harris MGR	1.50	.70	.15
□	148	Bob Johnson	1.50	.70	.15
□	149	Dick Nen	1.50	.70	.15
□	150	Rocky Colavito	2.00	.90	.20
□	151	Gary Wagner	1.50	.70	.15
□	152	Frank Malzone	1.75	.85	.17
□	153	Rico Carty	1.75	.85	.17
□	154	Chuck Hiller	1.50	.70	.15
□	155	Marcelino Lopez	1.50	.70	.15
□	156	Double Play Combo	1.75	.85	.17
		Dick Schofield			
		Hal Lanier			
□	157	Rene Lachemann	1.50	.70	.15
□	158	Jim Brewer	1.50	.70	.15
□	159	Chico Ruiz	1.50	.70	.15
□	160	Whitey Ford	6.00	2.80	.60
□	161	Jerry Lumpe	1.50	.70	.15
□	162	Lee Maye	1.50	.70	.15
□	163	Tito Francona	1.50	.70	.15
□	164	White Sox Rookies	1.50	.70	.15
		Tommie Agee			
		Marv Staehle			
□	165	Don Lock	1.50	.70	.15
□	166	Chris Krug	1.50	.70	.15
□	167	Boog Powell	2.00	.90	.20
□	168	Dan Osinski	1.50	.70	.15
□	169	Duke Sims	1.50	.70	.15
□	170	Cookie Rojas	1.50	.70	.15
□	171	Nick Willhite	1.50	.70	.15
□	172	Mets Team	1.75	.85	.17
□	173	Al Spangler	1.50	.70	.15
□	174	Ron Taylor	1.50	.70	.15
□	175	Bert Campaneris	2.00	.90	.20
□	176	Jim Davenport	1.50	.70	.15
□	177	Hector Lopez	1.50	.70	.15
□	178	Bob Tillman	1.50	.70	.15
□	179	Cards Rookies	1.75	.85	.17
		Dennis Aust			
		Bob Tolan			
□	180	Vada Pinson	2.00	.90	.20
□	181	Al Worthington	1.50	.70	.15
□	182	Jerry Lynch	1.50	.70	.15

			MINT	VG-E	F-G
☐	183	3rd Series Checklist	2.50	.40	.05
☐	184	Denis Menke	1.50	.70	.15
☐	185	Bob Buhl	1.50	.70	.15
☐	186	Ruben Amaro	1.50	.70	.15
☐	187	Chuck Dressen MGR	1.50	.70	.15
☐	188	Al Luplow	1.50	.70	.15
☐	189	John Roseboro	1.50	.70	.15
☐	190	Jimmie Hall	1.50	.70	.15
☐	191	Darrell Sutherland	1.50	.70	.15
☐	192	Vic Power	1.50	.70	.15
☐	193	Dave McNally	1.75	.85	.17
☐	194	Senators Team	1.75	.85	.17
☐	195	Joe Morgan	5.00	2.35	.50
☐	196	Don Pavletich	1.50	.70	.15

1967 O-Pee-Chee

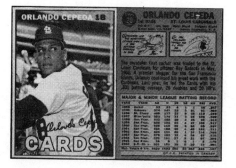

The cards in this 196 card set measure 2 1/2" by 3 1/2". The 1967 O-Pee-Chee series is very similar to the 1967 Topps regular set. The O-Pee-Chee cards are distinguished by the fact that they say "Printed in Canada" in the bottom right corner of the reverse. Each checklist card features a small circular picture of a popular player included in that series. Remember the prices below apply only to the O-Pee-Chee cards -- NOT to the 1967 Topps cards which are much more plentiful.

			MINT	VG-E	F-G
		COMPLETE SET (196)	350.00	150.00	35.00
		COMMON PLAYER (1-196)	1.25	.60	.12
☐	1	The Champs:	3.00	.75	.15
		Frank Robinson			
		Hank Bauer			
		Brooks Robinson			
☐	2	Jack Hamilton	1.25	.60	.12
☐	3	Duke Sims	1.25	.60	.12
☐	4	Hal Lanier	1.50	.70	.15
☐	5	Whitey Ford	5.00	2.35	.50
☐	6	Dick Simpson	1.25	.60	.12
☐	7	Don McMahon	1.25	.60	.12
☐	8	Chuck Harrison	1.25	.60	.12
☐	9	Ron Hansen	1.25	.60	.12
☐	10	Matty Alou	1.50	.70	.15
☐	11	Barry Moore	1.25	.60	.12
☐	12	Dodgers Rookies	1.25	.60	.12
		Jim Campanis			
		Bill Singer			
☐	13	Joe Sparma	1.25	.60	.12
☐	14	Phil Linz	1.25	.60	.12
☐	15	Earl Battey	1.25	.60	.12
☐	16	Bill Hands	1.25	.60	.12
☐	17	Jim Gosger	1.25	.60	.12
☐	18	Gene Oliver	1.25	.60	.12
☐	19	Jim McGlothlin	1.25	.60	.12
☐	20	Orlando Cepeda	2.00	.90	.20
☐	21	Dave Bristol MGR	1.25	.60	.12
☐	22	Gene Brabender	1.25	.60	.12
☐	23	Larry Elliot	1.25	.60	.12
☐	24	Bob Allen	1.25	.60	.12
☐	25	Elston Howard	1.75	.85	.17

			MINT	VG-E	F-G
☐	26	Bob Priddy	1.25	.60	.12
		(with traded line)			
☐	27	Bob Saverine	1.25	.60	.12
☐	28	Barry Latman	1.25	.60	.12
☐	29	Tommy McCraw	1.25	.60	.12
☐	30	Al Kaline	6.50	3.00	.60
☐	31	Jim Brewer	1.25	.60	.12
☐	32	Bob Bailey	1.25	.60	.12
☐	33	Athletic Rookies	1.75	.85	.17
		Sal Bando			
		Randy Schwartz			
☐	34	Pete Cimino	1.25	.60	.12
☐	35	Rico Carty	1.50	.70	.15
☐	36	Bob Tillman	1.25	.60	.12
☐	37	Rick Wise	1.25	.60	.12
☐	38	Bob Johnson	1.25	.60	.12
☐	39	Curt Simmons	1.25	.60	.12
☐	40	Rick Reichardt	1.25	.60	.12
☐	41	Joe Hoerner	1.25	.60	.12
☐	42	Mets Team	1.50	.70	.15
☐	43	Chico Salmon	1.25	.60	.12
☐	44	Joe Nuxhall	1.25	.60	.12
☐	45	Roger Maris	6.00	2.80	.60
☐	46	Lindy McDaniel	1.25	.60	.12
☐	47	Ken McMullen	1.25	.60	.12
☐	48	Bill Freehan	1.50	.70	.15
☐	49	Roy Face	1.50	.70	.15
☐	50	Tony Oliva	1.75	.85	.17
☐	51	Astros Rookies	1.25	.60	.12
		Dave Adlesh			
		Wes Bales			
☐	52	Dennis Higgins	1.25	.60	.12
☐	53	Clay Dalrymple	1.25	.60	.12
☐	54	Dick Green	1.25	.60	.12
☐	55	Don Drysdale	4.50	2.10	.45
☐	56	Jose Tartabull	1.25	.60	.12
☐	57	Pat Jarvis	1.25	.60	.12
☐	58	Paul Schaal	1.25	.60	.12
☐	59	Ralph Terry	1.25	.60	.12
☐	60	Luis Aparicio	3.00	1.40	.30
☐	61	Gordy Coleman	1.25	.60	.12
☐	62	1st Checklist	2.00	.40	.05
		Frank Robinson			
☐	63	Cards' Clubbers	1.75	.85	.17
		Lou Brock			
		Curt Flood			
☐	64	Fred Valentine	1.25	.60	.12
☐	65	Tom Haller	1.25	.60	.12
☐	66	Manny Mota	1.50	.70	.15
☐	67	Ken Berry	1.25	.60	.12
☐	68	Bob Buhl	1.25	.60	.12
☐	69	Vic Davalillo	1.25	.60	.12
☐	70	Ron Santo	1.50	.70	.15
☐	71	Camilo Pascual	1.25	.60	.12
☐	72	Tigers Rookies	1.25	.60	.12
		George Korince (Photo			
		actually John Brown)			
		John (Tom) Matchick			
☐	73	Rusty Staub	1.75	.85	.17
☐	74	Wes Stock	1.25	.60	.12
☐	75	George Scott	1.50	.70	.15
☐	76	Jim Barbieri	1.25	.60	.12
☐	77	Dooley Womack	1.25	.60	.12
☐	78	Pat Corrales	1.50	.70	.15
☐	79	Bubba Morton	1.25	.60	.12
☐	80	Jim Maloney	1.50	.70	.15
☐	81	Eddie Stanky MGR	1.25	.60	.12
☐	82	Steve Barber	1.25	.60	.12
☐	83	Ollie Brown	1.25	.60	.12
☐	84	Tommie Sisk	1.25	.60	.12
☐	85	Johnny Callison	1.25	.60	.12
☐	86	Mike McCormick	1.25	.60	.12
		(with traded line)			
☐	87	George Altman	1.25	.60	.12
☐	88	Mickey Lolich	1.75	.85	.17
☐	89	Felix Millan	1.25	.60	.12
☐	90	Jim Nash	1.25	.60	.12
☐	91	Johnny Lewis	1.25	.60	.12
☐	92	Ray Washburn	1.25	.60	.12
☐	93	Yankees Rookies	1.75	.85	.17
		Stan Bahnsen			
		Bobby Murcer			
☐	94	Ron Fairly	1.25	.60	.12
☐	95	Sonny Siebert	1.25	.60	.12
☐	96	Art Shamsky	1.25	.60	.12
☐	97	Mike Cuellar	1.50	.70	.15
☐	98	Rich Rollins	1.25	.60	.12
☐	99	Lee Stange	1.25	.60	.12
☐	100	Frank Robinson	4.50	2.10	.45
☐	101	Ken Johnson	1.25	.60	.12
☐	102	Phillies Team	1.50	.70	.15
☐	103	2nd Checklist	3.50	.60	.10
		Mickey Mantle			

□ 104 Minnie Rojas	1.25	.60	.12
□ 105 Ken Boyer	1.75	.85	.17
□ 106 Randy Hundley	1.25	.60	.12
□ 107 Joel Horlen	1.25	.60	.12
□ 108 Alex Johnson	1.25	.60	.12
□ 109 Tribe Thumpers	1.50	.70	.15
Rocky Colavito			
Leon Wagner			
□ 110 Jack Aker	1.25	.60	.12
□ 111 John Kennedy	1.25	.60	.12
□ 112 Dave Wickersham	1.25	.60	.12
□ 113 Dave Nicholson	1.25	.60	.12
□ 114 Jack Baldschun	1.25	.60	.12
□ 115 Paul Casanova	1.25	.60	.12
□ 116 Herman Franks MGR	1.25	.60	.12
□ 117 Darrell Brandon	1.25	.60	.12
□ 118 Bernie Allen	1.25	.60	.12
□ 119 Wade Blasingame	1.25	.60	.12
□ 120 Floyd Robinson	1.25	.60	.12
□ 121 Ed Bressoud	1.25	.60	.12
□ 122 George Brunet	1.25	.60	.12
□ 123 Pirates Rookies	1.25	.60	.12
Jim Price			
Luke Walker			
□ 124 Jim Stewart	1.25	.60	.12
□ 125 Moe Drabowsky	1.25	.60	.12
□ 126 Tony Taylor	1.25	.60	.12
□ 127 John O'Donoghue	1.25	.60	.12
□ 128 Ed Spiezio	1.25	.60	.12
□ 129 Phil Roof	1.25	.60	.12
□ 130 Phil Regan	1.25	.60	.12
□ 131 Yankees Team	1.50	.70	.15
□ 132 Ozzie Virgil	1.25	.60	.12
□ 133 Ron Kline	1.25	.60	.12
□ 134 Gates Brown	1.25	.60	.12
□ 135 Deron Johnson	1.25	.60	.12
□ 136 Carroll Sembera	1.25	.60	.12
□ 137 Twins Rookies	1.25	.60	.12
Ron Clark			
Jim Ollum			
□ 138 Dick Kelley	1.25	.60	.12
□ 139 Dalton Jones	1.25	.60	.12
□ 140 Willie Stargell	4.00	1.85	.40
□ 141 John Miller	1.25	.60	.12
□ 142 Jackie Brandt	1.25	.60	.12
□ 143 Sox Sockers	1.25	.60	.12
Pete Ward			
Don Buford			
□ 144 Bill Hepler	1.25	.60	.12
□ 145 Larry Brown	1.25	.60	.12
□ 146 Steve Carlton	30.00	14.00	3.00
□ 147 Tom Egan	1.25	.60	.12
□ 148 Adolfo Phillips	1.25	.60	.12
□ 149 Joe Moeller	1.25	.60	.12
□ 150 Mickey Mantle	55.00	22.00	5.00
□ 151 World Series Game 1	1.75	.85	.17
Moe mows down 11			
□ 152 World Series Game 2	2.00	.90	.20
Palmer blanks Dodgers			
□ 153 World Series Game 3	1.75	.85	.17
Blair's homer			
defeats L.A.			
□ 154 World Series Game 4	1.75	.85	.17
Orioles 4 straight			
□ 155 World Series Summary	1.75	.85	.17
Winners celebrate			
□ 156 Ron Herbel	1.25	.60	.12
□ 157 Danny Cater	1.25	.60	.12
□ 158 Jimmie Coker	1.25	.60	.12
□ 159 Bruce Howard	1.25	.60	.12
□ 160 Willie Davis	1.50	.70	.15
□ 161 Dick Williams MGR	1.50	.70	.15
□ 162 Billy O'Dell	1.25	.60	.12
□ 163 Vic Roznovsky	1.25	.60	.12
□ 164 Dwight Siebler	1.25	.60	.12
□ 165 Cleon Jones	1.25	.60	.12
□ 166 Eddie Mathews	4.00	1.85	.40
□ 167 Senators Rookies	1.25	.60	.12
Joe Coleman			
Tim Cullen			
□ 168 Ray Culp	1.25	.60	.12
□ 169 Horace Clarke	1.25	.60	.12
□ 170 Dick McAuliffe	1.25	.60	.12
□ 171 Calvin Koonce	1.25	.60	.12
□ 172 Bill Heath	1.25	.60	.12
□ 173 Cardinals Team	1.50	.70	.15
□ 174 Dick Radatz	1.25	.60	.12
□ 175 Bobby Knoop	1.25	.60	.12
□ 176 Sammy Ellis	1.25	.60	.12
□ 177 Tito Fuentes	1.25	.60	.12
□ 178 John Buzhardt	1.25	.60	.12
□ 179 Braves Rookies	1.25	.60	.12
Charles Vaughan			

	Cecil Upshaw			
□ 180	Curt Blefary	1.25	.60	.12
□ 181	Terry Fox	1.25	.60	.12
□ 182	Ed Charles	1.25	.60	.12
□ 183	Jim Pagliaroni	1.25	.60	.12
□ 184	George Thomas	1.25	.60	.12
□ 185	Ken Holtzman	1.50	.70	.15
□ 186	Mets Maulers	1.25	.60	.12
	Ed Kranepool			
	Ron Swoboda			
□ 187	Pedro Ramos	1.25	.60	.12
□ 188	Ken Harrelson	1.50	.70	.15
□ 189	Chuck Hinton	1.25	.60	.12
□ 190	Turk Farrell	1.25	.60	.12
□ 191	Checklist 3	2.50	.40	.05
	(Willie Mays)			
□ 192	Fred Gladding	1.25	.60	.12
□ 193	Jose Cardenal	1.25	.60	.12
□ 194	Bob Allison	1.25	.60	.12
□ 195	Al Jackson	1.25	.60	.12
□ 196	Johnny Romano	1.25	.60	.12

1968 O-Pee-Chee

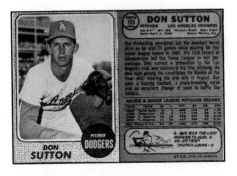

The cards in this 196 card set measure 2 1/2" by 3 1/2". The 1968 O-Pee-Chee set is very similar to the 1968 Topps regular set. O-Pee-Chee cards are distinguished by the fact that they say "Ptd. in Canada" on the bottom right of the reverse. The reverse also is printed in a different color scheme than the Topps issue. The front of each checklist card features a picture of a popular player inside a circle. Remember the prices below apply only to the O-Pee- Chee cards -- NOT to the 1968 Topps cards which are much more plentiful.

		MINT	VG-E	F-G
COMPLETE SET (196)		275.00	125.00	25.00
COMMON PLAYER (1-196)		.90	.40	.09
□	1 NL Batting Leaders	2.50	.75	.15
	Bob Clemente			
	Tony Gonzales			
	Matty Alou			
□	2 AL Batting Leaders	2.00	.90	.20
	Carl Yastrzemski			
	Frank Robinson			
	Al Kaline			
□	3 NL RBI Leaders	2.00	.90	.20
	Orlando Cepeda			
	Bob Clemente			
	Hank Aaron			
□	4 AL RBI Leaders	2.00	.90	.20
	Carl Yastrzemski			
	Harmon Killebrew			
	Frank Robinson			
□	5 NL Home Run Leaders	2.00	.90	.20
	Hank Aaron			
	Jim Wynn			
	Ron Santo			
	Willie McCovey			
□	6 NL Home Run Leaders	2.00	.90	.20

	Carl Yastrzemski				
	Harmon Killebrew				
	Frank Howard				
☐ 7	NL ERA Leaders	1.25	.60	.12	
	Phil Niekro				
	Jim Bunning				
	Chris Short				
☐ 8	AL ERA Leaders	1.00	.45	.10	
	Joe Horlen				
	Gary Peters				
	Sonny Siebert				
☐ 9	NL Pitching Leaders	1.00	.45	.10	
	Mike McCormick				
	Ferguson Jenkins				
	Jim Bunning				
	Claude Osteen				
☐ 10	NL Pitching Leaders	1.00	.45	.10	
	Jim Lonborg				
	Earl Wilson				
	Dean Chance				
☐ 11	NL Strikeout Leaders	1.25	.60	.12	
	Jim Bunning				
	Ferguson Jenkins				
	Gaylord Perry				
☐ 12	AL Strikeout Leaders	1.00	.45	.10	
	Jim Lonborg				
	Sam McDowell				
	Dean Chance				
☐ 13	Chuck Hartenstein	.90	.40	.09	
☐ 14	Jerry McNertney	.90	.40	.09	
☐ 15	Ron Hunt	.90	.40	.09	
☐ 16	Indians Rookies	1.50	.70	.15	
	Lou Piniella				
	Richie Scheinblum				
☐ 17	Dick Hall	.90	.40	.09	
☐ 18	Mike Hershberger	.90	.40	.09	
☐ 19	Juan Pizarro	.90	.40	.09	
☐ 20	Brooks Robinson	5.00	2.35	.50	
☐ 21	Ron Davis	.90	.40	.09	
☐ 22	Pat Dobson	.90	.40	.09	
☐ 23	Chico Cardenas	.90	.40	.09	
☐ 24	Bobby Locke	.90	.40	.09	
☐ 25	Julian Javier	.90	.40	.09	
☐ 26	Darrell Brandon	.90	.40	.09	
☐ 27	Gil Hodges MGR	2.50	1.15	.25	
☐ 28	Ted Uhlaender	.90	.40	.09	
☐ 29	Joe Verbanic	.90	.40	.09	
☐ 30	Joe Torre	1.25	.60	.12	
☐ 31	Ed Stroud	.90	.40	.09	
☐ 32	Joe Gibbon	.90	.40	.09	
☐ 33	Pete Ward	.90	.40	.09	
☐ 34	Al Ferrara	.90	.40	.09	
☐ 35	Steve Hargan	.90	.40	.09	
☐ 36	Pirates Rookies	.90	.40	.09	
	Bob Moose				
	Bob Robertson				
☐ 37	Billy Williams	2.00	.90	.20	
☐ 38	Tony Pierce	.90	.40	.09	
☐ 39	Cookie Rojas	.90	.40	.09	
☐ 40	Denny McLain	1.50	.70	.15	
☐ 41	Julio Gotay	.90	.40	.09	
☐ 42	Larry Haney	.90	.40	.09	
☐ 43	Gary Bell	.90	.40	.09	
☐ 44	Frank Kostro	.90	.40	.09	
☐ 45	Tom Seaver	25.00	11.00	2.50	
☐ 46	Dave Ricketts	.90	.40	.09	
☐ 47	Ralph Houk MGR	.90	.40	.09	
☐ 48	Ted Davidson	.90	.40	.09	
☐ 49	Ed Brinkman	.90	.40	.09	
☐ 50	Willie Mays	16.00	7.50	1.60	
☐ 51	Bob Locker	.90	.40	.09	
☐ 52	Hawk Taylor	.90	.40	.09	
☐ 53	Gene Alley	.90	.40	.09	
☐ 54	Stan Williams	.90	.40	.09	
☐ 55	Felipe Alou	1.00	.45	.10	
☐ 56	Orioles Rookies	.90	.40	.09	
	Dave Leonhard				
	Dave May				
☐ 57	Dan Schneider	.90	.40	.09	
☐ 58	Ed Mathews	3.00	1.40	.30	
☐ 59	Don Lock	.90	.40	.09	
☐ 60	Ken Holtzman	1.00	.45	.10	
☐ 61	Reggie Smith	1.25	.60	.12	
☐ 62	Chuck Dobson	.90	.40	.09	
☐ 63	Dick Kenworthy	.90	.40	.09	
☐ 64	Jim Merritt	.90	.40	.09	
☐ 65	John Roseboro	.90	.40	.09	
☐ 66	Casey Cox	.90	.40	.09	
☐ 67	Check List 1	1.50	.30	.05	
	Jim Kaat				
☐ 68	Ron Willis	.90	.40	.09	
☐ 69	Tom Tresh	1.00	.45	.10	
☐ 70	Bob Veale	.90	.40	.09	
☐ 71	Vern Fuller	.90	.40	.09	
☐ 72	Tommy John	2.00	.90	.20	
☐ 73	Jim Ray Hart	.90	.40	.09	
☐ 74	Milt Pappas	.90	.40	.09	
☐ 75	Don Mincher	.90	.40	.09	
☐ 76	Braves Rookies	.90	.40	.09	
	Jim Britton				
	Ron Reed				
☐ 77	Don Wilson	.90	.40	.09	
☐ 78	Jim Northrup	.90	.40	.09	
☐ 79	Ted Kubiak	.90	.40	.09	
☐ 80	Rod Carew	20.00	9.00	2.00	
☐ 81	Larry Jackson	.90	.40	.09	
☐ 82	Sam Bowens	.90	.40	.09	
☐ 83	John Stephenson	.90	.40	.09	
☐ 84	Bob Tolan	.90	.40	.09	
☐ 85	Gaylord Perry	3.00	1.40	.30	
☐ 86	Willie Stargell	3.00	1.40	.30	
☐ 87	Dick Williams MGR	.90	.40	.09	
☐ 88	Phil Regan	.90	.40	.09	
☐ 89	Jake Gibbs	.90	.40	.09	
☐ 90	Vada Pinson	1.25	.60	.12	
☐ 91	Jim Ollom	.90	.40	.09	
☐ 92	Ed Kranepool	.90	.40	.09	
☐ 93	Tony Cloninger	.90	.40	.09	
☐ 94	Lee Maye	.90	.40	.09	
☐ 95	Bob Aspromonte	.90	.40	.09	
☐ 96	Senator Rookies	.90	.40	.09	
	Frank Coggins				
	Dick Nold				
☐ 97	Tom Phoebus	.90	.40	.09	
☐ 98	Gary Sutherland	.90	.40	.09	
☐ 99	Rocky Colavito	1.25	.60	.12	
☐ 100	Bob Gibson	4.00	1.85	.40	
☐ 101	Glenn Beckert	.90	.40	.09	
☐ 102	Jose Cardenal	.90	.40	.09	
☐ 103	Don Sutton	2.00	.90	.20	
☐ 104	Dick Dietz	.90	.40	.09	
☐ 105	Al Downing	.90	.40	.09	
☐ 106	Dalton Jones	.90	.40	.09	
☐ 107	Check List 2	1.50	.30	.05	
	Juan Marichal				
☐ 108	Don Pavletich	.90	.40	.09	
☐ 109	Bert Campaneris	1.00	.45	.10	
☐ 110	Hank Aaron	16.00	7.50	1.60	
☐ 111	Rich Reese	.90	.40	.09	
☐ 112	Woody Fryman	.90	.40	.09	
☐ 113	Tigers Rookies	.90	.40	.09	
	Tom Matchick				
	Daryl Patterson				
☐ 114	Ron Swoboda	.90	.40	.09	
☐ 115	Sam McDowell	1.00	.45	.10	
☐ 116	Ken McMullen	.90	.40	.09	
☐ 117	Larry Jaster	.90	.40	.09	
☐ 118	Mark Belanger	1.00	.45	.10	
☐ 119	Ted Savage	.90	.40	.09	
☐ 120	Mel Stottlemyre	1.00	.45	.10	
☐ 121	Jimmie Hall	.90	.40	.09	
☐ 122	Gene Mauch MGR	1.00	.45	.10	
☐ 123	Jose Santiago	.90	.40	.09	
☐ 124	Nate Oliver	.90	.40	.09	
☐ 125	Joe Horlen	.90	.40	.09	
☐ 126	Bob Etheridge	.90	.40	.09	
☐ 127	Paul Lindblad	.90	.40	.09	
☐ 128	Astros Rookies	.90	.40	.09	
	Tom Dukes				
	Alonzo Harris				
☐ 129	Mickey Stanley	1.00	.45	.10	
☐ 130	Tony Perez	1.75	.85	.17	
☐ 131	Frank Bertaina	.90	.40	.09	
☐ 132	Bud Harrelson	.90	.40	.09	
☐ 133	Fred Whitfield	.90	.40	.09	
☐ 134	Pat Jarvis	.90	.40	.09	
☐ 135	Paul Blair	.90	.40	.09	
☐ 136	Randy Hundley	.90	.40	.09	
☐ 137	Twins Team	1.00	.45	.10	
☐ 138	Ruben Amaro	.90	.40	.09	
☐ 139	Chris Short	.90	.40	.09	
☐ 140	Tony Conigliaro	1.25	.60	.12	
☐ 141	Dal Maxvill	.90	.40	.09	
☐ 142	White Sox Rookies	.90	.40	.09	
	Buddy Bradford				
	Bill Voss				
☐ 143	Pete Cimino	.90	.40	.09	
☐ 144	Joe Morgan	3.00	1.40	.30	
☐ 145	Don Drysdale	3.50	1.65	.35	
☐ 146	Sal Bando	1.00	.45	.10	
☐ 147	Frank Linzy	.90	.40	.09	
☐ 148	Dave Bristol	.90	.40	.09	
☐ 149	Bob Saverine	.90	.40	.09	
☐ 150	Bob Clemente	15.00	7.00	1.50	

WORLD SERIES (151-158)

☐ 151	World Series Game 1:	2.50	1.15	.25

		MINT	VG-E	F-G
	Brock socks 4 hits in opener			
☐ 152	World Series Game 2: ..... Yaz smashes 2 homers	3.00	1.40	.30
☐ 153	World Series Game 3: ..... Briles cools off Boston	1.50	.70	.15
☐ 154	World Series Game 4: ..... Gibson hurls shutout	2.50	1.15	.25
☐ 155	World Series Game 5: ..... Lonborg wins again	1.50	.70	.15
☐ 156	World Series Game 6: ..... Petrocelli 2 homers	1.50	.70	.15
☐ 157	World Series Game 7: ..... St. Louis wins it	1.50	.70	.15
☐ 158	World Series Summary ... Cardinal celebrate	1.50	.70	.15
☐ 159	Don Kessinger	1.00	.45	.10
☐ 160	Earl Wilson	.90	.40	.09
☐ 161	Norm Miller	.90	.40	.09
☐ 162	Cards Rookies Hal Gilson Mike Torrez	1.25	.60	.12
☐ 163	Gene Brabender	.90	.40	.09
☐ 164	Ramon Webster	.90	.40	.09
☐ 165	Tony Oliva	1.50	.70	.15
☐ 166	Claude Raymond	.90	.40	.09
☐ 167	Elston Howard	1.50	.70	.15
☐ 168	Dodgers Team	1.25	.60	.12
☐ 169	Bob Bolin	.90	.40	.09
☐ 170	Jim Fregosi	1.00	.45	.10
☐ 171	Don Nottebart	.90	.40	.09
☐ 172	Walt Williams	.90	.40	.09
☐ 173	John Boozer	.90	.40	.09
☐ 174	Bob Tillman	.90	.40	.09
☐ 175	Maury Wills	1.50	.70	.15
☐ 176	Bob Allen	.90	.40	.09
☐ 177	Mets Rookies Jerry Koosman Nolan Ryan	60.00	27.00	6.00
☐ 178	Don Wert	.90	.40	.09
☐ 179	Bill Stoneman	.90	.40	.09
☐ 180	Curt Flood	1.00	.45	.10
☐ 181	Jerry Zimmerman	.90	.40	.09
☐ 182	Dave Guisti	.90	.40	.09
☐ 183	Bob Kennedy	.90	.40	.09
☐ 184	Lou Johnson	.90	.40	.09
☐ 185	Tom Haller	.90	.40	.09
☐ 186	Eddie Watt	.90	.40	.09
☐ 187	Sonny Jackson	.90	.40	.09
☐ 188	Cap Peterson	.90	.40	.09
☐ 189	Bill Landis	.90	.40	.09
☐ 190	Bill White	1.00	.45	.10
☐ 191	Dan Frisella	.90	.40	.09
☐ 192	Checklist 3 Carl Yastrzemski	2.50	.50	.05
☐ 193	Jack Hamilton	.90	.40	.09
☐ 194	Don Buford	.90	.40	.09
☐ 195	Joe Pepitone	1.00	.45	.10
☐ 196	Gary Nolan	.90	.40	.09

1969 O-Pee-Chee

The cards in this 218 card set measure 2 1/2" by 3 1/2". The 1969 O-Pee-Chee set is very similar to the 1969 Topps regular issue set. The O-Pee-Chee cards are distinguished by the fact that they say "Ptd. in Canada" on the bottom or side of the reverse. The dominant color on the reverse is a much richer color approaching purple. The front of each checklist card features a different popular player's picture inside a circle on the front of the checklist card. Remember the prices below apply only to the O-Pee-Chee cards -- NOT to the 1969 Topps cards which are much more plentiful.

		MINT	VG-E	F-G
COMPLETE SET (218)		275.00	125.00	25.00
COMMON PLAYER (1-218)		.90	.40	.09
☐ 1	AL Batting Leaders Carl Yastrzemski	2.50	.75	.15
	Danny Cater Tony Oliva			
☐ 2	NL Batting Leaders Pete Rose Matty Alou Felipe Alou	2.00	.90	.20
☐ 3	AL RBI Leaders Ken Harrelson Frank Howard Jim Northrup	1.25	.60	.12
☐ 4	NL RBI Leaders Willie McCovey Ron Santo Billy Williams	1.25	.60	.12
☐ 5	AL Home Run Leaders Frank Howard Willie Horton Ken Harrelson	1.25	.60	.12
☐ 6	NL Home Run Leaders Willie McCovey Richie Allen Ernie Banks	1.50	.70	.15
☐ 7	AL ERA Leaders Luis Tiant Sam McDowell Dave McNally	1.00	.45	.10
☐ 8	NL ERA Leaders Bob Gibson Bobby Bolin Bob Veale	1.00	.45	.10
☐ 9	AL Pitching Leaders Denny McLain Dave McNally Luis Tiant Mel Stottlemyre	1.00	.45	.10
☐ 10	NL Pitching Leaders Juan Marichal Bob Gibson Fergie Jenkins	1.75	.85	.17
☐ 11	AL Strikeout Leaders Sam McDowell Denny McLain Luis Tiant	1.00	.45	.10
☐ 12	NL Strikeout Leaders Bob Gibson Fergie Jenkins Bill Singer	1.00	.45	.10
☐ 13	Mickey Stanley	1.00	.45	.10
☐ 14	Al McBean	.90	.40	.09
☐ 15	Boog Powell	1.25	.60	.12
☐ 16	Giants Rookies Cesar Gutierrez Rich Robertson	.90	.40	.09
☐ 17	Mike Marshall	1.00	.45	.10
☐ 18	Dick Schofield	.90	.40	.09
☐ 19	Ken Suarez	.90	.40	.09
☐ 20	Ernie Banks	4.00	1.85	.40
☐ 21	Jose Santiago	.90	.40	.09
☐ 22	Jesus Alou	.90	.40	.09
☐ 23	Lew Krausse	.90	.40	.09
☐ 24	Walt Alston MGR	1.25	.60	.12
☐ 25	Roy White	.90	.40	.09
☐ 26	Clay Carroll	.90	.40	.09
☐ 27	Bernie Allen	.90	.40	.09
☐ 28	Mike Ryan	.90	.40	.09
☐ 29	Dave Morehead	.90	.40	.09
☐ 30	Bob Allison	.90	.40	.09
☐ 31	Mets Rookies Gary Gentry Amos Otis	1.50	.70	.15
☐ 32	Sammy Ellis	.90	.40	.09

☐ 33	Wayne Causey	.90	.40	.09
☐ 34	Gary Peters	.90	.40	.09
☐ 35	Joe Morgan	3.00	1.40	.30
☐ 36	Luke Walker	.90	.40	.09
☐ 37	Curt Motton	.90	.40	.09
☐ 38	Zoilo Versalles	.90	.40	.09
☐ 39	Dick Hughes	.90	.40	.09
☐ 40	Mayo Smith MGR	.90	.40	.09
☐ 41	Bob Barton	.90	.40	.09
☐ 42	Tommy Harper	.90	.40	.09
☐ 43	Joe Niekro	1.25	.60	.12
☐ 44	Danny Cater	.90	.40	.09
☐ 45	Maury Wills	1.50	.70	.15
☐ 46	Fritz Peterson	.90	.40	.09
☐ 47	Paul Popovich	.90	.40	.09
☐ 48	Brant Alyea	.90	.40	.09
☐ 49	Royals Rookies	.90	.40	.09
	Steve Jones			
	E. Rodriguez			
☐ 50	Bob Clemente	12.00	5.50	1.20
☐ 51	Woody Fryman	.90	.40	.09
☐ 52	Mike Andrews	.90	.40	.09
☐ 53	Sonny Jackson	.90	.40	.09
☐ 54	Cisco Carlos	.90	.40	.09
☐ 55	Jerry Grote	.90	.40	.09
☐ 56	Rich Reese	.90	.40	.09
☐ 57	Checklist 1	1.50	.30	.05
	Denny McLain			
☐ 58	Fred Gladding	.90	.40	.09
☐ 59	Jay Johnstone	.90	.40	.09
☐ 60	Nelson Briles	.90	.40	.09
☐ 61	Jimmie Hall	.90	.40	.09
☐ 62	Chico Salmon	.90	.40	.09
☐ 63	Jim Hickman	.90	.40	.09
☐ 64	Bill Monbouquette	.90	.40	.09
☐ 65	Willie Davis	1.00	.45	.10
☐ 66	Orioles Rookies	.90	.40	.09
	Mike Adamson			
	Merv Rettenmund			
☐ 67	Bill Stoneman	.90	.40	.09
☐ 68	Dave Duncan	.90	.40	.09
☐ 69	Steve Hamilton	.90	.40	.09
☐ 70	Tommy Helms	.90	.40	.09
☐ 71	Steve Whitaker	.90	.40	.09
☐ 72	Ron Taylor	.90	.40	.09
☐ 73	Johnny Briggs	.90	.40	.09
☐ 74	Preston Gomez	.90	.40	.09
☐ 75	Luis Aparicio	3.00	1.40	.30
☐ 76	Norm Miller	.90	.40	.09
☐ 77	Ron Perranoski	.90	.40	.09
☐ 78	Tom Satriano	.90	.40	.09
☐ 79	Milt Pappas	1.00	.45	.10
☐ 80	Norm Cash	1.25	.60	.12
☐ 81	Mel Queen	.90	.40	.09
☐ 82	Pirates Rookies	10.00	4.00	1.00
	Rich Hebner			
	Al Oliver			
☐ 83	Mike Ferraro	1.00	.45	.10
☐ 84	Bob Humphreys	.90	.40	.09
☐ 85	Lou Brock	5.00	2.35	.50
☐ 86	Pete Richert	.90	.40	.09
☐ 87	Horace Clarke	.90	.40	.09
☐ 88	Rich Nye	.90	.40	.09
☐ 89	Russ Gibson	.90	.40	.09
☐ 90	Jerry Koosman	1.25	.60	.12
☐ 91	Al Dark MGR	1.00	.45	.10
☐ 92	Jack Billingham	.90	.40	.09
☐ 93	Joe Foy	.90	.40	.09
☐ 94	Hank Aguirre	.90	.40	.09
☐ 95	Johnny Bench	30.00	14.00	3.00
☐ 96	Denver LeMaster	.90	.40	.09
☐ 97	Buddy Bradford	.90	.40	.09
☐ 98	Dave Giusti	.90	.40	.09
☐ 99	Twins Rookies	8.00	3.75	.80
	Danny Morris			
	Graig Nettles			
☐ 100	Hank Aaron	15.00	7.00	1.50
☐ 101	Daryl Patterson	.90	.40	.09
☐ 102	Jim Davenport	.90	.40	.09
☐ 103	Roger Repoz	.90	.40	.09
☐ 104	Steve Blass	.90	.40	.09
☐ 105	Rick Monday	1.00	.45	.10
☐ 106	Jim Hannan	.90	.40	.09
☐ 107	Checklist 2	1.50	.30	.05
	(Bob Gibson)			
☐ 108	Tony Taylor	.90	.40	.09
☐ 109	Jim Lonborg	1.00	.45	.10
☐ 110	Mike Shannon	1.00	.45	.10
☐ 111	Johnny Morris	.90	.40	.09
☐ 112	J.C. Martin	.90	.40	.09
☐ 113	Dave May	.90	.40	.09
☐ 114	Yankees Rookies	.90	.40	.09
	Alan Closter			

	John Cumberland			
☐ 115	Bill Hands	.90	.40	.09
☐ 116	Chuck Harrison	.90	.40	.09
☐ 117	Jim Fairey	.90	.40	.09
☐ 118	Stan Williams	.90	.40	.09
☐ 119	Doug Rader	1.00	.45	.10
☐ 120	Pete Rose	35.00	15.00	3.00
☐ 121	Joe Grzenda	.90	.40	.09
☐ 122	Ron Fairly	.90	.40	.09
☐ 123	Wilbur Wood	.90	.40	.09
☐ 124	Hank Bauer MGR	.90	.40	.09
☐ 125	Ray Sadecki	.90	.40	.09
☐ 126	Dick Tracewski	.90	.40	.09
☐ 127	Kevin Collins	.90	.40	.09
☐ 128	Tommie Aaron	.90	.40	.09
☐ 129	Bill McCool	.90	.40	.09
☐ 130	Carl Yastrzemski	20.00	9.00	2.00
☐ 131	Chris Cannizzaro	.90	.40	.09
☐ 132	Dave Baldwin	.90	.40	.09
☐ 133	Johnny Callison	.90	.40	.09
☐ 134	Jim Weaver	.90	.40	.09
☐ 135	Tommy Davis	1.25	.60	.12
☐ 136	Cards Rookies	1.00	.45	.10
	Steve Huntz			
	Mike Torrez			
☐ 137	Wally Bunker	.90	.40	.09
☐ 138	John Bateman	.90	.40	.09
☐ 139	Andy Kosco	.90	.40	.09
☐ 140	Jim Lefebvre	.90	.40	.09
☐ 141	Bill Dillman	.90	.40	.09
☐ 142	Woody Woodward	.90	.40	.09
☐ 143	Joe Nossek	.90	.40	.09
☐ 144	Bob Hendley	.90	.40	.09
☐ 145	Max Alvis	.90	.40	.09
☐ 146	Jim Perry	1.00	.45	.10
☐ 147	Leo Durocher MGR	1.25	.60	.12
☐ 148	Lee Stange	.90	.40	.09
☐ 149	Ollie Brown	.90	.40	.09
☐ 150	Denny McLain	1.25	.60	.12
☐ 151	Clay Dalrymple	2.50	1.15	.25
	(Catching, Phillies)			
☐ 152	Tommie Sisk	.90	.40	.09
☐ 153	Ed Brinkman	.90	.40	.09
☐ 154	Jim Britton	.90	.40	.09
☐ 155	Pete Ward	.90	.40	.09
☐ 156	Houston Rookies	.90	.40	.09
	Hal Gilson			
	Leon McFadden			
☐ 157	Bob Rodgers	.90	.40	.09
☐ 158	Joe Gibbon	.90	.40	.09
☐ 159	Jerry Adair	.90	.40	.09
☐ 160	Vada Pinson	1.25	.60	.12
☐ 161	John Purdin	.90	.40	.09
WORLD SERIES (162-169)				
☐ 162	World Series Game 1	2.50	1.15	.25
	Gibson fans 17			
☐ 163	World Series Game 2	1.50	.70	.15
	Tiger homers			
	deck the Cards			
☐ 164	World Series Game 3	1.50	.70	.15
	McCarver's homer			
☐ 165	World Series Game 4	2.50	1.15	.25
	Brock lead-off homer			
☐ 166	World Series Game 5	2.50	1.15	.25
	Kaline's key hit			
☐ 167	World Series Game 6	1.50	.70	.15
	Northrup grandslam			
☐ 168	World Series Game 7	2.50	1.15	.25
	Lolich outduels			
	Bob Gibson			
☐ 169	World Series Summary	1.50	.70	.15
	Tigers celebrate			
☐ 170	Frank Howard	1.25	.60	.12
☐ 171	Glenn Beckert	.90	.40	.09
☐ 172	Jerry Stephenson	.90	.40	.09
☐ 173	White Sox Rookies	.90	.40	.09
	Bob Christian			
	Gerry Nyman			
☐ 174	Grant Jackson	.90	.40	.09
☐ 175	Jim Bunning	1.50	.70	.15
☐ 176	Joe Azcue	.90	.40	.09
☐ 177	Ron Reed	.90	.40	.09
☐ 178	Ray Oyler	.90	.40	.09
☐ 179	Don Pavletich	.90	.40	.09
☐ 180	Willie Horton	1.00	.45	.10
☐ 181	Mel Nelson	.90	.40	.09
☐ 182	Bill Rigney MGR	.90	.40	.09
☐ 183	Don Shaw	.90	.40	.09
☐ 184	Roberto Pena	.90	.40	.09
☐ 185	Tom Phoebus	.90	.40	.09
☐ 186	John Edwards	.90	.40	.09
☐ 187	Leon Wagner	.90	.40	.09
☐ 188	Rick Wise	1.00	.45	.10

		MINT	VG-E	F-G
☐ 189	Red Sox Rookies	.90	.40	.09
	Joe Lahoud			
	John Thibodeau			
☐ 190	Willie Mays	15.00	7.00	1.50
☐ 191	Lindy McDaniel	.90	.40	.09
☐ 192	Jose Pagan	.90	.40	.09
☐ 193	Don Cardwell	.90	.40	.09
☐ 194	Ted Uhlaender	.90	.40	.09
☐ 195	John Odom	.90	.40	.09
☐ 196	Lum Harris MGR	.90	.40	.09
☐ 197	Dick Selma	.90	.40	.09
☐ 198	Willie Smith	.90	.40	.09
☐ 199	Jim French	.90	.40	.09
☐ 200	Bob Gibson	3.50	1.65	.35
☐ 201	Russ Snyder	.90	.40	.09
☐ 202	Don Wilson	.90	.40	.09
☐ 203	Dave Johnson	1.25	.60	.12
☐ 204	Jack Hiatt	.90	.40	.09
☐ 205	Rick Reichardt	.90	.40	.09
☐ 206	Phillies Rookies	1.00	.45	.10
	Larry Hisle			
	Barry Lersch			
☐ 207	Roy Face	1.00	.45	.10
☐ 208	Donn Clendenon	2.50	1.15	.25
	(Expos)			
☐ 209	Larry Haney	.90	.40	.09
	(reverse negative)			
☐ 210	Felix Millan	.90	.40	.09
☐ 211	Galen Cisco	.90	.40	.09
☐ 212	Tom Tresh	1.00	.45	.10
☐ 213	Gerry Arrigo	.90	.40	.09
☐ 214	Checklist 3	2.00	.40	.05
	With 69T deckle CL			
	on back (no player)			
☐ 215	Rico Petrocelli	1.00	.45	.10
☐ 216	Don Sutton	2.00	.90	.20
☐ 217	John Donaldson	.90	.40	.09
☐ 218	John Roseboro	.90	.40	.09

		MINT	VG-E	F-G
☐ 1	Rich Allen	2.00	.90	.20
☐ 2	Luis Aparicio	4.00	1.85	.40
☐ 3	Rod Carew	6.50	3.00	.65
☐ 4	Roberto Clemente	12.50	5.75	1.25
☐ 5	Curt Flood	1.50	.70	.15
☐ 6	Bill Freehan	1.50	.70	.15
☐ 7	Bob Gibson	4.00	1.85	.40
☐ 8	Ken Harrelson	1.50	.70	.15
☐ 9	Tommy Helms	1.50	.70	.15
☐ 10	Tom Haller	1.50	.70	.15
☐ 11	Willie Horton	1.50	.70	.15
☐ 12	Frank Howard	1.50	.70	.15
☐ 13	Willie McCovey	4.00	1.85	.40
☐ 14	Denny McLain	2.00	.90	.20
☐ 15	Juan Marichal	4.00	1.85	.40
☐ 16	Willie Mays	12.50	5.75	1.25
☐ 17	Boog Powell	1.50	.70	.15
☐ 18	Brooks Robinson	6.50	3.00	.65
☐ 19	Ron Santo	2.00	.90	.20
☐ 20	Rusty Staub	2.00	.90	.20
☐ 21	Mel Stottlemyre	1.50	.70	.15
☐ 22	Luis Tiant	1.50	.70	.15
☐ 23	Maury Wills	2.00	.90	.20
☐ 24	Carl Yastrzemski	12.50	5.75	1.25

1970 O-Pee-Chee

The cards in this 546 card set measure 2 1/2" by 3 1/2". The 1970 O-Pee-Chee set for 1970 has color photos surrounded by white frame lines and gray borders and is very similar to the corresponding Topps issue. The card stock is somewhat yellower on the reverse for the O-Pee-Chee cards. The backs have a blue biographical section and a yellow record section. All Star selections are featured on cards 450 to 469. The O-Pee-Chee cards can be distinguished from their Topps counterparts by the fact that they say "Printed in Canada" on the bottom of the reverse. The card backs are written in both French and English. Remember the prices below apply only to the O-Pee-Chee cards -- NOT to the 1970 Topps cards which are much more plentiful.

1969 O-Pee-Chee Deckle

This set is very similar to the U.S. deckle version produced by Topps. The cards are black and white, blank-backed, and unnumbered; they are numbered below according to alphabetical order. The facsimile autograph on the front of each card is written in black ink (instead of blue ink like the Topps issue). The cards measure 2 1/8" by 3 1/8" (slightly smaller than the American issue) and are cut with deckle edges. Remember the prices below apply only to the O-Pee-Chee cards -- NOT to the 1969 Topps Deckle cards which are much more plentiful.

	MINT	VG-E	F-G
COMPLETE SET (24)	80.00	37.00	8.00
COMMON PLAYER (1-24)	1.50	.70	.15

		MINT	VG-E	F-G
COMPLETE SET (546)		400.00	180.00	40.00
COMMON PLAYER (1-546)		.50	.22	.05
☐ 1	New York Mets Team	2.50	.50	.10
☐ 2	Diego Segui	.50	.22	.05
☐ 3	Darrel Chaney	.50	.22	.05
☐ 4	Tom Egan	.50	.22	.05
☐ 5	Wes Parker	.60	.28	.06
☐ 6	Grant Jackson	.50	.22	.05
☐ 7	Indians Rookies	.50	.22	.05
	Gary Boyd			
	Russ Nagelson			
☐ 8	Jose Martinez	.50	.22	.05
☐ 9	1st Checklist	1.00	.20	.05
☐ 10	Carl Yastrzemski	20.00	9.00	2.00

☐ 11	Nate Colbert	.50	.22	.05
☐ 12	John Hiller	.50	.22	.05
☐ 13	Jack Hiatt	.50	.22	.05
☐ 14	Hank Allen	.50	.22	.05
☐ 15	Larry Dierker	.50	.22	.05
☐ 16	Charlie Metro MGR	.50	.22	.05
☐ 17	Hoyt Wilhelm	2.50	1.15	.25
☐ 18	Carlos May	.50	.22	.05
☐ 19	John Boccabella	.50	.22	.05
☐ 20	Dave McNally	.60	.28	.06
☐ 21	A's Rookies	2.00	.90	.20
	Vida Blue			
	Gene Tenace			
☐ 22	Ray Washburn	.50	.22	.05
☐ 23	Bill Robinson	.50	.22	.05
☐ 24	Dick Selma	.50	.22	.05
☐ 25	Cesar Tovar	.50	.22	.05
☐ 26	Tug McGraw	.75	.35	.07
☐ 27	Chuck Hinton	.50	.22	.05
☐ 28	Billy Wilson	.50	.22	.05
☐ 29	Sandy Alomar	.50	.22	.05
☐ 30	Matty Alou	.60	.28	.06
☐ 31	Marty Pattin	.50	.22	.05
☐ 32	Harry Walker MGR	.50	.22	.05
☐ 33	Don Wert	.50	.22	.05
☐ 34	Willie Crawford	.50	.22	.05
☐ 35	Joe Horlen	.50	.22	.05
☐ 36	Red Rookies	.50	.22	.05
	Danny Breeden			
	Bernie Carbo			
☐ 37	Dick Drago	.50	.22	.05
☐ 38	Mack Jones	.50	.22	.05
☐ 39	Mike Nagy	.50	.22	.05
☐ 40	Rich Allen	.75	.35	.07
☐ 41	George Lauzerique	.50	.22	.05
☐ 42	Tito Fuentes	.50	.22	.05
☐ 43	Jack Aker	.50	.22	.05
☐ 44	Roberto Pena	.50	.22	.05
☐ 45	Dave Johnson	.60	.28	.06
☐ 46	Ken Rudolph	.50	.22	.05
☐ 47	Bob Miller	.50	.22	.05
☐ 48	Gil Garrido	.50	.22	.05
☐ 49	Tim Cullen	.50	.22	.05
☐ 50	Tommie Agee	.50	.22	.05
☐ 51	Bob Christian	.50	.22	.05
☐ 52	Bruce Dal Canton	.50	.22	.05
☐ 53	John Kennedy	.50	.22	.05
☐ 54	Jeff Torborg	.50	.22	.05
☐ 55	John Odom	.50	.22	.05
☐ 56	Phillies Rookies	.50	.22	.05
	Joe Lis			
	Scott Reid			
☐ 57	Pat Kelly	.50	.22	.05
☐ 58	Dave Marshall	.50	.22	.05
☐ 59	Dick Ellsworth	.50	.22	.05
☐ 60	Jim Wynn	.60	.28	.06
☐ 61	NL Batting Leaders	2.00	.90	.20
	Pete Rose			
	Bob Clemente			
	Cleon Jones			
☐ 62	AL Batting Leaders	1.00	.45	.10
	Rod Carew			
	Reggie Smith			
	Tony Oliva			
☐ 63	NL RBI Leaders	1.00	.45	.10
	Willie McCovey			
	Ron Santo			
	Tony Perez			
☐ 64	AL RBI Leaders	1.25	.60	.12
	Harmon Killebrew			
	Boog Powell			
	Reggie Jackson			
☐ 65	NL Home Run Leaders	1.50	.70	.15
	Willie McCovey			
	Hank Aaron			
	Lee May			
☐ 66	AL Home Run Leaders	1.00	.45	.10
	Harmon Killebrew			
	Frank Howard			
	Reggie Jackson			
☐ 67	NL ERA Leaders	2.00	.90	.20
	Juan Marichal			
	Steve Carlton			
	Bob Gibson			
☐ 68	AL ERA Leaders	1.00	.45	.10
	Dick Bosman			
	Jim Palmer			
	Mike Cuellar			
☐ 69	NL Pitching Leaders	2.00	.90	.20
	Tom Seaver			
	Phil Niekro			
	Fergie Jenkins			
	Juan Marichal			
☐ 70	AL Pitching Leaders	.75	.35	.07
	Dennis McLain			
	Mike Cuellar			
	Dave Boswell			
	Dave McNally			
	Jim Perry			
	Mel Stottlemyre			
☐ 71	NL Strikeout Leaders	1.00	.45	.10
	Fergie Jenkins			
	Bob Gibson			
	Bill Singer			
☐ 72	AL Strikeout Leaders	.75	.35	.07
	Sam McDowell			
	Mickey Lolich			
	Andy Messersmith			
☐ 73	Wayne Granger	.50	.22	.05
☐ 74	Angels Rookies	.50	.22	.05
	Greg Washburn			
	Wally Wolf			
☐ 75	Jim Kaat	1.25	.60	.12
☐ 76	Carl Taylor	.50	.22	.05
☐ 77	Frank Linzy	.50	.22	.05
☐ 78	Joe Lahoud	.50	.22	.05
☐ 79	Clay Kirby	.50	.22	.05
☐ 80	Don Kessinger	.60	.28	.06
☐ 81	Dave May	.50	.22	.05
☐ 82	Frank Fernandez	.50	.22	.05
☐ 83	Don Cardwell	.50	.22	.05
☐ 84	Paul Casanova	.50	.22	.05
☐ 85	Max Alvis	.50	.22	.05
☐ 86	Lum Harris MGR	.50	.22	.05
☐ 87	Steve Renko	.50	.22	.05
☐ 88	Pilots Rookies	.50	.22	.05
	Miguel Fuentes			
	Dick Baney			
☐ 89	Juan Rios	.50	.22	.05
☐ 90	Tim McCarver	.75	.35	.07
☐ 91	Rich Morales	.50	.22	.05
☐ 92	George Culver	.50	.22	.05
☐ 93	Rick Renick	.50	.22	.05
☐ 94	Fred Patek	.60	.28	.06
☐ 95	Earl Wilson	.50	.22	.05
☐ 96	Cardinals Rookies	2.00	.90	.20
	Leron Lee			
	Jerry Reuss			
☐ 97	Joe Moeller	.50	.22	.05
☐ 98	Gates Brown	.60	.28	.06
☐ 99	Bobby Pfeil	.50	.22	.05
☐ 100	Mel Stottlemyre	.60	.28	.06
☐ 101	Bobby Floyd	.50	.22	.05
☐ 102	Joe Rudi	.75	.35	.07
☐ 103	Frank Reberger	.50	.22	.05
☐ 104	Gerry Moses	.50	.22	.05
☐ 105	Tony Gonzalez	.50	.22	.05
☐ 106	Darold Knowles	.50	.22	.05
☐ 107	Bobby Etheridge	.50	.22	.05
☐ 108	Tom Burgmeier	.50	.22	.05
☐ 109	Expos Rookies	.50	.22	.05
	Garry Jestadt			
	Carl Morton			
☐ 110	Bob Moose	.50	.22	.05
☐ 111	Mike Hegan	.50	.22	.05
☐ 112	Dave Nelson	.50	.22	.05
☐ 113	Jim Ray	.50	.22	.05
☐ 114	Gene Michael	.75	.35	.07
☐ 115	Alex Johnson	.50	.22	.05
☐ 116	Sparky Lyle	.75	.35	.07
☐ 117	Don Young	.50	.22	.05
☐ 118	George Mitterwald	.50	.22	.05
☐ 119	Chuck Taylor	.50	.22	.05
☐ 120	Sal Bando	.60	.28	.06
☐ 121	Orioles Rookies	.50	.22	.05
	Fred Beene			
	Terry Crowley			
☐ 122	George Stone	.50	.22	.05
☐ 123	Don Gutteridge	.50	.22	.05
☐ 124	Larry Jaster	.50	.22	.05
☐ 125	Deron Johnson	.50	.22	.05
☐ 126	Marty Martinez	.50	.22	.05
☐ 127	Joe Coleman	.50	.22	.05
☐ 128	2nd Checklist	1.00	.20	.05
☐ 129	Jimmie Price	.50	.22	.05
☐ 130	Ollie Brown	.50	.22	.05
☐ 131	Dodgers Rookies	.50	.22	.05
	Ray Lamb			
	Bob Stinson			
☐ 132	Jim McGlothlin	.50	.22	.05
☐ 133	Clay Carroll	.50	.22	.05
☐ 134	Danny Walton	.50	.22	.05
☐ 135	Dick Dietz	.50	.22	.05
☐ 136	Steve Hargan	.50	.22	.05
☐ 137	Art Shamsky	.50	.22	.05
☐ 138	Joe Foy	.50	.22	.05

☐ 139	Rich Nye	.50	.22	.05	☐ 211	Ted Williams MGR	3.00	1.40	.30
☐ 140	Reggie Jackson	21.00	9.50	2.10	☐ 212	Al Santorini	.50	.22	.05
☐ 141	Pirates Rookies	.60	.28	.06	☐ 213	Andy Etchebarren	.50	.22	.05
	Dave Cash				☐ 214	Ken Boswell	.50	.22	.05
	Johnny Jeter				☐ 215	Reggie Smith	.75	.35	.07
☐ 142	Fritz Peterson	.50	.22	.05	☐ 216	Chuck Hartenstein	.50	.22	.05
☐ 143	Phil Gagliano	.50	.22	.05	☐ 217	Ron Hansen	.50	.22	.05
☐ 144	Ray Culp	.50	.22	.05	☐ 218	Ron Stone	.50	.22	.05
☐ 145	Rico Carty	.60	.28	.06	☐ 219	Jerry Kenney	.50	.22	.05
☐ 146	Danny Murphy	.50	.22	.05	☐ 220	Steve Carlton	12.00	5.50	1.20
☐ 147	Angel Hermoso	.50	.22	.05	☐ 221	Ron Brand	.50	.22	.05
☐ 148	Earl Weaver MGR	1.00	.45	.10	☐ 222	Jim Rooker	.50	.22	.05
☐ 149	Billy Champion	.50	.22	.05	☐ 223	Nate Oliver	.50	.22	.05
☐ 150	Harmon Killebrew	3.50	1.65	.35	☐ 224	Steve Barber	.50	.22	.05
☐ 151	Dave Roberts	.50	.22	.05	☐ 225	Lee May	.60	.28	.06
☐ 152	Ike Brown	.50	.22	.05	☐ 226	Ron Perranoski	.50	.22	.05
☐ 153	Gary Gentry	.50	.22	.05	☐ 227	Astros Rookies	.75	.35	.07
☐ 154	Senators Rookies	.50	.22	.05		John Mayberry			
	Jim Miles					Bob Watkins			
	Jan Dukes				☐ 228	Aurelio Rodriguez	.50	.22	.05
☐ 155	Denis Menke	.50	.22	.05	☐ 229	Rich Robertson	.50	.22	.05
☐ 156	Eddie Fisher	.50	.22	.05	☐ 230	Brooks Robinson	5.00	2.35	.50
☐ 157	Manny Mota	.60	.28	.06	☐ 231	Luis Tiant	.75	.35	.07
☐ 158	Jerry McNertney	.50	.22	.05	☐ 232	Bob Didier	.50	.22	.05
☐ 159	Tommy Helms	.50	.22	.05	☐ 233	Lew Krausse	.50	.22	.05
☐ 160	Phil Niekro	2.50	1.15	.25	☐ 234	Tommy Dean	.50	.22	.05
☐ 161	Richie Scheinblum	.50	.22	.05	☐ 235	Mike Epstein	.50	.22	.05
☐ 162	Jerry Johnson	.50	.22	.05	☐ 236	Bob Veale	.50	22	.05
☐ 163	Syd O'Brien	.50	.22	.05	☐ 237	Russ Gibson	.50	.22	.05
☐ 164	Ty Cline	.50	.22	.05	☐ 238	Jose Laboy	.50	.22	.05
☐ 165	Ed Kirkpatrick	.50	.22	.05	☐ 239	Ken Berry	.50	.22	.05
☐ 166	Al Oliver	2.50	1.15	.25	☐ 240	Fergie Jenkins	1.25	.60	.12
☐ 167	Bill Burbach	.50	.22	.05	☐ 241	Royals Rookies	.50	.22	.05
☐ 168	Dave Watkins	.50	.22	.05		Al Fitzmorris			
☐ 169	Tom Hall	.50	.22	.05		Scott Northey			
☐ 170	Billy Williams	2.00	.90	.20	☐ 242	Walter Alston MGR	.75	.35	.07
☐ 171	Jim Nash	.50	.22	.05	☐ 243	Joe Sparma	.50	.22	.05
☐ 172	Braves Rookies	.60	.28	.06	☐ 244	3rd Checklist	1.00	.20	.05
	Garry Hill				☐ 245	Leo Cardenas	.50	.22	
	Ralph Garr				☐ 246	Jim McAndrew	.50	.22	.05
☐ 173	Jim Hicks	.50	.22	.05	☐ 247	Lou Klimchock	.50	.22	.05
☐ 174	Ted Sizemore	.50	.22	.05	☐ 248	Jesus Alou	.50	.22	.05
☐ 175	Dick Bosman	.50	.22	.05	☐ 249	Bob Locker	.50	.22	.05
☐ 176	Jim Ray Hart	.50	.22	.05	☐ 250	Willie McCovey	5.00	2.35	.50
☐ 177	Jim Northrup	.60	.28	.06	☐ 251	Dick Schofield	.50	.22	.05
☐ 178	Denny Lemaster	.50	.22	.05	☐ 252	Lowell Palmer	.50	.22	.05
☐ 179	Ivan Murrell	.50	.22	.05	☐ 253	Ron Woods	.50	.22	.05
☐ 180	Tommy John	1.75	.85	.17	☐ 254	Camilo Pascual	.50	.22	.05
☐ 181	Sparky Anderson MGR	.75	.35	.07	☐ 255	Jim Spencer	.50	.22	.05
☐ 182	Dick Hall	.50	.22	.05	☐ 256	Vic Davalillo	.50	.22	.05
☐ 183	Jerry Grote	.50	.22	.05	☐ 257	Dennis Higgins	.50	.22	.05
☐ 184	Ray Fosse	.50	.22	.05	☐ 258	Paul Popovich	.50	.22	.05
☐ 185	Don Mincher	.50	.22	.05	☐ 259	Tommie Reynolds	.50	.22	.05
☐ 186	Rick Joseph	.50	.22	.05	☐ 260	Claude Osteen	.50	.22	.05
☐ 187	Mike Hedlund	.50	.22	.05	☐ 261	Curt Motton	.50	.22	.05
☐ 188	Manny Sanguillen	.60	.28	.06	☐ 262	Twins Rookies	.50	.22	.05
☐ 189	Yankees Rookies	20.00	9.00	2.00		Jerry Morales			
	Thurman Munson					Jim Williams			
	Dave McDonald				☐ 263	Duane Josephson	.50	.22	.05
☐ 190	Joe Torre	.75	.35	.07	☐ 264	Rich Hebner	.50	.22	.05
☐ 191	Vicente Romo	.50	.22	.05	☐ 265	Randy Hundley	.50	.22	.05
☐ 192	Jim Qualls	.50	.22	.05	☐ 266	Wally Bunker	.50	.22	.05
☐ 193	Mike Wegener	.50	.22	.05	☐ 267	Twins Rookies	.50	.22	.05
☐ 194	Chuck Manuel	.50	.22	.05		Herman Hill			
PLAYOFFS (195-202)						Paul Ratliff			
☐ 195	NL Playoff Game 1	1.50	.70	.15	☐ 268	Claude Raymond	.50	.22	.05
	Seaver wins opener				☐ 269	Cesar Gutierrez	.50	.22	.05
☐ 196	NL Playoff Game 2	.75	.35	.07	☐ 270	Chris Short	.50	.22	.05
	Mets show muscle				☐ 271	Greg Goossen	.50	.22	.05
☐ 197	NL Playoff Game 3	1.50	.70	.15	☐ 272	Hector Torres	.50	.22	.05
	Ryan saves the day				☐ 273	Ralph Houk MGR	.60	.28	.06
☐ 198	NL Playoff Summary	.75	.35	.07	☐ 274	Gerry Arrigo	.50	.22	.05
	Mets celebrate				☐ 275	Duke Sims	.50	.22	.05
☐ 199	AL Playoff Game 1	.75	.35	.07	☐ 276	Ron Hunt	.50	.22	.05
	Orioles win				☐ 277	Paul Doyle	.50	.22	.05
	squeaker (Cuellar)				☐ 278	Tommie Aaron	.50	.22	.05
☐ 200	AL Playoff Game 2	.75	.35	.07	☐ 279	Bill Lee	.60	.28	.06
	Powell scores				☐ 280	Donn Clendenon	.50	.22	.05
	winning run				☐ 281	Casey Cox	.50	.22	.05
☐ 201	AL Playoff Game 3	.75	.35	.07	☐ 282	Steve Huntz	.50	.22	.05
	Birds wrap it up				☐ 283	Angel Bravo	.50	.22	.05
☐ 202	AL Playoff Summary	.75	.35	.07	☐ 284	Jack Baldschun	.50	.22	.05
	Orioles celebrate				☐ 285	Paul Blair	.50	.22	.05
☐ 203	Rudy May	.50	.22	.05	☐ 286	Dodgers Rookies	4.00	1.85	.40
☐ 204	Len Gabrielson	.50	.22	.05		Jack Jenkins			
☐ 205	Bert Campaneris	.60	.28	.06		Bill Buckner			
☐ 206	Clete Boyer	.60	.28	.06	☐ 287	Fred Talbot	.50	.22	.05
☐ 207	Tigers Rookies	.50	.22	.05	☐ 288	Larry Hisle	.50	.22	.05
	Norman McRae				☐ 289	Gene Brabender	.50	.22	.05
	Bob Reed				☐ 290	Rod Carew	12.00	5.50	1.20
☐ 208	Fred Gladding	.50	.22	.05	☐ 291	Leo Durocher MGR	.75	.35	.07
☐ 209	Ken Suarez	.50	.22	.05	☐ 292	Eddie Leon	.50	.22	.05
☐ 210	Juan Marichal	3.00	1.40	.30	☐ 293	Bob Bailey	.50	.22	.05

☐ 294	Jose Azcue	.50	.22	.05
☐ 295	Cecil Upshaw	.50	.22	.05
☐ 296	Woody Woodward	.50	.22	.05
☐ 297	Curt Blefary	.50	.22	.05
☐ 298	Ken Henderson	.50	.22	.05
☐ 299	Buddy Bradford	.50	.22	.05
☐ 300	Tom Seaver	16.00	7.50	1.60
☐ 301	Chico Salmon	.50	.22	.05
☐ 302	Jeff James	.50	.22	.05
☐ 303	Brant Alyea	.50	.22	.05
☐ 304	Bill Russell	1.25	.60	.12

WORLD SERIES (305-310)

☐ 305	World Series Game 1	.75	.35	.07
	Buford leadoff homer			
☐ 306	World Series Game 2	.75	.35	.07
	Clendenon's homer			
	breaks ice			
☐ 307	World Series Game 3	.75	.35	.07
	Agee's catch			
	saves the day			
☐ 308	World Series Game 4	.75	.35	.07
	Martin's bunt			
	ends deadlock			
☐ 309	World Series Game 5	.75	.35	.07
	Koosman shuts door			
☐ 310	World Series Summary	.75	.35	.07
	Mets whoop it up			
☐ 311	Dick Green	.50	.22	.05
☐ 312	Mike Torrez	.60	.28	.06
☐ 313	Mayo Smith MGR	.50	.22	.05
☐ 314	Bill McCool	.50	.22	.05
☐ 315	Luis Aparicio	2.50	1.15	.25
☐ 316	Skip Guinn	.50	.22	.05
☐ 317	Red Sox Rookies	.50	.22	.05
	Billy Conigliaro			
	Luis Alvarado			
☐ 318	Willie Smith	.50	.22	.05
☐ 319	Clay Dalrymple	.50	.22	.05
☐ 320	Jim Maloney	.60	.28	.06
☐ 321	Lou Piniella	1.00	.45	.10
☐ 322	Luke Walker	.50	.22	.05
☐ 323	Wayne Comer	.50	.22	.05
☐ 324	Tony Taylor	.50	.22	.05
☐ 325	Dave Boswell	.50	.22	.05
☐ 326	Bill Voss	.50	.22	.05
☐ 327	Hal King	.50	.22	.05
☐ 328	George Brunet	.50	.22	.05
☐ 329	Chris Cannizzaro	.50	.22	.05
☐ 330	Lou Brock	4.00	1.85	.40
☐ 331	Chuck Dobson	.50	.22	.05
☐ 332	Bobby Wine	.50	.22	.05
☐ 333	Bobby Murcer	1.00	.45	.10
☐ 334	Phil Regan	.50	.22	.05
☐ 335	Bill Freehan	.60	.28	.06
☐ 336	Del Unser	.50	.22	.05
☐ 337	Mike McCormick	.50	.22	.05
☐ 338	Paul Schaal	.50	.22	.05
☐ 339	Johnny Edwards	.50	.22	.05
☐ 340	Tony Conigliaro	.75	.35	.07
☐ 341	Bill Sudakis	.50	.22	.05
☐ 342	Wilbur Wood	.50	.22	.05
☐ 343	4th Checklist	1.00	.20	.05
☐ 344	Marcelino Lopez	.50	.22	.05
☐ 345	Al Ferrara	.50	.22	.05
☐ 346	Red Schoendienst MGR	.60	.28	.06
☐ 347	Russ Snyder	.50	.22	.05
☐ 348	Mets Rookies	.50	.22	.05
	Mike Jorgensen			
	Jesse Hudson			
☐ 349	Steve Hamilton	.50	.22	.05
☐ 350	Roberto Clemente	15.00	7.00	1.50
☐ 351	Tom Murphy	.50	.22	.05
☐ 352	Bob Barton	.50	.22	.05
☐ 353	Stan Williams	.50	.22	.05
☐ 354	Amos Otis	.75	.35	.07
☐ 355	Doug Rader	.60	.28	.06
☐ 356	Fred Lasher	.50	.22	.05
☐ 357	Bob Burda	.50	.22	.05
☐ 358	Pedro Borbon	.50	.22	.05
☐ 359	Phil Roof	.50	.22	.05
☐ 360	Curt Flood	.60	.28	.06
☐ 361	Ray Jarvis	.50	.22	.05
☐ 362	Joe Hague	.50	.22	.05
☐ 363	Tom Shopay	.50	.22	.05
☐ 364	Dan McGinn	.50	.22	.05
☐ 365	Zoilo Versalles	.50	.22	.05
☐ 366	Barry Moore	.50	.22	.05
☐ 367	Mike Lum	.50	.22	.05
☐ 368	Ed Herrmann	.50	.22	.05
☐ 369	Alan Foster	.50	.22	.05
☐ 370	Tommy Harper	.50	.22	.05
☐ 371	Rod Gaspar	.50	.22	.05
☐ 372	Dave Guisti	.50	.22	.05

☐ 373	Roy White	.50	.22	.05
☐ 374	Tommie Sisk	.50	.22	.05
☐ 375	Johnny Callison	.50	.22	.05
☐ 376	Lefty Phillips	.50	.22	.05
☐ 377	Bill Butler	.50	.22	.05
☐ 378	Jim Davenport	.50	.22	.05
☐ 379	Tom Tischinski	.50	.22	.05
☐ 380	Tony Perez	1.50	.70	.15
☐ 381	Athletics Rookies	.50	.22	.05
	Bobby Brooks			
	Mike Olivo			
☐ 382	Jack DiLauro	.50	.22	.05
☐ 383	Mickey Stanley	.50	.22	.05
☐ 384	Gary Neibauer	.50	.22	.05
☐ 385	George Scott	.60	.28	.06
☐ 386	Bill Dillman	.50	.22	.05
☐ 387	Orioles Team	.75	.35	.07
☐ 388	Byron Browne	.50	.22	.05
☐ 389	Jim Shellenback	.50	.22	.05
☐ 390	Willie Davis	.75	.35	.07
☐ 391	Larry Brown	.50	.22	.05
☐ 392	Walt Hriniak	.50	.22	.05
☐ 393	John Gelnar	.50	.22	.05
☐ 394	Gil Hodges	2.50	1.15	.25
☐ 395	Walt Williams	.50	.22	.05
☐ 396	Steve Blass	.60	.28	.06
☐ 397	Roger Repoz	.50	.22	.05
☐ 398	Bill Stoneman	.50	.22	.05
☐ 399	Yankees Team	.75	.35	.07
☐ 400	Denny McLain	.75	.35	.07
☐ 401	Giants Rookies	.50	.22	.05
	John Harrell			
	Bernie Williams			
☐ 402	Ellie Rodriguez	.50	.22	.05
☐ 403	Jim Bunning	1.25	.60	.12
☐ 404	Rich Reese	.50	.22	.05
☐ 405	Bill Hands	.50	.22	.05
☐ 406	Mike Andrews	.50	.22	.05
☐ 407	Bob Watson	.60	.28	.06
☐ 408	Paul Lindblad	.50	.22	.05
☐ 409	Bob Tolan	.50	.22	.05
☐ 410	Boog Powell	1.25	.60	.12
☐ 411	Dodgers Team	.75	.35	.07
☐ 412	Larry Burchart	.50	.22	.05
☐ 413	Sonny Jackson	.50	.22	.05
☐ 414	Paul Edmondson	.50	.22	.05
☐ 415	Julian Javier	.50	.22	.05
☐ 416	Joe Verbanic	.50	.22	.05
☐ 417	John Bateman	.50	.22	.05
☐ 418	John Donaldson	.50	.22	.05
☐ 419	Ron Taylor	.50	.22	.05
☐ 420	Ken McMullen	.50	.22	.05
☐ 421	Pat Dobson	.60	.28	.06
☐ 422	Royals Team	.75	.35	.07
☐ 423	Jerry May	.50	.22	.05
☐ 424	Mike Kilkenny	.50	.22	.05
☐ 425	Bobby Bonds	1.00	.45	.10
☐ 426	Bill Rigney MGR	.50	.22	.05
☐ 427	Fred Norman	.50	.22	.05
☐ 428	Don Buford	.50	.22	.05
☐ 429	Cubs Rookies	.50	.22	.05
	Randy Bobb			
	Jim Cosman			
☐ 430	Andy Messersmith	.60	.28	.06
☐ 431	Ron Swoboda	.50	.22	.05
☐ 432	5th Checklist	1.00	.45	.10
☐ 433	Ron Bryant	.50	.22	.05
☐ 434	Felipe Alou	.60	.28	.06
☐ 435	Nelson Briles	.50	.22	.05
☐ 436	Phillies Team	.75	.35	.07
☐ 437	Danny Cater	.50	.22	.05
☐ 438	Pat Jarvis	.50	.22	.05
☐ 439	Lee Maye	.50	.22	.05
☐ 440	Bill Mazeroski	.75	.35	.07
☐ 441	John O'Donoghue	.50	.22	.05
☐ 442	Gene Mauch MGR	.60	.28	.06
☐ 443	Al Jackson	.50	.22	.05
☐ 444	White Sox Rookies	.50	.22	.05
	Billy Farmer			
	John Matias			
☐ 445	Vada Pinson	.75	.35	.07
☐ 446	Billy Grabarkewitz	.50	.22	.05
☐ 447	Lee Stange	.50	.22	.05
☐ 448	Astros Team	.75	.35	.07
☐ 449	Jim Palmer	7.50	3.50	.75

ALL-STARS (450-469)

☐ 450	Willie McCovey AS	2.50	1.15	.25
☐ 451	Boog Powell AS	.60	.28	.06
☐ 452	Felix Millan AS	.50	.22	.05
☐ 453	Rod Carew AS	3.00	1.40	.30
☐ 454	Ron Santo AS	.50	.22	.05
☐ 455	Brooks Robinson AS	2.50	1.15	.25
☐ 456	Don Kessinger AS	.50	.22	.05

☐ 457	Rico Petrocelli AS	.50	.22	.05
☐ 458	Pete Rose AS	7.50	3.50	.75
☐ 459	Reggie Jackson AS	5.00	2.35	.50
☐ 460	Matty Alou AS	.50	.22	.05
☐ 461	Carl Yastrzemski AS	4.00	1.85	.40
☐ 462	Hank Aaron AS	4.00	1.85	.40
☐ 463	Frank Robinson AS	2.50	1.15	.25
☐ 464	Johnny Bench AS	3.50	1.65	.35
☐ 465	Bill Freehan AS	.50	.22	.05
☐ 466	Juan Marichal AS	2.00	.90	.20
☐ 467	Denny McLain AS	.60	.28	.06
☐ 468	Jerry Koosman AS	.60	.28	.06
☐ 469	Sam McDowell AS	.50	.22	.05
☐ 470	Willie Stargell	3.50	1.65	.35
☐ 471	Chris Zachary	.50	.22	.05
☐ 472	Braves Team	.75	.35	.07
☐ 473	Don Bryant	.50	.22	.05
☐ 474	Dick Kelley	.50	.22	.05
☐ 475	Dick McAuliffe	.50	.22	.05
☐ 476	Don Shaw	.50	.22	.05
☐ 477	Orioles Rookies	.50	.22	.05
	Al Severinsen			
	Roger Freed			
☐ 478	Bob Heise	.50	.22	.05
☐ 479	Dick Woodson	.50	.22	.05
☐ 480	Glen Beckert	.50	.22	.05
☐ 481	Jose Tartabull	.50	.22	.05
☐ 482	Tom Hilgendorf	.50	.22	.05
☐ 483	Gail Hopkins	.50	.22	.05
☐ 484	Gary Nolan	.50	.22	.05
☐ 485	Jay Johnstone	.60	.28	.06
☐ 486	Terry Harmon	.50	.22	.05
☐ 487	Cisco Carlos	.50	.22	.05
☐ 488	J.C. Martin	.50	.22	.05
☐ 489	Eddie Kasko MGR	.50	.22	.05
☐ 490	Bill Singer	.50	.22	.05
☐ 491	Graig Nettles	2.50	1.15	.25
☐ 492	Astros Rookies	.50	.22	.05
	Keith Lampard			
	Scipio Spinks			
☐ 493	Lindy McDaniel	.50	.22	.05
☐ 494	Larry Stahl	.50	.22	.05
☐ 495	Dave Morehead	.50	.22	.05
☐ 496	Steve Whitaker	.50	.22	.05
☐ 497	Eddie Watt	.50	.22	.05
☐ 498	Al Weis	.50	.22	.05
☐ 499	Skip Lockwood	.50	.22	.05
☐ 500	Hank Aaron	15.00	7.00	1.50
☐ 501	White Sox Team	.75	.35	.07
☐ 502	Rollie Fingers	3.00	1.40	.30
☐ 503	Dal Maxvill	.50	.22	.05
☐ 504	Don Pavletich	.50	.22	.05
☐ 505	Ken Holtzman	.60	.28	.06
☐ 506	Ed Stroud	.50	.22	.05
☐ 507	Pat Corrales	.60	.28	.06
☐ 508	Joe Niekro	.75	.35	.07
☐ 509	Expos Team	.75	.35	.07
☐ 510	Tony Oliva	1.25	.60	.12
☐ 511	Joe Hoerner	.50	.22	.05
☐ 512	Billy Harris	.50	.22	.05
☐ 513	Preston Gomez MGR	.50	.22	.05
☐ 514	Steve Hovley	.50	.22	.05
☐ 515	Don Wilson	.50	.22	.05
☐ 516	Yankees Rookies	.50	.22	.05
	John Ellis			
	Jim Lyttle			
☐ 517	Joe Gibbon	.50	.22	.05
☐ 518	Bill Melton	.50	.22	.05
☐ 519	Don McMahon	.50	.22	.05
☐ 520	Willie Horton	.60	.28	.06
☐ 521	Cal Koonce	.50	.22	.05
☐ 522	Angels Team	.75	.35	.07
☐ 523	Jose Pena	.50	.22	.05
☐ 524	Alvin Dark MGR	.60	.28	.06
☐ 525	Jerry Adair	.50	.22	.05
☐ 526	Ron Herbel	.50	.22	.05
☐ 527	Don Bosch	.50	.22	.05
☐ 528	Elrod Hendricks	.50	.22	.05
☐ 529	Bob Aspromonte	.50	.22	.05
☐ 530	Bob Gibson	4.00	1.85	.40
☐ 531	Ron Clark	.50	.22	.05
☐ 532	Danny Murtaugh MGR	.50	.22	.05
☐ 533	Buzz Stephen	.50	.22	.05
☐ 534	Twins Team	.75	.35	.07
☐ 535	Andy Kosco	.50	.22	.05
☐ 536	Mike Kekich	.50	.22	.05
☐ 537	Joe Morgan	2.50	1.15	.25
☐ 538	Bob Humphreys	.50	.22	.05
☐ 539	Phillies Rookies	2.00	.90	.20
	Dennis Doyle			
	Larry Bowa			
☐ 540	Gary Peters	.50	.22	.05
☐ 541	Bill Heath	.50	.22	.05

☐ 542	6th Checklist	1.50	.30	.05
☐ 543	Clyde Wright	.50	.22	.05
☐ 544	Reds Team	1.00	.45	.10
☐ 545	Ken Harrelson	1.00	.45	.10
☐ 546	Ron Reed	.50	.22	.05

1971 O-Pee-Chee

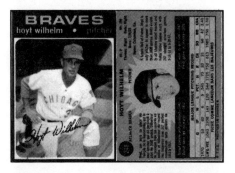

The cards in this 752 card set measure 2 1/2" by 3 1/2". The 1971 O-Pee-Chee set is a challenge to complete in "mint" condition because the black obverse border is easily scratched and damaged. The O-Pee-Chee cards seem to have been cut (into individual cards) not as sharply as the Topps cards; the borders frequently appear slightly frayed. An unusual feature of this set is that the player is also pictured in black and white on the back of the card. Cards 524-643 and the last series (644- 752) are somewhat scarce. The O-Pee-Chee cards can be distinguished from Topps cards by the "Printed in Canada" on the bottom of the reverse. The reverse color is yellow instead of the green found on the backs of the 1971 Topps cards. The card backs are written in both French and English, except for cards 524-752 which were printed in English only. There are several cards which are appear different from the corresponding Topps number on the obverse with a different pose or different team noted in bold type, i.e. "Recently Traded to ..." These changed cards are numbers 31, 32, 73, 144, 151, 161, 172, 182, 191, 202, 207, 248, 289, and 578. Remember, the prices below apply only to the O-Pee- Chee cards -- NOT Topps cards which are much more plentiful.

	MINT	VG-E	F-G
COMPLETE SET	600.00	275.00	60.00
COMMON PLAYER (1-523)	.40	.18	.04
COMMON PLAYER (524-643)	.65	.30	.06
COMMON PLAYER (644-752)	2.00	.90	.20

☐	1	Orioles Team	2.00	.40	.10
☐	2	Dock Ellis	.40	.18	.04
☐	3	Dick McAuliffe	.40	.18	.04
☐	4	Vic Davalillo	.40	.18	.04
☐	5	Thurman Munson	10.00	4.75	1.00
☐	6	Ed Spiezio	.40	.18	.04
☐	7	Jim Holt	.40	.18	.04
☐	8	Mike McQueen	.40	.18	.04
☐	9	George Scott	.50	.22	.05
☐	10	Claude Osteen	.50	.22	.05
☐	11	Elliott Maddox	.40	.18	.04
☐	12	Johnny Callison	.50	.22	.05
☐	13	White Sox Rookies	.40	.18	.04
		Charlie Brinkman			
		Dick Moloney			
☐	14	Dave Concepcion	4.00	1.85	.40
☐	15	Andy Messersmith	.50	.22	.05

☐ 16 Ken Singleton	2.00	.90	.20
☐ 17 Billy Sorrell	.40	.18	.04
☐ 18 Norm Miller	.40	.18	.04
☐ 19 Skip Pitlock	.40	.18	.04
☐ 20 Reggie Jackson	15.00	7.00	1.50
☐ 21 Dan McGinn	.40	.18	.04
☐ 22 Phil Roof	.40	.18	.04
☐ 23 Oscar Gamble	.50	.22	.05
☐ 24 Rich Hand	.40	.18	.04
☐ 25 Clarence Gaston	.40	.18	.04
☐ 26 Bert Blyleven	5.00	2.35	.50
☐ 27 Pirates Rookies	.40	.18	.04
Fred Cambria			
Gene Clines			
☐ 28 Ron Klimkowski	.40	.18	.04
☐ 29 Don Buford	.40	.18	.04
☐ 30 Phil Niekro	2.00	.90	.20
☐ 31 John Bateman	2.00	.90	.20
(different pose)			
☐ 32 Jerry Davanon	2.00	.90	.20
(Orioles)			
☐ 33 Del Unser	.40	.18	.04
☐ 34 Sandy Vance	.40	.18	.04
☐ 35 Lou Piniella	.75	.35	.07
☐ 36 Dean Chance	.50	.22	.05
☐ 37 Rich McKinney	.40	.18	.04
☐ 38 Jim Colborn	.40	.18	.04
☐ 39 Tiger Rookies	.40	.18	.04
Lerrin LaGrow			
Gene Lamont			
☐ 40 Lee May	.50	.22	.05
☐ 41 Rick Austin	.40	.18	.04
☐ 42 Boots Day	.40	.18	.04
☐ 43 Steve Kealey	.40	.18	.04
☐ 44 Johnny Edwards	.40	.18	.04
☐ 45 Jim Hunter	2.00	.90	.20
☐ 46 Dave Campbell	.40	.18	.04
☐ 47 Johnny Jeter	.40	.18	.04
☐ 48 Dave Baldwin	.40	.18	.04
☐ 49 Don Money	.40	.18	.04
☐ 50 Willie McCovey	3.50	1.65	.35
☐ 51 Steve Kline	.40	.18	.04
☐ 52 Braves Rookies	.50	.22	.05
Oscar Brown			
Earl Williams			
☐ 53 Paul Blair	.50	.22	.05
☐ 54 Checklist 1st Series	1.00	.20	.05
☐ 55 Steve Carlton	12.00	5.50	1.20
☐ 56 Duane Josephson	.40	.18	.04
☐ 57 Von Joshua	.40	.18	.04
☐ 58 Bill Lee	.50	.22	.05
☐ 59 Gene Mauch MGR	.50	.22	.05
☐ 60 Dick Bosman	.40	.18	.04
☐ 61 AL Batting Leaders	1.00	.45	.10
Alex Johnson			
Carl Yastrzemski			
Tony Oliva			
☐ 62 NL Batting Leaders	.60	.28	.06
Rico Carty			
Joe Torre			
Manny Sanguillen			
☐ 63 AL RBI Leaders	.75	.35	.07
Frank Robinson			
Tony Conigliaro			
Boog Powell			
☐ 64 NL RBI Leaders	.75	.35	.07
Johnny Bench			
Tony Perez			
Billy Williams			
☐ 65 AL HR Leaders	1.00	.45	.10
Frank Howard			
Harmon Killebrew			
Carl Yastrzemski			
☐ 66 NL HR Leaders	.75	.35	.07
Johnny Bench			
Billy Williams			
Tony Perez			
☐ 67 AL ERA Leaders	.60	.28	.06
Diego Segui			
Jim Palmer			
Clyde Wright			
☐ 68 NL ERA Leaders	.75	.35	.07
Tom Seaver			
Wayne Simpson			
Luke Walker			
☐ 69 AL Pitching Leaders	.60	.28	.06
Mike Cuellar			
Dave McNally			
Jim Perry			
☐ 70 NL Pitching Leaders	1.25	.60	.12
Bob Gibson			
Gaylord Perry			
Fergie Jenkins			

☐ 71 AL Strikeout Leaders	.60	.28	.06
Sam McDowell			
Mickey Lolich			
Bob Johnson			
☐ 72 NL Strikeout Leaders	1.25	.60	.12
Tom Seaver			
Bob Gibson			
Fergie Jenkins			
☐ 73 George Brunet	2.00	.90	.20
(Cardinals)			
☐ 74 Twins Rookies	.40	.18	.04
Pete Hamm			
Jim Nettles			
☐ 75 Gary Nolan	.40	.18	.04
☐ 76 Ted Savage	.40	.18	.04
☐ 77 Mike Compton	.40	.18	.04
☐ 78 Jim Spencer	.40	.18	.04
☐ 79 Wade Blasingame	.40	.18	.04
☐ 80 Bill Melton	.40	.18	.04
☐ 81 Felix Millan	.40	.18	.04
☐ 82 Casey Cox	.40	.18	.04
☐ 83 Met Rookies	.50	.22	.05
Tim Foli			
Randy Bobb			
☐ 84 Marcel Lachemann	.40	.18	.04
☐ 85 Bill Grabarkewitz	.40	.18	.04
☐ 86 Mike Kilkenny	.40	.18	.04
☐ 87 Jack Heidemann	.40	.18	.04
☐ 88 Hal King	.40	.18	.04
☐ 89 Ken Brett	.50	.22	.05
☐ 90 Joe Pepitone	.50	.22	.05
☐ 91 Bob Lemon MGR	1.00	.45	.10
☐ 92 Fred Wenz	.40	.18	.04
☐ 93 Senators Rookies	.40	.18	.04
Norm McRae			
Denny Riddleberger			
☐ 94 Don Hahn	.40	.18	.04
☐ 95 Luis Tiant	.60	.28	.06
☐ 96 Joe Hague	.40	.18	.04
☐ 97 Floyd Wicker	.40	.18	.04
☐ 98 Joe Decker	.40	.18	.04
☐ 99 Mark Belanger	.50	.22	.05
☐ 100 Pete Rose	35.00	16.50	3.50
☐ 101 Les Cain	.40	.18	.04
☐ 102 Astros Rookies	.50	.22	.05
Ken Forsch			
Larry Howard			
☐ 103 Rich Severinson	.40	.18	.04
☐ 104 Dan Frisella	.40	.18	.04
☐ 105 Tony Conigliaro	.60	.28	.06
☐ 106 Tom Dukes	.40	.18	.04
☐ 107 Roy Foster	.40	.18	.04
☐ 108 John Cumberland	.40	.18	.04
☐ 109 Steve Hovley	.40	.18	.04
☐ 110 Bill Mazeroski	.60	.28	.06
☐ 111 Yankee Rookies	.40	.18	.04
Loyd Colson			
Bobby Mitchell			
☐ 112 Manny Mota	.50	.22	.05
☐ 113 Jerry Crider	.40	.18	.04
☐ 114 Billy Conigliaro	.40	.18	.04
☐ 115 Donn Clendenon	.40	.18	.04
☐ 116 Ken Sanders	.40	.18	.04
☐ 117 Ted Simmons	5.00	2.35	.50
☐ 118 Cookie Rojas	.40	.18	.04
☐ 119 Frank Lucchesi MGR	.40	.18	.04
☐ 120 Willie Horton	.50	.22	.05
☐ 121 Cubs Rookies	.40	.18	.04
Jim Dunegan			
Roe Skidmore			
☐ 122 Eddie Watt	.40	.18	.04
☐ 123 Checklist 2nd Series	1.00	.20	.05
☐ 124 Don Gullett	.50	.22	.05
☐ 125 Ray Fosse	.40	.18	.04
☐ 126 Danny Coombs	.40	.18	.04
☐ 127 Danny Thompson	.40	.18	.04
☐ 128 Frank Johnson	.40	.18	.04
☐ 129 Aurelio Monteagudo	.40	.18	.04
☐ 130 Denis Menke	.40	.18	.04
☐ 131 Curt Blefary	.40	.18	.04
☐ 132 Jose Laboy	.40	.18	.04
☐ 133 Mickey Lolich	.75	.35	.07
☐ 134 Jose Arcia	.40	.18	.04
☐ 135 Rick Monday	.50	.22	.05
☐ 136 Duffy Dyer	.40	.18	.04
☐ 137 Marcelino Lopez	.40	.18	.04
☐ 138 Phillies Rookies	.50	.22	.05
Joe Lis			
Willie Montanez			
☐ 139 Paul Casanova	.40	.18	.04
☐ 140 Gaylord Perry	3.00	1.40	.30
☐ 141 Frank Quilici	.40	.18	.04
☐ 142 Mack Jones	.40	.18	.04

☐ 143	Steve Blass	.50	.22	.05
☐ 144	Jackie Hernandez	2.00	.90	.20
	(Pirates)			
☐ 145	Bill Singer	.40	.18	.04
☐ 146	Ralph Houk MGR	.50	.22	.05
☐ 147	Bob Priddy	.40	.18	.04
☐ 148	John Mayberry	.50	.22	.05
☐ 149	Mike Hershberger	.40	.18	.04
☐ 150	Sam McDowell	.50	.22	.05
☐ 151	Tommy Davis	2.00	.90	.20
	(Oakland A's)			
☐ 152	Angels Rookies	.40	.18	.04
	Lloyd Allen			
	Winston Llenas			
☐ 153	Gary Ross	.40	.18	.04
☐ 154	Cesar Gutierrez	.40	.18	.04
☐ 155	Ken Henderson	.40	.18	.04
☐ 156	Bart Johnson	.40	.18	.04
☐ 157	Bob Bailey	.40	.18	.04
☐ 158	Jerry Reuss	.60	.28	.06
☐ 159	Jarvis Tatum	.40	.18	.04
☐ 160	Tom Seaver	12.00	5.50	1.20
☐ 161	Ron Hunt	2.00	.90	.20
	(different pose)			
☐ 162	Jack Billingham	.40	.18	.04
☐ 163	Buck Martinez	.40	.18	.04
☐ 164	Reds Rookies:	.50	.22	.05
	Frank Duffy			
	Milt Wilcox			
☐ 165	Cesar Tovar	.40	.18	.04
☐ 166	Joe Hoerner	.40	.18	.04
☐ 167	Tom Grieve	.50	.22	.05
☐ 168	Bruce Dal Canton	.40	.18	.04
☐ 169	Ed Herrmann	.40	.18	.04
☐ 170	Mike Cuellar	.50	.22	.05
☐ 171	Bobby Wine	.40	.18	.04
☐ 172	Duke Sims	2.00	.90	.20
	(Dodgers)			
☐ 173	Gil Garrido	.40	.18	.04
☐ 174	Dave LaRoche	.40	.18	.04
☐ 175	Jim Hickman	.40	.18	.04
☐ 176	Red Sox Rookies	.40	.18	.04
	Bob Montgomery			
	Doug Griffin			
☐ 177	Hal McRae	.60	.28	.06
☐ 178	Dave Duncan	.40	.18	.04
☐ 179	Mike Corkins	.40	.18	.04
☐ 180	Al Kaline	4.00	1.85	.40
☐ 181	Hal Lanier	.50	.22	.05
☐ 182	Al Downing	2.00	.90	.20
	(Dodgers)			
☐ 183	Gil Hodges	2.00	.90	.20
☐ 184	Stan Bahnsen	.40	.18	.04
☐ 185	Julian Javier	.40	.18	.04
☐ 186	Bob Spence	.40	.18	.04
☐ 187	Ted Abernathy	.40	.18	.04
☐ 188	Dodgers Rookies	1.00	.45	.10
	Bob Valentine			
	Mike Strahler			
☐ 189	George Mitterwald	.40	.18	.04
☐ 190	Bob Tolan	.50	.22	.05
☐ 191	Mike Andrews	2.00	.90	.20
	(White Sox)			
☐ 192	Billy Wilson	.40	.18	.04
☐ 193	Bob Grich	2.00	.90	.20
☐ 194	Mike Lum	.40	.18	.04
PLAYOFFS (195-201)				
☐ 195	AL Playoff Game 1	.75	.35	.07
	Powell muscles Twins			
☐ 196	AL Playoff Game 2	.75	.35	.07
	McNally makes it			
	two straight			
☐ 197	AL Playoff Game 3	1.25	.60	.12
	Palmer mows 'em down			
☐ 198	AL Playoff Summary	.75	.35	.07
	Orioles Celebrate			
☐ 199	NL Playoff Game 1	.75	.35	.07
	Cline pinch-triple			
	decides it			
☐ 200	NL Playoff Game 2	.75	.35	.07
	Tolan scores for			
	third time			
☐ 201	NL Playoff Game 3	.75	.35	.07
	Cline scores			
	winning run			
☐ 202	Claude Raymond	2.00	.90	.20
	(different pose)			
☐ 203	Larry Gura	.75	.35	.07
☐ 204	Brewers Rookies	.40	.18	.04
	Bernie Smith			
	George Kopacz			
☐ 205	Gerry Moses	.40	.18	.04
☐ 206	Checklist 3rd Series	1.00	.20	.05

☐ 207	Alan Foster	2.00	.90	.20
	(Indians)			
☐ 208	Billy Martin	1.00	.45	.10
☐ 209	Steve Renko	.40	.18	.04
☐ 210	Rod Carew	12.00	5.50	1.20
☐ 211	Phil Hennigan	.40	.18	.04
☐ 212	Rich Hebner	.40	.18	.04
☐ 213	Frank Baker	.40	.18	.04
☐ 214	Al Ferrara	.40	.18	.04
☐ 215	Diego Segui	.40	.18	.04
☐ 216	Cardinals Rookies	.40	.18	.04
	Reggie Cleveland			
	Luis Melendez			
☐ 217	Ed Stroud	.40	.18	.04
☐ 218	Tony Cloninger	.40	.18	.04
☐ 219	Elrod Hendricks	.40	.18	.04
☐ 220	Ron Santo	.60	.28	.06
☐ 221	Dave Morehead	.40	.18	.04
☐ 222	Bob Watson	.50	.22	.05
☐ 223	Cecil Upshaw	.40	.18	.04
☐ 224	Alan Gallagher	.40	.18	.04
☐ 225	Gary Peters	.40	.18	.04
☐ 226	Bill Russell	.50	.22	.05
☐ 227	Floyd Weaver	.40	.18	.04
☐ 228	Wayne Garrett	.40	.18	.04
☐ 229	Jim Hannan	.40	.18	.04
☐ 230	Willie Stargell	3.00	1.40	.30
☐ 231	Indians Rookies	.50	.22	.05
	Vince Colbert			
	John Lowenstein			
☐ 232	John Strohmayer	.40	.18	.04
☐ 233	Larry Bowa	1.00	.45	.10
☐ 234	Jim Lyttle	.40	.18	.04
☐ 235	Nate Colbert	.40	.18	.04
☐ 236	Bob Humphreys	.40	.18	.04
☐ 237	Cesar Cedeno	1.50	.70	.15
☐ 238	Chuck Dobson	.40	.18	.04
☐ 239	Red Schoendienst MGR	.50	.22	.05
☐ 240	Clyde Wright	.40	.18	.04
☐ 241	Dave Nelson	.40	.18	.04
☐ 242	Jim Ray	.40	.18	.04
☐ 243	Carlos May	.40	.18	.04
☐ 244	Bob Tillman	.40	.18	.04
☐ 245	Jim Kaat	1.25	.60	.12
☐ 246	Tony Taylor	.40	.18	.04
☐ 247	Royals Rookies	.50	.22	.05
	Jerry Cram			
	Paul Splittorff			
☐ 248	Hoyt Wilhelm	5.00	2.35	.50
	(Braves)			
☐ 249	Chico Salmon	.40	.18	.04
☐ 250	Johnny Bench	15.00	7.00	1.50
☐ 251	Frank Reberger	.40	.18	.04
☐ 252	Eddie Leon	.40	.18	.04
☐ 253	Bill Sudakis	.40	.18	.04
☐ 254	Cal Koonce	.40	.18	.04
☐ 255	Bob Robertson	.40	.18	.04
☐ 256	Tony Gonzalez	.40	.18	.04
☐ 257	Nelson Briles	.40	.18	.04
☐ 258	Dick Green	.40	.18	.04
☐ 259	Dave Marshall	.40	.18	.04
☐ 260	Tommy Harper	.40	.18	.04
☐ 261	Darold Knowles	.40	.18	.04
☐ 262	Padres Rookies	.40	.18	.04
	Jim Williams			
	Dave Robinson			
☐ 263	John Ellis	.40	.18	.04
☐ 264	Joe Morgan	2.50	1.15	.25
☐ 265	Jim Northrup	.40	.18	.04
☐ 266	Bill Stoneman	.40	.18	.04
☐ 267	Rich Morales	.40	.18	.04
☐ 268	Phillies Team	.60	.28	.06
☐ 269	Gail Hopkins	.40	.18	.04
☐ 270	Rico Carty	.50	.22	.05
☐ 271	Bill Zepp	.40	.18	.04
☐ 272	Tommy Helms	.40	.18	.04
☐ 273	Pete Richert	.40	.18	.04
☐ 274	Ron Slocum	.40	.18	.04
☐ 275	Vada Pinson	.60	.28	.06
☐ 276	Giants Rookies	6.00	2.80	.60
	Mike Davison			
	George Foster			
☐ 277	Gary Waslewski	.40	.18	.04
☐ 278	Jerry Grote	.40	.18	.04
☐ 279	Lefty Phillips MGR	.40	.18	.04
☐ 280	Fergie Jenkins	1.25	.60	.12
☐ 281	Danny Walton	.40	.18	.04
☐ 282	Jose Pagan	.40	.18	.04
☐ 283	Dick Such	.40	.18	.04
☐ 284	Jim Gosger	.40	.18	.04
☐ 285	Sal Bando	.50	.22	.05
☐ 286	Jerry McNertney	.40	.18	.04
☐ 287	Mike Fiore	.40	.18	.04

288	Joe Moeller	.40	.18	.04
289	Rusty Staub	3.50	1.65	.35
	(different pose)			
290	Tony Oliva	1.00	.45	.10
291	George Culver	.40	.18	.04
292	Jay Johnstone	.50	.22	.05
293	Pat Corrales	.50	.22	.05
294	Steve Dunning	.40	.18	.04
295	Bobby Bonds	.75	.35	.07
296	Tom Timmermann	.40	.18	.04
297	Johnny Briggs	.40	.18	.04
298	Jim Nelson	.40	.18	.04
299	Ed Kirkpatrick	.40	.18	.04
300	Brooks Robinson	5.00	2.35	.50
301	Earl Wilson	.40	.18	.04
302	Phil Gagliano	.40	.18	.04
303	Lindy McDaniel	.40	.18	.04
304	Ron Brand	.40	.18	.04
305	Reggie Smith	.75	.35	.07
306	Jim Nash	.40	.18	.04
307	Don Wert	.40	.18	.04
308	Cardinals Team	.60	.28	.06
309	Dick Ellsworth	.40	.18	.07
310	Tommie Agee	.40	.18	.04
311	Lee Stange	.40	.18	.04
312	Harry Walker MGR	.40	.18	.04
313	Tom Hall	.40	.18	.04
314	Jeff Torborg	.40	.18	.04
315	Ron Fairly	.40	.18	.04
316	Fred Scherman	.40	.18	.04
317	Athletic Rookies	.40	.18	.04
	Jim Driscoll			
	Angel Mangual			
318	Rudy May	.40	.18	.04
319	Ty Cline	.40	.18	.04
320	Dave McNally	.50	.22	.05
321	Tom Matchick	.40	.18	.04
322	Jim Beauchamp	.40	.18	.04
323	Billy Champion	.40	.18	.04
324	Graig Nettles	2.00	.90	.20
325	Juan Marichal	3.00	1.40	.30
326	Richie Scheinblum	.40	.18	.04
WORLD SERIES (327-332)				
327	World Series Game 1	.75	.35	.07
	Powell homers to			
	opposite field			
328	World Series Game 2	.75	.35	.07
	Don Buford			
329	World Series Game 3	1.50	.70	.15
	Frank Robinson			
	shows muscle			
330	World Series Game 4	.75	.35	.07
	Reds stay alive			
331	World Series Game 5	1.50	.70	.15
	Brooks Robinson			
	commits robbery			
332	World Series Summary	.75	.35	.07
	Orioles Celebrate			
333	Clay Kirby	.40	.18	.04
334	Roberto Pena	.40	.18	.04
335	Jerry Koosman	.60	.28	.06
336	Tigers Team	.60	.28	.06
337	Jesus Alou	.40	.18	.04
338	Gene Tenace	.40	.18	.04
339	Wayne Simpson	.40	.18	.04
340	Rico Petrocelli	.50	.22	.05
341	Steve Garvey	40.00	18.00	4.00
342	Frank Tepedino	.40	.18	.04
343	Pirates Rookies	.40	.18	.04
	Ed Acosta			
	Milt May			
344	Ellie Rodriguez	.40	.18	.04
345	Joe Horlen	.40	.18	.04
346	Lum Harris MGR	.40	.18	.04
347	Ted Uhlaender	.40	.18	.04
348	Fred Norman	.40	.18	.04
349	Rich Reese	.40	.18	.04
350	Billy Williams	1.50	.70	.15
351	Jim Shellenback	.40	.18	.04
352	Denny Doyle	.40	.18	.04
353	Carl Taylor	.40	.18	.04
354	Don McMahon	.40	.18	.04
355	Bud Harrelson	.40	.18	.04
356	Bob Locker	.40	.18	.04
357	Reds Team	.75	.35	.07
358	Danny Cater	.40	.18	.04
359	Ron Reed	.40	.18	.04
360	Jim Fregosi	.50	.22	.05
361	Don Sutton	1.50	.70	.15
362	Orioles Rookies	.40	.18	.04
	Mike Adamson			
	Roger Freed			
363	Mike Nagy	.40	.18	.04
364	Tommy Dean	.40	.18	.04
365	Bob Johnson	.40	.18	.04
366	Ron Stone	.40	.18	.04
367	Dalton Jones	.40	.18	.04
368	Bob Veale	.40	.18	.04
369	Checklist 4th Series	1.00	.20	.05
370	Joe Torre	1.00	.45	.10
371	Jack Hiatt	.40	.18	.04
372	Lew Krausse	.40	.18	.04
373	Tom McCraw	.40	.18	.04
374	Clete Boyer	.50	.22	.05
375	Steve Hargan	.40	.18	.04
376	Expos Rookies	.40	.18	.04
	Clyde Mashore			
	Ernie McAnally			
377	Greg Garrett	.40	.18	.04
378	Tito Fuentes	.40	.18	.04
379	Wayne Granger	.40	.18	.04
380	Ted Williams MGR	3.00	1.40	.30
381	Fred Gladding	.40	.18	.04
382	Jake Gibbs	.40	.18	.04
383	Rod Gaspar	.40	.18	.04
384	Rollie Fingers	2.00	.90	.20
385	Maury Wills	1.00	.45	.10
386	Red Sox Team	.75	.35	.07
387	Ron Herbel	.40	.18	.04
388	Al Oliver	2.00	.90	.20
389	Ed Brinkman	.40	.18	.04
390	Glenn Beckert	.40	.18	.04
391	Twins Rookies	.40	.18	.04
	Steve Brye			
	Cotton Nash			
392	Grant Jackson	.40	.18	.04
393	Merv Rettenmund	.40	.18	.04
394	Clay Carroll	.40	.18	.04
395	Roy White	.40	.18	.04
396	Dick Schofield	.40	.18	.04
397	Alvin Dark MGR	.50	.22	.05
398	Howie Reed	.40	.18	.04
399	Jim French	.40	.18	.04
400	Hank Aaron	12.00	5.50	1.20
401	Tom Murphy	.40	.18	.04
402	Dodgers Team	.75	.35	.07
403	Joe Coleman	.40	.18	.04
404	Astros Rookies	.40	.18	.04
	Buddy Harris			
	Roger Metzger			
405	Leo Cardenas	.40	.18	.04
406	Ray Sadecki	.40	.18	.04
407	Joe Rudi	.50	.22	.05
408	Rafael Robles	.40	.18	.04
409	Don Pavletich	.40	.18	.04
410	Ken Holtzman	.50	.22	.05
411	George Spriggs	.40	.18	.04
412	Jerry Johnson	.40	.18	.04
413	Pat Kelly	.40	.18	.04
414	Woodie Fryman	.40	.18	.04
415	Mike Hegan	.40	.18	.04
416	Gene Alley	.40	.18	.04
417	Dick Hall	.40	.18	.04
418	Adolfo Phillips	.40	.18	.04
419	Ron Hansen	.40	.18	.04
420	Jim Merritt	.40	.18	.04
421	John Stephenson	.40	.18	.04
422	Frank Bertaina	.40	.18	.04
423	Tigers Rookies	.40	.18	.04
	Dennis Saunders			
	Tim Marting			
424	R. Rodriquez	.40	.18	.04
425	Doug Rader	.50	.22	.05
426	Chris Cannizzaro	.40	.18	.04
427	Bernie Allen	.40	.18	.04
428	Jim McAndrew	.40	.18	.04
429	Chuck Hinton	.40	.18	.04
430	Wes Parker	.50	.22	.05
431	Tom Burgmeier	.40	.18	.04
432	Bob Didier	.40	.18	.04
433	Skip Lockwood	.40	.18	.04
434	Gary Sutherland	.40	.18	.04
435	Jose Cardenal	.40	.18	.04
436	Wilbur Wood	.40	.18	.04
437	Danny Murtaugh MGR	.40	.18	.04
438	Mike McCormick	.40	.18	.04
439	Phillies Rookies	2.00	.90	.20
	Greg Luzinski			
	Scott Reid			
440	Bert Campaneris	.50	.22	.05
441	Milt Pappas	.50	.22	.05
442	Angels Team	.60	.28	.06
443	Rich Robertson	.40	.18	.04
444	Jimmie Price	.40	.18	.04
445	Art Shamsky	.40	.18	.04

☐ 446	Bobby Bolin	.40	.18	.04
☐ 447	Cesar Geronimo	.40	.18	.04
☐ 448	Dave Roberts	.40	.18	.04
☐ 449	Brant Alyea	.40	.18	.04
☐ 450	Bob Gibson	3.50	1.65	.35
☐ 451	Joe Keough	.40	.18	.04
☐ 452	John Boccabella	.40	.18	.04
☐ 453	Terry Crowley	.40	.18	.04
☐ 454	Mike Paul	.40	.18	.04
☐ 455	Don Kessinger	.50	.22	.05
☐ 456	Bob Meyer	.40	.18	.04
☐ 457	Willie Smith	.40	.18	.04
☐ 458	White Sox Rookies	.40	.18	.04
	Ron Lolich			
	Dave Lemonds			
☐ 459	Jim LeFebvre	.40	.18	.04
☐ 460	Fritz Peterson	.40	.18	.04
☐ 461	Jim Ray Hart	.40	.18	.04
☐ 462	Senators Team	.60	.28	.06
☐ 463	Tom Kelley	.40	.18	.04
☐ 464	Aurelio Rodriguez	.40	.18	.04
☐ 465	Tim McCarver	.60	.28	.06
☐ 466	Ken Berry	.40	.18	.04
☐ 467	Al Santorini	.40	.18	.04
☐ 468	Frank Fernandez	.40	.18	.04
☐ 469	Bob Aspromonte	.40	.18	.04
☐ 470	Bob Oliver	.40	.18	.04
☐ 471	Tom Griffin	.40	.18	.04
☐ 472	Ken Rudolph	.40	.18	.04
☐ 473	Gary Wagner	.40	.18	.04
☐ 474	Jim Fairey	.40	.18	.04
☐ 475	Ron Perranoski	.40	.18	.04
☐ 476	Dal Maxvill	.40	.18	.04
☐ 477	Earl Weaver MGR	1.00	.45	.10
☐ 478	Bernie Carbo	.40	.18	.04
☐ 479	Dennis Higgins	.40	.18	.04
☐ 480	Manny Sanguillen	.50	.22	.05
☐ 481	Daryl Patterson	.40	.18	.04
☐ 482	Padres Team	.60	.28	.06
☐ 483	Gene Michael	.50	.22	.05
☐ 484	Don Wilson	.40	.18	.04
☐ 485	Ken McMullen	.40	.18	.04
☐ 486	Steve Huntz	.40	.18	.04
☐ 487	Paul Schaal	.40	.18	.04
☐ 488	Jerry Stephenson	.40	.18	.04
☐ 489	Luis Alvarado	.40	.18	.04
☐ 490	Deron Johnson	.40	.18	.04
☐ 491	Jim Hardin	.40	.18	.04
☐ 492	Ken Boswell	.40	.18	.04
☐ 493	Dave May	.40	.18	.04
☐ 494	Braves Rookies	.50	.22	.05
	Ralph Garr			
	Rick Kester			
☐ 495	Felipe Alou	.50	.22	.05
☐ 496	Woody Woodward	.40	.18	.04
☐ 497	Horacio Pina	.40	.18	.04
☐ 498	John Kennedy	.40	.18	.04
☐ 499	Checklist 5th Series	1.00	.20	.05
☐ 500	Jim Perry	.60	.28	.06
☐ 501	Andy Etchebarren	.40	.18	.04
☐ 502	Cubs Team	.60	.28	.06
☐ 503	Gates Brown	.40	.18	.04
☐ 504	Ken Wright	.40	.18	.04
☐ 505	Ollie Brown	.40	.18	.04
☐ 506	Bobby Knoop	.40	.18	.04
☐ 507	George Stone	.40	.18	.04
☐ 508	Roger Repoz	.40	.18	.04
☐ 509	Jim Grant	.40	.18	.04
☐ 510	Ken Harrelson	.75	.35	.07
☐ 511	Chris Short	.40	.18	.04
☐ 512	Red Sox Rookies	.40	.18	.04
	Dick Mills			
	Mike Garman			
☐ 513	Nolan Ryan	10.00	4.75	1.00
☐ 514	Ron Woods	.40	.18	.04
☐ 515	Carl Morton	.40	.18	.04
☐ 516	Ted Kubiak	.40	.18	.04
☐ 517	Charlie Fox MGR	.40	.18	.04
☐ 518	Joe Grzenda	.40	.18	.04
☐ 519	Willie Crawford	.40	.18	.04
☐ 520	Tommy John	2.00	.90	.20
☐ 521	Leron Lee	.40	.18	.04
☐ 522	Twins Team	.60	.28	.06
☐ 523	John Odom	.40	.18	.04
☐ 524	Mickey Stanley	.65	.30	.06
☐ 525	Ernie Banks	7.50	3.50	.75
☐ 526	Ray Jarvis	.65	.30	.06
☐ 527	Cleon Jones	.65	.30	.06
☐ 528	Wally Bunker	.65	.30	.06
☐ 529	NL Rookie Infielders	2.50	1.15	.25
	Enzo Hernandez			
	Bill Buckner			
	Marty Perez			
☐ 530	Carl Yastrzemski	15.00	7.00	1.50
☐ 531	Mike Torrez	.75	.35	.07
☐ 532	Bill Rigney MGR	.65	.30	.06
☐ 533	Mike Ryan	.65	.30	.06
☐ 534	Luke Walker	.65	.30	.06
☐ 535	Curt Flood	.75	.35	.07
☐ 536	Claude Raymond	.65	.30	.06
☐ 537	Tom Egan	.65	.30	.06
☐ 538	Angel Bravo	.65	.30	.06
☐ 539	Larry Brown	.65	.30	.06
☐ 540	Larry Dierker	.65	.30	.06
☐ 541	Bob Burda	.65	.30	.06
☐ 542	Bob Miller	.65	.30	.06
☐ 543	Yankees Team	1.00	.45	.10
☐ 544	Vida Blue	2.50	1.15	.25
☐ 545	Dick Dietz	.65	.30	.06
☐ 546	John Matias	.65	.30	.06
☐ 547	Pat Dobson	.75	.35	.07
☐ 548	Don Mason	.65	.30	.06
☐ 549	Jim Brewer	.65	.30	.06
☐ 550	Harmon Killebrew	5.00	2.35	.50
☐ 551	Frank Linzy	.65	.30	.06
☐ 552	Buddy Bradford	.65	.30	.06
☐ 553	Kevin Collins	.65	.30	.06
☐ 554	Lowell Palmer	.65	.30	.06
☐ 555	Walt Williams	.65	.30	.06
☐ 556	Jim McGlothlin	.65	.30	.06
☐ 557	Tom Satriano	.65	.30	.06
☐ 558	Hector Torres	.65	.30	.06
☐ 559	AL Rookie Pitchers	.65	.30	.06
	Terry Cox			
	Bill Gogolewski			
	Gary Jones			
☐ 560	Rusty Staub	1.25	.60	.12
☐ 561	Syd O'Brien	.65	.30	.06
☐ 562	Dave Guisti	.65	.30	.06
☐ 563	Giants Team	1.00	.45	.10
☐ 564	Al Fitzmorris	.65	.30	.06
☐ 565	Jim Wynn	.75	.35	.07
☐ 566	Tim Cullen	.65	.30	.06
☐ 567	Walt Alston MGR	1.25	.60	.12
☐ 568	Sal Campisi	.65	.30	.06
☐ 569	Ivan Murrell	.65	.30	.06
☐ 570	Jim Palmer	7.50	3.50	.75
☐ 571	Ted Sizemore	.65	.30	.06
☐ 572	Jerry Kenney	.65	.30	.06
☐ 573	Ed Kranepool	.65	.30	.06
☐ 574	Jim Bunning	1.50	.70	.15
☐ 575	Bill Freehan	.75	.35	.07
☐ 576	Cubs Rookies	.65	.30	.06
	Adrian Garrett			
	Brock Davis			
	Garry Jestadt			
☐ 577	Jim Lonborg	.75	.35	.07
☐ 578	Eddie Kasko	2.50	1.15	.25
☐ 579	Marty Pattin	.65	.30	.06
☐ 580	Tony Perez	2.00	.90	.20
☐ 581	Roger Nelson	.65	.30	.06
☐ 582	Dave Cash	.65	.30	.06
☐ 583	Ron Cook	.65	.30	.06
☐ 584	Indians Team	1.00	.45	.10
☐ 585	Willie Davis	.75	.35	.07
☐ 586	Dick Woodson	.65	.30	.06
☐ 587	Sonny Jackson	.65	.30	.06
☐ 588	Tom Bradley	.65	.30	.06
☐ 589	Bob Barton	.65	.30	.06
☐ 590	Alex Johnson	.65	.30	.06
☐ 591	Jackie Brown	.75	.35	.07
☐ 592	Randy Hundley	.65	.30	.06
☐ 593	Jack Aker	.65	.30	.06
☐ 594	Cards Rookies	1.00	.45	.10
	Bob Chlupsa			
	Bob Stinson			
	Al Hrabosky			
☐ 595	Dave Johnson	1.00	.45	.10
☐ 596	Mike Jorgensen	.65	.30	.06
☐ 597	Ken Suarez	.65	.30	.06
☐ 598	Rick Wise	.75	.35	.07
☐ 599	Norm Cash	1.00	.45	.10
☐ 600	Willie Mays	16.00	7.50	1.60
☐ 601	Ken Tatum	.65	.30	.06
☐ 602	Marty Martinez	.65	.30	.06
☐ 603	Pirates Team	1.00	.45	.10
☐ 604	John Gelnar	.65	.30	.06
☐ 605	Orlando Cepeda	1.50	.70	.15
☐ 606	Chuck Taylor	.65	.30	.06
☐ 607	Paul Ratliff	.65	.30	.06
☐ 608	Mike Wegener	.65	.30	.06
☐ 609	Leo Durocher MGR	1.00	.45	.10
☐ 610	Amos Otis	.75	.35	.07
☐ 611	Tom Phoebus	.65	.30	.06
☐ 612	Indians Rookies	.65	.30	.06
	Lou Camilli			

Ted Ford
Steve Mingori

☐ 613	Pedro Borbon	.65	.30	.06
☐ 614	Billy Cowan	.65	.30	.06
☐ 615	Mel Stottlemyre	.75	.35	.07
☐ 616	Larry Hisle	.75	.35	.07
☐ 617	Clay Dalrymple	.65	.30	.06
☐ 618	Tug McGraw	1.00	.45	.10
☐ 619	Checklist 6th Series	1.50	.30	.05
☐ 620	Frank Howard	1.00	.45	.10
☐ 621	Ron Bryant	.65	.30	.06
☐ 622	Joe LaHoud	.65	.30	.06
☐ 623	Pat Jarvis	.65	.30	.06
☐ 624	Athletics Team	1.00	.45	.10
☐ 625	Lou Brock	7.50	3.50	.75
☐ 626	Freddie Patek	.65	.30	.06
☐ 627	Steve Hamilton	.65	.30	.06
☐ 628	John Bateman	.65	.30	.06
☐ 629	John Hiller	.65	.30	.06
☐ 630	Roberto Clemente	15.00	7.00	1.50
☐ 631	Eddie Fisher	.65	.30	.06
☐ 632	Darrel Chaney	.65	.30	.06
☐ 633	AL Rookie Outfielders	.65	.30	.06

Bobby Brooks
Pete Koegel
Scott Northey

☐ 634	Phil Regan	.65	.30	.06
☐ 635	Bobby Murcer	1.25	.60	.12
☐ 636	Denny LeMaster	.65	.30	.06
☐ 637	Dave Bristol MGR	.65	.30	.06
☐ 638	Stan Williams	.65	.30	.06
☐ 639	Tom Haller	.65	.30	.06
☐ 640	Frank Robinson	9.00	4.25	.90
☐ 641	Mets Team	1.50	.70	.15
☐ 642	Jim Roland	.65	.30	.06
☐ 643	Rick Reichardt	.65	.30	.06
☐ 644	Jim Stewart	2.00	.90	.20
☐ 645	Jim Maloney	2.00	.90	.20
☐ 646	Bobby Floyd	2.00	.90	.20
☐ 647	Juan Pizarro	2.00	.90	.20
☐ 648	Mets Rookies	2.50	1.15	.25

Rich Folkers
Ted Martinez
John Matlack

☐ 649	Sparky Lyle	2.50	1.15	.25
☐ 650	Rich Allen	4.00	1.85	.40
☐ 651	Jerry Robertson	2.00	.90	.20
☐ 652	Braves Team	2.50	1.15	.25
☐ 653	Russ Snyder	2.00	.90	.20
☐ 654	Don Shaw	2.00	.90	.20
☐ 655	Mike Epstein	2.00	.90	.20
☐ 656	Gerry Nyman	2.00	.90	.20
☐ 657	Jose Azcue	2.00	.90	.20
☐ 658	Paul Lindblad	2.00	.90	.20
☐ 659	Byron Browne	2.00	.90	.20
☐ 660	Ray Culp	2.00	.90	.20
☐ 661	Chuck Tanner MGR	2.50	1.15	.25
☐ 662	Mike Hedlund	2.00	.90	.20
☐ 663	Marv Staehle	2.00	.90	.20
☐ 664	Rookie Pitchers	2.00	.90	.20

Archie Reynolds
Bob Reynolds
Ken Reynolds

☐ 665	Ron Swoboda	2.00	.90	.20
☐ 666	Gene Brabender	2.00	.90	.20
☐ 667	Pete Ward	2.00	.90	.20
☐ 668	Gary Neibauer	2.00	.90	.20
☐ 669	Ike Brown	2.00	.90	.20
☐ 670	Bill Hands	2.00	.90	.20
☐ 671	Bill Voss	2.00	.90	.20
☐ 672	Ed Crosby	2.00	.90	.20
☐ 673	Gerry Janeski	2.00	.90	.20
☐ 674	Expos Team	2.50	1.15	.25
☐ 675	Dave Boswell	2.00	.90	.20
☐ 676	Tommie Reynolds	2.00	.90	.20
☐ 677	Jack DiLauro	2.00	.90	.20
☐ 678	George Thomas	2.00	.90	.20
☐ 679	Don O'Riley	2.00	.90	.20
☐ 680	Don Mincher	2.00	.90	.20
☐ 681	Bill Butler	2.00	.90	.20
☐ 682	Terry Harmon	2.00	.90	.20
☐ 683	Bill Burbach	2.00	.90	.20
☐ 684	Curt Motton	2.00	.90	.20
☐ 685	Moe Drabowsky	2.00	.90	.20
☐ 686	Chico Ruiz	2.00	.90	.20
☐ 687	Ron Taylor	2.00	.90	.20
☐ 688	Sparky Anderson MGR	2.50	1.15	.25
☐ 689	Frank Baker	2.00	.90	.20
☐ 690	Bob Moose	2.00	.90	.20
☐ 691	Bob Heise	2.00	.90	.20
☐ 692	AL Rookie Pitchers	2.00	.90	.20

Hal Haydel
Rogelio Moret

Wayne Twitchell

☐ 693	Jose Pena	2.00	.90	.20
☐ 694	Rick Renick	2.00	.90	.20
☐ 695	Joe Niekro	2.50	1.15	.25
☐ 696	Jerry Morales	2.00	.90	.20
☐ 697	Rickey Clark	2.00	.90	.20
☐ 698	Brewers Team	3.00	1.40	.30
☐ 699	Jim Britton	2.00	.90	.20
☐ 700	Boog Powell	3.00	1.40	.30
☐ 701	Bob Garibaldi	2.00	.90	.20
☐ 702	Milt Ramirez	2.00	.90	.20
☐ 703	Mike Kekich	2.00	.90	.20
☐ 704	J.C. Martin	2.00	.90	.20
☐ 705	Dick Selma	2.00	.90	.20
☐ 706	Joe Foy	2.00	.90	.20
☐ 707	Fred Lasher	2.00	.90	.20
☐ 708	Russ Nagelson	2.00	.90	.20
☐ 709	Rookie Outfielders	16.00	7.50	1.60

Dusty Baker
Don Baylor
Tom Paciorek

☐ 710	Sonny Siebert	2.00	.90	.20
☐ 711	Larry Stahl	2.00	.90	.20
☐ 712	Jose Martinez	2.00	.90	.20
☐ 713	Mike Marshall	2.50	1.15	.25
☐ 714	Dick Williams MGR	2.50	1.15	.25
☐ 715	Horace Clarke	2.00	.90	.20
☐ 716	Dave Leonhard	2.00	.90	.20
☐ 717	Tommie Aaron	2.00	.90	.20
☐ 718	Billy Wynne	2.00	.90	.20
☐ 719	Jerry May	2.00	.90	.20
☐ 720	Matty Alou	2.50	1.15	.25
☐ 721	John Morris	2.00	.90	.20
☐ 722	Astros Team	2.50	1.15	.25
☐ 723	Vicente Romo	2.00	.90	.20
☐ 724	Tom Tischinski	2.00	.90	.20
☐ 725	Gary Gentry	2.00	.90	.20
☐ 726	Paul Popovich	2.00	.90	.20
☐ 727	Ray Lamb	2.00	.90	.20
☐ 728	NL Rookie Outfielders	2.00	.90	.20

Wayne Redmond
Keith Lampard
Bernie Williams

☐ 729	Dick Billings	2.00	.90	.20
☐ 730	Jim Rooker	2.00	.90	.20
☐ 731	Jim Qualls	2.00	.90	.20
☐ 732	Bob Reed	2.00	.90	.20
☐ 733	Lee Maye	2.00	.90	.20
☐ 734	Rob Gardner	2.00	.90	.20
☐ 735	Mike Shannon	2.50	1.15	.25
☐ 736	Mel Queen	2.00	.90	.20
☐ 737	Preston Gomez MGR	2.00	.90	.20
☐ 738	Russ Gibson	2.00	.90	.20
☐ 739	Barry Lersch	2.00	.90	.20
☐ 740	Luis Aparicio	6.00	2.80	.60
☐ 741	Skip Guinn	2.00	.90	.20
☐ 742	Royals Team	3.00	1.40	.30
☐ 743	John O'Donoghue	2.00	.90	.20
☐ 744	Chuck Manuel	3.00	1.40	.30
☐ 745	Sandy Alomar	2.00	.90	.20
☐ 746	Andy Kosco	2.00	.90	.20
☐ 747	NL Rookie Pitchers	2.00	.90	.20

Al Severinsen
Scipio Spinks
Balor Moore

☐ 748	John Purdin	2.00	.90	.20
☐ 749	Ken Szotkiewicz	2.00	.90	.20
☐ 750	Denny McLain	2.50	1.15	.25
☐ 751	Al Weis	2.00	.90	.20
☐ 752	Dick Drago	2.00	.90	.20

1972 O-Pee-Chee

The cards in this 525 card set measure 2 1/2" by
3 1/2". The 1972 O-Pee-Chee set is very similar to
the 1972 Topps set. Features appearing for the first
time were "Boyhood Photos" (KP: 341-348 and
491-498) and "In Action" cards. The curved lines of
the color picture are a departure from the
rectangular designs of other years. The O-Pee-Chee
cards can be distinguished from Topps cards by the
"Printed in Canada" on the bottom of the reverse.
The reverse color is different from the color found

on the backs of the 1972 Topps cards. The card backs are written in both French and English. There is one card which is different from the corresponding Topps number on the obverse, number 465 Gil Hodges, which notes his death in April of 1972. Remember, the prices below apply only to the O-Pee-Chee cards -- NOT Topps cards which are much more plentiful.

		MINT	VG-E	F-G
	COMPLETE SET (525)	325.00	150.00	30.00
	COMMON PLAYER (1-525)	.40	.18	.04
☐ 1	Pirates Team	1.50	.50	.10
☐ 2	Ray Culp	.40	.18	.04
☐ 3	Bob Tolan	.40	.18	.04
☐ 4	Checklist 1st Series	1.00	.20	.05
☐ 5	John Bateman	.40	.18	.04
☐ 6	Fred Scherman	.40	.18	.04
☐ 7	Enzo Hernandez	.40	.18	.04
☐ 8	Ron Swoboda	.40	.18	.04
☐ 9	Stan Williams	.40	.18	.04
☐ 10	Amos Otis	.60	.28	.06
☐ 11	Bobby Valentine	.60	.28	.06
☐ 12	Jose Cardenal	.40	.18	.04
☐ 13	Joe Grzenda	.40	.18	.04
☐ 14	Phillies Rookies	.40	.18	.04
	Pete Koegel			
	Mike Anderson			
	Wayne Twitchell			
☐ 15	Walt Williams	.40	.18	.04
☐ 16	Mike Jorgensen	.40	.18	.04
☐ 17	Dave Duncan	.40	.18	.04
☐ 18	Juan Pizarro	.40	.18	.04
☐ 19	Billy Cowan	.40	.18	.04
☐ 20	Don Wilson	.40	.18	.04
☐ 21	Braves Team	.60	.28	.06
☐ 22	Rob Gardner	.40	.18	.04
☐ 23	Ted Kubiak	.40	.18	.04
☐ 24	Ted Ford	.40	.18	.04
☐ 25	Bill Singer	.40	.18	.04
☐ 26	Andy Etchebarren	.40	.18	.04
☐ 27	Bob Johnson	.40	.18	.04
☐ 28	Twins Rookies	.40	.18	.04
	Bob Gebhard			
	Steve Brye			
	Hal Haydel			
☐ 29	Bill Bonham	.40	.18	.04
☐ 30	Rico Petrocelli	.50	.22	.05
☐ 31	Cleon Jones	.40	.18	.04
☐ 32	Jones In Action	.40	.18	.04
☐ 33	Billy Martin	1.00	.45	.10
☐ 34	Martin In Action	.60	.28	.06
☐ 35	Jerry Johnson	.40	.18	.04
☐ 36	Johnson In Action	.40	.18	.04
☐ 37	Carl Yastrzemski	10.00	4.75	1.00
☐ 38	Yastrzemski In Action	5.00	2.35	.50
☐ 39	Bob Barton	.40	.18	.04
☐ 40	Barton In Action	.40	.18	.04
☐ 41	Tommy Davis	.50	.22	.05
☐ 42	Davis In Action	.40	.18	.04
☐ 43	Rick Wise	.40	.18	.04
☐ 44	Wise In Action	.40	.18	.04
☐ 45	Glenn Beckert	.40	.18	.04
☐ 46	Beckert In Action	.40	.18	.04
☐ 47	John Ellis	.40	.18	.04
☐ 48	Ellis In Action	.40	.18	.04
☐ 49	Willie Mays	10.00	4.75	1.00
☐ 50	Mays In Action	5.00	2.35	.50

☐ 51	Harmon Killebrew	2.00	.90	.20
☐ 52	Killebrew In Action	1.00	.45	.10
☐ 53	Bud Harrelson	.40	.18	.04
☐ 54	Harrelson In Action	.40	.18	.04
☐ 55	Clyde Wright	.40	.18	.04
☐ 56	Rich Chiles	.40	.18	.04
☐ 57	Bob Oliver	.40	.18	.04
☐ 58	Ernie McAnally	.40	.18	.04
☐ 59	Fred Stanley	.40	.18	.04
☐ 60	Manny Sanguillen	.50	.22	.05
☐ 61	Cubs Rookies	.60	.28	.06
	Burt Hooton			
	Gene Hiser			
	Earl Stephenson			
☐ 62	Angel Mangual	.40	.18	.04
☐ 63	Duke Sims	.40	.18	.04
☐ 64	Pete Broberg	.40	.18	.04
☐ 65	Cesar Cedeno	.60	.28	.06
☐ 66	Ray Corbin	.40	.18	.04
☐ 67	Red Schoendienst MGR	.50	.22	.05
☐ 68	Jim York	.40	.18	.04
☐ 69	Roger Freed	.40	.18	.04
☐ 70	Mike Cuellar	.50	.22	.05
☐ 71	Angels Team	.60	.28	.06
☐ 72	Bruce Kison	.60	.28	.06
☐ 73	Steve Huntz	.40	.18	.04
☐ 74	Cecil Upshaw	.40	.18	.04
☐ 75	Bert Campaneris	.50	.22	.05
☐ 76	Don Carrithers	.40	.18	.04
☐ 77	Ron Theobald	.40	.18	.04
☐ 78	Steve Arlin	.40	.18	.04
☐ 79	Red Sox Rookies	18.00	8.50	1.80
	Mike Garman			
	Cecil Cooper			
	Carlton Fisk			
☐ 80	Tony Perez	1.00	.45	.10
☐ 81	Mike Hedlund	.40	.18	.04
☐ 82	Ron Woods	.40	.18	.04
☐ 83	Dalton Jones	.40	.18	.04
☐ 84	Vince Colbert	.40	.18	.04
☐ 85	NL Batting Leaders:	.60	.28	.06
	Joe Torre			
	Ralph Garr			
	Glenn Beckert			
☐ 86	AL Batting Leaders:	.60	.28	.06
	Tony Oliva			
	Bobby Murcer			
	Merv Rettenmund			
☐ 87	NL RBI Leaders:	1.00	.45	.10
	Joe Torre			
	Willie Stargell			
	Hank Aaron			
☐ 88	AL RBI Leaders:	.75	.35	.07
	Harmon Killebrew			
	Frank Robinson			
	Reggie Smith			
☐ 89	NL Home Run Leaders:	1.00	.45	.10
	Willie Stargell			
	Hank Aaron			
	Lee May			
☐ 90	AL Home Run Leaders:	1.00	.45	.10
	Bill Melton			
	Norm Cash			
	Reggie Jackson			
☐ 91	NL ERA Leaders:	.75	.35	.07
	Tom Seaver			
	Dave Roberts			
	(photo actually			
	Danny Coombs)			
	Don Wilson			
☐ 92	AL ERA Leaders:	.75	.35	.07
	Vida Blue			
	Wilbur Wood			
	Jim Palmer			
☐ 93	NL Pitching Leaders:	1.00	.45	.10
	Fergie Jenkins			
	Steve Carlton			
	Al Downing			
	Tom Seaver			
☐ 94	AL Pitching Leaders:	.60	.28	.06
	Mickey Lolich			
	Vida Blue			
	Wilbur Wood			
☐ 95	NL Strikeout Leaders:	.75	.35	.07
	Tom Seaver			
	Fergie Jenkins			
	Bill Stoneman			
☐ 96	AL Strikeout Leaders:	.60	.28	.06
	Mickey Lolich			
	Vida Blue			
	Joe Coleman			
☐ 97	Tom Kelley	.40	.18	.04

☐ 98	Chuck Tanner MGR	.50	.22	.05
☐ 99	Ross Grimsley	.40	.18	.04
☐ 100	Frank Robinson	3.00	1.40	.30
☐ 101	Astros Rookies	1.25	.60	.12
	Bill Greif			
	J.R. Richard			
	Ray Busse			
☐ 102	Lloyd Allen	.40	.18	.04
☐ 103	Checklist 2nd Series	1.00	.20	.05
☐ 104	Toby Harrah	1.25	.60	.12
☐ 105	Gary Gentry	.40	.18	.04
☐ 106	Brewers Team	.60	.28	.06
☐ 107	Jose Cruz	2.50	1.15	.25
☐ 108	Gary Waslewski	.40	.18	.04
☐ 109	Jerry May	.40	.18	.04
☐ 110	Ron Hunt	.40	.18	.04
☐ 111	Jim Grant	.40	.18	.04
☐ 112	Greg Luzinski	1.00	.45	.10
☐ 113	Rogelio Moret	.40	.18	.04
☐ 114	Bill Buckner	1.00	.45	.10
☐ 115	Jim Fregosi	.50	.22	.05
☐ 116	Ed Farmer	.40	.18	.04
☐ 117	Cleo James	.40	.18	.04
☐ 118	Skip Lockwood	.40	.18	.04
☐ 119	Marty Perez	.40	.18	.04
☐ 120	Bill Freehan	.50	.22	.05
☐ 121	Ed Sprague	.40	.18	.04
☐ 122	Larry Biittner	.40	.18	.04
☐ 123	Ed Acosta	.40	.18	.04
☐ 124	Yankees Rookies	.40	.18	.04
	Alan Closter			
	Rusty Torres			
	Roger Hambright			
☐ 125	Dave Cash	.40	.18	.04
☐ 126	Bart Johnson	.40	.18	.04
☐ 127	Duffy Dyer	.40	.18	.04
☐ 128	Eddie Watt	.40	.18	.04
☐ 129	Charlie Fox MGR	.40	.18	.04
☐ 130	Bob Gibson	2.50	1.15	.25
☐ 131	Jim Nettles	.40	.18	.04
☐ 132	Joe Morgan	2.00	.90	.20
☐ 133	Joe Keough	.40	.18	.04
☐ 134	Carl Morton	.40	.18	.04
☐ 135	Vada Pinson	.60	.28	.06
☐ 136	Darrel Chaney	.40	.18	.04
☐ 137	Dick Williams MGR	.50	.22	.05
☐ 138	Mike Kekich	.40	.18	.04
☐ 139	Tim McCarver	.60	.28	.06
☐ 140	Pat Dobson	.50	.22	.05
☐ 141	Mets Rookies	.50	.22	.05
	Buzz Capra			
	Leroy Stanton			
	Jon Matlack			
☐ 142	Chris Chambliss	1.50	.70	.15
☐ 143	Garry Jestadt	.40	.18	.04
☐ 144	Marty Pattin	.40	.18	.04
☐ 145	Don Kessinger	.50	.22	.05
☐ 146	Steve Kealey	.40	.18	.04
☐ 147	Dave Kingman	4.00	1.85	.40
☐ 148	Dick Billings	.40	.18	.04
☐ 149	Gary Neibauer	.40	.18	.04
☐ 150	Norm Cash	.60	.28	.06
☐ 151	Jim Brewer	.40	.18	.04
☐ 152	Gene Clines	.40	.18	.04
☐ 153	Rick Auerbach	.40	.18	.04
☐ 154	Ted Simmons	1.25	.60	.12
☐ 155	Larry Dierker	.40	.18	.04
☐ 156	Twins Team	.60	.28	.06
☐ 157	Don Gullett	.50	.22	.05
☐ 158	Jerry Kenney	.40	.18	.04
☐ 159	John Boccabella	.40	.18	.04
☐ 160	Andy Messersmith	.50	.22	.05
☐ 161	Brock Davis	.40	.18	.04
☐ 162	Brewers Rookies	1.00	.45	.10
	Jerry Bell			
	Darrell Porter			
	Bob Reynolds			
	(Porter and Bell			
	photos switched)			
☐ 163	Tug McGraw	.60	.28	.06
☐ 164	McGraw In Action	.50	.22	.05
☐ 165	Chris Speier	.40	.18	.04
☐ 166	Speier In Action	.40	.18	.04
☐ 167	Deron Johnson	.40	.18	.04
☐ 168	Johnson In Action	.40	.18	.04
☐ 169	Vida Blue	.75	.35	.07
☐ 170	Blue In Action	.50	.22	.05
☐ 171	Darrell Evans	.75	.35	.07
☐ 172	Evans In Action	.50	.22	.05
☐ 173	Clay Kirby	.40	.18	.04
☐ 174	Kirby In Action	.40	.18	.04
☐ 175	Tom Haller	.40	.18	.04
☐ 176	Haller In Action	.40	.18	.04

☐ 177	Paul Schaal	.40	.18	.04
☐ 178	Schaal In Action	.40	.18	.04
☐ 179	Dock Ellis	.40	.18	.04
☐ 180	Ellis In Action	.40	.18	.04
☐ 181	Ed Kranepool	.40	.18	.04
☐ 182	Kranepool In Action	.40	.18	.04
☐ 183	Bill Melton	.40	.18	.04
☐ 184	Melton In Action	.40	.18	.04
☐ 185	Ron Bryant	.40	.18	.04
☐ 186	Bryant In Action	.40	.18	.04
☐ 187	Gates Brown	.40	.18	.04
☐ 188	Frank Lucchesi MGR	.40	.18	.04
☐ 189	Gene Tenace	.40	.18	.04
☐ 190	Dave Giusti	.40	.18	.04
☐ 191	Jeff Burroughs	.60	.28	.06
☐ 192	Cubs Team	.60	.28	.06
☐ 193	Kurt Bevacqua	.40	.18	.04
☐ 194	Fred Norman	.40	.18	.04
☐ 195	Orlando Cepeda	1.00	.45	.10
☐ 196	Mel Queen	.40	.18	.04
☐ 197	Johnny Briggs	.40	.18	.04
☐ 198	Dodgers Rookies	.75	.35	.07
	Charlie Hough			
	Bob O'Brien			
	Mike Strahler			
☐ 199	Mike Fiore	.40	.18	.04
☐ 200	Lou Brock	3.00	1.40	.30
☐ 201	Phil Roof	.40	.18	.04
☐ 202	Scipio Spinks	.40	.18	.04
☐ 203	Ron Blomberg	.40	.18	.04
☐ 204	Tommy Helms	.40	.18	.04
☐ 205	Dick Drago	.40	.18	.04
☐ 206	Dal Maxvill	.40	.18	.04
☐ 207	Tom Egan	.40	.18	.04
☐ 208	Milt Pappas	.40	.18	.04
☐ 209	Joe Rudi	.50	.22	.05
☐ 210	Denny McLain	.75	.35	.07
☐ 211	Gary Sutherland	.40	.18	.04
☐ 212	Grant Jackson	.40	.18	.04
☐ 213	Angels Rookies	.40	.18	.04
	Billy Parker			
	Art Kusnyer			
	Tom Silverio			
☐ 214	Mike McQueen	.40	.18	.04
☐ 215	Alex Johnson	.40	.18	.04
☐ 216	Joe Niekro	.60	.28	.06
☐ 217	Roger Metzger	.40	.18	.04
☐ 218	Eddie Kasko	.40	.18	.04
☐ 219	Rennie Stennett	.40	.18	.04
☐ 220	Jim Perry	.50	.22	.05
☐ 221	NL Playoffs:	.65	.30	.06
	Bucs champs			
☐ 222	AL Playoffs:	1.00	.45	.10
	Orioles champs			
	(Brooks Robinson)			
WORLD SERIES (223-230)				
☐ 223	World Series Game 1	.65	.30	.06
	(McNally pitching)			
☐ 224	World Series Game 2	.65	.30	.06
	(B. Robinson and			
	Belanger			
☐ 225	World Series Game 3	.65	.30	.06
	(Sanguillen scoring)			
☐ 226	World Series Game 4	2.00	.90	.20
	(Clemente on 2nd)			
☐ 227	World Series Game 5	.65	.30	.06
	(Briles pitching)			
☐ 228	World Series Game 6	.75	.35	.07
	(Frank Robinson and			
	Manny Sanguillen)			
☐ 229	World Series Game 7	.65	.30	.06
	(Blass pitching)			
☐ 230	World Series Summary	.65	.30	.06
	Pirates celebrate			
☐ 231	Casey Cox	.40	.18	.04
☐ 232	Giants Rookies	.40	.18	.04
	Chris Arnold			
	Jim Barr			
	Dave Rader			
☐ 233	Jay Johnstone	.50	.22	.05
☐ 234	Ron Taylor	.40	.18	.04
☐ 235	Merv Rettenmund	.40	.18	.04
☐ 236	Jim McGlothlin	.40	.18	.04
☐ 237	Yankees Team	.75	.35	.07
☐ 238	Leron Lee	.40	.18	.04
☐ 239	Tom Timmermann	.40	.18	.04
☐ 240	Rich Allen	1.00	.45	.10
☐ 241	Rollie Fingers	1.75	.85	.17
☐ 242	Don Mincher	.40	.18	.04
☐ 243	Frank Linzy	.40	.18	.04
☐ 244	Steve Braun	.40	.18	.04
☐ 245	Tommie Agee	.40	.18	.04
☐ 246	Tom Burgmeier	.40	.18	.04

☐ 247	Milt May	.40	.18	.04
☐ 248	Tom Bradley	.40	.18	.04
☐ 249	Garry Walker	.40	.18	.04
☐ 250	Boog Powell	.75	.35	.07
☐ 251	Checklist 3rd Series	1.00	.20	.05
☐ 252	Ken Reynolds	.40	.18	.04
☐ 253	Sandy Alomar	.40	.18	.04
☐ 254	Boots Day	.40	.18	.04
☐ 255	Jim Lonborg	.50	.22	.05
☐ 256	George Foster	1.75	.85	.17
☐ 257	Tigers Rookies	.40	.18	.04
	Jim Foor			
	Tim Hosley			
	Paul Jata			
☐ 258	Randy Hundley	.40	.18	.04
☐ 259	Sparky Lyle	.60	.28	.06
☐ 260	Ralph Garr	.50	.22	.05
☐ 261	Steve Mingori	.40	.18	.04
☐ 262	Padres Team	.60	.28	.06
☐ 263	Felipe Alou	.50	.22	.05
☐ 264	Tommy John	1.50	.70	.15
☐ 265	Wes Parker	.50	.22	.05
☐ 266	Bobby Bolin	.40	.18	.04
☐ 267	Dave Concepcion	1.50	.70	.15
☐ 268	A's Rookies	.40	.18	.04
	Dwain Anderson			
	Chris Floethe			
☐ 269	Don Hahn	.40	.18	.04
☐ 270	Jim Palmer	3.50	1.65	.35
☐ 271	Ken Rudolph	.40	.18	.04
☐ 272	Mickey Rivers	.75	.35	.07
☐ 273	Bobby Floyd	.40	.18	.04
☐ 274	Al Severinsen	.40	.18	.04
☐ 275	Cesar Tovar	.40	.18	.04
☐ 276	Gene Mauch MGR	.50	.22	.05
☐ 277	Elliot Maddox	.40	.18	.04
☐ 278	Dennis Higgins	.40	.18	.04
☐ 279	Larry Brown	.40	.18	.04
☐ 280	Willie McCovey	3.50	1.65	.35
☐ 281	Bill Parsons	.40	.18	.04
☐ 282	Astros Team	.60	.28	.06
☐ 283	Darrell Brandon	.40	.18	.04
☐ 284	Ike Brown	.40	.18	.04
☐ 285	Gaylord Perry	3.00	1.40	.30
☐ 286	Gene Alley	.40	.18	.04
☐ 287	Jim Hardin	.40	.18	.04
☐ 288	Johnny Jeter	.40	.18	.04
☐ 289	Syd O'Brien	.40	.18	.04
☐ 290	Sonny Siebert	.40	.18	.04
☐ 291	Hal McRae	.60	.28	.06
☐ 292	McRae In Action	.50	.22	.05
☐ 293	Danny Frisella	.40	.18	.04
☐ 294	Frisella In Action	.40	.18	.04
☐ 295	Dick Dietz	.40	.18	.04
☐ 296	Dietz In Action	.40	.18	.04
☐ 297	Claude Osteen	.40	.18	.04
☐ 298	Osteen In Action	.40	.18	.04
☐ 299	Hank Aaron	10.00	4.75	1.00
☐ 300	Aaron In Action	5.00	2.35	.50
☐ 301	George Mitterwald	.40	.18	.04
☐ 302	Mitterwald In Action	.40	.18	.04
☐ 303	Joe Pepitone	.50	.22	.05
☐ 304	Pepitone In Action	.40	.18	.04
☐ 305	Ken Boswell	.40	.18	.04
☐ 306	Boswell In Action	.40	.18	.04
☐ 307	Steve Renko	.40	.18	.04
☐ 308	Renko In Action	.40	.18	.04
☐ 309	Roberto Clemente	8.00	3.75	.80
☐ 310	Clemente In Action	4.00	1.85	.40
☐ 311	Clay Carroll	.40	.18	.04
☐ 312	Carroll In Action	.40	.18	.04
☐ 313	Luis Aparicio	2.00	.90	.20
☐ 314	Aparicio In Action	1.00	.45	.10
☐ 315	Paul Splittorff	.40	.18	.04
☐ 316	Cardinals Rookies	.50	.22	.05
	Jim Bibby			
	Jorge Roque			
	Santiago Guzman			
☐ 317	Rich Hand	.40	.18	.04
☐ 318	Sonny Jackson	.40	.18	.04
☐ 319	Aurelio Rodriguez	.40	.18	.04
☐ 320	Steve Blass	.50	.22	.05
☐ 321	Joe LaHoud	.40	.18	.04
☐ 322	Jose Pena	.40	.18	.04
☐ 323	Earl Weaver MGR	.60	.28	.06
☐ 324	Mike Ryan	.40	.18	.04
☐ 325	Mel Stottlemyre	.50	.22	.05
☐ 326	Pat Kelly	.40	.18	.04
☐ 327	Steve Stone	.75	.35	.07
☐ 328	Red Sox Team	.60	.28	.06
☐ 329	Roy Foster	.40	.18	.04
☐ 330	Jim Hunter	1.50	.70	.15
☐ 331	Stan Swanson	.40	.18	.04
☐ 332	Buck Martinez	.40	.18	.04
☐ 333	Steve Barber	.40	.18	.04
☐ 334	Rangers Rookies	.40	.18	.04
	Bill Fahey			
	Jim Mason			
	Tom Ragland			
☐ 335	Bill Hands	.40	.18	.04
☐ 336	Marty Martinez	.40	.18	.04
☐ 337	Mike Kilkenny	.40	.18	.04
☐ 338	Bob Grich	.75	.35	.07
☐ 339	Ron Cook	.40	.18	.04
☐ 340	Roy White	.50	.22	.05
KID PICTURES (341-348)				
☐ 341	KP: Joe Torre	.50	.22	.05
☐ 342	KP: Wilbur Wood	.40	.18	.04
☐ 343	KP: Willie Stargell	.60	.28	.06
☐ 344	KP: Dave McNally	.40	.18	.04
☐ 345	KP: Rick Wise	.40	.18	.04
☐ 346	KP: Jim Fregosi	.40	.18	.04
☐ 347	KP: Tom Seaver	1.00	.45	.10
☐ 348	KP: Sal Bando	.40	.18	.04
☐ 349	Al Fitzmorris	.40	.18	.04
☐ 350	Frank Howard	.60	.28	.06
☐ 351	Braves Rookies	.40	.18	.04
	Tom House			
	Rick Kester			
	Jimmy Britton			
☐ 352	Dave LaRoche	.40	.18	.04
☐ 353	Art Shamsky	.40	.18	.04
☐ 354	Tom Murphy	.40	.18	.04
☐ 355	Bob Watson	.50	.22	.05
☐ 356	Gerry Moses	.40	.18	.04
☐ 357	Woodie Fryman	.40	.18	.04
☐ 358	Sparky Anderson MGR	.60	.28	.06
☐ 359	Don Pavletich	.40	.18	.04
☐ 360	Dave Roberts	.40	.18	.04
☐ 361	Mike Andrews	.40	.18	.04
☐ 362	Mets Team	.75	.35	.07
☐ 363	Ron Klimkowski	.40	.18	.04
☐ 364	Johnny Callison	.50	.22	.05
☐ 365	Dick Bosman	.40	.18	.04
☐ 366	Jimmy Rosario	.40	.18	.04
☐ 367	Ron Perranoski	.40	.18	.04
☐ 368	Danny Thompson	.40	.18	.04
☐ 369	Jim LeFebvre	.40	.18	.04
☐ 370	Don Buford	.40	.18	.04
☐ 371	Denny LeMaster	.40	.18	.04
☐ 372	Royals Rookies	.40	.18	.04
	Lance Clemons			
	Monty Montgomery			
☐ 373	John Mayberry	.50	.22	.05
☐ 374	Jack Heidemann	.40	.18	.04
☐ 375	Reggie Cleveland	.40	.18	.04
☐ 376	Andy Kosco	.40	.18	.04
☐ 377	Terry Harmon	.40	.18	.04
☐ 378	Checklist 4th Series	1.00	.20	.05
☐ 379	Ken Berry	.40	.18	.04
☐ 380	Earl Williams	.40	.18	.04
☐ 381	White Sox Team	.60	.28	.06
☐ 382	Joe Gibbon	.40	.18	.04
☐ 383	Brant Alyea	.40	.18	.04
☐ 384	Dave Campbell	.40	.18	.04
☐ 385	Mickey Stanley	.40	.18	.04
☐ 386	Jim Colborn	.40	.18	.04
☐ 387	Horace Clarke	.40	.18	.04
☐ 388	Charlie Williams	.40	.18	.04
☐ 389	Bill Rigney MGR	.40	.18	.04
☐ 390	Willie Davis	.50	.22	.05
☐ 391	Ken Sanders	.40	.18	.04
☐ 392	Pirates Rookies	.75	.35	.07
	Fred Cambria			
	Richie Zisk			
☐ 393	Curt Motton	.40	.18	.04
☐ 394	Ken Forsch	.50	.22	.05
☐ 395	Matty Alou	.50	.22	.05
☐ 396	Paul Lindblad	.40	.18	.04
☐ 397	Phillies Team	.60	.28	.06
☐ 398	Larry Hisle	.50	.22	.05
☐ 399	Milt Wilcox	.50	.22	.05
☐ 400	Tony Oliva	1.00	.45	.10
☐ 401	Jim Nash	.40	.18	.04
☐ 402	Bobby Heise	.40	.18	.04
☐ 403	John Cumberland	.40	.18	.04
☐ 404	Jeff Torborg	.40	.18	.04
☐ 405	Ron Fairly	.40	.18	.04
☐ 406	George Hendrick	1.50	.70	.15
☐ 407	Chuck Taylor	.40	.18	.04
☐ 408	Jim Northrup	.50	.22	.05
☐ 409	Frank Baker	.40	.18	.04
☐ 410	Fergie Jenkins	1.00	.45	.10
☐ 411	Bob Montgomery	.40	.18	.04
☐ 412	Dick Kelley	.40	.18	.04
☐ 413	White Sox Rookies	.40	.18	.04

	Don Eddy			
	Dave Lemonds			
☐ 414	Bob Miller	.40	.18	.04
☐ 415	Cookie Rojas	.40	.18	.04
☐ 416	Johnny Edwards	.40	.18	.04
☐ 417	Tom Hall	.40	.18	.04
☐ 418	Tom Shopay	.40	.18	.04
☐ 419	Jim Spencer	.40	.18	.04
☐ 420	Steve Carlton	10.00	4.75	1.00
☐ 421	Ellie Rodriguez	.40	.18	.04
☐ 422	Ray Lamb	.40	.18	.04
☐ 423	Oscar Gamble	.50	.22	.05
☐ 424	Bill Gogolewski	.40	.18	.04
☐ 425	Ken Singleton	.60	.28	.06
☐ 426	Singleton In Action	.50	.22	.05
☐ 427	Tito Fuentes	.40	.18	.04
☐ 428	Fuentes In Action	.40	.18	.04
☐ 429	Bob Robertson	.40	.18	.04
☐ 430	Robertson In Action	.40	.18	.04
☐ 431	Clarence Gaston	.40	.18	.04
☐ 432	Gaston In Action	.40	.18	.04
☐ 433	Johnny Bench	11.00	5.25	1.10
☐ 434	Bench In Action	5.00	2.35	.50
☐ 435	Reggie Jackson	11.00	5.25	1.10
☐ 436	Jackson In Action	5.00	2.35	.50
☐ 437	Maury Wills	1.00	.45	.10
☐ 438	Wills In Action	.50	.22	.05
☐ 439	Billy Williams	1.50	.70	.15
☐ 440	Williams In Action	.75	.35	.07
☐ 441	Thurman Munson	7.00	3.25	.70
☐ 442	Munson In Action	3.50	1.65	.35
☐ 443	Ken Henderson	.40	.18	.04
☐ 444	Henderson In Action	.40	.18	.04
☐ 445	Tom Seaver	10.00	4.75	1.00
☐ 446	Seaver In Action	5.00	2.35	.50
☐ 447	Willie Stargell	2.50	1.15	.25
☐ 448	Stargell In Action	1.25	.60	.12
☐ 449	Bob Lemon MGR	.75	.35	.07
☐ 450	Mickey Lolich	.60	.28	.06
☐ 451	Tony LaRussa	.60	.28	.06
☐ 452	Ed Herrmann	.40	.18	.04
☐ 453	Barry Lersch	.40	.18	.04
☐ 454	A's Team	.60	.28	.06
☐ 455	Tommy Harper	.50	.22	.05
☐ 456	Mark Belanger	.50	.22	.05
☐ 457	Padres Rookies	.40	.18	.04
	Darcy Fast			
	Derrel Thomas			
	Mike Ivie			
☐ 458	Aurelio Monteagudo	.40	.18	.04
☐ 459	Rick Renick	.40	.18	.04
☐ 460	Al Downing	.40	.18	.04
☐ 461	Tim Cullen	.40	.18	.04
☐ 462	Rickey Clark	.40	.18	.04
☐ 463	Bernie Carbo	.40	.18	.04
☐ 464	Jim Roland	.40	.18	.04
☐ 465	Gil Hodges	7.50	3.50	.75
	(mentions his			
	death on 4/2/72)			
☐ 466	Norm Miller	.40	.18	.04
☐ 467	Steve Kline	.40	.18	.04
☐ 468	Richie Scheinblum	.40	.18	.04
☐ 469	Ron Herbel	.40	.18	.04
☐ 470	Ray Fosse	.40	.18	.04
☐ 471	Luke Walker	.40	.18	.04
☐ 472	Phil Gagliano	.40	.18	.04
☐ 473	Dan McGinn	.40	.18	.04
☐ 474	Orioles Rookies	2.00	.90	.20
	Don Baylor			
	Roric Harrison			
	Johnny Oates			
☐ 475	Gary Nolan	.40	.18	.04
☐ 476	Lee Richard	.40	.18	.04
☐ 477	Tom Phoebus	.40	.18	.04
☐ 478	Checklist 5th Series	1.00	.20	.05
☐ 479	Don Shaw	.40	.18	.04
☐ 480	Lee May	.50	.22	.05
☐ 481	Billy Conigliaro	.40	.18	.04
☐ 482	Joe Hoerner	.40	.18	.04
☐ 483	Ken Suarez	.40	.18	.04
☐ 484	Lum Harris MGR	.40	.18	.04
☐ 485	Phil Regan	.40	.18	.04
☐ 486	John Lowenstein	.40	.18	.04
☐ 487	Tigers Team	.60	.28	.06
☐ 488	Mike Nagy	.40	.18	.04
☐ 489	Expos Rookies	.40	.18	.04
	Terry Humphrey			
	Keith Lampard			
☐ 490	Dave McNally	.50	.22	.05
KID PICTURES (491-498)				
☐ 491	KP: Lou Piniella	.60	.28	.06
☐ 492	KP: Mel Stottlemyre	.40	.18	.04
☐ 493	KP: Bob Bailey	.40	.18	.04

☐ 494	KP: Willie Horton	.40	.18	.04
☐ 495	KP: Bill Melton	.40	.18	.04
☐ 496	KP: Bud Harrelson	.40	.18	.04
☐ 497	KP: Jim Perry	.40	.18	.04
☐ 498	KP: Brooks Robinson	1.00	.45	.10
☐ 499	Vicente Romo	.40	.18	.04
☐ 500	Joe Torre	.75	.35	.07
☐ 501	Pete Hamm	.40	.18	.04
☐ 502	Jackie Hernandez	.40	.18	.04
☐ 503	Gary Peters	.40	.18	.04
☐ 504	Ed Spiezio	.40	.18	.04
☐ 505	Mike Marshall	.50	.22	.05
☐ 506	Indians Rookies	.40	.18	.04
	Terry Ley			
	Jim Moyer			
	Dick Tidrow			
☐ 507	Fred Gladding	.40	.18	.04
☐ 508	Ellie Hendricks	.40	.18	.04
☐ 509	Don McMahon	.40	.18	.04
☐ 510	Ted Williams MGR	3.00	1.40	.30
☐ 511	Tony Taylor	.40	.18	.04
☐ 512	Paul Popovich	.40	.18	.04
☐ 513	Lindy McDaniel	.40	.18	.04
☐ 514	Ted Sizemore	.40	.18	.04
☐ 515	Bert Blyleven	2.00	.90	.20
☐ 516	Oscar Brown	.40	.18	.04
☐ 517	Ken Brett	.50	.22	.05
☐ 518	Wayne Garrett	.40	.18	.04
☐ 519	Ted Abernathy	.40	.18	.04
☐ 520	Larry Bowa	.75	.35	.07
☐ 521	Alan Foster	.40	.18	.04
☐ 522	Dodgers Team	1.00	.45	.10
☐ 523	Chuck Dobson	.40	.18	.04
☐ 524	Reds Rookies	.40	.18	.04
	Ed Armbrister			
	Mel Behney			
☐ 525	Carlos May	.40	.18	.04

1973 O-Pee-Chee

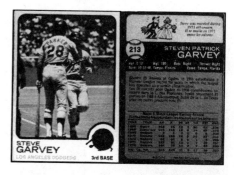

The cards in this 660 card set measure 2 1/2" by 3 1/2". The 1973 O-Pee-Chee set is indistinguishable from the 1973 Topps set on the obverse. However the reverses of the O-Pee-Chee cards are written in French and English and say "Printed in Canada" on the bottom. An "All-Time Leaders" series (471-478) appeared for the first time in this set. Kid pictures appeared again for the second year in a row (341-346). The backs appear to be more "yellow" than the Topps backs. Remember, the prices below apply only to the O-Pee-Chee cards -- NOT Topps cards which are much more plentiful.

	MINT	VG-E	F-G
COMPLETE SET	225.00	100.00	20.00
COMMON PLAYER (1-660)	.25	.10	.02
☐ 1 All-Time HR Leaders:	6.00	2.00	.40
714 Babe Ruth			
673 Hank Aaron			

654 Willie Mays

☐ 2	Rich Hebner	.25	.10	.02
☐ 3	Jim Lonborg	.25	.10	.02
☐ 4	John Milner	.25	.10	.02
☐ 5	Ed Brinkman	.25	.10	.02
☐ 6	Mac Scarce	.25	.10	.02
☐ 7	Texas Rangers Team	.35	.15	.03
☐ 8	Tom Hall	.25	.10	.02
☐ 9	Johnny Oates	.25	.10	.02
☐ 10	Don Sutton	1.00	.45	.10
☐ 11	Chris Chambliss	.35	.15	.03
☐ 12	Padres Manager:	.35	.15	.03
	Don Zimmer			
	Coaches: Dave Garcia			
	Johnny Podres			
	Bob Skinner			
	Whitey Wietelmann			
☐ 13	George Hendrick	.60	.28	.06
☐ 14	Sonny Siebert	.25	.10	.02
☐ 15	Ralph Garr	.25	.10	.02
☐ 16	Steve Braun	.25	.10	.02
☐ 17	Fred Gladding	.25	.10	.02
☐ 18	Leroy Stanton	.25	.10	.02
☐ 19	Tim Foli	.25	.10	.02
☐ 20	Stan Bahnsen	.25	.10	.02
☐ 21	Randy Hundley	.25	.10	.02
☐ 22	Ted Abernathy	.25	.10	.02
☐ 23	Dave Kingman	1.25	.60	.12
☐ 24	Al Santorini	.25	.10	.02
☐ 25	Roy White	.25	.10	.02
☐ 26	Pirates Team	.35	.15	.03
☐ 27	Bill Gogolewski	.25	.10	.02
☐ 28	Hal McRae	.35	.15	.03
☐ 29	Tony Taylor	.25	.10	.02
☐ 30	Tug McGraw	.50	.22	.05
☐ 31	Buddy Bell	2.50	1.15	.25
☐ 32	Fred Norman	.25	.10	.02
☐ 33	Jim Breazeale	.25	.10	.02
☐ 34	Pat Dobson	.25	.10	.02
☐ 35	Willie Davis	.35	.15	.03
☐ 36	Steve Barber	.25	.10	.02
☐ 37	Bill Robinson	.25	.10	.02
☐ 38	Mike Epstein	.25	.10	.02
☐ 39	Dave Roberts	.25	.10	.02
☐ 40	Reggie Smith	.50	.22	.05
☐ 41	Tom Walker	.25	.10	.02
☐ 42	Mike Andrews	.25	.10	.02
☐ 43	Randy Moffitt	.25	.10	.02
☐ 44	Rick Monday	.25	.10	.02
☐ 45	Ellie Rodriguez	.25	.10	.02
	(photo actually			
	John Felske)			
☐ 46	Lindy McDaniel	.25	.10	.02
☐ 47	Luis Melendez	.25	.10	.02
☐ 48	Paul Splittorff	.25	.10	.02
☐ 49	Minnesota Twins Mgr.	.35	.15	.03
	Frank Quilici			
	Coaches: Vern Morgan			
	Bob Rodgers			
	Ralph Rowe			
	Al Worthington			
☐ 50	Roberto Clemente	7.50	3.50	.75
☐ 51	Chuck Seelbach	.25	.10	.02
☐ 52	Denis Menke	.25	.10	.02
☐ 53	Steve Dunning	.25	.10	.02
☐ 54	Checklist 1st Series	.60	.10	.02
☐ 55	Jon Matlack	.35	.15	.03
☐ 56	Merv Rettenmund	.25	.10	.02
☐ 57	Derrel Thomas	.25	.10	.02
☐ 58	Mike Paul	.25	.10	.02
☐ 59	Steve Yeager	.50	.22	.05
☐ 60	Ken Holtzman	.35	.15	.03
☐ 61	Batting Leaders	1.00	.45	.10
	Billy Williams			
	Rod Carew			
☐ 62	Home Run Leaders	1.00	.45	.10
	Johnny Bench			
	Dick Allen			
☐ 63	RBI Leaders	1.00	.45	.10
	Johnny Bench			
	Dick Allen			
☐ 64	Stolen Base Leaders	.75	.35	.07
	Lou Brock			
	Bert Campaneris			
☐ 65	ERA Leaders	.75	.35	.07
	Steve Carlton			
	Luis Tiant			
☐ 66	Victory Leaders	1.00	.45	.10
	Steve Carlton			
	Gaylord Perry			
	Wilbur Wood			
☐ 67	Strikeout Leaders	2.00	.90	.20
	Steve Carlton			

Nolan Ryan

☐ 68	Leading Firemen	.35	.15	.03
	Clay Carroll			
	Sparky Lyle			
☐ 69	Phil Gagliano	.25	.10	.02
☐ 70	Milt Pappas	.25	.10	.02
☐ 71	Johnny Briggs	.25	.10	.02
☐ 72	Ron Reed	.25	.10	.02
☐ 73	Ed Herrmann	.25	.10	.02
☐ 74	Billy Champion	.25	.10	.02
☐ 75	Vada Pinson	.35	.15	.03
☐ 76	Doug Rader	.35	.15	.03
☐ 77	Mike Torrez	.35	.15	.03
☐ 78	Richie Scheinblum	.25	.10	.02
☐ 79	Jim Willoughby	.25	.10	.02
☐ 80	Tony Oliva	.60	.28	.06
☐ 81	Chicago Cubs MGR	.35	.15	.03
	Whitey Lockman			
	Coaches: Hank Aguirre			
	Ernie Banks			
	Larry Jansen			
	Pete Reiser			
☐ 82	Fritz Peterson	.25	.10	.02
☐ 83	Leron Lee	.25	.10	.02
☐ 84	Rollie Fingers	1.25	.60	.12
☐ 85	Ted Simmons	1.00	.45	.10
☐ 86	Tom McCraw	.25	.10	.02
☐ 87	Ken Boswell	.25	.10	.02
☐ 88	Mickey Stanley	.25	.10	.02
☐ 89	Jack Billingham	.25	.10	.02
☐ 90	Brooks Robinson	3.50	1.65	.35
☐ 91	Dodgers Team	.60	.28	.06
☐ 92	Jerry Bell	.25	.10	.02
☐ 93	Jesus Alou	.25	.10	.02
☐ 94	Dick Billings	.25	.10	.02
☐ 95	Steve Blass	.25	.10	.02
☐ 96	Doug Griffin	.25	.10	.02
☐ 97	Willie Montanez	.25	.10	.02
☐ 98	Dick Woodson	.25	.10	.02
☐ 99	Carl Taylor	.25	.10	.02
☐ 100	Hank Aaron	7.50	3.50	.75
☐ 101	Ken Henderson	.25	.10	.02
☐ 102	Rudy May	.25	.10	.02
☐ 103	Celerino Sanchez	.25	.10	.02
☐ 104	Reggie Cleveland	.25	.10	.02
☐ 105	Carlos May	.25	.10	.02
☐ 106	Terry Humphrey	.25	.10	.02
☐ 107	Phil Hennigan	.25	.10	.02
☐ 108	Bill Russell	.35	.15	.03
☐ 109	Doyle Alexander	.35	.15	.03
☐ 110	Bob Watson	.35	.15	.03
☐ 111	Dave Nelson	.25	.10	.02
☐ 112	Gary Ross	.25	.10	.02
☐ 113	Jerry Grote	.25	.10	.02
☐ 114	Lynn McGlothen	.25	.10	.02
☐ 115	Ron Santo	.40	.18	.04
☐ 116	Yankees Manager:	.40	.18	.04
	Ralph Houk			
	Coaches: Jim Hegan			
	Elston Howard			
	Dick Howser			
	Jim Turner			
☐ 117	Ramon Hernandez	.25	.10	.02
☐ 118	John Mayberry	.35	.15	.03
☐ 119	Larry Bowa	.50	.22	.05
☐ 120	Joe Coleman	.25	.10	.02
☐ 121	Dave Rader	.25	.10	.02
☐ 122	Jim Strickland	.25	.10	.02
☐ 123	Sandy Alomar	.25	.10	.02
☐ 124	Jim Hardin	.25	.10	.02
☐ 125	Ron Fairly	.25	.10	.02
☐ 126	Jim Brewer	.25	.10	.02
☐ 127	Brewers Team	.35	.15	.03
☐ 128	Ted Sizemore	.25	.10	.02
☐ 129	Terry Forster	.35	.15	.03
☐ 130	Pete Rose	15.00	7.00	1.50
☐ 131	Red Sox Manager	.35	.15	.03
	Eddie Kasko			
	Coaches: Doug Camilli			
	Don Lenhardt			
	Eddie Popowski			
	Lee Stange			
☐ 132	Matty Alou	.25	.10	.02
☐ 133	Dave Roberts	.25	.10	.02
☐ 134	Milt Wilcox	.25	.10	.02
☐ 135	Lee May	.35	.15	.03
☐ 136	Orioles Manager	.50	.22	.05
	Earl Weaver			
	Coaches:			
	George Bamberger			
	Jim Frey			
	Billy Hunter			
	George Staller			

☐ 137	Jim Beauchamp	.25	.10	.02
☐ 138	Horacio Pina	.25	.10	.02
☐ 139	Carmen Fanzone	.25	.10	.02
☐ 140	Lou Piniella	.50	.22	.05
☐ 141	Bruce Kison	.25	.10	.02
☐ 142	Thurman Munson	4.00	1.85	.40
☐ 143	John Curtis	.25	.10	.02
☐ 144	Marty Perez	.25	.10	.02
☐ 145	Bobby Bonds	.35	.15	.03
☐ 146	Woodie Fryman	.25	.10	.02
☐ 147	Mike Anderson	.25	.10	.02
☐ 148	Dave Goltz	.25	.10	.02
☐ 149	Ron Hunt	.25	.10	.02
☐ 150	Wilbur Wood	.25	.10	.02
☐ 151	Wes Parker	.35	.15	.03
☐ 152	Dave May	.25	.10	.02
☐ 153	Al Hrabosky	.35	.15	.03
☐ 154	Jeff Torborg	.25	.10	.02
☐ 155	Sal Bando	.35	.15	.03
☐ 156	Cesar Geronimo	.25	.10	.02
☐ 157	Denny Riddleberger	.25	.10	.02
☐ 158	Astros Team	.35	.15	.03
☐ 159	Clarence Gaston	.25	.10	.02
☐ 160	Jim Palmer	3.00	1.40	.30
☐ 161	Ted Martinez	.25	.10	.02
☐ 162	Pete Broberg	.25	.10	.02
☐ 163	Vic Davalillo	.25	.10	.02
☐ 164	Monty Montgomery	.25	.10	.02
☐ 165	Luis Aparicio	1.50	.70	.15
☐ 166	Terry Harmon	.25	.10	.02
☐ 167	Steve Stone	.35	.15	.03
☐ 168	Jim Northrup	.25	.10	.02
☐ 169	Ron Schueler	.25	.10	.02
☐ 170	Harmon Killebrew	2.00	.90	.20
☐ 171	Bernie Carbo	.25	.10	.02
☐ 172	Steve Kline	.25	.10	.02
☐ 173	Hal Breeden	.25	.10	.02
☐ 174	Rich Gossage	6.00	2.80	.60
☐ 175	Frank Robinson	3.00	1.40	.30
☐ 176	Chuck Taylor	.25	.10	.02
☐ 177	Bill Plummer	.25	.10	.02
☐ 178	Don Rose	.25	.10	.02
☐ 179	Oakland A's MGR:	.35	.15	.03

Dick Williams
Coaches: Jerry Adair
Vern Hoscheit
Irv Noren
Wes Stock

☐ 180	Fergie Jenkins	.90	.40	.09
☐ 181	Jack Brohamer	.25	.10	.02
☐ 182	Mike Caldwell	.35	.15	.03
☐ 183	Don Buford	.25	.10	.02
☐ 184	Jerry Koosman	.35	.15	.03
☐ 185	Jim Wynn	.35	.15	.03
☐ 186	Bill Fahey	.25	.10	.02
☐ 187	Luke Walker	.25	.10	.02
☐ 188	Cookie Rojas	.25	.10	.02
☐ 189	Greg Luzinski	.75	.35	.07
☐ 190	Bob Gibson	2.25	1.00	.22
☐ 191	Tigers Team	.40	.18	.04
☐ 192	Pat Jarvis	.25	.10	.02
☐ 193	Carlton Fisk	2.50	1.15	.25
☐ 194	Jorge Orta	.25	.10	.02
☐ 195	Clay Carroll	.25	.10	.02
☐ 196	Ken McMullen	.25	.10	.02
☐ 197	Ed Goodson	.25	.10	.02
☐ 198	Horace Clarke	.25	.10	.02
☐ 199	Bert Blyleven	1.00	.45	.10
☐ 200	Billy Williams	1.00	.45	.10
☐ 201	A.L. Playoffs	.60	.28	.06

A's over Tigers;
Hendrick scores
winning run

☐ 202	N.L. Playoffs	.60	.28	.06

Reds over Pirates
Foster's run decides

WORLD SERIES (203-210)

☐ 203	World Series Game 1	.60	.28	.06

Tenace the Menace

☐ 204	World Series Game 2	.60	.28	.06

A's two straight

☐ 205	World Series Game 3	.60	.28	.06

Reds win squeeker

☐ 206	World Series Game 4	.60	.28	.06

Tenace singles
in ninth

☐ 207	World Series Game 5	.60	.28	.06

Odom out at plate

☐ 208	World Series Game 6	.60	.28	.06

Red's slugging
ties series

☐ 209	World Series Game 7	.60	.28	.06

Campy stars

winning rally

☐ 210	World Series Summary	.60	.28	.06

World champions:
A's Win

☐ 211	Balor Moore	.25	.10	.02
☐ 212	Joe LaHoud	.25	.10	.02
☐ 213	Steve Garvey	8.00	3.75	.80
☐ 214	Steve Hamilton	.25	.10	.02
☐ 215	Dusty Baker	.60	.28	.06
☐ 216	Toby Harrah	.35	.15	.03
☐ 217	Don Wilson	.25	.10	.02
☐ 218	Aurelio Rodriguez	.25	.10	.02
☐ 219	Cardinals Team	.35	.15	.03
☐ 220	Nolan Ryan	4.50	2.10	.45
☐ 221	Fred Kendall	.25	.10	.02
☐ 222	Rob Gardner	.25	.10	.02
☐ 223	Bud Harrelson	.25	.10	.02
☐ 224	Bill Lee	.25	.10	.02
☐ 225	Al Oliver	1.25	.60	.12
☐ 226	Ray Fosse	.25	.10	.02
☐ 227	Wayne Twitchell	.25	.10	.02
☐ 228	Bobby Darwin	.25	.10	.02
☐ 229	Roric Harrison	.25	.10	.02
☐ 230	Joe Morgan	2.00	.90	.20
☐ 231	Bill Parsons	.25	.10	.02
☐ 232	Ken Singleton	.35	.15	.03
☐ 233	Ed Kirkpatrick	.25	.10	.02
☐ 234	Bill North	.25	.10	.02
☐ 235	Jim Hunter	1.25	.60	.12
☐ 236	Tito Fuentes	.25	.10	.02
☐ 237	Braves Manager	.50	.22	.05

Eddie Mathews
Coaches: Lew Burdette
Jim Busby
Roy Hartsfield
Ken Silvestri

☐ 238	Tony Muser	.25	.10	.02
☐ 239	Pete Richert	.25	.10	.02
☐ 240	Bobby Murcer	.50	.22	.05
☐ 241	Dwain Anderson	.25	.10	.02
☐ 242	George Culver	.25	.10	.02
☐ 243	Angels Team	.35	.15	.03
☐ 244	Ed Acosta	.25	.10	.02
☐ 245	Carl Yastrzemski	9.00	4.25	.90
☐ 246	Ken Sanders	.25	.10	.02
☐ 247	Del Unser	.25	.10	.02
☐ 248	Jerry Johnson	.25	.10	.02
☐ 249	Larry Biittner	.25	.10	.02
☐ 250	Manny Sanguillen	.35	.15	.03
☐ 251	Roger Nelson	.25	.10	.02
☐ 252	Giants Manager:	.25	.10	.02

Charlie Fox
Coaches:
Joe Amalfitano
Andy Gilbert
Don McMahon
John McNamara

☐ 253	Mark Belanger	.35	.15	.03
☐ 254	Bill Stoneman	.25	.10	.02
☐ 255	Reggie Jackson	9.00	4.25	.90
☐ 256	Chris Zachary	.25	.10	.02
☐ 257	N.Y. Mets Manager:	.60	.28	.06

Yogi Berra
Coaches: Roy McMillan
Joe Pignatano
Rube Walker
Eddie Yost

☐ 258	Tommy John	1.00	.45	.10
☐ 259	Jim Holt	.25	.10	.02
☐ 260	Gary Nolan	.25	.10	.02
☐ 261	Pat Kelly	.25	.10	.02
☐ 262	Jack Aker	.25	.10	.02
☐ 263	George Scott	.25	.10	.02
☐ 264	Checklist 2nd Series	.60	.10	.02
☐ 265	Gene Michael	.35	.15	.03
☐ 266	Mike Lum	.25	.10	.02
☐ 267	Lloyd Allen	.25	.10	.02
☐ 268	Jerry Morales	.25	.10	.02
☐ 269	Tim McCarver	.40	.18	.04
☐ 270	Luis Tiant	.35	.15	.03
☐ 271	Tom Hutton	.25	.10	.02
☐ 272	Ed Farmer	.25	.10	.02
☐ 273	Chris Speier	.25	.10	.02
☐ 274	Darold Knowles	.25	.10	.02
☐ 275	Tony Perez	.75	.35	.07
☐ 276	Joe Lovitto	.25	.10	.02
☐ 277	Bob Miller	.25	.10	.02
☐ 278	Orioles Team	.40	.18	.04
☐ 279	Mike Strahler	.25	.10	.02
☐ 280	Al Kaline	3.00	1.40	.30
☐ 281	Mike Jorgensen	.25	.10	.02
☐ 282	Steve Hovley	.25	.10	.02
☐ 283	Ray Sadecki	.25	.10	.02

☐ 284	Glenn Borgmann	.25	.10	.02
☐ 285	Don Kessinger	.35	.15	.03
☐ 286	Frank Linzy	.25	.10	.02
☐ 287	Eddie Leon	.25	.10	.02
☐ 288	Gary Gentry	.25	.10	.02
☐ 289	Bob Oliver	.25	.10	.02
☐ 290	Cesar Cedeno	.35	.15	.03
☐ 291	Rogelio Moret	.25	.10	.02
☐ 292	Jose Cruz	.60	.28	.06
☐ 293	Bernie Allen	.25	.10	.02
☐ 294	Steve Arlin	.25	.10	.02
☐ 295	Bert Campaneris	.35	.15	.03
☐ 296	Reds Manager:	.40	.18	.04
	Sparky Anderson			
	Coaches: Alex Grammas			
	Ted Kluszewski			
	George Scherger			
	Larry Shepard			
☐ 297	Walt Williams	.25	.10	.02
☐ 298	Ron Bryant	.25	.10	.02
☐ 299	Ted Ford	.25	.10	.02
☐ 300	Steve Carlton	7.00	3.25	.70
☐ 301	Billy Grabarkewitz	.25	.10	.02
☐ 302	Terry Crowley	.25	.10	.02
☐ 303	Nelson Briles	.25	.10	.02
☐ 304	Duke Sims	.25	.10	.02
☐ 305	Willie Mays	9.00	4.25	.90
☐ 306	Tom Burgmeier	.25	.10	.02
☐ 307	Boots Day	.25	.10	.02
☐ 308	Skip Lockwood	.25	.10	.02
☐ 309	Paul Popovich	.25	.10	.02
☐ 310	Dick Allen	.50	.22	.05
☐ 311	Joe Decker	.25	.10	.02
☐ 312	Oscar Brown	.25	.10	.02
☐ 313	Jim Ray	.25	.10	.02
☐ 314	Ron Swoboda	.25	.10	.02
☐ 315	John Odom	.25	.10	.02
☐ 316	Padres Team	.40	.18	.04
☐ 317	Danny Cater	.25	.10	.02
☐ 318	Jim McGlothlin	.25	.10	.02
☐ 319	Jim Spencer	.25	.10	.02
☐ 320	Lou Brock	3.00	1.40	.30
☐ 321	Rich Hinton	.25	.10	.02
☐ 322	Garry Maddox	.50	.22	.05
☐ 323	Tigers Manager:	.50	.22	.05
	Billy Martin			
	Coaches: Art Fowler			
	Charlie Silvera			
	Dick Tracewski			
☐ 324	Al Downing	.25	.10	.02
☐ 325	Boog Powell	.50	.22	.05
☐ 326	Darrell Brandon	.25	.10	.02
☐ 327	John Lowenstein	.25	.10	.02
☐ 328	Bill Bonham	.25	.10	.02
☐ 329	Ed Kranepool	.25	.10	.02
☐ 330	Rod Carew	7.00	3.25	.70
☐ 331	Carl Morton	.25	.10	.02
☐ 332	John Felske	.25	.10	.02
☐ 333	Gene Clines	.25	.10	.02
☐ 334	Freddie Patek	.25	.10	.02
☐ 335	Bob Tolan	.25	.10	.02
☐ 336	Tom Bradley	.25	.10	.02
☐ 337	Dave Duncan	.25	.10	.02
☐ 338	Checklist 3rd Series	.60	.10	.02
☐ 339	Dick Tidrow	.25	.10	.02
☐ 340	Nate Colbert	.25	.10	.02
KID PICTURES (341-346)				
☐ 341	KP: Jim Palmer	1.00	.45	.10
☐ 342	KP: Sam McDowell	.25	.10	.02
☐ 343	KP: Bobby Murcer	.35	.15	.03
☐ 344	KP: Jim Hunter	.50	.22	.05
☐ 345	KP: Chris Speier	.25	.10	.02
☐ 346	KP: Gaylord Perry	.50	.22	.05
☐ 347	Royals Team	.40	.18	.04
☐ 348	Rennie Stennett	.25	.10	.02
☐ 349	Dick McAuliffe	.25	.10	.02
☐ 350	Tom Seaver	7.00	3.25	.70
☐ 351	Jimmy Stewart	.25	.10	.02
☐ 352	Don Stanhouse	.25	.10	.02
☐ 353	Steve Brye	.25	.10	.02
☐ 354	Billy Parker	.25	.10	.02
☐ 355	Mike Marshall	.35	.15	.03
☐ 356	White Sox Manager	.35	.15	.03
	Chuck Tanner			
	Coaches: Joe Lonnett			
	Jim Mahoney			
	Al Monchak			
	Johnny Sain			
☐ 357	Ross Grimsley	.25	.10	.02
☐ 358	Jim Nettles	.25	.10	.02
☐ 359	Cecil Upshaw	.25	.10	.02
☐ 360	Joe Rudi	.35	.15	.03
	(photo actually			
	Gene Tenace)			
☐ 361	Fran Healy	.25	.10	.02
☐ 362	Eddie Watt	.25	.10	.02
☐ 363	Jackie Hernandez	.25	.10	.02
☐ 364	Rick Wise	.25	.10	.02
☐ 365	Rico Petrocelli	.35	.15	.03
☐ 366	Brock Davis	.25	.10	.02
☐ 367	Burt Hooton	.35	.15	.03
☐ 368	Bill Buckner	.65	.30	.06
☐ 369	Lerrin LaGrow	.25	.10	.02
☐ 370	Willie Stargell	2.00	.90	.20
☐ 371	Mike Kekich	.25	.10	.02
☐ 372	Oscar Gamble	.35	.15	.03
☐ 373	Clyde Wright	.25	.10	.02
☐ 374	Darrell Evans	.50	.22	.05
☐ 375	Larry Dierker	.25	.10	.02
☐ 376	Frank Duffy	.25	.10	.02
☐ 377	Expos Manager	.35	.15	.03
	Gene Mauch			
	Coaches: Dave Bristol			
	Larry Doby			
	Cal McLish			
	Jerry Zimmerman			
☐ 378	Lenny Randle	.25	.10	.02
☐ 379	Cy Acosta	.25	.10	.02
☐ 380	Johnny Bench	7.00	3.25	.70
☐ 381	Vicente Romo	.25	.10	.02
☐ 382	Mike Hegan	.25	.10	.02
☐ 383	Diego Segui	.25	.10	.02
☐ 384	Don Baylor	1.00	.45	.10
☐ 385	Jim Perry	.35	.15	.03
☐ 386	Don Money	.25	.10	.02
☐ 387	Jim Barr	.25	.10	.02
☐ 388	Ben Oglivie	.50	.22	.05
☐ 389	Mets Team	.75	.35	.07
☐ 390	Mickey Lolich	.50	.22	.05
☐ 391	Lee Lacy	.75	.35	.07
☐ 392	Dick Drago	.25	.10	.02
☐ 393	Jose Cardenal	.25	.10	.02
☐ 394	Sparky Lyle	.35	.15	.03
☐ 395	Roger Metzger	.25	.10	.02
☐ 396	Grant Jackson	.25	.10	.02
☐ 397	Dave Cash	.25	.10	.02
☐ 398	Rich Hand	.25	.10	.02
☐ 399	George Foster	1.50	.70	.15
☐ 400	Gaylord Perry	1.75	.85	.17
☐ 401	Clyde Mashore	.25	.10	.02
☐ 402	Jack Hiatt	.25	.10	.02
☐ 403	Sonny Jackson	.25	.10	.02
☐ 404	Chuck Brinkman	.25	.10	.02
☐ 405	Cesar Tovar	.25	.10	.02
☐ 406	Paul Lindblad	.25	.10	.02
☐ 407	Felix Millan	.25	.10	.02
☐ 408	Jim Colborn	.25	.10	.02
☐ 409	Ivan Murrell	.25	.10	.02
☐ 410	Willie McCovey	2.50	1.15	.25
☐ 411	Ray Corbin	.25	.10	.02
☐ 412	Manny Mota	.35	.15	.03
☐ 413	Tom Timmerman	.25	.10	.02
☐ 414	Ken Rudolph	.25	.10	.02
☐ 415	Marty Pattin	.25	.10	.02
☐ 416	Paul Schaal	.25	.10	.02
☐ 417	Scipio Spinks	.25	.10	.02
☐ 418	Bobby Grich	.40	.18	.04
☐ 419	Casey Cox	.25	.10	.02
☐ 420	Tommie Agee	.25	.10	.02
☐ 421	Angels Manager	.35	.15	.03
	Bobby Winkles			
	Coaches: Tom Morgan			
	Salty Parker			
	Jimmie Reese			
	John Roseboro			
☐ 422	Bob Robertson	.25	.10	.02
☐ 423	Johnny Jeter	.25	.10	.02
☐ 424	Denny Doyle	.25	.10	.02
☐ 425	Alex Johnson	.25	.10	.02
☐ 426	Dave LaRoche	.25	.10	.02
☐ 427	Rick Auerbach	.25	.10	.02
☐ 428	Wayne Simpson	.25	.10	.02
☐ 429	Jim Fairey	.25	.10	.02
☐ 430	Vida Blue	.45	.20	.04
☐ 431	Gerry Moses	.25	.10	.02
☐ 432	Dan Frisella	.25	.10	.02
☐ 433	Willie Horton	.35	.15	.03
☐ 434	Giants Team	.45	.20	.04
☐ 435	Rico Carty	.40	.18	.04
☐ 436	Jim McAndrew	.25	.10	.02
☐ 437	John Kennedy	.25	.10	.02
☐ 438	Enzo Hernandez	.25	.10	.02
☐ 439	Eddie Fisher	.25	.10	.02
☐ 440	Glenn Beckert	.25	.10	.02
☐ 441	Gail Hopkins	.25	.10	.02
☐ 442	Dick Dietz	.25	.10	.02

☐ 443 Danny Thompson	.25	.10	.02
☐ 444 Ken Brett	.35	.15	.03
☐ 445 Ken Berry	.25	.10	.02
☐ 446 Jerry Reuss	.40	.18	.04
☐ 447 Joe Hague	.25	.10	.02
☐ 448 John Hiller	.35	.15	.03
☐ 449 Indians Manager	.35	.15	.03
Ken Aspromonte			
Coaches:			
Rocky Colavito			
Joe Lutz			
Warren Spahn			
☐ 450 Joe Torre	.55	.25	.05
☐ 451 John Vuckovich	.25	.10	.02
☐ 452 Paul Casanova	.25	.10	.02
☐ 453 Checklist 4th Series	.60	.10	.02
☐ 454 Tom Haller	.25	.10	.02
☐ 455 Bill Melton	.25	.10	.02
☐ 456 Dick Green	.25	.10	.02
☐ 457 John Strohmayer	.25	.10	.02
☐ 458 Jim Mason	.25	.10	.02
☐ 459 Jimmy Howarth	.25	.10	.02
☐ 460 Bill Freehan	.35	.15	.03
☐ 461 Mike Corkins	.25	.10	.02
☐ 462 Ron Blomberg	.25	.10	.02
☐ 463 Ken Tatum	.25	.10	.02
☐ 464 Chicago Cubs Team	.40	.18	.04
☐ 465 Dave Giusti	.25	.10	.02
☐ 466 Jose Arcia	.25	.10	.02
☐ 467 Mike Ryan	.25	.10	.02
☐ 468 Tom Griffin	.25	.10	.02
☐ 469 Dan Monzon	.25	.10	.02
☐ 470 Mike Cuellar	.35	.15	.03
ALL-TIME LEADERS(471-478)			
☐ 471 Hits Leaders	2.00	.90	.20
Ty Cobb 4191			
☐ 472 Grand Slam Leaders	2.00	.90	.20
Lou Gehrig 23			
☐ 473 Total Bases Leaders	2.00	.90	.20
Hank Aaron 6172			
☐ 474 RBI Leaders	3.00	1.40	.30
Babe Ruth 2209			
☐ 475 Batting Leaders	2.00	.90	.20
Ty Cobb .367			
☐ 476 Shutout Leaders	1.00	.45	.10
Walter Johnson 113			
☐ 477 Victory Leaders	1.00	.45	.10
Cy Young 511			
☐ 478 Strikeout Leaders	1.00	.45	.10
Walter Johnson 3508			
☐ 479 Hal Lanier	.35	.15	.03
☐ 480 Juan Marichal	1.75	.85	.17
☐ 481 White Sox Team Card	.40	.18	.04
☐ 482 Rick Reuschel	.75	.35	.07
☐ 483 Dal Maxvill	.25	.10	.02
☐ 484 Ernie McAnally	.25	.10	.02
☐ 485 Norm Cash	.40	.18	.04
☐ 486 Phillies Manager	.35	.15	.03
Danny Ozark			
Coaches:			
Carroll Beringer			
Billy DeMars			
Ray Rippelmeyer			
Bobby Wine			
☐ 487 Bruce Dal Canton	.25	.10	.02
☐ 488 Dave Campbell	.25	.10	.02
☐ 489 Jeff Burroughs	.35	.15	.03
☐ 490 Claude Osteen	.25	.10	.02
☐ 491 Bob Montgomery	.25	.10	.02
☐ 492 Pedro Borbon	.25	.10	.02
☐ 493 Duffy Dyer	.25	.10	.02
☐ 494 Rich Morales	.25	.10	.02
☐ 495 Tommy Helms	.25	.10	.02
☐ 496 Ray Lamb	.25	.10	.02
☐ 497 Cardinals Manager	.35	.15	.03
Red Schoendienst			
Coaches: Vern Benson			
George Kissell			
Barney Schultz			
☐ 498 Graig Nettles	1.50	.70	.15
☐ 499 Bob Moose	.25	.10	.02
☐ 500 Oakland A's Team	.45	.20	.04
☐ 501 Larry Gura	.35	.15	.03
☐ 502 Bobby Valentine	.50	.22	.05
☐ 503 Phil Niekro	1.75	.85	.17
☐ 504 Earl Williams	.25	.10	.02
☐ 505 Bob Bailey	.25	.10	.02
☐ 506 Bart Johnson	.25	.10	.02
☐ 507 Darrel Chaney	.25	.10	.02
☐ 508 Gates Brown	.25	.10	.02
☐ 509 Jim Nash	.25	.10	.02
☐ 510 Amos Otis	.35	.15	.03
☐ 511 Sam McDowell	.35	.15	.03
☐ 512 Dalton Jones	.25	.10	.02
☐ 513 Dave Marshall	.25	.10	.02
☐ 514 Jerry Kenney	.25	.10	.02
☐ 515 Andy Messersmith	.35	.15	.03
☐ 516 Danny Walton	.25	.10	.02
☐ 517 Pirates Manager	.35	.15	.03
Bill Virdon			
Coaches: Don Leppert			
Bill Mazeroski			
Dave Ricketts			
Mel Wright			
☐ 518 Bob Veale	.25	.10	.02
☐ 519 John Edwards	.25	.10	.02
☐ 520 Mel Stottlemyre	.35	.15	.03
☐ 521 Atlanta Braves Team	.40	.18	.04
☐ 522 Leo Cardenas	.25	.10	.02
☐ 523 Wayne Granger	.25	.10	.02
☐ 524 Gene Tenace	.25	.10	.02
☐ 525 Jim Fregosi	.35	.15	.03
☐ 526 Ollie Brown	.25	.10	.02
☐ 527 Dan McGinn	.25	.10	.02
☐ 528 Paul Blair	.25	.10	.02
☐ 529 Milt May	.25	.10	.02
☐ 530 Jim Kaat	1.50	.70	.15
☐ 531 Ron Woods	.25	.10	.02
☐ 532 Steve Mingori	.25	.10	.02
☐ 533 Larry Stahl	.25	.10	.02
☐ 534 Dave Lemonds	.25	.10	.02
☐ 535 John Callison	.35	.15	.03
☐ 536 Phillies Team	.45	.20	.04
☐ 537 Bill Slayback	.25	.10	.02
☐ 538 Jim Ray Hart	.35	.15	.03
☐ 539 Tom Murphy	.25	.10	.02
☐ 540 Cleon Jones	.25	.10	.02
☐ 541 Bob Bolin	.25	.10	.02
☐ 542 Pat Corrales	.35	.15	.03
☐ 543 Alan Foster	.25	.10	.02
☐ 544 Von Joshua	.25	.10	.02
☐ 545 Orlando Cepeda	.90	.40	.09
☐ 546 Jim York	.25	.10	.02
☐ 547 Bobby Heise	.25	.10	.02
☐ 548 Don Durham	.25	.10	.02
☐ 549 Rangers Manager	.60	.28	.06
Whitey Herzog			
Coaches: Chuck Estrada			
Chuck Hiller			
Jackie Moore			
☐ 550 Dave Johnson	.75	.35	.07
☐ 551 Mike Kilkenny	.25	.10	.02
☐ 552 J.C. Martin	.25	.10	.02
☐ 553 Mickey Scott	.25	.10	.02
☐ 554 Dave Concepcion	.90	.40	.09
☐ 555 Bill Hands	.25	.10	.02
☐ 556 Yankees Team	.75	.35	.07
☐ 557 Bernie Williams	.25	.10	.02
☐ 558 Jerry May	.25	.10	.02
☐ 559 Barry Lersch	.25	.10	.02
☐ 560 Frank Howard	.50	.22	.05
☐ 561 Jim Geddes	.25	.10	.02
☐ 562 Wayne Garrett	.25	.10	.02
☐ 563 Larry Haney	.25	.10	.02
☐ 564 Mike Thompson	.25	.10	.02
☐ 565 Jim Hickman	.25	.10	.02
☐ 566 Lew Krausse	.25	.10	.02
☐ 567 Bob Fenwick	.25	.10	.02
☐ 568 Ray Newman	.25	.10	.02
☐ 569 Dodgers Manager	.60	.28	.06
Walt Alston			
Coaches: Red Adams			
Monty Basgall			
Jim Gilliam			
Tom Lasorda			
☐ 570 Bill Singer	.25	.10	.02
☐ 571 Rusty Torres	.25	.10	.02
☐ 572 Gary Sutherland	.25	.10	.02
☐ 573 Fred Beene	.25	.10	.02
☐ 574 Bob Didier	.25	.10	.02
☐ 575 Dock Ellis	.25	.10	.02
☐ 576 Expos Team	.45	.20	.04
☐ 577 Eric Soderholm	.25	.10	.02
☐ 578 Ken Wright	.25	.10	.02
☐ 579 Tom Grieve	.45	.20	.04
☐ 580 Joe Pepitone	.35	.15	.03
☐ 581 Steve Kealey	.25	.10	.02
☐ 582 Darrell Porter	.40	.18	.04
☐ 583 Bill Grief	.25	.10	.02
☐ 584 Chris Arnold	.25	.10	.02
☐ 585 Joe Niekro	.45	.20	.04
☐ 586 Bill Sudakis	.25	.10	.02
☐ 587 Rich McKinney	.25	.10	.02
☐ 588 Checklist 5th Series	2.00	.30	.05
☐ 589 Ken Forsch	.35	.15	.03
☐ 590 Deron Johnson	.25	.10	.02

☐ 591	Mike Hedlund	.25	.10	.02
☐ 592	John Boccabella	.25	.10	.02
☐ 593	Royals Manager	.35	.15	.03
	Jack McKeon			
	Coaches: Galen Cisco			
	Harry Dunlop			
	Charlie Lau			
☐ 594	Vic Harris	.25	.10	.02
☐ 595	Don Gullett	.35	.15	.03
☐ 596	Red Sox Team	.45	.20	.04
☐ 597	Mickey Rivers	.45	.20	.04
☐ 598	Phil Roof	.25	.10	.02
☐ 599	Ed Crosby	.25	.10	.02
☐ 600	Dave McNally	.35	.15	.03
☐ 601	Rookie Catchers	.35	.15	.03
	Sergio Robles			
	George Pena			
	Rick Stelmaszek			
☐ 602	Rookie Pitchers	.35	.15	.03
	Mel Behney			
	Ralph Garcia			
	Doug Rau			
☐ 603	Rookie 3rd Basemen	.35	.15	.03
	Terry Hughes			
	Bill McNulty			
	Ken Reitz			
☐ 604	Rookie Pitchers	.35	.15	.03
	Jesse Jefferson			
	Dennis O'Toole			
	Bob Strampe			
☐ 605	Rookie 1st Basemen	.35	.15	.03
	Enos Cabell			
	Pat Bourque			
	Gonzalo Marquez			
☐ 606	Rookie Outfielders	2.00	.90	.20
	Gary Matthews			
	Tom Paciorek			
	Jorge Roque			
☐ 607	Rookie Shortstops	.35	.15	.03
	Pepe Frias			
	Ray Busse			
	Mario Guerrero			
☐ 608	Rookie Pitchers	.50	.22	.05
	Steve Busby			
	Dick Colpaert			
	George Medich			
☐ 609	Rookie 2nd Basemen	2.50	1.15	.25
	Larvel Blanks			
	Pedro Garcia			
	Dave Lopes			
☐ 610	Rookie Pitchers	1.00	.45	.10
	Jimmy Freeman			
	Charlie Hough			
	Hank Webb			
☐ 611	Rookie Outfielders	1.00	.45	.10
	Rich Coggins			
	Jim Wohlford			
	Richie Zisk			
☐ 612	Rookie Pitchers	.35	.15	.03
	Steve Lawson			
	Bob Reynolds			
	Brent Strom			
☐ 613	Rookie Catchers	1.00	.45	.10
	Bob Boone			
	Skip Jutze			
	Mike Ivie			
☐ 614	Rookie Outfielders	6.00	2.80	.60
	Alonza Bumbry			
	Dwight Evans			
	Charlie Spikes			
☐ 615	Rookie 3rd Basemen	55.00	22.00	5.00
	Ron Cey			
	John Hilton			
	Mike Schmidt			
☐ 616	Rookie Pitchers	.35	.15	.03
	Norm Angelini			
	Steve Blateric			
	Mike Garman			
☐ 617	Rich Chiles	.25	.10	.02
☐ 618	Andy Etchebarren	.25	.10	.02
☐ 619	Billy Wilson	.25	.10	.02
☐ 620	Tommy Harper	.25	.10	.02
☐ 621	Joe Ferguson	.35	.15	.03
☐ 622	Larry Hisle	.35	.15	.03
☐ 623	Steve Renko	.25	.10	.02
☐ 624	Astros Manager	.50	.22	.05
	Leo Durocher			
	Coaches: Preston Gomez			
	Grady Hatton			
	Hub Kittle			
	Jim Owens			
☐ 625	Angel Mangual	.25	.10	.02

☐ 626	Bob Barton	.25	.10	.02
☐ 627	Luis Alvarado	.25	.10	.02
☐ 628	Jim Slaton	.35	.15	.03
☐ 629	Indians Team	.50	.22	.05
☐ 630	Denny McLain	.75	.35	.07
☐ 631	Tom Matchick	.25	.10	.02
☐ 632	Dick Selma	.25	.10	.02
☐ 633	Ike Brown	.25	.10	.02
☐ 634	Alan Closter	.25	.10	.02
☐ 635	Gene Alley	.35	.15	.03
☐ 636	Rickey Clark	.25	.10	.02
☐ 637	Norm Miller	.25	.10	.02
☐ 638	Ken Reynolds	.25	.10	.02
☐ 639	Willie Crawford	.25	.10	.02
☐ 640	Dick Bosman	.25	.10	.02
☐ 641	Reds Team	.50	.22	.05
☐ 642	Jose LaBoy	.25	.10	.02
☐ 643	Al Fitzmorris	.25	.10	.02
☐ 644	Jack Heidemann	.25	.10	.02
☐ 645	Bob Locker	.25	.10	.02
☐ 646	Brewers Manager	.45	.20	.04
	Del Crandall			
	Coaches: Harvey Kuenn			
	Joe Nossek			
	Bob Shaw			
	Jim Walton			
☐ 647	George Stone	.25	.10	.02
☐ 648	Tom Egan	.25	.10	.02
☐ 649	Rich Folkers	.25	.10	.02
☐ 650	Felipe Alou	.35	.15	.03
☐ 651	Don Carrithers	.25	.10	.02
☐ 652	Ted Kubiak	.25	.10	.02
☐ 653	Joe Hoerner	.25	.10	.02
☐ 654	Twins Team	.45	.20	.04
☐ 655	Clay Kirby	.25	.10	.02
☐ 656	John Ellis	.25	.10	.02
☐ 657	Bob Johnson	.25	.10	.02
☐ 658	Elliott Maddox	.25	.10	.02
☐ 659	Jose Pagan	.25	.10	.02
☐ 660	Fred Scherman	.35	.15	.03

1974 O-Pee-Chee

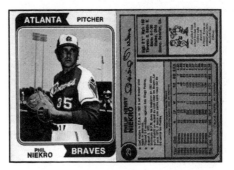

The cards in this 660 card set measure 2 1/2" by 3 1/2". The 1974 O-Pee-Chee cards are very similar to the 1974 Topps cards. Since the O-Pee-Chee cards were printed substantially later than the Topps cards, there was no "San Diego rumored moving to Washington" problem in the O-Pee-Chee set. The back color is golden yellow instead of green like the 1974 Topps. Backs are again written in French and English. There are a number of obverse differences between the two sets as well. They are numbers 3, 4, 5, 6, 7, 8, 9, 99, 166, and 196; the Aaron Specials generally feature two past cards per card instead of four as in the Topps. Remember, the prices below apply only to O-Pee-Chee cards -- they are NOT prices for Topps cards as they (Topps cards) are generally much more available.

		MINT	VG-E	F-G
	COMPLETE SET	225.00	100.00	20.00
	COMMON PLAYER (1-660)	.25	.10	.02
☐ 1	Hank Aaron	9.00	2.50	.50
	Complete ML record			
☐ 2	Aaron Special 54-57	3.00	1.40	.30
	Records on back			
☐ 3	Aaron Special 58-59	8.00	3.50	.75
☐ 4	Aaron Special 60-61	8.00	3.50	.75
☐ 5	Aaron Special 62-63	8.00	3.50	.75
☐ 6	Aaron Special 64-65	8.00	3.50	.75
☐ 7	Aaron Special 66-67	8.00	3.50	.75
☐ 8	Aaron Special 68-69	8.00	3.50	.75
☐ 9	Aaron Special 70-73	4.00	1.85	.40
	Milestone homers			
☐ 10	Johnny Bench	5.00	2.35	.50
☐ 11	Jim Bibby	.25	.10	.02
☐ 12	Dave May	.25	.10	.02
☐ 13	Tom Hilgendorf	.25	.10	.02
☐ 14	Paul Popovich	.25	.10	.02
☐ 15	Joe Torre	.50	.22	.05
☐ 16	Orioles Team	.35	.15	.03
☐ 17	Doug Bird	.25	.10	.02
☐ 18	Gary Thomasson	.25	.10	.02
☐ 19	Gerry Moses	.25	.10	.02
☐ 20	Nolan Ryan	3.50	1.65	.35
☐ 21	Bob Gallagher	.25	.10	.02
☐ 22	Cy Acosta	.25	.10	.02
☐ 23	Craig Robinson	.25	.10	.02
☐ 24	John Hiller	.25	.10	.02
☐ 25	Ken Singleton	.40	.18	.04
☐ 26	Bill Campbell	.25	.10	.02
☐ 27	George Scott	.35	.15	.03
☐ 28	Manny Sanguillen	.35	.15	.03
☐ 29	Phil Niekro	1.50	.70	.15
☐ 30	Bobby Bonds	.35	.15	.03
☐ 31	Astros Manager	.35	.15	.03
	Preston Gomez			
	Coaches: Roger Craig			
	Hub Kittle			
	Grady Hatton			
	Bob Lillis			
☐ 32	Johnny Grubb SD	.25	.10	.02
☐ 33	Don Newhauser	.25	.10	.02
☐ 34	Andy Kosco	.25	.10	.02
☐ 35	Gaylord Perry	1.75	.85	.17
☐ 36	Cardinals Team	.35	.15	.03
☐ 37	Dave Sells	.25	.10	.02
☐ 38	Don Kessinger	.35	.15	.03
☐ 39	Ken Suarez	.25	.10	.02
☐ 40	Jim Palmer	3.00	1.40	.30
☐ 41	Bobby Floyd	.25	.10	.02
☐ 42	Claude Osteen	.25	.10	.02
☐ 43	Jim Wynn	.25	.10	.02
☐ 44	Mel Stottlemyre	.25	.10	.02
☐ 45	Dave Johnson	.35	.15	.03
☐ 46	Pat Kelly	.25	.10	.02
☐ 47	Dick Ruthven	.25	.10	.02
☐ 48	Dick Sharon	.25	.10	.02
☐ 49	Steve Renko	.25	.10	.02
☐ 50	Rod Carew	4.50	2.10	.45
☐ 51	Bob Heise	.25	.10	.02
☐ 52	Al Oliver	1.00	.45	.10
☐ 53	Fred Kendall SD	.25	.10	.02
☐ 54	Elias Sosa	.25	.10	.02
☐ 55	Frank Robinson	2.25	1.00	.22
☐ 56	New York Mets Team	.50	.22	.05
☐ 57	Darold Knowles	.25	.10	.02
☐ 58	Charlie Spikes	.25	.10	.02
☐ 59	Ross Grimsley	.25	.10	.02
☐ 60	Lou Brock	2.25	1.00	.22
☐ 61	Luis Aparicio	1.50	.70	.15
☐ 62	Bob Locker	.25	.10	.02
☐ 63	Bill Sudakis	.25	.10	.02
☐ 64	Doug Rau	.25	.10	.02
☐ 65	Amos Otis	.35	.15	.03
☐ 66	Sparky Lyle	.35	.15	.03
☐ 67	Tommy Helms	.25	.10	.02
☐ 68	Grant Jackson	.25	.10	.02
☐ 69	Del Unser	.25	.10	.02
☐ 70	Dick Allen	.40	.18	.04
☐ 71	Dan Frisella	.25	.10	.02
☐ 72	Aurelio Rodriguez	.25	.10	.02
☐ 73	Mike Marshall	.35	.15	.03
☐ 74	Twins Team	.35	.15	.03
☐ 75	Jim Colborn	.25	.10	.02
☐ 76	Mickey Rivers	.35	.15	.03
☐ 77	Rich Troedson SD	.25	.10	.02
☐ 78	Giants Manager	.35	.15	.03
	Charlie Fox			

	Coaches: John McNamara			
	Joe Amalfitano			
	Andy Gilbert			
	Don McMahon			
☐ 79	Gene Tenace	.25	.10	.02
☐ 80	Tom Seaver	5.00	2.35	.50
☐ 81	Frank Duffy	.25	.10	.02
☐ 82	Dave Giusti	.25	.10	.02
☐ 83	Orlando Cepeda	.50	.22	.05
☐ 84	Rick Wise	.25	.10	.02
☐ 85	Joe Morgan	1.50	.70	.15
☐ 86	Joe Ferguson	.25	.10	.02
☐ 87	Fergie Jenkins	.75	.35	.07
☐ 88	Fred Patek	.25	.10	.02
☐ 89	Jackie Brown	.25	.10	.02
☐ 90	Bobby Murcer	.50	.22	.05
☐ 91	Ken Forsch	.25	.10	.02
☐ 92	Paul Blair	.25	.10	.02
☐ 93	Rod Gilbreath	.25	.10	.02
☐ 94	Tigers Team	.35	.15	.03
☐ 95	Steve Carlton	5.00	2.35	.50
☐ 96	Jerry Hairston	.25	.10	.02
☐ 97	Bob Bailey	.25	.10	.02
☐ 98	Bert Blyleven	.60	.28	.06
☐ 99	George Theodore	1.00	.45	.10
☐ 100	Willie Stargell	1.75	.85	.17
☐ 101	Bobby Valentine	.40	.18	.04
☐ 102	Bill Greif SD	.25	.10	.02
☐ 103	Sal Bando	.35	.15	.03
☐ 104	Ron Bryant	.25	.10	.02
☐ 105	Carlton Fisk	1.25	.60	.12
☐ 106	Harry Parker	.25	.10	.02
☐ 107	Alex Johnson	.25	.10	.02
☐ 108	Al Hrabosky	.35	.15	.03
☐ 109	Bobby Grich	.40	.18	.04
☐ 110	Billy Williams	.75	.35	.07
☐ 111	Clay Carroll	.25	.10	.02
☐ 112	Dave Lopes	.35	.15	.03
☐ 113	Dick Drago	.25	.10	.02
☐ 114	Angels Team	.35	.15	.03
☐ 115	Willie Horton	.35	.15	.03
☐ 116	Jerry Reuss	.35	.15	.03
☐ 117	Ron Blomberg	.25	.10	.02
☐ 118	Bill Lee	.35	.15	.03
☐ 119	Phillies Manager	.35	.15	.03
	Danny Ozark			
	Coaches:			
	Ray Rippelmeyer			
	Bobby Wine			
	Carroll Beringer			
	Billy DeMars			
☐ 120	Wilbur Wood	.25	.10	.02
☐ 121	Larry Lintz	.25	.10	.02
☐ 122	Jim Holt	.25	.10	.02
☐ 123	Nellie Briles	.25	.10	.02
☐ 124	Bobby Coluccio	.25	.10	.02
☐ 125	Nate Colbert SD	.25	.10	.02
☐ 126	Checklist 1	.60	.10	.02
☐ 127	Tom Paciorek	.25	.10	.02
☐ 128	John Ellis	.25	.10	.02
☐ 129	Chris Speier	.25	.10	.02
☐ 130	Reggie Jackson	6.00	2.80	.60
☐ 131	Bob Boone	.35	.15	.03
☐ 132	Felix Millan	.25	.10	.02
☐ 133	David Clyde	.25	.10	.02
☐ 134	Denis Menke	.25	.10	.02
☐ 135	Roy White	.25	.10	.02
☐ 136	Rick Reuschel	.35	.15	.03
☐ 137	Al Bumbry	.25	.10	.02
☐ 138	Eddie Brinkman	.25	.10	.02
☐ 139	Aurelio Monteagudo	.25	.10	.02
☐ 140	Darrell Evans	.40	.18	.04
☐ 141	Pat Bourque	.25	.10	.02
☐ 142	Pedro Garcia	.25	.10	.02
☐ 143	Dick Woodson	.25	.10	.02
☐ 144	Dodgers Manager	.50	.22	.05
	Walter Alston			
	Coaches: Tom Lasorda			
	Jim Gilliam			
	Red Adams			
	Monty Basgall			
☐ 145	Dock Ellis	.25	.10	.02
☐ 146	Ron Fairly	.25	.10	.02
☐ 147	Bart Johnson	.25	.10	.02
☐ 148	Dave Hilton SD	.25	.10	.02
☐ 149	Mac Scarce	.25	.10	.02
☐ 150	John Mayberry	.35	.15	.03
☐ 151	Diego Segui	.25	.10	.02
☐ 152	Oscar Gamble	.35	.15	.03
☐ 153	Jon Matlack	.35	.15	.03
☐ 154	Astros Team	.35	.15	.03
☐ 155	Bert Campaneris	.35	.15	.03

☐ 156 Randy Moffitt	.25	.10	.02
☐ 157 Vic Harris	.25	.10	.02
☐ 158 Jack Billingham	.25	.10	.02
☐ 159 Jim Ray Hart	.25	.10	.02
☐ 160 Brooks Robinson	2.25	1.00	.22
☐ 161 Ray Burris	.35	.15	.03
☐ 162 Bill Freehan	.35	.15	.03
☐ 163 Ken Berry	.25	.10	.02
☐ 164 Tom House	.35	.15	.03
☐ 165 Willie Davis	.35	.15	.03
☐ 166 Mickey Lolich	2.00	.90	.20
☐ 167 Luis Tiant	.35	.15	.03
☐ 168 Danny Thompson	.25	.10	.02
☐ 169 Steve Rogers	1.00	.45	.10
☐ 170 Bill Melton	.25	.10	.02
☐ 171 Eduardo Rodriguez	.25	.10	.02
☐ 172 Gene Clines	.25	.10	.02
☐ 173 Randy Jones SD	.45	.20	.04
☐ 174 Bill Robinson	.25	.10	.02
☐ 175 Reggie Cleveland	.25	.10	.02
☐ 176 John Lowenstein	.25	.10	.02
☐ 177 Dave Roberts	.25	.10	.02
☐ 178 Garry Maddox	.35	.15	.03
☐ 179 New York Mets Manager	.50	.22	.05
Yogi Berra			
Coaches: Rube Walker			
Eddie Yost			
Roy McMillan			
Joe Pignatano			
☐ 180 Ken Holtzman	.35	.15	.03
☐ 181 Cesar Geronimo	.25	.10	.02
☐ 182 Lindy McDaniel	.25	.10	.02
☐ 183 Johnny Oates	.25	.10	.02
☐ 184 Rangers Team	.35	.15	.03
☐ 185 Jose Cardenal	.25	.10	.02
☐ 186 Fred Scherman	.25	.10	.02
☐ 187 Don Baylor	.60	.28	.06
☐ 188 Rudy Meoli	.25	.10	.02
☐ 189 Jim Brewer	.25	.10	.02
☐ 190 Tony Oliva	.50	.22	.05
☐ 191 Al Fitzmorris	.25	.10	.02
☐ 192 Mario Guerrero	.25	.10	.02
☐ 193 Tom Walker	.25	.10	.02
☐ 194 Darrell Porter	.35	.15	.03
☐ 195 Carlos May	.25	.10	.02
☐ 196 Jim Hunter	4.00	1.85	.40
☐ 197 Vicente Romo SD	.25	.10	.02
☐ 198 Dave Cash	.25	.10	.02
☐ 199 Mike Kekich	.25	.10	.02
☐ 200 Cesar Cedeno	.35	.15	.03
LEADERS (201-208)			
☐ 201 Batting Leaders:	2.25	1.00	.22
Rod Carew			
Pete Rose			
☐ 202 Home Run Leaders:	1.25	.60	.12
Reggie Jackson			
Willie Stargell			
☐ 203 RBI Leaders:	1.25	.60	.12
Reggie Jackson			
Willie Stargell			
☐ 204 Stolen Base Leaders:	.60	.28	.06
Tommy Harper			
Lou Brock			
☐ 205 Victory Leaders:	.35	.15	.03
Wilbur Wood			
Ron Bryant			
☐ 206 ERA Leaders:	1.25	.60	.12
Jim Palmer			
Tom Seaver			
☐ 207 Strikeout Leaders:	1.25	.60	.12
Nolan Ryan			
Tom Seaver			
☐ 208 Leading Firemen:	.35	.15	.03
John Hiller			
Mike Marshall			
☐ 209 Ted Sizemore	.25	.10	.02
☐ 210 Bill Singer	.25	.10	.02
☐ 211 Chicago Cubs Team	.35	.15	.03
☐ 212 Rollie Fingers	1.00	.45	.10
☐ 213 Dave Rader	.25	.10	.02
☐ 214 Bill Grabarkewitz	.25	.10	.02
☐ 215 Al Kaline	2.50	1.15	.25
☐ 216 Ray Sadecki	.25	.10	.02
☐ 217 Tim Foli	.25	.10	.02
☐ 218 John Briggs	.25	.10	.02
☐ 219 Doug Griffin	.25	.10	.02
☐ 220 Don Sutton	1.00	.45	.10
☐ 221 White Sox Manager	.35	.15	.03
Chuck Tanner			
Coaches: Jim Mahoney			
Alex Monchak			
Johnny Sain			
Joe Lonnett			
☐ 222 Ramon Hernandez	.25	.10	.02
☐ 223 Jeff Burroughs	.35	.15	.03
☐ 224 Roger Metzger	.25	.10	.02
☐ 225 Paul Splittorff	.25	.10	.02
☐ 226 Padres Team Card SD	.40	.18	.04
☐ 227 Mike Lum	.25	.10	.02
☐ 228 Ted Kubiak	.25	.10	.02
☐ 229 Fritz Peterson	.25	.10	.02
☐ 230 Tony Perez	.60	.28	.06
☐ 231 Dick Tidrow	.25	.10	.02
☐ 232 Steve Brye	.25	.10	.02
☐ 233 Jim Barr	.25	.10	.02
☐ 234 John Milner	.25	.10	.02
☐ 235 Dave McNally	.35	.15	.03
☐ 236 Cardinals Manager	.35	.15	.03
Red Schoendienst			
Coaches: Barney Schultz			
George Kissell			
Johnny Lewis			
Vern Benson			
☐ 237 Ken Brett	.35	.15	.03
☐ 238 Fran Healy	.25	.10	.02
☐ 239 Bill Russell	.35	.15	.03
☐ 240 Joe Coleman	.25	.10	.02
☐ 241 Glenn Beckert SD	.25	.10	.02
☐ 242 Bill Gogolewski	.25	.10	.02
☐ 243 Bob Oliver	.25	.10	.02
☐ 244 Carl Morton	.25	.10	.02
☐ 245 Cleon Jones	.25	.10	.02
☐ 246 Athletics Team	.35	.15	.03
☐ 247 Rick Miller	.25	.10	.02
☐ 248 Tom Hall	.25	.10	.02
☐ 249 George Mitterwald	.25	.10	.02
☐ 250 Willie McCovey SD	3.00	1.40	.30
☐ 251 Graig Nettles	1.50	.70	.15
☐ 252 Dave Parker	10.00	4.75	1.00
☐ 253 John Boccabella	.25	.10	.02
☐ 254 Stan Bahnsen	.25	.10	.02
☐ 255 Larry Bowa	.40	.18	.04
☐ 256 Tom Griffin	.25	.10	.02
☐ 257 Buddy Bell	.75	.35	.07
☐ 258 Jerry Morales	.25	.10	.02
☐ 259 Bob Reynolds	.25	.10	.02
☐ 260 Ted Simmons	.75	.35	.07
☐ 261 Jerry Bell	.25	.10	.02
☐ 262 Ed Kirkpatrick	.25	.10	.02
☐ 263 Checklist 2	.60	.10	.02
☐ 264 Joe Rudi	.35	.15	.03
☐ 265 Tug McGraw	.40	.18	.04
☐ 266 Jim Northrup	.35	.15	.03
☐ 267 Andy Messersmith	.35	.15	.03
☐ 268 Tom Grieve	.35	.15	.03
☐ 269 Bob Johnson	.25	.10	.02
☐ 270 Ron Santo	.40	.18	.04
☐ 271 Bill Hands	.25	.10	.02
☐ 272 Paul Casanova	.25	.10	.02
☐ 273 Checklist 3	.60	.10	.02
☐ 274 Fred Beene	.25	.10	.02
☐ 275 Ron Hunt	.25	.10	.02
☐ 276 Angels Manager	.35	.15	.03
Bobby Winkles			
Coaches: John Roseboro			
Tom Morgan			
Jimmie Reese			
Salty Parker			
☐ 277 Gary Nolan	.25	.10	.02
☐ 278 Cookie Rojas	.25	.10	.02
☐ 279 Jim Crawford	.25	.10	.02
☐ 280 Carl Yastrzemski	7.50	3.50	.75
☐ 281 Giants Team	.35	.15	.03
☐ 282 Doyle Alexander	.25	.10	.02
☐ 283 Mike Schmidt	12.00	5.50	1.20
☐ 284 Dave Duncan	.25	.10	.02
☐ 285 Reggie Smith	.40	.18	.04
☐ 286 Tony Muser	.25	.10	.02
☐ 287 Clay Kirby	.25	.10	.02
☐ 288 Gorman Thomas	2.00	.90	.20
☐ 289 Rick Auerbach	.25	.10	.02
☐ 290 Vida Blue	.40	.18	.04
☐ 291 Don Hahn	.25	.10	.02
☐ 292 Chuck Seelbach	.25	.10	.02
☐ 293 Milt May	.25	.10	.02
☐ 294 Steve Foucault	.25	.10	.02
☐ 295 Rick Monday	.35	.15	.03
☐ 296 Ray Corbin	.25	.10	.02
☐ 297 Hal Breeden	.25	.10	.02
☐ 298 Roric Harrison	.25	.10	.02
☐ 299 Gene Michael	.35	.15	.03
☐ 300 Pete Rose	12.00	5.50	1.20
☐ 301 Bob Montgomery	.25	.10	.02
☐ 302 Rudy May	.25	.10	.02
☐ 303 George Hendrick	.40	.18	.04
☐ 304 Don Wilson	.25	.10	.02

☐ 305	Tito Fuentes	.25	.10	.02
☐ 306	Orioles Manager	.45	.20	.04
	Earl Weaver			
	Coaches: Jim Frey			
	George Bamberger			
	Billy Hunter			
	George Staller			
☐ 307	Luis Melendez	.25	.10	.02
☐ 308	Bruce Dal Canton	.25	.10	.02
☐ 309	Dave Roberts SD	.25	.10	.02
☐ 310	Terry Forster	.35	.15	.03
☐ 311	Jerry Grote	.25	.10	.02
☐ 312	Deron Johnson	.25	.10	.02
☐ 313	Barry Lersch	.25	.10	.02
☐ 314	Brewers Team	.35	.15	.03
☐ 315	Ron Cey	1.00	.45	.10
☐ 316	Jim Perry	.35	.15	.03
☐ 317	Richie Zisk	.35	.15	.03
☐ 318	Jim Merritt	.25	.10	.02
☐ 319	Randy Hundley	.25	.10	.02
☐ 320	Dusty Baker	.45	.20	.04
☐ 321	Steve Braun	.25	.10	.02
☐ 322	Ernie McAnally	.25	.10	.02
☐ 323	Richie Scheinblum	.25	.10	.02
☐ 324	Steve Kline	.25	.10	.02
☐ 325	Tommy Harper	.25	.10	.02
☐ 326	Reds Manager	.35	.15	.03
	Sparky Anderson			
	Coaches: Larry Shephard			
	George Scherger			
	Alex Grammas			
	Ted Kluszewski			
☐ 327	Tom Timmermann	.25	.10	.02
☐ 328	Skip Jutze	.25	.10	.02
☐ 329	Mark Belanger	.35	.15	.03
☐ 330	Juan Marichal	1.50	.70	.15
ALL-STARS (331-339)				
☐ 331	All-Star Catchers:	1.25	.60	.12
	Carlton Fisk			
	Johnny Bench			
☐ 332	All-Star 1B:	1.25	.60	.12
	Dick Allen			
	Hank Aaron			
☐ 333	All-Star 2B:	1.25	.60	.12
	Rod Carew			
	Joe Morgan			
☐ 334	All-Star 3B:	.80	.40	.08
	Brooks Robinson			
	Ron Santo			
☐ 335	All-Star SS:	.35	.15	.03
	Bert Campaneris			
	Chris Speier			
☐ 336	All-Star LF:	2.00	.90	.20
	Bobby Murcer			
	Pete Rose			
☐ 337	All-Star CF:	.35	.15	.03
	Amos Otis			
	Cesar Cedeno			
☐ 338	All-Star RF:	1.25	.60	.12
	Reggie Jackson			
	Billy Williams			
☐ 339	All-Star Pitchers:	.35	.15	.03
	Jim Hunter			
	Rick Wise			
☐ 340	Thurman Munson	4.00	1.85	.40
☐ 341	Dan Driessen	.40	.18	.04
☐ 342	Jim Lonborg	.35	.15	.03
☐ 343	Royals Team	.35	.15	.03
☐ 344	Mike Caldwell	.25	.10	.02
☐ 345	Bill North	.25	.10	.02
☐ 346	Ron Reed	.25	.10	.02
☐ 347	Sandy Alomar	.25	.10	.02
☐ 348	Pete Richert	.25	.10	.02
☐ 349	John Vukovich	.25	.10	.02
☐ 350	Bob Gibson	2.00	.90	.20
☐ 351	Dwight Evans	1.25	.60	.12
☐ 352	Bill Stoneman	.25	.10	.02
☐ 353	Rich Coggins	.25	.10	.02
☐ 354	Chicago Cubs Manager	.35	.15	.03
	Whitey Lockman			
	Coaches: J.C. Martin			
	Hank Aguirre			
	Al Spangler			
	Jim Marshall			
☐ 355	Dave Nelson	.25	.10	.02
☐ 356	Jerry Koosman	.40	.18	.04
☐ 357	Buddy Bradford	.25	.10	.02
☐ 358	Dal Maxvill	.25	.10	.02
☐ 359	Brent Strom	.25	.10	.02
☐ 360	Greg Luzinski	.75	.35	.07
☐ 361	Don Carrithers	.25	.10	.02
☐ 362	Hal King	.25	.10	.02

☐ 363	Yankees Team	.50	.22	.05
☐ 364	Cito Gaston SD	.25	.10	.02
☐ 365	Steve Busby	.35	.15	.03
☐ 366	Larry Hisle	.35	.15	.03
☐ 367	Norm Cash	.40	.18	.04
☐ 368	Manny Mota	.35	.15	.03
☐ 369	Paul Lindblad	.25	.10	.02
☐ 370	Bob Watson	.35	.15	.03
☐ 371	Jim Slaton	.25	.10	.02
☐ 372	Ken Reitz	.25	.10	.02
☐ 373	John Curtis	.25	.10	.02
☐ 374	Marty Perez	.25	.10	.02
☐ 375	Earl Williams	.25	.10	.02
☐ 376	Jorge Orta	.25	.10	.02
☐ 377	Ron Woods	.25	.10	.02
☐ 378	Burt Hooton	.25	.10	.02
☐ 379	Rangers Manager	.50	.22	.05
	Billy Martin			
	Coaches: Frank Lucchesi			
	Art Fowler			
	Charlie Silvera			
	Jackie Moore			
☐ 380	Bud Harrelson	.25	.10	.02
☐ 381	Charlie Sands	.25	.10	.02
☐ 382	Bob Moose	.25	.10	.02
☐ 383	Phillies Team	.35	.15	.03
☐ 384	Chris Chambliss	.35	.15	.03
☐ 385	Don Gullett	.25	.10	.02
☐ 386	Gary Matthews	.45	.20	.04
☐ 387	Rich Morales SD	.25	.10	.02
☐ 388	Phil Roof	.25	.10	.02
☐ 389	Gates Brown	.25	.10	.02
☐ 390	Lou Piniella	.50	.22	.05
☐ 391	Billy Champion	.25	.10	.02
☐ 392	Dick Green	.25	.10	.02
☐ 393	Orlando Pena	.25	.10	.02
☐ 394	Ken Henderson	.25	.10	.02
☐ 395	Doug Rader	.35	.15	.03
☐ 396	Tommy Davis	.35	.15	.03
☐ 397	George Stone	.25	.10	.02
☐ 398	Duke Sims	.25	.10	.02
☐ 399	Mike Paul	.25	.10	.02
☐ 400	Harmon Killebrew	2.00	.90	.20
☐ 401	Elliot Maddox	.25	.10	.02
☐ 402	Jim Rooker	.25	.10	.02
☐ 403	Red Sox Manager	.35	.15	.03
	Darrell Johnson			
	Coaches: Eddie Popowski			
	Lee Stange			
	Don Zimmer			
	Don Bryant			
☐ 404	Jim Howarth	.25	.10	.02
☐ 405	Ellie Rodriguez	.25	.10	.02
☐ 406	Steve Arlin	.25	.10	.02
☐ 407	Jim Wohlford	.25	.10	.02
☐ 408	Charlie Hough	.35	.15	.03
☐ 409	Ike Brown	.25	.10	.02
☐ 410	Pedro Borbon	.25	.10	.02
☐ 411	Frank Baker	.25	.10	.02
☐ 412	Chuck Taylor	.25	.10	.02
☐ 413	Don Money	.25	.10	.02
☐ 414	Checklist 4	.60	.10	.02
☐ 415	Gary Gentry	.25	.10	.02
☐ 416	White Sox Team	.35	.15	.03
☐ 417	Rich Folkers	.25	.10	.02
☐ 418	Walt Williams	.25	.10	.02
☐ 419	Wayne Twitchell	.25	.10	.02
☐ 420	Ray Fosse	.25	.10	.02
☐ 421	Dan Fife	.25	.10	.02
☐ 422	Gonzalo Marquez	.25	.10	.02
☐ 423	Fred Stanley	.25	.10	.02
☐ 424	Jim Beauchamp	.25	.10	.02
☐ 425	Pete Broberg	.25	.10	.02
☐ 426	Rennie Stennett	.25	.10	.02
☐ 427	Bobby Bolin	.25	.10	.02
☐ 428	Gary Sutherland	.25	.10	.02
☐ 429	Dick Lange	.25	.10	.02
☐ 430	Matty Alou	.35	.15	.03
☐ 431	Gene Garber	.35	.15	.03
☐ 432	Chris Arnold	.25	.10	.02
☐ 433	Lerrin LaGrow	.25	.10	.02
☐ 434	Ken McMullen	.25	.10	.02
☐ 435	Dave Concepcion	.50	.22	.05
☐ 436	Don Hood	.25	.10	.02
☐ 437	Jim Lyttle	.25	.10	.02
☐ 438	Ed Herrmann	.25	.10	.02
☐ 439	Norm Miller	.25	.10	.02
☐ 440	Jim Kaat	.75	.35	.07
☐ 441	Tom Ragland	.25	.10	.02
☐ 442	Alan Foster	.25	.10	.02
☐ 443	Tom Hutton	.25	.10	.02
☐ 444	Vic Davalillo	.25	.10	.02

☐ 445 George Medich	.25	.10	.02
☐ 446 Len Randle	.25	.10	.02
☐ 447 Twins Manager	.35	.15	.03
Frank Quilici			
Coaches: Ralph Rowe			
Bob Rodgers			
Vern Morgan			
☐ 448 Ron Hodges	.25	.10	.02
☐ 449 Tom McCraw	.25	.10	.02
☐ 450 Rich Hebner	.25	.10	.02
☐ 451 Tommy John	1.00	.45	.10
☐ 452 Gene Hiser	.25	.10	.02
☐ 453 Balor Moore	.25	.10	.02
☐ 454 Kurt Bevacqua	.25	.10	.02
☐ 455 Tom Bradley	.25	.10	.02
☐ 456 Dave Winfield	20.00	9.00	2.00
☐ 457 Chuck Goggin	.25	.10	.02
☐ 458 Jim Ray	.25	.10	.02
☐ 459 Reds Team	.35	.15	.03
☐ 460 Boog Powell	.50	.22	.05
☐ 461 John Odom	.25	.10	.02
☐ 462 Luis Alvarado	.25	.10	.02
☐ 463 Pat Dobson	.25	.10	.02
☐ 464 Jose Cruz	.50	.22	.05
☐ 465 Dick Bosman	.25	.10	.02
☐ 466 Dick Billings	.25	.10	.02
☐ 467 Winston Llenas	.25	.10	.02
☐ 468 Pepe Frias	.25	.10	.02
☐ 469 Joe Decker	.25	.10	.02
☐ 470 A.L. Playoffs:	1.50	.70	.15
A's over Orioles			
(Reggie Jackson)			
☐ 471 N.L. Playoffs:	.50	.22	.05
Mets over Reds			
(Matlack pitching)			
WORLD SERIES (472-479)			
☐ 472 World Series Game 1:	.50	.22	.05
(D.Knowles pitching)			
☐ 473 World Series Game 2:	1.50	.70	.15
(Willie Mays batting)			
☐ 474 World Series Game 3:	.50	.22	.05
(Campaneris stealing)			
☐ 475 World Series Game 4:	.50	.22	.05
(R.Staub batting)			
☐ 476 World Series Game 5:	.50	.22	.05
Cleon Jones scoring)			
☐ 477 World Series Game 6:	1.50	.70	.15
(Reggie Jackson)			
☐ 478 World Series Game 7:	.50	.22	.05
(Campaneris batting)			
☐ 479 World Series Summary:	.50	.22	.05
A's Celebrate; Win			
2nd cons. championship			
☐ 480 Willie Crawford	.25	.10	.02
☐ 481 Jerry Terrell	.25	.10	.02
☐ 482 Bob Didier	.25	.10	.02
☐ 483 Braves Team	.35	.15	.03
☐ 484 Carmen Fanzone	.25	.10	.02
☐ 485 Felipe Alou	.35	.15	.03
☐ 486 Steve Stone	.35	.15	.03
☐ 487 Ted Martinez	.25	.10	.02
☐ 488 Andy Etchebarren	.25	.10	.02
☐ 489 Pirates Manager	.35	.15	.03
Danny Murtaugh			
Coaches: Don Osborn			
Don Leppert			
Bill Mazeroski			
Bob Skinner			
☐ 490 Vada Pinson	.35	.15	.03
☐ 491 Roger Nelson	.25	.10	.02
☐ 492 Mike Rogodzinski	.25	.10	.02
☐ 493 Joe Hoerner	.25	.10	.02
☐ 494 Ed Goodson	.25	.10	.02
☐ 495 Dick McAuliffe	.25	.10	.02
☐ 496 Tom Murphy	.25	.10	.02
☐ 497 Bobby Mitchell	.25	.10	.02
☐ 498 Pat Corrales	.25	.10	.02
☐ 499 Rusty Torres	.25	.10	.02
☐ 500 Lee May	.35	.15	.03
☐ 501 Eddie Leon	.25	.10	.02
☐ 502 Dave LaRoche	.25	.10	.02
☐ 503 Eric Soderholm	.25	.10	.02
☐ 504 Joe Niekro	.35	.15	.03
☐ 505 Bill Buckner	.50	.22	.05
☐ 506 Ed Farmer	.25	.10	.02
☐ 507 Larry Stahl	.25	.10	.02
☐ 508 Expos Team	.35	.15	.03
☐ 509 Jesse Jefferson	.25	.10	.02
☐ 510 Wayne Garrett	.25	.10	.02
☐ 511 Toby Harrah	.35	.15	.03
☐ 512 Joe Lahoud	.25	.10	.02
☐ 513 Jim Campanis	.25	.10	.02
☐ 514 Paul Schaal	.25	.10	.02

☐ 515 Willie Montanez	.25	.10	.02
☐ 516 Horacio Pina	.25	.10	.02
☐ 517 Mike Hegan	.25	.10	.02
☐ 518 Derrel Thomas	.25	.10	.02
☐ 519 Bill Sharp	.25	.10	.02
☐ 520 Tim McCarver	.35	.15	.03
☐ 521 Indians Manager	.35	.15	.03
Ken Aspromonte			
Coaches: Clay Bryant			
Tony Pacheco			
☐ 522 J.R. Richard	.45	.20	.04
☐ 523 Cecil Cooper	2.25	1.00	.22
☐ 524 Bill Plummer	.25	.10	.02
☐ 525 Clyde Wright	.25	.10	.02
☐ 526 Frank Tepedino	.25	.10	.02
☐ 527 Bobby Darwin	.25	.10	.02
☐ 528 Bill Bonham	.25	.10	.02
☐ 529 Horace Clarke	.25	.10	.02
☐ 530 Mickey Stanley	.25	.10	.02
☐ 531 Expos Manager	.35	.15	.03
Gene Mauch			
Coaches: Dave Bristol			
Cal McLish			
Larry Doby			
Jerry Zimmerman			
☐ 532 Skip Lockwood	.25	.10	.02
☐ 533 Mike Phillips	.25	.10	.02
☐ 534 Eddie Watt	.25	.10	.02
☐ 535 Bob Tolan	.25	.10	.02
☐ 536 Duffy Dyer	.25	.10	.02
☐ 537 Steve Mingori	.25	.10	.02
☐ 538 Cesar Tovar	.25	.10	.02
☐ 539 Lloyd Allen	.25	.10	.02
☐ 540 Bob Robertson	.25	.10	.02
☐ 541 Indians Team	.35	.15	.03
☐ 542 Rich Gossage	1.75	.85	.17
☐ 543 Danny Cater	.25	.10	.02
☐ 544 Ron Schueler	.25	.10	.02
☐ 545 Billy Conigliaro	.25	.10	.02
☐ 546 Mike Corkins	.25	.10	.02
☐ 547 Glenn Borgmann	.25	.10	.02
☐ 548 Sonny Siebert	.25	.10	.02
☐ 549 Mike Jorgensen	.25	.10	.02
☐ 550 Sam McDowell	.35	.15	.03
☐ 551 Von Joshua	.25	.10	.02
☐ 552 Denny Doyle	.25	.10	.02
☐ 553 Jim Willoughby	.25	.10	.02
☐ 554 Tim Johnson	.25	.10	.02
☐ 555 Woody Fryman	.25	.10	.02
☐ 556 Dave Campbell	.25	.10	.02
☐ 557 Jim McGlothlin	.25	.10	.02
☐ 558 Bill Fahey	.25	.10	.02
☐ 559 Darrell Chaney	.25	.10	.02
☐ 560 Mike Cuellar	.35	.15	.03
☐ 561 Ed Kranepool	.25	.10	.02
☐ 562 Jack Aker	.25	.10	.02
☐ 563 Hal McRae	.35	.15	.03
☐ 564 Mike Ryan	.25	.10	.02
☐ 565 Milt Wilcox	.25	.10	.02
☐ 566 Jackie Hernandez	.25	.10	.02
☐ 567 Red Sox Team	.35	.15	.03
☐ 568 Mike Torrez	.35	.15	.03
☐ 569 Rick Dempsey	.35	.15	.03
☐ 570 Ralph Garr	.25	.10	.02
☐ 571 Rich Hand	.25	.10	.02
☐ 572 Enzo Hernandez	.25	.10	.02
☐ 573 Mike Adams	.25	.10	.02
☐ 574 Bill Parsons	.25	.10	.02
☐ 575 Steve Garvey	7.00	3.25	.70
☐ 576 Scipio Spinks	.25	.10	.02
☐ 577 Mike Sadek	.25	.10	.02
☐ 578 Ralph Houk MGR	.35	.15	.03
☐ 579 Cecil Upshaw	.25	.10	.02
☐ 580 Jim Spencer	.25	.10	.02
☐ 581 Fred Norman	.25	.10	.02
☐ 582 Bucky Dent	.50	.22	.05
☐ 583 Marty Pattin	.25	.10	.02
☐ 584 Ken Rudolph	.25	.10	.02
☐ 585 Merv Rettenmund	.25	.10	.02
☐ 586 Jack Brohamer	.25	.10	.02
☐ 587 Larry Christenson	.25	.10	.02
☐ 588 Hal Lanier	.35	.15	.03
☐ 589 Boots Day	.25	.10	.02
☐ 590 Roger Moret	.25	.10	.02
☐ 591 Sonny Jackson	.25	.10	.02
☐ 592 Ed Bane	.25	.10	.02
☐ 593 Steve Yeager	.35	.15	.03
☐ 594 Lee Stanton	.25	.10	.02
☐ 595 Steve Blass	.25	.10	.02
ROOKIES (596-608)			
☐ 596 Rookie Pitchers:	.35	.15	.03
Wayne Garland			
Fred Holdsworth			

Mark Littell
Dick Pole
☐ 597 Rookie Shortstops: .... .75 .35 .07
    Dave Chalk
    John Gamble
    Pete MacKanin
    Manny Trillo
☐ 598 Rookie Outfielders: .... 2.00 .90 .20
    Dave Augustine
    Ken Griffey
    Steve Ontiveros
    Jim Tyrone
☐ 599 Rookie Pitchers: .... .50 .22 .05
    Ron Diorio
    Dave Freisleben
    Frank Riccelli
    Greg Shanahan
☐ 600 Rookie Infielders: .... 7.00 3.25 .70
    Ron Cash
    Jim Cox
    Bill Madlock
    Reggie Sanders
☐ 601 Rookie Outfielders: .... .75 .35 .07
    Ed Armbrister
    Rich Bladt
    Brian Downing
    Bake McBride
☐ 602 Rookie Pitchers: .... .40 .18 .04
    Glen Abbott
    Rick Henninger
    Craig Swan
    Dan Vossler
☐ 603 Rookie Catchers: .... .35 .15 .03
    Barry Foote
    Tom Lundstedt
    Charlie Moore
    Sergio Robles
☐ 604 Rookie Infielders: .... 2.50 1.15 .25
    Terry Hughes
    John Knox
    Andy Thornton
    Frank White
☐ 605 Rookie Pitchers: .... .60 .28 .06
    Vic Albury
    Ken Frailing
    Kevin Kobel
    Frank Tanana
☐ 606 Rookie Outfielders: .... .35 .15 .03
    Jim Fuller
    Wilbur Howard
    Tommy Smith
    Otto Velez
☐ 607 Rookie Shortstops: .... .35 .15 .03
    Leo Foster
    Tom Heintzelman
    Dave Rosello
    Frank Taveras
☐ 608 Rookie Pitchers: .... .35 .15 .03
    Bob Apodaca
    Dick Baney
    John D'Acquisto
    Mike Wallace
☐ 609 Rico Petrocelli .... .35 .15 .03
☐ 610 Dave Kingman .... 1.00 .45 .10
☐ 611 Rich Stelmaszek .... .25 .10 .02
☐ 612 Luke Walker .... .25 .10 .02
☐ 613 Dan Monzon .... .25 .10 .02
☐ 614 Adrian Devine .... .25 .10 .02
☐ 615 John Jeter .... .25 .10 .02
☐ 616 Larry Gura .... .35 .15 .03
☐ 617 Ted Ford .... .25 .10 .02
☐ 618 Jim Mason .... .25 .10 .02
☐ 619 Mike Anderson .... .25 .10 .02
☐ 620 Al Downing .... .25 .10 .02
☐ 621 Bernie Carbo .... .25 .10 .02
☐ 622 Phil Gagliano .... .25 .10 .02
☐ 623 Celerino Sanchez .... .25 .10 .02
☐ 624 Bob Miller .... .25 .10 .02
☐ 625 Ollie Brown .... .25 .10 .02
☐ 626 Pirates Team .... .35 .15 .03
☐ 627 Carl Taylor .... .25 .10 .02
☐ 628 Ivan Murrell .... .25 .10 .02
☐ 629 Rusty Staub .... .50 .22 .05
☐ 630 Tommy Agee .... .25 .10 .02
☐ 631 Steve Barber .... .25 .10 .02
☐ 632 George Culver .... .25 .10 .02
☐ 633 Dave Hamilton .... .25 .10 .02
☐ 634 Braves Manager: .... .50 .22 .05
    Eddie Mathews
    Coaches: Herm Starrette
    Connie Ryan
    Jim Busby

Ken Silvestri
☐ 635 John Edwards .... .25 .10 .02
☐ 636 Dave Goltz .... .25 .10 .02
☐ 637 Checklist 5 .... .60 .10 .02
☐ 638 Ken Sanders .... .25 .10 .02
☐ 639 Joe Lovitto .... .25 .10 .02
☐ 640 Milt Pappas .... .25 .10 .02
☐ 641 Chuck Brinkman .... .25 .10 .02
☐ 642 Terry Harmon .... .25 .10 .02
☐ 643 Dodgers Team .... .50 .22 .05
☐ 644 Wayne Granger .... .25 .10 .02
☐ 645 Ken Boswell .... .25 .10 .02
☐ 646 George Foster .... 1.50 .70 .15
☐ 647 Juan Beniquez .... .50 .22 .05
☐ 648 Terry Crowley .... .25 .10 .02
☐ 649 Fernando Gonzalez .... .25 .10 .02
☐ 650 Mike Epstein .... .25 .10 .02
☐ 651 Leron Lee .... .25 .10 .02
☐ 652 Gail Hopkins .... .25 .10 .02
☐ 653 Bob Stinson .... .25 .10 .02
☐ 654 Jesus Alou .... .35 .15 .03
☐ 655 Mike Tyson .... .25 .10 .02
☐ 656 Adrian Garrett .... .25 .10 .02
☐ 657 Jim Shellenback .... .25 .10 .02
☐ 658 Lee Lacy .... .35 .15 .03
☐ 659 Joe Lis .... .25 .10 .02
☐ 660 Larry Dierker .... .35 .15 .03

1975 O-Pee-Chee

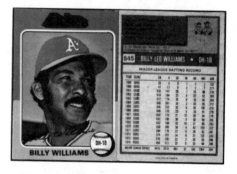

BILLY WILLIAMS

The cards in the 1975 O-Pee-Chee set are very similar to the 1975 Topps set. The cards in this 660 card set measure 2 1/2" by 3 1/2". The 660 card O-Pee-Chee set for 1975 was radically different in appearance from sets of the preceeding years. The most prominent change was the use of a two-color frame surrounding the picture area rather than a single, subdued color. A facsimile autograph appears on the picture, and the backs are printed in red and green on a yellow-vanilla card stock. Cards 189-212 depict the MVP's of both leagues from 1951 through 1974. The first six cards (1-6) feature players breaking records or achieving milestones during the previous season. Cards 306-313 picture league leaders in various statistical categories. Cards 459-466 depict the results of post-season action. Team cards feature a checklist back for players on that team. Backs are again written in French and English. Remember, the prices below apply only to O-Pee-Chee cards -- they are NOT prices for Topps cards as they (Topps cards) are generally much more available.

	MINT	VG-E	F-G
COMPLETE SET	250.00	110.00	25.00
COMMON PLAYER (1-660)	.20	.09	.02
☐ 1 RB: Hank Aaron	6.00	2.00	.40

		Sets Homer Mark				☐	82	Pat Kelly	.20	.09	.02
☐	2	RB: Lou Brock	1.25	.60	.12	☐	83	Jim Merritt	.20	.09	.02
		118 Stolen Bases				☐	84	Enzo Hernandez	.20	.09	.02
☐	3	RB: Bob Gibson	1.25	.60	.12	☐	85	Bill Bonham	.20	.09	.02
		3000th Strikeout				☐	86	Joe Lis	.20	.09	.02
☐	4	RB: Al Kaline	1.25	.60	.12	☐	87	George Foster	1.50	.70	.15
		3000 Hit Club				☐	88	Tom Egan	.20	.09	.02
☐	5	RB: Nolan Ryan	1.50	.70	.15	☐	89	Jim Ray	.20	.09	.02
		Fans 300 for				☐	90	Rusty Staub	.35	.15	.03
		3rd Year in a Row				☐	91	Dick Green	.20	.09	.02
☐	6	RB: Mike Marshall	.30	.12	.03	☐	92	Cecil Upshaw	.20	.09	.02
		Hurls 106 Games				☐	93	Dave Lopes	.35	.15	.03
☐	7	No Hit Pitchers:	.50	.22	.05	☐	94	Jim Lonborg	.25	.10	.02
		Steve Busby				☐	95	John Mayberry	.25	.10	.02
		Dick Bosman				☐	96	Mike Cosgrove	.20	.09	.02
		Nolan Ryan				☐	97	Earl Williams	.20	.09	.02
☐	8	Rogelio Moret	.20	.09	.02	☐	98	Rich Folkers	.20	.09	.02
☐	9	Frank Tepedino	.20	.09	.02	☐	99	Mike Hegan	.20	.09	.02
☐	10	Willie Davis	.25	.10	.02	☐	100	Willie Stargell	1.75	.85	.17
☐	11	Bill Melton	.20	.09	.02	☐	101	Expos: Team/Mgr.	.35	.10	.02
☐	12	David Clyde	.20	.09	.02			Gene Mauch			
☐	13	Gene Locklear	.20	.09	.02	☐	102	Joe Decker	.20	.09	.02
☐	14	Milt Wilcox	.20	.09	.02	☐	103	Rick Miller	.20	.09	.02
☐	15	Jose Cardenal	.20	.09	.02	☐	104	Bill Madlock	1.75	.85	.17
☐	16	Frank Tanana	.30	.12	.03	☐	105	Buzz Capra	.20	.09	.02
☐	17	Dave Concepcion	.50	.22	.05	☐	106	Mike Hargrove	.50	.22	.05
☐	18	Tigers: Team/Mgr.	.35	.10	.02	☐	107	Jim Barr	.20	.09	.02
		Ralph Houk				☐	108	Tom Hall	.20	.09	.02
☐	19	Jerry Koosman	.30	.12	.03	☐	109	George Hendrick	.35	.15	.03
☐	20	Thurman Munson	3.50	1.65	.35	☐	110	Wilbur Wood	.25	.10	.02
☐	21	Rollie Fingers	1.00	.45	.10	☐	111	Wayne Garrett	.20	.09	.02
☐	22	Dave Cash	.20	.09	.02	☐	112	Larry Hardy	.20	.09	.02
☐	23	Bill Russell	.25	.10	.02	☐	113	Elliott Maddox	.20	.09	.02
☐	24	Al Fitzmorris	.20	.09	.02	☐	114	Dick Lange	.20	.09	.02
☐	25	Lee May	.25	.10	.02	☐	115	Joe Ferguson	.20	.09	.02
☐	26	Dave McNally	.25	.10	.02	☐	116	Lerrin LaGrow	.20	.09	.02
☐	27	Ken Reitz	.20	.09	.02	☐	117	Orioles: Team/Mgr.	.50	.10	.02
☐	28	Tom Murphy	.20	.09	.02			Earl Weaver			
☐	29	Dave Parker	3.00	1.40	.30	☐	118	Mike Anderson	.20	.09	.02
☐	30	Bert Blyleven	.60	.28	.06	☐	119	Tommy Helms	.20	.09	.02
☐	31	Dave Rader	.20	.09	.02	☐	120	Steve Busby	.25	.10	.02
☐	32	Reggie Cleveland	.20	.09	.02			(photo actually			
☐	33	Dusty Baker	.40	.18	.04			Fran Healy)			
☐	34	Steve Renko	.20	.09	.02	☐	121	Bill North	.20	.09	.02
☐	35	Ron Santo	.35	.15	.03	☐	122	Al Hrabosky	.25	.10	.02
☐	36	Joe Lovitto	.20	.09	.02	☐	123	Johnny Briggs	.20	.09	.02
☐	37	Dave Freisleben	.20	.09	.02	☐	124	Jerry Reuss	.30	.12	.03
☐	38	Buddy Bell	.60	.28	.06	☐	125	Ken Singleton	.35	.15	.03
☐	39	Andy Thornton	.60	.28	.06	☐	126	Checklist 1-132	.60	.10	.02
☐	40	Bill Singer	.20	.09	.02	☐	127	Glenn Borgmann	.20	.09	.02
☐	41	Cesar Geronimo	.20	.09	.02	☐	128	Bill Lee	.25	.10	.02
☐	42	Joe Coleman	.20	.09	.02	☐	129	Rick Monday	.25	.10	.02
☐	43	Cleon Jones	.20	.09	.02	☐	130	Phil Niekro	1.00	.45	.10
☐	44	Pat Dobson	.25	.10	.02	☐	131	Toby Harrah	.25	.10	.02
☐	45	Joe Rudi	.25	.10	.02	☐	132	Randy Moffitt	.20	.09	.02
☐	46	Phillies: Team/Mgr	.35	.10	.02	☐	133	Dan Driessen	.20	.09	.02
		Danny Ozark				☐	134	Ron Hodges	.20	.09	.02
☐	47	Tommy John	1.00	.45	.10	☐	135	Charlie Spikes	.20	.09	.02
☐	48	Freddie Patek	.25	.10	.02	☐	136	Jim Mason	.20	.09	.02
☐	49	Larry Dierker	.25	.10	.02	☐	137	Terry Forster	.25	.10	.02
☐	50	Brooks Robinson	2.50	1.15	.25	☐	138	Del Unser	.20	.09	.02
☐	51	Bob Forsch	.25	.10	.02	☐	139	Horacio Pina	.20	.09	.02
☐	52	Darrell Porter	.25	.10	.02	☐	140	Steve Garvey	5.00	2.35	.50
☐	53	Dave Giusti	.20	.09	.02	☐	141	Mickey Stanley	.20	.09	.02
☐	54	Eric Soderholm	.20	.09	.02	☐	142	Bob Reynolds	.20	.09	.02
☐	55	Bobby Bonds	.35	.15	.03	☐	143	Cliff Johnson	.25	.10	.02
☐	56	Rick Wise	.25	.10	.02	☐	144	Jim Wohlford	.20	.09	.02
☐	57	Dave Johnson	.30	.12	.03	☐	145	Ken Holtzman	.25	.10	.02
☐	58	Chuck Taylor	.20	.09	.02	☐	146	Padres: Team/Mgr.	.35	.10	.02
☐	59	Ken Henderson	.20	.09	.02			John McNamara			
☐	60	Fergie Jenkins	.70	.32	.07	☐	147	Pedro Garcia	.20	.09	.02
☐	61	Dave Winfield	6.00	2.80	.60	☐	148	Jim Rooker	.20	.09	.02
☐	62	Fritz Peterson	.20	.09	.02	☐	149	Tim Foli	.20	.09	.02
☐	63	Steve Swisher	.20	.09	.02	☐	150	Bob Gibson	1.75	.85	.17
☐	64	Dave Chalk	.20	.09	.02	☐	151	Steve Brye	.20	.09	.02
☐	65	Don Gullett	.20	.09	.02	☐	152	Mario Guerrero	.20	.09	.02
☐	66	Willie Horton	.20	.09	.02	☐	153	Rick Reuschel	.25	.10	.02
☐	67	Tug McGraw	.30	.12	.03	☐	154	Mike Lum	.20	.09	.02
☐	68	Ron Blomberg	.20	.09	.02	☐	155	Jim Bibby	.25	.10	.02
☐	69	John Odom	.20	.09	.02	☐	156	Dave Kingman	1.00	.45	.10
☐	70	Mike Schmidt	10.00	4.75	1.00	☐	157	Pedro Borbon	.20	.09	.02
☐	71	Charlie Hough	.25	.10	.02	☐	158	Jerry Grote	.20	.09	.02
☐	72	Royals: Team/Mgr.	.35	.10	.02	☐	159	Steve Arlin	.20	.09	.02
		Jack McKeon				☐	160	Graig Nettles	1.25	.60	.12
☐	73	J.R. Richard	.35	.15	.03	☐	161	Stan Bahnsen	.20	.09	.02
☐	74	Mark Belanger	.25	.10	.02	☐	162	Willie Montanez	.20	.09	.02
☐	75	Ted Simmons	.70	.32	.07	☐	163	Jim Brewer	.20	.09	.02
☐	76	Ed Sprague	.20	.09	.02	☐	164	Mickey Rivers	.25	.10	.02
☐	77	Richie Zisk	.25	.10	.02	☐	165	Doug Rader	.25	.10	.02
☐	78	Ray Corbin	.20	.09	.02	☐	166	Woodie Fryman	.20	.09	.02
☐	79	Gary Matthews	.35	.15	.03	☐	167	Rich Coggins	.20	.09	.02
☐	80	Carlton Fisk	1.25	.60	.12	☐	168	Bill Greif	.20	.09	.02
☐	81	Ron Reed	.20	.09	.02	☐	169	Cookie Rojas	.20	.09	.02

☐170	Bert Campaneris	.30	.12	.03
☐171	Ed Kirkpatrick	.20	.09	.02
☐172	Red Sox: Team/Mgr.	.35	.10	.02
	Darrell Johnson			
☐173	Steve Rogers	.35	.15	.03
☐174	Bake McBride	.25	.10	.02
☐175	Don Money	.20	.09	.02
☐176	Burt Hooton	.20	.09	.02
☐177	Vic Correll	.20	.09	.02
☐178	Cesar Tovar	.20	.09	.02
☐179	Tom Bradley	.20	.09	.02
☐180	Joe Morgan	2.00	.90	.20
☐181	Fred Beene	.20	.09	.20
☐182	Don Hahn	.20	.09	.02
☐183	Mel Stottlemyre	.25	.10	.02
☐184	Jorge Orta	.20	.09	.02
☐185	Steve Carlton	4.50	2.10	.45
☐186	Willie Crawford	.20	.09	.02
☐187	Denny Doyle	.20	.09	.02
☐188	Tom Griffin	.20	.09	.02

MVP'S (189-212)

☐189	1951 MVP's:	1.00	.45	.10
	Larry (Yogi) Berra			
	Roy Campanella			
	(Campy never issued)			
☐190	1952 MVP's:	.30	.12	.03
	Bobby Shantz			
	Hank Bauer			
☐191	1953 MVP's:	.55	.25	.05
	Al Rosen			
	Roy Campanella			
☐192	1954 MVP's:	1.00	.45	.10
	Yogi Berra			
	Willie Mays			
☐193	1955 MVP's:	1.00	.45	.10
	Yogi Berra			
	Roy Campanella			
	(Campy never issued)			
☐194	1956 MVP's:	1.25	.60	.12
	Mickey Mantle			
	Don Newcombe			
☐195	1957 MVP's:	1.75	.85	.17
	Mickey Mantle			
	Hank Aaron			
☐196	1958 MVP's:	.55	.25	.05
	Jackie Jensen			
	Ernie Banks			
☐197	1959 MVP's:	.55	.25	.05
	Nellie Fox			
	Ernie Banks			
☐198	1960 MVP's:	.55	.25	.05
	Roger Maris			
	Dick Groat			
☐199	1961 MVP's:	.75	.35	.07
	Roger Maris			
	Frank Robinson			
☐200	1962 MVP's:	1.25	.60	.12
	Mickey Mantle			
	Maury Wills			
	(Wills never issued)			
☐201	1963 MVP's:	.55	.25	.05
	Elston Howard			
	Sandy Koufax			
☐202	1964 MVP's:	.55	.25	.05
	Brooks Robinson			
	Ken Boyer			
☐203	1965 MVP's:	.55	.25	.05
	Zoilo Versalles			
	Willie Mays			
☐204	1966 MVP's:	.75	.35	.07
	Frank Robinson			
	Bob Clemente			
☐205	1967 MVP's:	.75	.35	.07
	Carl Yastrzemski			
	Orlando Cepeda			
☐206	1968 MVP's:	.55	.25	.05
	Denny McLain			
	Bob Gibson			
☐207	1969 MVP's:	.65	.30	.06
	Harmon Killebrew			
	Willie McCovey			
☐208	1970 MVP's:	.55	.25	.05
	Boog Powell			
	Johnny Bench			
☐209	1971 MVP's:	.45	.20	.04
	Vida Blue			
	Joe Torre			
☐210	1972 MVP's:	.55	.25	.05
	Rich Allen			
	Johnny Bench			
☐211	1973 MVP's:	1.75	.85	.17
	Reggie Jackson			
	Pete Rose			
☐212	1974 MVP's:	.55	.25	.05
	Jeff Burroughs			
	Steve Garvey			
☐213	Oscar Gamble	.25	.10	.02
☐214	Harry Parker	.20	.09	.02
☐215	Bobby Valentine	.30	.12	.03
☐216	Giants: Team/Mgr.	.35	.10	.02
	Wes Westrum			
☐217	Lou Piniella	.40	.18	.04
☐218	Jerry Johnson	.20	.09	.02
☐219	Ed Herrmann	.20	.09	.02
☐220	Don Sutton	1.00	.45	.10
☐221	Aurelio Rodriguez	.20	.09	.02
☐222	Dan Spillner	.25	.10	.02
☐223	Robin Yount	15.00	7.00	1.50
☐224	Ramon Hernandez	.20	.09	.02
☐225	Bob Grich	.35	.15	.03
☐226	Bill Campbell	.20	.09	.02
☐227	Bob Watson	.25	.10	.02
☐228	George Brett	30.00	14.00	3.00
☐229	Barry Foote	.20	.09	.02
☐230	Jim Hunter	1.00	.45	.10
☐231	Mike Tyson	.20	.09	.02
☐232	Diego Segui	.20	.09	.02
☐233	Billy Grabarkewitz	.20	.09	.02
☐234	Tom Grieve	.30	.12	.03
☐235	Jack Billingham	.20	.09	.02
☐236	Angels: Team/Mgr.	.35	.10	.02
	Dick Williams			
☐237	Carl Morton	.20	.09	.02
☐238	Dave Duncan	.20	.09	.02
☐239	George Stone	.20	.09	.02
☐240	Garry Maddox	.25	.10	.02
☐241	Dick Tidrow	.20	.09	.02
☐242	Jay Johnstone	.25	.10	.02
☐243	Jim Kaat	.60	.28	.06
☐244	Bill Buckner	.50	.22	.05
☐245	Mickey Lolich	.35	.15	.03
☐246	Cardinals: Team/Mgr.	.35	.10	.02
	Red Schoendienst			
☐247	Enos Cabell	.20	.09	.02
☐248	Randy Jones	.25	.10	.02
☐249	Danny Thompson	.20	.09	.02
☐250	Ken Brett	.25	.10	.02
☐251	Fran Healy	.20	.09	.02
☐252	Fred Scherman	.20	.09	.02
☐253	Jesus Alou	.20	.09	.02
☐254	Mike Torrez	.25	.10	.02
☐255	Dwight Evans	.75	.35	.07
☐256	Billy Champion	.20	.09	.02
☐257	Checklist: 133-264	.60	.10	.02
☐258	Dave LaRoche	.20	.09	.02
☐259	Len Randle	.20	.09	.02
☐260	Johnny Bench	4.50	2.10	.45
☐261	Andy Hassler	.20	.09	.02
☐262	Rowland Office	.20	.09	.02
☐263	Jim Perry	.25	.10	.02
☐264	John Milner	.20	.09	.02
☐265	Ron Bryant	.20	.09	.02
☐266	Sandy Alomar	.20	.09	.02
☐267	Dick Ruthven	.20	.09	.02
☐268	Hal McRae	.30	.12	.03
☐269	Doug Rau	.20	.09	.02
☐270	Ron Fairly	.20	.09	.02
☐271	Jerry Moses	.20	.09	.02
☐272	Lynn McGlothen	.20	.09	.02
☐273	Steve Braun	.20	.09	.02
☐274	Vincente Romo	.20	.09	.02
☐275	Paul Blair	.25	.10	.02
☐276	White Sox Team/Mgr	.35	.10	.02
	Chuck Tanner			
☐277	Frank Taveras	.20	.09	.02
☐278	Paul Lindblad	.20	.09	.02
☐279	Milt May	.20	.09	.02
☐280	Carl Yastrzemski	5.00	2.35	.50
☐281	Jim Slaton	.20	.09	.02
☐282	Jerry Morales	.20	.09	.02
☐283	Steve Foucault	.20	.09	.02
☐284	Ken Griffey	.60	.28	.06
☐285	Ellie Rodriguez	.20	.09	.02
☐286	Mike Jorgensen	.20	.09	.02
☐287	Roric Harrison	.20	.09	.02
☐288	Bruce Ellingsen	.20	.09	.02
☐289	Ken Rudolph	.20	.09	.02
☐290	Jon Matlack	.25	.10	.02
☐291	Bill Sudakis	.20	.09	.02
☐292	Ron Schueler	.20	.09	.02
☐293	Dick Sharon	.20	.09	.02
☐294	Geoff Zahn	.25	.10	.02
☐295	Vada Pinson	.35	.15	.03
☐296	Alan Foster	.20	.09	.02
☐297	Craig Kusick	.20	.09	.02
☐298	Johnny Grubb	.25	.10	.02

299	Bucky Dent	.30	.12	.03
300	Reggie Jackson	6.00	2.80	.60
301	Dave Roberts	.20	.09	.02
302	Rick Burleson	.60	.28	.06
303	Grant Jackson	.20	.09	.02
304	Pirates: Team/Mgr. Danny Murtaugh	.35	.10	.02
305	Jim Colborn	.20	.09	.02
	LEADERS (306-313)			
306	Batting Leaders: Rod Carew Ralph Garr	.55	.25	.05
307	Home Run Leaders: Dick Allen Mike Schmidt	.75	.35	.07
308	RBI Leaders: Jeff Burroughs Johnny Bench	.55	.25	.05
309	Stolen Base Leaders: Bill North Lou Brock	.55	.25	.05
310	Victory Leaders: Jim Hunter Fergie Jenkins Andy Messersmith Phil Niekro	.55	.25	.05
311	ERA Leaders: Jim Hunter Buzz Capra	.35	.15	.03
312	Strikeout Leaders: Nolan Ryan Steve Carlton	1.25	.60	.12
313	Leading Firemen: Terry Forster Mike Marshall	.30	.12	.03
314	Buck Martinez	.20	.09	.02
315	Don Kessinger	.25	.10	.02
316	Jackie Brown	.20	.09	.02
317	Joe LaHoud	.20	.09	.02
318	Ernie McAnally	.20	.09	.02
319	Johnny Oates	.20	.09	.02
320	Pete Rose	12.00	5.50	1.20
321	Rudy May	.20	.09	.02
322	Ed Goodson	.20	.09	.02
323	Fred Holdsworth	.20	.09	.02
324	Ed Kranepool	.20	.09	.02
325	Tony Oliva	.50	.22	.05
326	Wayne Twitchell	.20	.09	.02
327	Jerry Hairston	.20	.09	.02
328	Sonny Siebert	.20	.09	.02
329	Ted Kubiak	.20	.09	.02
330	Mike Marshall	.25	.10	.02
331	Indians: Team/Mgr. Frank Robinson	.45	.10	.02
332	Fred Kendall	.20	.09	.02
333	Dick Drago	.20	.09	.02
334	Greg Gross	.20	.09	.02
335	Jim Palmer	2.50	1.15	.25
336	Rennie Stennett	.20	.09	.02
337	Kevin Kobel	.20	.09	.02
338	Rick Stelmaszek	.20	.09	.02
339	Jim Fregosi	.30	.12	.03
340	Paul Splittorff	.20	.09	.02
341	Hal Breeden	.20	.09	.02
342	Leroy Stanton	.20	.09	.02
343	Danny Frisella	.20	.09	.02
344	Ben Oglivie	.30	.12	.03
345	Clay Carroll	.20	.09	.02
346	Bobby Darwin	.20	.09	.02
347	Mike Caldwell	.25	.10	.02
348	Tony Muser	.20	.09	.02
349	Ray Sadecki	.20	.09	.02
350	Bobby Murcer	.45	.20	.04
351	Bob Boone	.25	.10	.02
352	Darold Knowles	.20	.09	.02
353	Luis Melendez	.20	.09	.02
354	Dick Bosman	.20	.09	.02
355	Chris Cannizzaro	.20	.09	.02
356	Rico Petrocelli	.25	.10	.02
357	Ken Forsch	.25	.10	.02
358	Al Bumbry	.20	.09	.02
359	Paul Popovich	.20	.09	.02
360	George Scott	.25	.10	.02
361	Dodgers: Team/Mgr. Walter Alston	.45	.10	.02
362	Steve Hargan	.20	.09	.02
363	Carmen Fanzone	.20	.09	.02
364	Doug Bird	.20	.09	.02
365	Bob Bailey	.20	.09	.02
366	Ken Sanders	.20	.09	.02
367	Craig Robinson	.20	.09	.02
368	Vic Albury	.20	.09	.02
369	Merv Rettenmund	.20	.09	.02
370	Tom Seaver	4.00	1.85	.40
371	Gates Brown	.25	.10	.02
372	John D'Acquisto	.20	.09	.02
373	Bill Sharp	.20	.09	.02
374	Eddie Watt	.20	.09	.02
375	Roy White	.25	.10	.02
376	Steve Yeager	.25	.10	.02
377	Tom Hilgendorf	.20	.09	.02
378	Derrel Thomas	.20	.09	.02
379	Bernie Carbo	.20	.09	.02
380	Sal Bando	.25	.10	.02
381	John Curtis	.20	.09	.02
382	Don Baylor	.75	.35	.07
383	Jim York	.20	.09	.02
384	Brewers: Team/Mgr. Del Crandall	.35	.10	.02
385	Dock Ellis	.20	.09	.02
386	Checklist: 265-396	.60	.10	.02
387	Jim Spencer	.20	.09	.02
388	Steve Stone	.25	.10	.02
389	Tony Solaita	.20	.09	.02
390	Ron Cey	.70	.32	.07
391	Don DeMola	.20	.09	.02
392	Bruce Bochte	.60	.28	.06
393	Gary Gentry	.20	.09	.02
394	Larvell Blanks	.20	.09	.02
395	Bud Harrelson	.20	.09	.02
396	Fred Norman	.20	.09	.02
397	Bill Freehan	.25	.10	.02
398	Elias Sosa	.20	.09	.02
399	Terry Harmon	.20	.09	.02
400	Dick Allen	.35	.15	.03
401	Mike Wallace	.20	.09	.02
402	Bob Tolan	.20	.09	.02
403	Tom Buskey	.20	.09	.02
404	Ted Sizemore	.20	.09	.02
405	John Montague	.20	.09	.02
406	Bob Gallagher	.20	.09	.02
407	Herb Washington	.20	.09	.02
408	Clyde Wright	.20	.09	.02
409	Bob Robertson	.20	.09	.02
410	Mike Cueller (sic, Cuellar)	.25	.10	.02
411	George Mitterwald	.20	.09	.02
412	Bill Hands	.20	.09	.02
413	Marty Pattin	.20	.09	.02
414	Manny Mota	.25	.10	.02
415	John Hiller	.25	.10	.02
416	Larry Lintz	.20	.09	.02
417	Skip Lockwood	.20	.09	.02
418	Leo Foster	.20	.09	.02
419	Dave Goltz	.20	.09	.02
420	Larry Bowa	.35	.15	.03
421	Mets: Team/Mgr Yogi Berra	.50	.10	.02
422	Brian Downing	.25	.10	.02
423	Clay Kirby	.20	.09	.02
424	John Lowenstein	.20	.09	.02
425	Tito Fuentes	.20	.09	.02
426	George Medich	.20	.09	.02
427	Clarence Gaston	.20	.09	.02
428	Dave Hamilton	.20	.09	.02
429	Jim Dwyer	.20	.09	.02
430	Luis Tiant	.30	.12	.03
431	Rod Gilbreath	.20	.09	.02
432	Ken Berry	.20	.09	.02
433	Larry Demery	.20	.09	.02
434	Bob Locker	.20	.09	.02
435	Dave Nelson	.20	.09	.02
436	Ken Frailing	.20	.09	.02
437	Al Cowens	.40	.18	.04
438	Don Carrithers	.20	.09	.02
439	Ed Brinkman	.20	.09	.02
440	Andy Messersmith	.25	.10	.02
441	Bobby Heise	.20	.09	.02
442	Maximino Leon	.20	.09	.02
443	Twins: Team/Mgr. Frank Quilici	.35	.10	.02
444	Gene Garber	.20	.09	.02
445	Felix Millan	.20	.09	.02
446	Bart Johnson	.20	.09	.02
447	Terry Crowley	.20	.09	.02
448	Frank Duffy	.20	.09	.02
449	Charlie Williams	.20	.09	.02
450	Willie McCovey	2.00	.90	.20
451	Rick Dempsey	.30	.12	.03
452	Angel Mangual	.20	.09	.02
453	Claude Osteen	.25	.10	.02
454	Doug Griffin	.20	.09	.02
455	Don Wilson	.20	.09	.02
456	Bob Coluccio	.20	.09	.02
457	Mario Mendoza	.20	.09	.02
458	Ross Grimsley	.20	.09	.02

☐ 459 1974 AL Champs: A's over Orioles (Second base action pictured)	.30	.12	.03
☐ 460 1974 NL Champs: Dodgers over Pirates (Taveras and Garvey at second base)	.50	.22	.05
WORLD SERIES (461-466)			
☐ 461 World Series Game 1 (Reggie Jackson)	1.25	.60	.12
☐ 462 World Series Game 2 (Dodger dugout)	.30	.12	.03
☐ 463 World Series Game 3 (Fingers pitching)	.50	.22	.05
☐ 464 World Series Game 4 (A's batter)	.30	.12	.03
☐ 465 World Series Game 5 (Rudi rounding third)	.30	.12	.03
☐ 466 World Series Summary: A's do it again Win 3rd straight (A's group)	.30	.12	.03
☐ 467 Ed Halicki	.20	.09	.02
☐ 468 Bobby Mitchell	.20	.09	.02
☐ 469 Tom Dettore	.20	.09	.02
☐ 470 Jeff Burroughs	.25	.10	.02
☐ 471 Bob Stinson	.20	.09	.02
☐ 472 Bruce Dal Canton	.20	.09	.02
☐ 473 Ken McMullen	.20	.09	.02
☐ 474 Luke Walker	.20	.09	.02
☐ 475 Darrell Evans	.40	.18	.04
☐ 476 Eduardo Figueroa	.20	.09	.02
☐ 477 Tom Hutton	.20	.09	.02
☐ 478 Tom Burgmeier	.20	.09	.02
☐ 479 Ken Boswell	.20	.09	.02
☐ 480 Carlos May	.20	.09	.02
☐ 481 Will McEnaney	.20	.09	.02
☐ 482 Tom McCraw	.20	.09	.02
☐ 483 Steve Ontiveros	.20	.09	.02
☐ 484 Glenn Beckert	.20	.09	.02
☐ 485 Sparky Lyle	.30	.12	.03
☐ 486 Ray Fosse	.20	.09	.02
☐ 487 Astros: Team/Mgr. Preston Gomez	.35	.10	.02
☐ 488 Bill Travers	.20	.09	.02
☐ 489 Cecil Cooper	1.50	.70	.15
☐ 490 Reggie Smith	.35	.15	.03
☐ 491 Doyle Alexander	.25	.10	.02
☐ 492 Rich Hebner	.20	.09	.02
☐ 493 Don Stanhouse	.20	.09	.02
☐ 494 Pete LaCock	.20	.09	.02
☐ 495 Nelson Briles	.20	.09	.02
☐ 496 Pepe Frias	.20	.09	.02
☐ 497 Jim Nettles	.20	.09	.02
☐ 498 Al Downing	.20	.09	.02
☐ 499 Marty Perez	.20	.09	.02
☐ 500 Nolan Ryan	3.50	1.65	.35
☐ 501 Bill Robinson	.20	.09	.02
☐ 502 Pat Bourque	.20	.09	.02
☐ 503 Fred Stanley	.20	.09	.02
☐ 504 Buddy Bradford	.20	.09	.02
☐ 505 Chris Speier	.20	.09	.02
☐ 506 Leron Lee	.20	.09	.02
☐ 507 Tom Carroll	.20	.09	.02
☐ 508 Bob Hansen	.20	.09	.02
☐ 509 Dave Hilton	.20	.09	.02
☐ 510 Vida Blue	.35	.15	.03
☐ 511 Rangers: Team/Mgr. Billy Martin	.40	.10	.02
☐ 512 Larry Milbourne	.20	.09	.02
☐ 513 Dick Pole	.20	.09	.02
☐ 514 Jose Cruz	.50	.22	.05
☐ 515 Manny Sanguillen	.25	.10	.02
☐ 516 Don Hood	.20	.09	.02
☐ 517 Checklist: 397-528	.60	.10	.02
☐ 518 Leo Cardenas	.20	.09	.02
☐ 519 Jim Todd	.20	.09	.02
☐ 520 Amos Otis	.30	.12	.03
☐ 521 Dennis Blair	.20	.09	.02
☐ 522 Gary Sutherland	.20	.09	.02
☐ 523 Tom Paciorek	.20	.09	.02
☐ 524 John Doherty	.20	.09	.02
☐ 525 Tom House	.25	.10	.02
☐ 526 Larry Hisle	.25	.10	.02
☐ 527 Mac Scarce	.20	.09	.02
☐ 528 Eddie Leon	.20	.09	.02
☐ 529 Gary Thomasson	.20	.09	.02
☐ 530 Gaylord Perry	1.50	.70	.15
☐ 531 Reds: Team/Mgr. Sparky Anderson	.45	.10	.02
☐ 532 Gorman Thomas	1.00	.45	.10
☐ 533 Rudy Meoli	.20	.09	.02
☐ 534 Alex Johnson	.20	.09	.02
☐ 535 Gene Tenace	.20	.09	.02
☐ 536 Bob Moose	.20	.09	.02
☐ 537 Tommy Harper	.20	.09	.02
☐ 538 Duffy Dyer	.20	.09	.02
☐ 539 Jesse Jefferson	.20	.09	.02
☐ 540 Lou Brock	2.00	.90	.20
☐ 541 Roger Metzger	.20	.09	.02
☐ 542 Pete Broberg	.20	.09	.02
☐ 543 Larry Biittner	.20	.09	.02
☐ 544 Steve Mingori	.20	.09	.02
☐ 545 Billy Williams	.75	.35	.07
☐ 546 John Knox	.20	.09	.02
☐ 547 Von Joshua	.20	.09	.02
☐ 548 Charlie Sands	.20	.09	.02
☐ 549 Bill Butler	.20	.09	.02
☐ 550 Ralph Garr	.20	.09	.02
☐ 551 Larry Christenson	.20	.09	.02
☐ 552 Jack Brohamer	.20	.09	.02
☐ 553 John Boccabella	.20	.09	.02
☐ 554 Rich Gossage	1.25	.60	.12
☐ 555 Al Oliver	.90	.40	.09
☐ 556 Tim Johnson	.20	.09	.02
☐ 557 Larry Gura	.25	.10	.02
☐ 558 Dave Roberts	.20	.09	.02
☐ 559 Bob Montgomery	.20	.09	.02
☐ 560 Tony Perez	.75	.35	.07
☐ 561 A's: Team/Mgr. Alvin Dark	.35	.10	.02
☐ 562 Gary Nolan	.20	.09	.02
☐ 563 Wilbur Howard	.20	.09	.02
☐ 564 Tommy Davis	.25	.10	.02
☐ 565 Joe Torre	.50	.22	.05
☐ 566 Ray Burris	.20	.09	.02
☐ 567 Jim Sundberg	.75	.35	.07
☐ 568 Dale Murray	.20	.09	.02
☐ 569 Frank White	.50	.22	.05
☐ 570 Jim Wynn	.25	.10	.02
☐ 571 Dave Lemanczyk	.20	.09	.02
☐ 572 Roger Nelson	.20	.09	.02
☐ 573 Orlando Pena	.20	.09	.02
☐ 574 Tony Taylor	.20	.09	.02
☐ 575 Gene Clines	.20	.09	.02
☐ 576 Phil Roof	.20	.09	.02
☐ 577 John Morris	.20	.09	.02
☐ 578 Dave Tomlin	.20	.09	.02
☐ 579 Skip Pitlock	.20	.09	.02
☐ 580 Frank Robinson	2.00	.90	.20
☐ 581 Darrel Chaney	.20	.09	.02
☐ 582 Eduardo Rodriguez	.20	.09	.02
☐ 583 Andy Etchebarren	.20	.09	.02
☐ 584 Mike Garman	.20	.09	.02
☐ 585 Chris Chambliss	.30	.12	.03
☐ 586 Tim McCarver	.30	.12	.03
☐ 587 Chris Ward	.20	.09	.02
☐ 588 Rick Auerbach	.20	.09	.02
☐ 589 Braves: Team/Mgr. Clyde King	.35	.10	.02
☐ 590 Cesar Cedeno	.30	.12	.03
☐ 591 Glenn Abbott	.20	.09	.02
☐ 592 Balor Moore	.20	.09	.02
☐ 593 Gene Lamont	.20	.09	.02
☐ 594 Jim Fuller	.20	.09	.02
☐ 595 Joe Niekro	.35	.15	.03
☐ 596 Ollie Brown	.20	.09	.02
☐ 597 Winston Llenas	.20	.09	.02
☐ 598 Bruce Kison	.20	.09	.02
☐ 599 Nate Colbert	.20	.09	.02
☐ 600 Rod Carew	4.50	2.10	.45
☐ 601 Juan Beniquez	.25	.10	.02
☐ 602 John Vukovich	.20	.09	.02
☐ 603 Lew Krausse	.20	.09	.02
☐ 604 Oscar Zamora	.20	.09	.02
☐ 605 John Ellis	.20	.09	.02
☐ 606 Bruce Miller	.20	.09	.02
☐ 607 Jim Holt	.20	.09	.02
☐ 608 Gene Michael	.25	.10	.02
☐ 609 Ellie Hendricks	.20	.09	.02
☐ 610 Ron Hunt	.20	.09	.02
☐ 611 Yankees: Team/Mgr. Bill Virdon	.50	.10	.02
☐ 612 Terry Hughes	.20	.09	.02
☐ 613 Bill Parsons	.20	.09	.02
ROOKIES (614-624)			
☐ 614 Rookie Pitchers: Jack Kucek Dyar Miller Vern Ruhle Paul Siebert	.25	.10	.02
☐ 615 Rookie Pitchers: Pat Darcy Dennis Leonard Tom Underwood	1.00	.45	.10

	Hank Webb			
☐ 616	Rookie Outfielders: 18.00	8.50	1.80
	Dave Augustine		
	Pepe Mangual		
	Jim Rice		
	John Scott		
☐ 617	Rookie Infielders: 2.00	.90	.20
	Mike Cubbage		
	Doug DeCinces		
	Reggie Sanders		
	Manny Trillo		
☐ 618	Rookie Pitchers: 2.00	.90	.20
	Jamie Easterly		
	Tom Johnson		
	Scott McGregor		
	Rick Rhoden		
☐ 619	Rookie Outfielders: .... .25	.10	.02
	Benny Ayala		
	Nyls Nyman		
	Tommy Smith		
	Jerry Turner		
☐ 620	Rookie Catcher/OF: 18.00	8.50	1.80
	Gary Carter		
	Marc Hill		
	Danny Meyer		
	Leon Roberts		
☐ 621	Rookie Pitchers: 1.50	.70	.15
	John Denny		
	Rawly Eastwick		
	Jim Kern		
	Juan Veintidos		
☐ 622	Rookie Outfielders: 9.00	4.25	.90
	Ed Armbrister		
	Fred Lynn		
	Tom Poquette		
	Terry Whitfield		
☐ 623	Rookie Infielders: 10.00	4.75	1.00
	Phil Garner		
	Keith Hernandez		
	Bob Sheldon		
	Tom Veryzer		
☐ 624	Rookie Pitchers: .... .25	.10	.02
	Doug Konieczny		
	Gary Lavelle		
	Jim Otten		
	Eddie Solomon		
☐ 625	Boog Powell .... .45	.20	.04
☐ 626	Larry Haney .... .20	.09	.02
	(photo actually		
	Dave Duncan)		
☐ 627	Tom Walker .... .20	.09	.02
☐ 628	Ron LeFlore .... .50	.22	.05
☐ 629	Joe Hoerner .... .20	.09	.02
☐ 630	Greg Luzinski .... .50	.22	.05
☐ 631	Lee Lacy .... .30	.12	.03
☐ 632	Morris Nettles .... .20	.09	.02
☐ 633	Paul Casanova .... .20	.09	.02
☐ 634	Cy Acosta .... .20	.09	.02
☐ 635	Chuck Dobson .... .20	.09	.02
☐ 636	Charlie Moore .... .20	.09	.02
☐ 637	Ted Martinez .... .20	.09	.02
☐ 638	Cubs: Team/Mgr. .... .35	.10	.02
	Jim Marshall		
☐ 639	Steve Kline .... .20	.09	.02
☐ 640	Harmon Killebrew 1.75	.85	.17
☐ 641	Jim Northrup .... .25	.10	.02
☐ 642	Mike Phillips .... .20	.09	.02
☐ 643	Brent Strom .... .20	.09	.02
☐ 644	Bill Fahey .... .20	.09	.02
☐ 645	Danny Cater .... .20	.09	.02
☐ 646	Checklist: 529-660 .... .60	.10	.02
☐ 647	Claudell Washington 1.50	.70	.15
☐ 648	Dave Pagan .... .20	.09	.02
☐ 649	Jack Heidemann .... .20	.09	.02
☐ 650	Dave May .... .20	.09	.02
☐ 651	John Morlan .... .20	.09	.02
☐ 652	Lindy McDaniel .... .20	.09	.02
☐ 653	Lee Richard .... .20	.09	.02
☐ 654	Jerry Terrell .... .20	.09	.02
☐ 655	Rico Carty .... .25	.10	.02
☐ 656	Bill Plummer .... .20	.09	.02
☐ 657	Bob Oliver .... .20	.09	.02
☐ 658	Vic Harris .... .20	.09	.02
☐ 659	Bob Apodaca .... .20	.09	.02
☐ 660	Hank Aaron 7.50	3.50	.75

1976 O-Pee-Chee

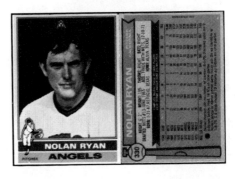

The 1976 O-Pee-Chee set of 660 cards (measuring 2 1/2" by 3 1/2") is known for its sharp color photographs and interesting presentation of subjects. The cards in the 1976 O- Pee-Chee set are very similar to the 1976 Topps set. A "Father and Son" series (66-70) spotlights five Major Leaguers whose fathers also made the "Big Show". Other series include "All Time All Stars" (341-350) and "Record Breakers" from the previous season (1-6). The backs are printed in red and green on a yellow-vanilla card stock and "Ptd. in Canada" is printed on the backs of the cards. Team cards feature a checklist back for players on that team. Backs are again written in French and English. Remember, the prices below apply only to O-Pee-Chee cards -- they are NOT prices for Topps cards as they (Topps cards) are generally much more available.

		MINT	VG-E	F-G
COMPLETE SET	....	150.00	70.00	15.00
COMMON PLAYER (1-660)	....	.20	.09	.02
☐ 1	RB: Hank Aaron	5.00	2.00	.40
	Most RBI's 2262			
☐ 2	RB: Bobby Bonds	.30	.12	.03
	Most leadoff homers 32;			
	Plus 3 Seasons of			
	30 HR's and 30 SB's			
☐ 3	RB: Mickey Lolich	.30	.12	.03
	Lefthander Most			
	Strikeouts 2679			
☐ 4	RB: Dave Lopes	.30	.12	.03
	Most consecutive			
	SB attempts, 38			
☐ 5	RB: Tom Seaver	1.25	.60	.12
	Most cons. seasons			
	with 200 SO's, 8			
☐ 6	RB: Rennie Stennett	.25	.10	.02
	Most hits in a 9			
	inning game, 7			
☐ 7	Jim Umbarger	.20	.09	.02
☐ 8	Tito Fuentes	.20	.09	.02
☐ 9	Paul Lindblad	.20	.09	.02
☐ 10	Lou Brock	1.75	.85	.17
☐ 11	Jim Hughes	.20	.09	.02
☐ 12	Richie Zisk	.25	.10	.02
☐ 13	John Wockenfuss	.20	.09	.02
☐ 14	Gene Garber	.25	.10	.02
☐ 15	George Scott	.25	.10	.02
☐ 16	Bob Apodaca	.20	.09	.02
☐ 17	New York Yankees Team	.50	.10	.02
☐ 18	Dale Murray	.20	.09	.02
☐ 19	George Brett	8.00	3.75	.80
☐ 20	Bob Watson	.25	.10	.02
☐ 21	Dave Laroche	.20	.09	.02
☐ 22	Bill Russell	.25	.10	.02
☐ 23	Brian Downing	.25	.10	.02
☐ 24	Cesar Geronimo	.20	.09	.02
☐ 25	Mike Torrez	.25	.10	.02
☐ 26	Andy Thornton	.30	.12	.03
☐ 27	Ed Figueroa	.20	.09	.02
☐ 28	Dusty Baker	.30	.12	.03

☐ 29	Rick Burleson	.30	.12	.03
☐ 30	John Montefusco	.30	.12	.03
☐ 31	Len Randle	.20	.09	.02
☐ 32	Danny Frisella	.20	.09	.02
☐ 33	Bill North	.20	.09	.02
☐ 34	Mike Garman	.20	.09	.02
☐ 35	Tony Oliva	.40	.18	.04
☐ 36	Frank Taveras	.20	.09	.02
☐ 37	John Hiller	.25	.10	.02
☐ 38	Garry Maddox	.25	.10	.02
☐ 39	Pete Broberg	.20	.09	.02
☐ 40	Dave Kingman	.75	.35	.07
☐ 41	Tippy Martinez	.50	.22	.05
☐ 42	Barry Foote	.20	.09	.02
☐ 43	Paul Splittorff	.25	.10	.02
☐ 44	Doug Rader	.25	.10	.02
☐ 45	Boog Powell	.40	.18	.04
☐ 46	Dodgers Team	.50	.10	.02
☐ 47	Jesse Jefferson	.20	.09	.02
☐ 48	Dave Concepcion	.40	.18	.04
☐ 49	Dave Duncan	.20	.09	.02
☐ 50	Fred Lynn	1.75	.85	.17
☐ 51	Ray Burris	.20	.09	.02
☐ 52	Dave Chalk	.20	.09	.02
☐ 53	Mike Beard	.20	.09	.02
☐ 54	Dave Radar	.20	.09	.02
☐ 55	Gaylord Perry	1.25	.60	.12
☐ 56	Bob Tolan	.20	.09	.02
☐ 57	Phil Garner	.30	.12	.03
☐ 58	Ron Reed	.20	.09	.02
☐ 59	Larry Hisle	.25	.10	.02
☐ 60	Jerry Reuss	.30	.12	.03
☐ 61	Ron LeFlore	.25	.10	.02
☐ 62	Johnny Oates	.20	.09	.02
☐ 63	Bobby Darwin	.20	.09	.02
☐ 64	Jerry Koosman	.30	.12	.03
☐ 65	Chris Chambliss	.25	.10	.02

FATHER/SON CARDS (66-70)

☐ 66	Father and Son: Gus Bell / Buddy Bell	.35	.15	.03
☐ 67	Father and Son: Ray Boone / Bob Boone	.25	.10	.02
☐ 68	Father and Son: Joe Coleman / Joe Coleman Jr.	.25	.10	.02
☐ 69	Father and Son: Jim Hegan / Mike Hegan	.25	.10	.02
☐ 70	Father and Son: Roy Smalley / Roy Smalley Jr.	.25	.10	.02
☐ 71	Steve Rogers	.30	.12	.03
☐ 72	Hal McRae	.30	.12	.03
☐ 73	Orioles Team	.50	.10	.02
☐ 74	Oscar Gamble	.25	.10	.02
☐ 75	Larry Dierker	.20	.09	.02
☐ 76	Willie Crawford	.20	.09	.02
☐ 77	Pedro Borbon	.20	.09	.02
☐ 78	Cecil Cooper	1.00	.45	.10
☐ 79	Jerry Morales	.20	.09	.02
☐ 80	Jim Kaat	.50	.22	.05
☐ 81	Darrell Evans	.40	.18	.04
☐ 82	Von Joshua	.20	.09	.02
☐ 83	Jim Spencer	.20	.09	.02
☐ 84	Brent Strom	.20	.09	.02
☐ 85	Mickey Rivers	.25	.10	.02
☐ 86	Mike Tyson	.20	.09	.02
☐ 87	Tom Burgmeier	.20	.09	.02
☐ 88	Duffy Dyer	.20	.09	.02
☐ 89	Vern Ruhle	.20	.09	.02
☐ 90	Sal Bando	.25	.10	.02
☐ 91	Tom Hutton	.20	.09	.02
☐ 92	Eduardo Rodriguez	.20	.09	.02
☐ 93	Mike Phillips	.20	.09	.02
☐ 94	Jim Dwyer	.20	.09	.02
☐ 95	Brooks Robinson	2.00	.90	.20
☐ 96	Doug Bird	.20	.09	.02
☐ 97	Wilbur Howard	.20	.09	.02
☐ 98	Dennis Eckersley	1.00	.45	.10
☐ 99	Lee Lacy	.30	.12	.03
☐ 100	Jim Hunter	.80	.40	.08
☐ 101	Pete LaCock	.20	.09	.02
☐ 102	Jim Willoughby	.20	.09	.02
☐ 103	Biff Pocoroba	.20	.09	.02
☐ 104	Reds Team	.50	.10	.02
☐ 105	Gary Lavelle	.25	.10	.02
☐ 106	Tom Grieve	.25	.10	.02
☐ 107	Dave Roberts	.20	.09	.02
☐ 108	Don Kirkwood	.20	.09	.02
☐ 109	Larry Lintz	.20	.09	.02
☐ 110	Carlos May	.20	.09	.02
☐ 111	Danny Thompson	.20	.09	.02
☐ 112	Kent Tekulve	.75	.35	.07
☐ 113	Gary Sutherland	.20	.09	.02
☐ 114	Jay Johnstone	.25	.10	.02
☐ 115	Ken Holtzman	.25	.10	.02
☐ 116	Charlie Moore	.20	.09	.02
☐ 117	Mike Jorgensen	.20	.09	.02
☐ 118	Red Sox Team	.50	.10	.02
☐ 119	Checklist 1-132	.50	.10	.02
☐ 120	Rusty Staub	.35	.15	.03
☐ 121	Tony Solaita	.20	.09	.02
☐ 122	Mike Cosgrove	.20	.09	.02
☐ 123	Walt Williams	.20	.09	.02
☐ 124	Doug Rau	.20	.09	.02
☐ 125	Don Baylor	.60	.28	.06
☐ 126	Tom Dettore	.20	.09	.02
☐ 127	Larvell Blanks	.20	.09	.02
☐ 128	Ken Griffey	.35	.15	.03
☐ 129	Andy Etchebarren	.20	.09	.02
☐ 130	Luis Tiant	.30	.12	.03
☐ 131	Bill Stein	.20	.09	.02
☐ 132	Don Hood	.20	.09	.02
☐ 133	Gary Matthews	.30	.12	.03
☐ 134	Mike Ivie	.20	.09	.02
☐ 135	Bake McBride	.25	.10	.02
☐ 136	Dave Goltz	.20	.09	.02
☐ 137	Bill Robinson	.20	.09	.02
☐ 138	Lerrin LaGrow	.20	.09	.02
☐ 139	Gorman Thomas	.50	.22	.05
☐ 140	Vida Blue	.35	.15	.03
☐ 141	Larry Parrish	1.50	.70	.15
☐ 142	Dick Drago	.20	.09	.02
☐ 143	Jerry Grote	.20	.09	.02
☐ 144	Al Fitzmorris	.20	.09	.02
☐ 145	Larry Bowa	.35	.15	.03
☐ 146	George Medich	.20	.09	.02
☐ 147	Astros Team	.35	.10	.02
☐ 148	Stan Thomas	.20	.09	.02
☐ 149	Tommy Davis	.25	.10	.02
☐ 150	Steve Garvey	4.00	1.85	.40
☐ 151	Bill Bonham	.20	.09	.02
☐ 152	Leroy Stanton	.20	.09	.02
☐ 153	Buzz Capra	.20	.09	.02
☐ 154	Bucky Dent	.25	.10	.02
☐ 155	Jack Billingham	.20	.09	.02
☐ 156	Rico Carty	.25	.10	.02
☐ 157	Mike Caldwell	.25	.10	.02
☐ 158	Ken Reitz	.20	.09	.02
☐ 159	Jerry Terrell	.20	.09	.02
☐ 160	Dave Winfield	4.00	1.85	.40
☐ 161	Bruce Kison	.20	.09	.02
☐ 162	Jack Pierce	.20	.09	.02
☐ 163	Jim Slaton	.20	.09	.02
☐ 164	Pepe Mangual	.20	.09	.02
☐ 165	Gene Tenace	.20	.09	.02
☐ 166	Skip Lockwood	.20	.09	.02
☐ 167	Freddie Patek	.20	.09	.02
☐ 168	Tom Hilgendorf	.20	.09	.02
☐ 169	Graig Nettles	1.00	.45	.10
☐ 170	Rick Wise	.20	.09	.02
☐ 171	Greg Gross	.20	.09	.02
☐ 172	Rangers Team	.35	.10	.02
☐ 173	Steve Swisher	.20	.09	.02
☐ 174	Charlie Hough	.25	.10	.02
☐ 175	Ken Singleton	.35	.15	.03
☐ 176	Dick Lange	.20	.09	.02
☐ 177	Marty Perez	.20	.09	.02
☐ 178	Tom Buskey	.20	.09	.02
☐ 179	George Foster	1.50	.70	.15
☐ 180	Rich Gossage	1.25	.60	.12
☐ 181	Willie Montanez	.20	.09	.02
☐ 182	Harry Rasmussen	.20	.09	.02
☐ 183	Steve Braun	.20	.09	.02
☐ 184	Bill Greif	.20	.09	.02
☐ 185	Dave Parker	2.00	.90	.20
☐ 186	Tom Walker	.20	.09	.02
☐ 187	Pedro Garcia	.20	.09	.02
☐ 188	Fred Scherman	.20	.09	.02
☐ 189	Claudell Washington	.35	.15	.03
☐ 190	Jon Matlack	.25	.10	.02

LEADERS (191-205)

#				
☐ 191	NL Batting Leaders: Bill Madlock / Ted Simmons / Manny Sanguillen	.40	.18	.04
☐ 192	AL Batting Leaders: Rod Carew / Fred Lynn / Thurman Munson	1.25	.60	.12
☐ 193	NL Home Run Leaders: Mike Schmidt / Dave Kingman / Greg Luzinski	.65	.30	.06

194	AL Home Run Leaders: ... Reggie Jackson / George Scott / John Mayberry	.65	.30	.06
195	NL RBI Leaders: Greg Luzinski / Johnny Bench / Tony Perez	.45	.20	.04
196	AL RBI Leaders: George Scott / John Mayberry / Fred Lynn	.40	.18	.04
197	NL Steals Leaders: Dave Lopes / Joe Morgan / Lou Brock	.65	.30	.06
198	AL Steals Leaders: Mickey Rivers / Claudell Washington / Amos Otis	.25	.10	.02
199	NL Victory Leaders: Tom Seaver / Randy Jones / Andy Messersmith	.45	.20	.04
200	AL Victory Leaders: Jim Hunter / Jim Palmer / Vida Blue	.60	.28	.06
201	NL ERA Leaders: Randy Jones / Andy Messersmith / Tom Seaver	.45	.20	.04
202	AL ERA Leaders: Jim Palmer / Jim Hunter / Dennis Eckersley	.50	.22	.05
203	NL Strikeout Leaders: .... Tom Seaver / John Montefusco / Andy Messersmith	.45	.20	.04
204	AL Strikeout Leaders: .... Frank Tanana / Bert Blyleven / Gaylord Perry	.40	.18	.04
205	Leading Firemen: Al Hrabosky / Rich Gossage	.25	.10	.02
206	Manny Trillo	.25	.10	.02
207	Andy Hassler	.20	.09	.02
208	Mike Lum	.20	.09	.02
209	Alan Ashby	.25	.10	.02
210	Lee May	.25	.10	.02
211	Clay Carroll	.20	.09	.02
212	Pat Kelly	.20	.09	.02
213	Dave Heaverlo	.20	.09	.02
214	Eric Soderholm	.20	.09	.02
215	Reggie Smith	.35	.15	.03
216	Expos Team	.35	.10	.02
217	Dave Freisleben	.20	.09	.02
218	John Knox	.20	.09	.02
219	Tom Murphy	.20	.09	.02
220	Manny Sanguillen	.25	.10	.02
221	Jim Todd	.20	.09	.02
222	Wayne Garrett	.20	.09	.02
223	Ollie Brown	.20	.09	.02
224	Jim York	.20	.09	.02
225	Roy White	.25	.10	.02
226	Jim Sundberg	.25	.10	.02
227	Oscar Zamora	.20	.09	.02
228	John Hale	.20	.09	.02
229	Jerry Remy	.30	.12	.03
230	Carl Yastrzemski	5.00	2.35	.50
231	Tom House	.25	.10	.02
232	Frank Duffy	.20	.09	.02
233	Grant Jackson	.20	.09	.02
234	Mike Sadek	.20	.09	.02
235	Bert Blyleven	.50	.22	.05
236	Royals Team	.35	.10	.02
237	Dave Hamilton	.20	.09	.02
238	Larry Biittner	.20	.09	.02
239	John Curtis	.20	.09	.02
240	Pete Rose	12.00	5.50	1.20
241	Hector Torres	.20	.09	.02
242	Dan Meyer	.20	.09	.02
243	Jim Rooker	.20	.09	.02
244	Bill Sharp	.20	.09	.02
245	Felix Millan	.20	.09	.02
246	Cesar Tovar	.20	.09	.02
247	Terry Harmon	.20	.09	.02
248	Dick Tidrow	.20	.09	.02
249	Cliff Johnson	.25	.10	.02
250	Fergie Jenkins	.45	.20	.04
251	Rick Monday	.25	.10	.02
252	Tim Nordbrook	.20	.09	.02
253	Bill Buckner	.40	.18	.04
254	Rudy Meoli	.20	.09	.02
255	Fritz Peterson	.20	.09	.02
256	Rowland Office	.20	.09	.02
257	Ross Grimsley	.20	.09	.02
258	Nyls Nyman	.20	.09	.02
259	Darrel Chaney	.20	.09	.02
260	Steve Busby	.25	.10	.02
261	Gary Thomasson	.20	.09	.02
262	Checklist: 133-264	.50	.10	.02
263	Lyman Bostock	.50	.22	.05
264	Steve Renko	.20	.09	.02
265	Willie Davis	.25	.10	.02
266	Alan Foster	.20	.09	.02
267	Aurelio Rodriguez	.20	.09	.02
268	Del Unser	.20	.09	.02
269	Rick Austin	.20	.09	.02
270	Willie Stargell	1.50	.70	.15
271	Jim Lonborg	.25	.10	.02
272	Rick Dempsey	.30	.12	.03
273	Joe Niekro	.30	.12	.03
274	Tommy Harper	.25	.10	.02
275	Rick Manning	.25	.10	.02
276	Mickey Scott	.20	.09	.02
277	Cubs Team	.35	.10	.02
278	Bernie Carbo	.20	.09	.02
279	Roy Howell	.20	.09	.02
280	Burt Hooten	.20	.09	.02
281	Dave May	.20	.09	.02
282	Dan Osborn	.20	.09	.02
283	Merv Rettenmund	.20	.09	.02
284	Steve Ontiveros	.20	.09	.02
285	Mike Cuellar	.25	.10	.02
286	Jim Wohlford	.20	.09	.02
287	Pete Mackanin	.20	.09	.02
288	Bill Campbell	.25	.10	.02
289	Enzo Hernandez	.20	.09	.02
290	Ted Simmons	.60	.28	.06
291	Ken Sanders	.20	.09	.02
292	Leon Roberts	.20	.09	.02
293	Bill Castro	.20	.09	.02
294	Ed Kirkpatrick	.20	.09	.02
295	Dave Cash	.20	.09	.02
296	Pat Dobson	.25	.10	.02
297	Roger Metzger	.20	.09	.02
298	Dick Bosman	.20	.09	.02
299	Champ Summers	.20	.09	.02
300	Johnny Bench	3.50	1.65	.35
301	Jackie Brown	.20	.09	.02
302	Rick Miller	.20	.09	.02
303	Steve Foucault	.20	.09	.02
304	Angels Team	.35	.10	.02
305	Andy Messersmith	.25	.10	.02
306	Rod Gilbreath	.20	.09	.02
307	Al Bumbry	.20	.09	.02
308	Jim Barr	.20	.09	.02
309	Bill Melton	.20	.09	.02
310	Randy Jones	.25	.10	.02
311	Cookie Rojas	.20	.09	.02
312	Don Carrithers	.20	.09	.02
313	Dan Ford	.25	.10	.02
314	Ed Kranepool	.25	.10	.02
315	Al Hrabosky	.25	.10	.02
316	Robin Yount	5.00	2.35	.50
317	John Candelaria	1.50	.70	.15
318	Bob Boone	.25	.10	.02
319	Larry Gura	.25	.10	.02
320	Willie Horton	.25	.10	.02
321	Jose Cruz	.40	.18	.04
322	Glenn Abbott	.20	.09	.02
323	Rob Sperring	.20	.09	.02
324	Jim Bibby	.25	.10	.02
325	Tony Perez	.50	.22	.05
326	Dick Pole	.20	.09	.02
327	Dave Moates	.20	.09	.02
328	Carl Morton	.20	.09	.02
329	Joe Ferguson	.20	.09	.02
330	Nolan Ryan	3.00	1.40	.30
331	Padres Team	.35	.10	.02
332	Charlie Williams	.20	.09	.02
333	Bob Coluccio	.20	.09	.02
334	Dennis Leonard	.35	.15	.03
335	Bob Grich	.35	.15	.03
336	Vic Albury	.20	.09	.02
337	Bud Harrelson	.20	.09	.02
338	Bob Bailey	.20	.09	.02
339	John Denny	.50	.22	.05
340	Jim Rice	5.00	2.35	.50

ALL-TIME GREATS

341	All-Time 1B: Lou Gehrig	1.75	.85	.17
342	All-Time 2B:	1.00	.45	.10

	Rogers Hornsby				☐ 427	Kurt Bevacqua	.20	.09	.02
☐ 343	All-Time 3B:	.60	.28	.06	☐ 428	Jim Crawford	.20	.09	.02
	Pie Traynor				☐ 429	Fred Stanley	.20	.09	.02
☐ 344	All-Time SS:	1.00	.45	.10	☐ 430	Jose Cardenal	.20	.09	.02
	Honus Wagner				☐ 431	Dick Ruthven	.20	.09	.02
☐ 345	All-Time OF:	2.75	1.25	.27	☐ 432	Tom Veryzer	.20	.09	.02
	Babe Ruth				☐ 433	Rick Waits	.25	.10	.02
☐ 346	All-Time OF:	1.75	.85	.17	☐ 434	Morris Nettles	.20	.09	.02
	Ty Cobb				☐ 435	Phil Niekro	1.00	.45	.10
☐ 347	All-Time OF:	1.75	.85	.17	☐ 436	Bill Fahey	.20	.09	.02
	Ted Williams				☐ 437	Terry Forster	.25	.10	.02
☐ 348	All-Time C:	.60	.28	.06	☐ 438	Doug DeCinces	.65	.30	.06
	Mickey Cochrane				☐ 439	Rick Rhoden	.35	.15	.03
☐ 349	All-Time RHP:	1.00	.45	.10	☐ 440	John Mayberry	.25	.10	.02
	Walter Johnson				☐ 441	Gary Carter	6.00	2.80	.60
☐ 350	All-Time LHP:	.75	.35	.07	☐ 442	Hank Webb	.20	.09	.02
	Lefty Grove				☐ 443	Giants Team	.35	.10	.02
☐ 351	Randy Hundley	.20	.09	.02	☐ 444	Gary Nolan	.20	.09	.02
☐ 352	Dave Giusti	.20	.09	.02	☐ 445	Rico Petrocelli	.25	.10	.02
☐ 353	Sixto Lezcano	.30	.12	.03	☐ 446	Larry Haney	.20	.09	.02
☐ 354	Ron Blomberg	.20	.09	.02	☐ 447	Gene Locklear	.20	.09	.02
☐ 355	Steve Carlton	3.50	1.65	.35	☐ 448	Tom Johnson	.20	.09	.02
☐ 356	Ted Martinez	.20	.09	.02	☐ 449	Bob Robertson	.20	.09	.02
☐ 357	Ken Forsch	.25	.10	.02	☐ 450	Jim Palmer	2.50	1.15	.25
☐ 358	Buddy Bell	.35	.15	.03	☐ 451	Buddy Bradford	.20	.09	.02
☐ 359	Rick Reuschel	.25	.10	.02	☐ 452	Tom Hausman	.20	.09	.02
☐ 360	Jeff Burroughs	.25	.10	.02	☐ 453	Lou Piniella	.35	.15	.03
☐ 361	Tigers Team	.40	.10	.02	☐ 454	Tom Griffin	.20	.09	.02
☐ 362	Will McEnaney	.20	.09	.02	☐ 455	Dick Allen	.35	.15	.03
☐ 363	Dave Collins	1.25	.60	.12	☐ 456	Joe Coleman	.20	.09	.02
☐ 364	Elias Sosa	.20	.09	.02	☐ 457	Ed Crosby	.20	.09	.02
☐ 365	Carlton Fisk	1.00	.45	.10	☐ 458	Earl Williams	.20	.09	.02
☐ 366	Bobby Valentine	.30	.12	.03	☐ 459	Jim Brewer	.20	.09	.02
☐ 367	Bruce Miller	.20	.09	.02	☐ 460	Cesar Cedeno	.30	.12	.03
☐ 368	Wilbur Wood	.20	.09	.02	☐ 461	NL and AL Champs:	.40	.18	.04
☐ 369	Frank White	.35	.15	.03		Reds sweep Bucs			
☐ 370	Ron Cey	.65	.30	.06		Bosox surprise A's			
☐ 371	Ellie Hendricks	.20	.09	.02	☐ 462	'75 World Series:	.40	.18	.04
☐ 372	Rick Baldwin	.20	.09	.02		Reds Champs			
☐ 373	Johnny Briggs	.20	.09	.02	☐ 463	Steve Hargan	.20	.09	.02
☐ 374	Dan Warthen	.20	.09	.02	☐ 464	Ken Henderson	.20	.09	.02
☐ 375	Ron Fairly	.20	.09	.02	☐ 465	Mike Marshall	.25	.10	.02
☐ 376	Rich Hebner	.20	.09	.02	☐ 466	Bob Stinson	.20	.09	.02
☐ 377	Mike Hegan	.20	.09	.02	☐ 467	Woodie Fryman	.20	.09	.02
☐ 378	Steve Stone	.25	.10	.02	☐ 468	Jesus Alou	.20	.09	.02
☐ 379	Ken Boswell	.20	.09	.02	☐ 469	Rawley Eastwick	.20	.09	.02
☐ 380	Bobby Bonds	.30	.12	.03	☐ 470	Bobby Murcer	.40	.18	.04
☐ 381	Denny Doyle	.20	.09	.02	☐ 471	Jim Burton	.20	.09	.02
☐ 382	Matt Alexander	.20	.09	.02	☐ 472	Bob Davis	.20	.09	.02
☐ 383	John Ellis	.20	.09	.02	☐ 473	Paul Blair	.25	.10	.02
☐ 384	Phillies Team	.35	.10	.02	☐ 474	Ray Corbin	.20	.09	.02
☐ 385	Mickey Lolich	.35	.15	.03	☐ 475	Joe Rudi	.25	.10	.02
☐ 386	Ed Goodson	.20	.09	.02	☐ 476	Bob Moose	.20	.09	.02
☐ 387	Mike Miley	.20	.09	.02	☐ 477	Indians Team	.35	.10	.02
☐ 388	Stan Perzanowski	.20	.09	.02	☐ 478	Lynn McGlothen	.20	.09	.02
☐ 389	Glenn Adams	.20	.09	.02	☐ 479	Bobby Mitchell	.20	.09	.02
☐ 390	Don Gullett	.25	.10	.02	☐ 480	Mike Schmidt	6.00	2.80	.60
☐ 391	Jerry Hairston	.20	.09	.02	☐ 481	Rudy May	.20	.09	.02
☐ 392	Checklist 265-396	.50	.10	.02	☐ 482	Tim Hosley	.20	.09	.02
☐ 393	Paul Mitchell	.20	.09	.02	☐ 483	Mickey Stanley	.20	.09	.02
☐ 394	Fran Healy	.20	.09	.02	☐ 484	Eric Raich	.20	.09	.02
☐ 395	Jim Wynn	.25	.10	.02	☐ 485	Mike Hargrove	.25	.10	.02
☐ 396	Bill Lee	.25	.10	.02	☐ 486	Bruce Dal Canton	.20	.09	.02
☐ 397	Tim Foli	.20	.09	.02	☐ 487	Leron Lee	.20	.09	.02
☐ 398	Dave Tomlin	.20	.09	.02	☐ 488	Claude Osteen	.25	.10	.02
☐ 399	Luis Melendez	.20	.09	.02	☐ 489	Skip Jutze	.20	.09	.02
☐ 400	Rod Carew	3.50	1.65	.35	☐ 490	Frank Tanana	.30	.12	.03
☐ 401	Ken Brett	.25	.10	.02	☐ 491	Terry Crowley	.20	.09	.02
☐ 402	Don Money	.20	.09	.02	☐ 492	Martin Pattin	.20	.09	.02
☐ 403	Geoff Zahn	.20	.09	.02	☐ 493	Derrel Thomas	.20	.09	.02
☐ 404	Enos Cabell	.20	.09	.02	☐ 494	Craig Swan	.25	.10	.02
☐ 405	Rollie Fingers	.80	.40	.08	☐ 495	Nate Colbert	.20	.09	.02
☐ 406	Ed Herrmann	.20	.09	.02	☐ 496	Juan Beniquez	.25	.10	.02
☐ 407	Tom Underwood	.20	.09	.02	☐ 497	Joe McIntosh	.20	.09	.02
☐ 408	Charlie Spikes	.20	.09	.02	☐ 498	Glenn Borgmann	.20	.09	.02
☐ 409	Dave Lemanczyk	.20	.09	.02	☐ 499	Mario Guerrero	.20	.09	.02
☐ 410	Ralph Garr	.20	.09	.02	☐ 500	Reggie Jackson	5.00	2.35	.50
☐ 411	Bill Singer	.20	.09	.02	☐ 501	Billy Champion	.20	.09	.02
☐ 412	Toby Harrah	.25	.10	.02	☐ 502	Tim McCarver	.30	.12	.03
☐ 413	Pete Varney	.20	.09	.02	☐ 503	Elliott Maddox	.20	.09	.02
☐ 414	Wayne Garland	.20	.09	.02	☐ 504	Pirates Team	.35	.10	.02
☐ 415	Vada Pinson	.35	.15	.03	☐ 505	Mark Belanger	.25	.10	.02
☐ 416	Tommy John	.75	.35	.07	☐ 506	George Mitterwald	.20	.09	.02
☐ 417	Gene Clines	.20	.09	.02	☐ 507	Ray Bare	.20	.09	.02
☐ 418	Jose Morales	.20	.09	.02	☐ 508	Duane Kuiper	.20	.09	.02
☐ 419	Reggie Cleveland	.20	.09	.02	☐ 509	Bill Hands	.20	.09	.02
☐ 420	Joe Morgan	2.00	.90	.20	☐ 510	Amos Otis	.30	.12	.03
☐ 421	A's Team	.35	.10	.02	☐ 511	Jamie Easterley	.20	.09	.02
☐ 422	Johnny Grubb	.20	.09	.02	☐ 512	Ellie Rodriguez	.20	.09	.02
☐ 423	Ed Halicki	.20	.09	.02	☐ 513	Bart Johnson	.20	.09	.02
☐ 424	Phil Roof	.20	.09	.02	☐ 514	Dan Driessen	.25	.10	.02
☐ 425	Rennie Stennett	.20	.09	.02	☐ 515	Steve Yeager	.25	.10	.02
☐ 426	Bob Forsch	.25	.10	.02	☐ 516	Wayne Granger	.20	.09	.02

☐ 517	John Milner	.20	.09	.02
☐ 518	Doug Flynn	.20	.09	.02
☐ 519	Steve Brye	.20	.09	.02
☐ 520	Willie McCovey	1.50	.70	.15
☐ 521	Jim Colborn	.20	.09	.02
☐ 522	Ted Sizemore	.20	.09	.02
☐ 523	Bob Montgomery	.20	.09	.02
☐ 524	Pete Falcone	.20	.09	.02
☐ 525	Billy Williams	.65	.30	.06
☐ 526	Checklist 397-528	.50	.10	.02
☐ 527	Mike Anderson	.20	.09	.02
☐ 528	Dock Ellis	.20	.09	.02
☐ 529	Deron Johnson	.20	.09	.02
☐ 530	Don Sutton	.80	.40	.08
☐ 531	New York Mets Team	.50	.10	.02
☐ 532	Milt May	.20	.09	.02
☐ 533	Lee Richard	.20	.09	.02
☐ 534	Stan Bahnsen	.20	.09	.02
☐ 535	Dave Nelson	.20	.09	.02
☐ 536	Mike Thompson	.20	.09	.02
☐ 537	Tony Muser	.20	.09	.02
☐ 538	Pat Darcy	.20	.09	.02
☐ 539	John Balaz	.20	.09	.02
☐ 540	Bill Freehan	.30	.12	.03
☐ 541	Steve Mingori	.20	.09	.02
☐ 542	Keith Hernandez	3.50	1.65	.35
☐ 543	Wayne Twitchell	.20	.09	.02
☐ 544	Pepe Frias	.20	.09	.02
☐ 545	Sparky Lyle	.30	.12	.03
☐ 546	Dave Rosello	.20	.09	.02
☐ 547	Roric Harrison	.20	.09	.02
☐ 548	Manny Mota	.25	.10	.02
☐ 549	Randy Tate	.20	.09	.02
☐ 550	Hank Aaron	5.00	2.35	.50
☐ 551	Jerry DaVanon	.20	.09	.02
☐ 552	Terry Humphrey	.20	.09	.02
☐ 553	Randy Moffitt	.20	.09	.02
☐ 554	Ray Fosse	.20	.09	.02
☐ 555	Dyar Miller	.20	.09	.02
☐ 556	Twins Team	.35	.10	.02
☐ 557	Dan Spillner	.20	.09	.02
☐ 558	Clarence Gaston	.20	.09	.02
☐ 559	Clyde Wright	.20	.09	.02
☐ 560	Jorge Orta	.20	.09	.02
☐ 561	Tom Carroll	.20	.09	.02
☐ 562	Adrian Garrett	.20	.09	.02
☐ 563	Larry Demery	.20	.09	.02
☐ 564	Bubble Gum Champ: Kurt Bevacqua	.25	.10	.02
☐ 565	Tug McGraw	.30	.12	.03
☐ 566	Ken McMullen	.20	.09	.02
☐ 567	George Stone	.20	.09	.02
☐ 568	Rob Andrews	.20	.09	.02
☐ 569	Nelson Briles	.20	.09	.02
☐ 570	George Hendrick	.30	.12	.03
☐ 571	Don DeMola	.20	.09	.02
☐ 572	Rich Coggins	.20	.09	.02
☐ 573	Bill Travers	.20	.09	.02
☐ 574	Don Kessinger	.25	.10	.02
☐ 575	Dwight Evans	.50	.22	.05
☐ 576	Maximino Leon	.20	.09	.02
☐ 577	Marc Hill	.20	.09	.02
☐ 578	Ted Kubiak	.20	.09	.02
☐ 579	Clay Kirby	.20	.09	.02
☐ 580	Bert Campaneris	.30	.12	.03
☐ 581	Cardinals Team	.50	.10	.02
☐ 582	Mike Kekich	.20	.09	.02
☐ 583	Tommy Helms	.20	.09	.02
☐ 584	Stan Wall	.20	.09	.02
☐ 585	Joe Torre	.40	.18	.04
☐ 586	Ron Schueler	.20	.09	.02
☐ 587	Leo Cardenas	.20	.09	.02
☐ 588	Kevin Kobel	.20	.09	.02
☐ 589	Rookie Pitchers: Santo Alcala Mike Flanagan Joe Pactwa Pablo Torrealba	1.50	.70	.15
☐ 590	Rookie Outfielders: Henry Cruz Chet Lemon Ellis Valentine Terry Whitfield	1.50	.70	.15
☐ 591	Rookie Pitchers: Steve Grilli Craig Mitchell Jose Sosa George Throop	.25	.10	.02
☐ 592	Rookie Infielders: Willie Randolph Dave McKay Jerry Royster Roy Staiger	1.50	.70	.15
☐ 593	Rookie Pitchers: Larry Anderson Ken Crosby Mark Littell Butch Metzger	.25	.10	.02
☐ 594	Rookie Catchers/OF: Andy Merchant Ed Ott Royle Stillman Jerry White	.25	.10	.02
☐ 595	Rookie Pitchers: Art DeFillipis Randy Lerch Sid Monge Steve Barr	.25	.10	.02
☐ 596	Rookie Infielders: Craig Reynolds Lamar Johnson Johnnie LeMaster Jerry Manuel	.45	.20	.04
☐ 597	Rookie Pitchers: Don Aase Jack Kucek Frank LaCorte Mike Pazik	1.00	.45	.10
☐ 598	Rookie Outfielders: Hector Cruz Jamie Quirk Jerry Turner Joe Wallis	.25	.10	.02
☐ 599	Rookie Pitchers: Rob Dressler Ron Guidry Bob McClure Pat Zachry	8.00	3.75	.80
☐ 600	Tom Seaver	3.50	1.65	.35
☐ 601	Ken Rudolph	.20	.09	.02
☐ 602	Doug Konieczny	.20	.09	.02
☐ 603	Jim Holt	.20	.09	.02
☐ 604	Joe Lovitto	.20	.09	.02
☐ 605	Al Downing	.20	.09	.02
☐ 606	Brewers Team	.35	.10	.02
☐ 607	Rich Hinton	.20	.09	.02
☐ 608	Vic Correll	.20	.09	.02
☐ 609	Fred Norman	.20	.09	.02
☐ 610	Greg Luzinski	.40	.18	.04
☐ 611	Rich Folkers	.20	.09	.02
☐ 612	Joe Lahoud	.20	.09	.02
☐ 613	Tim Johnson	.20	.09	.02
☐ 614	Fernando Arroyo	.20	.09	.02
☐ 615	Mike Cubbage	.20	.09	.02
☐ 616	Buck Martinez	.20	.09	.02
☐ 617	Darold Knowles	.20	.09	.02
☐ 618	Jack Brohamer	.20	.09	.02
☐ 619	Bill Butler	.20	.09	.02
☐ 620	Al Oliver	.75	.35	.07
☐ 621	Tom Hall	.20	.09	.02
☐ 622	Rick Auerbach	.20	.09	.02
☐ 623	Bob Allietta	.20	.09	.02
☐ 624	Tony Taylor	.20	.09	.02
☐ 625	J.R. Richard	.30	.12	.03
☐ 626	Bob Sheldon	.20	.09	.02
☐ 627	Bill Plummer	.20	.09	.02
☐ 628	John D'Acquisto	.20	.09	.02
☐ 629	Sandy Alomar	.20	.09	.02
☐ 630	Chris Speier	.20	.09	.02
☐ 631	Braves Team	.35	.10	.02
☐ 632	Rogelio Moret	.20	.09	.02
☐ 633	John Stearns	.25	.10	.02
☐ 634	Larry Christenson	.20	.09	.02
☐ 635	Jim Fregosi	.25	.10	.02
☐ 636	Joe Decker	.20	.09	.02
☐ 637	Bruce Bochte	.25	.10	.02
☐ 638	Doyle Alexander	.25	.10	.02
☐ 639	Fred Kendall	.20	.09	.02
☐ 640	Bill Madlock	1.00	.45	.10
☐ 641	Tom Paciorek	.20	.09	.02
☐ 642	Dennis Blair	.20	.09	.02
☐ 643	Checklist 529-660	.50	.10	.02
☐ 644	Tom Bradley	.20	.09	.02
☐ 645	Darrell Porter	.25	.10	.02
☐ 646	John Lowenstein	.20	.09	.02
☐ 647	Ramon Hernandez	.20	.09	.02
☐ 648	Al Cowens	.25	.10	.02
☐ 649	Dave Roberts	.20	.09	.02
☐ 650	Thurman Munson	3.50	1.65	.35
☐ 651	John Odom	.20	.09	.02
☐ 652	Ed Armbrister	.20	.09	.02
☐ 653	Mike Norris	.25	.10	.02
☐ 654	Doug Griffin	.20	.09	.02
☐ 655	Mike Vail	.20	.09	.02
☐ 656	White Sox Team	.35	.10	.02
☐ 657	Roy Smalley	.40	.18	.04

			MINT	VG-E	F-G
☐	658	Jerry Johnson	.20	.09	.02
☐	659	Ben Oglivie	.30	.12	.03
☐	660	Dave Lopes	.50	.22	.05

1977 O-Pee-Chee

The 1977 O-Pee-chee set of 264 is not only much smaller numerically than its American counterpart, but also contains many different poses and is loaded with players from the two Canadian teams. The reverse biography is printed in English only, but the card has a different color stock than the American version, is numbered differently and is clearly marked O-Pee-Chee on the back.

			MINT	VG-E	F-G
	COMPLETE SET		65.00	27.00	6.00
	COMMON PLAYER (1-264)		.12	.05	.01
☐	1	Batting Leaders: George Brett Bill Madlock	1.00	.30	.06
☐	2	Home Run Leaders: Graig Nettles Mike Schmidt	.60	.28	.06
☐	3	RBI Leaders: Lee May George Foster	.25	.10	.02
☐	4	Stolen Base Leaders: Bill North Dave Lopes	.20	.09	.02
☐	5	Victory Leaders: Jim Palmer Randy Jones	.30	.12	.03
☐	6	Strikeout Leaders: Nolan Ryan Tom Seaver	1.00	.45	.10
☐	7	ERA Leaders: Mark Fidrych John Denny	.20	.09	.02
☐	8	Leading Firemen: Bill Campbell Rawly Eastwick	.20	.09	.02
☐	9	Mike Jorgensen	.12	.05	.01
☐	10	Jim Hunter	.75	.35	.07
☐	11	Ken Griffey	.20	.09	.02
☐	12	Bill Campbell	.12	.05	.01
☐	13	Otto Velez	.12	.05	.01
☐	14	Milt May	.12	.05	.01
☐	15	Dennis Eckersley	.20	.09	.02
☐	16	John Mayberry	.16	.07	.01
☐	17	Larry Bowa	.25	.10	.02
☐	18	Don Carrithers	.12	.05	.01
☐	19	Ken Singleton	.25	.10	.02
☐	20	Bill Stein	.12	.05	.01
☐	21	Ken Brett	.16	.07	.01
☐	22	Gary Woods	.12	.05	.01
☐	23	Steve Swisher	.12	.05	.01
☐	24	Don Sutton	.75	.35	.07
☐	25	Willie Stargell	1.50	.70	.15
☐	26	Jerry Koosman	.20	.09	.02
☐	27	Del Unser	.12	.05	.01
☐	28	Bob Grich	.25	.10	.02
☐	29	Jim Slaton	.12	.05	.01
☐	30	Thurman Munson	2.50	1.15	.25
☐	31	Dan Driessen	.16	.07	.01
☐	32	Tom Bruno	.12	.05	.01
☐	33	Larry Hisle	.16	.07	.01
☐	34	Phil Garner	.16	.07	.01
☐	35	Mike Hargrove	.16	.07	.01
☐	36	Jackie Brown	.12	.05	.01
☐	37	Carl Yastrzemski	3.50	1.65	.35
☐	38	Dave Roberts	.12	.05	.01
☐	39	Ray Fosse	.12	.05	.01
☐	40	Dave McKay	.12	.05	.01
☐	41	Paul Splittorff	.16	.07	.01
☐	42	Garry Maddox	.16	.07	.01
☐	43	Phil Niekro	.75	.35	.07
☐	44	Roger Metzger	.12	.05	.01
☐	45	Gary Carter	3.50	1.65	.35
☐	46	Jim Spencer	.12	.05	.01
☐	47	Ross Grimsley	.12	.05	.01
☐	48	Bob Bailor	.12	.05	.01
☐	49	Chris Chambliss	.16	.07	.01
☐	50	Will McEnaney	.12	.05	.01
☐	51	Lou Brock	1.50	.70	.15
☐	52	Rollie Fingers	.60	.28	.06
☐	53	Chris Speier	.12	.05	.01
☐	54	Bombo Rivera	.12	.05	.01
☐	55	Pete Broberg	.12	.05	.01
☐	56	Bill Madlock	.90	.40	.09
☐	57	Rick Rhoden	.20	.09	.02
☐	58	Blue Jays: Coaches	.20	.09	.02
☐	59	John Candelaria	.20	.09	.02
☐	60	Ed Kranepool	.16	.07	.01
☐	61	Dave LaRoche	.12	.05	.01
☐	62	Jim Rice	3.50	1.65	.35
☐	63	Don Stanhouse	.12	.05	.01
☐	64	Jason Thompson	.75	.35	.07
☐	65	Nolan Ryan	2.50	1.15	.25
☐	66	Tom Poquette	.12	.05	.01
☐	67	Leon Hooten	.12	.05	.01
☐	68	Bob Boone	.16	.07	.01
☐	69	Mickey Rivers	.20	.09	.02
☐	70	Gary Nolan	.12	.05	.01
☐	71	Sixto Lezcano	.12	.05	.01
☐	72	Larry Parrish	.25	.10	.02
☐	73	Dave Goltz	.12	.05	.01
☐	74	Bert Campaneris	.20	.09	.02
☐	75	Vida Blue	.30	.12	.03
☐	76	Rick Cerone	.16	.07	.01
☐	77	Ralph Garr	.16	.07	.01
☐	78	Ken Forsch	.16	.07	.01
☐	79	Willie Montanez	.12	.05	.01
☐	80	Jim Palmer	2.00	.90	.20
☐	81	Jerry White	.12	.05	.01
☐	82	Gene Tenace	.12	.05	.01
☐	83	Bobby Murcer	.30	.12	.03
☐	84	Garry Templeton	1.25	.60	.12
☐	85	Bill Singer	.12	.05	.01
☐	86	Buddy Bell	.30	.12	.03
☐	87	Luis Tiant	.20	.09	.02
☐	88	Rusty Staub	.30	.12	.03
☐	89	Sparky Lyle	.25	.10	.02
☐	90	Jose Morales	.12	.05	.01
☐	91	Dennis Leonard	.20	.09	.02
☐	92	Tommy Smith	.12	.05	.01
☐	93	Steve Carlton	3.50	1.65	.35
☐	94	John Scott	.12	.05	.01
☐	95	Bill Bonham	.12	.05	.01
☐	96	Dave Lopes	.20	.09	.02
☐	97	Jerry Reuss	.20	.09	.02
☐	98	Dave Kingman	.50	.22	.05
☐	99	Dan Warthen	.12	.05	.01
☐	100	Johnny Bench	2.50	1.15	.25
☐	101	Bert Blyleven	.40	.18	.04
☐	102	Cecil Cooper	.75	.35	.07
☐	103	Mike Willis	.12	.05	.01
☐	104	Dan Ford	.16	.07	.01
☐	105	Frank Tanana	.20	.09	.02
☐	106	Bill North	.12	.05	.01
☐	107	Joe Ferguson	.12	.05	.01
☐	108	Dick Williams MGR	.16	.07	.01
☐	109	John Denny	.20	.09	.02
☐	110	Willie Randolph	.25	.10	.02
☐	111	Reggie Cleveland	.12	.05	.01
☐	112	Doug Howard	.12	.05	.01
☐	113	Randy Jones	.16	.07	.01
☐	114	Rico Carty	.16	.07	.01
☐	115	Mark Fidrych	.35	.15	.03
☐	116	Darrell Porter	.25	.10	.02
☐	117	Wayne Garrett	.12	.05	.01
☐	118	Greg Luzinski	.40	.18	.04
☐	119	Jim Barr	.12	.05	.01
☐	120	George Foster	.90	.40	.09
☐	121	Phil Roof	.12	.05	.01

☐ 122	Bucky Dent	.20	.09	.02
☐ 123	Steve Braun	.12	.05	.01
☐ 124	Checklist: 1-132	.40	.08	.01
☐ 125	Lee May	.16	.07	.01
☐ 126	Woodie Fryman	.12	.05	.01
☐ 127	Jose Cardenal	.12	.05	.01
☐ 128	Doug Rau	.12	.05	.01
☐ 129	Rennie Stennett	.12	.05	.01
☐ 130	Pete Vuckovich	.50	.22	.05
☐ 131	Cesar Cedeno	.25	.10	.02
☐ 132	Jon Matlack	.16	.07	.01
☐ 133	Don Baylor	.40	.18	.04
☐ 134	Darrel Chaney	.12	.05	.01
☐ 135	Tony Perez	.45	.20	.04
☐ 136	Aurelio Rodriguez	.12	.05	.01
☐ 137	Carlton Fisk	.75	.35	.07
☐ 138	Wayne Garland	.12	.05	.01
☐ 139	Dave Hilton	.12	.05	.01
☐ 140	Rawly Eastwick	.12	.05	.01
☐ 141	Amos Otis	.20	.09	.02
☐ 142	Tug McGraw	.25	.10	.02
☐ 143	Rod Carew	3.00	1.40	.30
☐ 144	Mike Torrez	.16	.07	.01
☐ 145	Sal Bando	.20	.09	.02
☐ 146	Dock Ellis	.12	.05	.01
☐ 147	Jose Cruz	.30	.12	.03
☐ 148	Alan Ashby	.16	.07	.01
☐ 149	Gaylord Perry	1.00	.45	.10
☐ 150	Keith Hernandez	2.00	.90	.20
☐ 151	Dave Pagan	.12	.05	.01
☐ 152	Richie Zisk	.16	.07	.01
☐ 153	Steve Rogers	.30	.12	.03
☐ 154	Mark Belanger	.16	.07	.01
☐ 155	Andy Messersmith	.16	.07	.01
☐ 156	Dave Winfield	2.50	1.15	.25
☐ 157	Chuck Hartenstein	.12	.05	.01
☐ 158	Manny Trillo	.16	.07	.01
☐ 159	Steve Yeager	.16	.07	.01
☐ 160	Cesar Geronimo	.12	.05	.01
☐ 161	Jim Rooker	.12	.05	.01
☐ 162	Tim Foli	.12	.05	.01
☐ 163	Fred Lynn	1.50	.70	.15
☐ 164	Ed Figueroa	.12	.05	.01
☐ 165	Johnny Grubb	.12	.05	.01
☐ 166	Pedro Garcia	.12	.05	.01
☐ 167	Ron LeFlore	.16	.07	.01
☐ 168	Rich Hebner	.12	.05	.01
☐ 169	Larry Herndon	.12	.07	.01
☐ 170	George Brett	5.00	2.35	.50
☐ 171	Joe Kerrigan	.12	.05	.01
☐ 172	Bud Harrelson	.12	.05	.01
☐ 173	Bobby Bonds	.25	.10	.02
☐ 174	Bill Travers	.12	.05	.01
☐ 175	John Lowenstein	.12	.05	.01
☐ 176	Butch Wynegar	.20	.09	.02
☐ 177	Pete Falcone	.12	.05	.01
☐ 178	Claudell Washington	.16	.07	.01
☐ 179	Checklist: 133-264	.40	.08	.01
☐ 180	Dave Cash	.12	.05	.01
☐ 181	Fred Norman	.12	.05	.01
☐ 182	Roy White	.16	.07	.01
☐ 183	Marty Perez	.12	.05	.01
☐ 184	Jesse Jefferson	.12	.05	.01
☐ 185	Jim Sundberg	.20	.09	.02
☐ 186	Dan Meyer	.12	.05	.01
☐ 187	Fergie Jenkins	.40	.18	.04
☐ 188	Tom Veryzer	.12	.05	.01
☐ 189	Dennis Blair	.12	.05	.01
☐ 190	Rick Manning	.12	.05	.01
☐ 191	Doug Bird	.12	.05	.01
☐ 192	Al Bumbry	.12	.05	.01
☐ 193	Dave Roberts	.12	.05	.01
☐ 194	Larry Christenson	.12	.05	.01
☐ 195	Chet Lemon	.30	.12	.03
☐ 196	Ted Simmons	.60	.28	.06
☐ 197	Ray Burris	.12	.05	.01
☐ 198	Expos: Coaches	.20	.09	.02
☐ 199	Ron Cey	.35	.15	.03
☐ 200	Reggie Jackson	3.50	1.65	.35
☐ 201	Pat Zachry	.12	.05	.01
☐ 202	Doug Ault	.12	.05	.01
☐ 203	Al Oliver	.75	.35	.07
☐ 204	Robin Yount	3.00	1.40	.30
☐ 205	Tom Seaver	2.50	1.15	.25
☐ 206	Joe Rudi	.16	.07	.01
☐ 207	Barry Foote	.12	.05	.01
☐ 208	Toby Harrah	.16	.07	.01
☐ 209	Jeff Burroughs	.16	.07	.01
☐ 210	George Scott	.16	.07	.01
☐ 211	Jim Mason	.12	.05	.01
☐ 212	Vern Ruhle	.12	.05	.01
☐ 213	Fred Kendall	.12	.05	.01
☐ 214	Rick Reuschel	.20	.09	.02
☐ 215	Hal McRae	.20	.09	.02
☐ 216	Chip Lang	.12	.05	.01
☐ 217	Graig Nettles	.75	.35	.07
☐ 218	George Hendrick	.25	.10	.02
☐ 219	Glenn Abbott	.12	.05	.01
☐ 220	Joe Morgan	1.25	.60	.12
☐ 221	Sam Ewing	.12	.05	.01
☐ 222	George Medich	.12	.05	.01
☐ 223	Reggie Smith	.30	.12	.03
☐ 224	Dave Hamilton	.12	.05	.01
☐ 225	Pepe Frias	.12	.05	.01
☐ 226	Jay Johnstone	.16	.07	.01
☐ 227	J.R. Richard	.30	.12	.03
☐ 228	Doug DeCinces	.35	.15	.03
☐ 229	Dave Lemanczyk	.12	.05	.01
☐ 230	Rick Monday	.16	.07	.01
☐ 231	Manny Sanguillen	.16	.07	.01
☐ 232	John Montefusco	.16	.07	.01
☐ 233	Duane Kuiper	.12	.05	.01
☐ 234	Ellis Valentine	.16	.07	.01
☐ 235	Dick Tidrow	.12	.05	.01
☐ 236	Ben Oglivie	.25	.10	.02
☐ 237	Rick Burleson	.20	.09	.02
☐ 238	Roy Hartsfield MGR	.12	.05	.01
☐ 239	Lyman Bostock	.30	.12	.03
☐ 240	Pete Rose	6.00	2.80	.60
☐ 241	Mike Ivie	.12	.05	.01
☐ 242	Dave Parker	1.50	.70	.15
☐ 243	Bill Greif	.12	.05	.01
☐ 244	Freddie Patek	.12	.05	.01
☐ 245	Mike Schmidt	4.00	1.85	.40
☐ 246	Brian Downing	.16	.07	.01
☐ 247	Steve Hargan	.12	.05	.01
☐ 248	Dave Collins	.20	.09	.02
☐ 249	Felix Millan	.12	.05	.01
☐ 250	Don Gullett	.16	.07	.01
☐ 251	Jerry Royster	.12	.05	.01
☐ 252	Earl Williams	.12	.05	.01
☐ 253	Frank Duffy	.12	.05	.01
☐ 254	Tippy Martinez	.16	.07	.01
☐ 255	Steve Garvey	3.00	1.40	.30
☐ 256	Alvis Woods	.12	.05	.01
☐ 257	John Hiller	.16	.07	.01
☐ 258	Dave Concepcion	.35	.15	.03
☐ 259	Dwight Evans	.45	.20	.04
☐ 260	Pete MacKanin	.12	.05	.01
☐ 261	RB: George Brett Most Consec. Games Three Or More Hits	1.50	.70	.15
☐ 262	RB: Minnie Minoso Oldest Player To Hit Safely	.25	.10	.02
☐ 263	RB: Jose Morales, Most Pinch-hits, Season	.20	.09	.02
☐ 264	RB: Nolan Ryan, Most Seasons 300 Or More Strikeouts	1.00	.45	.10

1978 O-Pee-Chee

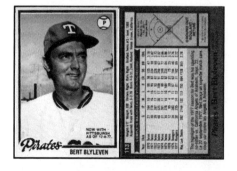

BERT BLYLEVEN

The 1978 O-Pee-Chee set of 242 cards follows the
pattern set in 1977 as this Canadian issue differs
from the Topps set of this year by the inclusion of
many more players from the two Canadian teams.

The backs are in both French and English. The asterisked cards have an extra line on the front indicating team change. Double printed (DP) cards are noted in the checklist below.

		MINT	VG-E	F-G
	COMPLETE SET	30.00	14.00	3.00
	COMMON PLAYER (1-242)	.07	.03	.01
☐ 1	Batting Leaders Dave Parker Rod Carew	.50	.15	.03
☐ 2	Home Run Leaders DP George Foster Jim Rice	.10	.04	.01
☐ 3	RBI Leaders George Foster Larry Hisle	.15	.06	.01
☐ 4	Stolen Base Leaders DP Frank Taveras Freddie Patek	.07	.03	.01
☐ 5	Victory Leaders Steve Carlton Dave Goltz Dennis Leonard Jim Palmer	.35	.15	.03
☐ 6	Strikeout Leaders DP Phil Niekro Nolan Ryan	.10	.04	.01
☐ 7	ERA Leaders DP John Candelaria Frank Tanana	.07	.03	.01
☐ 8	Firemen Leaders Rollie Fingers Bill Campbell	.15	.06	.01
☐ 9	Steve Rogers DP	.10	.04	.01
☐ 10	Graig Nettles DP	.15	.06	.01
☐ 11	Doug Capilla	.07	.03	.01
☐ 12	George Scott	.10	.04	.01
☐ 13	Gary Woods	.07	.03	.01
☐ 14	Tom Veryzer *	.10	.04	.01
☐ 15	Wayne Garland	.07	.03	.01
☐ 16	Amos Otis	.10	.04	.01
☐ 17	Larry Christenson	.07	.03	.01
☐ 18	Dave Cash	.07	.03	.01
☐ 19	Jim Barr	.07	.03	.01
☐ 20	Ruppert Jones	.10	.04	.01
☐ 21	Eric Soderholm	.07	.03	.01
☐ 22	Jesse Jefferson	.07	.03	.01
☐ 23	Jerry Morales	.07	.03	.01
☐ 24	Doug Rau	.07	.03	.01
☐ 25	Rennie Stennett	.07	.03	.01
☐ 26	Lee Mazzilli	.15	.06	.01
☐ 27	Dick Williams MGR	.10	.04	.01
☐ 28	Joe Rudi	.10	.04	.01
☐ 29	Robin Yount	1.50	.70	.15
☐ 30	Don Gullett DP	.07	.03	.01
☐ 31	Roy Howell DP	.05	.02	.00
☐ 32	Cesar Geronimo	.07	.03	.01
☐ 33	Rick Langford DP	.05	.02	.00
☐ 34	Dan Ford	.10	.04	.01
☐ 35	Gene Tenace	.07	.03	.01
☐ 36	Santo Alcala	.07	.03	.01
☐ 37	Rick Burleson	.12	.05	.01
☐ 38	Dave Rozema	.07	.03	.01
☐ 39	Duane Kuiper	.07	.03	.01
☐ 40	Ron Fairly *	.10	.04	.01
☐ 41	Dennis Leonard	.15	.06	.01
☐ 42	Greg Luzinski	.30	.12	.03
☐ 43	Willie Montanez *	.10	.04	.01
☐ 44	Enos Cabell	.07	.03	.01
☐ 45	Ellis Valentine	.12	.05	.01
☐ 46	Steve Stone	.15	.06	.01
☐ 47	Lee May DP	.07	.03	.01
☐ 48	Roy White	.10	.04	.01
☐ 49	Jerry Garvin	.07	.03	.01
☐ 50	Johnny Bench	1.50	.70	.15
☐ 51	Garry Templeton	.35	.15	.03
☐ 52	Doyle Alexander	.10	.04	.01
☐ 53	Steve Henderson	.10	.04	.01
☐ 54	Stan Bahnsen	.07	.03	.01
☐ 55	Dan Meyer	.07	.03	.01
☐ 56	Rick Reuschel	.10	.04	.01
☐ 57	Reggie Smith	.25	.10	.02
☐ 58	Blue Jays Team DP	.10	.04	.01
☐ 59	John Montefusco	.10	.04	.01
☐ 60	Dave Parker	1.25	.60	.12
☐ 61	Jim Bibby	.10	.04	.01
☐ 62	Fred Lynn	.75	.35	.07
☐ 63	Jose Morales	.07	.03	.01
☐ 64	Aurelio Rodriguez	.07	.03	.01
☐ 65	Frank Tanana	.12	.05	.01
☐ 66	Darrell Porter	.12	.05	.01
☐ 67	Otto Velez	.10	.04	.01
☐ 68	Larry Bowa	.20	.09	.02
☐ 69	Jim Hunter	.50	.22	.05
☐ 70	George Foster	.75	.35	.07
☐ 71	Cecil Cooper DP	.15	.06	.01
☐ 72	Gary Alexander DP	.05	.02	.00
☐ 73	Paul Thormodsgard	.07	.03	.01
☐ 74	Toby Harrah	.12	.05	.01
☐ 75	Mitchell Page	.10	.04	.01
☐ 76	Alan Ashby	.07	.03	.01
☐ 77	Jorge Orta	.07	.03	.01
☐ 78	Dave Winfield	1.50	.70	.15
☐ 79	Andy Messersmith *	.10	.04	.01
☐ 80	Ken Singleton	.25	.10	.02
☐ 81	Will McEnaney	.07	.03	.01
☐ 82	Lou Piniella	.20	.09	.02
☐ 83	Bob Forsch	.10	.04	.01
☐ 84	Dan Driessen	.10	.04	.01
☐ 85	Dave Lemanczyk	.07	.03	.01
☐ 86	Paul Dade	.07	.03	.01
☐ 87	Bill Campbell	.10	.04	.01
☐ 88	Ron LeFlore	.12	.05	.01
☐ 89	Bill Madlock	.75	.35	.07
☐ 90	Tony Perez DP	.15	.06	.01
☐ 91	Freddie Patek	.07	.03	.01
☐ 92	Glenn Abbott	.07	.03	.01
☐ 93	Garry Maddox	.10	.04	.01
☐ 94	Steve Staggs	.07	.03	.01
☐ 95	Bobby Murcer	.20	.09	.02
☐ 96	Don Sutton	.60	.28	.06
☐ 97	Al Oliver *	.75	.35	.07
☐ 98	Jon Matlack *	.12	.05	.01
☐ 99	Sam Mejias	.07	.03	.01
☐ 100	Pete Rose DP	3.00	1.40	.30
☐ 101	Randy Jones	.10	.04	.01
☐ 102	Sixto Lezcano	.10	.04	.01
☐ 103	Jim Clancy DP	.07	.03	.01
☐ 104	Butch Wynegar	.12	.05	.01
☐ 105	Nolan Ryan	1.50	.70	.15
☐ 106	Wayne Gross	.07	.03	.01
☐ 107	Bob Watson	.10	.04	.01
☐ 108	Joe Kerrigan *	.10	.04	.01
☐ 109	Keith Hernandez	1.50	.70	.15
☐ 110	Reggie Jackson	2.25	1.00	.22
☐ 111	Denny Doyle	.07	.03	.01
☐ 112	Sam Ewing	.07	.03	.01
☐ 113	Bert Blyleven *	.30	.12	.03
☐ 114	Andre Thornton	.15	.06	.01
☐ 115	Milt May	.07	.03	.01
☐ 116	Jim Colborn	.07	.03	.01
☐ 117	Warren Cromartie	.10	.04	.01
☐ 118	Ted Sizemore	.07	.03	.01
☐ 119	Checklist 1-121	.35	.05	.01
☐ 120	Tom Seaver	1.50	.70	.15
☐ 121	Luis Gomez	.07	.03	.01
☐ 122	Jim Spencer *	.10	.04	.01
☐ 123	Leroy Stanton	.07	.03	.01
☐ 124	Luis Tiant	.15	.06	.01
☐ 125	Mark Belanger	.10	.04	.01
☐ 126	Jackie Brown	.07	.03	.01
☐ 127	Bill Buckner	.20	.09	.02
☐ 128	Bill Robinson	.07	.03	.01
☐ 129	Rick Cerone	.10	.04	.01
☐ 130	Ron Cey	.20	.09	.02
☐ 131	Jose Cruz	.20	.09	.02
☐ 132	Len Randle DP	.05	.02	.00
☐ 133	Bob Grich	.15	.06	.01
☐ 134	Jeff Burroughs	.10	.04	.01
☐ 135	Gary Carter	2.00	.90	.20
☐ 136	Milt Wilcox	.10	.04	.01
☐ 137	Carl Yastrzemski	2.00	.90	.20
☐ 138	Dennis Eckersley	.12	.05	.01
☐ 139	Tim Nordbrook	.07	.03	.01
☐ 140	Ken Griffey	.15	.06	.01
☐ 141	Bob Boone	.12	.05	.01
☐ 142	Dave Goltz DP	.07	.03	.01
☐ 143	Al Cowens	.10	.04	.01
☐ 144	Bill Atkinson	.07	.03	.01
☐ 145	Chris Chambliss	.10	.04	.01
☐ 146	Jim Slaton *	.10	.04	.01
☐ 147	Bill Stein	.07	.03	.01
☐ 148	Bob Bailor	.07	.03	.01
☐ 149	J.R. Richard	.20	.09	.02
☐ 150	Ted Simmons	.45	.20	.04
☐ 151	Rick Manning	.07	.03	.01
☐ 152	Lerrin LaGrow	.07	.03	.01
☐ 153	Larry Parrish	.20	.09	.02
☐ 154	Eddie Murray	18.00	8.50	1.80
☐ 155	Phil Niekro	.60	.28	.06
☐ 156	Bake McBride	.10	.04	.01
☐ 157	Pete Vuckovich	.12	.05	.01
☐ 158	Ivan DeJesus	.07	.03	.01

☐ 159 Rick Rhoden	.12	.05	.01
☐ 160 Joe Morgan	1.00	.45	.10
☐ 161 Ed Ott	.07	.03	.01
☐ 162 Don Stanhouse	.07	.03	.01
☐ 163 Jim Rice	2.00	.90	.20
☐ 164 Bucky Dent	.12	.05	.01
☐ 165 Jim Kern	.07	.03	.01
☐ 166 Doug Rader	.10	.04	.01
☐ 167 Steve Kemp	.20	.09	.02
☐ 168 John Mayberry	.10	.04	.01
☐ 169 Tim Foli *	.10	.04	.01
☐ 170 Steve Carlton	1.50	.70	.15
☐ 171 Pepe Frias	.07	.03	.01
☐ 172 Pat Zachry	.07	.03	.01
☐ 173 Don Baylor	.40	.18	.04
☐ 174 Sal Bando DP	.07	.03	.01
☐ 175 Alvis Woods	.07	.03	.01
☐ 176 Mike Hargrove	.10	.04	.01
☐ 177 Vida Blue	.25	.10	.02
☐ 178 George Hendrick	.20	.09	.02
☐ 179 Jim Palmer	1.25	.60	.12
☐ 180 Andre Dawson	1.25	.60	.12
☐ 181 Paul Moskau	.07	.03	.01
☐ 182 Mickey Rivers	.10	.04	.01
☐ 183 Checklist 122-242	.35	.05	.01
☐ 184 Jerry Johnson	.07	.03	.01
☐ 185 Willie McCovey	1.00	.45	.10
☐ 186 Enrique Romo	.07	.03	.01
☐ 187 Butch Hobson	.10	.04	.01
☐ 188 Rusty Staub	.25	.10	.02
☐ 189 Wayne Twitchell	.07	.03	.01
☐ 190 Steve Garvey	2.00	.90	.20
☐ 191 Rick Waits	.10	.04	.01
☐ 192 Doug DeCinces	.25	.10	.02
☐ 193 Tom Murphy	.07	.03	.01
☐ 194 Rich Hebner	.07	.03	.01
☐ 195 Ralph Garr	.10	.04	.01
☐ 196 Bruce Sutter	.60	.28	.06
☐ 197 Tom Poquette	.07	.03	.01
☐ 198 Wayne Garrett	.07	.03	.01
☐ 199 Pedro Borbon	.07	.03	.01
☐ 200 Thurman Munson	1.50	.70	.15
☐ 201 Rollie Fingers	.50	.22	.05
☐ 202 Doug Ault	.07	.03	.01
☐ 203 Phil Garner DP	.07	.03	.01
☐ 204 Lou Brock	1.00	.45	.10
☐ 205 Ed Kranepool	.10	.04	.01
☐ 206 Bobby Bonds *	.20	.09	.02
☐ 207 Expos Team DP	.15	.06	.01
☐ 208 Bump Wills	.07	.03	.01
☐ 209 Gary Matthews	.15	.06	.01
☐ 210 Carlton Fisk	.75	.35	.07
☐ 211 Jeff Byrd	.07	.03	.01
☐ 212 Jason Thompson	.15	.06	.01
☐ 213 Larvell Blanks	.07	.03	.01
☐ 214 Sparky Lyle	.15	.06	.01
☐ 215 George Brett	3.50	1.65	.35
☐ 216 Del Unser	.07	.03	.01
☐ 217 Manny Trillo	.10	.04	.01
☐ 218 Roy Hartsfield MGR	.07	.03	.01
☐ 219 Carlos Lopez	.07	.03	.01
☐ 220 Dave Concepcion	.20	.09	.02
☐ 221 John Candelaria	.12	.05	.01
☐ 222 Dave Lopes	.15	.06	.01
☐ 223 Tim Blackwell DP *	.07	.03	.01
☐ 224 Chet Lemon	.15	.06	.01
☐ 225 Mike Schmidt	3.00	1.40	.30
☐ 226 Cesar Cedeno	.15	.06	.01
☐ 227 Mike Willis	.07	.03	.01
☐ 228 Willie Randolph	.15	.06	.01
☐ 229 Doug Bair	.10	.04	.01
☐ 230 Rod Carew	1.50	.70	.15
☐ 231 Mike Flanagan	.15	.06	.01
☐ 232 Chris Speier	.07	.03	.01
☐ 233 Don Aase *	.25	.10	.02
☐ 234 Buddy Bell	.25	.10	.02
☐ 235 Mark Fidrych	.20	.09	.02
☐ 236 RB: Lou Brock Most Steals, Lifetime	.40	.18	.04
☐ 237 RB: Sparky Lyle Most Games Pure Relief, Lifetime	.15	.06	.01
☐ 238 RB: Willie McCovey Most Times 2 HR's in Inning, Lifetime	.50	.22	.05
☐ 239 RB: Brooks Robinson Most Consecutive Seasons with one club	.60	.28	.06
☐ 240 RB: Pete Rose Most Hits, Switch- hitter, Lifetime	1.25	.60	.12
☐ 241 RB: Nolan Ryan Most games 10 or More	.75	.35	.07

Strikeouts, Lifetime

☐ 242 RB: Reggie Jackson .... 1.00 .45 .10
Most Homers, One
World Series

1979 O-Pee-Chee

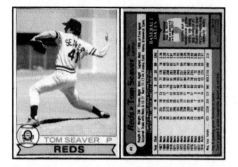

The 1979 O-Pee-Chee set was the largest (374) original baseball card set issued (up to that time) by O-Pee-Chee. The fronts have an O-Pee-Chee logo in the lower left corner comparable to the Topps logo on the 1979 American Set. The asterisked cards have an extra line on the front indicating team change. Double printed (DP) cards are noted in the checklist below.

		MINT	VG-E	F-G
COMPLETE SET		26.00	12.00	2.00
COMMON PLAYER (1-374)		.06	.02	.00
☐	1 Lee May	.15	.06	.01
☐	2 Dick Drago	.06	.02	.00
☐	3 Paul Dade	.06	.02	.00
☐	4 Ross Grimsley	.06	.02	.00
☐	5 Joe Morgan DP	.15	.06	.01
☐	6 Kevin Kobel	.06	.02	.00
☐	7 Terry Forster	.12	.05	.01
☐	8 Paul Molitor	.60	.28	.06
☐	9 Steve Carlton	1.50	.70	.15
☐	10 Dave Goltz	.06	.02	.00
☐	11 Dave Winfield	1.50	.70	.15
☐	12 Dave Rozema	.06	.02	.00
☐	13 Ed Figueroa	.06	.02	.00
☐	14 Alan Ashby	.09	.04	.01
☐	15 Dale Murphy	3.50	1.65	.35
☐	16 Dennis Eckersley	.12	.05	.01
☐	17 Ron Blomberg	.06	.02	.00
☐	18 Wayne Twitchell	.06	.02	.00
☐	19 Al Hrabosky	.09	.04	.01
☐	20 Fred Norman	.06	.02	.00
☐	21 Steve Garvey DP	.75	.35	.07
☐	22 Willie Stargell	.90	.40	.09
☐	23 John Hale	.06	.02	.00
☐	24 Mickey Rivers	.09	.04	.01
☐	25 Jack Brohamer	.06	.02	.00
☐	26 Tom Underwood	.06	.02	.00
☐	27 Mark Belanger	.09	.04	.01
☐	28 Elliott Maddox	.06	.02	.00
☐	29 John Candelaria	.12	.05	.01
☐	30 Shane Rawley	.60	.28	.06
☐	31 Steve Yeager	.09	.04	.01
☐	32 Warren Cromartie	.09	.04	.01
☐	33 Jason Thompson	.12	.05	.01
☐	34 Roger Erickson	.06	.02	.00
☐	35 Gary Matthews	.15	.06	.01
☐	36 Pete Falcone	.06	.02	.00
☐	37 Dick Tidrow	.06	.02	.00
☐	38 Bob Boone	.09	.04	.01
☐	39 Jim Bibby	.09	.04	.01
☐	40 Len Barker	.09	.04	.01
☐	41 Robin Yount	1.25	.60	.12
☐	42 Sam Mejias	.06	.02	.00
☐	43 Ray Burris	.06	.02	.00

☐ 44	Tom Seaver DP	.65	.30	.06
☐ 45	Roy Howell	.06	.02	.00
☐ 46	Jim Todd	.06	.02	.00
☐ 47	Frank Duffy	.06	.02	.00
☐ 48	Joel Youngblood	.06	.02	.00
☐ 49	Vida Blue	.20	.09	.02
☐ 50	Cliff Johnson	.09	.04	.01
☐ 51	Nolan Ryan	1.25	.60	.12
☐ 52	Ozzie Smith	2.00	.90	.20
☐ 53	Jim Sundberg	.09	.04	.01
☐ 54	Mike Paxton	.06	.02	.00
☐ 55	Lou Whitaker	1.25	.60	.12
☐ 56	Dan Schatzeder	.06	.02	.00
☐ 57	Rick Burleson	.12	.05	.01
☐ 58	Doug Bair	.09	.04	.01
☐ 59	Ted Martinez	.06	.02	.00
☐ 60	Bob Watson	.09	.04	.01
☐ 61	Jim Clancy	.06	.02	.00
☐ 62	Rowland Office	.06	.02	.00
☐ 63	Bobby Murcer	.20	.09	.02
☐ 64	Don Gullett	.09	.04	.01
☐ 65	Tom Paciorek	.06	.02	.00
☐ 66	Rick Rhoden	.09	.04	.01
☐ 67	Duane Kuiper	.06	.02	.00
☐ 68	Bruce Boisclair	.06	.02	.00
☐ 69	Manny Sarmiento	.06	.02	.00
☐ 70	Wayne Cage	.06	.02	.00
☐ 71	John Hiller	.09	.04	.01
☐ 72	Rick Cerone	.09	.04	.01
☐ 73	Dwight Evans	.35	.15	.03
☐ 74	Buddy Solomon	.06	.02	.00
☐ 75	Roy White	.09	.04	.01
☐ 76	Mike Flanagan	.12	.05	.01
☐ 77	Tom Johnson	.06	.02	.00
☐ 78	Glenn Burke	.06	.02	.00
☐ 79	Frank Taveras	.06	.02	.00
☐ 80	Don Sutton	.45	.20	.04
☐ 81	Leon Roberts	.06	.02	.00
☐ 82	George Hendrick	.15	.06	.01
☐ 83	Aurelio Rodriguez	.06	.02	.00
☐ 84	Ron Reed	.06	.02	.00
☐ 85	Alvis Woods	.06	.02	.00
☐ 86	Jim Beattie DP	.06	.02	.00
☐ 87	Larry Hisle	.09	.04	.01
☐ 88	Mike Garman	.06	.02	.00
☐ 89	Tim Johnson	.06	.02	.00
☐ 90	Paul Splittorff	.09	.04	.01
☐ 91	Darrel Chaney	.06	.02	.00
☐ 92	Mike Torrez	.09	.04	.01
☐ 93	Eric Soderholm	.06	.02	.00
☐ 94	Ron Cey	.18	.08	.01
☐ 95	Randy Jones	.09	.04	.01
☐ 96	Bill Madlock	.45	.20	.04
☐ 97	Steve Kemp DP	.10	.04	.01
☐ 98	Bob Apodaca	.06	.02	.00
☐ 99	Johnny Grubb	.06	.02	.00
☐ 100	Larry Milbourne	.06	.02	.00
☐ 101	Johnny Bench DP	.65	.30	.06
☐ 102	Dave Lemanczyk	.06	.02	.00
☐ 103	Reggie Cleveland	.06	.02	.00
☐ 104	Larry Bowa	.15	.06	.01
☐ 105	Denny Martinez	.06	.02	.00
☐ 106	Bill Travers	.06	.02	.00
☐ 107	Willie McCovey	.90	.40	.09
☐ 108	Wilbur Wood	.09	.04	.01
☐ 109	Dennis Leonard	.12	.05	.01
☐ 110	Roy Smalley	.09	.04	.01
☐ 111	Cesar Geronimo	.06	.02	.00
☐ 112	Jesse Jefferson	.06	.02	.00
☐ 113	Dave Revering	.06	.02	.00
☐ 114	Rich Gossage	.50	.22	.05
☐ 115	Steve Stone	.12	.05	.01
☐ 116	Doug Flynn	.06	.02	.00
☐ 117	Bob Forsch	.09	.04	.01
☐ 118	Paul Mitchell	.06	.02	.00
☐ 119	Toby Harrah	.09	.04	.01
☐ 120	Steve Rogers	.15	.06	.01
☐ 121	Checklist 1-125 DP	.15	.03	.00
☐ 122	Balor Moore	.06	.02	.00
☐ 123	Rick Reuschel	.09	.04	.01
☐ 124	Jeff Burroughs	.09	.04	.01
☐ 125	Willie Randolph	.15	.06	.01
☐ 126	Bob Stinson	.06	.02	.00
☐ 127	Rick Wise	.09	.04	.01
☐ 128	Luis Gomez	.06	.02	.00
☐ 129	Tommy John	.35	.15	.03
☐ 130	Richie Zisk	.09	.04	.01
☐ 131	Mario Guerrero	.06	.02	.00
☐ 132	Oscar Gamble	.09	.04	.01
☐ 133	Don Money	.06	.02	.00
☐ 134	Joe Rudi	.09	.04	.01
☐ 135	Woodie Fryman	.06	.02	.00
☐ 136	Butch Hobson	.09	.04	.01
☐ 137	Jim Colborn	.06	.02	.00
☐ 138	Tom Grieve	.09	.04	.01
☐ 139	Andy Messersmith	.12	.05	.01
☐ 140	Andre Thornton	.15	.06	.01
☐ 141	Kevin Kravec	.06	.02	.00
☐ 142	Bobby Bonds	.15	.06	.01
☐ 143	Jose Cruz	.20	.09	.02
☐ 144	Dave Lopes	.15	.06	.01
☐ 145	Jerry Garvin	.06	.02	.00
☐ 146	Pepe Frias	.06	.02	.00
☐ 147	Mitchell Page	.06	.02	.00
☐ 148	Ted Sizemore	.06	.02	.00
☐ 149	Rich Gale	.06	.02	.00
☐ 150	Steve Ontiveros	.06	.02	.00
☐ 151	Rod Carew	1.25	.60	.12
☐ 152	Lary Sorensen DP	.06	.02	.00
☐ 153	Willie Montanez	.06	.02	.00
☐ 154	Floyd Bannister	.12	.05	.01
☐ 155	Bert Blyleven	.25	.10	.02
☐ 156	Ralph Garr	.09	.04	.01
☐ 157	Thurman Munson	1.25	.60	.12
☐ 158	Bob Robertson	.06	.02	.00
☐ 159	Jon Matlack	.09	.04	.01
☐ 160	Carl Yastrzemski	1.75	.85	.17
☐ 161	Gaylord Perry	.60	.28	.06
☐ 162	Mike Tyson	.06	.02	.00
☐ 163	Cecil Cooper	.50	.22	.05
☐ 164	Pedro Borbon	.06	.02	.00
☐ 165	Art Howe DP	.06	.02	.00
☐ 166	Joe Coleman	.06	.02	.00
☐ 167	George Brett	2.00	.90	.20
☐ 168	Gary Alexander	.06	.02	.00
☐ 169	Chet Lemon	.12	.05	.01
☐ 170	Craig Swan	.09	.04	.01
☐ 171	Chris Chambliss	.09	.04	.01
☐ 172	John Montague	.06	.02	.00
☐ 173	Ron Jackson	.06	.02	.00
☐ 174	Jim Palmer	1.00	.45	.10
☐ 175	Willie Upshaw	1.50	.70	.15
☐ 176	Tug McGraw	.12	.05	.01
☐ 177	Bill Buckner	.20	.09	.02
☐ 178	Doug Rau	.06	.02	.00
☐ 179	Andre Dawson	1.25	.60	.12
☐ 180	Jim Wright	.06	.02	.00
☐ 181	Garry Templeton	.20	.09	.02
☐ 182	Bill Bonham	.06	.02	.00
☐ 183	Lee Mazzilli	.09	.04	.01
☐ 184	Alan Trammell	1.25	.60	.12
☐ 185	Amos Otis	.12	.05	.01
☐ 186	Tom Dixon	.06	.02	.00
☐ 187	Mike Cubbage	.06	.02	.00
☐ 188	Sparky Lyle	.15	.06	.01
☐ 189	Juan Bernhardt	.06	.02	.00
☐ 190	Bump Wills	.25	.10	.02
☐ 191	Dave Kingman	.35	.15	.03
☐ 192	Lamar Johnson	.06	.02	.00
☐ 193	Lance Rautzhan	.06	.02	.00
☐ 194	Ed Herrmann	.06	.02	.00
☐ 195	Bill Campbell	.09	.04	.01
☐ 196	Gorman Thomas	.25	.10	.02
☐ 197	Paul Moskau	.06	.02	.00
☐ 198	Dale Murray	.06	.02	.00
☐ 199	John Mayberry	.09	.04	.01
☐ 200	Phil Garner	.09	.04	.01
☐ 201	Dan Ford	.09	.04	.01
☐ 202	Gary Thomasson	.06	.02	.00
☐ 203	Rollie Fingers	.40	.18	.04
☐ 204	Al Oliver	.40	.18	.04
☐ 205	Doug Ault	.06	.02	.00
☐ 206	Scott McGregor	.09	.04	.01
☐ 207	Dave Cash	.06	.02	.00
☐ 208	Bill Plummer	.06	.02	.00
☐ 209	Ivan DeJesus	.06	.02	.00
☐ 210	Jim Rice	1.50	.70	.15
☐ 211	Ray Knight	.12	.05	.01
☐ 212	Paul Hartzell	.06	.02	.00
☐ 213	Tim Foli	.06	.02	.00
☐ 214	Butch Wynegar DP	.06	.02	.00
☐ 215	Darrell Evans	.15	.06	.01
☐ 216	Ken Griffey	.15	.06	.01
☐ 217	Doug DeCinces	.20	.09	.02
☐ 218	Ruppert Jones	.12	.05	.01
☐ 219	Bob Montgomery	.06	.02	.00
☐ 220	Rick Manning	.06	.02	.00
☐ 221	Chris Speier	.06	.02	.00
☐ 222	Bobby Valentine	.15	.06	.01
☐ 223	Dave Parker	.90	.40	.09
☐ 224	Larry Biittner	.06	.02	.00
☐ 225	Ken Clay	.06	.02	.00
☐ 226	Gene Tenace	.06	.02	.00
☐ 227	Frank White	.15	.06	.01
☐ 228	Rusty Staub	.20	.09	.02
☐ 229	Lee Lacy	.12	.05	.01

☐ 230 Doyle Alexander	.09	.04	.01
☐ 231 Bruce Bochte	.09	.04	.01
☐ 232 Steve Henderson	.09	.04	.01
☐ 233 Jim Lonborg	.09	.04	.01
☐ 234 Dave Concepcion	.20	.09	.02
☐ 235 Jerry Morales	.06	.02	.00
☐ 236 Len Randle	.06	.02	.00
☐ 237 Bill Lee DP	.06	.02	.00
☐ 238 Bruce Sutter	.50	.22	.05
☐ 239 Jim Essian	.06	.02	.00
☐ 240 Graig Nettles	.40	.18	.04
☐ 241 Otto Velez	.09	.04	.01
☐ 242 Checklist 126-250 DP	.15	.03	.00
☐ 243 Reggie Smith	.15	.06	.01
☐ 244 Stan Bahnsen DP	.06	.02	.00
☐ 245 Garry Maddox DP	.06	.02	.00
☐ 246 Joaquin Andujar	.20	.09	.02
☐ 247 Dan Driessen	.09	.04	.01
☐ 248 Bob Grich	.15	.06	.01
☐ 249 Fred Lynn	.60	.28	.06
☐ 250 Skip Lockwood	.06	.02	.00
☐ 251 Craig Reynolds	.09	.04	.01
☐ 252 Willie Horton	.09	.04	.01
☐ 253 Rick Waits	.06	.02	.00
☐ 254 Bucky Dent	.12	.05	.01
☐ 255 Bob Knepper	.20	.09	.02
☐ 256 Miguel Dilone	.06	.02	.00
☐ 257 Bob Owchinko	.06	.02	.00
☐ 258 Al Cowens	.09	.04	.01
☐ 259 Bob Bailor	.06	.02	.00
☐ 260 Larry Christenson	.06	.02	.00
☐ 261 Tony Perez	.30	.12	.03
☐ 262 Blue Jays Checklist	.20	.06	.01
☐ 263 Glenn Abbott	.06	.02	.00
☐ 264 Ron Guidry	.60	.28	.06
☐ 265 Ed Kranepool	.09	.04	.01
☐ 266 Charlie Hough	.09	.04	.01
☐ 267 Ted Simmons	.35	.15	.03
☐ 268 Jack Clark	.60	.28	.06
☐ 269 Enos Cabell	.06	.02	.00
☐ 270 Gary Carter	1.50	.70	.15
☐ 271 Sam Ewing	.06	.02	.00
☐ 272 Tom Burgmeier	.06	.02	.00
☐ 273 Freddie Patek	.06	.02	.00
☐ 274 Frank Tanana	.09	.04	.01
☐ 275 Leroy Stanton	.06	.02	.00
☐ 276 Ken Forsch	.09	.04	.01
☐ 277 Ellis Valentine	.09	.04	.01
☐ 278 Greg Luzinski	.25	.10	.02
☐ 279 Rick Bosetti	.06	.02	.00
☐ 280 John Stearns	.09	.04	.01
☐ 281 Enrique Romo	.06	.02	.00
☐ 282 Bob Bailey	.06	.02	.00
☐ 283 Sal Bando	.09	.04	.01
☐ 284 Matt Keough	.09	.04	.01
☐ 285 Biff Pocoroba	.06	.02	.00
☐ 286 Mike Lum	.06	.02	.00
☐ 287 Jay Johnstone	.09	.04	.01
☐ 288 John Montefusco	.09	.04	.01
☐ 289 Ed Ott	.06	.02	.00
☐ 290 Dusty Baker	.20	.09	.02
☐ 291 Rico Carty	.12	.05	.01
☐ 292 Nino Espinosa	.06	.02	.00
☐ 293 Rich Hebner	.06	.02	.00
☐ 294 Cesar Cedeno	.15	.06	.01
☐ 295 Darrell Porter	.12	.05	.01
☐ 296 Rod Gilbreath	.06	.02	.00
☐ 297 Jim Kern	.06	.02	.00
☐ 298 Claudell Washington	.12	.05	.01
☐ 299 Luis Tiant	.15	.06	.01
☐ 300 Mike Parrott	.06	.02	.00
☐ 301 Pete Broberg	.06	.02	.00
☐ 302 Greg Gross	.06	.02	.00
☐ 303 Darold Knowles	.06	.02	.00
☐ 304 Paul Blair	.09	.04	.01
☐ 305 Julio Cruz	.09	.04	.01
☐ 306 Hal McRae	.12	.05	.01
☐ 307 Ken Reitz	.06	.02	.00
☐ 308 Tom Murphy	.06	.02	.00
☐ 309 Terry Whitfield	.06	.02	.00
☐ 310 J.R. Richard	.20	.09	.02
☐ 311 Mike Hargrove	.09	.04	.01
☐ 312 Rick Dempsey	.09	.04	.01
☐ 313 Phil Niekro	.60	.28	.06
☐ 314 Bob Stanley	.12	.05	.01
☐ 315 Jim Spencer	.06	.02	.00
☐ 316 George Foster	.60	.28	.06
☐ 317 Dave LaRoche	.06	.02	.00
☐ 318 Rudy May	.06	.02	.00
☐ 319 Jeff Newman	.06	.02	.00
☐ 320 Rick Monday DP	.06	.02	.00
☐ 321 Omar Moreno	.09	.04	.01
☐ 322 Dave McKay	.06	.02	.00

☐ 323 Mike Schmidt	2.25	1.00	.22
☐ 324 Ken Singleton	.20	.09	.02
☐ 325 Jerry Remy	.06	.02	.00
☐ 326 Bert Campaneris	.12	.05	.01
☐ 327 Pat Zachry	.06	.02	.00
☐ 328 Larry Herndon	.12	.05	.01
☐ 329 Mark Fidrych	.15	.06	.01
☐ 330 Del Unser	.06	.02	.00
☐ 331 Gene Garber	.06	.02	.00
☐ 332 Bake McBride	.09	.04	.01
☐ 333 Jorge Orta	.06	.02	.00
☐ 334 Don Kirkwood	.06	.02	.00
☐ 335 Don Baylor	.50	.22	.05
☐ 336 Bill Robinson	.06	.02	.00
☐ 337 Manny Trillo	.09	.04	.01
☐ 338 Eddie Murray	3.00	1.40	.30
☐ 339 Tom Hausman	.06	.02	.00
☐ 340 George Scott DP	.06	.02	.00
☐ 341 Rick Sweet	.06	.02	.00
☐ 342 Lou Piniella	.15	.06	.01
☐ 343 Pete Rose	3.00	1.40	.30
☐ 344 Stan Papi	.06	.02	.00
☐ 345 Jerry Koosman	.12	.05	.01
☐ 346 Hosken Powell	.06	.02	.00
☐ 347 George Medich	.09	.04	.01
☐ 348 Ron LeFlore DP	.06	.02	.00
☐ 349 Expos Team Checklist	.20	.06	.01
☐ 350 Lou Brock	1.00	.45	.10
☐ 351 Bill North	.06	.02	.00
☐ 352 Jim Hunter DP	.15	.06	.01
☐ 353 Checklist 251-374 DP	.15	.03	.00
☐ 354 Ed Halicki	.06	.02	.00
☐ 355 Tom Hutton	.06	.02	.00
☐ 356 Mike Caldwell	.09	.04	.01
☐ 357 Larry Parrish	.15	.06	.01
☐ 358 Geoff Zahn	.09	.04	.01
☐ 359 Derrel Thomas	.06	.02	.00
☐ 360 Carlton Fisk	.50	.22	.05
☐ 361 John Henry Johnson	.06	.02	.00
☐ 362 Dave Chalk	.06	.02	.00
☐ 363 Dan Meyer DP	.06	.02	.00
☐ 364 Sixto Lezcano	.06	.02	.00
☐ 365 Rennie Stennett	.06	.02	.00
☐ 366 Mike Willis	.06	.02	.00
☐ 367 Buddy Bell DP	.09	.04	.01
☐ 368 Mickey Stanley	.06	.02	.00
☐ 369 Dave Radar	.06	.02	.00
☐ 370 Burt Hooton	.09	.04	.01
☐ 371 Keith Hernandez	1.00	.45	.10
☐ 372 Bill Stein	.06	.02	.00
☐ 373 Hal Dues	.06	.02	.00
☐ 374 Reggie Jackson DP	.75	.35	.07

1980 O-Pee-Chee

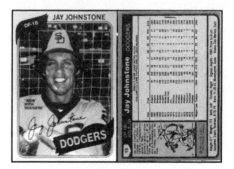

The 1980 baseball set issued by O-Pee-Chee for distribution in Canada contains 374 cards. They are printed on white stock rather than the gray stock used by Topps. The backs contain biographies in both English and French. Cards marked with an asterisk in the checklist denote players with the line "Now with (new team name)" on the front. Color changes, to correspond to the new team are apparent on the pennant, name and frame on the front. Double printed (DP) cards are noted in the checklist below.

	MINT	VG-E	F-G
COMPLETE SET	55.00	25.00	5.00
COMMON PLAYER (1-374)	.08	.03	.01

		MINT	VG-E	F-G
☐	1 Craig Swan	.15	.05	.01
☐	2 Denny Martinez	.08	.03	.01
☐	3 Dave Cash *	.08	.03	.01
☐	4 Bruce Sutter	.35	.15	.03
☐	5 Ron Jackson	.08	.03	.01
☐	6 Balor Moore	.08	.03	.01
☐	7 Dan Ford	.08	.03	.01
☐	8 Pat Putnam	.08	.03	.01
☐	9 Derrel Thomas	.08	.03	.01
☐	10 Jim Slaton	.08	.03	.01
☐	11 Lee Mazzilli	.12	.05	.01
☐	12 Del Unser	.08	.03	.01
☐	13 Mark Wagner	.08	.03	.01
☐	14 Vida Blue	.20	.09	.02
☐	15 Jay Johnstone	.12	.05	.01
☐	16 Julio Cruz DP	.08	.03	.01
☐	17 Tony Scott	.08	.03	.01
☐	18 Jeff Newman DP	.05	.02	.00
☐	19 Luis Tiant	.15	.06	.01
☐	20 Carlton Fisk	.50	.22	.05
☐	21 Dave Palmer	.35	.15	.03
☐	22 Bombo Rivera	.08	.03	.01
☐	23 Bill Fahey	.08	.03	.01
☐	24 Frank White	.15	.06	.01
☐	25 Rico Carty	.12	.05	.01
☐	26 Bill Bonham DP	.05	.02	.00
☐	27 Rick Miller	.08	.03	.01
☐	28 J.R. Richard	.15	.06	.01
☐	29 Joe Ferguson DP	.08	.03	.01
☐	30 Bill Madlock	.50	.22	.05
☐	31 Pete Vuckovich	.15	.06	.01
☐	32 Doug Flynn	.08	.03	.01
☐	33 Bucky Dent	.15	.06	.01
☐	34 Mike Ivie	.08	.03	.01
☐	35 Bob Stanley	.15	.06	.01
☐	36 Al Bumbry	.08	.03	.01
☐	37 Gary Carter	1.25	.60	.12
☐	38 John Milner DP	.05	.02	.00
☐	39 Sid Monge	.08	.03	.01
☐	40 Bill Russell	.12	.05	.01
☐	41 John Stearns	.12	.05	.01
☐	42 Dave Stieb	3.00	1.40	.30
☐	43 Ruppert Jones *	.12	.05	.01
☐	44 Bob Owchinko	.08	.03	.01
☐	45 Ron LeFlore *	.12	.05	.01
☐	46 Ted Sizemore	.08	.03	.01
☐	47 Ted Simmons	.35	.15	.03
☐	48 Pepe Frias *	.08	.03	.01
☐	49 Ken Landreaux	.15	.06	.01
☐	50 Manny Trillo	.12	.05	.01
☐	51 Rick Dempsey	.12	.05	.01
☐	52 Cecil Cooper	.40	.18	.04
☐	53 Bill Lee	.12	.05	.01
☐	54 Victor Cruz	.08	.03	.01
☐	55 Johnny Bench	1.00	.45	.10
☐	56 Rich Dauer	.08	.03	.01
☐	57 Frank Tanana	.12	.05	.01
☐	58 Francisco Barrios	.08	.03	.01
☐	59 Bob Horner	.90	.40	.09
☐	60 Fred Lynn DP	.30	.12	.03
☐	61 Bob Knepper	.15	.06	.01
☐	62 Sparky Lyle	.15	.06	.01
☐	63 Larry Cox	.08	.03	.01
☐	64 Dock Ellis *	.08	.03	.01
☐	65 Phil Garner	.12	.05	.01
☐	66 Greg Luzinski	.25	.10	.02
☐	67 Checklist 1-125	.20	.05	.01
☐	68 Dave Lemanczyk	.08	.03	.01
☐	69 Tony Perez *	.35	.15	.03
☐	70 Gary Thomasson	.08	.03	.01
☐	71 Craig Reynolds	.08	.03	.01
☐	72 Amos Otis	.15	.06	.01
☐	73 Biff Pocoroba	.08	.03	.01
☐	74 Matt Keough	.08	.03	.01
☐	75 Bill Buckner	.20	.09	.02
☐	76 John Castino	.12	.05	.01
☐	77 Rich Gossage	.50	.22	.05
☐	78 Gary Alexander	.08	.03	.01
☐	79 Phil Huffman	.08	.03	.01
☐	80 Bruce Bochte	.12	.05	.01
☐	81 Darrell Evans	.20	.09	.02
☐	82 Terry Puhl	.12	.05	.01
☐	83 Jason Thompson	.15	.06	.01
☐	84 Lary Sorenson	.08	.03	.01
☐	85 Jerry Remy	.08	.03	.01
☐	86 Tony Brizzolara	.08	.03	.01
☐	87 Willie Wilson DP	.20	.09	.02
☐	88 Eddie Murray	2.50	1.15	.25
☐	89 Larry Christenson	.08	.03	.01
☐	90 Bob Randall	.08	.03	.01
☐	91 Greg Pryor	.08	.03	.01
☐	92 Glenn Abbott	.08	.03	.01
☐	93 Jack Clark	.50	.22	.05
☐	94 Rick Waits	.08	.03	.01
☐	95 Luis Gomez *	.08	.03	.01
☐	96 Burt Hooton	.08	.03	.01
☐	97 John Henry Johnson	.08	.03	.01
☐	98 Ray Knight	.15	.06	.01
☐	99 Rick Reuschel	.12	.05	.01
☐	100 Champ Summers	.08	.03	.01
☐	101 Ron Davis	.25	.10	.02
☐	102 Warren Cromartie	.08	.03	.01
☐	103 Ken Reitz	.08	.03	.01
☐	104 Hal McRae	.15	.06	.01
☐	105 Alan Ashby	.08	.03	.01
☐	106 Kevin Kobel	.08	.03	.01
☐	107 Buddy Bell	.18	.08	.01
☐	108 Dave Goltz *	.12	.05	.01
☐	109 John Montefusco	.08	.03	.01
☐	110 Lance Parrish	1.00	.45	.10
☐	111 Mike LaCoss	.08	.03	.01
☐	112 Jim Rice	1.50	.70	.15
☐	113 Steve Carlton	1.50	.70	.15
☐	114 Sixto Lezcano	.08	.03	.01
☐	115 Ed Halicki	.08	.03	.01
☐	116 Jose Morales	.08	.03	.01
☐	117 Dave Concepcion	.18	.08	.01
☐	118 Joe Cannon	.08	.03	.01
☐	119 Willie Montanez *	.08	.03	.01
☐	120 Lou Piniella	.18	.08	.01
☐	121 Bill Stein	.08	.03	.01
☐	122 Dave Winfield	1.25	.60	.12
☐	123 Alan Trammell	.75	.35	.07
☐	124 Andre Dawson	.90	.40	.09
☐	125 Marc Hill	.08	.03	.01
☐	126 Don Aase	.15	.06	.01
☐	127 Dave Kingman	.35	.15	.03
☐	128 Checklist 126-250	.25	.05	.01
☐	129 Dennis Lamp	.08	.03	.01
☐	130 Phil Niekro	.40	.18	.04
☐	131 Tim Foli DP	.05	.02	.00
☐	132 Jim Clancy	.08	.03	.01
☐	133 Bill Atkinson *	.08	.03	.01
☐	134 Paul Dade DP	.05	.02	.00
☐	135 Dusty Baker	.15	.06	.01
☐	136 Al Oliver	.30	.12	.03
☐	137 Dave Chalk	.08	.03	.01
☐	138 Bill Robinson	.08	.03	.01
☐	139 Robin Yount	1.00	.45	.10
☐	140 Dan Schatzeder *	.12	.05	.01
☐	141 Mike Schmidt DP	.75	.35	.07
☐	142 Ralph Garr *	.12	.05	.01
☐	143 Dale Murphy	3.00	1.40	.30
☐	144 Jerry Koosman	.12	.05	.01
☐	145 Tom Veryzer	.08	.03	.01
☐	146 Rick Bosetti	.08	.03	.01
☐	147 Jim Spencer	.08	.03	.01
☐	148 Gaylord Perry	.45	.20	.04
☐	149 Paul Blair	.08	.03	.01
☐	150 Don Baylor	.30	.12	.03
☐	151 Dave Rozema	.08	.03	.01
☐	152 Steve Garvey	1.50	.70	.15
☐	153 Elias Sosa	.08	.03	.01
☐	154 Larry Gura	.12	.05	.01
☐	155 Tim Johnson	.08	.03	.01
☐	156 Steve Henderson	.08	.03	.01
☐	157 Ron Guidry	.50	.22	.05
☐	158 Mike Edwards	.08	.03	.01
☐	159 Butch Wynegar	.12	.05	.01
☐	160 Randy Jones	.12	.05	.01
☐	161 Denny Walling	.08	.03	.01
☐	162 Mike Hargrove	.12	.05	.01
☐	163 Dave Parker	.75	.35	.07
☐	164 Roger Metzger	.08	.03	.01
☐	165 Johnny Grubb	.08	.03	.01
☐	166 Steve Kemp	.15	.06	.01
☐	167 Bob Lacey	.08	.03	.01
☐	168 Chris Speier	.08	.03	.01
☐	169 Dennis Eckersley	.12	.05	.01
☐	170 Keith Hernandez	.90	.40	.09
☐	171 Claudell Washington	.12	.05	.01
☐	172 Tom Underwood *	.08	.03	.01
☐	173 Dan Driessen	.12	.05	.01
☐	174 Al Cowens *	.12	.05	.01
☐	175 Rich Hebner *	.08	.03	.01
☐	176 Willie McCovey	.75	.35	.07
☐	177 Carney Lansford	.30	.12	.03

☐ 178	Ken Singleton	.25	.10	.02	☐ 271	Steve Rogers	.15	.06	.01
☐ 179	Jim Essian	.08	.03	.01	☐ 272	Jim Morrison	.08	.03	.01
☐ 180	Mike Vail	.08	.03	.01	☐ 273	Clint Hurdle	.08	.03	.01
☐ 181	Randy Lerch	.08	.03	.01	☐ 274	Dale Murray	.08	.03	.01
☐ 182	Larry Parrish	.15	.06	.01	☐ 275	Jim Barr	.08	.03	.01
☐ 183	Checklist 251-374	.25	.05	.01	☐ 276	Jim Sundberg DP	.08	.03	.01
☐ 184	George Hendrick	.18	.08	.01	☐ 277	Willie Horton	.12	.05	.01
☐ 185	Bob Davis	.08	.03	.01	☐ 278	Andre Thornton	.15	.06	.01
☐ 186	Gary Matthews	.15	.06	.01	☐ 279	Bob Forsch	.12	.05	.01
☐ 187	Lou Whitaker	.75	.35	.07	☐ 280	Joe Strain	.08	.03	.01
☐ 188	Darrell Porter DP	.08	.03	.01	☐ 281	Rudy May *	.08	.03	.01
☐ 189	Wayne Gross	.08	.03	.01	☐ 282	Pete Rose	3.00	1.40	.30
☐ 190	Bobby Murcer	.20	.09	.02	☐ 283	Jeff Burroughs	.12	.05	.01
☐ 191	Willie Aikens *	.25	.10	.02	☐ 284	Rick Langford	.08	.03	.01
☐ 192	Jim Kern	.08	.03	.01	☐ 285	Ken Griffey	.15	.06	.01
☐ 193	Cesar Cedeno	.15	.06	.01	☐ 286	Bill Nahorodny *	.08	.03	.01
☐ 194	Joel Youngblood	.08	.03	.01	☐ 287	Art Howe	.08	.03	.01
☐ 195	Ross Grimsley	.08	.03	.01	☐ 288	Ed Figueroa	.08	.03	.01
☐ 196	Jerry Mumphrey *	.12	.05	.01	☐ 289	Joe Rudi	.12	.05	.01
☐ 197	Kevin Bell	.08	.03	.01	☐ 290	Alfredo Griffin	.15	.06	.01
☐ 198	Garry Maddox	.12	.05	.01	☐ 291	Dave Lopes	.15	.06	.01
☐ 199	Dave Freisleben	.08	.03	.01	☐ 292	Rick Manning	.08	.03	.01
☐ 200	Ed Ott	.08	.03	.01	☐ 293	Dennis Leonard	.12	.05	.01
☐ 201	Enos Cabell	.08	.03	.01	☐ 294	Bud Harrelson	.08	.03	.01
☐ 202	Pete LaCock	.08	.03	.01	☐ 295	Skip Lockwood *	.08	.03	.01
☐ 203	Fergie Jenkins	.30	.12	.03	☐ 296	Roy Smalley	.12	.05	.01
☐ 204	Milt Wilcox	.12	.05	.01	☐ 297	Kent Tekulve	.12	.05	.01
☐ 205	Ozzie Smith	.50	.22	.05	☐ 298	Scot Thompson	.08	.03	.01
☐ 206	Ellis Valentine	.12	.05	.01	☐ 299	Ken Kravec	.08	.03	.01
☐ 207	Dan Meyer	.08	.03	.01	☐ 300	Blue Jays Checklist	.20	.05	.01
☐ 208	Barry Foote	.08	.03	.01	☐ 301	Scott Sanderson	.12	.05	.01
☐ 209	George Foster	.50	.22	.05	☐ 302	Charlie Moore	.08	.03	.01
☐ 210	Dwight Evans	.35	.15	.03	☐ 303	Nolan Ryan *	1.00	.45	.10
☐ 211	Paul Molitor	.35	.15	.03	☐ 304	Bob Bailor	.08	.03	.01
☐ 212	Tony Solaita	.08	.03	.01	☐ 305	Bob Stinson	.08	.03	.01
☐ 213	Bill North	.08	.03	.01	☐ 306	Al Hrabosky *	.12	.05	.01
☐ 214	Paul Splittorf	.12	.05	.01	☐ 307	Mitchell Page	.08	.03	.01
☐ 215	Bobby Bonds *	.18	.08	.01	☐ 308	Garry Templeton	.20	.09	.02
☐ 216	Butch Hobson	.08	.03	.01	☐ 309	Chet Lemon	.15	.06	.01
☐ 217	Mark Belanger	.12	.05	.01	☐ 310	Jim Palmer	.75	.35	.07
☐ 218	Grant Jackson	.08	.03	.01	☐ 311	Rick Cerone	.12	.05	.01
☐ 219	Tom Hutton DP	.05	.02	.00	☐ 312	Jon Matlack	.12	.05	.01
☐ 220	Pat Zachry	.08	.03	.01	☐ 313	Don Money	.08	.03	.01
☐ 221	Duane Kuiper	.08	.03	.01	☐ 314	Reggie Jackson	1.50	.70	.15
☐ 222	Larry Hisle DP	.08	.03	.01	☐ 315	Brian Downing	.08	.03	.01
☐ 223	Mike Krukow	.12	.05	.01	☐ 316	Woodie Fryman	.08	.03	.01
☐ 224	Johnnie LeMaster	.08	.03	.01	☐ 317	Alan Bannister	.08	.03	.01
☐ 225	Billy Almon *	.08	.03	.01	☐ 318	Ron Reed	.08	.03	.01
☐ 226	Joe Niekro	.15	.06	.01	☐ 319	Willie Stargell	.60	.28	.06
☐ 227	Dave Revering	.08	.03	.01	☐ 320	Jerry Garvin DP	.05	.02	.00
☐ 228	Don Sutton	.40	.18	.04	☐ 321	Cliff Johnson	.08	.03	.01
☐ 229	John Hiller	.12	.05	.01	☐ 322	Doug DeCinces	.20	.09	.02
☐ 230	Alvis Woods	.08	.03	.01	☐ 323	Gene Richards	.08	.03	.01
☐ 231	Mark Fidrych	.15	.06	.01	☐ 324	Joaquin Andujar	.25	.10	.02
☐ 232	Duffy Dyer	.08	.03	.01	☐ 325	Richie Zisk	.12	.05	.01
☐ 233	Nino Espinosa	.08	.03	.01	☐ 326	Bob Grich	.18	.08	.01
☐ 234	Doug Bair	.08	.03	.01	☐ 327	Gorman Thomas	.20	.09	.02
☐ 235	George Brett	2.50	1.15	.25	☐ 328	Chris Chambliss	.12	.05	.01
☐ 236	Mike Torrez	.12	.05	.01	☐ 329	Blue Jays Prospects:	.12	.05	.01
☐ 237	Frank Taveras	.08	.03	.01		Butch Edge			
☐ 238	Bert Blyleven	.25	.10	.02		Pat Kelly			
☐ 239	Willie Randolph	.15	.06	.01		Ted Wilborn			
☐ 240	Mike Sadek DP	.05	.02	.00	☐ 330	Larry Bowa	.15	.06	.01
☐ 241	Jerry Royster	.08	.03	.01	☐ 331	Barry Bonnell *	.12	.05	.01
☐ 242	John Denny *	.20	.09	.02	☐ 332	John Candelaria	.12	.05	.01
☐ 243	Rick Monday	.12	.05	.01	☐ 333	Toby Harrah	.12	.05	.01
☐ 244	Jesse Jefferson	.08	.03	.01	☐ 334	Larry Biittner	.08	.03	.01
☐ 245	Aurelio Rodriguez *	.08	.03	.01	☐ 335	Mike Flanagan	.12	.05	.01
☐ 246	Bob Boone	.12	.05	.01	☐ 336	Ed Kranepool	.08	.03	.01
☐ 247	Cesar Geronimo	.08	.03	.01	☐ 337	Ken Forsch DP	.08	.03	.01
☐ 248	Bob Shirley	.08	.03	.01	☐ 338	John Mayberry	.12	.05	.01
☐ 249	Expos Checklist	.20	.05	.01	☐ 339	Rick Burleson	.12	.05	.01
☐ 250	Bob Watson *	.12	.05	.01	☐ 340	Milt May *	.08	.03	.01
☐ 251	Mickey Rivers	.12	.05	.01	☐ 341	Roy White	.12	.05	.01
☐ 252	Mike Tyson * DP	.05	.02	.00	☐ 342	Joe Morgan	.60	.28	.06
☐ 253	Wayne Nordhagen	.08	.03	.01	☐ 343	Rollie Fingers	.35	.15	.03
☐ 254	Roy Howell	.08	.03	.01	☐ 344	Mario Mendoza	.08	.03	.01
☐ 255	Lee May	.12	.05	.01	☐ 345	Stan Bahnsen	.08	.03	.01
☐ 256	Jerry Martin	.08	.03	.01	☐ 346	Tug McGraw	.15	.06	.01
☐ 257	Bake McBride	.12	.05	.01	☐ 347	Rusty Staub	.15	.06	.01
☐ 258	Silvio Martinez	.08	.03	.01	☐ 348	Tommy John	.30	.12	.03
☐ 259	Jim Mason	.08	.03	.01	☐ 349	Ivan DeJesus	.08	.03	.01
☐ 260	Tom Seaver	1.00	.45	.10	☐ 350	Reggie Smith	.18	.08	.01
☐ 261	Rick Wortham DP	.05	.02	.00	☐ 351	Expos Prospects	.30	.12	.03
☐ 262	Mike Cubbage	.08	.03	.01		Tony Bernazard			
☐ 263	Gene Garber	.12	.05	.01		Randy Miller			
☐ 264	Bert Campaneris	.15	.06	.01		John Tamargo			
☐ 265	Tom Buskey	.08	.03	.01	☐ 352	Floyd Bannister	.12	.05	.01
☐ 266	Leon Roberts	.08	.03	.01	☐ 353	Rod Carew DP	.50	.22	.05
☐ 267	Ron Cey	.25	.10	.02	☐ 354	Otto Velez	.08	.03	.01
☐ 268	Steve Ontiveros	.08	.03	.01	☐ 355	Gene Tenace	.08	.03	.01
☐ 269	Mike Caldwell	.12	.05	.01	☐ 356	Freddie Patek *	.08	.03	.01
☐ 270	Nelson Norman	.08	.03	.01	☐ 357	Elliott Maddox	.08	.03	.01

☐	358	Pat Underwood	.08	.03	.01
☐	359	Graig Nettles	.25	.10	.02
☐	360	Rodney Scott	.08	.03	.01
☐	361	Terry Whitfield	.08	.03	.01
☐	362	Fred Norman *	.08	.03	.01
☐	363	Sal Bando	.12	.05	.01
☐	364	Greg Gross	.08	.03	.01
☐	365	Carl Yastrzemski DP	.60	.28	.06
☐	366	Paul Hartzell	.08	.03	.01
☐	367	Jose Cruz	.20	.09	.02
☐	368	Shane Rawley	.15	.06	.01
☐	369	Jerry White	.08	.03	.01
☐	370	Rick Wise *	.12	.05	.01
☐	371	Steve Yeager	.12	.05	.01
☐	372	Omar Moreno	.08	.03	.01
☐	373	Bump Wills	.08	.03	.01
☐	374	Craig Kusick *	.08	.03	.01

1981 O-Pee-Chee

The O-Pee-Chee baseball series for 1981 consists of 374 cards, with a major emphasis placed on the members of the Blue Jays and Expos. The biography found on the reverse of each card is given in both French and English. In cases where a player changed teams or was traded before press time, a small line of print on the obverse makes note of the change. These cards are asterisked in the checklist below. Double printed (DP) cards are noted in the checklist below.

			MINT	VG-E	F-G
	COMPLETE SET		24.00	11.00	2.00
	COMMON PLAYER		.05	.02	.00
☐	1	Frank Pastore	.05	.02	.00
☐	2	Phil Huffman	.05	.02	.00
☐	3	Len Barker	.08	.03	.01
☐	4	Robin Yount	.45	.20	.04
☐	5	Dave Stieb	.15	.06	.01
☐	6	Gary Carter	.65	.30	.06
☐	7	Butch Hobson *	.05	.02	.00
☐	8	Lance Parrish	.35	.15	.03
☐	9	Bruce Sutter *	.25	.10	.02
☐	10	Mike Flanagan	.08	.03	.01
☐	11	Paul Mirabella	.05	.02	.00
☐	12	Craig Reynolds	.05	.02	.00
☐	13	Joe Charboneau	.08	.03	.01
☐	14	Dan Driessen	.05	.02	.00
☐	15	Larry Parrish	.10	.04	.01
☐	16	Ron Davis	.05	.02	.00
☐	17	Cliff Johnson *	.08	.03	.01
☐	18	Bruce Bochte	.05	.02	.00
☐	19	Jim Clancy	.08	.03	.01
☐	20	Bill Russell	.08	.03	.01
☐	21	Ron Oester	.05	.02	.00
☐	22	Danny Darwin	.05	.02	.00
☐	23	Willie Aikens	.08	.03	.01
☐	24	Don Stanhouse	.05	.02	.00
☐	25	Sixto Lezcano *	.08	.03	.01
☐	26	U.L. Washington	.05	.02	.00
☐	27	Champ Summers DP	.05	.02	.00

☐	28	Enrique Romo	.05	.02	.00
☐	29	Gene Tenace	.05	.02	.00
☐	30	Jack Clark	.20	.09	.02
☐	31	Checklist 1-125 DP	.08	.01	.00
☐	32	Ken Oberkfell	.05	.02	.00
☐	33	Rick Honeycutt *	.10	.04	.01
☐	34	Al Bumbry	.05	.02	.00
☐	35	John Tamargo DP	.03	.01	.00
☐	36	Ed Farmer	.05	.02	.00
☐	37	Gary Roenicke	.08	.03	.01
☐	38	Tim Foli DP	.03	.01	.00
☐	39	Eddie Murray	1.25	.60	.12
☐	40	Roy Howell *	.05	.02	.00
☐	41	Bill Gullickson	.30	.12	.03
☐	42	Jerry White DP	.03	.01	.00
☐	43	Tim Blackwell	.05	.02	.00
☐	44	Steve Henderson	.05	.02	.00
☐	45	Enos Cabell *	.05	.02	.00
☐	46	Rick Bossetti	.05	.02	.00
☐	47	Bill North	.05	.02	.00
☐	48	Rich Gossage	.25	.10	.02
☐	49	Bob Shirley *	.05	.02	.00
☐	50	Dave Lopes	.10	.04	.01
☐	51	Shane Rawley	.10	.04	.01
☐	52	Lloyd Moseby	1.50	.70	.15
☐	53	Burt Hooton	.05	.02	.00
☐	54	Ivan DeJesus	.05	.02	.00
☐	55	Mike Norris	.08	.03	.01
☐	56	Del Unser	.05	.02	.00
☐	57	Dave Revering	.05	.02	.00
☐	58	Joel Youngblood	.05	.02	.00
☐	59	Steve McCatty	.05	.02	.00
☐	60	Willie Randolph	.10	.04	.01
☐	61	Butch Wynegar	.08	.03	.01
☐	62	Gary Lavelle	.05	.02	.00
☐	63	Willie Montanez	.05	.02	.00
☐	64	Terry Puhl	.08	.03	.01
☐	65	Scott McGregor	.08	.03	.01
☐	66	Buddy Bell	.12	.05	.01
☐	67	Toby Harrah	.08	.03	.01
☐	68	Jim Rice	.65	.30	.06
☐	69	Darrell Evans	.15	.06	.01
☐	70	Al Oliver DP	.10	.04	.01
☐	71	Hal Dues	.05	.02	.00
☐	72	Barry Evans DP	.03	.01	.00
☐	73	Doug Bair	.05	.02	.00
☐	74	Mike Hargrove	.05	.02	.00
☐	75	Reggie Smith	.10	.04	.01
☐	76	Mario Mendoza *	.05	.02	.00
☐	77	Mike Barlow	.05	.02	.00
☐	78	Garth Iorg	.05	.02	.00
☐	79	Jeff Reardon	.75	.35	.07
☐	80	Roger Erickson	.05	.02	.00
☐	81	Dave Stapleton	.10	.04	.01
☐	82	Barry Bonnell	.08	.03	.01
☐	83	Dave Concepcion	.12	.05	.01
☐	84	Johnnie Lemaster	.05	.02	.00
☐	85	Mike Caldwell	.08	.03	.01
☐	86	Wayne Gross	.05	.02	.00
☐	87	Rick Camp	.05	.02	.00
☐	88	Joe Lefebvre	.10	.04	.01
☐	89	Darrell Jackson	.05	.02	.00
☐	90	Bake McBride	.08	.03	.01
☐	91	Tim Stoddard DP	.05	.02	.00
☐	92	Mike Easler	.15	.06	.01
☐	93	Jim Bibby	.08	.03	.01
☐	94	Kent Tekulve	.08	.03	.01
☐	95	Jim Sundberg	.08	.03	.01
☐	96	Tommy John	.25	.10	.02
☐	97	Chris Speier	.05	.02	.00
☐	98	Clint Hurdle	.05	.02	.00
☐	99	Phil Garner	.08	.03	.01
☐	100	Rod Carew	.75	.35	.07
☐	101	Steve Stone	.08	.03	.01
☐	102	Joe Niekro	.10	.04	.01
☐	103	Jerry Martin *	.05	.02	.00
☐	104	Ron LeFlore DP *	.05	.02	.00
☐	105	Jose Cruz	.12	.05	.01
☐	106	Don Money	.05	.02	.00
☐	107	Bobby Brown	.05	.02	.00
☐	108	Larry Herndon	.08	.03	.01
☐	109	Dennis Eckersley	.08	.03	.01
☐	110	Carl Yastrzemski	1.00	.45	.10
☐	111	Greg Minton	.08	.03	.01
☐	112	Dan Schatzeder	.08	.03	.01
☐	113	George Brett	1.75	.85	.17
☐	114	Tom Underwood	.05	.02	.00
☐	115	Roy Smalley *	.08	.03	.01
☐	116	Carlton Fisk	.35	.15	.03
☐	117	Pete Falcone	.05	.02	.00
☐	118	Dale Murphy	2.00	.90	.20
☐	119	Tippy Martinez	.08	.03	.01
☐	120	Larry Bowa	.12	.05	.01

☐ 121	Julio Cruz	.05	.02	.00
☐ 122	Jim Gantner	.08	.03	.01
☐ 123	Al Cowens	.08	.03	.01
☐ 124	Jerry Garvin	.05	.02	.00
☐ 125	Andre Dawson	.40	.18	.04
☐ 126	Charlie Leibrandt	.60	.28	.06
☐ 127	Willie Stargell	.35	.15	.03
☐ 128	Andre Thornton	.10	.04	.01
☐ 129	Art Howe	.05	.02	.00
☐ 130	Larry Gura	.08	.03	.01
☐ 131	Jerry Remy	.05	.02	.00
☐ 132	Rick Dempsey	.10	.04	.01
☐ 133	Alan Trammell DP	.15	.06	.01
☐ 134	Mike LaCoss	.05	.02	.00
☐ 135	Gorman Thomas	.15	.06	.01
☐ 136	Expos Future Stars	3.00	1.40	.30
	Tim Raines			
	Roberto Ramos			
	Bobby Pate			
☐ 137	Bill Madlock	.25	.10	.02
☐ 138	Rich Dotson DP	.25	.10	.02
☐ 139	Oscar Gamble	.08	.03	.01
☐ 140	Bob Forsch	.08	.03	.01
☐ 141	Miguel Dilone	.05	.02	.00
☐ 142	Jackson Todd	.05	.02	.00
☐ 143	Dan Meyer	.05	.02	.00
☐ 144	Gary Templeton	.15	.06	.01
☐ 145	Mickey Rivers	.08	.03	.01
☐ 146	Alan Ashby	.05	.02	.00
☐ 147	Dale Berra	.08	.03	.01
☐ 148	Randy Jones *	.08	.03	.01
☐ 149	Joe Nolan	.05	.02	.00
☐ 150	Mark Fidrych	.12	.05	.01
☐ 151	Tony Armas	.15	.06	.01
☐ 152	Steve Kemp	.10	.04	.01
☐ 153	Jerry Reuss	.10	.04	.01
☐ 154	Rick Langford	.05	.02	.00
☐ 155	Chris Chambliss	.08	.03	.01
☐ 156	Bob McClure	.05	.02	.00
☐ 157	John Wathan	.05	.02	.00
☐ 158	John Curtis	.05	.02	.00
☐ 159	Steve Howe	.12	.05	.01
☐ 160	Garry Maddox	.08	.03	.01
☐ 161	Dan Graham	.05	.02	.00
☐ 162	Doug Corbett	.08	.03	.01
☐ 163	Rob Dressler	.05	.02	.00
☐ 164	Bucky Dent	.08	.03	.01
☐ 165	Alvis Woods	.05	.02	.00
☐ 166	Floyd Bannister	.12	.05	.01
☐ 167	Lee Mazilli	.08	.03	.01
☐ 168	Don Robinson DP	.05	.02	.00
☐ 169	John Mayberry	.08	.03	.01
☐ 170	Woodie Fryman	.05	.02	.00
☐ 171	Gene Richards	.05	.02	.00
☐ 172	Rick Burleson *	.10	.04	.01
☐ 173	Bump Wills	.05	.02	.00
☐ 174	Glenn Abbott	.05	.02	.00
☐ 175	Dave Collins	.08	.03	.01
☐ 176	Mike Krukow	.08	.03	.01
☐ 177	Rick Monday	.08	.03	.01
☐ 178	Dave Parker	.35	.15	.03
☐ 179	Rudy May	.05	.02	.00
☐ 180	Pete Rose	2.50	1.15	.25
☐ 181	Elias Sosa	.05	.02	.00
☐ 182	Bob Grich	.12	.05	.01
☐ 183	Fred Norman	.05	.02	.00
☐ 184	Jim Dwyer *	.05	.02	.00
☐ 185	Dennis Leonard	.12	.05	.01
☐ 186	Gary Matthews	.12	.05	.01
☐ 187	Ron Hassey DP	.05	.02	.00
☐ 188	Doug DeCinces	.15	.06	.01
☐ 189	Craig Swan	.05	.02	.00
☐ 190	Cesar Cedeno	.12	.05	.01
☐ 191	Rick Sutcliffe	.35	.15	.03
☐ 192	Kiko Garcia	.05	.02	.00
☐ 193	Pete Vuckovich *	.10	.04	.01
☐ 194	Tony Bernazard *	.10	.04	.01
☐ 195	Keith Hernandez	.45	.20	.04
☐ 196	Jerry Mumphrey	.05	.02	.00
☐ 197	Jim Kern	.05	.02	.00
☐ 198	Jerry Dybzinski	.05	.02	.00
☐ 199	Ken Lowenstein	.05	.02	.00
☐ 200	George Foster	.25	.10	.02
☐ 201	Phil Niekro	.25	.10	.02
☐ 202	Bill Buckner	.15	.06	.01
☐ 203	Steve Carlton	.75	.35	.07
☐ 204	John D'Acquisto *	.05	.02	.00
☐ 205	Rick Reuschel	.08	.03	.01
☐ 206	Dan Quisenberry	.40	.18	.04
☐ 207	Mike Schmidt DP	.60	.28	.06
☐ 208	Bob Watson	.08	.03	.01
☐ 209	Jim Spencer	.05	.02	.00
☐ 210	Jim Palmer	.40	.18	.04

☐ 211	Derrel Thomas	.05	.02	.00
☐ 212	Steve Nicosia	.05	.02	.00
☐ 213	Omar Moreno	.05	.02	.00
☐ 214	Richie Zisk *	.10	.04	.01
☐ 215	Larry Hisle	.08	.03	.01
☐ 216	Mike Torrez	.08	.03	.01
☐ 217	Rich Hebner	.05	.02	.00
☐ 218	Britt Burns	.35	.15	.03
☐ 219	Ken Landreaux	.08	.03	.01
☐ 220	Tom Seaver	.60	.28	.06
☐ 221	Bob Davis *	.05	.02	.00
☐ 222	Jorge Orta	.05	.02	.00
☐ 223	Bobby Bonds	.12	.05	.01
☐ 224	Pat Zachry	.05	.02	.00
☐ 225	Ruppert Jones	.08	.03	.01
☐ 226	Duane Kuiper	.05	.02	.00
☐ 227	Rodney Scott	.05	.02	.00
☐ 228	Tom Paciorek	.05	.02	.00
☐ 229	Rollie Fingers *	.25	.10	.02
☐ 230	George Hendrick	.12	.05	.01
☐ 231	Tony Perez	.18	.08	.01
☐ 232	Grant Jackson	.05	.02	.00
☐ 233	Damaso Garcia	.75	.35	.07
☐ 234	Lou Whitaker	.25	.10	.02
☐ 235	Scott Sanderson	.08	.03	.01
☐ 236	Mike Ivie	.05	.02	.00
☐ 237	Charlie Moore	.05	.02	.00
☐ 238	Blue Jays Rookies	.15	.06	.01
	Luis Leal			
	Brian Milner			
	Ken Schrom			
☐ 239	Rick Miller DP *	.05	.02	.00
☐ 240	Nolan Ryan	.50	.22	.05
☐ 241	Checklist 126-250 DP	.08	.01	.00
☐ 242	Chet Lemon	.10	.04	.01
☐ 243	Dave Palmer	.08	.03	.01
☐ 244	Ellis Valentine	.08	.03	.01
☐ 245	Carney Lansford *	.15	.06	.01
☐ 246	Ed Ott DP	.03	.01	.00
☐ 247	Glenn Hubbard DP	.03	.01	.00
☐ 248	Joey McLaughlin	.05	.02	.00
☐ 249	Jerry Narron	.05	.02	.00
☐ 250	Ron Guidry	.30	.12	.03
☐ 251	Steve Garvey	.80	.40	.08
☐ 252	Victor Cruz	.05	.02	.00
☐ 253	Bobby Murcer	.15	.06	.01
☐ 254	Ozzie Smith	.20	.09	.02
☐ 255	John Stearns	.05	.02	.00
☐ 256	Bill Campbell	.05	.02	.00
☐ 257	Rennie Stennett	.05	.02	.00
☐ 258	Rick Waits	.05	.02	.00
☐ 259	Gary Lucas	.05	.02	.00
☐ 260	Ron Cey	.15	.06	.01
☐ 261	Rickey Henderson	1.25	.60	.12
☐ 262	Sammy Stewart	.05	.02	.00
☐ 263	Brian Downing	.05	.02	.00
☐ 264	Mark Bomback	.05	.02	.00
☐ 265	John Candelaria	.08	.03	.01
☐ 266	Rennie Martin	.05	.02	.00
☐ 267	Stan Bahnsen	.05	.02	.00
☐ 268	Expos Team Checklist	.10	.02	.01
☐ 269	Ken Forsch	.08	.03	.01
☐ 270	Greg Luzinski	.18	.08	.01
☐ 271	Ron Jackson	.05	.02	.00
☐ 272	Wayne Garland	.05	.02	.00
☐ 273	Milt May	.05	.02	.00
☐ 274	Rick Wise	.08	.03	.01
☐ 275	Dwight Evans	.18	.08	.01
☐ 276	Sal Bando	.08	.03	.01
☐ 277	Alfredo Griffin	.12	.05	.01
☐ 278	Rick Sofield	.05	.02	.00
☐ 279	Bob Knepper *	.15	.06	.01
☐ 280	Ken Griffey	.12	.05	.01
☐ 281	Ken Singleton	.12	.05	.01
☐ 282	Ernie Whitt	.05	.02	.00
☐ 283	Billy Sample	.05	.02	.00
☐ 284	Jack Morris	.40	.18	.04
☐ 285	Dick Ruthven	.05	.02	.00
☐ 286	Johnny Bench	.50	.22	.05
☐ 287	Dave Smith	.10	.04	.01
☐ 288	Amos Otis	.12	.05	.01
☐ 289	Dave Goltz	.05	.02	.00
☐ 290	Bob Boone DP	.05	.02	.00
☐ 291	Aurelio Lopez	.05	.02	.00
☐ 292	Tom Hume	.05	.02	.00
☐ 293	Charlie Lea	.20	.09	.02
☐ 294	Bert Blyleven *	.15	.06	.01
☐ 295	Hal McRae	.08	.03	.01
☐ 296	Bob Stanley	.08	.03	.01
☐ 297	Bob Bailor *	.05	.02	.00
☐ 298	Jerry Koosman	.10	.04	.01
☐ 299	Eliott Maddox *	.05	.02	.00
☐ 300	Paul Molitor	.15	.06	.01

□ 301	Matt Keough	.05	.02	.00
□ 302	Pat Putnam	.05	.02	.00
□ 303	Dan Ford	.05	.02	.00
□ 304	John Castino	.08	.03	.01
□ 305	Barry Foote	.05	.02	.00
□ 306	Lou Piniella	.12	.05	.01
□ 307	Gene Garber	.08	.03	.01
□ 308	Rick Manning	.05	.02	.00
□ 309	Don Baylor	.15	.06	.01
□ 310	Vida Blue DP	.08	.03	.01
□ 311	Doug Flynn	.05	.02	.00
□ 312	Rick Rhoden	.08	.03	.01
□ 313	Fred Lynn *	.30	.12	.03
□ 314	Rich Dauer	.05	.02	.00
□ 315	Kirk Gibson	2.25	1.00	.22
□ 316	Ken Reitz *	.05	.02	.00
□ 317	Lonnie Smith	.10	.04	.01
□ 318	Steve Yeager	.08	.03	.01
□ 319	Rowland Office	.05	.02	.00
□ 320	Tom Burgmeier *	.05	.02	.00
□ 321	Leon Durham *	1.50	.70	.15
□ 322	Neil Allen	.08	.03	.01
□ 323	Ray Burris *	.05	.02	.00
□ 324	Mike Willis	.05	.02	.00
□ 325	Ray Knight	.10	.04	.01
□ 326	Rafael Landestoy	.05	.02	.00
□ 327	Moose Haas	.08	.03	.01
□ 328	Ross Baumgarten	.05	.02	.00
□ 329	Joaquin Andujar	.15	.06	.01
□ 330	Frank White	.15	.06	.01
□ 331	Blue Jays Checklist	.10	.03	.01
□ 332	Dick Drago	.05	.02	.00
□ 333	Sid Monge	.05	.02	.00
□ 334	Joe Sambito	.08	.03	.01
□ 335	Rick Cerone	.08	.03	.01
□ 336	Eddie Whitson	.08	.03	.01
□ 337	Sparky Lyle	.10	.04	.01
□ 338	Checklist 251-374	.20	.04	.01
□ 339	Jon Matlack	.08	.03	.01
□ 340	Ben Oglivie	.10	.04	.01
□ 341	Dwayne Murphy	.12	.05	.01
□ 342	Terry Crowley	.05	.02	.00
□ 343	Frank Taveras	.05	.02	.00
□ 344	Steve Rogers	.15	.06	.01
□ 345	Warren Cromartie	.08	.03	.01
□ 346	Bill Caudill	.10	.04	.01
□ 347	Harold Baines	2.25	1.00	.22
□ 348	Frank Lacorte	.05	.02	.00
□ 349	Glenn Hoffman	.10	.04	.01
□ 350	J.R. Richard	.12	.05	.01
□ 351	Otto Velez	.05	.02	.00
□ 352	Ted Simmons *	.20	.09	.02
□ 353	Terry Kennedy *	.12	.05	.01
□ 354	Al Hrabosky	.08	.03	.01
□ 355	Bob Horner	.25	.10	.02
□ 356	Cecil Cooper	.25	.10	.02
□ 357	Bob Welch	.10	.04	.01
□ 358	Paul Moskau	.05	.02	.00
□ 359	Dave Rader *	.05	.02	.00
□ 360	Willie Wilson	.15	.06	.01
□ 361	Dave Kingman DP	.08	.03	.01
□ 362	Joe Rudi *	.08	.03	.01
□ 363	Rich Gale	.05	.02	.00
□ 364	Steve Trout	.05	.02	.00
□ 365	Graig Nettles DP	.08	.03	.01
□ 366	Lamar Johnson	.05	.02	.00
□ 367	Denny Martinez	.05	.02	.00
□ 368	Manny Trillo	.08	.03	.01
□ 369	Frank Tanana *	.08	.03	.01
□ 370	Reggie Jackson	.90	.40	.09
□ 371	Bill Lee	.08	.03	.01
□ 372	Jay Johnstone	.08	.03	.01
□ 373	Jason Thompson	.08	.03	.01
□ 374	Tom Hutton	.05	.02	.00

Montreal Expos
third base **LARRY PARRISH** troisième-but
Card Number 4 of 24 - Carte Numéro 4 de 24
© 1981 O-Pee-Chee Co. Ltd. Printed in Canada - imprimé au Canada

French and English. A distinctive red (Expos) or blue (Blue Jays) border surrounds the player photo.

		MINT	VG-E	F-G
COMPLETE SET		3.50	1.65	.35
COMMON PLAYER		.10	.04	.01
MONTREAL EXPOS (1-12)				
□ 1	Willie Montanez	.10	.04	.01
□ 2	Rodney Scott	.10	.04	.01
□ 3	Chris Speier	.10	.04	.01
□ 4	Larry Parrish	.15	.06	.01
□ 5	Warren Cromartie	.10	.04	.01
□ 6	Andre Dawson	.35	.15	.03
□ 7	Ellis Valentine	.10	.04	.01
□ 8	Gary Carter	.75	.35	.07
□ 9	Steve Rogers	.15	.06	.01
□ 10	Woodie Fryman	.10	.04	.01
□ 11	Jerry White	.10	.04	.01
□ 12	Scott Sanderson	.10	.04	.01
TORONTO BLUE JAYS (13-24)				
□ 13	John Mayberry	.15	.06	.01
□ 14	Damasa Garcia (sic, Damaso)	.20	.09	.02
□ 15	Alfredo Griffin	.15	.06	.01
□ 16	Garth Iorg	.10	.04	.01
□ 17	Alvis Woods	.10	.04	.01
□ 18	Rick Bosetti	.10	.04	.01
□ 19	Barry Bonnell	.10	.04	.01
□ 20	Ernie Whitt	.10	.04	.01
□ 21	Jim Clancy	.15	.06	.01
□ 22	Dave Stieb	.25	.10	.02
□ 23	Otto Velez	.10	.04	.01
□ 24	Lloyd Moseby	.35	.15	.03

1981 O-Pee-Chee Posters

The 24 full-color posters in the 1981 O-Pee-Chee poster insert set were inserted inside the regular wax packs and feature players of the Montreal Expos and the Toronto Blue Jays. These posters are typically found with two folds and measure approximately 4 7/8" by 6 7/8". The posters are blank-backed and are numbered at the bottom in

1982 O-Pee-Chee

The 396 cards in the 1982 O-Pee-Chee baseball card set are the largest "original" set total ever printed by this Canadian firm; the previous high was 374 in 1979, 1980, and 1981. The set contains virtually the same pictures for the players also featured in the 1982 Topps issue, but the photos appear brighter.

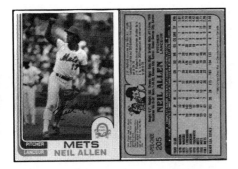

Once again, players who have changed teams will be found with traded lines inside the picture area. There is an emphasis on the two Canadian major league teams and every card shows the player position in both English and French. The reverses have blue print on green and are also bilingual. The O-Pee-Chee logo appears on the front of every card. Super Action (SA) cards are indicated in the checklist below.

		MINT	VG-E	F-G
COMPLETE SET		21.00	9.50	2.10
COMMON PLAYER		.04	.02	.00

☐	1	Dan Spillner	.08	.02	.00
☐	2	Ken Singleton	.12	.05	.01
☐	3	John Candelaria	.08	.03	.01
☐	4	Frank Tanana	.08	.03	.01
☐	5	Reggie Smith	.10	.04	.01
☐	6	Rick Monday	.06	.02	.00
☐	7	Scott Sanderson	.06	.02	.00
☐	8	Rich Dauer	.04	.02	.00
☐	9	Ron Guidry	.25	.10	.02
☐	10	SA: Ron Guidry	.15	.06	.01
☐	11	Tom Brookens	.04	.02	.00
☐	12	Moose Haas	.06	.02	.00
☐	13	Chet Lemon	.08	.03	.01
☐	14	Steve Howe	.06	.02	.00
☐	15	Ellis Valentine	.06	.02	.00
☐	16	Toby Harrah	.06	.02	.00
☐	17	Darrell Evans	.10	.04	.01
☐	18	Johnny Bench	.50	.22	.05
☐	19	Ernie Whitt	.04	.02	.00
☐	20	Garry Maddox	.06	.02	.00
☐	21	Graig Nettles	.15	.06	.01
☐	22	Al Oliver	.15	.06	.01
☐	23	Bob Boone	.06	.02	.00
☐	24	Pete Rose	1.50	.70	.15
☐	25	Jerry Remy	.04	.02	.00
☐	26	Jorge Orta	.04	.02	.00
☐	27	Bobby Bonds	.10	.04	.01
☐	28	Jim Clancy	.06	.02	.00
☐	29	Dwayne Murphy	.08	.03	.01
☐	30	Tom Seaver	.50	.22	.05
☐	31	SA: Tom Seaver	.25	.10	.02
☐	32	Claudell Washington	.08	.03	.01
☐	33	Bob Shirley	.04	.02	.00
☐	34	Bob Forsch	.06	.02	.00
☐	35	Willie Aikens	.06	.02	.00
☐	36	Rod Carew	.50	.22	.05
☐	37	Willie Randolph	.08	.03	.01
☐	38	Charlie Lea	.06	.02	.00
☐	39	Lou Whitaker	.15	.06	.01
☐	40	Dave Parker	.35	.15	.03
☐	41	SA: Dave Parker	.15	.06	.01
☐	42	Mark Belanger	.06	.02	.00
☐	43	Rick Langford	.04	.02	.00
☐	44	Rollie Fingers	.20	.09	.02
☐	45	Rick Cerone	.06	.02	.00
☐	46	Johnny Wockenfuss	.04	.02	.00
☐	47	Jack Morris	.25	.10	.02
☐	48	Cesar Cedeno	.12	.05	.01
☐	49	Alvis Woods	.04	.02	.00
☐	50	Buddy Bell	.12	.05	.01
☐	51	Mickey Rivers	.06	.02	.00
☐	52	Steve Rogers	.12	.05	.01
☐	53	Toronto Blue Jays	.10	.03	.01
☐	54	Ron Hassey	.04	.02	.00

☐	55	Rick Burleson	.08	.03	.01
☐	56	Harold Baines	.30	.12	.03
☐	57	Craig Reynolds	.04	.02	.00
☐	58	Carlton Fisk	.20	.09	.02
☐	59	Jim Kern	.04	.02	.00
☐	60	Tony Armas	.10	.04	.01
☐	61	Warren Cromartie	.06	.02	.00
☐	62	Graig Nettles	.12	.05	.01
☐	63	Jerry Koosman	.08	.03	.01
☐	64	Pat Zachry	.04	.02	.00
☐	65	Terry Kennedy	.10	.04	.01
☐	66	Richie Zisk	.06	.02	.00
☐	67	Rich Gale	.04	.02	.00
☐	68	Steve Carlton	.50	.22	.05
☐	69	Greg Luzinski	.15	.06	.01
☐	70	Tim Raines	.50	.22	.05
☐	71	Roy Lee Jackson	.04	.02	.00
☐	72	Carl Yastrzemski	.75	.35	.07
☐	73	John Castino	.06	.02	.00
☐	74	Joe Niekro	.10	.04	.01
☐	75	Tommy John	.20	.09	.02
☐	76	Dave Winfield	.50	.22	.05
☐	77	Miguel Dilone	.04	.02	.00
☐	78	Gary Gray	.04	.02	.00
☐	79	Tom Hume	.04	.02	.00
☐	80	Jim Palmer	.30	.12	.03
☐	81	SA: Jim Palmer	.15	.06	.01
☐	82	Vida Blue	.10	.04	.01
☐	83	Garth Iorg	.04	.02	.00
☐	84	Rennie Stennett	.04	.02	.00
☐	85	Dave Lopes	.08	.03	.01
☐	86	Dave Concepcion	.12	.05	.01
☐	87	Matt Keough	.04	.02	.00
☐	88	Jim Spencer	.04	.02	.00
☐	89	Steve Henderson	.04	.02	.00
☐	90	Nolan Ryan	.40	.18	.04
☐	91	Carney Lansford	.10	.04	.01
☐	92	Bake McBride	.06	.02	.00
☐	93	Dave Stapleton	.04	.02	.00
☐	94	Montreal Expos	.10	.03	.01
☐	95	Ozzie Smith	.15	.06	.01
☐	96	Rich Hebner	.04	.02	.00
☐	97	Tim Foli	.04	.02	.00
☐	98	Darrell Porter	.06	.02	.00
☐	99	Barry Bonnell	.06	.02	.00
☐	100	Mike Schmidt	.75	.35	.07
☐	101	SA: Mike Schmidt	.30	.12	.03
☐	102	Dan Briggs	.04	.02	.00
☐	103	Al Cowens	.06	.02	.00
☐	104	Grant Jackson	.04	.02	.00
☐	105	Kirk Gibson	.30	.12	.03
☐	106	Dan Schatzeder	.06	.02	.00
☐	107	Juan Berenguer	.04	.02	.00
☐	108	Jack Morris	.30	.12	.03
☐	109	Dave Revering	.04	.02	.00
☐	110	Carlton Fisk	.20	.09	.02
☐	111	SA: Carlton Fisk	.15	.06	.01
☐	112	Billy Sample	.04	.02	.00
☐	113	Steve McCatty	.04	.02	.00
☐	114	Ken Landreaux	.06	.02	.00
☐	115	Gaylord Perry	.20	.09	.02
☐	116	Elias Sosa	.04	.02	.00
☐	117	Rich Gossage	.20	.09	.02
☐	118	Montreal Expos	.10	.03	.01
☐	119	Billy Almon	.04	.02	.00
☐	120	Gary Lucas	.04	.02	.00
☐	121	Ken Oberkfell	.04	.02	.00
☐	122	Steve Carlton	.40	.18	.04
☐	123	Jeff Reardon	.15	.06	.01
☐	124	Bill Buckner	.12	.05	.01
☐	125	Danny Ainge	.10	.04	.01
☐	126	Paul Splittorff	.06	.02	.00
☐	127	Lonnie Smith	.08	.03	.01
☐	128	Rudy May	.04	.02	.00
☐	129	Checklist 1-132	.10	.02	.00
☐	130	Julio Cruz	.04	.02	.00
☐	131	Stan Bahnsen	.04	.02	.00
☐	132	Pete Vuckovich	.06	.02	.00
☐	133	Luis Salazar	.04	.02	.00
☐	134	Dan Ford	.04	.02	.00
☐	135	Denny Martinez	.04	.02	.00
☐	136	Lary Sorensen	.04	.02	.00
☐	137	Fergie Jenkins	.12	.05	.01
☐	138	Rick Camp	.04	.02	.00
☐	139	Wayne Nordhagen	.04	.02	.00
☐	140	Ron LeFlore	.06	.02	.00
☐	141	Rick Sutcliffe	.20	.09	.02
☐	142	Rick Waits	.04	.02	.00
☐	143	Mookie Wilson	.10	.04	.01
☐	144	Greg Minton	.06	.02	.00
☐	145	Bob Horner	.20	.09	.02
☐	146	Joe Morgan	.20	.09	.02
☐	147	Larry Gura	.06	.02	.00

☐ 148	Alfredo Griffin	.08	.03	.01
☐ 149	Pat Putnam	.04	.02	.00
☐ 150	Ted Simmons	.15	.06	.01
☐ 151	Gary Matthews	.10	.04	.01
☐ 152	Greg Luzinski	.15	.06	.01
☐ 153	Mike Flanagan	.08	.03	.01
☐ 154	Jim Morrison	.04	.02	.00
☐ 155	Otto Velez	.04	.02	.00
☐ 156	Frank White	.10	.04	.01
☐ 157	Doug Corbett	.06	.02	.00
☐ 158	Brian Downing	.06	.02	.00
☐ 159	Willie Randolph	.08	.03	.01
☐ 160	Luis Tiant	.10	.04	.01
☐ 161	Andre Thornton	.08	.03	.01
☐ 162	Amos Otis	.08	.03	.01
☐ 163	Paul Mirabella	.04	.02	.00
☐ 164	Bert Blyleven	.12	.05	.01
☐ 165	Rowland Office	.04	.02	.00
☐ 166	Gene Tenace	.04	.02	.00
☐ 167	Cecil Cooper	.15	.06	.01
☐ 168	Bruce Benedict	.04	.02	.00
☐ 169	Mark Clear	.06	.02	.00
☐ 170	Jim Bibby	.06	.02	.00
☐ 171	Ken Griffey	.10	.04	.01
☐ 172	Bill Gullickson	.06	.02	.00
☐ 173	Mike Scioscia	.06	.02	.00
☐ 174	Doug DeCinces	.12	.05	.01
☐ 175	Jerry Mumphrey	.04	.02	.00
☐ 176	Rollie Fingers	.20	.09	.02
☐ 177	George Foster	.20	.09	.02
☐ 178	Mitchell Page	.04	.02	.00
☐ 179	Steve Garvey	.50	.22	.05
☐ 180	SA: Steve Garvey	.25	.10	.02
☐ 181	Woodie Fryman	.04	.02	.00
☐ 182	Larry Herndon	.06	.02	.00
☐ 183	Frank White	.10	.04	.01
☐ 184	Alan Ashby	.04	.02	.00
☐ 185	Phil Niekro	.18	.08	.01
☐ 186	Leon Roberts	.04	.02	.00
☐ 187	Rod Carew	.40	.18	.04
☐ 188	Willie Stargell	.20	.09	.02
☐ 189	Joel Youngblood	.04	.02	.00
☐ 190	J.R. Richard	.10	.04	.01
☐ 191	Tim Wallach	.75	.35	.07
☐ 192	Broderick Perkins	.04	.02	.00
☐ 193	Johnny Grubb	.04	.02	.00
☐ 194	Larry Bowa	.10	.04	.01
☐ 195	Paul Molitor	.12	.05	.01
☐ 196	Willie Upshaw	.15	.06	.01
☐ 197	Roy Smalley	.06	.02	.00
☐ 198	Chris Speier	.04	.02	.00
☐ 199	Don Aase	.08	.03	.01
☐ 200	George Brett	1.00	.45	.10
☐ 201	SA: George Brett	.40	.18	.04
☐ 202	Rick Manning	.04	.02	.00
☐ 203	Toronto Blue Jays	.10	.03	.01
☐ 204	Rick Reuschel	.06	.02	.00
☐ 205	Neil Allen	.06	.02	.00
☐ 206	Leon Durham	.15	.06	.01
☐ 207	Jim Gantner	.06	.02	.00
☐ 208	Joe Morgan	.15	.06	.01
☐ 209	Gary Lavelle	.04	.02	.00
☐ 210	Keith Hernandez	.30	.12	.03
☐ 211	Joe Charboneau	.06	.02	.00
☐ 212	Mario Mendoza	.04	.02	.00
☐ 213	Willie Randolph	.08	.03	.01
☐ 214	Lance Parrish	.25	.10	.02
☐ 215	Mike Krukow	.06	.02	.00
☐ 216	Ron Cey	.10	.04	.01
☐ 217	Ruppert Jones	.06	.02	.00
☐ 218	Dave Lopes	.06	.02	.00
☐ 219	Steve Yeager	.06	.02	.00
☐ 220	Manny Trillo	.06	.02	.00
☐ 221	Dave Concepcion	.10	.04	.01
☐ 222	Butch Wynegar	.06	.02	.00
☐ 223	Lloyd Moseby	.15	.06	.01
☐ 224	Bruce Bochte	.04	.02	.00
☐ 225	Ed Ott	.04	.02	.00
☐ 226	Checklist 133-264	.10	.02	.00
☐ 227	Ray Burris	.04	.02	.00
☐ 228	Reggie Smith	.08	.03	.01
☐ 229	Oscar Gamble	.06	.02	.00
☐ 230	Willie Wilson	.15	.06	.01
☐ 231	Brian Kingman	.04	.02	.00
☐ 232	John Stearns	.04	.02	.00
☐ 233	Duane Kuiper	.04	.02	.00
☐ 234	Don Baylor	.15	.06	.01
☐ 235	Mike Easler	.08	.03	.01
☐ 236	Lou Piniella	.10	.04	.01
☐ 237	Robin Yount	.35	.15	.03
☐ 238	Kevin Saucier	.04	.02	.00
☐ 239	Jon Matlack	.06	.02	.00
☐ 240	Bucky Dent	.08	.03	.01
☐ 241	SA: Bucky Dent	.06	.02	.00
☐ 242	Milt May	.04	.02	.00
☐ 243	Lee Mazzilli	.06	.02	.00
☐ 244	Gary Carter	.40	.18	.04
☐ 245	Ken Reitz	.04	.02	.00
☐ 246	Scott McGregor	.06	.02	.00
☐ 247	Pedro Guerrero	.45	.20	.04
☐ 248	Art Howe	.04	.02	.00
☐ 249	Dick Tidrow	.04	.02	.00
☐ 250	Tug McGraw	.08	.03	.01
☐ 251	Fred Lynn	.25	.10	.02
☐ 252	SA: Fred Lynn	.15	.06	.01
☐ 253	Gene Richards	.04	.02	.00
☐ 254	Jorge Bell	1.50	.70	.15
☐ 255	Tony Perez	.15	.06	.01
☐ 256	SA: Tony Perez	.10	.04	.01
☐ 257	Rich Dotson	.06	.02	.00
☐ 258	Bo Diaz	.06	.02	.00
☐ 259	Rodney Scott	.04	.02	.00
☐ 260	Bruce Sutter	.18	.08	.01
☐ 261	George Brett	.75	.35	.07
☐ 262	Rick Dempsey	.08	.03	.01
☐ 263	Mike Phillips	.04	.02	.00
☐ 264	Jerry Garvin	.04	.02	.00
☐ 265	Al Bumbry	.04	.02	.00
☐ 266	Hubie Brooks	.25	.10	.02
☐ 267	Vida Blue	.10	.04	.01
☐ 268	Rickey Henderson	.50	.22	.05
☐ 269	Rick Peters	.04	.02	.00
☐ 270	Rusty Staub	.08	.03	.01
☐ 271	Sixto Lezcano	.06	.02	.00
☐ 272	Bump Wills	.04	.02	.00
☐ 273	Gary Allenson	.04	.02	.00
☐ 274	Randy Jones	.06	.02	.00
☐ 275	Bob Watson	.06	.02	.00
☐ 276	Dave Kingman	.15	.06	.01
☐ 277	Terry Puhl	.06	.02	.00
☐ 278	Jerry Reuss	.08	.03	.01
☐ 279	Sammy Stewart	.04	.02	.00
☐ 280	Ben Oglivie	.08	.03	.01
☐ 281	Kent Tekulve	.08	.03	.01
☐ 282	Ken Macha	.04	.02	.00
☐ 283	Ron Davis	.06	.02	.00
☐ 284	Bob Grich	.10	.04	.01
☐ 285	Sparky Lyle	.10	.04	.01
☐ 286	Rich Gossage	.18	.08	.01
☐ 287	Dennis Eckersley	.08	.03	.01
☐ 288	Garry Templeton	.12	.05	.01
☐ 289	Bob Stanley	.06	.02	.00
☐ 290	Ken Singleton	.12	.05	.01
☐ 291	Mickey Hatcher	.04	.02	.00
☐ 292	Dave Palmer	.06	.02	.00
☐ 293	Damaso Garcia	.10	.04	.01
☐ 294	Don Money	.04	.02	.00
☐ 295	George Hendrick	.08	.03	.01
☐ 296	Steve Kemp	.10	.04	.01
☐ 297	Dave Smith	.08	.03	.01
☐ 298	Bucky Dent	.08	.03	.01
☐ 299	Steve Trout	.06	.02	.00
☐ 300	Reggie Jackson	.60	.28	.06
☐ 301	SA: Reggie Jackson	.25	.10	.02
☐ 302	Doug Flynn	.04	.02	.00
☐ 303	Wayne Gross	.04	.02	.00
☐ 304	Johnny Bench	.40	.18	.04
☐ 305	Don Sutton	.20	.09	.02
☐ 306	SA: Don Sutton	.10	.04	.01
☐ 307	Mark Bomback	.04	.02	.00
☐ 308	Charlie Moore	.04	.02	.00
☐ 309	Jeff Burroughs	.06	.02	.00
☐ 310	Mike Hargrove	.06	.02	.00
☐ 311	Enos Cabell	.04	.02	.00
☐ 312	Lenny Randle	.04	.02	.00
☐ 313	Ivan DeJesus	.04	.02	.00
☐ 314	Buck Martinez	.04	.02	.00
☐ 315	Burt Hooton	.04	.02	.00
☐ 316	Scott McGregor	.06	.02	.00
☐ 317	Dick Ruthven	.04	.02	.00
☐ 318	Mike Heath	.04	.02	.00
☐ 319	Ray Knight	.08	.03	.01
☐ 320	Chris Chambliss	.06	.02	.00
☐ 321	SA: Chris Chambliss	.04	.02	.00
☐ 322	Ross Baumgarten	.04	.02	.00
☐ 323	Bill Lee	.06	.02	.00
☐ 324	Gorman Thomas	.12	.05	.01
☐ 325	Jose Cruz	.10	.04	.01
☐ 326	Al Oliver	.15	.06	.01
☐ 327	Jackson Todd	.04	.02	.00
☐ 328	Ed Farmer	.04	.02	.00
☐ 329	U.L. Washington	.04	.02	.00
☐ 330	Ken Griffey	.10	.04	.01
☐ 331	John Milner	.04	.02	.00
☐ 332	Don Robinson	.06	.02	.00
☐ 333	Cliff Johnson	.04	.02	.00

☐ 334	Fernando Valenzuela	.50	.22	.05	
☐ 335	Jim Sundberg	.06	.02	.00	
☐ 336	George Foster	.15	.06	.01	

NL ALL-STARS (337-347)

☐ 337	Pete Rose AS	.50	.22	.05
☐ 338	Dave Lopes AS	.06	.02	.00
☐ 339	Mike Schmidt AS	.30	.12	.03
☐ 340	Dave Concepcion AS	.06	.02	.00
☐ 341	Andre Dawson AS	.15	.06	.01
☐ 342	George Foster AS	.12	.05	.01
☐ 343	Dave Parker AS	.15	.06	.01
☐ 344	Gary Carter AS	.20	.09	.02
☐ 345	Fernando Valenzuela AS .	.20	.09	.02
☐ 346	Tom Seaver AS	.20	.09	.02
☐ 347	Bruce Sutter AS	.10	.04	.01
☐ 348	Darrell Porter	.06	.02	.00
☐ 349	Dave Collins	.06	.02	.00
☐ 350	Amos Otis	.08	.03	.01
☐ 351	Frank Taveras	.04	.02	.00
☐ 352	Dave Winfield	.40	.18	.04
☐ 353	Larry Parrish	.08	.03	.01
☐ 354	Roberto Ramos	.04	.02	.00
☐ 355	Dwight Evans	.12	.05	.01
☐ 356	Mickey Rivers	.06	.02	.00
☐ 357	Butch Hobson	.04	.02	.00
☐ 358	Carl Yastrzemski	.40	.18	.04
☐ 359	Ron Jackson	.04	.02	.00
☐ 360	Len Barker	.06	.02	.00
☐ 361	Pete Rose	1.00	.45	.10
☐ 362	Kevin Hickey	.04	.02	.00
☐ 363	Rod Carew	.40	.18	.04
☐ 364	Hector Cruz	.04	.02	.00
☐ 365	Bill Madlock	.15	.06	.01
☐ 366	Jim Rice	.30	.12	.03
☐ 367	Ron Cey	.10	.04	.01
☐ 368	Luis Leal	.06	.02	.00
☐ 369	Dennis Leonard	.08	.03	.01
☐ 370	Mike Norris	.06	.02	.00
☐ 371	Tom Paciorek	.04	.02	.00
☐ 372	Willie Stargell	.15	.06	.01
☐ 373	Dan Driessen	.06	.02	.00
☐ 374	Larry Bowa	.10	.04	.01
☐ 375	Dusty Baker	.10	.04	.01
☐ 376	Joey McLaughlin	.04	.02	.00
☐ 377	Reggie Jackson	.45	.20	.04
☐ 378	Mike Caldwell	.06	.02	.00
☐ 379	Andre Dawson	.20	.09	.02
☐ 380	Dave Stieb	.20	.09	.02
☐ 381	Alan Trammell	.15	.06	.01
☐ 382	John Mayberry	.06	.02	.00
☐ 383	John Wathan	.04	.02	.00
☐ 384	Hal McRae	.08	.03	.01
☐ 385	Ken Forsch	.06	.02	.00
☐ 386	Jerry White	.04	.02	.00
☐ 387	Tom Veryzer	.04	.02	.00
☐ 388	Joe Rudi	.06	.02	.00
☐ 389	Bob Knepper	.10	.04	.01
☐ 390	Eddie Murray	.75	.35	.07
☐ 391	Dale Murphy	.75	.35	.07
☐ 392	Bob Boone	.06	.02	.00
☐ 393	Al Hrabosky	.06	.02	.00
☐ 394	Checklist 265-396	.10	.02	.00
☐ 395	Omar Moreno	.04	.02	.00
☐ 396	Rich Gossage	.15	.06	.01

☐ 2	Damaso Garcia	.20	.09	.02
☐ 3	Ernie Whitt	.10	.04	.01
☐ 4	Lloyd Moseby	.35	.15	.03
☐ 5	Alvis Woods	.10	.04	.01
☐ 6	Dave Stieb	.25	.10	.02
☐ 7	Roy Lee Jackson	.15	.06	.01
☐ 8	Joey McLaughlin	.10	.04	.01
☐ 9	Luis Leal	.10	.04	.01
☐ 10	Aurelio Rodriguez	.10	.04	.01
☐ 11	Otto Velez	.10	.04	.01
☐ 12	Juan Berenger	.15	.06	.01
	(sic, Berenguer)			

MONTREAL EXPOS (13-24)

☐ 13	Warren Cromartie	.10	.04	.01
☐ 14	Rodney Scott	.10	.04	.01
☐ 15	Larry Parrish	.15	.06	.01
☐ 16	Gary Carter	.75	.35	.07
☐ 17	Tim Raines	.75	.35	.07
☐ 18	Andre Dawson	.35	.15	.03
☐ 19	Terry Francona	.15	.06	.01
☐ 20	Steve Rogers	.15	.06	.01
☐ 21	Bill Gullickson	.15	.06	.01
☐ 22	Scott Sanderson	.10	.04	.01
☐ 23	Jeff Reardon	.20	.09	.02
☐ 24	Jerry White	.10	.04	.01

1982 O-Pee-Chee Posters

The 24 full-color posters in the 1982 O-Pee-Chee poster insert set were inserted inside the regular wax packs and feature players of the Montreal Expos and the Toronto Blue Jays. These posters are typically found with two folds and measure approximately 4 7/8" by 6 7/8". The posters are blank-backed and are numbered at the bottom in French and English. A distinctive red (Blue Jays) or blue (Expos) border surrounds the player photo.

	MINT	VG-E	F-G
COMPLETE SET	3.50	1.65	.35
COMMON PLAYER	.10	.04	.01

TORONTO BLUE JAYS (1-12)

☐ 1	John Mayberry	.15	.06	.01

1983 O-Pee-Chee

The 396 cards in the 1983 O-Pee-Chee baseball card set are again very similar to the Topps set of the same year. They are the same size (2 1/2" by 3 1/2") and contain virtually the same pictures for the players also featured in the 1983 Topps American issue. Once again, players who have changed teams will be found with traded lines inside the picture area. Super Veteran (SV) cards are featured as in the Topps set. There is an emphasis on the two Canadian major league teams and every card shows the player position in both English and French. The reverses are also bilingual. The O-Pee-Chee logo

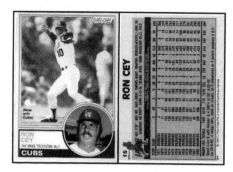

appears on the front of every card.

		MINT	VG-E	F-G
COMPLETE SET		18.00	8.00	1.50
COMMON PLAYER (1-396)		.03	.01	.00

☐ 1	Rusty Staub	.12	.03	.01
☐ 2	Larry Parrish	.08	.03	.01
☐ 3	George Brett	.60	.28	.06
☐ 4	Carl Yastrzemski	.45	.20	.04
☐ 5	SV: Al Oliver	.08	.03	.01
☐ 6	Bill Virdon MGR	.04	.02	.00
☐ 7	Gene Richards	.04	.02	.00
☐ 8	Steve Balboni	.10	.04	.01
☐ 9	Joey McLaughlin	.04	.02	.00
☐ 10	Gorman Thomas	.10	.04	.01
☐ 11	Chris Chambliss	.06	.02	.00
☐ 12	Ray Burris	.03	.01	.00
☐ 13	Larry Herndon	.03	.01	.00
☐ 14	Ozzie Smith	.15	.06	.01
☐ 15	Ron Cey	.10	.04	.01
☐ 16	Willie Wilson	.15	.06	.01
☐ 17	Kent Tekulve	.06	.02	.00
☐ 18	SV: Kent Tekulve	.03	.01	.00
☐ 19	Oscar Gamble	.06	.02	.00
☐ 20	Carlton Fisk	.15	.06	.01
☐ 21	Dale Murphy AS	.25	.10	.02
☐ 22	Randy Lerch	.03	.01	.00
☐ 23	Dale Murphy	.60	.28	.06
☐ 24	Steve Mura	.03	.01	.00
☐ 25	Hal McRae	.06	.02	.00
☐ 26	Dennis Lamp	.03	.01	.00
☐ 27	Ron Washington	.03	.01	.00
☐ 28	Bruce Bochte	.03	.01	.00
☐ 29	Randy Jones	.06	.02	.00
☐ 30	Jim Rice	.25	.10	.02
☐ 31	Bill Gullickson	.06	.02	.00
☐ 32	Dave Concepcion AS	.06	.02	.00
☐ 33	SV: Ted Simmons	.10	.04	.01
☐ 34	Bobby Cox MGR	.03	.01	.00
☐ 35	Rollie Fingers	.18	.08	.01
☐ 36	SV: Rollie Fingers	.10	.04	.01
☐ 37	Mike Hargrove	.06	.02	.00
☐ 38	Roy Smalley	.06	.02	.00
☐ 39	Terry Puhl	.06	.02	.00
☐ 40	Fernando Valenzuela	.25	.10	.02
☐ 41	Garry Maddox	.06	.02	.00
☐ 42	Dale Murray	.03	.01	.00
☐ 43	Bob Dernier	.06	.02	.00
☐ 44	Don Robinson	.06	.02	.00
☐ 45	John Mayberry	.06	.02	.00
☐ 46	Richard Dotson	.06	.02	.00
☐ 47	Wayne Nordhagen	.03	.01	.00
☐ 48	Lary Sorenson	.03	.01	.00
☐ 49	Willie McGee	2.50	1.15	.25
☐ 50	Bob Horner	.20	.09	.02
☐ 51	SV: Rusty Staub	.08	.03	.01
☐ 52	Tom Seaver	.25	.10	.02
☐ 53	Chet Lemon	.06	.02	.00
☐ 54	Scott Sanderson	.06	.02	.00
☐ 55	Mookie Wilson	.06	.02	.00
☐ 56	Reggie Jackson	.40	.18	.04
☐ 57	Tim Blackwell	.03	.01	.00
☐ 58	Keith Moreland	.06	.02	.00
☐ 59	Alvis Woods	.03	.01	.00
☐ 60	Johnny Bench	.35	.15	.03
☐ 61	SV: Johnny Bench	.20	.09	.02
☐ 62	Jim Gott	.08	.03	.01
☐ 63	Rick Monday	.06	.02	.00
☐ 64	Gary Matthews	.08	.03	.01
☐ 65	Jack Morris	.20	.09	.02
☐ 66	Lou Whitaker	.15	.06	.01
☐ 67	U.L. Washington	.03	.01	.00
☐ 68	Eric Show	.10	.04	.01
☐ 69	Lee Lacy	.06	.02	.00
☐ 70	Steve Carlton	.30	.12	.03
☐ 71	SV: Steve Carlton	.15	.06	.01
☐ 72	Tom Paciorek	.03	.01	.00
☐ 73	Manny Trillo	.06	.02	.00
☐ 74	SV: Tony Perez	.08	.03	.01
☐ 75	Amos Otis	.10	.04	.01
☐ 76	Rick Mahler	.06	.02	.00
☐ 77	Hosken Powell	.03	.01	.00
☐ 78	Bill Caudill	.06	.02	.00
☐ 79	Dan Petry	.15	.06	.01
☐ 80	George Foster	.15	.06	.01
☐ 81	Joe Morgan	.20	.09	.02
☐ 82	Burt Hooten	.03	.01	.00
☐ 83	Ryne Sandberg	4.00	1.85	.40
☐ 84	Alan Ashby	.03	.01	.00
☐ 85	Keith Moreland	.06	.02	.00
☐ 86	Tom Hume	.03	.01	.00
☐ 87	Dennis Leonard	.08	.03	.01
☐ 88	Jim Gantner	.06	.02	.00
☐ 89	Leon Roberts	.03	.01	.00
☐ 90	Jerry Reuss	.06	.02	.00
☐ 91	Ben Oglivie	.06	.02	.00
☐ 92	SV: Sparky Lyle	.06	.02	.00
☐ 93	John Castino	.03	.01	.00
☐ 94	Phil Niekro	.15	.06	.01
☐ 95	Alan Trammell	.15	.06	.01
☐ 96	Gaylord Perry	.15	.06	.01
☐ 97	Tom Herr	.08	.03	.01
☐ 98	Vance Law	.03	.01	.00
☐ 99	Dickie Noles	.03	.01	.00
☐ 100	Pete Rose	1.00	.45	.10
☐ 101	SV: Pete Rose	.40	.18	.04
☐ 102	Dave Concepcion	.10	.04	.01
☐ 103	Darrell Porter	.06	.02	.00
☐ 104	Ron Guidry	.20	.09	.02
☐ 105	Don Baylor	.10	.04	.01
☐ 106	Steve Rogers AS	.08	.03	.01
☐ 107	Greg Minton	.06	.02	.00
☐ 108	Glenn Hoffman	.03	.01	.00
☐ 109	Luis Leal	.06	.02	.00
☐ 110	Ken Griffey	.10	.04	.01
☐ 111	Montreal Expos	.10	.03	.01
☐ 112	Luis Pujols	.03	.01	.00
☐ 113	Julio Cruz	.03	.01	.00
☐ 114	Jim Slaton	.03	.01	.00
☐ 115	Chili Davis	.10	.04	.01
☐ 116	Pedro Guerrero	.25	.10	.02
☐ 117	Mike Ivie	.03	.01	.00
☐ 118	Chris Welsh	.03	.01	.00
☐ 119	Frank Pastore	.03	.01	.00
☐ 120	Len Barker	.06	.02	.00
☐ 121	Chris Speier	.03	.01	.00
☐ 122	Bob Murcer	.08	.03	.01
☐ 123	Bill Russell	.06	.02	.00
☐ 124	Lloyd Moseby	.12	.05	.01
☐ 125	Leon Durham	.12	.05	.01
☐ 126	SV: Carl Yastrzemski	.25	.10	.02
☐ 127	John Candelaria	.06	.02	.00
☐ 128	Phil Garner	.06	.02	.00
☐ 129	Checklist 1-132	.10	.02	.00
☐ 130	Dave Stieb	.20	.09	.02
☐ 131	Geoff Zahn	.03	.01	.00
☐ 132	Todd Cruz	.03	.01	.00
☐ 133	Tony Pena	.10	.04	.01
☐ 134	Hubie Brooks	.20	.09	.02
☐ 135	Dwight Evans	.10	.04	.01
☐ 136	Willie Aikens	.06	.02	.00
☐ 137	Woodie Fryman	.03	.01	.00
☐ 138	Rick Dempsey	.06	.02	.00
☐ 139	Bruce Berenyi	.03	.01	.00
☐ 140	Willie Randolph	.06	.02	.00
☐ 141	Eddie Murray	.75	.35	.07
☐ 142	Mike Caldwell	.06	.02	.00
☐ 143	Tony Gwynn	3.50	1.65	.35
☐ 144	SV: Tommy John	.10	.04	.01
☐ 145	Don Sutton	.20	.09	.02
☐ 146	SV: Don Sutton	.10	.04	.01
☐ 147	Rick Manning	.03	.01	.00
☐ 148	George Hendrick	.08	.03	.01
☐ 149	Johnny Ray	.12	.05	.01
☐ 150	Bruce Sutter	.15	.06	.01
☐ 151	SV: Bruce Sutter	.08	.03	.01
☐ 152	Jay Johnstone	.06	.02	.00
☐ 153	Jerry Koosman	.08	.03	.01
☐ 154	Johnnie LeMaster	.03	.01	.00
☐ 155	Dan Quisenberry	.20	.09	.02
☐ 156	Luis Salazar	.03	.01	.00
☐ 157	Steve Bedrosian	.10	.04	.01
☐ 158	Jim Sundberg	.06	.02	.00

☐ 159	SV: Gaylord Perry	.12	.05	.01
☐ 160	Dave Kingman	.12	.05	.01
☐ 161	SV: Dave Kingman	.08	.03	.01
☐ 162	Mark Clear	.06	.02	.00
☐ 163	Cal Ripken	1.00	.45	.10
☐ 164	Dave Palmer	.06	.02	.00
☐ 165	Dan Driessen	.06	.02	.00
☐ 166	Tug McGraw	.08	.03	.01
☐ 167	Denny Martinez	.03	.01	.00
☐ 168	Juan Eichelberger	.03	.01	.00
☐ 169	Doug Flynn	.03	.01	.00
☐ 170	Steve Howe	.06	.02	.00
☐ 171	Frank White	.10	.04	.01
☐ 172	Mike Flanagan	.06	.02	.00
☐ 173	Andre Dawson AS	.12	.05	.01
☐ 174	Manny Trillo AS	.06	.02	.00
☐ 175	Bo Diaz	.03	.01	.00
☐ 176	Dave Righetti	.15	.06	.01
☐ 177	Harold Baines	.20	.09	.02
☐ 178	Vida Blue	.10	.04	.01
☐ 179	SV: Luis Tiant	.06	.02	.00
☐ 180	Rickey Henderson	.50	.22	.05
☐ 181	Rick Rhoden	.06	.02	.00
☐ 182	Fred Lynn	.25	.10	.02
☐ 183	Ed Vande Berg	.08	.03	.01
☐ 184	Dwayne Murphy	.06	.02	.00
☐ 185	Tim Lollar	.03	.01	.00
☐ 186	Dave Tobik	.03	.01	.00
☐ 187	SV: Tug McGraw	.06	.02	.00
☐ 188	Rick Miller	.03	.01	.00
☐ 189	Dan Schatzeder	.06	.02	.00
☐ 190	Cecil Cooper	.12	.05	.01
☐ 191	Jim Beattie	.03	.01	.00
☐ 192	Rich Dauer	.03	.01	.00
☐ 193	Al Cowens	.06	.02	.00
☐ 194	Roy Lee Jackson	.03	.01	.00
☐ 195	Mike Gates	.03	.01	.00
☐ 196	Tommy John	.20	.09	.02
☐ 197	Bob Forsch	.06	.02	.00
☐ 198	Steve Garvey	.40	.18	.04
☐ 199	Brad Mills	.04	.02	.00
☐ 200	Rod Carew	.35	.15	.03
☐ 201	SV: Rod Carew	.20	.09	.02
☐ 202	Toronto Blue Jays	.10	.03	.01
☐ 203	Floyd Bannister	.06	.02	.00
☐ 204	Bruce Benedict	.03	.01	.00
☐ 205	Dave Parker	.25	.10	.02
☐ 206	Ken Oberkfell	.03	.01	.00
☐ 207	SV: Graig Nettles	.08	.03	.01
☐ 208	Sparky Lyle	.08	.03	.01
☐ 209	Jason Thompson	.06	.02	.00
☐ 210	Jack Clark	.15	.06	.01
☐ 211	Jim Kaat	.12	.05	.01
☐ 212	John Stearns	.03	.01	.00
☐ 213	Tom Burgmeier	.03	.01	.00
☐ 214	Jerry White	.03	.01	.00
☐ 215	Mario Soto	.08	.03	.01
☐ 216	Scott McGregor	.06	.02	.00
☐ 217	Tim Stoddard	.03	.01	.00
☐ 218	Bill Laskey	.03	.01	.00
☐ 219	SV: Reggie Jackson	.25	.10	.02
☐ 220	Dusty Baker	.10	.04	.01
☐ 221	Joe Niekro	.08	.03	.01
☐ 222	Damaso Garcia	.08	.03	.01
☐ 223	John Montefusco	.03	.01	.00
☐ 224	Mickey Rivers	.06	.02	.00
☐ 225	Enos Cabell	.03	.01	.00
☐ 226	LaMarr Hoyt	.10	.04	.01
☐ 227	Tim Raines	.35	.15	.03
☐ 228	Joaquin Andujar	.15	.06	.01
☐ 229	Tim Wallach	.12	.05	.01
☐ 230	Fergie Jenkins	.12	.05	.01
☐ 231	SV: Fergie Jenkins	.08	.03	.01
☐ 232	Tom Brunansky	.25	.10	.02
☐ 233	Ivan DeJesus	.03	.01	.00
☐ 234	Bryn Smith	.06	.02	.00
☐ 235	Claudell Washington	.08	.03	.01
☐ 236	Steve Renko	.03	.01	.00
☐ 237	Dan Norman	.03	.01	.00
☐ 238	Cesar Cedeno	.10	.04	.01
☐ 239	Dave Stapleton	.03	.01	.00
☐ 240	Rich Gossage	.15	.06	.01
☐ 241	SV: Rich Gossage	.10	.04	.01
☐ 242	Bob Stanley	.06	.02	.00
☐ 243	Rich Gale	.03	.01	.00
☐ 244	Sixto Lezcano	.03	.01	.00
☐ 245	Steve Sax	.15	.06	.01
☐ 246	Jerry Mumphrey	.03	.01	.00
☐ 247	Dave Smith	.06	.02	.00
☐ 248	Bake McBride	.06	.02	.00
☐ 249	Checklist 133-264	.10	.02	.00
☐ 250	Bill Buckner	.12	.05	.01
☐ 251	Kent Hrbek	.25	.10	.02
☐ 252	Gene Tenace	.03	.01	.00
☐ 253	Charlie Lea	.06	.02	.00
☐ 254	Rick Cerone	.06	.02	.00
☐ 255	Gene Garber	.03	.01	.00
☐ 256	SV: Gene Garber	.03	.01	.00
☐ 257	Jesse Barfield	.30	.12	.03
☐ 258	Dave Winfield	.35	.15	.03
☐ 259	Don Money	.03	.01	.00
☐ 260	Steve Kemp	.08	.03	.01
☐ 261	Steve Yeager	.06	.02	.00
☐ 262	Keith Hernandez	.25	.10	.02
☐ 263	Tippy Martinez	.03	.01	.00
☐ 264	SV: Joe Morgan	.10	.04	.01
☐ 265	Joel Youngblood	.03	.01	.00
☐ 266	Bruce Sutter AS	.10	.04	.01
☐ 267	Terry Francona	.06	.02	.00
☐ 268	Neil Allen	.06	.02	.00
☐ 269	Ron Oester	.03	.01	.00
☐ 270	Dennis Eckersley	.06	.02	.00
☐ 271	Dale Berra	.06	.02	.00
☐ 272	Al Bumbry	.03	.01	.00
☐ 273	Lonnie Smith	.08	.03	.01
☐ 274	Terry Kennedy	.08	.03	.01
☐ 275	Ray Knight	.08	.03	.01
☐ 276	Mike Norris	.06	.02	.00
☐ 277	Rance Mulliniks	.06	.02	.00
☐ 278	Dan Spillner	.03	.01	.00
☐ 279	Bucky Dent	.08	.03	.01
☐ 280	Bert Blyleven	.12	.05	.01
☐ 281	Barry Bonnell	.03	.01	.00
☐ 282	Reggie Smith	.08	.03	.01
☐ 283	SV: Reggie Smith	.06	.02	.00
☐ 284	Ted Simmons	.12	.05	.01
☐ 285	Lance Parrish	.20	.09	.02
☐ 286	Larry Christenson	.03	.01	.00
☐ 287	Ruppert Jones	.06	.02	.00
☐ 288	Bob Welch	.06	.02	.00
☐ 289	John Wathan	.03	.01	.00
☐ 290	Jeff Reardon	.08	.03	.01
☐ 291	Dave Revering	.03	.01	.00
☐ 292	Craig Swan	.03	.01	.00
☐ 293	Graig Nettles	.15	.06	.01
☐ 294	Alfredo Griffin	.08	.03	.01
☐ 295	Jerry Remy	.03	.01	.00
☐ 296	Joe Sambito	.06	.02	.00
☐ 297	Ron LeFlore	.06	.02	.00
☐ 298	Brian Downing	.03	.01	.00
☐ 299	Jim Palmer	.25	.10	.02
☐ 300	Mike Schmidt	.35	.15	.03
☐ 301	SV: Mike Schmidt	.20	.09	.02
☐ 302	Ernie Whitt	.03	.01	.00
☐ 303	Andre Dawson	.20	.09	.02
☐ 304	SV: Bobby Murcer	.06	.02	.00
☐ 305	Larry Bowa	.08	.03	.01
☐ 306	Lee Mazzilli	.06	.02	.00
☐ 307	Lou Piniella	.08	.03	.01
☐ 308	Buck Martinez	.03	.01	.00
☐ 309	Jerry Martin	.03	.01	.00
☐ 310	Greg Luzinski	.12	.05	.01
☐ 311	Al Oliver	.15	.06	.01
☐ 312	Mike Torrez	.06	.02	.00
☐ 313	Dick Ruthven	.03	.01	.00
☐ 314	Gary Carter AS	.20	.09	.02
☐ 315	Rick Burleson	.06	.02	.00
☐ 316	SV: Phil Niekro	.12	.05	.01
☐ 317	Moose Haas	.06	.02	.00
☐ 318	Carney Lansford	.10	.04	.01
☐ 319	Tim Foli	.03	.01	.00
☐ 320	Steve Rogers	.08	.03	.01
☐ 321	Kirk Gibson	.25	.10	.02
☐ 322	Glenn Hubbard	.03	.01	.00
☐ 323	Luis DeLeon	.03	.01	.00
☐ 324	Mike Marshall	.15	.06	.01
☐ 325	Von Hayes	.15	.06	.01
☐ 326	Garth Iorg	.03	.01	.00
☐ 327	Jose Cruz	.10	.04	.01
☐ 328	SV: Jim Palmer	.12	.05	.01
☐ 329	Darrell Evans	.10	.04	.01
☐ 330	Buddy Bell	.10	.04	.01
☐ 331	Mike Krukow	.06	.02	.00
☐ 332	Omar Moreno	.03	.01	.00
☐ 333	Dave Laroche	.03	.01	.00
☐ 334	SV: Dave LaRoche	.03	.01	.00
☐ 335	Bill Madlock	.12	.05	.01
☐ 336	Garry Templeton	.08	.03	.01
☐ 337	John Lowenstein	.03	.01	.00
☐ 338	Willie Upshaw	.08	.03	.01
☐ 339	Dave Hostetler	.06	.02	.00
☐ 340	Larry Gura	.06	.02	.00
☐ 341	Doug DeCinces	.10	.04	.01
☐ 342	Mike Schmidt AS	.20	.09	.02
☐ 343	Charlie Hough	.06	.02	.00
☐ 344	Andre Thornton	.08	.03	.01

☐ 345	Jim Clancy	.06	.02	.00
☐ 346	Ken Forsch	.06	.02	.00
☐ 347	Sammy Stewart	.03	.01	.00
☐ 348	Alan Bannister	.03	.01	.00
☐ 349	Checklist 265-396	.10	.02	.00
☐ 350	Robin Yount	.30	.12	.03
☐ 351	Warren Cromartie	.06	.02	.00
☐ 352	Tim Raines AS	.12	.05	.01
☐ 353	Tony Armas	.10	.04	.01
☐ 354	SV: Tom Seaver	.15	.06	.01
☐ 355	Tony Perez	.15	.06	.01
☐ 356	Toby Harrah	.06	.02	.00
☐ 357	Dan Ford	.03	.01	.00
☐ 358	Charlie Puleo	.03	.01	.00
☐ 359	Dave Collins	.06	.02	.00
☐ 360	Nolan Ryan	.30	.12	.03
☐ 361	SV: Nolan Ryan	.15	.06	.01
☐ 362	Bill Almon	.03	.01	.00
☐ 363	Eddie Milner	.03	.01	.00
☐ 364	Gary Lucas	.03	.01	.00
☐ 365	Dave Lopes	.06	.02	.00
☐ 366	Bob Boone	.06	.02	.00
☐ 367	Biff Pocoroba	.03	.01	.00
☐ 368	Richie Zisk	.06	.02	.00
☐ 369	Tony Bernazard	.06	.02	.00
☐ 370	Gary Carter	.30	.12	.03
☐ 371	Paul Molitor	.10	.04	.01
☐ 372	Art Howe	.03	.01	.00
☐ 373	Pete Rose AS	.25	.10	.02
☐ 374	Glenn Adams	.03	.01	.00
☐ 375	Pete Vukovich	.06	.02	.00
☐ 376	Gary Lavelle	.03	.01	.00
☐ 377	Lee May	.06	.02	.00
☐ 378	SV: Lee May	.03	.01	.00
☐ 379	Butch Wynegar	.06	.02	.00
☐ 380	Ron Davis	.06	.02	.00
☐ 381	Bob Grich	.08	.03	.01
☐ 382	Gary Roenicke	.03	.01	.00
☐ 383	Jim Kaat	.10	.04	.01
☐ 384	Steve Carlton AS	.15	.06	.01
☐ 385	Mike Easler	.08	.03	.01
☐ 386	Rod Carew AS	.15	.06	.01
☐ 387	Bobby Grich AS	.06	.02	.00
☐ 388	George Brett AS	.20	.09	.02
☐ 389	Robin Yount AS	.15	.06	.01
☐ 390	Reggie Jackson AS	.15	.06	.01
☐ 391	Rickey Henderson AS	.15	.06	.01
☐ 392	Fred Lynn AS	.10	.04	.01
☐ 393	Carlton Fisk AS	.10	.04	.01
☐ 394	Pete Vukovich AS	.06	.02	.00
☐ 395	Larry Gura AS	.06	.02	.00
☐ 396	Dan Quisenberry AS	.08	.03	.01

1984 O-Pee-Chee

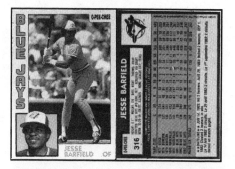

The 396 cards in the 1984 O-Pee-Chee baseball card set are again very similar to the Topps set of the same year. They are the same size (2 1/2" by 3 1/2") and contain virtually the same pictures for the players also featured in the 1984 Topps American issue. Once again, players who have changed teams will be found with traded lines inside the picture area. There is an emphasis on the two Canadian major league teams and every card shows the player position in both English and French. The reverses are also bilingual. The O-Pee-Chee logo appears on the front of every card.

		MINT	VG-E	F-G
COMPLETE SET		18.00	8.00	1.50
COMMON PLAYER (1-396)		.03	.01	.00

☐ 1	Pascual Perez	.07	.01	.00
☐ 2	Cal Ripken	.50	.22	.05
☐ 3	Lloyd Moseby	.10	.04	.01
☐ 4	Mel Hall	.10	.04	.01
☐ 5	Willie Wilson	.12	.05	.01
☐ 6	Mike Morgan	.03	.01	.00
☐ 7	Gary Lucas	.03	.01	.00
☐ 8	Don Mattingly	8.00	3.75	.80
☐ 9	Jim Gott	.06	.02	.00
☐ 10	Robin Yount	.30	.12	.03
☐ 11	Joey McLaughlin	.03	.01	.00
☐ 12	Billy Sample	.03	.01	.00
☐ 13	Oscar Gamble	.06	.02	.00
☐ 14	Bill Russell	.06	.02	.00
☐ 15	Burt Hooton	.03	.01	.00
☐ 16	Omar Moreno	.03	.01	.00
☐ 17	Dave Lopes	.06	.02	.00
☐ 18	Dale Berra	.03	.01	.00
☐ 19	Rance Mulliniks	.03	.01	.00
☐ 20	Greg Luzinski	.10	.04	.01
☐ 21	Doug Sisk	.10	.04	.01
☐ 22	Don Robinson	.06	.02	.00
☐ 23	Keith Moreland	.06	.02	.00
☐ 24	Richard Dotson	.06	.02	.00
☐ 25	Glenn Hubbard	.03	.01	.00
☐ 26	Rod Carew	.30	.12	.03
☐ 27	Alan Wiggins	.06	.02	.00
☐ 28	Frank Viola	.08	.03	.01
☐ 29	Phil Niekro	.15	.06	.01
☐ 30	Wade Boggs	.90	.40	.09
☐ 31	Dave Parker	.25	.10	.02
☐ 32	Bobby Ramos	.03	.01	.00
☐ 33	Tom Burgmeier	.03	.01	.00
☐ 34	Eddie Milner	.03	.01	.00
☐ 35	Don Sutton	.15	.06	.01
☐ 36	Glenn Wilson	.10	.04	.01
☐ 37	Mike Krukow	.06	.02	.00
☐ 38	Dave Collins	.06	.02	.00
☐ 39	Garth Lorg	.03	.01	.00
☐ 40	Dusty Baker	.08	.03	.01
☐ 41	Tony Bernazard	.06	.02	.00
☐ 42	Claudell Washington	.06	.02	.00
☐ 43	Cecil Cooper	.12	.05	.01
☐ 44	Dan Driessen	.06	.02	.00
☐ 45	Jerry Mumphrey	.03	.01	.00
☐ 46	Rick Rhoden	.06	.02	.00
☐ 47	Rudy Law	.03	.01	.00
☐ 48	Julio Franco	.12	.05	.01
☐ 49	Mike Norris	.06	.02	.00
☐ 50	Chris Chambliss	.06	.02	.00
☐ 51	Pete Falcone	.03	.01	.00
☐ 52	Mike Marshall	.15	.06	.01
☐ 53	Amos Otis	.08	.03	.01
☐ 54	Jesse Orosco	.08	.03	.01
☐ 55	Dave Concepcion	.10	.04	.01
☐ 56	Gary Allenson	.03	.01	.00
☐ 57	Dan Schatzeder	.03	.01	.00
☐ 58	Jerry Remy	.03	.01	.00
☐ 59	Carney Lansford	.10	.04	.01
☐ 60	Paul Molitor	.10	.04	.01
☐ 61	Chris Codiroli	.03	.01	.00
☐ 62	Dave Hostetler	.03	.01	.00
☐ 63	Ed VandeBerg	.03	.01	.00
☐ 64	Ryne Sandberg	.40	.18	.04
☐ 65	Kirk Gibson	.25	.10	.02
☐ 66	Nolan Ryan	.25	.10	.02
☐ 67	Gary Ward	.06	.02	.00
☐ 68	Luis Salazar	.03	.01	.00
☐ 69	Dan Quisenberry	.15	.06	.01
☐ 70	Gary Matthews	.06	.02	.00
☐ 71	Pete O'Brien	.50	.22	.05
☐ 72	John Wathan	.03	.01	.00
☐ 73	Jody Davis	.10	.04	.01
☐ 74	Kent Tekulve	.06	.02	.00
☐ 75	Bob Forsch	.06	.02	.00
☐ 76	Alfredo Griffin	.06	.02	.00
☐ 77	Bryn Smith	.06	.02	.00
☐ 78	Mike Torrez	.06	.02	.00
☐ 79	Mike Hargrove	.06	.02	.00
☐ 80	Steve Rogers	.08	.03	.01
☐ 81	Bake McBride	.06	.02	.00
☐ 82	Doug DeCinces	.10	.04	.01
☐ 83	Richie Zisk	.06	.02	.00

☐	84	Randy Bush	.03	.01	.00
☐	85	Atlee Hammaker	.06	.02	.00
☐	86	Chet Lemon	.06	.02	.00
☐	87	Frank Pastore	.03	.01	.00
☐	88	Alan Trammell	.15	.06	.01
☐	89	Terry Francona	.06	.02	.00
☐	90	Pedro Guerrero	.25	.10	.02
☐	91	Dan Spillner	.03	.01	.00
☐	92	Lloyd Moseby	.10	.04	.01
☐	93	Bob Knepper	.10	.04	.01
☐	94	Ted Simmons	.10	.04	.01
☐	95	Aurelio Lopez	.03	.01	.00
☐	96	Bill Buckner	.10	.04	.01
☐	97	LaMarr Hoyt	.10	.04	.01
☐	98	Tom Brunansky	.15	.06	.01
☐	99	Ron Oester	.03	.01	.00
☐	100	Reggie Jackson	.40	.18	.04
☐	101	Ron Davis	.06	.02	.00
☐	102	Ken Oberkfell	.03	.01	.00
☐	103	Dwayne Murphy	.08	.03	.01
☐	104	Jim Slaton	.03	.01	.00
☐	105	Tony Armas	.10	.04	.01
☐	106	Ernie Whitt	.03	.01	.00
☐	107	Johnnie LeMaster	.03	.01	.00
☐	108	Randy Moffitt	.03	.01	.00
☐	109	Terry Forster	.06	.02	.00
☐	110	Ron Guidry	.20	.09	.02
☐	111	Bill Virdon MGR	.03	.01	.00
☐	112	Doyle Alexander	.06	.02	.00
☐	113	Lonnie Smith	.06	.02	.00
☐	114	Checklist	.08	.01	.00
☐	115	Andre Thornton	.08	.03	.01
☐	116	Jeff Reardon	.08	.03	.01
☐	117	Tom Herr	.08	.03	.01
☐	118	Charlie Hough	.06	.02	.00
☐	119	Phil Garner	.06	.02	.00
☐	120	Keith Hernandez	.25	.10	.02
☐	121	Rich Gossage	.15	.06	.01
☐	122	Ted Simmons	.10	.04	.01
☐	123	Butch Wynegar	.06	.02	.00
☐	124	Damaso Garcia	.08	.03	.01
☐	125	Britt Burns	.06	.02	.00
☐	126	Bert Blyleven	.10	.04	.01
☐	127	Carlton Fisk	.12	.05	.01
☐	128	Rick Manning	.03	.01	.00
☐	129	Bill Laskey	.03	.01	.00
☐	130	Ozzie Smith	.12	.05	.01
☐	131	Bo Diaz	.03	.01	.00
☐	132	Tom Paciorek	.03	.01	.00
☐	133	Dave Rozema	.03	.01	.00
☐	134	Dave Stieb	.15	.06	.01
☐	135	Brian Downing	.03	.01	.00
☐	136	Rick Camp	.03	.01	.00
☐	137	Willie Aikens	.06	.02	.00
☐	138	Charlie Moore	.03	.01	.00
☐	139	George Frazier	.03	.01	.00
☐	140	Storm Davis	.08	.03	.01
☐	141	Glenn Hoffman	.03	.01	.00
☐	142	Charlie Lea	.06	.02	.00
☐	143	Mike Vail	.03	.01	.00
☐	144	Steve Sax	.12	.05	.01
☐	145	Gary Lavelle	.03	.01	.00
☐	146	Gorman Thomas	.12	.05	.01
☐	147	Dan Petry	.12	.05	.01
☐	148	Mark Clear	.06	.02	.00
☐	149	Dave Beard	.03	.01	.00
☐	150	Dale Murphy	.50	.22	.05
☐	151	Steve Trout	.06	.02	.00
☐	152	Tony Pena	.10	.04	.01
☐	153	Geoff Zahn	.03	.01	.00
☐	154	Dave Henderson	.06	.02	.00
☐	155	Frank White	.08	.03	.01
☐	156	Dick Ruthven	.03	.01	.00
☐	157	Gary Gaetti	.08	.03	.01
☐	158	Lance Parrish	.20	.09	.02
☐	159	Joe Price	.03	.01	.00
☐	160	Mario Soto	.06	.02	.00
☐	161	Tug McGraw	.06	.02	.00
☐	162	Bob Ojeda	.08	.03	.01
☐	163	George Hendrick	.06	.02	.00
☐	164	Scott Sanderson	.06	.02	.00
☐	165	Ken Singleton	.08	.03	.01
☐	166	Terry Kennedy	.08	.03	.01
☐	167	Gene Garber	.03	.01	.00
☐	168	Juan Bonilla	.03	.01	.00
☐	169	Larry Parrish	.06	.02	.00
☐	170	Jerry Reuss	.06	.02	.00
☐	171	John Tudor	.12	.05	.01
☐	172	Dave Kingman	.35	.15	.03
☐	173	Garry Templeton	.08	.03	.01
☐	174	Bob Boone	.06	.02	.00
☐	175	Graig Nettles	.12	.05	.01
☐	176	Lee Smith	.08	.03	.01
☐	177	LaMarr Hoyt	.08	.03	.01
☐	178	Bill Krueger	.03	.01	.00
☐	179	Buck Martinez	.03	.01	.00
☐	180	Manny Trillo	.06	.02	.00
☐	181	Lou Whitaker	.15	.06	.01
☐	182	Darryl Strawberry	4.00	1.85	.40
☐	183	Neil Allen	.06	.02	.00
☐	184	Jim Rice	.30	.12	.03
☐	185	Sixto Lezcano	.03	.01	.00
☐	186	Tom Hume	.03	.01	.00
☐	187	Garry Maddox	.06	.02	.00
☐	188	Bryan Little	.03	.01	.00
☐	189	Jose Cruz	.10	.04	.01
☐	190	Ben Oglivie	.06	.02	.00
☐	191	Cesar Cedeno	.08	.03	.01
☐	192	Nick Esasky	.25	.10	.02
☐	193	Ken Forsch	.03	.01	.00
☐	194	Jim Palmer	.25	.10	.02
☐	195	Jack Morris	.20	.09	.02
☐	196	Steve Howe	.03	.01	.00
☐	197	Harold Baines	.15	.06	.01
☐	198	Bill Doran	.45	.20	.04
☐	199	Willie Hernandez	.12	.05	.01
☐	200	Andre Dawson	.20	.09	.02
☐	201	Bruce Kison	.03	.01	.00
☐	202	Bobby Cox MGR	.03	.01	.00
☐	203	Matt Keough	.03	.01	.00
☐	204	Ron Guidry	.20	.09	.02
☐	205	Greg Minton	.03	.01	.00
☐	206	Al Holland	.03	.01	.00
☐	207	Luis Leal	.03	.01	.00
☐	208	Jose Oquendo	.03	.01	.00
☐	209	Leon Durham	.12	.05	.01
☐	210	Joe Morgan	.15	.06	.01
☐	211	Lou Whitaker	.15	.06	.01
☐	212	George Brett	.35	.15	.03
☐	213	Bruce Hurst	.06	.02	.00
☐	214	Steve Carlton	.30	.12	.03
☐	215	Tippy Martinez	.03	.01	.00
☐	216	Ken Landreaux	.06	.02	.00
☐	217	Alan Ashby	.03	.01	.00
☐	218	Dennis Eckersley	.06	.02	.00
☐	219	Craig McMurtry	.06	.02	.00
☐	220	Fernando Valenzuela	.25	.10	.02
☐	221	Cliff Johnson	.03	.01	.00
☐	222	Rick Honeycutt	.06	.02	.00
☐	223	George Brett	.35	.15	.03
☐	224	Rusty Staub	.08	.03	.01
☐	225	Lee Mazzilli	.06	.02	.00
☐	226	Pat Putnam	.03	.01	.00
☐	227	Bob Welch	.06	.02	.00
☐	228	Rick Cerone	.03	.01	.00
☐	229	Lee Lacy	.06	.02	.00
☐	230	Rickey Henderson	.35	.15	.03
☐	231	Gary Redus	.25	.10	.02
☐	232	Tim Wallach	.10	.04	.01
☐	233	Checklist	.08	.01	.00
☐	234	Rafael Ramirez	.03	.01	.00
☐	235	Matt Young	.12	.05	.01
☐	236	Ellis Valentine	.06	.02	.00
☐	237	John Castino	.03	.01	.00
☐	238	Eric Show	.03	.01	.00
☐	239	Bob Horner	.15	.06	.01
☐	240	Eddie Murray	.40	.18	.04
☐	241	Billy Almon	.03	.01	.00
☐	242	Greg Brock	.06	.02	.00
☐	243	Bruce Sutter	.12	.05	.01
☐	244	Dwight Evans	.10	.04	.01
☐	245	Rick Sutcliffe	.12	.05	.01
☐	246	Terry Crowley	.03	.01	.00
☐	247	Fred Lynn	.15	.06	.01
☐	248	Bill Dawley	.03	.01	.00
☐	249	Dave Stapleton	.03	.01	.00
☐	250	Bill Madlock	.12	.05	.01
☐	251	Jim Sundberg	.06	.02	.00
☐	252	Steve Yeager	.06	.02	.00
☐	253	Jim Wohlford	.03	.01	.00
☐	254	Shane Rawley	.06	.02	.00
☐	255	Bruce Benedict	.03	.01	.00
☐	256	Dave Geisel	.03	.01	.00
☐	257	Julio Cruz	.03	.01	.00
☐	258	Luis Sanchez	.03	.01	.00
☐	259	Von Hayes	.10	.04	.01
☐	260	Scott McGregor	.06	.02	.00
☐	261	Tom Seaver	.25	.10	.02
☐	262	Doug Flynn	.03	.01	.00
☐	263	Wayne Gross	.03	.01	.00
☐	264	Larry Gura	.06	.02	.00
☐	265	John Montefusco	.03	.01	.00
☐	266	Dave Winfield	.35	.15	.03
☐	267	Tim Lollar	.03	.01	.00
☐	268	Ron Washington	.03	.01	.00
☐	269	Mickey Rivers	.06	.02	.00

☐ 270	Mookie Wilson	.06	.02	.00
☐ 271	Moose Haas	.06	.02	.00
☐ 272	Rick Dempsey	.06	.02	.00
☐ 273	Dan Quisenberry	.15	.06	.01
☐ 274	Steve Henderson	.03	.01	.00
☐ 275	Len Matuszek	.03	.01	.00
☐ 276	Frank Tanana	.06	.02	.00
☐ 277	Dave Righetti	.12	.05	.01
☐ 278	Jorge Bell	.15	.06	.01
☐ 279	Ivan DeJesus	.03	.01	.00
☐ 280	Floyd Bannister	.06	.02	.00
☐ 281	Dale Murray	.03	.01	.00
☐ 282	Andre Robertson	.03	.01	.00
☐ 283	Rollie Fingers	.15	.06	.01
☐ 284	Tommy John	.15	.06	.01
☐ 285	Darrell Porter	.06	.02	.00
☐ 286	Lary Sorensen	.03	.01	.00
☐ 287	Warren Cromartie	.03	.01	.00
☐ 288	Jim Beattie	.03	.01	.00
☐ 289	Blue Jay Checklist	.08	.02	.00
☐ 290	Dave Dravecky	.08	.03	.01
☐ 291	Eddie Murray	.40	.18	.04
☐ 292	Greg Bargar	.03	.01	.00
☐ 293	Tom Underwood	.03	.01	.00
☐ 294	U.L. Washington	.03	.01	.00
☐ 295	Mike Flanagan	.06	.02	.00
☐ 296	Rich Gedman	.08	.03	.01
☐ 297	Bruce Berenyi	.03	.01	.00
☐ 298	Jim Gantner	.06	.02	.00
☐ 299	Bill Caudill	.06	.02	.00
☐ 300	Pete Rose	.50	.22	.05
☐ 301	Steve Kemp	.08	.03	.01
☐ 302	Barry Bonnell	.03	.01	.00
☐ 303	Joel Youngblood	.03	.01	.00
☐ 304	Rick Langford	.03	.01	.00
☐ 305	Roy Smalley	.06	.02	.00
☐ 306	Ken Griffey	.08	.03	.01
☐ 307	Al Oliver	.12	.05	.01
☐ 308	Ron Hassey	.03	.01	.00
☐ 309	Len Barker	.06	.02	.00
☐ 310	Willie McGee	.25	.10	.02
☐ 311	Jerry Koosman	.08	.03	.01
☐ 312	Jorge Orta	.03	.01	.00
☐ 313	Pete Vuckovich	.06	.02	.00
☐ 314	George Wright	.06	.02	.00
☐ 315	Bob Grich	.10	.04	.01
☐ 316	Jesse Barfield	.20	.09	.02
☐ 317	Willie Upshaw	.08	.03	.01
☐ 318	Bill Gullickson	.06	.02	.00
☐ 319	Ray Burris	.03	.01	.00
☐ 320	Bob Stanley	.06	.02	.00
☐ 321	Ray Knight	.08	.03	.01
☐ 322	Ken Schrom	.06	.02	.00
☐ 323	Johnny Ray	.12	.05	.01
☐ 324	Brian Giles	.03	.01	.00
☐ 325	Darrell Evans	.08	.03	.01
☐ 326	Mike Caldwell	.06	.02	.00
☐ 327	Ruppert Jones	.06	.02	.00
☐ 328	Chris Speier	.03	.01	.00
☐ 329	Bobby Castillo	.03	.01	.00
☐ 330	John Candelaria	.06	.02	.00
☐ 331	Bucky Dent	.06	.02	.00
☐ 332	Expos Checklist	.08	.02	.00
☐ 333	Larry Herndon	.03	.01	.00
☐ 334	Chuck Rainey	.03	.01	.00
☐ 335	Don Baylor	.10	.04	.01
☐ 336	Bob James	.08	.03	.01
☐ 337	Jim Clancy	.06	.02	.00
☐ 338	Duane Kuiper	.03	.01	.00
☐ 339	Roy Lee Jackson	.03	.01	.00
☐ 340	Hal McRae	.06	.02	.00
☐ 341	Larry McWilliams	.03	.01	.00
☐ 342	Tim Foli	.03	.01	.00
☐ 343	Fergie Jenkins	.10	.04	.01
☐ 344	Dickie Thon	.06	.02	.00
☐ 345	Kent Hrbek	.20	.09	.02
☐ 346	Larry Bowa	.08	.03	.01
☐ 347	Buddy Bell	.08	.03	.01
☐ 348	Toby Harrah	.06	.02	.00
☐ 349	Dan Ford	.03	.01	.00
☐ 350	George Foster	.15	.06	.01
☐ 351	Lou Piniella	.08	.03	.01
☐ 352	Dave Stewart	.03	.01	.00
☐ 353	Mike Easler	.06	.02	.00
☐ 354	Jeff Burroughs	.06	.02	.00
☐ 355	Jason Thompson	.06	.02	.00
☐ 356	Glenn Abbott	.03	.01	.00
☐ 357	Ron Cey	.10	.04	.01
☐ 358	Bob Dernier	.03	.01	.00
☐ 359	Jim Acker	.03	.01	.00
☐ 360	Willie Randolph	.06	.02	.00
☐ 361	Mike Schmidt	.35	.15	.03
☐ 362	David Green	.03	.01	.00

☐ 363	Cal Ripken	.40	.18	.04
☐ 364	Jim Rice	.25	.10	.02
☐ 365	Steve Bedrosian	.06	.02	.00
☐ 366	Gary Carter	.30	.12	.03
☐ 367	Chili Davis	.12	.05	.01
☐ 368	Hubie Brooks	.15	.06	.01
☐ 369	Steve McCatty	.03	.01	.00
☐ 370	Tim Raines	.25	.10	.02
☐ 371	Joaquin Andujar	.12	.05	.01
☐ 372	Gary Roenicke	.03	.01	.00
☐ 373	Ron Kittle	.12	.05	.01
☐ 374	Rich Dauer	.03	.01	.00
☐ 375	Dennis Leonard	.08	.03	.01
☐ 376	Rick Burleson	.06	.02	.00
☐ 377	Eric Rasmussen	.03	.01	.00
☐ 378	Dave Winfield	.30	.12	.03
☐ 379	Checklist	.08	.01	.00
☐ 380	Steve Garvey	.35	.15	.03
☐ 381	Jack Clark	.12	.05	.01
☐ 382	Odell Jones	.03	.01	.00
☐ 383	Terry Puhl	.06	.02	.00
☐ 384	Joe Niekro	.08	.03	.01
☐ 385	Tony Perez	.10	.04	.01
NL ALL-STARS (386-396)				
☐ 386	George Hendrick AS	.06	.02	.00
☐ 387	Johnny Ray AS	.06	.02	.00
☐ 388	Mike Schmidt AS	.20	.09	.02
☐ 389	Ozzie Smith AS	.08	.03	.01
☐ 390	Tim Raines AS	.15	.06	.01
☐ 391	Dale Murphy AS	.20	.09	.02
☐ 392	Andre Dawson AS	.10	.04	.01
☐ 393	Gary Carter AS	.15	.06	.01
☐ 394	Steve Rogers AS	.06	.02	.00
☐ 395	Steve Carlton AS	.15	.06	.01
☐ 396	Jesse Orosco AS	.06	.02	.00

1985 O-Pee-Chee

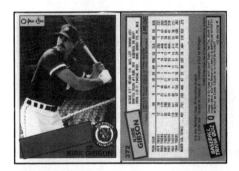

The 396 cards in the 1985 O-Pee-Chee baseball card set are again very similar to the Topps set of the same year. They are the same size (2 1/2" by 3 1/2") and contain virtually the same pictures for the players also featured in the 1985 Topps American issue. Once again, players who have changed teams will be found with traded lines inside the picture area. There is an emphasis on the two Canadian major league teams and every card shows the player position in both English and French. The reverses are also bilingual. The O-Pee-Chee logo appears on the front of every card.

		MINT	VG-E	F-G
COMPLETE SET		18.00	8.50	1.80
COMMON PLAYER (1-396)		.03	.01	.00
☐ 1	Tom Seaver	.40	.15	.03
☐ 2	Gary Lavelle	.03	.01	.00
☐ 3	Tim Wallach	.10	.04	.01
☐ 4	Jim Wohlford	.03	.01	.00
☐ 5	Jeff Robinson	.03	.01	.00
☐ 6	Willie Wilson	.15	.06	.01
☐ 7	Cliff Johnson	.03	.01	.00

☐	8	Willie Randolph	.05	.02	.00	☐ 101	Jim Acker	.03	.01	.00
☐	9	Larry Herndon	.03	.01	.00	☐ 102	Jim Sundberg	.05	.02	.00
☐	10	Kirby Puckett	1.00	.45	.10	☐ 103	Ozzie Virgil	.05	.02	.00
☐	11	Mookie Wilson	.06	.02	.00	☐ 104	Mike Fitzgerald	.05	.02	.00
☐	12	Dave Lopes	.06	.02	.00	☐ 105	Ron Kittle	.12	.05	.01
☐	13	Tim Lollar	.03	.01	.00	☐ 106	Pasqual Perez	.05	.02	.00
☐	14	Chris Bando	.03	.01	.00	☐ 107	Barry Bonnell	.03	.01	.00
☐	15	Jerry Koosman	.07	.03	.01	☐ 108	Lou Whitaker	.15	.06	.01
☐	16	Bobby Meacham	.05	.02	.00	☐ 109	Gary Roenicke	.05	.02	.00
☐	17	Mike Scott	.08	.03	.01	☐ 110	Alejandro Pena	.06	.02	.00
☐	18	Rich Gedman	.07	.03	.01	☐ 111	Doug DeCinces	.09	.04	.01
☐	19	George Frazier	.03	.01	.00	☐ 112	Doug Flynn	.03	.01	.00
☐	20	Chet Lemon	.05	.02	.00	☐ 113	Tom Herr	.09	.04	.01
☐	21	Dave Concepcion	.08	.03	.01	☐ 114	Bob James	.06	.02	.00
☐	22	Jason Thompson	.05	.02	.00	☐ 115	Rickey Henderson	.45	.20	.04
☐	23	Bret Saberhagen	1.00	.45	.10	☐ 116	Pete Rose	.75	.35	.07
☐	24	Jesse Barfield	.15	.06	.01	☐ 117	Greg Gross	.03	.01	.00
☐	25	Steve Bedrosian	.05	.02	.00	☐ 118	Eric Show	.05	.02	.00
☐	26	Roy Smalley	.05	.02	.00	☐ 119	Buck Martinez	.03	.01	.00
☐	27	Bruce Berenyi	.03	.01	.00	☐ 120	Steve Kemp	.07	.03	.01
☐	28	Butch Wynegar	.03	.01	.00	☐ 121	Checklist 1-132	.07	.01	.00
☐	29	Alan Ashby	.03	.01	.00	☐ 122	Tom Brunansky	.15	.06	.01
☐	30	Cal Ripken	.45	.20	.04	☐ 123	Dave Kingman	.12	.05	.01
☐	31	Luis Leal	.03	.01	.00	☐ 124	Garry Templeton	.09	.04	.01
☐	32	Dave Dravecky	.06	.02	.00	☐ 125	Kent Tekulve	.05	.02	.00
☐	33	Tito Landrum	.03	.01	.00	☐ 126	Darryl Strawberry	.40	.18	.04
☐	34	Pedro Guerrero	.20	.09	.02	☐ 127	Mark Gubicza	.15	.06	.01
☐	35	Graig Nettles	.10	.04	.01	☐ 128	Ernie Whitt	.03	.01	.00
☐	36	Fred Breining	.03	.01	.00	☐ 129	Don Robinson	.05	.02	.00
☐	37	Roy Lee Jackson	.03	.01	.00	☐ 130	Al Oliver	.10	.04	.01
☐	38	Steve Henderson	.03	.01	.00	☐ 131	Mario Soto	.07	.03	.01
☐	39	Gary Pettis	.07	.03	.01	☐ 132	Jeff Leonard	.06	.02	.00
☐	40	Phil Niekro	.15	.06	.01	☐ 133	Andre Dawson	.20	.09	.02
☐	41	Dwight Gooden	7.00	3.25	.70	☐ 134	Bruce Hurst	.05	.02	.00
☐	42	Luis Sanchez	.03	.01	.00	☐ 135	Bobby Cox MGR	.03	.01	.00
☐	43	Lee Smith	.06	.02	.00	☐ 136	Matt Young	.05	.02	.00
☐	44	Dickie Thon	.05	.02	.00	☐ 137	Bob Forsch	.05	.02	.00
☐	45	Greg Minton	.05	.02	.00	☐ 138	Ron Darling	.25	.10	.02
☐	46	Mike Flanagan	.06	.02	.00	☐ 139	Steve Trout	.05	.02	.00
☐	47	Bud Black	.05	.02	.00	☐ 140	Geoff Zahn	.03	.01	.00
☐	48	Tony Fernandez	.12	.05	.01	☐ 141	Ken Forsch	.03	.01	.00
☐	49	Carlton Fisk	.15	.06	.01	☐ 142	Jerry Willard	.03	.01	.00
☐	50	John Candelaria	.06	.02	.00	☐ 143	Bill Gullickson	.05	.02	.00
☐	51	Bob Watson	.05	.02	.00	☐ 144	Mike Mason	.05	.02	.00
☐	52	Rick Leach	.03	.01	.00	☐ 145	Alvin Davis	.60	.28	.06
☐	53	Rick Rhoden	.06	.02	.00	☐ 146	Gary Redus	.06	.02	.00
☐	54	Cesar Cedeno	.07	.03	.01	☐ 147	Willie Aikens	.05	.02	.00
☐	55	Frank Tanana	.05	.02	.00	☐ 148	Steve Yeager	.05	.02	.00
☐	56	Larry Bowa	.07	.03	.01	☐ 149	Dickie Noles	.03	.01	.00
☐	57	Willie McGee	.25	.10	.02	☐ 150	Jim Rice	.25	.10	.02
☐	58	Rich Dauer	.03	.01	.00	☐ 151	Moose Haas	.05	.02	.00
☐	59	Jorge Bell	.15	.06	.01	☐ 152	Steve Balboni	.06	.02	.00
☐	60	George Hendrick	.06	.02	.00	☐ 153	Frank LaCorte	.03	.01	.00
☐	61	Donnie Moore	.05	.02	.00	☐ 154	Argenis Salazar	.03	.01	.00
☐	62	Mike Ramsey	.03	.01	.00	☐ 155	Bob Grich	.07	.03	.01
☐	63	Nolan Ryan	.25	.10	.02	☐ 156	Craig Reynolds	.03	.01	.00
☐	64	Mark Bailey	.05	.02	.00	☐ 157	Bill Madlock	.09	.04	.01
☐	65	Bill Buckner	.08	.03	.01	☐ 158	Pat Tabler	.05	.02	.00
☐	66	Jerry Reuss	.05	.02	.00	☐ 159	Don Slaught	.05	.02	.00
☐	67	Mike Schmidt	.35	.15	.03	☐ 160	Lance Parrish	.20	.09	.02
☐	68	Von Hayes	.10	.04	.01	☐ 161	Ken Schrom	.05	.02	.00
☐	69	Phil Bradley	.75	.35	.07	☐ 162	Wally Backman	.07	.03	.01
☐	70	Don Baylor	.10	.04	.01	☐ 163	Dennis Eckersley	.06	.02	.00
☐	71	Julio Cruz	.03	.01	.00	☐ 164	Dave Collins	.05	.02	.00
☐	72	Rick Sutcliffe	.12	.05	.01	☐ 165	Dusty Baker	.06	.02	.00
☐	73	Storm Davis	.06	.02	.00	☐ 166	Claudell Washington	.06	.02	.00
☐	74	Mike Krukow	.05	.02	.00	☐ 167	Rick Camp	.03	.01	.00
☐	75	Willie Upshaw	.08	.03	.01	☐ 168	Garth Iorg	.03	.01	.00
☐	76	Craig Lefferts	.03	.01	.00	☐ 169	Shane Rawley	.06	.02	.00
☐	77	Lloyd Moseby	.12	.05	.01	☐ 170	George Foster	.14	.06	.01
☐	78	Ron Davis	.03	.01	.00	☐ 171	Tony Bernazard	.05	.02	.00
☐	79	Rick Mahler	.05	.02	.00	☐ 172	Don Sutton	.15	.06	.01
☐	80	Keith Hernandez	.25	.10	.02	☐ 173	Jerry Remy	.05	.02	.00
☐	81	Vance Law	.03	.01	.00	☐ 174	Rick Honeycutt	.05	.02	.00
☐	82	Joe Price	.03	.01	.00	☐ 175	Dave Parker	.15	.06	.01
☐	83	Dennis Lamp	.03	.01	.00	☐ 176	Buddy Bell	.10	.04	.01
☐	84	Gary Ward	.05	.02	.00	☐ 177	Steve Garvey	.35	.15	.03
☐	85	Mike Marshall	.12	.05	.01	☐ 178	Miguel Dilone	.03	.01	.00
☐	86	Marvell Wynne	.05	.02	.00	☐ 179	Tommy John	.12	.05	.01
☐	87	David Green	.05	.02	.00	☐ 180	Dave Winfield	.30	.12	.03
☐	88	Bryn Smith	.05	.02	.00	☐ 181	Alan Trammell	.18	.08	.01
☐	89	Sixto Lezcano	.03	.01	.00	☐ 182	Rollie Fingers	.15	.06	.01
☐	90	Rich Gossage	.15	.06	.01	☐ 183	Larry McWilliams	.03	.01	.00
☐	91	Jeff Burroughs	.03	.01	.00	☐ 184	Carmen Castillo	.03	.01	.00
☐	92	Bobby Brown	.03	.01	.00	☐ 185	Al Holland	.03	.01	.00
☐	93	Oscar Gamble	.05	.02	.00	☐ 186	Jerry Mumphrey	.03	.01	.00
☐	94	Rick Dempsey	.06	.02	.00	☐ 187	Chris Chambliss	.05	.02	.00
☐	95	Jose Cruz	.09	.04	.01	☐ 188	Jim Clancy	.05	.02	.00
☐	96	Johnny Ray	.10	.04	.01	☐ 189	Glenn Wilson	.10	.04	.01
☐	97	Joel Youngblood	.03	.01	.00	☐ 190	Rusty Staub	.07	.03	.01
☐	98	Eddie Whitson	.05	.02	.00	☐ 191	Ozzie Smith	.12	.05	.01
☐	99	Milt Wilcox	.03	.01	.00	☐ 192	Howard Johnson	.05	.02	.00
☐	100	George Brett	.45	.20	.04	☐ 193	Jimmy Key	.25	.10	.02

☐ 194 Terry Kennedy	.07	.03	.01
☐ 195 Glenn Hubbard	.03	.01	.00
☐ 196 Pete O'Brien	.07	.03	.01
☐ 197 Keith Moreland	.05	.02	.00
☐ 198 Eddie Milner	.03	.01	.00
☐ 199 Dave Engle	.05	.02	.00
☐ 200 Reggie Jackson	.35	.15	.03
☐ 201 Burt Hooton	.03	.01	.00
☐ 202 Gorman Thomas	.08	.03	.01
☐ 203 Larry Parrish	.07	.03	.01
☐ 204 Bob Stanley	.05	.02	.00
☐ 205 Steve Rogers	.06	.02	.00
☐ 206 Phil Garner	.05	.02	.00
☐ 207 Ed VandeBerg	.05	.02	.00
☐ 208 Jack Clark	.15	.06	.01
☐ 209 Bill Campbell	.05	.02	.00
☐ 210 Gary Matthews	.06	.02	.00
☐ 211 Dave Palmer	.05	.02	.00
☐ 212 Tony Perez	.11	.05	.01
☐ 213 Sammy Stewart	.03	.01	.00
☐ 214 John Tudor	.10	.04	.01
☐ 215 Bob Brenly	.06	.02	.00
☐ 216 Jim Gantner	.05	.02	.00
☐ 217 Bryan Clark	.03	.01	.00
☐ 218 Doyle Alexander	.05	.02	.00
☐ 219 Bo Diaz	.05	.02	.00
☐ 220 Fred Lynn	.15	.06	.01
☐ 221 Eddie Murray	.45	.20	.04
☐ 222 Hubie Brooks	.15	.06	.01
☐ 223 Tom Hume	.03	.01	.00
☐ 224 Al Cowens	.05	.02	.00
☐ 225 Mike Boddicker	.08	.03	.01
☐ 226 Len Matuszek	.03	.01	.00
☐ 227 Danny Darwin	.03	.01	.00
☐ 228 Scott McGregor	.06	.02	.00
☐ 229 Dave LaPoint	.03	.01	.00
☐ 230 Gary Carter	.35	.15	.03
☐ 231 Joaquin Andujar	.10	.04	.01
☐ 232 Rafael Ramirez	.03	.01	.00
☐ 233 Wayne Gross	.03	.01	.00
☐ 234 Neil Allen	.05	.02	.00
☐ 235 Gary Maddox	.05	.02	.00
☐ 236 Mark Thurmond	.05	.02	.00
☐ 237 Julio Franco	.10	.04	.01
☐ 238 Ray Burris	.03	.01	.00
☐ 239 Tim Teufel	.06	.02	.00
☐ 240 Dave Stieb	.20	.09	.02
☐ 241 Brett Butler	.09	.04	.01
☐ 242 Greg Brock	.06	.02	.00
☐ 243 Barbaro Garbey	.03	.01	.00
☐ 244 Greg Walker	.12	.05	.01
☐ 245 Chili Davis	.10	.04	.01
☐ 246 Darrell Porter	.05	.02	.00
☐ 247 Tippy Martinez	.05	.02	.00
☐ 248 Terry Forster	.07	.03	.01
☐ 249 Harold Baines	.15	.06	.01
☐ 250 Jesse Orosco	.06	.02	.00
☐ 251 Brad Gulden	.03	.01	.00
☐ 252 Mike Hargrove	.05	.02	.00
☐ 253 Nick Esasky	.06	.02	.00
☐ 254 Frank Williams	.03	.01	.00
☐ 255 Lonnie Smith	.06	.02	.00
☐ 256 Daryl Sconiers	.03	.01	.00
☐ 257 Bryan Little	.03	.01	.00
☐ 258 Terry Francona	.05	.02	.00
☐ 259 Mark Langston	.25	.10	.02
☐ 260 Dave Righetti	.12	.05	.01
☐ 261 Checklist 133-264	.07	.01	.00
☐ 262 Bob Horner	.15	.06	.01
☐ 263 Mel Hall	.10	.04	.01
☐ 264 John Shelby	.05	.02	.00
☐ 265 Juan Samuel	.15	.06	.01
☐ 266 Frank Viola	.06	.02	.00
☐ 267 Jim Fanning MGR	.03	.01	.00
☐ 268 Dick Ruthven	.03	.01	.00
☐ 269 Bobby Ramos	.03	.01	.00
☐ 270 Dan Quisenberry	.15	.06	.01
☐ 271 Dwight Evans	.10	.04	.01
☐ 272 Andre Thornton	.07	.03	.01
☐ 273 Orel Hershiser	.90	.40	.09
☐ 274 Ray Knight	.07	.03	.01
☐ 275 Bill Caudill	.05	.02	.00
☐ 276 Charlie Hough	.05	.02	.00
☐ 277 Tim Raines	.25	.10	.02
☐ 278 Mike Squires	.03	.01	.00
☐ 279 Alex Trevino	.03	.01	.00
☐ 280 Ron Romanick	.15	.06	.01
☐ 281 Tom Niedenfuer	.06	.02	.00
☐ 282 Mike Stenhouse	.05	.02	.00
☐ 283 Terry Puhl	.05	.02	.00
☐ 284 Hal McRae	.06	.02	.00
☐ 285 Dan Driessen	.05	.02	.00
☐ 286 Rudy Law	.03	.01	.00

☐ 287 Walt Terrell	.06	.02	.00
☐ 288 Jeff Kunkel	.10	.04	.01
☐ 289 Bob Knepper	.08	.03	.01
☐ 290 Cecil Cooper	.10	.04	.01
☐ 291 Bob Welch	.06	.02	.00
☐ 292 Frank Pastore	.03	.01	.00
☐ 293 Dan Schatzeder	.03	.01	.00
☐ 294 Tom Nieto	.03	.01	.00
☐ 295 Joe Niekro	.08	.03	.01
☐ 296 Ryne Sandberg	.40	.18	.04
☐ 297 Gary Lucas	.03	.01	.00
☐ 298 John Castino	.03	.01	.00
☐ 299 Bill Doran	.07	.03	.01
☐ 300 Rod Carew	.30	.12	.03
☐ 301 John Montefusco	.05	.02	.00
☐ 302 Johnnie LeMaster	.03	.01	.00
☐ 303 Jim Beattie	.03	.01	.00
☐ 304 Gary Gaetti	.07	.03	.01
☐ 305 Dale Berra	.05	.02	.00
☐ 306 Rick Reuschel	.05	.02	.00
☐ 307 Ken Oberkfell	.03	.01	.00
☐ 308 Kent Hrbek	.20	.09	.02
☐ 309 Mike Witt	.10	.04	.01
☐ 310 Manny Trillo	.05	.02	.00
☐ 311 Jim Gott	.03	.01	.00
☐ 312 LaMarr Hoyt	.09	.04	.01
☐ 313 Dave Schmidt	.03	.01	.00
☐ 314 Ron Oester	.05	.02	.00
☐ 315 Doug Sisk	.03	.01	.00
☐ 316 John Lowenstein	.03	.01	.00
☐ 317 Derrell Thomas	.03	.01	.00
☐ 318 Ted Simmons	.09	.04	.01
☐ 319 Darrell Evans	.08	.03	.01
☐ 320 Dale Murphy	.45	.20	.04
☐ 321 Ricky Horton	.06	.02	.00
☐ 322 Ken Phelps	.05	.02	.00
☐ 323 Lee Mazzilli	.05	.02	.00
☐ 324 Don Mattingly	.90	.40	.09
☐ 325 John Denny	.06	.02	.00
☐ 326 Ken Singleton	.08	.03	.01
☐ 327 Brook Jacoby	.15	.06	.01
☐ 328 Greg Luzinski	.08	.03	.01
☐ 329 Bob Ojeda	.08	.03	.01
☐ 330 Leon Durham	.12	.05	.01
☐ 331 Bill Laskey	.05	.02	.00
☐ 332 Ben Oglivie	.05	.02	.00
☐ 333 Willie Hernandez	.12	.05	.01
☐ 334 Bob Dernier	.05	.02	.00
☐ 335 Bruce Benedict	.03	.01	.00
☐ 336 Rance Mulliniks	.03	.01	.00
☐ 337 Rick Cerone	.05	.02	.00
☐ 338 Britt Burns	.06	.02	.00
☐ 339 Danny Heep	.03	.01	.00
☐ 340 Robin Yount	.25	.10	.02
☐ 341 Andy Van Slyke	.07	.03	.01
☐ 342 Curt Wilkerson	.03	.01	.00
☐ 343 Bill Russell	.05	.02	.00
☐ 344 Dave Henderson	.06	.02	.00
☐ 345 Charlie Lea	.06	.02	.00
☐ 346 Terry Pendleton	.20	.09	.02
☐ 347 Carney Lansford	.09	.04	.01
☐ 348 Bob Boone	.05	.02	.00
☐ 349 Mike Easler	.06	.02	.00
☐ 350 Wade Boggs	.75	.35	.07
☐ 351 Atlee Hammaker	.05	.02	.00
☐ 352 Joe Morgan	.15	.06	.01
☐ 353 Damaso Garcia	.09	.04	.01
☐ 354 Floyd Bannister	.05	.02	.00
☐ 355 Bert Blyleven	.10	.04	.01
☐ 356 John Butcher	.03	.01	.00
☐ 357 Fernando Valenzuela	.30	.12	.03
☐ 358 Tony Pena	.10	.04	.01
☐ 359 Mike Smithson	.03	.01	.00
☐ 360 Steve Carlton	.25	.10	.02
☐ 361 Alfredo Griffin	.05	.02	.00
☐ 362 Craig McMurtry	.03	.01	.00
☐ 363 Bill Dawley	.05	.02	.00
☐ 364 Richard Dotson	.06	.02	.00
☐ 365 Carmelo Martinez	.06	.02	.00
☐ 366 Ron Cey	.09	.04	.01
☐ 367 Tony Scott	.03	.01	.00
☐ 368 Dave Bergman	.03	.01	.00
☐ 369 Steve Sax	.12	.05	.01
☐ 370 Bruce Sutter	.12	.05	.01
☐ 371 Mickey Rivers	.05	.02	.00
☐ 372 Kirk Gibson	.20	.09	.02
☐ 373 Scott Sanderson	.05	.02	.00
☐ 374 Brian Downing	.03	.01	.00
☐ 375 Jeff Reardon	.08	.03	.01
☐ 376 Frank DiPino	.05	.02	.00
☐ 377 Checklist 265-396	.07	.01	.00
☐ 378 Alan Wiggins	.06	.02	.00
☐ 379 Charles Hudson	.05	.02	.00

☐ 380 Ken Griffey	.07	.03	.01
☐ 381 Tom Paciorek	.03	.01	.00
☐ 382 Jack Morris	.16	.07	.01
☐ 383 Tony Gwynn	.30	.12	.03
☐ 384 Jody Davis	.09	.04	.01
☐ 385 Jose DeLeon	.05	.02	.00
☐ 386 Bob Kearney	.03	.01	.00
☐ 387 George Wright	.03	.01	.00
☐ 388 Ron Guidry	.15	.06	.01
☐ 389 Rick Manning	.03	.01	.00
☐ 390 Sid Fernandez	.25	.10	.02
☐ 391 Bruce Bochte	.05	.02	.00
☐ 392 Dan Petry	.10	.04	.01
☐ 393 Tim Stoddard	.03	.01	.00
☐ 394 Tony Armas	.10	.04	.01
☐ 395 Paul Molitor	.10	.04	.01
☐ 396 Mike Heath	.05	.02	.00

☐ 10 Charlie Lea	.15	.06	.01
☐ 11 Steve Rogers	.15	.06	.01
☐ 12 Jeff Reardon	.20	.09	.02
TORONTO BLUE JAYS (13-24)			
☐ 13 Buck Martinez	.10	.04	.01
☐ 14 Willie Upshaw	.20	.09	.02
☐ 15 Domaso Garcia	.20	.09	.02
(sic, Damaso)			
☐ 16 Tony Fernandez	.35	.15	.03
☐ 17 Rance Mulliniks	.10	.04	.01
☐ 18 Jorge Bell	.35	.15	.03
☐ 19 Lloyd Moseby	.35	.15	.03
☐ 20 Jesse Barfield	.35	.15	.03
☐ 21 Doyle Alexander	.15	.06	.01
☐ 22 Dave Stieb	.25	.10	.02
☐ 23 Bill Caudill	.15	.06	.01
☐ 24 Gary Lavelle	.10	.04	.01

1985 O-Pee-Chee Posters

Poster Number 5 of 24 - Affiche No 5 de 24
© 1985 O-Pee-Chee Co. Ltd. Printed in Canada - Imprimé au Canada

The 24 full-color posters in the 1985 O-Pee-Chee poster insert set were inserted inside the regular wax packs and feature players of the Montreal Expos and the Toronto Blue Jays. These posters are typically found with two folds and measure approximately 4 7/8" by 6 7/8". The posters are blank-backed and are numbered at the bottom in French and English. A distinctive blue (Blue Jays) or red (Expos) border surrounds the player photo.

	MINT	VG-E	F-G
COMPLETE SET	3.50	1.65	.35
COMMON PLAYER	.10	.04	.01
MONTREAL EXPOS (1-12)			
☐ 1 Mike Fitzgerald	.15	.06	.01
☐ 2 Dan Driessen	.10	.04	.01
☐ 3 Dave Palmer	.15	.06	.01
☐ 4 U.L. Washington	.10	.04	.01
☐ 5 Hubie Brooks	.50	.22	.05
☐ 6 Tim Wallach	.25	.10	.02
☐ 7 Tim Raines	.75	.35	.07
☐ 8 Herm Winningham	.15	.06	.01
☐ 9 Andre Dawson	.35	.15	.03

1986 O-Pee-Chee

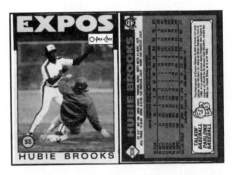

The 396 cards in the 1986 O-Pee-Chee baseball card set are again very similar to the Topps set of the same year. They are the same size (2 1/2" by 3 1/2") and contain virtually the same pictures for the players also featured in the 1986 Topps American issue. Once again, players who have changed teams will be found with traded lines inside the picture area. There is an emphasis on the two Canadian major league teams and every card shows the player position in both English and French. The reverses are also bilingual. The O-Pee-Chee logo appears on the front of every card.

	MINT	VG-E	F-G
COMPLETE SET	12.50	5.75	1.25
COMMON PLAYER (1-396)	.03	.01	.00
☐ 1 Pete Rose	.75	.25	.05
☐ 2 Ken Landreaux	.05	.02	.00
☐ 3 Rob Picciolo	.03	.01	.00
☐ 4 Steve Garvey	.25	.10	.02
☐ 5 Andy Hawkins	.03	.01	.00
☐ 6 Rudy Law	.03	.01	.00
☐ 7 Lonnie Smith	.05	.02	.00
☐ 8 Dwayne Murphy	.07	.03	.01
☐ 9 Moose Haas	.05	.02	.00
☐ 10 Tony Gwynn	.20	.09	.02
☐ 11 Bob Ojeda	.07	.03	.01
☐ 12 Jose Uribe	.05	.02	.00
☐ 13 Bob Kearney	.03	.01	.00
☐ 14 Julio Cruz	.03	.01	.00
☐ 15 Eddie Whitson	.03	.01	.00
☐ 16 Rick Schu	.06	.02	.00
☐ 17 Mike Stenhouse	.03	.01	.00
☐ 18 Lou Thornton	.05	.02	.00
☐ 19 Ryne Sandberg	.25	.10	.02
☐ 20 Lou Whitaker	.15	.06	.01
☐ 21 Mark Brouhard	.03	.01	.00
☐ 22 Gary Lavelle	.03	.01	.00
☐ 23 Manny Lee	.05	.02	.00
☐ 24 Don Slaught	.05	.02	.00
☐ 25 Willie Wilson	.12	.05	.01

□	#	Name			
□	26	Mike Marshall	.12	.05	.01
□	27	Ray Knight	.07	.03	.01
□	28	Mario Soto	.06	.02	.00
□	29	Dave Anderson	.03	.01	.00
□	30	Eddie Murray	.35	.15	.03
□	31	Dusty Baker	.06	.02	.00
□	32	Steve Yeager	.05	.02	.00
□	33	Andy Van Slyke	.06	.02	.00
□	34	Dave Righetti	.12	.05	.01
□	35	Jeff Reardon	.08	.03	.01
□	36	Burt Hooton	.03	.01	.00
□	37	Johnny Ray	.09	.04	.01
□	38	Glenn Hoffman	.03	.01	.00
□	39	Rick Mahler	.05	.02	.00
□	40	Ken Griffey	.07	.03	.01
□	41	Brad Wellman	.03	.01	.00
□	42	Joe Hesketh	.06	.02	.00
□	43	Mark Salas	.15	.06	.01
□	44	Jorge Orta	.03	.01	.00
□	45	Damaso Garcia	.08	.03	.01
□	46	Jim Acker	.03	.01	.00
□	47	Bill Madlock	.10	.04	.01
□	48	Bill Almon	.03	.01	.00
□	49	Rick Manning	.03	.01	.00
□	50	Dan Quisenberry	.12	.05	.01
□	51	Jim Gantner	.05	.02	.00
□	52	Kevin Bass	.09	.04	.01
□	53	Len Dykstra	.60	.28	.06
□	54	John Franco	.06	.02	.00
□	55	Fred Lynn	.15	.06	.01
□	56	Jim Morrison	.03	.01	.00
□	57	Bill Doran	.08	.03	.01
□	58	Leon Durham	.10	.04	.01
□	59	Andre Thornton	.07	.03	.01
□	60	Dwight Evans	.09	.04	.01
□	61	Larry Herndon	.03	.01	.00
□	62	Bob Boone	.05	.02	.00
□	63	Kent Hrbek	.16	.07	.01
□	64	Floyd Bannister	.05	.02	.00
□	65	Harold Baines	.16	.07	.01
□	66	Pat Tabler	.05	.02	.00
□	67	Carmelo Martinez	.05	.02	.00
□	68	Ed Lynch	.03	.01	.00
□	69	George Foster	.12	.05	.01
□	70	Dave Winfield	.25	.10	.02
□	71	Ken Schrom	.05	.02	.00
□	72	Toby Harrah	.05	.02	.00
□	73	Jackie Gutierrez	.03	.01	.00
□	74	Rance Mulliniks	.03	.01	.00
□	75	Jose DeLeon	.03	.01	.00
□	76	Ron Romanick	.03	.01	.00
□	77	Charlie Leibrandt	.06	.02	.00
□	78	Bruce Benedict	.03	.01	.00
□	79	Dave Schmidt	.03	.01	.00
□	80	Darryl Strawberry	.35	.15	.03
□	81	Wayne Krenchicki	.03	.01	.00
□	82	Tippy Martinez	.03	.01	.00
□	83	Phil Garner	.05	.02	.00
□	84	Darrell Porter	.05	.02	.00
□	85	Tony Perez	.09	.04	.01
□	86	Tom Waddell	.03	.01	.00
□	87	Tim Hulett	.05	.02	.00
□	88	Barbaro Garbey	.03	.01	.00
□	89	Randy St. Claire	.03	.01	.00
□	90	Garry Templeton	.08	.03	.01
□	91	Tim Teufel	.06	.02	.00
□	92	Al Cowens	.05	.02	.00
□	93	Scot Thompson	.03	.01	.00
□	94	Tom Herr	.08	.03	.01
□	95	Ozzie Virgil	.05	.02	.00
□	96	Jose Cruz	.08	.03	.01
□	97	Gary Gaetti	.08	.03	.01
□	98	Roger Clemens	.60	.28	.06
□	99	Vance Law	.03	.01	.00
□	100	Nolan Ryan	.20	.09	.02
□	101	Mike Smithson	.03	.01	.00
□	102	Raphael Santana	.03	.01	.00
□	103	Darrell Evans	.08	.03	.01
□	104	Rich Gossage	.15	.06	.01
□	105	Gary Ward	.05	.02	.00
□	106	Jim Gott	.03	.01	.00
□	107	Rafael Ramirez	.03	.01	.00
□	108	Ted Power	.03	.01	.00
□	109	Ron Guidry	.15	.06	.01
□	110	Scott McGregor	.06	.02	.00
□	111	Mike Scioscia	.05	.02	.00
□	112	Glen Hubbard	.03	.01	.00
□	113	U.L. Washington	.03	.01	.00
□	114	Al Oliver	.09	.04	.01
□	115	Jay Howell	.05	.02	.00
□	116	Brook Jacoby	.09	.04	.01
□	117	Willie McGee	.20	.09	.02
□	118	Jerry Royster	.03	.01	.00
□	119	Barry Bonnell	.03	.01	.00
□	120	Steve Carlton	.25	.10	.02
□	121	Alfredo Griffin	.05	.02	.00
□	122	David Green	.03	.01	.00
□	123	Greg Walker	.10	.04	.01
□	124	Frank Tanana	.06	.02	.00
□	125	Dave Lopes	.05	.02	.00
□	126	Mike Krukow	.05	.02	.00
□	127	Jack Howell	.20	.09	.02
□	128	Herm Winningham	.05	.02	.00
□	130	Alan Trammell	.15	.06	.01
□	131	Checklist 1-132	.07	.01	.00
□	132	Razor Shines	.03	.01	.00
□	133	Bruce Sutter	.12	.05	.01
□	134	Carney Lansford	.08	.03	.01
□	135	Joe Niekro	.08	.03	.01
□	136	Ernie Whitt	.03	.01	.00
□	137	Charlie Moore	.03	.01	.00
□	138	Mel Hall	.08	.03	.01
□	139	Roger McDowell	.35	.15	.03
□	140	John Candelaria	.06	.02	.00
□	141	Bob Rodgers MGR	.03	.01	.00
□	142	Manny Trillo	.05	.02	.00
□	143	Dave Palmer	.05	.02	.00
□	144	Robin Yount	.20	.09	.02
□	145	Pedro Guerrero	.20	.09	.02
□	146	Von Hayes	.09	.04	.01
□	147	Lance Parrish	.18	.08	.01
□	148	Mike Heath	.03	.01	.00
□	149	Brett Butler	.08	.03	.01
□	150	Joaquin Andujar	.10	.04	.01
□	151	Graig Nettles	.12	.05	.01
□	152	Pete Vuckovich	.05	.02	.00
□	153	Jason Thompson	.05	.02	.00
□	154	Bert Roberge	.03	.01	.00
□	155	Bob Grich	.07	.03	.01
□	156	Roy Smalley	.05	.02	.00
□	157	Ron Hassey	.03	.01	.00
□	158	Bob Stanley	.05	.02	.00
□	159	Orel Hershiser	.20	.09	.02
□	160	Chet Lemon	.06	.02	.00
□	161	Terry Puhl	.05	.02	.00
□	162	Dave Lapoint	.05	.02	.00
□	163	Onix Concepcion	.03	.01	.00
□	164	Steve Balboni	.06	.02	.00
□	165	Mike Davis	.06	.02	.00
□	166	Dickie Thon	.05	.02	.00
□	167	Zane Smith	.12	.05	.01
□	168	Jeff Burroughs	.05	.02	.00
□	169	Alex Trevino	.03	.01	.00
□	170	Gary Carter	.30	.12	.03
□	171	Tito Landrum	.03	.01	.00
□	172	Sammy Stewart	.03	.01	.00
□	173	Wayne Gross	.03	.01	.00
□	174	Britt Burns	.05	.02	.00
□	175	Steve Sax	.10	.04	.01
□	176	Jody Davis	.08	.03	.01
□	177	Joel Youngblood	.03	.01	.00
□	178	Fernando Valenzuela	.25	.10	.02
□	179	Storm Davis	.06	.02	.00
□	180	Don Mattingly	.80	.40	.08
□	181	Steve Bedrosian	.05	.02	.00
□	182	Jesse Orosco	.06	.02	.00
□	183	Gary Roenicke	.03	.01	.00
□	184	Don Baylor	.09	.04	.01
□	185	Rollie Fingers	.12	.05	.01
□	186	Ruppert Jones	.05	.02	.00
□	187	Scott Fletcher	.05	.02	.00
□	188	Bob Dernier	.05	.02	.00
□	189	Mike Mason	.03	.01	.00
□	190	George Hendrick	.06	.02	.00
□	191	Wally Backman	.07	.03	.01
□	192	Oddibe McDowell	.20	.09	.02
□	193	Bruce Hurst	.05	.02	.00
□	194	Ron Cey	.09	.04	.01
□	195	Dave Concepcion	.08	.03	.01
□	196	Doyle Alexander	.05	.02	.00
□	197	Dale Murray	.03	.01	.00
□	198	Mark Langston	.08	.03	.01
□	199	Dennis Eckersley	.06	.02	.00
□	200	Mike Schmidt	.30	.12	.03
□	201	Nick Esasky	.05	.02	.00
□	202	Ken Dayley	.05	.02	.00
□	203	Rick Cerone	.05	.02	.00
□	204	Larry McWilliams	.03	.01	.00
□	205	Brian Downing	.03	.01	.00
□	206	Danny Darwin	.03	.01	.00
□	207	Bill Caudill	.05	.02	.00
□	208	Dave Rozema	.03	.01	.00
□	209	Eric Show	.03	.01	.00
□	210	Brad Komminsk	.05	.02	.00
□	211	Chris Bando	.03	.01	.00
□	212	Chris Speier	.03	.01	.00

☐ 213	Jim Clancy	.05	.02	.00
☐ 214	Randy Bush	.03	.01	.00
☐ 215	Frank White	.06	.02	.00
☐ 216	Dan Petry	.09	.04	.01
☐ 217	Tim Wallach	.09	.04	.01
☐ 218	Mitch Webster	.25	.10	.02
☐ 219	Dennis Lamp	.03	.01	.00
☐ 220	Bob Horner	.15	.06	.01
☐ 221	Dave Henderson	.05	.02	.00
☐ 222	Dave Smith	.05	.02	.00
☐ 223	Willie Upshaw	.07	.03	.01
☐ 224	Cesar Cedeno	.07	.03	.01
☐ 225	Ron Darling	.16	.07	.01
☐ 226	Lee Lacy	.06	.02	.00
☐ 227	John Tudor	.08	.03	.01
☐ 228	Jim Presley	.20	.09	.02
☐ 229	Bill Gullickson	.05	.02	.00
☐ 230	Terry Kennedy	.07	.03	.01
☐ 231	Bob Knepper	.08	.03	.01
☐ 232	Rick Rhoden	.06	.02	.00
☐ 233	Richard Dotson	.06	.02	.00
☐ 234	Jesse Barfield	.18	.08	.01
☐ 235	Butch Wynegar	.05	.02	.00
☐ 236	Jerry Reuss	.05	.02	.00
☐ 237	Juan Samuel	.09	.04	.01
☐ 238	Larry Parrish	.06	.02	.00
☐ 239	Bill Buckner	.08	.03	.01
☐ 240	Pat Sheridan	.03	.01	.00
☐ 241	Tony Fernandez	.10	.04	.01
☐ 242	Rich Thompson	.03	.01	.00
☐ 243	Rickey Henderson	.35	.15	.03
☐ 244	Craig Lefferts	.03	.01	.00
☐ 245	Jim Sundberg	.05	.02	.00
☐ 246	Phil Niekro	.15	.06	.01
☐ 247	Terry Harper	.03	.01	.00
☐ 248	Spike Owen	.05	.02	.00
☐ 249	Brett Saberhagen	.20	.09	.02
☐ 250	Dwight Gooden	1.25	.60	.12
☐ 251	Rich Dauer	.03	.01	.00
☐ 252	Keith Hernandez	.20	.09	.02
☐ 253	Bo Diaz	.03	.01	.00
☐ 254	Ozzie Guillen	.25	.10	.02
☐ 255	Tony Armas	.08	.03	.01
☐ 256	Andre Dawson	.20	.09	.02
☐ 257	Doug DeCinces	.07	.03	.01
☐ 258	Tim Burke	.15	.06	.01
☐ 259	Dennis Boyd	.08	.03	.01
☐ 260	Tony Pena	.09	.04	.01
☐ 261	Sal Butera	.03	.01	.00
☐ 262	Wade Boggs	.60	.28	.06
☐ 263	Checklist 133-264	.07	.01	.00
☐ 264	Ron Oester	.05	.02	.00
☐ 265	Ron Davis	.05	.02	.00
☐ 266	Keith Moreland	.05	.02	.00
☐ 267	Paul Molitor	.09	.04	.01
☐ 268	John Denny	.07	.03	.01
☐ 269	Frank Viola	.06	.02	.00
☐ 270	Jack Morris	.15	.06	.01
☐ 271	Dave Collins	.05	.02	.00
☐ 272	Bert Blyleven	.10	.04	.01
☐ 273	Jerry Willard	.03	.01	.00
☐ 274	Matt Young	.05	.02	.00
☐ 275	Charlie Hough	.05	.02	.00
☐ 276	Dave Dravecky	.06	.02	.00
☐ 277	Garth Iorg	.03	.01	.00
☐ 278	Hal McRae	.05	.02	.00
☐ 279	Curt Wilkerson	.03	.01	.00
☐ 280	Tim Raines	.20	.09	.02
☐ 281	Bill Laskey	.03	.01	.00
☐ 282	Jerry Mumphrey	.03	.01	.00
☐ 283	Pat Clements	.12	.05	.01
☐ 284	Bob James	.03	.01	.00
☐ 285	Buddy Bell	.09	.04	.01
☐ 286	Tom Brookens	.03	.01	.00
☐ 287	Dave Parker	.16	.07	.01
☐ 288	Ron Kittle	.10	.04	.01
☐ 289	Johnnie LeMaster	.03	.01	.00
☐ 290	Carlton Fisk	.15	.06	.01
☐ 291	Jimmy Key	.08	.03	.01
☐ 292	Gary Matthews	.06	.02	.00
☐ 293	Marvell Wynne	.05	.02	.00
☐ 294	Danny Cox	.05	.02	.00
☐ 295	Kirk Gibson	.18	.08	.01
☐ 296	Mariano Duncan	.18	.08	.01
☐ 297	Ozzie Smith	.12	.05	.01
☐ 298	Craig Reynolds	.03	.01	.00
☐ 299	Bryn Smith	.05	.02	.00
☐ 300	George Brett	.35	.15	.03
☐ 301	Walt Terrell	.06	.02	.00
☐ 302	Greg Gross	.03	.01	.00
☐ 303	Claudell Washington	.06	.02	.00
☐ 304	Howard Johnson	.05	.02	.00
☐ 305	Phil Bradley	.15	.06	.01

☐ 306	R.J. Reynolds	.06	.02	.00
☐ 307	Bob Brenly	.05	.02	.00
☐ 308	Hubie Brooks	.15	.06	.01
☐ 309	Alvin Davis	.15	.06	.01
☐ 310	Donnie Hill	.03	.01	.00
☐ 311	Dick Schofield	.03	.01	.00
☐ 312	Tom Filer	.05	.02	.00
☐ 313	Mike Fitzgerald	.05	.02	.00
☐ 314	Marty Barrett	.05	.02	.00
☐ 315	Mookie Wilson	.05	.02	.00
☐ 316	Alan Knicely	.03	.01	.00
☐ 317	Ed Romero	.03	.01	.00
☐ 318	Glenn Wilson	.08	.03	.01
☐ 319	Bud Black	.05	.02	.00
☐ 320	Jim Rice	.20	.09	.02
☐ 321	Terry Pendleton	.06	.02	.00
☐ 322	Dave Kingman	.10	.04	.01
☐ 323	Gary Pettis	.07	.03	.01
☐ 324	Dan Schatzeder	.03	.01	.00
☐ 325	Juan Beniquez	.05	.02	.00
☐ 326	Kent Tekulve	.06	.02	.00
☐ 327	Mike Pagliarulo	.35	.15	.03
☐ 328	Pete O'Brien	.07	.03	.01
☐ 329	Kirby Puckett	.35	.15	.03
☐ 330	Rick Sutcliffe	.12	.05	.01
☐ 331	Alan Ashby	.03	.01	.00
☐ 332	Willie Randolph	.07	.03	.01
☐ 333	Tom Henke	.05	.02	.00
☐ 334	Ken Oberkfell	.03	.01	.00
☐ 335	Don Sutton	.15	.06	.01
☐ 336	Dan Gladden	.06	.02	.00
☐ 337	George Vukovich	.03	.01	.00
☐ 338	Jorge Bell	.15	.06	.01
☐ 339	Jim Dwyer	.03	.01	.00
☐ 340	Cal Ripken	.30	.12	.03
☐ 341	Willie Hernandez	.10	.04	.01
☐ 342	Gary Redus	.06	.02	.00
☐ 343	Jerry Koosman	.07	.03	.01
☐ 344	Jim Wohlford	.03	.01	.00
☐ 345	Donnie Moore	.05	.02	.00
☐ 346	Floyd Youmans	.50	.22	.05
☐ 347	Gorman Thomas	.09	.04	.01
☐ 348	Cliff Johnson	.03	.01	.00
☐ 349	Ken Howell	.05	.02	.00
☐ 350	Jack Clark	.12	.05	.01
☐ 351	Gary Lucas	.03	.01	.00
☐ 352	Bob Clark	.03	.01	.00
☐ 353	Dave Stieb	.15	.06	.01
☐ 354	Tony Bernazard	.05	.02	.00
☐ 355	Lee Smith	.06	.02	.00
☐ 356	Mickey Hatcher	.03	.01	.00
☐ 357	Ed Vandeberg	.03	.01	.00
☐ 358	Rick Dempsey	.06	.02	.00
☐ 359	Bobby Cox MGR	.03	.01	.00
☐ 360	Lloyd Moseby	.12	.05	.01
☐ 361	Shane Rawley	.06	.02	.00
☐ 362	Garry Maddox	.05	.02	.00
☐ 363	Buck Martinez	.03	.01	.00
☐ 364	Ed Nunez	.05	.02	.00
☐ 365	Luis Leal	.03	.01	.00
☐ 366	Dale Berra	.03	.01	.00
☐ 367	Mike Boddicker	.08	.03	.01
☐ 368	Greg Brock	.06	.02	.00
☐ 369	Al Holland	.03	.01	.00
☐ 370	Vince Coleman	1.25	.60	.12
☐ 371	Rod Carew	.25	.10	.02
☐ 372	Ben Oglivie	.05	.02	.00
☐ 373	Lee Mazzilli	.05	.02	.00
☐ 374	Terry Francona	.05	.02	.00
☐ 375	Rich Gedman	.07	.03	.01
☐ 376	Charlie Lea	.05	.02	.00
☐ 377	Joe Carter	.12	.05	.01
☐ 378	Bruce Bochte	.03	.01	.00
☐ 379	Bobby Meacham	.03	.01	.00
☐ 380	LaMarr Hoyt	.07	.03	.01
☐ 381	Jeff Leonard	.06	.02	.00
☐ 382	Ivan Calderon	.20	.09	.02
☐ 383	Chris Brown	.60	.28	.06
☐ 384	Steve Trout	.05	.02	.00
☐ 385	Cecil Cooper	.09	.04	.01
☐ 386	Cecil Fielder	.15	.06	.01
☐ 387	Tim Flannery	.03	.01	.00
☐ 388	Chris Codiroli	.03	.01	.00
☐ 389	Glenn Davis	.35	.15	.03
☐ 390	Tom Seaver	.25	.10	.02
☐ 391	Julio Franco	.08	.03	.01
☐ 392	Tom Brunansky	.10	.04	.01
☐ 393	Rob Wilfong	.03	.01	.00
☐ 394	Reggie Jackson	.30	.12	.03
☐ 395	Scott Garrelts	.07	.03	.01
☐ 396	Checklist 265-396	.08	.01	.00

1986 Provigo Expos

The cards are found in (lightly perforated) panels of three (two player cards and an advertising card. The panel of three measures 7 1/2" by 3 3/8" whereas each individual card measures 2 1/2" by 3 3/8". An album is available to hold the cards in the set; however in order to use the album, the cards must be separated into individuals. Cards are numbered on the back as well as prominently displaying the player's uniform number on the front of the card. The cards are attractive and the backs feature blue and red printing on a white card stock. Biographical information on the backs of the cards is written in French and English.

		MINT	VG-E	F-G
COMPLETE SET		6.50	3.00	.65
COMMON PLAYER		.20	.09	.02
☐ 1	Hubie Brooks	.60	.25	.05
☐ 2	Dann Bilardello	.20	.09	.02
☐ 3	Buck Rogers MGR	.20	.09	.02
☐ 4	Andy McGaffigan	.20	.09	.02
☐ 5	Mitch Webster	.50	.20	.04
☐ 6	Jim Wohlford	.20	.09	.02
☐ 7	Tim Raines	.60	.28	.06
☐ 8	Jay Tibbs	.20	.09	.02
☐ 9	Andre Dawson	.60	.25	.05
☐ 10	Andres Gallarraga	.40	.18	.04
☐ 11	Tim Wallach	.50	.20	.04
☐ 12	Dan Schatzeder	.20	.09	.02
☐ 13	Jeff Reardon	.30	.12	.03
☐ 14	Coaching Staff:	.20	.09	.02
	Joe Kerrigan			
	Bobby Winkles			
	Larry Bearnarth			
☐ 15	Jason Thompson	.20	.09	.02
☐ 16	Bert Roberge	.20	.09	.02
☐ 17	Tim Burke	.30	.12	.03
☐ 18	Al Newman	.20	.09	.02
☐ 19	Bryn Smith	.20	.09	.02
☐ 20	Wayne Krenchicki	.20	.09	.02
☐ 21	Joe Hesketh	.30	.12	.03
☐ 22	Herman Winningham	.20	.09	.02
☐ 23	Vance Law	.20	.09	.02
☐ 24	Floyd Youmans	.50	.20	.04
☐ 25	Jeff Parrett	.20	.09	.02
☐ 26	Mike Fitzgerald	.20	.09	.02
☐ 27	Youppi (Mascot)	.20	.09	.02
☐ 28	Coaching Staff:	.20	.09	.02
	Rick Renick			
	Ron Hansen			
	Ken Macha			

1983 Stuart Expos

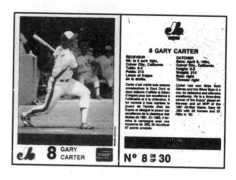

This set consists of 30 cards each measuring 2 1/2" by 3 1/2" featuring players of the Montreal Expos. Cards are numbered on the back and also show each player's uniform number on the front. The backs feature red and blue print on off-white card stock. The biographies on the back are written in both French and English.

		MINT	VG-E	F-G
COMPLETE SET		8.00	3.75	.80
COMMON PLAYER		.20	.09	.02
☐ 1	Bill Virdon MGR	.30	.12	.03
☐ 2	Woodie Fryman	.20	.09	.02
☐ 3	Vern Rapp COACH	.20	.09	.02
☐ 4	Andre Dawson	.60	.28	.06
☐ 5	Jeff Reardon	.40	.18	.04
☐ 6	Al Oliver	.50	.22	.05
☐ 7	Doug Flynn	.20	.09	.02
☐ 8	Gary Carter	1.00	.45	.10
☐ 9	Tim Raines	1.00	.45	.10
☐ 10	Steve Rogers	.30	.12	.03
☐ 11	Billy DeMars COACH	.20	.09	.02
☐ 12	Tim Wallach	.50	.22	.05
☐ 13	Galen Cisco COACH	.20	.09	.02
☐ 14	Terry Francona	.30	.12	.03
☐ 15	Bill Gullickson	.30	.12	.03
☐ 16	Ray Burris	.20	.09	.02
☐ 17	Scott Sanderson	.30	.12	.03
☐ 18	Warren Cromartie	.30	.12	.03
☐ 19	Jerry White	.20	.09	.02
☐ 20	Bobby Ramos	.20	.09	.02
☐ 21	Jim Wohlford	.20	.09	.02
☐ 22	Dan Schatzeder	.20	.09	.02
☐ 23	Charlie Lea	.30	.12	.03
☐ 24	Brian Little	.20	.09	.02
☐ 25	Mel Wright COACH	.20	.09	.02
☐ 26	Tim Blackwell	.20	.09	.02
☐ 27	Chris Speier	.20	.09	.02
☐ 28	Randy Lerch	.20	.09	.02
☐ 29	Bryn Smith	.30	.12	.03
☐ 30	Brad Mills	.20	.09	.02

1984 Stuart Expos

This set consists of 40 cards each measuring 2 1/2" by 3 1/2" featuring players of the Montreal Expos. Cards are numbered on the back and also show each player's uniform number on the front. This set is distinguished from the previous year by the red border around the picture on the obverse. The backs feature red and blue print on white card stock. The biographies on the back are written in both French and English. An album was also available for holding the cards; the album is gray, white, blue, and

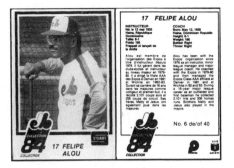

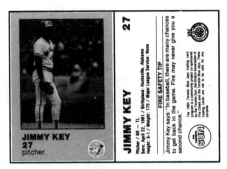

red and contains two-pocket plastic pages.

		MINT	VG-E	F-G
COMPLETE SET		25.00	11.00	2.50
COMMON PLAYER (1-20)		.20	.09	.02
COMMON PLAYER (21-40)		.40	.18	.04

			MINT	VG-E	F-G
☐	1	Youppi (Mascot)	.20	.09	.02
☐	2	Bill Virdon MGR	.30	.12	.03
☐	3	Billy DeMars COACH	.20	.09	.02
☐	4	Galen Cisco COACH	.20	.09	.02
☐	5	Russ Nixon COACH	.20	.09	.02
☐	6	Felipe Alou COACH	.30	.12	.03
☐	7	Dan Schatzeder	.20	.09	.02
☐	8	Charlie Lea	.30	.12	.03
☐	9	Roberto Ramos	.20	.09	.02
☐	10	Bob James	.30	.12	.03
☐	11	Andre Dawson	.50	.22	.05
☐	12	Gary Lucas	.20	.09	.02
☐	13	Jeff Reardon	.40	.18	.04
☐	14	Tim Wallach	.40	.18	.04
☐	15	Gary Carter	.75	.35	.07
☐	16	Tim Gullickson	.30	.12	.03
☐	17	Pete Rose	2.00	.90	.20
☐	18	Terry Francona	.30	.12	.03
☐	19	Steve Rogers	.30	.12	.03
☐	20	Tim Raines	.75	.35	.07
☐	21	Bryn Smith	.50	.22	.05
☐	22	Greg Harris	.50	.22	.05
☐	23	David Palmer	.50	.22	.05
☐	24	Jim Wohlford	.40	.18	.04
☐	25	Miguel Dilone	.40	.18	.04
☐	26	Mike Stenhouse	.40	.18	.04
☐	27	Chris Speier	.40	.18	.04
☐	28	Derrel Thomas	.40	.18	.04
☐	29	Doug Flynn	.40	.18	.04
☐	30	Bryan Little	.40	.18	.04
☐	31	Argenis Salazar	.40	.18	.04
☐	32	Mike Fuentes	.40	.18	.04
☐	33	Joe Kerrigan	.40	.18	.04
☐	34	Andy McGaffigan	.40	.18	.04
☐	35	Fred Breining	.40	.18	.04
☐	36	Expo '83 All Stars	1.50	.70	.15
		Gary Carter			
		Andre Dawson			
		Tim Raines			
		Steve Rogers			
☐	37	Co-Players of the Year	1.50	.70	.15
		Andre Dawson			
		Tim Raines			
☐	38	Coaching Staff	.40	.18	.04
☐	39	Expos Team Photo	.40	.18	.04
☐	40	Checklist Card	.40	.18	.04

1984 Toronto Fire

This attractive, blue bordered, 35 card set features Toronto Blue Jays, their coaches and manager. The cards (measuring 2 1/2" by 3 1/2") are numbered only by uniform number, and the backs contain player biographical data, a Fire Safety Tip emanating from that player and the logos of the sponsoring

Toronto Sun and Ontario Association of Fire Chiefs. The cards are unnumbered on the back but they contain the player's uniform number on the front of the card. Below cards are conveniently numbered in alphabetical order.

			MINT	VG-E	F-G
COMPLETE SET			8.00	3.75	.80
COMMON PLAYER			.20	.09	.02

			MINT	VG-E	F-G
☐	1	Jim Acker	.20	.09	.02
☐	2	Willie Aikens	.20	.09	.02
☐	3	Doyle Alexander	.25	.10	.02
☐	4	Jesse Barfield	.75	.35	.07
☐	5	George Bell	.75	.35	.07
☐	6	Jim Clancy	.30	.12	.03
☐	7	Bryan Clark	.20	.09	.02
☐	8	Stan Clarke	.20	.09	.02
☐	9	Dave Collins	.30	.12	.03
☐	10	Bobby Cox MGR	.25	.10	.02
☐	11	Tony Fernandez	.60	.28	.06
☐	12	Damaso Garcia	.40	.18	.04
☐	13	Cito Gaston COACH	.20	.09	.02
☐	14	Jim Gott	.20	.09	.02
☐	15	Alfredo Griffin	.30	.12	.03
☐	16	Kelly Gruber	.30	.12	.03
☐	17	Garth Iorg	.20	.09	.02
☐	18	Roy Lee Jackson	.20	.09	.02
☐	19	Cliff Johnson	.20	.09	.02
☐	20	Jimmy Key	.35	.15	.03
☐	21	Dennis Lamp	.20	.09	.02
☐	22	Rick Leach	.20	.09	.02
☐	23	Luis Leal	.20	.09	.02
☐	24	Buck Martinez	.20	.09	.02
☐	25	Lloyd Moseby	.60	.28	.06
☐	26	Rance Mulliniks	.20	.09	.02
☐	27	Billy Smith COACH	.20	.09	.02
☐	28	Dave Stieb	.60	.28	.06
☐	29	John Sullivan COACH	.20	.09	.02
☐	30	Willie Upshaw	.50	.22	.05
☐	31	Mitch Webster	.50	.20	.04
☐	32	Ernie Whitt	.20	.09	.02
☐	33	Al Widmar COACH	.20	.09	.02
☐	34	Jim Williams COACH	.25	.10	.02
☐	35	Blue Jays Logo	.20	.09	.02

1985 Toronto Fire

This attractive, blue bordered, 36 card set features Toronto Blue Jays, their coaches and manager. The cards (measuring 2 1/2" by 3 1/2") are numbered only by uniform number, and the backs contain player biographical data, a Fire Safety Tip emanating from that player and the logos of the sponsoring Toronto Star, Ministry of the Solicitor General, Midas Muffler, and the Ontario Association of Fire Chiefs. The cards are unnumbered on the back but they contain the player's uniform number on the front of the card. Below cards are conveniently

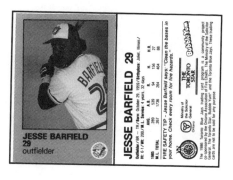

numbered in alphabetical order.

	MINT	VG-E	F-G
COMPLETE SET	7.00	3.25	.70
COMMON PLAYER	.20	.09	.02

		MINT	VG-E	F-G
☐ 1	Jim Acker	.20	.09	.02
☐ 2	Willie Aikens	.20	.09	.02
☐ 3	Doyle Alexander	.25	.10	.02
☐ 4	Jesse Barfield	.75	.35	.07
☐ 5	George Bell	.75	.35	.07
☐ 6	Jeff Burroughs	.25	.10	.02
☐ 7	Bill Caudill	.25	.10	.02
☐ 8	Jim Clancy	.25	.10	.02
☐ 9	Bobby Cox MGR	.20	.09	.02
☐ 10	Tony Fernandez	.60	.28	.06
☐ 11	Damaso Garcia	.40	.18	.04
☐ 12	Cito Gaston COACH	.20	.09	.02
☐ 13	Kelly Gruber	.20	.09	.02
☐ 14	Tom Henke	.25	.10	.02
☐ 15	Garth Iorg	.20	.09	.02
☐ 16	Jimmy Key	.35	.15	.03
☐ 17	Dennis Lamp	.20	.09	.02
☐ 18	Gary Lavelle	.20	.09	.02
☐ 19	Luis Leal	.20	.09	.02
☐ 20	Manny Lee	.20	.09	.02
☐ 21	Buck Martinez	.20	.09	.02
☐ 22	Len Matuszek	.20	.09	.02
☐ 23	Lloyd Moseby	.50	.22	.05
☐ 24	Rance Mulliniks	.20	.09	.02
☐ 25	Ron Musselman	.20	.09	.02
☐ 26	Billy Smith COACH	.20	.09	.02
☐ 27	Dave Stieb	.50	.22	.05
☐ 28	John Sullivan COACH	.20	.09	.02
☐ 29	Lou Thornton	.20	.09	.02
☐ 30	Willie Upshaw	.40	.18	.04
☐ 31	Mitch Webster	.40	.18	.04
☐ 32	Ernie Whitt	.20	.09	.02
☐ 33	Al Widmar COACH	.20	.09	.02
☐ 34	Jimy Williams COACH	.20	.09	.02
☐ 35	Blue Jays LOGO (unnumbered, checklist back)	.20	.09	.02
☐ 36	Blue Jays Team Photo (schedule on back)	.20	.09	.02

numbered in alphabetical order.

	MINT	VG-E	F-G
COMPLETE SET	7.00	3.25	.70
COMMON PLAYER	.20	.09	.02

		MINT	VG-E	F-G
☐ 1	Jim Acker	.20	.09	.02
☐ 2	Doyle Alexander	.25	.10	.02
☐ 3	Jesse Barfield	.75	.35	.07
☐ 4	George Bell	.75	.35	.07
☐ 5	Bill Caudill	.25	.10	.02
☐ 6	Jim Clancy	.25	.10	.02
☐ 7	Steve Davis	.25	.10	.02
☐ 8	Mark Eichhorn	.40	.18	.04
☐ 9	Tony Fernandez	.50	.22	.05
☐ 10	Cecil Fielder	.25	.10	.02
☐ 11	Tom Filer	.25	.10	.02
☐ 12	Damaso Garcia	.40	.18	.04
☐ 13	Cito Gaston COACH	.20	.09	.02
☐ 14	Don Gordon	.20	.09	.02
☐ 15	Kelly Gruber	.20	.09	.02
☐ 16	Jeff Hearron	.20	.09	.02
☐ 17	Tom Henke	.25	.10	.02
☐ 18	Garth Iorg	.20	.09	.02
☐ 19	Cliff Johnson	.20	.09	.02
☐ 20	Jimmy Key	.35	.15	.03
☐ 21	Dennis Lamp	.20	.09	.02
☐ 22	Gary Lavelle	.20	.09	.02
☐ 23	Rick Leach	.20	.09	.02
☐ 24	Buck Martinez	.20	.09	.02
☐ 25	John McLaren COACH	.20	.09	.02
☐ 26	Lloyd Moseby	.50	.22	.05
☐ 27	Rance Mulliniks	.20	.09	.02
☐ 28	Billy Smith COACH	.20	.09	.02
☐ 29	Dave Stieb	.50	.22	.05
☐ 30	John Sullivan COACH	.20	.09	.02
☐ 31	Willie Upshaw	.40	.18	.04
☐ 32	Ernie Whitt	.20	.09	.02
☐ 33	Al Widmar COACH	.20	.09	.02
☐ 34	Jimy Williams MGR	.20	.09	.02
☐ 35	Blue Jays LOGO (Won-Lost Record)	.20	.09	.02
☐ 36	Blue Jays Team Photo (checklist back)	.20	.09	.02

1986 Toronto Fire

This attractive, blue bordered, 36 card set features Toronto Blue Jays, their coaches and manager. The cards (measuring 2 1/2" by 3 1/2") are numbered only by uniform number, and the backs contain player biographical data, a Fire Safety Tip emanating from that player and the logos of the sponsoring Toronto Star, Ministry of the Solicitor General, Bubble Yum, and the Ontario Association of Fire Chiefs. The cards are unnumbered on the back but they contain the player's uniform number on the front of the card. Below cards are conveniently

1974 Weston Expos

This large size (approximately 3 1/2" by 5 1/2") set of ten cards features exclusively players of the Montreal Expos. The card fronts feature a color photo inside a thin white border with a facsimile autograph in black ink. The backs feature two sets of biography and statistics, one in English and one in French. The cards are not numbered except to the extent that the player's uniform number is prominently displayed on the card back. The player's uniforms and caps have been airbrushed to remove the Expos insignia whereever it may have

29	KEN SINGLETON — Right Field

Bats: Throws Ht. Wt. Date and Place of Birth
L/R Right 6-4 213 6/10/47 New York, N.Y.

1973 Batting Record

G	AB	R	H	2B	3B	HR	RBI	AVE.
162	560	100	169	26	2	23	103	.302
R	186	23	55	10	1	8	34	.296
L	374	77	114	16	1	15	69	.305

Ken bats left or right handed. He holds the Expos
team record for having batted in 103 runs and
crossing the plate 100 times.

Get your EXPOS trading cards free inside
specially marked packages of
39c B. B. BATS
Collect the whole lot

29	KEN SINGLETON — Champ Droit

Bâton: Lancer Tail Pds. Date au lieu de naissance
G/D Droitier 6-4 213 10/6/47 New York, N.Y.

Record au bâton pour 1973

P	AB	P	C.S.	2B	3B	C.C	P.P.	MOY
162	560	100	169	26	2	23	103	.302
D	186	23	55	10	1	8	34	.296
G	374	77	114	16	1	15	69	.305

Ken peut frapper des deux côtés, gauche ou droit.
Il détient le record des Expos pour point produit
avec 103 et la mème a compté 100 points.

Obtenez votre carte des EXPOS gratuitement
à l'intérieur d'emballages spécialement marqués
de 39c B. B. BATS
Collectionnez la série complète.

COPYRIGHT PRO STAR PROMOTIONS INC.

KEN SINGLETON

appeared.

	MINT	VG-E	F-G
COMPLETE SET	4.00	1.85	.40
COMMON PLAYER	.35	.15	.03
☐ 3 Bob Bailey	.35	.15	.03
☐ 8 Boots Day	.35	.15	.03
☐ 12 John Boccabella	.35	.15	.03
☐ 16 Mike Jorgensen	.35	.15	.03
☐ 18 Steve Renko	.35	.15	.03
☐ 19 Tim Foli	.35	.15	.03
☐ 21 Ernie McAnally	.35	.15	.03
☐ 26 Bill Stoneman	.45	.20	.04
☐ 29 Ken Singleton	.75	.35	.07
☐ 33 Ron Hunt	.35	.15	.03

1955 Armour Coins

The front of each of the plastic baseball "coins" in
this set contains a raised profile of a ballplayer. Each
plastic coin measures 1 1/2" in diameter. Although
similar in design to the 1959 and 1960 issues by
Armour, the 1955 set is distinguished by a number
of details: the full team name under the profile, the
listing of birthplace and date and batting and
throwing preferences on the back and, of course,
the 1954 batting or won-loss record located on the
reverse. The coins are not numbered and come in
colors of black, blue, blue-green, green, orange, red,
and yellow. Mantle and Kuenn exist in two variations
each. The set price below includes both variations.

	MINT	VG-E	F-G
COMPLETE SET	250.00	110.00	25.00
COMMON PLAYER	2.50	1.15	.25
☐ 1 Johnny Antonelli	2.50	1.15	.25
☐ 2 Yogi Berra	12.00	5.50	1.20
☐ 3 Del Crandall	2.50	1.15	.25
☐ 4 Larry Doby	4.00	1.85	.40
☐ 5 Jim Finigan	2.50	1.15	.25
☐ 6 Whitey Ford	10.00	4.75	1.00
☐ 7 Jim Gilliam	4.00	1.85	.40
☐ 8 Harvey Haddix	2.50	1.15	.25
☐ 9 Ron Jackson	2.50	1.15	.25

☐ 10 Jackie Jensen	4.00	1.85	.40
☐ 11 Ted Kluszewski	4.00	1.85	.40
☐ 12A Harvey Kuenn (reg.)	6.00	2.80	.60
☐ 12B Harvey Kuenn (cond.)	25.00	11.00	2.50
☐ 13A Mickey Mantel ERR (sic, Mantle)	35.00	16.50	3.50
☐ 13B Mickey Mantle COR	125.00	57.00	12.50
☐ 14 Don Mueller	2.50	1.15	.25
☐ 15 Pee Wee Reese	10.00	4.75	1.00
☐ 16 Allie Reynolds	4.00	1.85	.40
☐ 17 Al Rosen	4.00	1.85	.40
☐ 18 Curt Simmons	2.50	1.15	.25
☐ 19 Duke Snider	15.00	7.00	1.50
☐ 20 Warren Spahn	12.00	5.50	1.20
☐ 21 Frank Thomas	2.50	1.15	.25
☐ 22 Virgil Trucks	2.50	1.15	.25
☐ 23 Robert Turley	2.50	1.15	.25
☐ 24 Mickey Vernon	2.50	1.15	.25

1959 Armour Coins

There are 20 coins in the 1959 Armour set, 10 from
each league. Each coin measures 1 1/2" in
diameter. In contrast to the 1955 set produced by
this company, the raised profiles are not as finely
detailed and the lettering is larger. In addition, the
team nickname (for example, "Redlegs") is listed
below the profile, and the reverse does not record
birth date and place or batting and throwing
preferences. The coins are not numbered and are
found in colors of dark and pale blue, dark and pale
green, orange, red, and pale yellow.

	MINT	VG-E	F-G
COMPLETE SET	90.00	40.00	8.00
COMMON PLAYER	2.25	1.00	.22
☐ 1 Hank Aaron	22.00	9.50	2.10
☐ 2 Johnny Antonelli	2.25	1.00	.22
☐ 3 Richie Ashburn	4.00	1.85	.40
☐ 4 Ernie Banks	9.00	4.00	.85
☐ 5 Don Blasingame	2.25	1.00	.22
☐ 6 Bob Cerv	2.25	1.00	.22
☐ 7 Del Crandall	2.25	1.00	.22
☐ 8 Whitey Ford	9.00	4.00	.85
☐ 9 Nellie Fox	4.00	1.85	.40
☐ 10 Jackie Jensen	3.00	1.40	.30
☐ 11 Harvey Kuenn	4.00	1.85	.40
☐ 12 Frank Malzone	2.25	1.00	.22
☐ 13 Johnny Podres	3.00	1.40	.30
☐ 14 Frank Robinson	9.00	4.00	.85
☐ 15 Roy Sievers	2.25	1.00	.22
☐ 16 Bob Skinner	2.25	1.00	.22
☐ 17 Frank Thomas	2.25	1.00	.22
☐ 18 Gus Triandos	2.25	1.00	.22
☐ 19 Bob Turley	2.25	1.00	.22
☐ 20 Mickey Vernon	2.25	1.00	.22

1960 Armour Coins

Although the 20 plastic baseball player coins produced by Armour in 1960 were identical in style to those of the 1959 set, there was quite a turnover in personnel. Thirteen new subjects were depicted, with Aaron, Banks, Crandall, Ford, Fox, Malzone, and Triandos the only returnees. The coins are the same size as the previous year, 1 1/2" in diameter. The reverse of these unnumbered coins lists the 1959 record for each individual. They are found in the following colors: two shades of blue, two shades of green, orange, red, salmon, tan, and yellow. The complete set price below includes all variations. The Daley coin is regarded by serious Armour collectors as being quite scarce.

	MINT	VG-E	F-G
COMPLETE SET	650.00	300.00	60.00
COMMON PLAYER	2.25	1.00	.22
☐ 1A Hank Aaron (Milwaukee)	40.00	18.00	4.00
☐ 1B Hank Aaron (Braves)	21.00	9.00	2.00
☐ 2 Bob Allison	2.25	1.00	.22
☐ 3 Ernie Banks	9.00	4.00	.85
☐ 4 Ken Boyer	4.00	1.85	.40
☐ 5 Rocky Colavito	4.00	1.85	.40
☐ 6 Gene Conley	2.25	1.00	.22
☐ 7 Del Crandall	2.25	1.00	.22
☐ 8 Bud Daley	500.00	225.00	50.00
☐ 9 Don Drysdale	8.00	3.50	.75
☐ 10 Whitey Ford	9.00	4.00	.85
☐ 11 Nellie Fox	4.00	1.85	.40
☐ 12 Al Kaline	9.00	4.00	.85
☐ 13A Frank Malzone (Boston)	20.00	9.00	2.00
☐ 13B Frank Malzone (Red Sox)	4.00	1.85	.40
☐ 14 Mickey Mantle	35.00	16.50	3.50
☐ 15 Eddie Mathews	8.00	3.50	.75
☐ 16 Willie Mays	21.00	9.00	2.00
☐ 17 Vada Pinson	4.00	1.85	.40
☐ 18 Dick Stuart	2.25	1.00	.22
☐ 19 Gus Triandos	2.25	1.00	.22
☐ 20 Early Wynn	6.50	3.00	.65

1985 Cain's Tiger Discs

This set of discs was distributed by Cain's Potato Chips in 1985 to commemorate the Tigers' World Championship in 1984. Each disc measures 2 3/4" in diameter. Each disc has a distinctive yellow border on the front. Inside this yellow border is a full color photo of the player with his hat on. The statistics on back of the disc give the player's 1984 pitching or hitting record as well as his vital statistics. The discs are not numbered; hence they are listed below in alphabetical order.

	MINT	VG-E	F-G
COMPLETE SET	6.00	2.80	.60
COMMON PLAYER	.20	.09	.02
☐ 1 Doug Bair	.20	.09	.02
☐ 2 Juan Berenguer	.20	.09	.02
☐ 3 Dave Bergman	.20	.09	.02
☐ 4 Tom Brookens	.20	.09	.02
☐ 5 Marty Castillo	.20	.09	.02
☐ 6 Darrell Evans	.30	.12	.03
☐ 7 Barbaro Garbey	.20	.09	.02
☐ 8 Kirk Gibson	.60	.28	.06
☐ 9 John Grubb	.20	.09	.02
☐ 10 Willie Hernandez	.40	.18	.04
☐ 11 Larry Herndon	.20	.09	.02
☐ 12 Chet Lemon	.30	.12	.03
☐ 13 Aurelio Lopez	.20	.09	.02
☐ 14 Jack Morris	.50	.22	.05
☐ 15 Lance Parrish	.60	.28	.06
☐ 16 Dan Petry	.30	.12	.03
☐ 17 Bill Scherrer	.20	.09	.02
☐ 18 Alan Trammell	.50	.22	.05
☐ 19 Lou Whitaker	.50	.22	.05
☐ 20 Milt Wilcox	.20	.09	.02

1969 Citgo Metal Coins

This set of metal coins was distributed at Citgo stations in 1969 to commemorate the 100th anniversary of professional baseball. Each metal coin measures 1" in diameter. Although the coins are not numbered, they are arranged in the checklist below according to numbers found on a display card (which could be obtained from the company via mail). Each coin depicts a ballplayer in a raised portrait; the brass-like metal plating is often found discolored due to oxidation.

	MINT	VG-E	F-G
COMPLETE SET	50.00	22.00	5.00
COMMON PLAYER	.50	.22	.05
☐ 1 Denny McLain	.75	.35	.07
☐ 2 Dave McNally	.60	.28	.06
☐ 3 Jim Lonborg	.60	.28	.06
☐ 4 Harmon Killebrew	4.00	1.85	.40
☐ 5 Mel Stottlemyre	.60	.28	.06
☐ 6 Willie Horton	.60	.28	.06
☐ 7 Jim Fregosi	.60	.28	.06
☐ 8 Rico Petrocelli	.50	.22	.05

		MINT	VG-E	F-G
☐ 9	Stan Bahnsen	.50	.22	.05
☐ 10	Frank Howard	.75	.35	.07
☐ 11	Joe Torre	.75	.35	.07
☐ 12	Jerry Koosman	.60	.28	.06
☐ 13	Ron Santo	.75	.35	.07
☐ 14	Pete Rose	20.00	9.00	2.00
☐ 15	Rusty Staub	.75	.35	.07
☐ 16	Henry Aaron	10.00	4.75	1.00
☐ 17	Richie Allen	.75	.35	.07
☐ 18	Ron Swoboda	.50	.22	.05
☐ 19	Willie McCovey	5.00	2.35	.50
☐ 20	Jim Bunning	1.00	.45	.10

1976 Crane Discs

Produced under the auspices of Michael Schlecter Associates (MSA) in 1976, the ballplayer-on-disc format was distributed by a number of different advertisers -- such as Crane's, Isaly's and Towne Club -- and can be found in various regions of the country.

		MINT	VG-E	F-G
COMPLETE SET		5.00	2.00	.40
COMMON PLAYER (1-70)		.04	.02	.00
☐ 1	Hank Aaron	.50	.22	.05
☐ 2	Johnny Bench	.40	.18	.04
☐ 3	Vida Blue	.06	.02	.00
☐ 4	Larry Bowa	.06	.02	.00
☐ 5	Lou Brock	.30	.12	.03
☐ 6	Jeff Burroughs	.04	.02	.00
☐ 7	John Candelaria	.04	.02	.00
☐ 8	Jose Cardenal	.04	.02	.00
☐ 9	Rod Carew	.30	.12	.03

☐ 10	Steve Carlton	.30	.12	.03
☐ 11	Dave Cash	.04	.02	.00
☐ 12	Cesar Cedeno	.06	.02	.00
☐ 13	Ron Cey	.06	.02	.00
☐ 14	Carlton Fisk	.10	.04	.01
☐ 15	Tito Fuentes	.04	.02	.00
☐ 16	Steve Garvey	.40	.18	.04
☐ 17	Ken Griffey	.06	.02	.00
☐ 18	Don Gullett	.04	.02	.00
☐ 19	Willie Horton	.04	.02	.00
☐ 20	Al Hrabosky	.04	.02	.00
☐ 21	Catfish Hunter	.15	.06	.01
☐ 22	Reggie Jackson	.40	.18	.04
☐ 23	Randy Jones	.04	.02	.00
☐ 24	Jim Kaat	.06	.02	.00
☐ 25	Don Kessinger	.04	.02	.00
☐ 26	Dave Kingman	.08	.03	.01
☐ 27	Jerry Koosman	.06	.02	.00
☐ 28	Mickey Lolich	.06	.02	.00
☐ 29	Greg Luzinski	.08	.03	.01
☐ 30	Fred Lynn	.15	.06	.01
☐ 31	Bill Madlock	.08	.03	.01
☐ 32	Carlos May	.04	.02	.00
☐ 33	John Mayberry	.04	.02	.00
☐ 34	Bake McBride	.04	.02	.00
☐ 35	Doc Medich	.04	.02	.00
☐ 36	Andy Messersmith	.05	.02	.00
☐ 37	Rick Monday	.04	.02	.00
☐ 38	John Montefusco	.04	.02	.00
☐ 39	Jerry Morales	.04	.02	.00
☐ 40	Joe Morgan	.20	.09	.02
☐ 41	Thurman Munson	.30	.12	.03
☐ 42	Bobby Murcer	.06	.02	.00
☐ 43	Al Oliver	.10	.04	.01
☐ 44	Jim Palmer	.25	.10	.02
☐ 45	Dave Parker	.15	.06	.01
☐ 46	Tony Perez	.10	.04	.01
☐ 47	Jerry Reuss	.06	.02	.00
☐ 48	Brooks Robinson	.30	.12	.03
☐ 49	Frank Robinson	.25	.10	.02
☐ 50	Steve Rogers	.06	.02	.00
☐ 51	Pete Rose	.75	.35	.07
☐ 52	Nolan Ryan	.30	.12	.03
☐ 53	Manny Sanguillen	.04	.02	.00
☐ 54	Mike Schmidt	.40	.18	.04
☐ 55	Tom Seaver	.30	.12	.03
☐ 56	Ted Simmons	.10	.04	.01
☐ 57	Reggie Smith	.06	.02	.00
☐ 58	Willie Stargell	.20	.09	.02
☐ 59	Rusty Staub	.06	.02	.00
☐ 60	Rennie Stennett	.04	.02	.00
☐ 61	Don Sutton	.15	.06	.01
☐ 62	Andy Thornton	.06	.02	.00
☐ 63	Luis Tiant	.06	.02	.00
☐ 64	Joe Torre	.08	.03	.01
☐ 65	Mike Tyson	.04	.02	.00
☐ 66	Bob Watson	.06	.02	.00
☐ 67	Wilbur Wood	.04	.02	.00
☐ 68	Jimmy Wynn	.04	.02	.00
☐ 69	Carl Yastrzemski	.50	.22	.05
☐ 70	Richie Zisk	.06	.02	.00

1910 Domino Discs

These discs were issued by Sweet Caporal Cigarettes and consist of a metal rim around cardboard. The discs come in a variety of colors: black, blue, brown, green, and red. The player's picture, name, and team are on the front whereas the back shows a domino. Each disc is approximately 1 1/16" in diameter. The ACC designation for this set is PX7. Many variations exist. The set price below does not include variations.

		MINT	VG-E	F-G
	COMPLETE SET	2000.00	900.00	200.00
	COMMON PLAYER	10.00	4.75	1.00
☐ 1	Leon (Red) Ames	10.00	4.75	1.00
☐ 2	James Archer	10.00	4.75	1.00
☐ 3	James (Pepper) Austin	10.00	4.75	1.00
☐ 4	Frank Baker	20.00	9.00	2.00
☐ 5	Neal Ball	10.00	4.75	1.00
☐ 6	Cy Barger	10.00	4.75	1.00
☐ 7	Jack Barry	10.00	4.75	1.00
☐ 8	John Bates	10.00	4.75	1.00
☐ 9	Beals Becker	10.00	4.75	1.00
☐ 10	George Bell	10.00	4.75	1.00
☐ 11	Chief Bender	20.00	9.00	2.00
☐ 12	William Bergen	10.00	4.75	1.00
☐ 13	Bob Bescher	10.00	4.75	1.00
☐ 14	Dode Birmingham	10.00	4.75	1.00
☐ 15	Roger Bresnahan	20.00	9.00	2.00
☐ 16	Albert Bridwell	10.00	4.75	1.00
☐ 17	Mordecai Brown	20.00	9.00	2.00
☐ 18	Robert Byrne	10.00	4.75	1.00
☐ 19	James (Nixey) Callahan	10.00	4.75	1.00
☐ 20	Howard Camnitz	10.00	4.75	1.00
☐ 21	William Carrigan	10.00	4.75	1.00
☐ 22	Frank Chance	25.00	11.00	2.50
☐ 23	Hal Chase	15.00	7.00	1.50
☐ 24	Ed Cicotte	12.00	5.50	1.20
☐ 25	Fred Clarke	20.00	9.00	2.00
☐ 26	Ty Cobb	150.00	70.00	15.00
☐ 27	Eddie Collins	25.00	11.00	2.50
☐ 28	Doc Crandall	10.00	4.75	1.00
☐ 29	William Cree	10.00	4.75	1.00
☐ 30	Bill Dahlen	12.00	5.50	1.20
☐ 31	Delahanty	12.00	5.50	1.20
☐ 32	Devlin	10.00	4.75	1.00
☐ 33	Josh Devore	10.00	4.75	1.00
☐ 34	Dooin	10.00	4.75	1.00
☐ 35	Doolan	10.00	4.75	1.00
☐ 36	Dougherty	10.00	4.75	1.00
☐ 37	Downey	10.00	4.75	1.00
☐ 38	Doyle	10.00	4.75	1.00
☐ 39	Louis Drucke	10.00	4.75	1.00
☐ 40	Engle	10.00	4.75	1.00
☐ 41	Erwin	10.00	4.75	1.00
☐ 42	Evans	10.00	4.75	1.00
☐ 43	Johnny Evers	20.00	9.00	2.00
☐ 44	Ferguson	10.00	4.75	1.00
☐ 45	Ford	10.00	4.75	1.00
☐ 46	Fromme	10.00	4.75	1.00
☐ 47	Gaspar	10.00	4.75	1.00
☐ 48	Gibson	10.00	4.75	1.00
☐ 49	Grant	10.00	4.75	1.00
☐ 50	Clark Griffith	20.00	9.00	2.00
☐ 51	Groom	10.00	4.75	1.00
☐ 52	Harmon	10.00	4.75	1.00
☐ 53	Hartsel	10.00	4.75	1.00
☐ 54	Hauser	10.00	4.75	1.00
☐ 55	Hoblitzel	10.00	4.75	1.00
☐ 56	Hoffman	10.00	4.75	1.00
☐ 57	Miller Huggins	25.00	11.00	2.50
☐ 58	Hummell	10.00	4.75	1.00
☐ 59	Hugh Jennings	25.00	11.00	2.50
☐ 60	Walter Johnson	75.00	35.00	7.50
☐ 61	Karger	10.00	4.75	1.00
☐ 62A	John Knight Washington Senators	15.00	7.00	1.50
☐ 62B	John Knight New York Yankees	15.00	7.00	1.50
☐ 63	Konetchy	10.00	4.75	1.00
☐ 64	Krause	10.00	4.75	1.00
☐ 65	Napoleon Lajoie	50.00	22.00	5.00
☐ 66	Laporte	10.00	4.75	1.00
☐ 67	Leach	10.00	4.75	1.00
☐ 68	Leever	10.00	4.75	1.00
☐ 69	Leifield	10.00	4.75	1.00
☐ 70	Livingston	10.00	4.75	1.00
☐ 71	Lobert	10.00	4.75	1.00
☐ 72	Lord	10.00	4.75	1.00
☐ 73	Maddox	10.00	4.75	1.00
☐ 74	McGee	10.00	4.75	1.00
☐ 75	Rube Marquard	20.00	9.00	2.00
☐ 76	Christy Mathewson	75.00	35.00	7.50
☐ 77	Mattern	10.00	4.75	1.00
☐ 78	McBride	10.00	4.75	1.00
☐ 79	John McGraw	30.00	14.00	3.00
☐ 80	McLean	10.00	4.75	1.00
☐ 81	John McIntire	10.00	4.75	1.00
☐ 82	Matthew McIntyre	10.00	4.75	1.00
☐ 83	Fred Merkle	10.00	4.75	1.00
☐ 84	Meyers	10.00	4.75	1.00
☐ 85	Milan	10.00	4.75	1.00
☐ 86	Miller	10.00	4.75	1.00
☐ 87	Mitchell	10.00	4.75	1.00
☐ 88A	Pat Moran Chicago Cubs	15.00	7.00	1.50
☐ 88B	Pat Moran Philadelphia Phillies	15.00	7.00	1.50
☐ 89	Mullen	10.00	4.75	1.00
☐ 90	Murphy	10.00	4.75	1.00
☐ 91	Murray	10.00	4.75	1.00
☐ 92	Needham	10.00	4.75	1.00
☐ 93	Oakes	10.00	4.75	1.00
☐ 94	Oldring	10.00	4.75	1.00
☐ 95	Parent	10.00	4.75	1.00
☐ 96	Dode Paskert	10.00	4.75	1.00
☐ 97	Pelty	10.00	4.75	1.00
☐ 98	Phelps	10.00	4.75	1.00
☐ 99	Deacon Phillippe	12.00	5.50	1.20
☐ 100	Quinn	10.00	4.75	1.00
☐ 101	Ed Reulbach	12.00	5.50	1.20
☐ 102	Richie	10.00	4.75	1.00
☐ 103	Rowan	10.00	4.75	1.00
☐ 104	Nap Rucker	10.00	4.75	1.00
☐ 105A	Doc Scanlan Brooklyn Superbas	15.00	7.00	1.50
☐ 105B	Doc Scanlan Philadelphia Phillies	15.00	7.00	1.50
☐ 106	Germany Schaefer	10.00	4.75	1.00
☐ 107	Schmidt	10.00	4.75	1.00
☐ 108	Schulte	10.00	4.75	1.00
☐ 109	Jimmy Sheckard	10.00	4.75	1.00
☐ 110	Smith	10.00	4.75	1.00
☐ 111	Tris Speaker	50.00	22.00	5.00
☐ 112	Stovall	10.00	4.75	1.00
☐ 113A	Gabby Street Washington Senators	15.00	7.00	1.50
☐ 113B	Gabby Street New York Yankees	15.00	7.00	1.50
☐ 114	Suggs	10.00	4.75	1.00
☐ 115	Thomas	10.00	4.75	1.00
☐ 116	Joe Tinker	20.00	9.00	2.00
☐ 117	Titus	10.00	4.75	1.00
☐ 118	Turner	10.00	4.75	1.00
☐ 119	Heine Wagner	12.00	5.50	1.20
☐ 120	Bobby Wallace	20.00	9.00	2.00
☐ 121	Ed Walsh	20.00	9.00	2.00
☐ 122	Warhop	10.00	4.75	1.00
☐ 123	Wheat	20.00	9.00	2.00
☐ 124	White	10.00	4.75	1.00
☐ 125	John (Chief) Wilson New York Giants	10.00	4.75	1.00
☐ 126	Arthur Wilson Pittsburgh Pirates	10.00	4.75	1.00
☐ 127	Hooks Wiltse	10.00	4.75	1.00
☐ 128	Wolter	10.00	4.75	1.00
☐ 129	Cy Young	50.00	22.00	5.00

Doubleheader Pins

These metal discs were issued by Gum, Inc. circa 1933. The player's picture, name, and team are on the front whereas the back is blank. Also on the front is a "1" or a "2". The wrapper says, "Put 1 and 2 together and make a Double Header." Each disc is approximately 1 1/4" in diameter. The ACC designation for this set is PX3.

	MINT	VG-E	F-G
COMPLETE SET	650.00	300.00	50.00
COMMON PLAYER	12.00	5.50	1.20

		MINT	VG-E	F-G
☐	1 "Sparky" Adams 1	12.00	5.50	1.20
☐	2 Dale Alexander 2	12.00	5.50	1.20
☐	3 Earl Averill	20.00	9.00	2.00
☐	4 Dick Bartell 1	12.00	5.50	1.20
☐	5 Walter Berger 2	12.00	5.50	1.20
☐	6 "Sunny"Jim Bottomley 2	20.00	9.00	2.00
☐	7 "Lefty" Brandt	12.00	5.50	1.20
☐	8 Owen T. Carroll 1	12.00	5.50	1.20
☐	9 "Lefty" Clark 2	12.00	5.50	1.20
☐	10 Mickey Cochrane 2	30.00	14.00	3.00
☐	11 Joe Cronin	25.00	11.00	2.50
☐	12 Jimmy Dykes 2	12.00	5.50	1.20
☐	13 George Earnshaw 1	12.00	5.50	1.20
☐	14 Wes Ferrell 1	12.00	5.50	1.20
☐	15 Neal Finn	12.00	5.50	1.20
☐	16 Lew Fonseca 1	12.00	5.50	1.20
☐	17 Jimmy Foxx 2	50.00	22.00	5.00
☐	18 Frankie Frisch 1	30.00	14.00	3.00
☐	19 "Chick" Fullis 1	12.00	5.50	1.20
☐	20 Charley Gehringer 1	30.00	14.00	3.00
☐	21 "Goose Goslin 1	20.00	9.00	2.00
☐	22 Johnny Hodapp 2	12.00	5.50	1.20
☐	23 Frank Hogan 2	12.00	5.50	1.20
☐	24 Si Johnson 2	12.00	5.50	1.20
☐	25 Joe Judge 2	12.00	5.50	1.20
☐	26 "Chuck" Klein 1	25.00	11.00	2.50
☐	27 Al Lopez 1	20.00	9.00	2.00
☐	28 Ray Lucas 1	12.00	5.50	1.20
☐	29 Red Lucas 1	12.00	5.50	1.20
☐	30 Ted Lyons 2	20.00	9.00	2.00
☐	31 "Firpo" Marberry 1	12.00	5.50	1.20
☐	32 Oscar Melillo 2	12.00	5.50	1.20
☐	33 Lefty O'Doul 1	12.00	5.50	1.20
☐	34 George Pipgras 1	12.00	5.50	1.20
☐	35 Flint Rhem 1	12.00	5.50	1.20
☐	36 Sam Rice 1	20.00	9.00	2.00
☐	37 "Muddy" Ruel 1	12.00	5.50	1.20
☐	38 Harry Seibold 1	12.00	5.50	1.20
☐	39 Al Simmons 1	25.00	11.00	2.50
☐	40 Joe Vosmik 1	12.00	5.50	1.20
☐	41 Gerald Walker	12.00	5.50	1.20
☐	42 "Pinky" Whitney 2	12.00	5.50	1.20
☐	43 Hack Wilson	25.00	11.00	2.50

1986 KAS Cardinals Discs

WILLIE McGEE
ST. LOUIS CARDINALS
OUTFIELD

This set of discs was distributed by KAS in 1986 to commemorate the Cardinal's "almost" World Championship in 1985. Each disc measures 2 3/4" in diameter. Each disc has a white border on the front. Inside this white border is a full color photo of the player with his hat airbrushed to erase the team logo on ther hat. The statistics on back of the

disc give the player's 1984 pitching or hitting record as well as his vital statistics. The discs are numbered on the back.

	MINT	VG-E	F-G
COMPLETE SET	10.00	4.75	1' 0
COMMON PLAYER	.30	.12	.03

		MINT	VG-E	F-G
☐	1 Vince Coleman	1.50	.70	.15
☐	2 Ken Dayley	.30	.12	.03
☐	3 Tito Landrum	.30	.12	.03
☐	4 Steve Braun	.30	.12	.03
☐	5 Danny Cox	.40	.18	.04
☐	6 Bob Forsch	.40	.18	.04
☐	7 Ozzie Smith	.75	.35	.07
☐	8 Brian Harper	.30	.12	.03
☐	9 Jack Clark	.50	.22	.05
☐	10 Todd Worrell	.50	.22	.05
☐	11 Joaquin Andujar	.50	.22	.05
☐	12 Tom Nieto	.30	.12	.03
☐	13 Kurt Kepshire	.30	.12	.03
☐	14 Terry Pendleton	.40	.18	.04
☐	15 Tom Herr	.40	.18	.04
☐	16 Darrell Porter	.40	.18	.04
☐	17 John Tudor	.50	.22	.05
☐	18 Jeff Lahti	.30	.12	.03
☐	19 Andy Van Slyke	.40	.18	.04
☐	20 Willie McGee	.75	.35	.07

1986 Kitty Clover Discs

GEORGE BRETT
KANSAS CITY ROYALS
INFIELD

This set of discs was distributed by Kitty Clover in 1986 to commemorate the Royals' World Championship in 1985. Each disc measures 2 3/4" in diameter. Each disc has a white border on the front. Inside this white border is a full color photo of the player with his hat on. However the hat's team emblem has been deleted from the picture. The statistics on back of the disc give the player's 1985 pitching or hitting record as well as his vital statistics. The discs are numbered on the back.

	MINT	VG-E	F-G
COMPLETE SET	10.00	4.75	1.00
COMMON PLAYER	.30	.12	.03

		MINT	VG-E	F-G
☐	1 Lonnie Smith	.40	.18	.04
☐	2 Buddy Biancalana	.40	.18	.04
☐	3 Bret Saberhagen	1.00	.45	.10
☐	4 Hal McRae	.40	.18	.04
☐	5 Onix Concepcion	.30	.12	.03
☐	6 Jorge Orta	.30	.12	.03
☐	7 Bud Black	.40	.18	.04
☐	8 Dan Quisenberry	.60	.28	.06
☐	9 Dane Iorg	.30	.12	.03
☐	10 Charlie Leibrandt	.40	.18	.04
☐	11 Pat Sheridan	.30	.12	.03
☐	12 John Wathan	.30	.12	.03
☐	13 Frank White	.40	.18	.04

☐ 14	Darryl Motley	.30	.12	.03
☐ 15	Willie Wilson	.50	.22	.05
☐ 16	Danny Jackson	.40	.18	.04
☐ 17	Steve Balboni	.40	.18	.04
☐ 18	Jim Sundberg	.40	.18	.04
☐ 19	Mark Gubicza	.40	.18	.04
☐ 20	George Brett	1.50	.70	.15

1965 Old London Coins

1977 Pepsi Discs

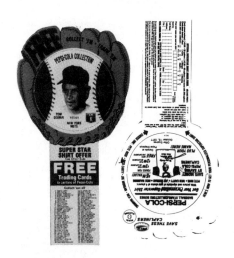

The Old London set of metal baseball coins was distributed in that company's snack products in 1965. The coin was produced for Old London by Space Magic, Ltd. a Canadian firm which manufactured similar sets in 1964 and 1971. Each metal coin measures 1 1/2" in diameter. The silver-colored backs contain the company logo and a short biographical sketch of the player. Each team is represented by two ballplayers, except for the Mets (1) and the Cardinals (3) -- Tracy Stallard was traded from the former to the latter.

	MINT	VG-E	F-G
COMPLETE SET	325.00	150.00	30.00
COMMON PLAYER	3.00	1.40	.30

☐ 1	Hank Aaron	40.00	18.00	4.00
☐ 2	Richie Allen	5.00	2.35	.50
☐ 3	Ernie Banks	20.00	9.00	2.00
☐ 4	Ken Boyer	5.00	2.35	.50
☐ 5	Jim Bunning	7.50	3.50	.75
☐ 6	Orlando Cepeda	5.00	2.35	.50
☐ 7	Willie Davis	4.00	1.85	.40
☐ 8	Ron Fairly	3.00	1.40	.30
☐ 9	Dick Farrell	3.00	1.40	.30
☐ 10	Bob Friend	3.00	1.40	.30
☐ 11	Dick Groat	4.00	1.85	.40
☐ 12	Ron Hunt	3.00	1.40	.30
☐ 13	Ken Johnson	3.00	1.40	.30
☐ 14	Willie Mays	40.00	18.00	4.00
☐ 15	Bill Mazeroski	5.00	2.35	.50
☐ 16	Vada Pinson	5.00	2.35	.50
☐ 17	Frank Robinson	20.00	9.00	2.00
☐ 18	Tracy Stallard	3.00	1.40	.30
☐ 19	Joe Torre	5.00	2.35	.50
☐ 20	Billy Williams	7.50	3.50	.75
☐ 21	Bob Allison	3.00	1.40	.30
☐ 22	Dean Chance	3.00	1.40	.30
☐ 23	Rocky Colavito	5.00	2.35	.50
☐ 24	Vic Davalillo	3.00	1.40	.30
☐ 25	Jim Fregosi	4.00	1.85	.40
☐ 26	Chuck Hinton	3.00	1.40	.30
☐ 27	Al Kaline	20.00	9.00	2.00
☐ 28	Harmon Killebrew	15.00	7.00	1.50
☐ 29	Don Lock	3.00	1.40	.30
☐ 30	Mickey Mantle	60.00	27.00	6.00
☐ 31	Roger Maris	15.00	7.00	1.50
☐ 32	Gary Peters	3.00	1.40	.30
☐ 33	Boog Powell	5.00	2.35	.50
☐ 34	Dick Radatz	3.00	1.40	.30
☐ 35	Brooks Robinson	20.00	9.00	2.00
☐ 36	Leon Wagner	3.00	1.40	.30
☐ 37	Pete Ward	3.00	1.40	.30
☐ 38	Dave Wickersham	3.00	1.40	.30
☐ 39	John Wyatt	3.00	1.40	.30
☐ 40	Carl Yastrzemski	40.00	18.00	4.00

These discs actually form the middle of a glove-shaped tab which was inserted in cartons of Pepsi-Cola during a baseball related promotion. The disc itself measures 3 3/8" in diameter the glove tab is approximately 9" tall. The backs of the discs and the tab tell how you can get a personalized superstar shirt of Pete Rose, Rico Carty, Joe Morgan, or Rick Manning by sending in Pepsi cap liners. The players are shown in "generic" hats, i.e., the team logos have been airbrushed. This set was sanctioned by the Major League Baseball Players Association. The set is quite heavy in Cleveland Indians and Cincinnati Reds.

	MINT	VG-E	F-G
COMPLETE SET	8.00	3.75	.80
COMMON PLAYER (1-72)	.04	.02	.00

☐ 1	Robin Yount	.40	.18	.04
☐ 2	Rod Carew	.40	.18	.04
☐ 3	Butch Wynegar	.04	.02	.00
☐ 4	Manny Sanguillen	.04	.02	.00
☐ 5	Mike Hargrove	.04	.02	.00
☐ 6	Larvel Blanks	.04	.02	.00
☐ 7	Jim Kern	.04	.02	.00
☐ 8	Pat Dobson	.04	.02	.00
☐ 9	Rico Carty	.06	.02	.00
☐ 10	John Grubb	.04	.02	.00
☐ 11	Buddy Bell	.10	.04	.01
☐ 12	Rick Manning	.06	.02	.00
☐ 13	Dennis Eckersley	.06	.02	.00
☐ 14	Wayne Garland	.04	.02	.00
☐ 15	Dave Laroche	.04	.02	.00
☐ 16	Rick Waits	.04	.02	.00
☐ 17	Ray Fosse	.04	.02	.00
☐ 18	Frank Duffy	.04	.02	.00
☐ 19	Duane Kuiper	.04	.02	.00
☐ 20	Jim Palmer	.25	.10	.02
☐ 21	Fred Lynn	.20	.09	.02
☐ 22	Carlton Fisk	.10	.04	.01
☐ 23	Carl Yastrzemski	.60	.28	.06
☐ 24	Nolan Ryan	.40	.18	.04
☐ 25	Bobby Grich	.08	.03	.01
☐ 26	Ralph Garr	.04	.02	.00
☐ 27	Richie Zisk	.04	.02	.00
☐ 28	Ron LeFlore	.04	.02	.00
☐ 29	Rusty Staub	.08	.03	.01
☐ 30	Mark Fidrych	.08	.03	.01
☐ 31	Willie Horton	.06	.02	.00
☐ 32	George Brett	.60	.28	.06
☐ 33	Amos Otis	.06	.02	.00
☐ 34	Reggie Jackson	.50	.22	.05
☐ 35	Don Gullett	.04	.02	.00
☐ 36	Thurman Munson	.30	.12	.03

☐ 37 Al Hrabosky	.04	.02	.00
☐ 38 Mike Tyson	.04	.02	.00
☐ 39 Gene Tenace	.04	.02	.00
☐ 40 George Hendrick	.06	.02	.00
☐ 41 Chris Speier	.04	.02	.00
☐ 42 John Montefusco	.04	.02	.00
☐ 43 Pete Rose	1.00	.45	.10
☐ 44 Johnny Bench	.40	.18	.04
☐ 45 Dan Driessen	.04	.02	.00
☐ 46 Joe Morgan	.25	.10	.02
☐ 47 Dave Concepcion	.08	.03	.01
☐ 48 George Foster	.15	.06	.01
☐ 49 Cesar Geronimo	.04	.02	.00
☐ 50 Ken Griffey	.06	.02	.00
☐ 51 Gary Nolan	.04	.02	.00
☐ 52 Santo Alcala	.04	.02	.00
☐ 53 Jack Billingham	.04	.02	.00
☐ 54 Pedro Borbon	.04	.02	.00
☐ 55 Rawly Eastwick	.04	.02	.00
☐ 56 Fred Norman	.04	.02	.00
☐ 57 Pat Zachry	.04	.02	.00
☐ 58 Jeff Burroughs	.06	.02	.00
☐ 59 Manny Trillo	.06	.02	.00
☐ 60 Bob Watson	.06	.02	.00
☐ 61 Steve Garvey	.50	.22	.05
☐ 62 Don Sutton	.15	.06	.01
☐ 63 John Candelaria	.06	.02	.00
☐ 64 Willie Stargell	.25	.10	.02
☐ 65 Jerry Reuss	.06	.02	.00
☐ 66 Dave Cash	.04	.02	.00
☐ 67 Tom Seaver	.40	.18	.04
☐ 68 Jon Matlack	.06	.02	.00
☐ 69 Dave Kingman	.15	.06	.01
☐ 70 Mike Schmidt	.50	.22	.05
☐ 71 Jay Johnstone	.04	.02	.00
☐ 72 Greg Luzinski	.10	.04	.01

1962 Salada Plastic Coins

There are 221 different players in the 1962 plastic baseball coins marketed in Salada Tea and Junket Pudding mixes. Each plastic coin measures 1 3/8" in diameter. The initial production run consisted of 10 representatives from each of the 18 major league teams. A subsequent run added 20 players from the Mets and the Colt 45's and also dropped 21 of the original subjects, who were replaced by 21 new players assigned higher numbers. The "coin" itself is made of one-color plastic (light or dark) blue, black, orange, red or white) which has a color portrait printed on paper inserted into the obverse serface. A 10-coin, shield-like holder was available for each team. The complete set price below includes all variations.

	MINT	VG-E	F-G
COMPLETE SET	4000.00	1800.00	400.00
COMMON PLAYER (1-180)	1.50	.70	.15
COMMON PLAYER (181-221)	3.00	1.40	.30

☐ 1 Jim Gentile	1.50	.70	.15
☐ 2 Billy Pierce	100.00	45.00	10.00
☐ 3 Chico Fernandez	1.50	.70	.15
☐ 4 Tom Brewer	20.00	9.00	2.00
☐ 5 Woody Held	1.50	.70	.15
☐ 6 Ray Herbert	20.00	9.00	2.00
☐ 7A Ken Aspromonte (Angels)	5.00	2.35	.50

☐ 7B Ken Aspromonte (Cleveland)	2.50	1.15	.25
☐ 8 Whitey Ford	15.00	7.00	1.50
☐ 9A Jim Lemon (red buttons) (does not exist)	.00	.00	.00
☐ 9B Jim Lemon (white buttons)	1.50	.70	.15
☐ 10 Billy Klaus	1.50	.70	.15
☐ 11 Steve Barber	20.00	9.00	2.00
☐ 12 Nellie Fox	5.00	2.35	.50
☐ 13 Jim Bunning	4.00	1.85	.40
☐ 14 Frank Malzone	1.50	.70	.15
☐ 15 Tito Francona	1.50	.70	.15
☐ 16 Bobby Del Greco	1.50	.70	.15
☐ 17A Steve Bilko (red buttons)	5.00	2.35	.50
☐ 17B Steve Bilko (white buttons)	2.50	1.15	.25
☐ 18 Tony Kubek	40.00	18.00	4.00
☐ 19 Earl Battey	1.50	.70	.15
☐ 20 Chuck Cottier	1.50	.70	.15
☐ 21 Willie Tasby	1.50	.70	.15
☐ 22 Bob Allison	2.50	1.15	.25
☐ 23 Roger Maris	20.00	9.00	2.00
☐ 24A Earl Averill (red buttons)	5.00	2.35	.50
☐ 24B Earl Averill (white buttons)	2.50	1.15	.25
☐ 25 Jerry Lumpe	1.50	.70	.15
☐ 26 Jim Grant	20.00	9.00	2.00
☐ 27 Carl Yastrzemski	50.00	22.00	5.00
☐ 28 Rocky Colavito	2.50	1.15	.25
☐ 29 Al Smith	1.50	.70	.15
☐ 30 Jim Busby	20.00	9.00	2.00
☐ 31 Dick Howser	2.50	1.15	.25
☐ 32 Jim Perry	2.50	1.15	.25
☐ 33 Yogi Berra	20.00	9.00	2.00
☐ 34A Ken Hamlin (red buttons)	5.00	2.35	.50
☐ 34B Ken Hamlin (white buttons)	2.50	1.15	.25
☐ 35 Dale Long	1.50	.70	.15
☐ 36 Harmon Killebrew	15.00	7.00	1.50
☐ 37 Hal Brown	1.50	.70	.15
☐ 38A Gary Geiger (O on hat)	500.00	225.00	50.00
☐ 38B Gary Geiger (no O on hat)	2.50	1.15	.25
☐ 39A Minnie Minoso (White Sox)	25.00	11.00	2.50
☐ 39B Minnie Minoso (Cardinals)	15.00	7.00	1.50
☐ 40 Brooks Robinson	30.00	14.00	3.00
☐ 41 Mickey Mantle	60.00	27.00	6.00
☐ 42 Bennie Daniels	1.50	.70	.15
☐ 43 Billy Martin	3.00	1.40	.30
☐ 44 Vic Power	1.50	.70	.15
☐ 45 Joe Pignatano	1.50	.70	.15
☐ 46A Ryne Duren (red buttons)	5.00	2.35	.50
☐ 46B Ryne Duren (white buttons)	2.50	1.15	.25
☐ 47A Pete Runnels (2nd base)	6.00	2.80	.60
☐ 47B Pete Runnels (1st base)	3.00	1.40	.30
☐ 48A Dick Williams (name right)	750.00	350.00	75.00
☐ 48B Dick Williams (name left)	5.00	2.35	.50
☐ 49 Jim Landis	1.50	.70	.15
☐ 50 Steve Boros	1.50	.70	.15
☐ 51A Zoilo Versalles (red buttons)	5.00	2.35	.50
☐ 51B Zoilo Versalles (white buttons)	2.50	1.15	.25
☐ 52 Johnny Temple (Indians)	8.00	3.75	.80
☐ 52 Johnny Temple (Orioles)	4.00	1.85	.40
☐ 53A Jackie Brandt (Oriole)	5.00	2.35	.50
☐ 53B Jackie Brandt (Orioles)	750.00	350.00	75.00
☐ 54 Denny McLain	2.50	1.15	.25
☐ 55 Sherm Lollar	1.50	.70	.15
☐ 56 Gene Stephens	1.50	.70	.15
☐ 57A Leon Wagner (red buttons)	5.00	2.35	.50
☐ 57B Leon Wagner (white buttons)	2.50	1.15	.25
☐ 58 Frank Lary	1.50	.70	.15

☐ 59	Bill Skowron	2.50	1.15	.25
☐ 60	Vic Wertz	20.00	9.00	2.00
☐ 61	Willie Kirkland	1.50	.70	.15
☐ 62	Leo Posada	1.50	.70	.15
☐ 63A	Albie Pearson (red buttons)	5.00	2.35	.50
☐ 63B	Albie Pearson (white buttons)	2.50	1.15	.25
☐ 64	Bobby Richardson	5.00	2.35	.50
☐ 65A	Marv Breeding (Shortstop)	6.00	2.80	.60
☐ 65B	Marv Breeding (2nd Base)	3.00	1.40	.30
☐ 66	Roy Sievers	75.00	35.00	7.50
☐ 67	Al Kaline	25.00	11.00	2.50
☐ 68A	Don Buddin (Red Sox)	6.00	2.80	.60
☐ 68B	Don Buddin (Colt .45's)	3.00	1.40	.30
☐ 69A	Lenny Green (red buttons)	5.00	2.35	.50
☐ 69B	Lenny Green (white buttons)	2.50	1.15	.25
☐ 70	Gene Green	20.00	9.00	2.00
☐ 71	Luis Aparicio	6.00	2.80	.60
☐ 72	Norm Cash	2.50	1.15	.25
☐ 73	Jackie Jensen	20.00	9.00	2.00
☐ 74	Bubba Phillips	1.50	.70	.15
☐ 75	James Archer	1.50	.70	.15
☐ 76A	Ken Hunt (red buttons)	5.00	2.35	.50
☐ 76B	Ken Hunt (white buttons)	2.50	1.15	.25
☐ 77	Ralph Terry	2.50	1.15	.25
☐ 78	Camilo Pascual	1.50	.70	.15
☐ 79	Marty Keough	20.00	9.00	2.00
☐ 80	Clete Boyer	2.50	1.15	.25
☐ 81	Jim Pagliaroni	1.50	.70	.15
☐ 82A	Gene Leek (red buttons)	5.00	2.35	.50
☐ 82B	Gene Leek (white buttons)	2.50	1.15	.25
☐ 83	Jake Wood	1.50	.70	.15
☐ 84	Coot Veal	20.00	9.00	2.00
☐ 85	Norm Siebern	1.50	.70	.15
☐ 86A	Andy Carey (White Sox)	30.00	14.00	3.00
☐ 86B	Andy Carey (Phillies)	4.00	1.85	.40
☐ 87A	Bill Tuttle (red buttons)	5.00	2.35	.50
☐ 87B	Bill Tuttle (white buttons)	2.50	1.15	.25
☐ 88A	Jimmy Piersall (Indians)	6.00	2.80	.60
☐ 88B	Jimmy Piersall (Senators)	3.00	1.40	.30
☐ 89	Ron Hansen	30.00	14.00	3.00
☐ 90A	Chuck Stobbs (red buttons)	5.00	2.35	.50
☐ 90B	Chuck Stobbs (white buttons)	2.50	1.15	.25
☐ 91A	Ken McBride (red buttons)	5.00	2.35	.50
☐ 91B	Ken McBride (white buttons)	2.50	1.15	.25
☐ 92	Bill Bruton	1.50	.70	.15
☐ 93	Gus Triandos	1.50	.70	.15
☐ 94	John Romano	1.50	.70	.15
☐ 95	Frank Howard	2.50	1.15	.25
☐ 96	Gene Woodling	1.50	.70	.15
☐ 97A	Early Wynn (pitching)	30.00	14.00	3.00
☐ 97B	Early Wynn (portrait)	15.00	7.00	1.50
☐ 98	Milt Pappas	1.50	.70	.15
☐ 99	Bill Monboquette	1.50	.70	.15
☐ 100	Wayne Causey	1.50	.70	.15
☐ 101	Don Elston	1.50	.70	.15
☐ 102A	Charlie Neal (Dodgers)	6.00	2.80	.60
☐ 102B	Charlie Neal (Mets)	3.00	1.40	.30
☐ 103	Don Blasingame	1.50	.70	.15
☐ 104	Frank Thomas	20.00	9.00	2.00
☐ 105	Wes Covington	1.50	.70	.15
☐ 106	Chuck Hiller	1.50	.70	.15
☐ 107	Don Hoak	1.50	.70	.15
☐ 108A	Bob Lillis (Cardinals)	12.00	5.50	1.20
☐ 108B	Bob Lillis (Colt .45's)	3.00	1.40	.30
☐ 109	Sandy Koufax	20.00	9.00	2.00
☐ 110	Jerry Coleman	1.50	.70	.15
☐ 111	Eddie Matthews (sic, Mathews)	12.00	5.50	1.20
☐ 112	Art Mahaffey	1.50	.70	.15
☐ 113A	Ed Bailey (red buttons)	9.00	4.25	.90
☐ 113B	Ed Bailey (white buttons)	2.50	1.15	.25
☐ 114	Smokey Burgess	1.50	.70	.15
☐ 115	Bill White	1.50	.70	.15
☐ 116	Ed Bouchee	20.00	9.00	2.00
☐ 117	Bob Buhl	1.50	.70	.15
☐ 118	Vada Pinson	2.50	1.15	.25
☐ 119	Carl Sawatski	1.50	.70	.15
☐ 120	Dick Stuart	1.50	.70	.15
☐ 121	Harvey Kuenn	30.00	14.00	3.00
☐ 122	Pancho Herrera	1.50	.70	.15
☐ 123A	Don Zimmer (Cubs)	6.00	2.80	.60
☐ 123B	Don Zimmer (Mets)	3.00	1.40	.30
☐ 124	Wally Moon	1.50	.70	.15
☐ 125	Joe Adcock	1.50	.70	.15
☐ 126	Joey Jay	1.50	.70	.15
☐ 127A	Maury Wills (blue number 3)	8.00	3.75	.80
☐ 127B	Maury Wills (red number 3)	8.00	3.75	.80
☐ 128	George Altman	1.50	.70	.15
☐ 129A	John Buzhardt (Phillies)	6.00	2.80	.60
☐ 129B	John Buzhardt (White Sox)	3.00	1.40	.30
☐ 130	Felipe Alou	1.50	.70	.15
☐ 131	Bill Mazeroski	2.50	1.15	.25
☐ 132	Ernie Broglio	1.50	.70	.15
☐ 133	Johnny Roseboro	1.50	.70	.15
☐ 134	Mike McCormick	1.50	.70	.15
☐ 135A	Charlie Smith (Philadelphia)	6.00	2.80	.60
☐ 135B	Charlie Smith (White Sox)	3.00	1.40	.30
☐ 136	Ron Santo	2.50	1.15	.25
☐ 137	Gene Freese	1.50	.70	.15
☐ 138	Dick Groat	2.50	1.15	.25
☐ 139	Curt Flood	2.50	1.15	.25
☐ 140	Frank Bolling	1.50	.70	.15
☐ 141	Clay Dalrymple	1.50	.70	.15
☐ 142	Willie McCovey	20.00	9.00	2.00
☐ 143	Bob Skinner	1.50	.70	.15
☐ 144	Lindy McDaniel	1.50	.70	.15
☐ 145	Glenn Hobbie	1.50	.70	.15
☐ 146A	Gil Hodges (Dodgers)	30.00	14.00	3.00
☐ 146B	Gil Hodges (Mets)	15.00	7.00	1.50
☐ 147	Eddie Kasko	1.50	.70	.15
☐ 148	Gino Cimoli	60.00	27.00	6.00
☐ 149	Willie Mays	50.00	22.00	5.00
☐ 150	Bob Clemente	40.00	18.00	4.00
☐ 151	Red Schoendienst	2.50	1.15	.25
☐ 152	Joe Torre	2.50	1.15	.25
☐ 153	Bob Purkey	1.50	.70	.15
☐ 154A	Tommy Davis (Outfield)	5.00	2.35	.50
☐ 154B	Tommy Davis (3rd Base)	2.50	1.15	.25
☐ 155A	Andre Rodgers (Shortstop)	5.00	2.35	.50
☐ 155B	Andre Rodgers (1st Base)	2.50	1.15	.25
☐ 156	Tony Taylor	1.50	.70	.15
☐ 157	Bob Friend	1.50	.70	.15
☐ 158A	Gus Bell (Reds)	6.00	2.80	.60
☐ 158B	Gus Bell (Mets)	3.00	1.40	.30
☐ 159	Roy McMillan	1.50	.70	.15
☐ 160	Carl Warwick	1.50	.70	.15
☐ 161	Willie Davis	1.50	.70	.15
☐ 162	Sam Jones	50.00	22.00	5.00
☐ 163	Ruben Amaro	1.50	.70	.15
☐ 164	Sammy Taylor	1.50	.70	.15
☐ 165	Frank Robinson	20.00	9.00	2.00
☐ 166	Lew Burdette	2.50	1.15	.25
☐ 167	Ken Boyer	2.50	1.15	.25
☐ 168	Bill Virdon	2.50	1.15	.25
☐ 169	Jim Davenport	1.50	.70	.15
☐ 170	Don Demeter	1.50	.70	.15
☐ 171	Richie Ashburn	30.00	14.00	3.00
☐ 172	Johnny Podres	2.50	1.15	.25
☐ 173A	Joe Cunningham (Cardinals)	30.00	14.00	3.00

☐ 173B	Joe Cunningham (White Sox)	15.00	7.00	1.50
☐ 174	Elroy Face	1.50	.70	.15
☐ 175	Orlando Cepeda	2.50	1.15	.25
☐ 176A	Bobby Gene Smith (Philadelphia)	6.00	2.80	.60
☐ 176B	Bobby Gene Smith (Mets)	3.00	1.40	.30
☐ 177A	Ernie Banks (Outfield)	30.00	14.00	3.00
☐ 177B	Ernie Banks (Shortstop)	15.00	7.00	1.50
☐ 178A	Daryl Spencer (3rd Base)	6.00	2.80	.60
☐ 178B	Daryl Spencer (1st Base)	3.00	1.40	.30
☐ 179	Bob Schmidt	20.00	9.00	2.00
☐ 180	Henry Aaron	50.00	22.00	5.00
☐ 181	Hobie Landrith	3.00	1.40	.30
☐ 182A	Ed Broussard (sic, Bressoud)	250.00	110.00	25.00
☐ 182B	Ed Bressoud (correct)	15.00	7.00	1.50
☐ 183	Felix Mantilla	3.00	1.40	.30
☐ 184	Dick Farrell	3.00	1.40	.30
☐ 185	Bob Miller	3.00	1.40	.30
☐ 186	Don Taussig	3.00	1.40	.30
☐ 187	Pumpsie Green	3.00	1.40	.30
☐ 188	Bobby Shantz	3.00	1.40	.30
☐ 189	Roger Craig	4.00	1.85	.40
☐ 190	Hal Smith	3.00	1.40	.30
☐ 191	Johnny Edwards	3.00	1.40	.30
☐ 192	John DeMerit	3.00	1.40	.30
☐ 193	Joe Amalfitano	3.00	1.40	.30
☐ 194	Norm Larker	3.00	1.40	.30
☐ 195	Al Heist	3.00	1.40	.30
☐ 196	Al Spangler	3.00	1.40	.30
☐ 197	Alex Grammas	3.00	1.40	.30
☐ 198	Jerry Lynch	3.00	1.40	.30
☐ 199	Jim McKnight	3.00	1.40	.30
☐ 200	Jose Pagen (sic, Pagan)	3.00	1.40	.30
☐ 201	Jim Gilliam	10.00	4.75	1.00
☐ 202	Art Ditmar	3.00	1.40	.30
☐ 203	Bud Daley	3.00	1.40	.30
☐ 204	John Callison	4.00	1.85	.40
☐ 205	Stu Miller	3.00	1.40	.30
☐ 206	Russ Snyder	3.00	1.40	.30
☐ 207	Billy Williams	15.00	7.00	1.50
☐ 208	Walt Bond	3.00	1.40	.30
☐ 209	Joe Koppe	3.00	1.40	.30
☐ 210	Don Schwall	15.00	7.00	1.50
☐ 211	Billy Gardner	3.00	1.40	.30
☐ 212	Chuck Estrada	3.00	1.40	.30
☐ 213	Gary Bell	3.00	1.40	.30
☐ 214	Floyd Robinson	3.00	1.40	.30
☐ 215	Duke Snider	30.00	14.00	3.00
☐ 216	Lee Maye	3.00	1.40	.30
☐ 217	Howie Bedell	3.00	1.40	.30
☐ 218	Bob Will	3.00	1.40	.30
☐ 219	Dick Green	10.00	4.75	1.00
☐ 220	Carroll Hardy	3.00	1.40	.30
☐ 221	Danny O'Connell	3.00	1.40	.30

1963 Salada Metal Coins

The 1963 baseball coin set distributed by Salada Tea and Junket Pudding marked a drastic change from the set of the previous year. The coins were made of metal, rather than plastic, with conspicuous red rims for National League players and blue rims for their American League counterparts. Each coin measures 1 1/2" in diameter. The subject's portrait was printed in color on the front, with his name,

position, team and 1962 statistics listed on the back. Also on the reverse is located the coin number and the line "Save and Trade 63 All Star Baseball Coins."

		MINT	VG-E	F-G
COMPLETE SET		275.00	120.00	27.00
COMMON PLAYER		2.50	1.15	.25
☐ 1	Don Drysdale	12.50	5.50	1.25
☐ 2	Dick Farrell	2.50	1.15	.25
☐ 3	Bob Gibson	15.00	7.00	1.50
☐ 4	Sandy Koufax	25.00	11.00	2.50
☐ 5	Juan Marichal	12.50	5.75	1.25
☐ 6	Bob Purkey	2.50	1.15	.25
☐ 7	Bob Shaw	2.50	1.15	.25
☐ 8	Warren Spahn	15.00	7.00	1.50
☐ 9	Johnny Podres	2.50	1.15	.25
☐ 10	Art Mahaffey	2.50	1.15	.25
☐ 11	Del Crandall	2.50	1.15	.25
☐ 12	John Roseboro	2.50	1.15	.25
☐ 13	Orlando Cepeda	3.50	1.65	.35
☐ 14	Bill Mazeroski	3.50	1.65	.35
☐ 15	Ken Boyer	3.50	1.65	.35
☐ 16	Dick Groat	3.50	1.65	.35
☐ 17	Ernie Banks	15.00	7.00	1.50
☐ 18	Frank Bolling	2.50	1.15	.25
☐ 19	Jim Davenport	2.50	1.15	.25
☐ 20	Maury Wills	5.00	2.35	.50
☐ 21	Willie Davis	2.50	1.15	.25
☐ 22	Willie Mays	35.00	16.50	3.50
☐ 23	Bob Clemente	30.00	14.00	3.00
☐ 24	Henry Aaron	35.00	16.50	3.50
☐ 25	Matty Alou	2.50	1.15	.25
☐ 26	John Callison	2.50	1.15	.25
☐ 27	Richie Ashburn	5.00	2.35	.50
☐ 28	Eddie Mathews	15.00	7.00	1.50
☐ 29	Frank Robinson	15.00	7.00	1.50
☐ 30	Billy Williams	12.00	5.50	1.20
☐ 31	George Altman	2.50	1.15	.25
☐ 32	Hank Aguirre	2.50	1.15	.25
☐ 33	Jim Bunning	5.00	2.35	.50
☐ 34	Dick Donovan	2.50	1.15	.25
☐ 35	Bill Monbouquette	2.50	1.15	.25
☐ 36	Camilo Pascual	2.50	1.15	.25
☐ 37	Dave Stenhouse	2.50	1.15	.25
☐ 38	Ralph Terry	2.50	1.15	.25
☐ 39	Hoyt Wilhelm	10.00	4.75	1.00
☐ 40	Jim Kaat	5.00	2.35	.50
☐ 41	Ken McBride	2.50	1.15	.25
☐ 42	Ray Herbert	2.50	1.15	.25
☐ 43	Milt Pappas	2.50	1.15	.25
☐ 44	Earl Battey	2.50	1.15	.25
☐ 45	Elston Howard	3.50	1.65	.35
☐ 46	John Romano	2.50	1.15	.25
☐ 47	Jim Gentile	2.50	1.15	.25
☐ 48	Billy Moran	2.50	1.15	.25
☐ 49	Rich Rollins	2.50	1.15	.25
☐ 50	Luis Aparicio	10.00	4.75	1.00
☐ 51	Norm Siebern	2.50	1.15	.25
☐ 52	Bobby Richardson	5.00	2.35	.50
☐ 53	Brooks Robinson	25.00	11.00	2.50
☐ 54	Tom Tresh	3.50	1.65	.35
☐ 55	Leon Wagner	2.50	1.15	.25
☐ 56	Mickey Mantle	60.00	27.00	6.00
☐ 57	Roger Maris	20.00	9.00	2.00
☐ 58	Rocky Colavito	5.00	2.35	.50
☐ 59	Frank Thomas	2.50	1.15	.25
☐ 60	Jim Landis	2.50	1.15	.25
☐ 61	Pete Runnels	2.50	1.15	.25
☐ 62	Yogi Berra	25.00	11.00	2.50
☐ 63	Al Kaline	25.00	11.00	2.50

1983 Seven-Eleven Coins

The coins in this 12 coin set measure 1 3/4" diameter. This set of action coins was released by 7-11 stores in the Los Angeles area. Given out with large Slurpee drinks, the set features Los Angeles Dodgers (blue background) and California Angels (red background) on plastic discs. The fronts feature two pictures (portrait and action) of each player, each of which can be seen by moving the coin slightly to one side or another. Brief statistics fill the backs of these coins. The coins are numbered by

uniform number on the front; in addition, an individual coin number can be found on the back.

	MINT	VG-E	F-G
COMPLETE SET	10.00	4.75	1.00
COMMON PLAYER	.50	.22	.05
☐ 1 Rod Carew California Angels 29	1.50	.70	.15
☐ 2 Steve Sax Los Angeles Dodgers 3	1.00	.45	.10
☐ 3 Fred Lynn California Angels 19	1.00	.45	.10
☐ 4 Pedro Guerrero Los Angeles Dodgers 28	1.50	.70	.15
☐ 5 Reggie Jackson California Angels 44	2.00	.90	.20
☐ 6 Dusty Baker Los Angeles Dodgers 12	.50	.22	.05
☐ 7 Doug DeCinces California Angels 11	.60	.28	.06
☐ 8 Fernando Valenzuela Los Angeles Dodgers 34	2.00	.90	.20
☐ 9 Tommy John California Angels 25	1.00	.45	.10
☐10 Rick Monday Los Angeles Dodgers 16	.50	.22	.05
☐11 Bobby Grich California Angels 4	.60	.28	.06
☐12 Greg Brock Los Angeles Dodgers 9	.60	.28	.06

1984 Seven-Eleven Coins

The coins in this 72 coin set measure 1 3/4" diameter. For the second year in a row, 7-11 issued sets of coins (officially called Slurpee Discs). The fronts feature two pictures (portrait and action) of each player, each of which can be seen by moving the coin slightly to one side or another. There were, in effect, three different sets of 24 coins corresponding to an east, central, and west region. Of the total 72 coins, only 60 different players appear. Six players appear in all three sets. The repeat players are Andre Dawson, Robin Yount, Dale Murphy, George Brett, Mike Schmidt, and Eddie Murray. Each team is represented by at least one player, and as one might expect, players within the three groups favor the teams of the geographical

location in which that particular group was issued. Coins are numbered on the back, which is different from the uniform number which is on the front of the coin.

	MINT	VG-E	F-G
COMPLETE SET (72)	40.00	18.00	4.00
COMMON PLAYER	.50	.22	.05
EAST (E) PLAYERS			
☐ 1E Andre Dawson	.60	.28	.06
☐ 2E Robin Yount	.60	.28	.06
☐ 3E Dale Murphy	1.00	.45	.10
☐ 4E Mike Schmidt	1.00	.45	.10
☐ 5E George Brett	1.00	.45	.10
☐ 6E Eddie Murray	1.00	.45	.10
☐ 7E Dave Winfield	1.00	.45	.10
☐ 8E Tom Seaver	1.00	.45	.10
☐ 9E Mike Boddicker	.60	.28	.06
☐10E Wade Boggs	2.00	.90	.20
☐11E Bill Madlock	.60	.28	.06
☐12E Steve Carlton	1.00	.45	.10
☐13E Dave Stieb	.60	.28	.06
☐14E Cal Ripken	1.00	.45	.10
☐15E Jim Rice	.75	.35	.07
☐16E Ron Guidry	.60	.28	.06
☐17E Darryl Strawberry	2.00	.90	.20
☐18E Tony Pena	.60	.28	.06
☐19E John Denny	.50	.22	.05
☐20E Tim Raines	1.00	.45	.10
☐21E Rick Dempsey	.50	.22	.05
☐22E Rich Gossage	.60	.28	.06
☐23E Gary Matthews	.50	.22	.05
☐24E Keith Hernandez	.75	.35	.07
CENTRAL (C) PLAYERS			
☐ 1C Andre Dawson	.60	.28	.06
☐ 2C Robin Yount	.60	.28	.06
☐ 3C Dale Murphy	1.00	.45	.10
☐ 4C Mike Schmidt	1.00	.45	.10
☐ 5C George Brett	1.00	.45	.10
☐ 6C Eddie Murray	1.00	.45	.10
☐ 7C Bruce Sutter	.60	.28	.06
☐ 8C Cecil Cooper	.60	.28	.06
☐ 9C Willie McGee	.75	.35	.07
☐10C Mike Hargrove	.50	.22	.05
☐11C Kent Hrbek	1.00	.45	.10
☐12C Carlton Fisk	.60	.28	.06
☐13C Mario Soto	.60	.28	.06
☐14C Lonnie Smith	.50	.22	.05
☐15C Gary Carter	1.00	.45	.10
☐16C Lou Whitaker	.60	.28	.06
☐17C Ron Kittle	.75	.35	.07
☐18C Paul Molitor	.60	.28	.06
☐19C Ozzie Smith	.75	.35	.07
☐20C Fergie Jenkins	.50	.22	.05
☐21C Ted Simmons	.50	.22	.05
☐22C Pete Rose	2.50	1.15	.25
☐23C LaMarr Hoyt	.50	.22	.05
☐24C Dan Quisenberry	.60	.28	.06
WEST (W) PLAYERS			
☐ 1W Andre Dawson	.60	.28	.06
☐ 2W Robin Yount	.60	.28	.06
☐ 3W Dale Murphy	1.00	.45	.10
☐ 4W Mike Schmidt	1.00	.45	.10
☐ 5W George Brett	1.00	.45	.10
☐ 6W Eddie Murray	1.00	.45	.10
☐ 7W Steve Garvey	1.50	.70	.15
☐ 8W Rod Carew	1.00	.45	.10
☐ 9W Fernando Valenzuela	1.00	.45	.10
☐10W Bob Horner	.75	.35	.07
☐11W Buddy Bell	.60	.28	.06
☐12W Reggie Jackson	1.50	.70	.15
☐13W Nolan Ryan	1.00	.45	.10
☐14W Pedro Guerrero	.75	.35	.07
☐15W Atlee Hammaker	.50	.22	.05
☐16W Fred Lynn	.75	.35	.07
☐17W Terry Kennedy	.50	.22	.05
☐18W Dusty Baker	.50	.22	.05
☐19W Jose Cruz	.60	.28	.06
☐20W Steve Rogers	.50	.22	.05
☐21W Rickey Henderson	1.50	.70	.15
☐22W Steve Sax	.75	.35	.07
☐23W Dickie Thon	.50	.22	.05
☐24W Matt Young	.50	.22	.05

1985 Seven-Eleven Coins

These "3-D" type coins are very similar to those of the preceding years except that in 1985 Seven Eleven issued six subsets. The subsets are Central, Detroit, Eastern, Great Lakes, Southeast, and Western. Each of the six subsets contains 16 coins except for the Tigers set which contains only 14 and was distributed in somwewhat smaller supply. Each coin measures 1 3/4" in diameter.

	MINT	VG-E	F-G
COMPLETE SET (94)	60.00	27.00	6.00
COMMON PLAYER	.50	.22	.05

CENTRAL (C) PLAYERS
☐	1C Nolan Ryan	1.00	.45	.10
☐	2C George Brett	1.50	.70	.15
☐	3C Dave Winfield	1.00	.45	.10
☐	4C Mike Schmidt	1.00	.45	.10
☐	5C Bruce Sutter	.50	.22	.05
☐	6C Joaquin Andujar	.50	.22	.05
☐	7C Willie Hernandez	.60	.28	.06
☐	8C Wade Boggs	2.00	.90	.20
☐	9C Gary Carter	1.00	.45	.10
☐	10C Jose Cruz	.60	.28	.06
☐	11C Kent Hrbek	.75	.35	.07
☐	12C Reggie Jackson	1.50	.70	.15
☐	13C Lance Parrish	.75	.35	.07
☐	14C Terry Puhl	.50	.22	.05
☐	15C Dan Quisenberry	.60	.28	.06
☐	16C Ozzie Smith	.75	.35	.07

DETROIT (D) PLAYERS
☐	1D Lou Whitaker	.75	.35	.07
☐	2D Sparky Anderson	.60	.28	.06
☐	3D Darrell Evans	.60	.28	.06
☐	4D Larry Herndon	.50	.22	.05
☐	5D Dave Rozema	.50	.22	.05
☐	6D Milt Wilcox	.50	.22	.05
☐	7D Dan Petry	.60	.28	.06
☐	8D Alan Trammell	.75	.35	.07
☐	9D Aurelio Lopez	.50	.22	.05
☐	10D Willie Hernandez	.60	.28	.06
☐	11D Chet Lemon	.60	.28	.06
☐	12D Jack Morris	.75	.35	.07
☐	13D Kirk Gibson	1.00	.45	.10
☐	14D Lance Parrish	1.00	.45	.10

EAST (E) PLAYERS
☐	1E Eddie Murray	1.50	.70	.15
☐	2E George Brett	1.50	.70	.15
☐	3E Steve Carlton	1.00	.45	.10
☐	4E Jim Rice	.75	.35	.07
☐	5E Dave Winfield	1.00	.45	.10
☐	6E Mike Boddicker	.60	.28	.06
☐	7E Wade Boggs	2.00	.90	.20
☐	8E Dwight Evans	.60	.28	.06
☐	9E Dwight Gooden	2.50	1.15	.25
☐	10E Keith Hernandez	.75	.35	.07
☐	11E Bill Madlock	.60	.28	.06
☐	12E Don Mattingly	2.50	1.15	.25
☐	13E Dave Righetti	.75	.35	.07
☐	14E Cal Ripken Jr.	1.00	.45	.10
☐	15E Juan Samuel	.75	.35	.07
☐	16E Mike Schmidt	1.50	.70	.15

GREAT LAKES (G)
☐	1G Willie Hernandez	.60	.28	.06
☐	2G George Brett	1.50	.70	.15
☐	3G Dave Winfield	1.00	.45	.10
☐	4G Eddie Murray	1.50	.70	.15
☐	5G Bruce Sutter	.60	.28	.06
☐	6G Harold Baines	.75	.35	.07
☐	7G Bert Blyleven	.60	.28	.06

☐	8G Leon Durham	.60	.28	.06
☐	9G Chet Lemon	.50	.22	.05
☐	10G Pete Rose	2.50	1.15	.25
☐	11G Ryne Sandberg	1.00	.45	.10
☐	12G Tom Seaver	1.00	.45	.10
☐	13G Mario Soto	.60	.28	.06
☐	14G Rick Sutcliffe	.60	.28	.06
☐	15G Alan Trammell	.75	.35	.07
☐	16G Robin Yount	1.00	.45	.10

SOUTHEAST (S)
☐	1S Dale Murphy	1.50	.70	.15
☐	2S Steve Carlton	1.00	.45	.10
☐	3S Nolan Ryan	1.00	.45	.10
☐	4S Bruce Sutter	.60	.28	.06
☐	5S Dave Winfield	1.00	.45	.10
☐	6S Steve Bedrosian	.50	.22	.05
☐	7S Andre Dawson	.75	.35	.07
☐	8S Kirk Gibson	1.00	.45	.10
☐	9S Fred Lynn	.75	.35	.07
☐	10S Gary Matthews	.50	.22	.05
☐	11S Phil Niekro	.75	.35	.07
☐	12S Tim Raines	.75	.35	.07
☐	13S Darryl Strawberry	2.00	.90	.20
☐	14S Dave Stieb	.60	.28	.06
☐	15S Willie Upshaw	.60	.28	.06
☐	16S Lou Whitaker	.75	.35	.07

WEST (W) PLAYERS
☐	1W Mike Schmidt	1.50	.70	.15
☐	2W Jim Rice	.75	.35	.07
☐	3W Dale Murphy	1.50	.70	.15
☐	4W Eddie Murray	1.50	.70	.15
☐	5W Dave Winfield	1.00	.45	.10
☐	6W Rod Carew	1.00	.45	.10
☐	7W Alvin Davis	.75	.35	.07
☐	8W Steve Garvey	1.50	.70	.15
☐	9W Rich Gossage	.75	.35	.07
☐	10W Pedro Guerrero	.75	.35	.07
☐	11W Tony Gwynn	1.00	.45	.10
☐	12W Rickey Henderson	1.50	.70	.15
☐	13W Reggie Jackson	1.50	.70	.15
☐	14W Jeff Leonard	.60	.28	.06
☐	15W Alejandro Pena	.50	.22	.05
☐	16W Fernando Valenzuela	1.00	.45	.10

1986 Seven-Eleven Coins

Four subsets of 16 coins each were distributed regionally by the Seven-Eleven chain of convenience stores. The first eight coins in each region are the same; the last eight (9- 16) in each region were apparently selected to showcase players from that area. Except for Dwight Gooden all other coins feature three players on each card depending on how you tilt the coin to see one of the three players. The three players are typically related by position. Each coin measures 1 3/4" in diameter.

	MINT	VG-E	F-G
COMPLETE SET (64)	40.00	18.00	4.00
COMMON PLAYER	.50	.22	.05

CENTRAL (C) PLAYERS
☐	1C Dwight Gooden	2.00	.90	.20
☐	2C Wade Boggs George Brett Pete Rose	2.00	.90	.20
☐	3C Keith Hernandez Don Mattingly	1.00	.45	.10

Cal Ripken
☐ 4C Harold Baines .... .75 .35 .07
 Pedro Guerrero
 Dave Parker
☐ 5C Dale Murphy .... 1.00 .45 .10
 Jim Rice
 Mike Schmidt
☐ 6C Ron Guidry .... .75 .35 .07
 Bret Saberhagen
 Fernando Valenzuela
☐ 7C Goose Gossage .... .60 .28 .06
 Dan Quisenberry
 Bruce Sutter
☐ 8C Steve Carlton .... 1.00 .45 .10
 Nolan Ryan
 Tom Seaver
☐ 9C Keith Hernandez .... .75 .35 .07
 Ryne Sandberg
 Robin Yount
☐ 10C Bert Blyleven .... .60 .28 .06
 Jack Morris
 Rick Sutcliffe
☐ 11C Rollie Fingers .... .50 .22 .05
 Bob James
 Lee Smith
☐ 12C Carlton Fisk .... .60 .28 .06
 Lance Parrish
 Tony Pena
☐ 13C Shawon Dunston .... .60 .28 .06
 Ozzie Guillen
 Earnie Riles
☐ 14C Brett Butler .... .60 .28 .06
 Chet Lemon
 Willie Wilson
☐ 15C Tom Brunansky .... .50 .22 .05
 Cecil Cooper
 Darrell Evans
☐ 16C Kirk Gibson .... .60 .28 .06
 Paul Molitor
 Greg Walker

EAST (E) PLAYERS
☐ 1E Dwight Gooden .... 2.00 .90 .20
☐ 2E Wade Boggs .... 2.00 .90 .20
 George Brett
 Pete Rose
☐ 3E Keith Hernandez .... 1.00 .45 .10
 Don Mattingly
 Cal Ripken
☐ 4E Harold Baines .... .75 .35 .07
 Pedro Guerrero
 Dave Parker
☐ 5E Dale Murphy .... 1.00 .45 .10
 Jim Rice
 Mike Schmidt
☐ 6E Ron Guidry .... .75 .35 .07
 Bret Saberhagen
 Fernando Valenzuela
☐ 7E Goose Gossage .... .60 .28 .06
 Dan Quisenberry
 Bruce Sutter
☐ 8E Steve Carlton .... 1.00 .45 .10
 Nolan Ryan
 Tom Seaver
☐ 9E Steve Lyons .... .60 .28 .06
 Rick Schu
 Larry Sheets
☐ 10E Jeff Reardon .... .50 .22 .05
 Dave Righetti
 Bob Stanley
☐ 11E George Bell .... 1.00 .45 .10
 Darryl Strawberry
 Dave Winfield
☐ 12E Rickey Henderson .... 1.00 .45 .10
 Tim Raines
 Juan Samuel
☐ 13E Andre Dawson .... .75 .35 .07
 Dwight Evans
 Eddie Murray
☐ 14E Mike Boddicker .... .60 .28 .06
 Ron Darling
 Dave Stieb
☐ 15E Tim Burke .... .60 .28 .06
 Brian Fisher
 Roger McDowell
☐ 16E Jesse Barfield .... .75 .35 .07
 Gary Carter
 Fred Lynn

SOUTHERN (S) PLAYERS
☐ 1S Dwight Gooden .... 2.00 .90 .20
☐ 2S Wade Boggs .... 2.00 .90 .20
 George Brett
 Pete Rose
☐ 3S Keith Hernandez .... 1.00 .45 .10

Don Mattingly
Cal Ripken
☐ 4S Harold Baines .... .75 .35 .07
 Pedro Guerrero
 Dave Parker
☐ 5S Dale Murphy .... 1.00 .45 .10
 Jim Rice
 Mike Schmidt
☐ 6S Ron Guidry .... .75 .35 .07
 Bret Saberhagen
 Fernando Valenzuela
☐ 7S Goose Gossage .... .60 .28 .06
 Dan Quisenberry
 Bruce Sutter
☐ 8S Steve Carlton .... 1.00 .45 .10
 Nolan Ryan
 Tom Seaver
☐ 9S Vince Coleman .... 2.00 .90 .20
 Eric Davis
 Oddibe McDowell
☐ 10S Buddy Bell .... .60 .28 .06
 Ozzie Smith
 Lou Whitaker
☐ 11S Mike Scott .... .60 .28 .06
 Mario Soto
 John Tudor
☐ 12S Jeff Lahti .... .50 .22 .05
 Ted Power
 Dave Smith
☐ 13S Jack Clark .... .60 .28 .06
 Jose Cruz
 Bob Horner
☐ 14S Bill Doran .... .60 .28 .06
 Tommy Herr
 Ron Oester
☐ 15S Tom Browning .... .60 .28 .06
 Joe Hesketh
 Todd Worrell
☐ 16S Willie McGee .... 1.50 .70 .15
 Jerry Mumphrey
 Pete Rose

WESTERN (W) PLAYERS
☐ 1W Dwight Gooden .... 2.00 .90 .20
☐ 2W Wade Boggs .... 2.00 .90 .20
 George Brett
 Pete Rose
☐ 3W Keith Hernandez .... 1.00 .45 .10
 Don Mattingly
 Cal Ripken
☐ 4W Harold Baines .... .75 .35 .07
 Pedro Guerrero
 Dave Parker
☐ 5W Dale Murphy .... 1.00 .45 .10
 Jim Rice
 Mike Schmidt
☐ 6W Ron Guidry .... .75 .35 .07
 Bret Saberhagen
 Fernando Valenzuela
☐ 7W Goose Gossage .... .60 .28 .06
 Dan Quisenberry
 Bruce Sutter
☐ 8W Steve Carlton .... 1.00 .45 .10
 Nolan Ryan
 Tom Seaver
☐ 9W Reggie Jackson .... .75 .35 .07
 Dave Kingman
 Gorman Thomas
☐ 10W Rod Carew .... 1.00 .45 .10
 Tony Gwynn
 Carney Lansford
☐ 11W Phil Bradley .... .60 .28 .06
 Mike Marshall
 Graig Nettles
☐ 12W Andy Hawkins .... .60 .28 .06
 Orel Hershiser
 Mike Witt
☐ 13W Chris Brown .... .75 .35 .07
 Ivan Calderon
 Mariano Duncan
☐ 14W Steve Garvey .... .75 .35 .07
 Bill Madlock
 Jim Presley
☐ 15W Jay Howell .... .50 .22 .05
 Donnie Moore
 Edwin Nunez
☐ 16W Karl Best .... .50 .22 .05
 Stewart Cliburn
 Steve Ontiveros

1964 Topps Metal Coins

is set of 164 unnumbered coins issued in 1964 is
metimes divided into two sets -- the regular series
-120) and the all-star series (121-164). Each
etal coin is 1 1/2" in diameter. The regular series
atures gold and silver coins with a full color photo
the player, including the background of the photo.
e player's name, team and position are delineated
the coin front. The back includes the line "Collect
e entire set of 120 all-stars". The all-star series
ntains a full color cutout photo of the player on
solid background. The fronts feature the line "
964 All-stars" along with the name only of the
ayer. The backs contain the line "Collect all 44
ecial stars". Mantle, Causey, and Hinton appear
two variations each. The complete set price below
ludes all variations.

	MINT	VG-E	F-G
MPLETE SET	375.00	150.00	30.00
MMON PLAYER	.60	.28	.06
1 Don Zimmer	.75	.35	.07
2 Jim Wynn	.75	.35	.07
3 Johnny Orsino	.60	.28	.06
4 Jim Bouton	.90	.40	.09
5 Dick Groat	.90	.40	.09
6 Leon Wagner	.60	.28	.06
7 Frank Malzone	.60	.28	.06
8 Steve Barber	.60	.28	.06
9 Johnny Romano	.60	.28	.06
10 Tom Tresh	.75	.35	.07
11 Felipe Alou	.75	.35	.07
12 Dick Stuart	.75	.35	.07
13 Claude Osteen	.75	.35	.07
14 Juan Pizarro	.60	.28	.06
15 Donn Clendenon	.60	.28	.06
16 Jimmie Hall	.60	.28	.06
17 Al Jackson	.60	.28	.06
18 Brooks Robinson	10.00	4.75	1.00
19 Bob Allison	.75	.35	.07
20 Ed Roebuck	.60	.28	.06
21 Pete Ward	.60	.28	.06
22 Willie McCovey	8.00	3.75	.80
23 Elston Howard	1.50	.70	.15
24 Diego Segui	.60	.28	.06
25 Ken Boyer	1.50	.70	.15
26 Carl Yastrzemski	15.00	7.00	1.50
27 Bill Mazeroski	1.00	.45	.10
28 Jerry Lumpe	.60	.28	.06
29 Woody Held	.60	.28	.06
30 Dick Radatz	.60	.28	.06
31 Luis Aparicio	5.00	2.35	.50
32 Dave Nicholson	.60	.28	.06
33 Eddie Mathews	8.00	3.75	.80
34 Don Drysdale	8.00	3.75	.80
35 Ray Culp	.60	.28	.06
36 Juan Marichal	8.00	3.75	.80
37 Frank Robinson	8.00	3.75	.80

☐ 38	Chuck Hinton	.60	.28	.06
☐ 39	Floyd Robinson	.60	.28	.06
☐ 40	Tommy Harper	.60	.28	.06
☐ 41	Ron Hansen	.60	.28	.06
☐ 42	Ernie Banks	10.00	4.75	1.00
☐ 43	Jesse Gonder	.60	.28	.06
☐ 44	Stan Williams	.60	.28	.06
☐ 45	Vada Pinson	1.00	.45	.10
☐ 46	Rocky Colavito	1.50	.70	.15
☐ 47	Bill Monbouquette	.60	.28	.06
☐ 48	Max Alvis	.60	.28	.06
☐ 49	Norm Siebern	.60	.28	.06
☐ 50	John Callison	.75	.35	.07
☐ 51	Rich Rollins	.60	.28	.06
☐ 52	Ken McBride	.60	.28	.06
☐ 53	Don Lock	.60	.28	.06
☐ 54	Ron Fairly	.60	.28	.06
☐ 55	Bob Clemente	15.00	7.00	1.50
☐ 56	Dick Ellsworth	.60	.28	.06
☐ 57	Tommy Davis	.90	.40	.09
☐ 58	Tony Gonzalez	.60	.28	.06
☐ 59	Bob Gibson	8.00	3.75	.80
☐ 60	Jim Maloney	.75	.35	.07
☐ 61	Frank Howard	.90	.40	.09
☐ 62	Jim Pagliaroni	.60	.28	.06
☐ 63	Orlando Cepeda	1.50	.70	.15
☐ 64	Ron Perranoski	.60	.28	.06
☐ 65	Curt Flood	.90	.40	.09
☐ 66	Alvin McBean	.60	.28	.06
☐ 67	Dean Chance	.60	.28	.06
☐ 68	Ron Santo	1.00	.45	.10
☐ 69	Jack Baldschun	.60	.28	.06
☐ 70	Milt Pappas	.75	.35	.07
☐ 71	Gary Peters	.60	.28	.06
☐ 72	Bobby Richardson	1.50	.70	.15
☐ 73	Frank Thomas	.60	.28	.06
☐ 74	Hank Aguirre	.60	.28	.06
☐ 75	Carlton Willey	.60	.28	.06
☐ 76	Camilo Pascual	.60	.28	.06
☐ 77	Bob Friend	.60	.28	.06
☐ 78	Bill White	.90	.40	.09
☐ 79	Norm Cash	.90	.40	.09
☐ 80	Willie Mays	15.00	7.00	1.50
☐ 81	Leon Carmel	.60	.28	.06
☐ 82	Pete Rose	25.00	11.00	2.50
☐ 83	Henry Aaron	15.00	7.00	1.50
☐ 84	Bob Aspromonte	.60	.28	.06
☐ 85	Jim O'Toole	.60	.28	.06
☐ 86	Vic Davalillo	.60	.28	.06
☐ 87	Bill Freehan	.75	.35	.07
☐ 88	Warren Spahn	8.00	3.75	.80
☐ 89	Ken Hunt	.60	.28	.06
☐ 90	Denis Menke	.60	.28	.06
☐ 91	Dick Farrell	.60	.28	.06
☐ 92	Jim Hickman	.60	.28	.06
☐ 93	Jim Bunning	1.50	.70	.15
☐ 94	Bob Hendley	.60	.28	.06
☐ 95	Ernie Broglio	.60	.28	.06
☐ 96	Rusty Staub	1.00	.45	.10
☐ 97	Lou Brock	8.00	3.75	.80
☐ 98	Jim Fregosi	.90	.40	.09
☐ 99	Jim Grant	.60	.28	.06
☐ 100	Al Kaline	10.00	4.75	1.00
☐ 101	Earl Battey	.60	.28	.06
☐ 102	Wayne Causey	.60	.28	.06
☐ 103	Chuck Schilling	.60	.28	.06
☐ 104	Boog Powell	1.00	.45	.10
☐ 105	Dave Wickersham	.60	.28	.06
☐ 106	Sandy Koufax	12.00	5.50	1.20
☐ 107	John Bateman	.60	.28	.06
☐ 108	Ed Brinkman	.60	.28	.06
☐ 109	Al Downing	.60	.28	.06
☐ 110	Joe Azcue	.60	.28	.06
☐ 111	Albie Pearson	.60	.28	.06
☐ 112	Harmon Killebrew	8.00	3.75	.80
☐ 113	Tony Taylor	.60	.28	.06
☐ 114	Larry Jackson	.60	.28	.06
☐ 115	Billy O'Dell	.60	.28	.06
☐ 116	Don Demeter	.60	.28	.06
☐ 117	Ed Charles	.60	.28	.06
☐ 118	Joe Torre	1.50	.70	.15
☐ 119	Don Nottebart	.60	.28	.06
☐ 120	Mickey Mantle	25.00	11.00	2.50
ALL-STARS (121-164)				
☐ 121	Joe Pepitone	.60	.28	.06
☐ 122	Dick Stuart	.60	.28	.06
☐ 123	Bobby Richardson	1.50	.70	.15
☐ 124	Jerry Lumpe	.60	.28	.06
☐ 125	Brooks Robinson	10.00	4.75	1.00
☐ 126	Frank Malzone	.75	.35	.07
☐ 127	Luis Aparicio	5.00	2.35	.50
☐ 128	Jim Fregosi	1.00	.45	.10
☐ 129	Al Kaline	10.00	4.75	1.00

☐ 130	Leon Wagner	.60	.28	.06
☐ 131A	Mickey Mantle (right handed)	25.00	11.00	2.50
☐ 131B	Mickey Mantle (left handed)	25.00	11.00	2.50
☐ 132	Albie Pearson	.60	.28	.06
☐ 133	Harmon Killebrew	6.00	2.80	.60
☐ 134	Carl Yastrzemski	15.00	7.00	1.50
☐ 135	Frank Howard	.90	.40	.09
☐ 136	Earl Battey	.60	.28	.06
☐ 137	Camilo Pascual	.60	.28	.06
☐ 138	Jim Bouton	.90	.40	.09
☐ 139	Whitey Ford	8.00	3.75	.80
☐ 140	Gary Peters	.60	.28	.06
☐ 141	Bill White	.75	.35	.07
☐ 142	Orlando Cepeda	1.00	.45	.10
☐ 143	Bill Mazeroski	.90	.40	.09
☐ 144	Tony Taylor	.60	.28	.06
☐ 145	Ken Boyer	1.00	.45	.10
☐ 146	Ron Santo	.90	.40	.09
☐ 147	Dick Groat	.75	.35	.07
☐ 148	Roy McMillan	.60	.28	.06
☐ 149	Henry Aaron	15.00	7.00	1.50
☐ 150	Bob Clemente	12.00	5.50	1.20
☐ 151	Willie Mays	15.00	7.00	1.50
☐ 152	Vada Pinson	1.00	.45	.10
☐ 153	Willie Davis	.75	.35	.07
☐ 154	Frank Robinson	8.00	3.75	.80
☐ 155	Joe Torre	1.50	.70	.15
☐ 156	Tim McCarver	1.00	.45	.10
☐ 157	Juan Marichal	6.00	2.80	.60
☐ 158	Jim Maloney	.75	.35	.07
☐ 159	Sandy Koufax	10.00	4.75	1.00
☐ 160	Warren Spahn	8.00	3.75	.80
☐ 161A	Wayne Causey National League	10.00	4.75	1.00
☐ 161B	Wayne Causey American League	.60	.28	.06
☐ 162A	Chuck Hinton National League	10.00	4.75	1.00
☐ 162B	Chuck Hinton American League	.60	.28	.06
☐ 163	Bob Aspromonte	.60	.28	.06
☐ 164	Ron Hunt	.60	.28	.06

1971 Topps Metal Coins

This full color set of 153 coins contains the photo of the player surrounded by a colored band, which contains the player's name, his team, his position and several stars. The backs contain the coin number, short biographical data, and the line "Collect the entire set of 153 coins." The set was evidently produced in three groups of 51 as coins 1-51 have brass backs, coins 52-102 have chrome backs, and coins 103-153 have blue backs. Each coin measures 1 1/2" in diameter.

		MINT	VG-E	F-G
COMPLETE SET		200.00	90.00	20.00
COMMON PLAYER		.40	.18	.04
☐ 1	Clarence Gaston	.40	.18	.04
☐ 2	Dave Johnson	.60	.28	.06
☐ 3	Jim Bunning	.75	.35	.07
☐ 4	Jim Spencer	.40	.18	.04
☐ 5	Felix Millan	.40	.18	.04
☐ 6	Gerry Moses	.40	.18	.04
☐ 7	Fergie Jenkins	.60	.28	.06
☐ 8	Felipe Alou	.60	.28	.06

☐ 9	Jim McGlothlin	.40	.18	.04
☐ 10	Dick McAuliffe	.40	.18	.04
☐ 11	Joe Torre	.90	.40	.09
☐ 12	Jim Perry	.60	.28	.06
☐ 13	Bobby Bonds	.75	.35	.07
☐ 14	Danny Cater	.40	.18	.04
☐ 15	Bill Mazeroski	.75	.35	.07
☐ 16	Luis Aparicio	2.50	1.15	.25
☐ 17	Doug Rader	.50	.22	.05
☐ 18	Vada Pinson	.75	.35	.07
☐ 19	John Bateman	.40	.18	.04
☐ 20	Lew Krausse	.40	.18	.04
☐ 21	Billy Grabarkewitz	.40	.18	.04
☐ 22	Frank Howard	.60	.28	.06
☐ 23	Jerry Koosman	.60	.28	.06
☐ 24	Rod Carew	7.50	3.50	.75
☐ 25	Al Ferrara	.40	.18	.04
☐ 26	Dave McNally	.50	.22	.05
☐ 27	Jim Hickman	.40	.18	.04
☐ 28	Sandy Alomar	.40	.18	.04
☐ 29	Lee May	.50	.22	.05
☐ 30	Rico Petrocelli	.50	.22	.05
☐ 31	Don Money	.40	.18	.04
☐ 32	Jim Rooker	.40	.18	.04
☐ 33	Dick Dietz	.40	.18	.04
☐ 34	Roy White	.50	.22	.05
☐ 35	Carl Morton	.40	.18	.04
☐ 36	Walt Williams	.40	.18	.04
☐ 37	Phil Niekro	1.50	.70	.15
☐ 38	Bill Freehan	.50	.22	.05
☐ 39	Julian Javier	.40	.18	.04
☐ 40	Rick Monday	.50	.22	.05
☐ 41	Don Wilson	.40	.18	.04
☐ 42	Ray Fosse	.40	.18	.04
☐ 43	Art Shamsky	.40	.18	.04
☐ 44	Ted Savage	.40	.18	.04
☐ 45	Claude Osteen	.50	.22	.05
☐ 46	Ed Brinkman	.40	.18	.04
☐ 47	Matty Alou	.50	.22	.05
☐ 48	Al Oliver	.75	.35	.07
☐ 49	Danny Coombs	.40	.18	.04
☐ 50	Frank Robinson	5.00	2.35	.50
☐ 51	Randy Hundley	.40	.18	.04
☐ 52	Ceasar Tovar	.40	.18	.04
☐ 53	Wayne Simpson	.40	.18	.04
☐ 54	Bobby Murcer	.75	.35	.07
☐ 55	Carl Taylor	.40	.18	.04
☐ 56	Tommy John	1.00	.45	.10
☐ 57	Willie McCovey	5.00	2.35	.50
☐ 58	Carl Yastrzemski	12.00	5.50	1.20
☐ 59	Bob Bailey	.40	.18	.04
☐ 60	Clyde Wright	.40	.18	.04
☐ 61	Orlando Cepeda	1.00	.45	.10
☐ 62	Al Kaline	6.00	2.80	.60
☐ 63	Bob Gibson	5.00	2.35	.50
☐ 64	Bert Campaneris	.60	.28	.06
☐ 65	Ted Sizemore	.40	.18	.04
☐ 66	Duke Sims	.40	.18	.04
☐ 67	Bud Harrelson	.40	.18	.04
☐ 68	Gerald McNertney	.40	.18	.04
☐ 69	Jim Wynn	.50	.22	.05
☐ 70	Ken Bosman	.40	.18	.04
☐ 71	Roberto Clemente	10.00	4.75	1.00
☐ 72	Rich Reese	.40	.18	.04
☐ 73	Gaylord Perry	1.50	.70	.15
☐ 74	Boog Powell	.90	.40	.09
☐ 75	Billy Williams	1.50	.70	.15
☐ 76	Bill Melton	.50	.22	.05
☐ 77	Nate Colbert	.40	.18	.04
☐ 78	Reggie Smith	.60	.28	.06
☐ 79	Deron Johnson	.40	.18	.04
☐ 80	Jim Hunter	1.50	.70	.15
☐ 81	Bobby Tolan	.40	.18	.04
☐ 82	Jim Northrup	.50	.22	.05
☐ 83	Ron Fairly	.50	.22	.05
☐ 84	Alex Johnson	.40	.18	.04
☐ 85	Pat Jarvis	.40	.18	.04
☐ 86	Sam McDowell	.50	.22	.05
☐ 87	Lou Brock	6.00	2.80	.60
☐ 88	Danny Walton	.40	.18	.04
☐ 89	Denis Menke	.50	.22	.05
☐ 90	Jim Palmer	4.00	1.85	.40
☐ 91	Tommy Agee	.50	.22	.05
☐ 92	Duane Josephson	.40	.18	.04
☐ 93	Tommy Davis	.60	.28	.06
☐ 94	Mel Stottlemyre	.60	.28	.06
☐ 95	Ron Santo	.90	.40	.09
☐ 96	Amos Otis	.60	.28	.06
☐ 97	Ken Henderson	.40	.18	.04
☐ 98	George Scott	.50	.22	.05
☐ 99	Dock Ellis	.40	.18	.04
☐ 100	Harmon Killebrew	5.00	2.35	.50
☐ 101	Pete Rose	20.00	9.00	2.00

☐ 102 Rick Reichardt	.40	.18	.04
☐ 103 Cleon Jones	.40	.18	.04
☐ 104 Ron Perranoski	.40	.18	.04
☐ 105 Tony Perez	1.00	.45	.10
☐ 106 Mickey Lolich	.75	.35	.07
☐ 107 Tim McCarver	.60	.28	.06
☐ 108 Reggie Jackson	10.00	4.75	1.00
☐ 109 Chris Cannizzaro	.40	.18	.04
☐ 110 Steve Hargan	.40	.18	.04
☐ 111 Rusty Staub	.75	.35	.07
☐ 112 Andy Messersmith	.50	.22	.05
☐ 113 Rico Carty	.60	.28	.06
☐ 114 Brooks Robinson	6.00	2.80	.60
☐ 115 Steve Carlton	6.00	2.80	.60
☐ 116 Mike Hegan	.40	.18	.04
☐ 117 Joe Morgan	4.00	1.85	.40
☐ 118 Thurman Munson	5.00	2.35	.50
☐ 119 Don Kessinger	.50	.22	.05
☐ 120 Joel Horlen	.40	.18	.04
☐ 121 Wes Parker	.50	.22	.05
☐ 122 Sonny Siebert	.40	.18	.04
☐ 123 Willie Stargell	2.50	1.15	.25
☐ 124 Aurelio Rodriguez	.40	.18	.04
☐ 125 Juan Marichal	4.00	1.85	.40
☐ 126 Mike Epstein	.40	.18	.04
☐ 127 Tom Seaver	7.50	3.50	.75
☐ 128 Tony Oliva	1.00	.45	.10
☐ 129 Jim Merritt	.40	.18	.04
☐ 130 Willie Horton	.50	.22	.05
☐ 131 Rick Wise	.40	.18	.04
☐ 132 Sal Bando	.75	.35	.07
☐ 133 Gates Brown	.40	.18	.04
☐ 134 Bud Harrelson	.50	.22	.05
☐ 135 Mack Jones	.40	.18	.04
☐ 136 Jim Fregosi	.60	.28	.06
☐ 137 Hank Aaron	10.00	4.75	1.00
☐ 138 Fritz Peterson	.40	.18	.04
☐ 139 Joe Hague	.40	.18	.04
☐ 140 Tommy Harper	.40	.18	.04
☐ 141 Larry Dierker	.40	.18	.04
☐ 142 Tony Conigliaro	.60	.28	.06
☐ 143 Glenn Beckert	.40	.18	.04
☐ 144 Carlos May	.40	.18	.04
☐ 145 Don Sutton	1.50	.70	.15
☐ 146 Paul Casanova	.40	.18	.04
☐ 147 Bob Moose	.40	.18	.04
☐ 148 Chico Cardenas	.40	.18	.04
☐ 149 Johnny Bench	7.50	3.50	.75
☐ 150 Mike Cuellar	.50	.22	.05
☐ 151 Donn Clendenon	.40	.18	.04
☐ 152 Lou Piniella	1.00	.45	.10
☐ 153 Willie Mays	10.00	4.75	1.00

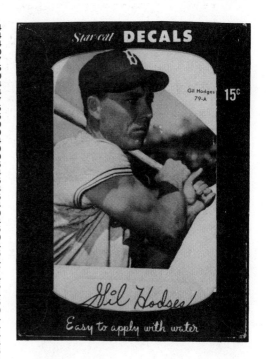

1952 Star Cal Large

Type One of the Star Cal Decal set, issued in 1952, contains (theoretically) the cards listed in the checklist below. Each decal sheet measures 4 1/8" by 6 1/8". When the decals have been taken from the paper wrapper, a checklist of existing decals is revealed on the wrapper. The set was issued by the Meyercord Company of Chicago and carries a catalog designation of W625-1.

	MINT	VG-E	F-G
COMPLETE SET	1800.00	800.00	150.00
COMMON CARD	10.00	4.75	1.00
☐ 70A Allie Reynolds	12.00	5.50	1.20
☐ 70B Ed Lopat	12.00	5.50	1.20
☐ 70C Yogi Berra	40.00	18.00	4.00
☐ 70D Vic Raschi	12.00	5.50	1.20
☐ 70E Jerry Coleman	10.00	4.75	1.00
☐ 70F Phil Rizzuto	25.00	11.00	2.50
☐ 70G Mickey Mantle	500.00	225.00	50.00
☐ 71A Mel Parnell	10.00	4.75	1.00
☐ 71B Ted Williams	90.00	42.00	9.00
☐ 71C Ted Williams	90.00	42.00	9.00
☐ 71D Vern Stephens	10.00	4.75	1.00

☐ 71E Billy Goodman	10.00	4.75	1.00
☐ 71F Dom DiMaggio	15.00	7.00	1.50
☐ 71G Dick Gernert	10.00	4.75	1.00
☐ 71H Hoot Evers	10.00	4.75	1.00
☐ 72A George Kell	20.00	9.00	2.00
☐ 72B Hal Newhouser	15.00	7.00	1.50
☐ 72C Hoot Evers	10.00	4.75	1.00
☐ 72D Vic Wertz	10.00	4.75	1.00
☐ 72E Fred Hutchinson	10.00	4.75	1.00
☐ 72F Bill Groth	10.00	4.75	1.00
☐ 73A Al Zarilla	10.00	4.75	1.00
☐ 73B Billy Pierce	12.00	5.50	1.20
☐ 73C Eddie Robinson	10.00	4.75	1.00
☐ 73D Chico Carrasquel	10.00	4.75	1.00
☐ 73E Minnie Minoso	12.00	5.50	1.20
☐ 73F Jim Busby	10.00	4.75	1.00
☐ 73G Nellie Fox	15.00	7.00	1.50
☐ 73H Sam Mele	10.00	4.75	1.00
☐ 74A Larry Doby	12.00	5.50	1.20
☐ 74B Al Rosen	15.00	7.00	1.50
☐ 74C Bob Lemon	20.00	9.00	2.00
☐ 74D Jim Hegan	10.00	4.75	1.00
☐ 74E Bob Feller	40.00	18.00	4.00
☐ 74F Dale Mitchell	10.00	4.75	1.00
☐ 75A Ned Garver	10.00	4.75	1.00
☐ 76A Gus Zernial	10.00	4.75	1.00
☐ 76B Ferris Fain	10.00	4.75	1.00
☐ 77A Richie Ashburn	15.00	7.00	1.50
☐ 77B Ralph Kiner	20.00	9.00	2.00
☐ 78A Bobby Thomson	12.00	5.50	1.20
☐ 78B Alvin Dark	12.00	5.50	1.20
☐ 78C Sal Maglie	12.00	5.50	1.20
☐ 78D Larry Jansen	10.00	4.75	1.00
☐ 78E Willie Mays	150.00	70.00	15.00
☐ 78F Monte Irvin	20.00	9.00	2.00
☐ 78G Whitey Lockman	10.00	4.75	1.00
☐ 79A Gil Hodges	25.00	11.00	2.50
☐ 79B Pee Wee Reese	30.00	14.00	3.00
☐ 79C Roy Campanella	90.00	42.00	9.00
☐ 79D Don Newcombe	15.00	7.00	1.50
☐ 79E Duke Snider	60.00	27.00	6.00
☐ 79F Preacher Roe	15.00	7.00	1.50
☐ 79G Jackie Robinson	90.00	42.00	9.00
☐ 80A Eddie Miksis	10.00	4.75	1.00
☐ 80B Dutch Leonard	10.00	4.75	1.00
☐ 80C Randy Jackson	10.00	4.75	1.00
☐ 80D Bob Rush	10.00	4.75	1.00
☐ 80E Hank Sauer	10.00	4.75	1.00
☐ 80F Phil Cavarretta	10.00	4.75	1.00

☐ 80G	Warren Hacker	10.00	4.75	1.00
☐ 81A	Red Schoendienst	12.00	5.50	1.20
☐ 81B	Wally Westlake	10.00	4.75	1.00
☐ 81C	Cliff Chambers	10.00	4.75	1.00
☐ 81D	Enos Slaughter	20.00	9.00	2.00
☐ 81E	Stan Musial	60.00	27.00	6.00
☐ 81F	Stan Musial	60.00	27.00	6.00
☐ 81G	Jerry Staley	10.00	4.75	1.00

1952 Star Cal Small

Type Two of the Star Cal Decal set features a decal package half the size of the W625-1 set, each sheet contains two decals, each of which is approximately half the size of the large decal found in the W625-1 set. Each decal package (sheet) measures 3 1/16" by 4 1/8". The set was issued by the Meyercord Company of Chicago and carries a catalog designation of W625-2. The checklist below features two players per "card".

	MINT	VG-E	F-G
COMPLETE SET	500.00	225.00	50.00
COMMON CARD	10.00	4.75	1.00

☐ 84A	Allie Reynolds and Vic Raschi	12.00	5.50	1.20
☐ 84B	Ed Lopat and Yogi Berra	20.00	9.00	2.00
☐ 84C	Phil Rizzuto and Jerry Coleman	15.00	7.00	1.50
☐ 85A	Ted Williams and Ted Williams	75.00	35.00	7.50
☐ 85B	Dom DiMaggio and Mel Parnell	12.00	5.50	1.20
☐ 85C	Vern Stephens and Billy Goodman	10.00	4.75	1.00
☐ 86A	George Kell and Hal Newhouser	20.00	9.00	2.00
☐ 86B	Hoot Evers and Vic Wertz	10.00	4.75	1.00
☐ 86C	Bill Groth and Fred Hutchinson	10.00	4.75	1.00
☐ 87A	Eddie Robinson and Eddie Robinson	10.00	4.75	1.00
☐ 87B	Chico Carrasquel and Minnie Minoso	10.00	4.75	1.00

☐ 87C	Billy Pierce and Nellie Fox	15.00	7.00	1.50
☐ 87D	Al Zarilla and Jim Busby	10.00	4.75	1.00
☐ 88A	Bob Lemon and Jim Hegan	15.00	7.00	1.50
☐ 88B	Larry Doby and Bob Feller	25.00	11.00	2.50
☐ 88C	Dale Mitchell and Al Rosen	12.00	5.50	1.20
☐ 89A	Ned Garver and Ned Garver	10.00	4.75	1.00
☐ 89B	Ferris Fain and Gus Zernial	10.00	4.75	1.00
☐ 89C	Richie Ashburn and Richie Ashburn	15.00	7.00	1.50
☐ 89D	Ralph Kiner and Ralph Kiner	18.00	8.50	1.80
☐ 90A	Willie Mays and Monty Irvin	75.00	35.00	7.50
☐ 90B	Larry Jansen and Sal Maglie	10.00	4.75	1.00
☐ 90C	Bobby Thomson and Al Dark	12.00	5.50	1.20
☐ 91A	Gil Hodges and Pee Wee Reese	25.00	11.00	2.50
☐ 91B	Roy Campanella and Jackie Robinson	75.00	35.00	7.50
☐ 91C	Duke Snider and Preacher Roe	30.00	14.00	3.00
☐ 92A	Phil Cavarretta and Dutch Leonard	10.00	4.75	1.00
☐ 92B	Randy Jackson and Eddie Miksis	10.00	4.75	1.00
☐ 92C	Bob Rush and Hank Sauer	10.00	4.75	1.00
☐ 93A	Stan Musial and Stan Musial	60.00	27.00	6.00
☐ 93B	Red Schoendienst and Enos Slaughter	18.00	8.50	1.80
☐ 93C	Cliff Chambers and Wally Westlake	10.00	4.75	1.00

1969 Topps Decal Inserts

The 1969 Topps Decal Inserts are a set of 48 unnumbered decals issued as inserts in packages of 1969 Topps regular issue cards. Each decal is approximately 1" by 1 1/2" although including the plain backing the measurement is 1 3/4" by 2 1/8". The decals appear to be miniature versions of the Topps regular issue of that year. The copyright notice on the side indicates that these decals were produced in the United Kingdom. Most of the players on the decals are stars.

		MINT	VG-E	F-G
COMPLETE SET		100.00	45.00	10.00
COMMON PLAYER (1-48)		.75	.35	.07

			MINT	VG-E	F-G
☐	1	Hank Aaron	10.00	4.75	1.00
☐	2	Richie Allen	1.00	.45	.10
☐	3	Felipe Alou	.90	.40	.09
☐	4	Matty Alou	.75	.35	.07
☐	5	Luis Aparicio	2.00	.90	.20
☐	6	Bob Clemente	10.00	4.75	1.00
☐	7	Donn Clendenon	.75	.35	.07
☐	8	Tommy Davis	.90	.40	.09
☐	9	Don Drysdale	4.00	1.85	.40
☐	10	Joe Foy	.75	.35	.07
☐	11	Jim Fregosi	.90	.40	.09
☐	12	Bob Gibson	4.00	1.85	.40
☐	13	Tony Gonzalez	.75	.35	.07
☐	14	Tom Haller	.75	.35	.07
☐	15	Ken Harrelson	.90	.40	.09
☐	16	Tommy Helms	.75	.35	.07
☐	17	Willie Horton	.90	.40	.09
☐	18	Frank Howard	.90	.40	.09
☐	19	Fergie Jenkins	1.50	.70	.15
☐	20	Harmon Killebrew	4.00	1.85	.40
☐	21	Jerry Koosman	.90	.40	.09
☐	22	Tim McCarver	.90	.40	.09
☐	23	Willie McCovey	4.00	1.85	.40
☐	24	Sam McDowell	.90	.40	.09
☐	25	Denny McLain	.90	.40	.09
☐	26	Dave McNally	.90	.40	.09
☐	27	Mickey Mantle	20.00	9.00	2.00
☐	28	Willie Mays	10.00	4.75	1.00
☐	29	Reggie Jackson	10.00	4.75	1.00
☐	30	Don Mincher	.75	.35	.07
☐	31	Rick Monday	.90	.40	.09
☐	32	Tony Oliva	1.50	.70	.15
☐	33	Camilo Pascual	.75	.35	.07
☐	34	Rick Reichardt	.75	.35	.07
☐	35	Pete Rose	20.00	9.00	2.00
☐	36	Frank Robinson	4.00	1.85	.40
☐	37	Ron Santo	.90	.40	.09
☐	38	Dick Selma	.75	.35	.07
☐	39	Tom Seaver	7.50	3.50	.75
☐	40	Chris Short	.75	.35	.07
☐	41	Rusty Staub	.90	.40	.09
☐	42	Mel Stottlemyre	.90	.40	.09
☐	43	Luis Tiant	.90	.40	.09
☐	44	Pete Ward	.75	.35	.07
☐	45	Hoyt Wilhelm	3.00	1.40	.30
☐	46	Maury Wills	1.50	.70	.15
☐	47	Jim Wynn	.75	.35	.07
☐	48	Carl Yastrzemski	10.00	4.75	1.00

1921-1924 Exhibits

Although the Exhibit Supply Company issued 64 cards in 1921 and 128 cards in each of the following three years, the category of 1921-24 was created because of the large number of pictures found repeated in all four years. Each exhibit card measures 3 3/8" by 5 3/8". The cards of 1921 are characterized by ornate hand-lettered names while the cards of 1922-24 have players' names hand-written in a plainer style. Also for 1921 cards, the abbreviation used for the junior circuit was "Am.L." In contrast, cards of the 1922-24 period have the American League abbreviated "A.L." All the cards in the 1921-24 category are black and white and have blank backs; some have white borders measuring approximately 3/16" in width. There is some mislabeling of pictures, incorrect assignment of proper names, and many misspellings. Some of the cards have a horizontal (HOR) orientation.

		MINT	VG-E	F-G
COMPLETE SET		2400.00	1100.00	200.00
COMMON PLAYER		8.00	3.75	.80

			MINT	VG-E	F-G
☐	1	Chas. B. Adams	8.00	3.75	.80
☐	2	Grover C. Alexander	25.00	11.00	2.50
☐	3	James Bagby	8.00	3.75	.80
☐	4	J. Frank Baker	16.00	7.50	1.60
☐	5	David Bancroft	16.00	7.50	1.60
☐	6	Walter Barbare	8.00	3.75	.80
☐	7	Turner Barber	8.00	3.75	.80
☐	8	Clyde Barnhart	8.00	3.75	.80
☐	9	John Bassler	8.00	3.75	.80
☐	10	Carlson L. Bigbee	8.00	3.75	.80
☐	11	Ray Blades	8.00	3.75	.80
☐	12	Sam Bohne	8.00	3.75	.80
☐	13	James Bottomley	16.00	7.50	1.60
☐	14	Geo. Burns (Cinn) portrait	8.00	3.75	.80
☐	15	Geo. J. Burns (New York NL)	8.00	3.75	.80
☐	16	George Burns (Boston AL)	8.00	3.75	.80
☐	17	George Burns (Cleveland)	8.00	3.75	.80
☐	18	Joe Bush	8.00	3.75	.80
☐	19	Owen Bush	8.00	3.75	.80
☐	20	Leon Cadore	8.00	3.75	.80
☐	21	Max G. Carey	16.00	7.50	1.60
☐	22	Jim Caveney	8.00	3.75	.80
☐	23	Dan Clark	8.00	3.75	.80
☐	24	Ty R. Cobb	100.00	45.00	10.00
☐	25	Eddie T. Collins	20.00	9.00	2.00
☐	26	John Collins	8.00	3.75	.80
☐	27	Wilbur Cooper	8.00	3.75	.80
☐	28	Stanley Coveleskie	16.00	7.50	1.60
☐	29	Walton E. Cruise	8.00	3.75	.80
☐	30	George Cutshaw	8.00	3.75	.80
☐	31	Dave Danforth	8.00	3.75	.80
☐	32	Jacob E. Daubert	8.00	3.75	.80
☐	33	George Dauss	8.00	3.75	.80
☐	34	Charles A. Deal	8.00	3.75	.80
☐	35	Bill Doak (Brooklyn)	8.00	3.75	.80
☐	36	Bill Doak (St. Louis NL)	8.00	3.75	.80
☐	37	Joe Dugan (Boston AL)	8.00	3.75	.80
☐	38	Joe A. Dugan (New York AL)	8.00	3.75	.80
☐	39	Joe A. Dugan (Philadelphia AL)	8.00	3.75	.80
☐	40	Pat Duncan	8.00	3.75	.80
☐	41	James Dykes	8.00	3.75	.80
☐	42	Howard J. Ehmke (Boston AL)	8.00	3.75	.80
☐	43	Howard Ehmke (Detroit) (with border)	8.00	3.75	.80
☐	44	Wm. Evans	9.00	4.25	.90
☐	45	U.C. Red Faber	16.00	7.50	1.60
☐	46	Bib Falk	8.00	3.75	.80

☐ 47	Dana Fillingim	8.00	3.75	.80
☐ 48	Ira Flagstead (Boston AL)	8.00	3.75	.80
☐ 49	A. Fletcher	8.00	3.75	.80
☐ 50	J.F. Fournier (Brooklyn)	8.00	3.75	.80
☐ 51	J.F. Fournier (St. Louis NL)	8.00	3.75	.80
☐ 52	Howard Freigau	8.00	3.75	.80
☐ 53	Frank F. Frisch	25.00	11.00	2.50
☐ 54	C.E. Galloway	8.00	3.75	.80
☐ 55	W.L. Gardner (Cleveland)	8.00	3.75	.80
☐ 56	Joe Genewich	8.00	3.75	.80
☐ 57	Wally Gerber	8.00	3.75	.80
☐ 58	Mike Gonzales	8.00	3.75	.80
☐ 59	H.M. "Hank" Gowdy (Boston NL)	8.00	3.75	.80
☐ 60	H.M. "Hank" Gowdy (New York NL)	8.00	3.75	.80
☐ 61	Burleigh A. Grimes	16.00	7.50	1.60
☐ 62	Ray Grimes	8.00	3.75	.80
☐ 63	Charles Grimm	10.00	4.75	1.00
☐ 64	Heinie Groh (Cincinnati)	10.00	4.75	1.00
☐ 65	Heinie Groh (New York NL)	10.00	4.75	1.00
☐ 66	Jesse Haines	16.00	7.50	1.60
☐ 67	Chas. L. Hartnett	16.00	7.50	1.60
☐ 68	George Harper	8.00	3.75	.80
☐ 69	Sam Harris	8.00	3.75	.80
☐ 70	Slim Harris	8.00	3.75	.80
☐ 71	Clifton Heathcote	8.00	3.75	.80
☐ 72	Harry Heilmann	16.00	7.50	1.60
☐ 73	Andy High	8.00	3.75	.80
☐ 74	Umpire Hildebrand	8.00	3.75	.80
☐ 75	Walter L. Holke (Boston NL)	8.00	3.75	.80
☐ 76	Walter L. Holke (Philadelphia NL)	8.00	3.75	.80
☐ 77	Chas. J. Hollocher	8.00	3.75	.80
☐ 78	Rogers Hornsby	35.00	16.50	3.50
☐ 79	Wilbert Hubbell	8.00	3.75	.80
☐ 80	Bill Jacobson	8.00	3.75	.80
☐ 81	Charles D. Jamieson	8.00	3.75	.80
☐ 82	E.R. Johnson	8.00	3.75	.80
☐ 83	James H. Johnson	8.00	3.75	.80
☐ 84	Walter P. Johnson	50.00	22.00	5.00
☐ 85	Sam P. Jones	8.00	3.75	.80
☐ 86	Joe Judge	8.00	3.75	.80
☐ 87	Willie Kamm	8.00	3.75	.80
☐ 88	Tony Kaufman	8.00	3.75	.80
☐ 89	George L. Kelly	16.00	7.50	1.60
☐ 90	Dick Kerr	8.00	3.75	.80
☐ 91	William L. Killefer	8.00	3.75	.80
☐ 92	Bill Klem (Umpire)	16.00	7.50	1.60
☐ 93	Ed Konetchy	8.00	3.75	.80
☐ 94	John "Doc" Lavan	8.00	3.75	.80
☐ 95	Dudley Lee	8.00	3.75	.80
☐ 96	Harry Liebold (Boston AL)	8.00	3.75	.80
☐ 97	Harry Liebold (Washington) (with border)	8.00	3.75	.80
☐ 98	Adolph Luque	8.00	3.75	.80
☐ 99	Walter Mails	8.00	3.75	.80
☐ 100	Geo. Maisel	8.00	3.75	.80
☐ 101	Walt. J. Maranville	16.00	7.50	1.60
☐ 102	W.C. (Wid) Matthews	8.00	3.75	.80
☐ 103	Carl W. Mays	8.00	3.75	.80
☐ 104	John McGraw	25.00	11.00	2.50
☐ 105	J. Stuffy McInnis (Boston AL)	8.00	3.75	.80
☐ 106	J. Stuffy McInnis (Boston NL)	8.00	3.75	.80
☐ 107	Lee Meadows	8.00	3.75	.80
☐ 108	Clyde Milan	8.00	3.75	.80
☐ 109	Ed (Bing) Miller	8.00	3.75	.80
☐ 110	Hack Miller	8.00	3.75	.80
☐ 111	Umpire Moriarty	8.00	3.75	.80
☐ 112	Johnny Morrison	8.00	3.75	.80
☐ 113	John A. Mostil	8.00	3.75	.80
☐ 114	Robert Meusel	8.00	3.75	.80
☐ 115	Harry Myers	8.00	3.75	.80
☐ 116	Rollie C. Naylor	8.00	3.75	.80
☐ 117	A. Earl Neale	10.00	4.75	1.00
☐ 118	Arthur Nehf	8.00	3.75	.80
☐ 119	Joe Oeschger	8.00	3.75	.80
☐ 120	Ivan M. Olson	8.00	3.75	.80
☐ 121	Geo. O'Neil	8.00	3.75	.80
☐ 122	S.F. "Steve" O'Neil	8.00	3.75	.80
☐ 123	J.F. O'Neill	8.00	3.75	.80
☐ 124	Ernest Padgett	8.00	3.75	.80
☐ 125	Roger Peckinpaugh (New York AL) (with border)	8.00	3.75	.80
☐ 126	Peckinpaugh (Washington)	8.00	3.75	.80
☐ 127	Ralph "Cy" Perkins	8.00	3.75	.80
☐ 128	Val Picinich (Boston AL)	8.00	3.75	.80
☐ 129	Val Picinich (Washington)	8.00	3.75	.80
☐ 130	Bill Piercy (light background)	8.00	3.75	.80
☐ 131	Bill Piercy (dark background)	8.00	3.75	.80
☐ 132	Herman Pillett	8.00	3.75	.80
☐ 133	Wally Pipp	10.00	4.75	1.00
☐ 134	Raymond R. Powell (light background)	8.00	3.75	.80
☐ 135	Raymond R. Powell (dark background)	8.00	3.75	.80
☐ 136	Del Pratt (Detroit)	8.00	3.75	.80
☐ 137	Derrill Pratt (Boston AL)	8.00	3.75	.80
☐ 138	Joe "Goldie" Rapp	8.00	3.75	.80
☐ 139	Walter Reuther	8.00	3.75	.80
☐ 140	Edgar S. Rice	16.00	7.50	1.60
☐ 141	Umpire Rigler	8.00	3.75	.80
☐ 142	E. E. Rigney	8.00	3.75	.80
☐ 143	Jimmy Ring	8.00	3.75	.80
☐ 144	Eppa Rixey	16.00	7.50	1.60
☐ 145	Chas. Robertson	8.00	3.75	.80
☐ 146	Eddie Rommel	8.00	3.75	.80
☐ 147	Muddy Ruel	8.00	3.75	.80
☐ 148	George H. Babe Ruth	150.00	70.00	15.00
☐ 149	George H. Babe Ruth (with border)	150.00	70.00	15.00
☐ 150	J. H. Sand	8.00	3.75	.80
☐ 151	Ray W. Schalk	16.00	7.50	1.60
☐ 152	Wallie Schang	8.00	3.75	.80
☐ 153	Everett Scott (Boston AL)	8.00	3.75	.80
☐ 154	Everett Scott (New York AL)	8.00	3.75	.80
☐ 155	Harry Severeid	8.00	3.75	.80
☐ 156	Joseph Sewell	16.00	7.50	1.60
☐ 157	H.S. Shanks	8.00	3.75	.80
☐ 158	Earl Sheely	8.00	3.75	.80
☐ 159	Urban Shocker	8.00	3.75	.80
☐ 160	Al Simmons	20.00	9.00	2.00
☐ 161	George H. Sisler	25.00	11.00	2.50
☐ 162	Earl Smith (New York NL) (with border)	8.00	3.75	.80
☐ 163	Earl Smith (New York NL) (2/3 shot)	8.00	3.75	.80
☐ 164	Elmer Smith (Boston AL)	8.00	3.75	.80
☐ 165	Jack Smith	8.00	3.75	.80
☐ 166	R.E. Smith	8.00	3.75	.80
☐ 167	Sherrod Smith (Brooklyn)	8.00	3.75	.80
☐ 168	Sherrod Smith (Cleveland)	8.00	3.75	.80
☐ 169	Frank Snyder	8.00	3.75	.80
☐ 170	Allan Sothoron	8.00	3.75	.80
☐ 171	Tris Speaker	35.00	16.50	3.50
☐ 172	Arnold Statz	8.00	3.75	.80
☐ 173	Casey Stengel	35.00	16.50	3.50
☐ 174	J.R. Stevenson	8.00	3.75	.80
☐ 175	Milton Stock	8.00	3.75	.80
☐ 176	James Tierney (Boston NL)	8.00	3.75	.80
☐ 177	James Tierney (Pittsburgh)	8.00	3.75	.80
☐ 178	John Tobin	8.00	3.75	.80
☐ 179	George Toporcer	8.00	3.75	.80
☐ 180	Robert Veach	8.00	3.75	.80
☐ 181	Clarence (Tillie) Walker	8.00	3.75	.80
☐ 182	Curtis Walker	8.00	3.75	.80
☐ 183	Aaron Ward	8.00	3.75	.80
☐ 184	Zack D. Wheat	16.00	7.50	1.60
☐ 185	Geo. B. Whitted	8.00	3.75	.80
☐ 186	Cy Williams	8.00	3.75	.80
☐ 187	Kenneth R. Williams	8.00	3.75	.80
☐ 188	Ivy B. Wingo	8.00	3.75	.80
☐ 189	Joe Wood	10.00	4.75	1.00
☐ 190	L. Woodall	8.00	3.75	.80
☐ 191	Russell G. Wrightstone	8.00	3.75	.80
☐ 192	Moses Yellowhorse	8.00	3.75	.80

☐ 193 Ross Youngs 16.00   7.50   1.60

1925 Exhibits

The most dramatic change in the 1925 series from that of the preceding group was the printed legend which appeared for the first time in this printing. The subject's name, position, team, and the line "(Made in U.S.A.)" appear on four separate lines in a bottom corner, enclosed in a small white box. The name of the player is printed in large capitals while the other lines are of a smaller type size. The cards are black and white, have plain backs, and are unnumbered. Each exhibit card measures 3 3/8" by 5 3/8". There are 128 cards in the set and numerous misspellings exist. Note: the card marked "Robert Veach" does not picture that player, but is thought to contain a photo of Ernest Vache. A few of the cards are presented in a horizontal (HOR) format. Players are in alphabetical order by team: Boston NL 1-8, Brooklyn 9-16, Chicago 17-24, Cincinnati 25-32, New York 33-40, Philadelphia 41-48, Pittsburgh 49-56, St. Louis 57-64, Boston AL 65-72, Chicago 73-80, Cleveland 81-88, Detroit 89-96, New York 97-104, Philadelphia 105-112, St. Louis 113-120, Washington 121- 128.

	MINT	VG-E	F-G
COMPLETE SET	2700.00	1250.00	250.00
COMMON PLAYER	15.00	7.00	1.50

BOSTON BEES

☐	1	David Bancroft	30.00	14.00	3.00
☐	2	Jesse Barnes	15.00	7.00	1.50
☐	3	Lawrence Benton	15.00	7.00	1.50
☐	4	Maurice Burrus	15.00	7.00	1.50
☐	5	Joseph Genewich	15.00	7.00	1.50
☐	6	Frank Gibson	15.00	7.00	1.50
☐	7	David Harris	15.00	7.00	1.50
☐	8	George O'Neil	15.00	7.00	1.50

BROOKLYN DODGERS

☐	9	John H. Deberry	15.00	7.00	1.50
☐	10	Decatur	15.00	7.00	1.50
☐	11	Jacques F. Fournier	15.00	7.00	1.50
☐	12	Burleigh A. Grimes	30.00	14.00	3.00
☐	13	James H. Johnson (sic, Johnston)	15.00	7.00	1.50
☐	14	Milton J. Stock	15.00	7.00	1.50
☐	15	A.C. Dazzy Vance	30.00	14.00	3.00
☐	16	Zack Wheat	30.00	14.00	3.00

CHICAGO CUBS

☐	17	Sparky Adams	15.00	7.00	1.50
☐	18	Grover C. Alexander	45.00	20.00	4.50
☐	19	John Brooks	15.00	7.00	1.50
☐	20	Howard Freigau	15.00	7.00	1.50
☐	21	Charles Grimm	18.00	8.50	1.80
☐	22	Leo Hartnett	30.00	14.00	3.00
☐	23	Walter Maranville	30.00	14.00	3.00
☐	24	A.J. Weis	15.00	7.00	1.50

CINCINNATI REDS

☐	25	Raymond Bressler	15.00	7.00	1.50
☐	26	Hugh M. Critz	15.00	7.00	1.50
☐	27	Peter Donohue	15.00	7.00	1.50
☐	28	Charles Dressen	18.00	8.50	1.80
☐	29	John (Stuffy) McInnes (McInnis)	18.00	8.50	1.80
☐	30	Eppa Rixey	30.00	14.00	3.00
☐	31	Ed. Roush	30.00	14.00	3.00
☐	32	Ivy Wingo	15.00	7.00	1.50

NEW YORK GIANTS

☐	33	Frank Frisch	45.00	20.00	4.50
☐	34	Heine Groh	18.00	8.50	1.80
☐	35	Travis C. Jackson	30.00	14.00	3.00
☐	36	Emil Meusel	15.00	7.00	1.50
☐	37	Arthur Nehf	15.00	7.00	1.50
☐	38	Frank Snyder	15.00	7.00	1.50
☐	39	Wm. H. Southworth	15.00	7.00	1.50
☐	40	William Terry	45.00	20.00	4.50

PHILADELPHIA PHILLIES

☐	41	George Harper	15.00	7.00	1.50
☐	42	Nelson Hawks	15.00	7.00	1.50
☐	43	Walter Henline	15.00	7.00	1.50
☐	44	Walter Holke	15.00	7.00	1.50
☐	45	Wilbur Hubbell	15.00	7.00	1.50
☐	46	John Mokan	15.00	7.00	1.50
☐	47	John Sand	15.00	7.00	1.50
☐	48	Fred Williams	15.00	7.00	1.50

PITTSBURGH PIRATES

☐	49	Carson Bigbee	15.00	7.00	1.50
☐	50	Max Carey	30.00	14.00	3.00
☐	51	Hazen Cuyler	30.00	14.00	3.00
☐	52	George Grantham	15.00	7.00	1.50
☐	53	Ray Kremer	15.00	7.00	1.50
☐	54	Earl Smith	15.00	7.00	1.50
☐	55	Harold Traynor	35.00	16.50	3.50
☐	56	Glenn Wright	15.00	7.00	1.50

ST. LOUIS CARDINALS

☐	57	Lester Bell HOR	15.00	7.00	1.50
☐	58	Raymond Blates (sic, Blades)	15.00	7.00	1.50
☐	59	James Bottomly (sic, Bottomley)	30.00	14.00	3.00
☐	60	Max Flack	15.00	7.00	1.50
☐	61	Rogers Hornsby	60.00	27.00	6.00
☐	62	Clarence Mueller	15.00	7.00	1.50
☐	63	William Sherdell	15.00	7.00	1.50
☐	64	George Toporcer	15.00	7.00	1.50

BOSTON RED SOX

☐	65	Howard Ehmke	15.00	7.00	1.50
☐	66	Ira Flagstead	15.00	7.00	1.50
☐	67	I. Valentine Picinich	15.00	7.00	1.50
☐	68	John Quinn	15.00	7.00	1.50
☐	69	Charles Ruffing	30.00	14.00	3.00
☐	70	Philip Todt	15.00	7.00	1.50
☐	71	Robert Veach	15.00	7.00	1.50
☐	72	William Wambsganss	15.00	7.00	1.50

CHICAGO WHITE SOX

☐	73	Eddie Collins	30.00	14.00	3.00
☐	74	Bib Falk	15.00	7.00	1.50
☐	75	Harry Hooper	30.00	14.00	3.00
☐	76	Willie Kamm	15.00	7.00	1.50
☐	77	I.M. Davis	15.00	7.00	1.50
☐	78	Ray Shalk (Schalk)	30.00	14.00	3.00
☐	79	Earl Sheely	15.00	7.00	1.50
☐	80	Hollis Thurston	15.00	7.00	1.50

CLEVELAND INDIANS

☐	81	Wilson Fewster	15.00	7.00	1.50
☐	82	Charles Jamieson	15.00	7.00	1.50
☐	83	Walter Lutzke	15.00	7.00	1.50
☐	84	Glenn Myatt	15.00	7.00	1.50
☐	85	Joseph Sewell	30.00	14.00	3.00
☐	86	Sherrod Smith	15.00	7.00	1.50
☐	87	Tristram Speaker	60.00	27.00	6.00
☐	88	Homer Summa	15.00	7.00	1.50

DETROIT TIGERS

☐	89	John Bassler	15.00	7.00	1.50
☐	90	Tyrus Cobb	200.00	90.00	20.00
☐	91	George Dauss	15.00	7.00	1.50
☐	92	Harry Heilmann	30.00	14.00	3.00
☐	93	Frank O'Rourke	15.00	7.00	1.50

			MINT	VG-E	F-G
☐	94	Emory Rigney	15.00	7.00	1.50
☐	95	Al Wings (Wingo) HOR	15.00	7.00	1.50
☐	96	Larry Woodall	15.00	7.00	1.50

NEW YORK GIANTS

☐	97	Henry L. Gehrig	200.00	90.00	20.00
☐	98	Robert W. Muesel			
		(sic, Meusel)	18.00	8.50	1.80
☐	99	Walter C. Pipp	18.00	8.50	1.80
☐	100	George H. Babe Ruth	300.00	130.00	30.00
☐	101	Walter H. Shang			
		(sic, Schang)	15.00	7.00	1.50
☐	102	J.R. Shawkey	15.00	7.00	1.50
☐	103	Urban J. Shocker	15.00	7.00	1.50
☐	104	Aaron Ward	15.00	7.00	1.50

PHILADELPHIA A'S

☐	105	Max Bishop	15.00	7.00	1.50
☐	106	James J. Dykes	18.00	8.50	1.80
☐	107	Samuel Gray	15.00	7.00	1.50
☐	108	Samuel Hale	15.00	7.00	1.50
☐	109	Edmund (Bind) Miller			
		(sic, Bing)	15.00	7.00	1.50
☐	110	Ralph Perkins	15.00	7.00	1.50
☐	111	Edwin Rommel	15.00	7.00	1.50
☐	112	Frank Welch	15.00	7.00	1.50

ST. LOUIS BROWNS

☐	113	Walter Gerber	15.00	7.00	1.50
☐	114	William Jacobson	15.00	7.00	1.50
☐	115	Martin McManus	15.00	7.00	1.50
☐	116	Henry Severid			
		(sic, Severeid)	15.00	7.00	1.50
☐	117	George Sissler			
		(sic, Sisler)	45.00	20.00	4.50
☐	118	John Tobin	15.00	7.00	1.50
☐	119	Kenneth Williams	15.00	7.00	1.50
☐	120	Ernest Wingard	15.00	7.00	1.50

WASHINGTON SENATORS

☐	121	Oswald Bluege	15.00	7.00	1.50
☐	122	Stanley Coveleski	30.00	14.00	3.00
☐	123	Leon Goslin	30.00	14.00	3.00
☐	124	Stanley Harris	30.00	14.00	3.00
☐	125	Walter Johnson	90.00	42.00	9.00
☐	126	Joseph Judge	18.00	8.50	1.80
☐	127	Earl McNeely	15.00	7.00	1.50
☐	128	Harold Ruel	15.00	7.00	1.50

1926 Exhibits

The year 1926 marked the last of the 128-card sets produced by Exhibit Supply. Of this number, 70 cards are identical to those issued in 1925 but are easily identified because of the new blue-gray color introduced in 1926. Another 21 cards use 1925 pictures but contain the line "Ex. Sup. Co., U.S.A."; these are marked with an asterisk in the checklist below. The 37 photos new to this set have an unboxed legend and carry the new company line. Bischoff is incorrectly placed with Boston, N.L. (should be A.L.); the picture of Galloway is reversed; the photos of Hunnefield and Thomas are erroneously exchanged. Each exhibit card measures 3 3/8" by 5 3/8". Players are in alphabetical order by team: Boston NL 1-8, Brooklyn 9-16, Chicago 17-24, Cincinnati 25-32, New York 33-40, Philadelphia 41-48, Pittsburgh 49-56, St. Louis 57-64, Boston AL 65-72, Chicago 73-80, Cleveland 81-88, Detroit 89-96, New York 97-104, Philadelphia 105-112, St. Louis 113-120, Washington 121-128.

	MINT	VG-E	F-G
COMPLETE SET	2700.00	1250.00	250.00
COMMON PLAYER	15.00	7.00	1.50

BOSTON BEES

☐	1	Lawrence Benton *	15.00	7.00	1.50
☐	2	Andrew High *	15.00	7.00	1.50
☐	3	Maurice Burrus *	15.00	7.00	1.50
☐	4	David Bancroft *	30.00	14.00	3.00
☐	5	Joseph Genewich *	15.00	7.00	1.50
☐	6	Bernie F. Neis *	15.00	7.00	1.50
☐	7	Edward Taylor	15.00	7.00	1.50
☐	8	J. Taylor *	15.00	7.00	1.50

BROOKLYN DODGERS

☐	9	John Butler *	15.00	7.00	1.50
☐	10	Jacques F. Furnier			
		(sic, Fournier) *	15.00	7.00	1.50
☐	11	Burleigh A.Grimes *	30.00	14.00	3.00
☐	12	Wilson Fewster *	15.00	7.00	1.50
☐	13	Douglas McWeeny *	15.00	7.00	1.50
☐	14	George O'Neil *	15.00	7.00	1.50
☐	15	Walter Maranville *	30.00	14.00	3.00
☐	16	Zach Wheat *	30.00	14.00	3.00

CHICAGO CUBS

☐	17	Sparky Adams	15.00	7.00	1.50
☐	18	J. Fred Blake *	15.00	7.00	1.50
☐	19	James E. Cooney *	15.00	7.00	1.50
☐	20	Howard Freigau	15.00	7.00	1.50
☐	21	Charles Grimm	18.00	8.50	1.80
☐	22	Leo Hartnett	30.00	14.00	3.00
☐	23	C.E. Heathcote *	15.00	7.00	1.50
☐	24	Joseph M. Munson *	15.00	7.00	1.50

CINCINNATI REDS

☐	25	Raymond Bressler	15.00	7.00	1.50
☐	26	Hugh M. Critz	15.00	7.00	1.50
☐	27	Peter Donohue	15.00	7.00	1.50
☐	28	Charles Dressen	18.00	8.50	1.80
☐	29	Walter C. Pipp *	18.00	8.50	1.80
☐	30	Eppa Rixey	30.00	14.00	3.00
☐	31	Ed. Roush	30.00	14.00	3.00
☐	32	Ivy Wingo	15.00	7.00	1.50

NEW YORK GIANTS

☐	33	Edward S. Farrell *	15.00	7.00	1.50
☐	34	Frank Frisch *	45.00	20.00	4.50
☐	35	Frank Snyder *	15.00	7.00	1.50
☐	36	Fredrick Lindstrom			
		(sic, Frederick) *	30.00	14.00	3.00
☐	37	Hugh A.McQuillan *	15.00	7.00	1.50
☐	38	Emil Musel *			
		(sic, Meusel)	15.00	7.00	1.50
☐	39	James J. Ring *	15.00	7.00	1.50
☐	40	William Terry *	45.00	20.00	4.50

PHILADELPHIA PHILLIES

☐	41	John M. Bentley *	15.00	7.00	1.50
☐	42	Bernard Friberg *	15.00	7.00	1.50
☐	43	George Harper	15.00	7.00	1.50
☐	44	Walter Henline *	15.00	7.00	1.50
☐	45	Clarence Huber *	15.00	7.00	1.50
☐	46	John Makan *			
		(sic, Mokan)	15.00	7.00	1.50
☐	47	John Sand *	15.00	7.00	1.50
☐	48	Russell Wrigtstone			
		(sic, Wrightstone) *	15.00	7.00	1.50

PITTSBURGH PIRATES
☐ 49	Carson Bigbee	15.00	7.00	1.50
☐ 50	Max Carey	30.00	14.00	3.00
☐ 51	Hazen Cuyler	30.00	14.00	3.00
☐ 52	George Grantham	15.00	7.00	1.50
☐ 53	Ray Kremer	15.00	7.00	1.50
☐ 54	Earl Smith	15.00	7.00	1.50
☐ 55	Harold Traynor	35.00	16.50	3.50
☐ 56	Glen Wright	15.00	7.00	1.50

ST. LOUIS CARDINALS
☐ 57	Lester Bell *	15.00	7.00	1.50
☐ 58	Raymond Blates (sic, Blades)	15.00	7.00	1.50
☐ 59	James Bottomly (sic, Bottomley)	30.00	14.00	3.00
☐ 60	Rogers Hornsby	60.00	27.00	6.00
☐ 61	Clarence Mueller	15.00	7.00	1.50
☐ 62	Robert O'Farrell *	15.00	7.00	1.50
☐ 63	William Sherdell	15.00	7.00	1.50
☐ 64	George Torporcer	15.00	7.00	1.50

BOSTON RED SOX
☐ 65	Ira Flagstead	15.00	7.00	1.50
☐ 66	Fred Haney *	15.00	7.00	1.50
☐ 67	Ramon Herrera *	15.00	7.00	1.50
☐ 68	John Quinn	15.00	7.00	1.50
☐ 69	Emory Rigney *	15.00	7.00	1.50
☐ 70	Charles Ruffing	30.00	14.00	3.00
☐ 71	Philip Todt	15.00	7.00	1.50
☐ 72	Fred Wingfield *	15.00	7.00	1.50

CHICAGO WHITE SOX
☐ 73	Ted Blankenship *	15.00	7.00	1.50
☐ 74	Eddie Collins	30.00	14.00	3.00
☐ 75	Bib Falk	15.00	7.00	1.50
☐ 76	Wm. Hunnefield * (sic, Tommy Thomas)	15.00	7.00	1.50
☐ 77	Willie Kamm	15.00	7.00	1.50
☐ 78	Ray Shalk (Schalk)	30.00	14.00	3.00
☐ 79	Earl Sheely	15.00	7.00	1.50
☐ 80	Hollis Thurston	15.00	7.00	1.50

CLEVELAND INDIANS
☐ 81	Geo. H. Burns * HOR	15.00	7.00	1.50
☐ 82	Walter Lutzke	15.00	7.00	1.50
☐ 83	Glenn Myatt	15.00	7.00	1.50
☐ 84	Joseph Sewell	30.00	14.00	3.00
☐ 85	Sherrod Smith	15.00	7.00	1.50
☐ 86	Tristram Speaker	60.00	27.00	6.00
☐ 87	Fred Spurgeon *	15.00	7.00	1.50
☐ 88	Homer Summa	15.00	7.00	1.50

DETROIT TIGERS
☐ 89	John Bassler	15.00	7.00	1.50
☐ 90	Lucerne Blue * (sic, Luzerne)	15.00	7.00	1.50
☐ 91	Tyrus Cobb	200.00	90.00	20.00
☐ 92	George Dauss	15.00	7.00	1.50
☐ 93	Harry Heilmann	30.00	14.00	3.00
☐ 94	Frank O'Rourke	15.00	7.00	1.50
☐ 95	Charles Gehringer (batting)	45.00	20.00	4.50
☐ 96	John Warner *	15.00	7.00	1.50

NEW YORK YANKEES
☐ 97	Patrick T.Collins *	15.00	7.00	1.50
☐ 98	Earl B. Combs *	30.00	14.00	3.00
☐ 99	Henry L. Gehrig	200.00	90.00	20.00
☐ 100	Anthony Lazzeri *	21.00	9.50	2.10
☐ 101	Robert W. Muesel (sic, Meusel)	18.00	8.50	1.80
☐ 102	Geo. H. Babe Ruth	300.00	130.00	30.00
☐ 103	J. R. Shawkey	15.00	7.00	1.50
☐ 104	Urban J. Shocker	15.00	7.00	1.50

PHILADELPHIA A'S
☐ 105	Max Bishop	15.00	7.00	1.50
☐ 106	Joseph Galloway *	15.00	7.00	1.50
☐ 107	James J. Dykes *	15.00	7.00	1.50
☐ 108	Joseph Hauser *	15.00	7.00	1.50
☐ 109	Edmund (Bind) Miller (sic, Bing)	15.00	7.00	1.50
☐ 110	Ralph Perkins	15.00	7.00	1.50
☐ 111	Edwin Rommel	15.00	7.00	1.50
☐ 112	Wm. Wambsganss *	15.00	7.00	1.50

ST. LOUIS BROWNS
☐ 113	Wm. Hargrave *	15.00	7.00	1.50
☐ 114	William Jacobson	15.00	7.00	1.50
☐ 115	Martin McManus	15.00	7.00	1.50
☐ 116	Oscar Melillo *	15.00	7.00	1.50
☐ 117	Walter Gerber	15.00	7.00	1.50
☐ 118	George Sissler (sic, Sisler)	45.00	20.00	4.50
☐ 119	Kenneth Williams	15.00	7.00	1.50
☐ 120	Ernest Wingard	15.00	7.00	1.50

WASHINGTON SENATORS
☐ 121	Oswald Bluege	15.00	7.00	1.50
☐ 122	Stanley Coveleski	30.00	14.00	3.00
☐ 123	Leon Goslin	30.00	14.00	3.00
☐ 124	Stanley Harris	30.00	14.00	3.00
☐ 125	Walter Johnson	90.00	42.00	9.00
☐ 126	Joseph Judge	18.00	8.50	1.80
☐ 127	Earl McNeely	15.00	7.00	1.50
☐ 128	Harold Ruel	15.00	7.00	1.50

1927 Exhibits

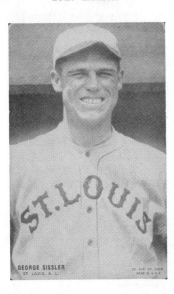

Two innovations characterize the 64-card set produced by Exhibit Supply Company for 1927. The first was a radical departure from the color scheme of previous sets marked by this year's light green hue. The second was the installation of the divided legend, whereby the player's name (all caps) and team were set in one corner, and the lines "Ex. Sup. Co., Chgo." and "Made in U.S.A." were set in the other. All the photos employed in this set were taken from the previous issues in 1925 and 1926, although 13 players appear with new teams. The usual misspellings and incorrect labeling of names and initials occurs throughout the set. Note: Genewich and Hunnefield have a different style of print, and Myatt is missing the right side of the legend. Each card measures 3 3/8" by 5 3/8". Players are listed in alphabetical order by team: Boston NL 1-4, Brooklyn 5- 8, Chicago 9-12, Cincinnati 13-16, New York 17-20, Philadelphia 21-24, Pittsburgh 25-28, St. Louis 29-32, Boston AL 33-36, Chicago 37-40, Cleveland 41-44, Detroit 45-48, New York 49-52, Philadelphia 53-56, St. Louis 57-60, Washington 61-64.

	MINT	VG-E	F-G
COMPLETE SET	700.00	320.00	70.00
COMMON PLAYER	8.00	3.75	.80

BOSTON BEES
☐ 1	David Bancroft	16.00	7.50	1.60
☐ 2	Joseph Genewich	8.00	3.75	.80
☐ 3	Andrew High	8.00	3.75	.80
☐ 4	J. Taylor	8.00	3.75	.80

BROOKLYN DODGERS
☐ 5	John Buttler (Butler)	8.00	3.75	.80
☐ 6	Wilson Fewster	8.00	3.75	.80
☐ 7	Burleigh A. Grimes	16.00	7.50	1.60
☐ 8	Walter Henline	8.00	3.75	.80

CHICAGO CUBS
☐ 9	Sparky Adams	8.00	3.75	.80

☐ 10	Charles Grimm	10.00	4.75	1.00
☐ 11	Leo Hartnett	16.00	7.50	1.60
☐ 12	Clifton Heathcote	8.00	3.75	.80
CINCINNATI REDS				
☐ 13	Raymond Bressler	8.00	3.75	.80
☐ 14	Walter C. Pipp	10.00	4.75	1.00
☐ 15	Eppa Rixey	16.00	7.50	1.60
☐ 16	Ivy Wingo	8.00	3.75	.80
NEW YORK GIANTS				
☐ 17	John M. Bentley	8.00	3.75	.80
☐ 18	George Harper	8.00	3.75	.80
☐ 19	Rogers Hornsby	35.00	16.50	3.50
☐ 20	Fredrick Lindstrom	16.00	7.50	1.60
PHILADELPHIA PHILLIES				
☐ 21	A. R. Decatur	8.00	3.75	.80
☐ 22	John "Stuffy" McInnes (sic, McInnis)	8.00	3.75	.80
☐ 23	John Mokan	8.00	3.75	.80
☐ 24	Russell Wrightstone	8.00	3.75	.80
PITTSBURGH PIRATES				
☐ 25	Hazen Cuyler	16.00	7.50	1.60
☐ 26	Ray Kremer	8.00	3.75	.80
☐ 27	Earl Smith	8.00	3.75	.80
☐ 28	Harold Traynor	16.00	7.50	1.60
ST. LOUIS CARDINALS				
☐ 29	Grover C. Alexander	25.00	11.00	2.50
☐ 30	James Bottomly (sic, Bottomley)	16.00	7.50	1.60
☐ 31	Robert O'Farrell	8.00	3.75	.80
☐ 32	Wm. H. Southworth	8.00	3.75	.80
BOSTON RED SOX				
☐ 33	Ira Flagstead	8.00	3.75	.80
☐ 34	Fred Haney	8.00	3.75	.80
☐ 35	Philip Todt	8.00	3.75	.80
☐ 36	Fred Wingfield	8.00	3.75	.80
CHICAGO WHITE SOX				
☐ 37	Fred Blankenship (sic, Ted)	8.00	3.75	.80
☐ 38	Wm. Hunnefield (sic, Tommy Thomas)	8.00	3.75	.80
☐ 39	Willie Kamm	8.00	3.75	.80
☐ 40	Ray Schalk	16.00	7.50	1.60
CLEVELAND INDIANS				
☐ 41	Geo. H. Burns HOR	8.00	3.75	.80
☐ 42	Walter Lutzke	8.00	3.75	.80
☐ 43	Glenn Myatt	8.00	3.75	.80
☐ 44	Bernie Neis	8.00	3.75	.80
DETROIT TIGERS				
☐ 45	John Bassler	8.00	3.75	.80
☐ 46	George Daus * (sic, Dauss)	8.00	3.75	.80
☐ 47	Charles Gehringer	25.00	11.00	2.50
☐ 48	Harry Heilman (sic, Heilmann)	16.00	7.50	1.60
NEW YORK YANKEES				
☐ 49	Henry L. Gehrig	100.00	45.00	10.00
☐ 50	Anthony Lazzeri	10.00	4.75	1.00
☐ 51	Robert W. Muesel (sic, Meusel)	10.00	4.75	1.00
☐ 52	Geo.H. Babe Ruth	150.00	70.00	15.00
PHILADELPHIA A'S				
☐ 53	Tyrus Cobb	100.00	45.00	10.00
☐ 54	Eddie Collins	16.00	7.50	1.60
☐ 55	William Wambsganns (sic, Wambsganss)	8.00	3.75	.80
☐ 56	Zach Wheat	16.00	7.50	1.60
ST. LOUIS BROWNS				
☐ 57	Wm. Hargrave	8.00	3.75	.80
☐ 58	Kenneth Williams	8.00	3.75	.80
☐ 59	George Sissler (sic, Sisler)	25.00	11.00	2.50
☐ 60	Ernest Wingard	8.00	3.75	.80
WASHINGTON SENATORS				
☐ 61	Leon Goslin	16.00	7.50	1.60
☐ 62	Walter Johnson	50.00	22.00	5.00
☐ 63	Harold Ruel	8.00	3.75	.80
☐ 64	Tristam Speaker (sic, Tristram)	35.00	16.50	3.50

1928 Exhibits

In contrast to the green color of the preceding year, the 64 Exhibit cards of 1928 are blue in color. Each card measures 3 3/8" by 5 3/8". They may be found with blank backs, or postcard backs

LOU GEHRIG
NEW YORK A. L.

EX. SUP. CO. CHGO.
MADE IN U.S.A.

containing a small premium offer clip-off in one corner. The use of the divided legend was continued, with the Roush card being unique in the set as it also cites his position. Of the 64 players in the set, 24 appear for the first time, while 12 of the holdovers show new poses. In addition, four players are shown with new team affiliations. The remaining 24 cards are identical to those issued in 1927 except for color. Once again, there is at least one mistaken identity and many misspellings and wrong names. A few of the cards are presented horizontally (HOR). Players are listed below in alphabetical order by team: Boston NL 1-4, Brooklyn 5-8, Chicago 9-12, Cincinnati 13-16, New York 17- 20, Philadelphia 21-24, Pittsburgh 25-28, St. Louis 29-32, Boston AL 33-36, Chicago 37-40, Cleveland 41-44, Detroit 45-48, New York 49-52, Philadelphia 53-56, St. Louis 57-60, Washington 61-64.

		MINT	VG-E	F-G
COMPLETE SET		700.00	320.00	70.00
COMMON PLAYER		8.00	3.75	.80
BOSTON BEES				
☐ 1	Edward Brown	8.00	3.75	.80
☐ 2	Rogers Hornsby HOR	35.00	16.50	3.50
☐ 3	Robert Smith	8.00	3.75	.80
☐ 4	J. Taylor	8.00	3.75	.80
BROOKLYN DODGERS				
☐ 5	David Bancroft	16.00	7.50	1.60
☐ 6	Max G. Carey	16.00	7.50	1.60
☐ 7	Charles R. Hargraves	8.00	3.75	.80
☐ 8	Arthur "Dazzy" Vance	16.00	7.50	1.60
CHICAGO CUBS				
☐ 9	E. English	8.00	3.75	.80
☐ 10	Leo Hartnett	16.00	7.50	1.60
☐ 11	A. C. Root	8.00	3.75	.80
☐ 12	L. R. (Hack) Wilson	25.00	11.00	2.50
CINCINNATI REDS				
☐ 13	Hugh M. Critz	8.00	3.75	.80
☐ 14	Eugene Hargrave	8.00	3.75	.80
☐ 15	Adolph Luque	8.00	3.75	.80
☐ 16	William A. Zitzmann	8.00	3.75	.80
NEW YORK GIANTS				
☐ 17	Virgil Barnes	8.00	3.75	.80
☐ 18	J. Francis Hogan	8.00	3.75	.80
☐ 19	Fredrick Lindstrom (sic, Frederick)	16.00	7.50	1.60
☐ 20	Edd. Roush, Outfield	16.00	7.50	1.60
PHILADELPHIA PHILLIES				
☐ 21	Fred Leach	8.00	3.75	.80
☐ 22	James Ring	8.00	3.75	.80

☐ 23	Henry Sand HOR	8.00	3.75	.80
☐ 24	Fred Williams	8.00	3.75	.80

PITTSBURGH PIRATES

☐ 25	Ray Kremer	8.00	3.75	.80
☐ 26	Earl Smith	8.00	3.75	.80
☐ 27	Paul Waner	16.00	7.50	1.60
☐ 28	Glenn Wright	8.00	3.75	.80

ST. LOUIS CARDINALS

☐ 29	Grover C. Alexander (no emblem)	25.00	11.00	2.50
☐ 30	Francis R. Blades	8.00	3.75	.80
☐ 31	Frank Frisch	25.00	11.00	2.50
☐ 32	James Wilson	8.00	3.75	.80

BOSTON RED SOX

☐ 33	Ira Flagstead	8.00	3.75	.80
☐ 34	Bryan "Slim" Harriss	8.00	3.75	.80
☐ 35	Fred Hoffman	8.00	3.75	.80
☐ 36	Philip Todt	8.00	3.75	.80

CHICAGO WHITE SOX

☐ 37	Chalmer W. Cissell HOR	8.00	3.75	.80
☐ 38	Bib Falk	8.00	3.75	.80
☐ 39	Theodore Lyons	16.00	7.50	1.60
☐ 40	Harry McCurdy	8.00	3.75	.80

CLEVELAND INDIANS

☐ 41	Chas. Jamieson	8.00	3.75	.80
☐ 42	Glenn Myatt	8.00	3.75	.80
☐ 43	Joseph Sewell	16.00	7.50	1.60
☐ 44	Geo. Uhle	8.00	3.75	.80

DETROIT TIGERS

☐ 45	Robert Fothergill	8.00	3.75	.80
☐ 46	Jack Tavener HOR	8.00	3.75	.80
☐ 47	Earl G. Whitehill	8.00	3.75	.80
☐ 48	Lawrence Woodall	8.00	3.75	.80

NEW YORK YANKEES

☐ 49	Pat Collins	8.00	3.75	.80
☐ 50	Lou Gehrig	100.00	45.00	10.00
☐ 51	Geo. H. "Babe" Ruth	150.00	70.00	15.00
☐ 52	Urban J. Shocker	8.00	3.75	.80

PHILADELPHIA A'S

☐ 53	Gordon S. Cochrane	25.00	11.00	2.50
☐ 54	Howard Ehmke	8.00	3.75	.80
☐ 55	Joseph Hauser	8.00	3.75	.80
☐ 56	Al. Simmons	20.00	9.00	2.00

ST. LOUIS BROWNS

☐ 57	L.A. Blue	8.00	3.75	.80
☐ 58	John Ogden (sic, Warren Ogden)	8.00	3.75	.80
☐ 59	Walter Shang (sic, Schang)	8.00	3.75	.80
☐ 60	Fred Schulte	8.00	3.75	.80

WASHINGTON SENATORS

☐ 61	Leon Goslin	16.00	7.50	1.60
☐ 62	Stanley Harris	16.00	7.50	1.60
☐ 63	Sam Jones	8.00	3.75	.80
☐ 64	Harold Ruel	8.00	3.75	.80

1928 PCL Exhibits

Exhibit card collectors speculate that this 32- card set, produced in 1928, was distributed regionally, in California only, in conjunction with the Exhibit Company's regular series of major league players. The cards are blue in color (as are the major league cards) and contain pictures of ball players from the six California teams of the PCL. There are no cards known for Portland and Seattle (and given that 32 cards is the exact length of a one-half sheet printing, none can be expected to appear). The cards have plain backs and carry a divided legend (two lines on each side) on the front. Several names are misspelled, several more are wrongly assigned ("Carl" instead of "Walter" Berger), and the Hollywood team name should read "Sheiks". Several of the cards are oriented horizontally (HOR). Each card measures 3 3/8" by 5 3/8". The American Card Catalog designation for this set is W465.

	MINT	VG-E	F-G
COMPLETE SET	1250.00	600.00	100.00

COMMON PLAYER	40.00	18.00	4.00
☐ 1 "Buzz" Arlett	40.00	18.00	4.00
☐ 2 Earl Averill	100.00	45.00	10.00
☐ 3 Carl Berger (Walter, sic)	50.00	22.00	5.00
☐ 4 "Ping" Bodie	40.00	18.00	4.00
☐ 5 Carl Dittmar HOR	40.00	18.00	4.00
☐ 6 Jack Penton	40.00	18.00	4.00
☐ 7 Neal "Mickey" Finn (Cornelius, sic)	40.00	18.00	4.00
☐ 8 Tony Governor	40.00	18.00	4.00
☐ 9 Truck Hannah HOR	40.00	18.00	4.00
☐ 10 Mickey Heath HOR	40.00	18.00	4.00
☐ 11 Wally Hood	40.00	18.00	4.00
☐ 12 Fuzzy Hufft	40.00	18.00	4.00
☐ 13 Snead Jolly (Smead Jolley, sic)	40.00	18.00	4.00
☐ 14 Bobby "Ducky" Jones	40.00	18.00	4.00
☐ 15 Rudy Kallio	40.00	18.00	4.00
☐ 16 Johnny Kerr HOR	40.00	18.00	4.00
☐ 17 Harry Krause	40.00	18.00	4.00
☐ 18 Lynford H. Larry (sic, Lary)	40.00	18.00	4.00
☐ 19 Dudley Lee	40.00	18.00	4.00
☐ 20 Walter "Duster" Mails	40.00	18.00	4.00
☐ 21 Jimmy Reese	50.00	22.00	5.00
☐ 22 Dusty Rhodes	40.00	18.00	4.00
☐ 23 Hal Rhyne	40.00	18.00	4.00
☐ 24 Hank Severied (Severeid, sic)	40.00	18.00	4.00
☐ 25 Earl Sheely	40.00	18.00	4.00
☐ 26 Frank Shellenback	40.00	18.00	4.00
☐ 27 Gordon Slade	40.00	18.00	4.00
☐ 28 Hollis Thurston	40.00	18.00	4.00
☐ 29 Babe Twombly	40.00	18.00	4.00
☐ 30 Earl "Tex" Weathersby	40.00	18.00	4.00
☐ 31 Ray French	40.00	18.00	4.00
☐ 32 Ray Keating	40.00	18.00	4.00

1929-1930 Four in One Exhibits

The years 1929-30 marked the initial appearance of the Exhibit Company's famous "Four-In-One" design. Each of the 32 cards depict four players from one team, with a total of 128 players shown (eight from each of 16 major league teams). Each of these exhibit cards measures 3 3/8" by 5 3/8". The

MARK KOENIG
NEW YORK A. L.

GEO. H. "BABE" RUTH
NEW YORK A. L.

LEO DUROCHER
NEW YORK A. L.

HENRY L. GEHRIG
NEW YORK A. L.

player's names and teams are located under each picture in dark blue or white print. All the reverses are post card style with the premium clip-off across one corner. There are 11 color combinations known for the fronts. The backs may be uncolored, red (black/red front), or yellow (blue/yellow front). The card labeled "Babe Herman" actually depicts Jesse Petty. The ACC designation is W463-1.

		MINT	VG-E	F-G
	COMPLETE SET	750.00	300.00	60.00
	COMMON PLAYER	16.00	7.50	1.60
☐ 1	Pat Collins	24.00	11.00	2.40
	Joe Dugan			
	Edward Farrel			
	(sic, Farrell)			
	George Sisler			
☐ 2	Lance Richbourg	16.00	7.50	1.60
	Fred Maguire			
	Robert Smith			
	George Harper			
☐ 3	D'Arcy Flowers	20.00	9.00	2.00
	Arthur "Dazzy" Vance			
	Nick Cullop			
	Harvey Hendrick			
☐ 4	Floyd C. Herman	20.00	9.00	2.00
	David Bancroft			
	John H. Deberry			
	Del L. Bisonette			
	(sic, Bissonette)			
☐ 5	Leo Hartnett	60.00	27.00	6.00
	C.E. Beck			
	L.R. (Hack) Wilson			
	Rogers Hornsby			
☐ 6	C.H. Root	20.00	9.00	2.00
	Hazen Cuyler			
	E. English			
	C.J. Grimm			
☐ 7	H.M. Critz	20.00	9.00	2.00
	W.C. Walker			
	George L. Kelly			
	V.J. Picinich			
☐ 8	E.V. Purdy	16.00	7.50	1.60
	C.A. Pittenger			
	C.F. Lucas			
	H.E. Ford			
☐ 9	L. Benton	30.00	14.00	3.00
	Melvin Ott			
	William Terry			
	Andrew Reese			
☐ 10	J.F. Hogan	24.00	11.00	2.40
	Travis C. Jackson			
	J.D. Welsh			
	Fred Lindstrom			
☐ 11	Frank O'Doul	16.00	7.50	1.60
	Bernard Friberg			
	Fresco Thompson			
	Donald Hurst			
☐ 12	Cy Williams	16.00	7.50	1.60
	A. C. Whitney			
	Ray Benge			
	Lester L. Sweetland			
☐ 13	Earl J. Adams	20.00	9.00	2.00
	R. Bartell			
	Harold Traynor			
	Earl Sheely			
☐ 14	Lloyd Waner	24.00	11.00	2.40
	Charles R. Hargreaves			
	Ray Kremer			
	Paul Waner			
☐ 15	Grover C. Alexander	50.00	22.00	5.00
	James Wilson			
	Frank Frisch			
	James Bottomly			
	(sic, Bottomley)			
☐ 16	Fred G. Haney	20.00	9.00	2.00
	Chas. J. Hafey			
	Taylor Douthit			
	Chas. M. Gilbert			
	(sic, Gelbert)			
☐ 17	J.A. Heving	20.00	9.00	2.00
	J. Rothrock			
	Charles H. Ruffing			
	R.R. (R.E.) Reeves			
☐ 18	P.J. Todt	16.00	7.50	1.60
	H. Rhyne			
	W.W. Regan			
	D. Taitt			
☐ 19	Chalmer W. Cissell	16.00	7.50	1.60
	John W. Clancy			
	John L. Kerr			
	Willie Kamm			
☐ 20	Alex Metzler	16.00	7.50	1.60
	Alphonse Thomas			
	Carl Reynolds			
	Martin G. Autrey			
	(sic, Autry)			
☐ 21	L.A. Fonseca	20.00	9.00	2.00
	Joe Sewell			
	Carl Lind			
	J. Tavener			
☐ 22	K. Holloway	20.00	9.00	2.00
	Bibb A. Falk			
	Luke Sewell			
	Earl Averill			
☐ 23	Dale Alexander	24.00	11.00	2.40
	G. F. McManus			
	H. F. Rice			
	C. Gehringer			
☐ 24	M. J. Shea	20.00	9.00	2.00
	G. E. Uhle			
	Harry E. Heilman			
	(sic, Heilmann)			
	C. N. Richardson			
☐ 25	Waite Hoyt	35.00	16.50	3.50
	Anthony Lazzeri			
	Benny Bengough			
	Earl B. Coombs			
	(sic, Combs)			
☐ 26	Mark Koenig	250.00	150.00	35.00
	Geo. H. "Babe" Ruth			
	Leo Durocher			
	Henry L. Gehrig			
☐ 27	Jimmy Foxx	75.00	35.00	7.50
	Gordon S. Cochrane			
	Robert M. Grove			
	George Haas			
☐ 28	Homer Summa	16.00	7.50	1.60
	James Dykes			
	Samuel Hale			
	Max Bishop			
☐ 29	Heine Manush	20.00	9.00	2.00
	W.H. Shang			
	(sic, Schang)			
	S. Gray			
	R. Kress			
☐ 30	Oscar Melillo	16.00	7.50	1.60
	F.O. Rourke			
	(sic, O'Rourke)			
	L.A. Blue			
	F. Schulte			
☐ 31	Leon Goslin	20.00	9.00	2.00
	Oswald Bluege			
	Harold Ruel			
	Joseph Judge			

□ 32 Sam Rice	20.00	9.00	2.00

Jack Hayes
Sam P. Jones
Chas. M. Myer

1931-32 Four in One Exhibits

The collector should refer to the checklists when trying to determine the year of issue of any "Four-In-One" set because the checklist (showing the players as they are, appear in groups of four) and the card color will ultimately provide the right clues. Some of the colors of the previous issue -- black on green, orange, red or yellow, and blue on white -- are repeated in this series, but the 1931-32 cards are distinguishable by the combinations of players which appear. Each card measures 3 3/8" by 5 3/8". The backs contain a description of attainable "Free Prizes" for coupons. The backs also contain the clip-off premium coupon. There are numerous misspellings, as usual, in the set. The ACC designation for this set is W463-2.

	MINT	VG-E	F-G
COMPLETE SET	1250.00	600.00	100.00
COMMON PLAYER	25.00	11.00	2.50
□ 1 Walter Maranville	30.00	14.00	3.00

J.T. Zachary
Alfred Spohrer
Randolph Moore

□ 2 Lance Richbourg	25.00	11.00	2.50

Fred Maguire
Earl Sheely
Walter Berger

□ 3 D'Arcy Flowers	30.00	14.00	3.00

Arthur "Dazzy" Vance
Frank O'Doul
Fresco Thompson

□ 4 Floyd C. Herman	25.00	11.00	2.50

Glenn Wright
Jack Quinn
Del L. Bisonette

□ 5 Leo Hartnett	75.00	35.00	7.50

J.R. Stevenson
(sic, Stephenson)
L.R. (Hack) Wilson

Rogers Hornsby

□ 6 C.H. Root	30.00	14.00	3.00

Hazen Cuyler
E. English
C.J. Grimm

□ 7 Les Durocher	40.00	18.00	4.00

(sic, Leo)
W.C. Walker
Harry Heilmann
Nick Cullop

□ 8 W. Roettger	25.00	11.00	2.50

Gooch
C.F. Lucas
H.E. Ford

□ 9 J.F. Hogan	35.00	16.50	3.50

Travis C. Jackson
H.M. Critz
Fred Lindstrom

□ 10 Robert O'Farrell	50.00	22.00	5.00

Melvin Ott
William Terry
Fred Fitzsimmons

□ 11 Chuck Klein	30.00	14.00	3.00

A.C. Whitney
Ray Benge
Buzz Arlett

□ 12 Harry McCurdy	25.00	11.00	2.50

Bernard Friberg
Richard Bartell
Donald Hurst

□ 13 Adam Comorosky	35.00	16.50	3.50

Gus Suhr
Harold Traynor
T.J. Thevenow

□ 14 Lloyd Waner	35.00	16.50	3.50

George Grantham
Ray Kremer
Paul Waner

□ 15 Earl J. Adams	45.00	20.00	4.50

James Wilson
Frank Frisch
James Bottomly
(sic, Bottomley)

□ 16 Bill Hallahan	30.00	14.00	3.00

Chas. J. Hafey
Taylor Douthit
Chas. M. Gilbert
(sic, Gelbert)

□ 17 Chas. Berry	25.00	11.00	2.50

J. Rothrock
Robt. Reeves
R.R. Reeves (R.E.)

□ 18 E.W. Webb	25.00	11.00	2.50

H. Rhyne
Bill Sweeney
D. MacFayden

□ 19 Luke L. Appling	35.00	16.50	3.50

Ted Lyons
Chalmer W. Cissell
Willie Kamm

□ 20 Smead Jolley	25.00	11.00	2.50

L.A. Blue
Carl Reynolds
Henry Tate

□ 21 Hunnefield	25.00	11.00	2.50

J. Goldman
Ed Morgan
Wes Ferrell

□ 22 L.A. Fonseca	30.00	14.00	3.00

B.A. Falk
Luke Sewell
Earl Averill

□ 23 Dale Alexander	35.00	16.50	3.50

G.F. McManus
G.E. Uhle
C. Gehringer

□ 24 Wallie Schang	30.00	14.00	3.00

E. Funk
Mark Koenig
Waite Hoyt

□ 25 W. Dickey	75.00	35.00	7.50

Anthony Lazzeri
Herb Pennock
Earl B. Coombs
(sic, Combs)

□ 26 Lyn Lary	400.00	180.00	40.00

Geo. H. Babe Ruth
James Reese
Henry L. Gehrig

□ 27 John Boley	30.00	14.00	3.00

James Dykes
E.J. Miller
Al Simmons

☐ 28	Jimmy Foxx	100.00	45.00	10.00
	Gordon S. Cochrane			
	Robert M. Grove			
	George Haas			
☐ 29	O. Melillo	30.00	14.00	3.00
	F.O. Rourke			
	(sic, O'Rourke)			
	Leon Goslin			
	F. Schulte			
☐ 30	W. Stewart	30.00	14.00	3.00
	Richard Farrell			
	(sic, Ferrell)			
	S. Gray			
	R. Kress			
☐ 31	Roy Spencer	40.00	18.00	4.00
	Heine Manush			
	Joe Cronin			
	Fred Marberry			
☐ 32	O. Bluege	30.00	14.00	3.00
	Joe Judge			
	Sam Rice			
	C. Myer			

1933 Four in One Exhibits

The physical dimensions of the cardboard sheet used by the Exhibit Supply Company in printing their card sets over the years allows the following correlation to be made when one establishes that 32 of the standard-sized cards (3 3/8" by 5 3/8") are printed per sheet. Sets of 128 cards are equal to four sheets, 64 cards to two sheets, 32 cards to one sheet, and 16 cards to one-half sheet. Whether it was economics, the Depression, or simplicity of operation which caused the company to change their set totals in a descending order since 1922, in 1933. The first of a series of 16-card sets was released. The fronts of these cards are black green, orange, red, or yellow; the backs are blank. The catalog designation for this set is W463-3.

	MINT	VG-E	F-G
COMPLETE SET	700.00	300.00	60.00
COMMON PLAYER	25.00	11.00	2.50

☐ 1	Lance Richbourg	25.00	11.00	2.50
	Fred Maguire			
	Earl Sheely			
	Walter Berger			

☐ 2	Vincent Lopez (Al)	35.00	16.50	3.50
	Glenn Wright			
	Arthur Dazzy Vance			
	Frank O'Doul			
☐ 3	J.R. Stephenson	25.00	11.00	2.50
	C.J. Grimm			
	E. English			
	C.H. Root			
☐ 4	Taylor Douthit	30.00	14.00	3.00
	George Grantham			
	G. F. Lucas			
	Chas. Hafey			
☐ 5	Fred Fitzsimmons	30.00	14.00	3.00
	H. M. Critz			
	Fred Lindstrom			
	Robert O'Farrell			
☐ 6	Chuck Klein	30.00	14.00	3.00
	Ray Benge			
	Richard Bartell			
	Donald Hurst			
☐ 7	Tom J. Thevenow	35.00	16.50	3.50
	Paul Waner			
	Gus Suhr			
	Lloyd Waner			
☐ 8	Earl J. Adams	35.00	16.50	3.50
	Frank Frisch			
	Bill Halloran			
	Chas. Gelbert			
☐ 9	D. MacFayden	25.00	11.00	2.50
	E. W. Webb			
	H. Rhyne			
	Chas. Berry			
☐ 10	Charles Berry	30.00	14.00	3.00
	Bob Seeds			
	C.A. Blue			
	Ted Lyons			
☐ 11	Wes Ferrell	30.00	14.00	3.00
	Luke Sewell			
	Ed Morgan			
	Earl Averill			
☐ 12	"Muddy" Ruel	35.00	16.50	3.50
	G.E. Uhle			
	Jonathon Stone			
	C. Gehringer			
☐ 13	George H."Babe" Ruth	300.00	130.00	30.00
	Herb Pennock			
	Anthony Lazzeri			
	W. Dickey			
☐ 14	Mickey Cochrane	100.00	45.00	10.00
	Jimmy Foxx			
	Al Simmons			
	Robert M. Grove			
☐ 15	Richard Farrell	35.00	16.50	3.50
	(sic, Ferrell)			
	O. Melillo			
	Leon Goslin			
	S. Grey			
☐ 16	H. Manush	30.00	14.00	3.00
	F. Marberry			
	J. Judge			
	Roy Spencer			

1934 Four in One Exhibits

The emergence of the bubble gum card producers in 1933-34 may have motivated Exhibit Supply to make a special effort to provide a "quality" set for 1934. The new 16-card series was printed in colors of blue, brown, olive green and violet -- all in softer tones than used in previous years. No less than 25 players appeared on cards for the first time, and another 16 were given entirely new poses. For the first time in the history of the Exhibit baseball series, there were no spelling errors. However, perfection is rarely attained in any endeavor, and the "bugaboo" of 1934 was the labeling of Al Lopez as Vincent Lopez (famous band leader and prognosticator). The cards have plain backs. Each card measures 3 3/8" by 5 3/8". The ACC designation for this set is W463-4.

		MINT	VG-E	F-G
	COMPLETE SET	700.00	320.00	70.00
	COMMON PLAYER	16.00	7.50	1.60
☐ 1	Bill Urbansky Ed Brandt Walter Berger Frank Hogan	16.00	7.50	1.60
☐ 2	Vincent Lopez (Al) Glenn Wright Sam Leslie Leonard Koenecke	20.00	9.00	2.00
☐ 3	Chas. Klein C.J. Grimm E. English Lon Warneke	20.00	9.00	2.00
☐ 4	Botchi Lombardi Tony Piet Jimmy Bottomley Chas. J. Hafey	35.00	16.50	3.50
☐ 5	Blondy Ryan Bill Terry Carl Hubbell Mel Ott	60.00	27.00	6.00
☐ 6	Jimmy Wilson Wesley Schulmerich Richard Bartell Donald Hurst	16.00	7.50	1.60
☐ 7	T.J. Thevenow Paul Waner Pie Traynor Lloyd Waner	35.00	16.50	3.50
☐ 8	Pepper Martin Frank Frisch Bill Hallahan John Rothrock	25.00	11.00	2.50
☐ 9	Lefty Grove Roy Johnson Bill Cissell Rick Ferrell	35.00	16.50	3.50
☐ 10	Luke Appling Al Simmons Evar Swanson George Earnshaw	30.00	14.00	3.00
☐ 11	Wes Ferrell Frank Pytlak Willie Kamm Earl Averill	20.00	9.00	2.00
☐ 12	Mickey Cochrane Goose Goslin Fred Marberry C. Gehringer	50.00	22.00	5.00
☐ 13	Geo.H. "Babe" Ruth Vernon Gomez Lou Gehrig W. Dickey	400.00	180.00	40.00
☐ 14	Mickey Cochrane Jimmy Foxx Al Simmons	100.00	45.00	10.00

☐ 15	Robert M. Grove Irving Burns O. Melillo Irving Hadley Rollie Hemsley	16.00	7.50	1.60
☐ 16	Heine Manush Alvin Crowder Joe Cronin Joe Kuhel	25.00	11.00	2.50

1935 Four in One Exhibits

The year 1935 marked the return of the 16-card Exhibit series to a simple slate blue color. Babe Ruth appears with Boston, N.L., the last time his card would be made while he was playing, after being included in every Exhibit series since 1921. Of the 64 players pictured, 17 are shown for the first time, while 11 of the returnees are graced with new poses. The infamous "Vincent Lopez" card returns with this set, and the photo purportedly showing Tony Cuccinello is really that of George Puccinello. The cards have plain backs. The ACC designation is W463-5. The cards measure 3 3/8" by 5 3/8".

		MINT	VG-E	F-G
	COMPLETE SET	450.00	200.00	45.00
	COMMON PLAYER	16.00	7.50	1.60
☐ 1	"Babe" Ruth Frank Hogan Walter Berger Ed Brandt	225.00	100.00	22.00
☐ 2	Van Mungo Vincent Lopez (Al) Dan Taylor Tony Cuccinello	20.00	9.00	2.00
☐ 3	Chas. Klein C. J. Grimm Lon Warneke Gabby Hartnett	30.00	14.00	3.00
☐ 4	Botchi Lombardi Paul Derringer Jimmy Bottomley Chas. J. Hafey	35.00	16.50	3.50
☐ 5	Hughie Critz Bill Terry Carl Hubbell	60.00	27.00	6.00

	Mel Ott		
☐ 6	Jimmy Wilson 16.00	7.50	1.60
	Phil Collins		
	John "Blondy" Ryan		
	Geo. Watkins		
☐ 7	Paul Waner 35.00	16.50	3.50
	Pie Traynor		
	Guy Bush		
	Floyd Vaughn		
☐ 8	Pepper Martin 100.00	45.00	10.00
	Frank Frisch		
	Jerome "Dizzy" Dean		
	Paul Dean		
☐ 9	Lefty Grove 60.00	27.00	6.00
	Billy Werber		
	Joe Cronin		
	Rick Ferrell		
☐10	Al Simmons 30.00	14.00	3.00
	Jimmy Dykes		
	Ted Lyons		
	Henry Bonura		
☐11	Mel Harder 20.00	9.00	2.00
	Hal Trosky		
	Willie Kamm		
	Earl Averill		
☐12	Mickey Cochrane 40.00	18.00	4.00
	Goose Goslin		
	Linwood Rowe		
	(sic, Lynwood)		
	C. Gehringer		
☐13	Tony Lazzeri 150.00	70.00	15.00
	Vernon Gomez		
	Lou Gehrig		
	W. Dickey		
☐14	Slug Mahaffey 30.00	14.00	3.00
	Jimmy Foxx		
	George Cramer		
	Bob Johnson		
☐15	Irving Burns 16.00	7.50	1.60
	Oscar Melillo		
	L. N. Newson		
	Rollie Hemsley		
☐16	Buddy Meyer (Myer) 20.00	9.00	2.00
	Earl Whitehill		
	H. Manush		
	Fred Schulte		

1936 Four in One Exhibits

In 1936, the 16-card Exhibit set retained the "slate" or blue-gray color of the preceding year, but also added an olive green hue to the set. The cards are blank-backed, but for the first time since the "Four-In-One" design was introduced in 1929, a line reading "Ptd. in U.S.A." was placed in the bottom border on the obverse. The set contains 16 players making their debut in Exhibit cards, while nine holdovers have new poses. The photos of George Puccinelli was correctly identified and placed with Philadelphia, A.L. The ACC designation is W463-6. The cards measure 3 3/8" by 5 3/8".

	MINT	VG-E	F-G
COMPLETE SET	600.00	275.00	60.00
COMMON PLAYER	16.00	7.50	1.60
☐ 1 Bill Urbanski	16.00	7.50	1.60
Pinky Whitney			
Walter Berger			
Danny MacFayden			
☐ 2 Van Mungo	20.00	9.00	2.00
Stan Bordagaray			
Fred Lindstrom			
Dutch Brandt			
☐ 3 Billy Herman	25.00	11.00	2.50
Augie Galan			
Lon Warneke			
Gabby Hartnett			
☐ 4 Botchie Lombardi	20.00	9.00	2.00
Paul Derringer			
Babe Herman			
Alex Kampouris			

☐ 5 Gus. Mancuso	60.00	27.00	6.00
Bill Terry			
Carl Hubbell			
Mel Ott			
☐ 6 Jimmy Wilson	16.00	7.50	1.60
Curt Davis			
Dolph Camilli			
Johnny Moore			
☐ 7 Paul Waner	35.00	16.50	3.50
Pie Traynor			
Guy Bush			
Floyd Vaughn			
☐ 8 Joe "Ducky" Medwick	100.00	45.00	10.00
Frank Frisch			
Jerome "Dizzy" Dean			
Paul Dean			
☐ 9 Lefty Grove	100.00	45.00	10.00
Jimmy Foxx			
Joe Cronin			
Rick Ferrell			
☐10 Luke Appling	30.00	14.00	3.00
Jimmy Dykes			
Ted Lyons			
Henry Bonura			
☐11 Mel Harder	20.00	9.00	2.00
Hal Trosky			
Joe Vosmik			
Earl Averill			
☐12 Mickey Cochrane	50.00	22.00	5.00
Goose Goslin			
Linwood Rowe			
(sic, Lynwood)			
C. Gehringer			
☐13 Tony Lazzeri	150.00	70.00	15.00
Vernon Gomez			
Lou Gehrig			
Red Ruffing			
☐14 Charles Berry	16.00	7.50	1.60
Puccinelli			
Frank Higgins			
Bob Johnson			
☐15 Harland Clift	16.00	7.50	1.60
Sammy West			
Paul Andrews			
Rollie Hemsley			
☐16 Buddy Meyer (Myer)	16.00	7.50	1.60
Earl Whitehill			
Ossie Bluege			
L.N. Newsom			

1937 Four in One Exhibits

It would appear that Exhibit Supply was merely "flip-flopping" color schemes during the three year period 1935-37. In 1935, the cards were blue-gray; in 1936, the cards were either blue-gray or green; now, in 1937, the cards appear in green only. As with the previous set, the name and team of each player is printed in two or three lines under his picture, the "Ptd. in U.S.A." line appears in the bottom border (missing on some cards), and the backs are blank. The ACC designation is W463-7. The cards measure 3 3/8" by 5 3/8".

		MINT	VG-E	F-G
	COMPLETE SET	700.00	325.00	70.00
	COMMON PLAYER	16.00	7.50	1.60
☐ 1	Bill Urbanski Alfonso Lopez Walter Berger Danny MacFayden	20.00	9.00	2.00
☐ 2	Van Mungo E. English Johnny Moore (Philadelphia NL) Gordon Phelps	16.00	7.50	1.60
☐ 3	Billy Herman Augie Galan Bill Lee Gabby Hartnett	25.00	11.00	2.50
☐ 4	Botchi Lombardi Paul Derringer Lew Riggs Phil Weintraub	20.00	9.00	2.00
☐ 5	Gus Mancuso Sam Leslie Carl Hubbell Mel Ott	50.00	22.00	5.00
☐ 6	Pinky Whitney Wm. Walters Dolph Camilli Johnny Moore	16.00	7.50	1.60
☐ 7	Paul Waner Gus Suhr Cy Blanton Floyd Vaughn	25.00	11.00	2.50
☐ 8	Joe "Duck" Medwick Lon Warneke Jerome "Dizzy" Dean Stuart Martin	75.00	35.00	7.50
☐ 9	Lefty Grove	100.00	45.00	10.00
	Jimmy Foxx Joe Cronin Dick Ferrell			
☐ 10	Luke Appling Jimmy Dykes Vernon Kennedy Henry Bonura	20.00	9.00	2.00
☐ 11	Bob Feller Hal Trosky Frank Pytlak Earl Averill	60.00	27.00	6.00
☐ 12	Mickey Cochrane Goose Goslin Linwood Rowe C. Gehringer	45.00	20.00	4.50
☐ 13	Tony Lazzeri Vernon Gomez Lou Gehrig Joe DiMaggio	250.00	110.00	25.00
☐ 14	Billy Weber (sic, Werber) Harry Kelly (sic, Kelley) Wallace Moses Bob Johnson	16.00	7.50	1.60
☐ 15	Harland Clift Sammy West Orval Hildebrand Rollie Hemsley	16.00	7.50	1.60
☐ 16	Buddy Meyer (Myer) Jonathan Stone Joe Kuhel L.N. Newsom	16.00	7.50	1.60

1938 Four in One Exhibits

The 1938 set of 16 cards demonstrated the fact that one consistent "quality" of Exhibit Supply sets is their inconsistency. For example, the card of Tony Cuccinello once again contains the photo of George Puccinelli, a mistake first made in 1935, corrected in 1936, and now made again in 1938. The set is also rife with name and spelling errors. Of the 64 players depicted, 12 are new arrivals and three are returnees with new poses. Another ten retained their 1937 photos but were designated new team affiliations. The cards have blank backs. The set was the last to employ the "Four-In-One" format. The ACC designation is W463-8. The cards measure 3 3/8" by 5 3/8".

	MINT	VG-E	F-G
COMPLETE SET	850.00	400.00	75.00
COMMON PLAYER	25.00	11.00	2.50
□ 1 Tony Cuccinello	30.00	14.00	3.00
(sic, Geo. Puccinelli)			
Roy Johnson			
Vince DiMaggio			
Danny MacFayden			
□ 2 Van Mungo	30.00	14.00	3.00
Leo Durocher			
Dolph Camilli			
Gordon Phelps			
□ 3 Billy Herman	90.00	42.00	9.00
Augie Galan			
Jerome "Dizzy" Dean			
Gabby Hartnett			
□ 4 Dutch Lombardi	30.00	14.00	3.00
Paul Derringer			
Lew Riggs			
Ival Goodman			
□ 5 Hank Leiber	60.00	27.00	6.00
Jim Ripple			
Carl Hubbell			
Mel Ott			
□ 6 Pinky Whitney	30.00	14.00	3.00
Wm. Walters			
Chas. Klein			
Morris Arnovich			
□ 7 Paul Waner	35.00	16.50	3.50
Gus Suhr			
Cy Blanton			
Floyd Vaughn			
□ 8 Joe "Ducky" Medwick	45.00	20.00	4.50
Lon Warneke			
John Mize			
Stuart Martin			
□ 9 Lefty Grove	90.00	42.00	9.00
Jimmy Foxx			
Joe Cronin			
Joe Vosmik			
□ 10 Luke Appling	35.00	16.50	3.50
Luke Sewell			
Mike Kreevich			
Ted Lyons			
□ 11 Bob Feller	60.00	27.00	6.00
Hal Trosky			
Odell Hale			
Earl Averill			
□ 12 Hank Greenberg	60.00	27.00	6.00
Rudy York			
Tom Bridges			
C. Gehringer			
□ 13 W. Dickey	300.00	130.00	30.00
Vernon Gomez			
Lou Gehrig			
Joe DiMaggio			
□ 14 Billy Weber	25.00	11.00	2.50
(sic, Werber)			
Harry Kelly			
(sic, Kelley)			
Wallace Moses			
Bob Johnson			
□ 15 Harland Clift	25.00	11.00	2.50
Sammy West			
Beau Bell			
L.N. Newsom			
□ 16 Buddy Meyer (Myer)	30.00	14.00	3.00
Jonathan Stone			
Wes Ferrell			
Rick Ferrell			

1939-1946 Salutation Exhibits

This collection of 81 exhibit cards shares a common style: the "Personal Greeting" or "Salutation". The specific greeting varies from card to card -- "Yours truly, Best wishes, etc." -- as does the location of the exhibit identification (lower left, LL, or lower right, LR). Some players appear with different teams and

there are occasional misspellings. Each card measures 3 3/8" by 5 3/8".

	MINT	VG-E	F-G
COMPLETE SET	2100.00	1000.00	200.00
COMMON PLAYER	2.00	.90	.20
□ 1 Luke Appling (LL)	5.00	2.35	.50
Sincerely Yours			
□ 2 Luke Appling (LR)	4.00	1.85	.40
Sincerely Yours			
□ 3 Earl Averill	250.00	110.00	25.00
Very Best Wishes			
□ 4 Charles "Red" Barrett	2.00	.90	.20
Yours Truly			
□ 5 Henry "Hank" Borowy	2.00	.90	.20
Sincerely Yours			
□ 6 Lou Boudreau	4.00	1.85	.40
Sincerely			
□ 7 Adolf Camilli	15.00	7.00	1.50
Very Truly Yours			
□ 8 Phil Cavaretta	2.00	.90	.20
Cordially Yours			
□ 9 Harland Clift	10.00	4.75	1.00
Very Truly Yours			
□ 10 Tony Cuccinello	20.00	9.00	2.00
Very Best Wishes			
□ 11 Dizzy Dean	25.00	11.00	2.50
Sincerely			
□ 12 Paul Derringer	2.00	.90	.20
Yours Truly			
□ 13 Bill Dickey (LR)	16.00	7.50	1.60
Cordially Yours			
□ 14 Bill Dickey (LL)	16.00	7.50	1.60
Cordially Yours			
□ 15 Joe DiMaggio	25.00	11.00	2.50
Cordially			
□ 16 Bob Elliott	2.00	.90	.20
Truly Yours			
□ 17 Bob Feller	30.00	14.00	3.00
Best Wishes			
□ 18 Bob Feller	10.00	4.75	1.00
Yours Truly			
□ 19 Dave Ferriss	2.00	.90	.20
Best of Luck			
□ 20 Jimmy Foxx	60.00	27.00	6.00
Sincerely			
□ 21 Lou Gehrig	250.00	110.00	25.00
Sincerely			
□ 22 Charlie Gehringer	25.00	11.00	2.50
Yours Truly			
□ 23 Vernon Gomez	60.00	27.00	6.00
Sincerely			
□ 24 Joe Gordon (Cleveland)	20.00	9.00	2.00
Sincerely			
□ 25 Joe Gordon (New York)	2.00	.90	.20
Sincerely			

☐ 26 Hank Greenberg	12.00	5.50	1.20
Truly Yours			
☐ 27 Henry Greenberg	50.00	22.00	5.00
Very Truly Yours			
☐ 28 Robert Grove	35.00	16.50	3.50
Cordially Yours			
☐ 29 Gabby Hartnett	200.00	90.00	20.00
Cordially			
☐ 30 Buddy Hassett	10.00	4.75	1.00
Yours Truly			
☐ 31 Jeff Heath	10.00	4.75	1.00
Best Wishes			
☐ 32 Jeff Heath (Small	2.00	.90	.20
Pic) Best Wishes			
☐ 33 Kirby Higbe	10.00	4.75	1.00
Sincerely			
☐ 34 Tommy Holmes	2.00	.90	.20
Yours Truly			
☐ 35 Tommy Holmes	60.00	27.00	6.00
Sincerely Yours			
☐ 36 Carl Hubbell	16.00	7.50	1.60
Best Wishes			
☐ 37 Bob Johnson	10.00	4.75	1.00
Yours Truly			
☐ 38 Charles Keller	2.00	.90	.20
Best Wishes			
☐ 39 Ken Keltner	25.00	11.00	2.50
Sincerly (sic)			
☐ 40 Chuck Klein	75.00	35.00	7.50
Yours Truly			
☐ 41 Mike Kreevich	50.00	22.00	5.00
Sincerely			
☐ 42 Joe Kuhel	10.00	4.75	1.00
Truly Yours			
☐ 43 Bill Lee	10.00	4.75	1.00
Cordially Yours			
☐ 44 Ernie Lombardi (1/2 B)	100.00	45.00	10.00
Cordially			
☐ 45 Ernie Lombardi	4.00	1.85	.40
Cordially Yours			
☐ 46 Marty Marion	4.00	1.85	.40
Best Wishes			
☐ 47 Merrill May	10.00	4.75	1.00
Best Wishes			
☐ 48 Frank McCormick (LL)	10.00	4.75	1.00
Sincerely			
☐ 49 Frank McCormick (LR)	2.00	.90	.20
Sincerely			
☐ 50 George McQuinn (LL)	10.00	4.75	1.00
Yours Truly			
☐ 51 George McQuinn (LR)	4.00	1.85	.40
Yours Truly			
☐ 52 Joe Medwick	16.00	7.50	1.60
Very Best Wishes			
☐ 53 Johnny Mize (LL)	12.00	5.50	1.20
Yours Truly			
☐ 54 Johnny Mize (LR)	5.00	2.35	.50
Yours Truly			
☐ 55 Hugh Mulcahy	50.00	22.00	5.00
Cordially			
☐ 56 Hal Newhouser	4.00	1.85	.40
Best Wishes			
☐ 57 Louis (Buck) Newsom	2.00	.90	.20
Sincerely			
☐ 58 Buck Newson (sic)	125.00	57.00	12.50
Very Best Wishes			
☐ 59 Mel Ott (LL)	40.00	18.00	4.00
Sincerely Yours			
☐ 60 Mel Ott (LR)	16.00	7.50	1.60
Sincerely Yours			
☐ 61 Andy Pafko	2.00	.90	.20
Sincerely Yours			
☐ 62 Andy Pafko	2.00	.90	.20
Yours Truly			
☐ 63 Claude Passeau	2.00	.90	.20
Sincerely			
☐ 64 Howard Pollett (LL)	10.00	4.75	1.00
Best Wishes			
☐ 65 Howard Pollett (LR)	2.00	.90	.20
Best Wishes			
☐ 66 Pete Reiser (LL)	50.00	22.00	5.00
Truly Yours			
☐ 67 Pete Reiser (LR)	2.00	.90	.20
Truly Yours			
☐ 68 Johnny Rizzo	100.00	45.00	10.00
Sincerely Yours			
☐ 69 Glen Russell	100.00	45.00	10.00
Sincerely			
☐ 70 George Stirnweiss	2.00	.90	.20
Yours Truly			
☐ 71 Cecil Travis	10.00	4.75	1.00
Best Wishes			
☐ 72 Paul Trout	2.00	.90	.20

Truly Yours			
☐ 73 Johnny Vander Meer	12.00	5.50	1.20
Cordially Yours			
☐ 74 Arky Vaughan	15.00	7.00	1.50
Best Wishes			
☐ 75 Fred "Dixie" Walker	2.00	.90	.20
("D" on Hat)			
Yours Truly			
☐ 76 Fred "Dixie" Walker	30.00	14.00	3.00
Cap blanked out			
Yours Truly			
☐ 77 Bucky Walters	2.00	.90	.20
Sincerely Yours			
☐ 78 Lon Warneke	10.00	4.75	1.00
Very Truly Yours			
☐ 79 Ted Williams (9)	125.00	57.00	12.50
Sincerely			
☐ 80 Ted Williams	16.00	7.50	1.60
Sincerely Yours			
☐ 81 Rudy York	2.00	.90	.20
Cordially			

1947-1966 Exhibits

This grouping encompasses a wide time span but displays a common design. The following players have been illegally reprinted in mass quantities on a thinner-than-original cardboard which is also characterized by a dark gray back: Aaron, Ford, Fox, Hodges, Elston Howard, Mantle, Mays, Musial, Newcombe, Reese, Spahn, and Ted Williams. Each card measures 3 3/8" by 5 3/8". In the checklist below SIG refers to signature and SCR refers to script name on card. The abbreviations POR (portrait), BAT (batting), and FIE (fielding) are also used below. There are many levels of scarcity within this "set," essentially based on which year(s) the player's card was printed. The Mickey Mantle portrait card, for example, was only printed in 1966, the last year of production. Those scarce cards which were only produced one year are noted parenthetically below by the year(s) of issue.

		MINT	VG-E	F-G
COMPLETE SET		2100.00	900.00	200.00
COMMON PLAYER		.75	.35	.07
☐	1 Hank Aaron	7.50	3.50	.75
☐	2A Joe Adcock SCR	1.50	.70	.15
☐	2B Joe Adcock SIG	1.50	.70	.15
☐	3 Max Alvis (1966)	10.00	4.75	1.00
☐	4A Johnny Antonelli	.75	.35	.07
	(Braves)			
☐	4B Johnny Antonelli	1.50	.70	.15
	(Giants)			
☐	5A Luis Aparicio POR	3.50	1.65	.35
☐	5B Luis Aparicio BAT	15.00	7.00	1.50
	(1964)			
☐	6 Luke Appling	3.50	1.65	.35
☐	7A Richie Ashburn	3.00	1.40	.30
	(Phillies)			
☐	7B Ritchie Ashburn	1.50	.70	.15
	(sic, Richie)			
☐	7C Richie Ashburn			
	(Cubs) (1961)	7.50	3.50	.75
☐	8 Bob Aspromonte	2.00	.90	.20
	(1964 and 1966)			
☐	9 Toby Atwell	1.50	.70	.15
☐	10A Ed Bailey (1961)			
	(Cincinnati cap)	3.00	1.40	.30
☐	10B Ed Bailey (no cap)	.75	.35	.07
☐	11 Gene Baker	.75	.35	.07
☐	12A Ernie Banks SCR	10.00	4.75	1.00
☐	12B Ernie Banks SIG	5.00	2.35	.50
☐	12C Ernie Banks POR	10.00	4.75	1.00
	(1964 and 1966)			
☐	13 Steve Barber	2.00	.90	.20
	(1964 and 1966)			
☐	14 Earl Battey	2.00	.90	.20
	(1964 and 1966)			

☐ 15	Matt Batts	1.50	.70	.15
☐ 16A	Hank Bauer (New York cap)	1.50	.70	.15
☐ 16B	Hank Bauer (1961) (plain cap)	3.50	1.65	.35
☐ 17	Frank Baumholtz	1.50	.70	.15
☐ 18	Gene Bearden	1.50	.70	.15
☐ 19	Joe Beggs (1947)	7.50	3.50	.75
☐ 20A	Yogi Berra	6.00	2.80	.60
☐ 20B	Larry "Yogi" Berra (1964 and 1966)	12.00	5.50	1.20
☐ 21	Steve Bilko	1.50	.70	.15
☐ 22A	Ewell Blackwell (foot up)	1.50	.70	.15
☐ 22B	Ewell Blackwell POR	1.50	.70	.15
☐ 23A	Don Blasingame (St. Louis cap)	1.50	.70	.15
☐ 23B	Don Blasingame (plain cap) (1961)	3.00	1.40	.30
☐ 24	Ken Boyer (1964 and 1966)	3.50	1.65	.35
☐ 25	Ralph Branca	3.00	1.40	.30
☐ 26	Jackie Brandt (1961)	25.00	11.00	2.50
☐ 27	Harry Brecheen	.75	.35	.07
☐ 28	Tom Brewer (1960 and 1961)	1.50	.70	.15
☐ 29	Lou Brissie	1.50	.70	.15
☐ 30	Bill Bruton	.75	.35	.07
☐ 31A	Lew Burdette (side view)	1.50	.70	.15
☐ 31B	Lew Burdette (1964) (facing)	5.00	2.35	.50
☐ 32	Johnny Callison (1964 and 1966)	2.00	.90	.20
☐ 33	Roy Campanella	8.00	3.75	.80
☐ 34A	Chico Carrasquel (White Sox)	.75	.35	.07
☐ 34B	Chico Carrasquel (plain cap)	3.50	1.65	.35
☐ 35	George Case (1947)	7.50	3.50	.75
☐ 36	Hugh Casey	1.50	.70	.15
☐ 37	Norm Cash (1964 and 1966)	4.00	1.85	.40
☐ 38A	Orlando Cepeda POR (1960 and 1961)	3.00	1.40	.30
☐ 38B	Orlando Cepeda BAT (1964 and 1966)	4.00	1.85	.40
☐ 39A	Bob Cerv (1960) (A's uniform)	2.00	.90	.20
☐ 39B	Bob Cerv (1961) (plain uniform)	9.00	4.25	.90
☐ 40	Dean Chance (1964 and 1966)	2.00	.90	.20
☐ 41	Spud Chandler (1947)	7.50	3.50	.75
☐ 42	Tom Cheney (1964 and 1966)	2.00	.90	.20
☐ 43	Bubba Church	1.50	.70	.15
☐ 44	Roberto Clemente	9.00	4.25	.90
☐ 45A	Rocky Colavito POR (1961)	9.00	4.25	.90
☐ 45B	Rocky Colavito BAT (1964)	5.00	2.35	.50
☐ 46	Choo Choo Coleman (1964 and 1966)	4.00	1.85	.40
☐ 47	Gordy Coleman (1964 and 1966)	5.00	2.35	.50
☐ 48	Jerry Coleman	1.50	.70	.15
☐ 49	Mort Cooper (1947)	7.50	3.50	.75
☐ 50	Walker Cooper (found with or without "Made in USA")	1.50	.70	.15
☐ 51	Roger Craig (1964 and 1966)	4.00	1.85	.40
☐ 52	Delmar Crandall	.75	.35	.07
☐ 53A	Joe Cunningham POR (1964)	5.00	2.35	.50
☐ 53B	Joe Cunningham BAT (1961)	10.00	4.75	1.00
☐ 54	Guy Curtright (1947) (sic, Cartwright)	7.50	3.50	.75
☐ 55	Bud Daley (1961)	20.00	9.00	2.00
☐ 56A	Alvin Dark (Boston cap)	1.50	.70	.15
☐ 56B	Alvin Dark (New York cap)	1.50	.70	.15
☐ 56C	Alvin Dark (Cubs) (1960)	3.00	1.40	.30
☐ 57	Murray Dickson	1.50	.70	.15
☐ 58	Bob Dillinger	1.50	.70	.15
☐ 59	Dom DiMaggio (1947)	9.00	4.25	.90
☐ 60	Joe Dobson	1.50	.70	.15
☐ 61	Larry Doby	1.50	.70	.15
☐ 62	Bobby Doerr	5.00	2.35	.50
☐ 63A	Dick Donovan (Braves, plain cap)	1.50	.70	.15
☐ 63B	Dick Donovan (White Sox)	1.50	.70	.15
☐ 64	Walter Dropo	.75	.35	.07
☐ 65A	Don Drysdale POR (1960 and 1961)	20.00	9.00	2.00
☐ 65B	Don Drysdale (1964) (portrait 1/2)	20.00	9.00	2.00
☐ 66	Luke Easter	1.50	.70	.15
☐ 67	Bruce Edwards	1.50	.70	.15
☐ 68	Del Ennis	.75	.35	.07
☐ 69	Al Evans	1.50	.70	.15
☐ 70	Walter Evers	1.50	.70	.15
☐ 71A	Ferris Fain FIE	3.00	1.40	.30
☐ 71B	Ferris Fain POR	1.50	.70	.15
☐ 72	Dick Farrell (1964 and 1966)	2.00	.90	.20
☐ 73A	Whitey Ford (no glove, throwing)	4.00	1.85	.40
☐ 73B	Whitey Ford POR (1964)	35.00	16.50	3.50
☐ 73C	Ed "Whitey" Ford (glove on shoulder) (1964 and 1966)	10.00	4.75	1.00
☐ 74	Dick Fowler	3.00	1.40	.30

75	Nelson Fox	1.50	.70	.15
76	Tito Francona (1964 and 1966)	2.00	.90	.20
77	Bob Friend	.75	.35	.07
78	Carl Furillo	3.00	1.40	.30
79	Augie Galan	1.50	.70	.15
80	Jim Gentile (1964 and 1966)	2.00	.90	.20
81	Tony Gonzalez (1964 and 1966)	2.00	.90	.20
82A	Billy Goodman FIE (fielding)	1.50	.70	.15
82B	Billy Goodman BAT (1960 and 1961)	2.50	1.15	.25
83	Ted Greengrass (sic, Jim)	1.50	.70	.15
84	Dick Groat	1.50	.70	.15
85	Steve Gromek	1.50	.70	.15
86	Johnny Groth	.75	.35	.07
87	Orval Grove (1947)	7.50	3.50	.75
88A	Frank Gustine (Pirates)	1.50	.70	.15
88B	Frank Gustine (Cubs)	1.50	.70	.15
89	Berthold Haas (1950)	5.00	2.35	.50
90	Grady Hatton	1.50	.70	.15
91	Jim Hegan	.75	.35	.07
92	Tom Henrich	2.50	1.15	.25
93	Ray Herbert (1964)	9.00	4.25	.90
94	Gene Hermanski	1.50	.70	.15
95	Whitey Herzog (1960 and 1961)	2.00	.90	.20
96	Kirby Higbe (1947)	7.50	3.50	.75
97	Chuck Hinton (1964 and 1966)	2.00	.90	.20
98	Don Hoak (1964)	9.00	4.25	.90
99A	Gil Hodges (Brooklyn cap)	5.00	2.35	.50
99B	Gil Hodges (Los Angeles cap)	5.00	2.35	.50
100	Johnny Hopp (1947)	7.50	3.50	.75
101	Elston Howard (1960 and 1961)	2.00	.90	.20
102	Frank Howard (1964 and 1966)	4.00	1.85	.40
103	Ken Hubbs (1964)	20.00	9.00	2.00
104	Tex Hughson (1947)	7.50	3.50	.75
105	Fred Hutchinson (1950)	3.00	1.40	.30
106	Monte Irvin	4.00	1.85	.40
107	Joey Jay (1964 and 1966)	2.00	.90	.20
108	Jackie Jensen (1960)	10.00	4.75	1.00
109	Sam Jethroe	1.50	.70	.15
110	Bill Johnson (1950)	3.00	1.40	.30
111	Walter Judnich (1947)	7.50	3.50	.75
112A	Al Kaline SCR (kneeling)	7.50	3.50	.75
112B	Al Kaline SIG POR	7.50	3.50	.75
113	George Kell	4.00	1.85	.40
114	Charley Keller	3.00	1.40	.30
115	Alex Kellner	.75	.35	.07
116	Kenn Keltner (sic, Ken)	1.50	.70	.15
117A	Harmon Killebrew (pin-stripes, batting) (1960 and 1961)	9.00	4.25	.90
117B	Harmon Killibrew (sic, Killebrew) POR (1966)	20.00	9.00	2.00
117C	Harmon Killebrew (throwing) (1964 and 1966)	9.00	4.25	.90
118	Ellis Kinder	1.50	.70	.15
119	Ralph Kiner	4.00	1.85	.40
120	Billy Klaus (1960)	7.50	3.50	.75
121A	Ted Kluszewski (Reds)	1.50	.70	.15
121B	Ted Kluszewski (Pirates)	1.50	.70	.15
121C	Ted Kluszewski (plain uniform) (1960 and 1961)	5.00	2.35	.50
122	Don Kolloway (1950)	3.00	1.40	.30
123	Jim Konstanty	1.50	.70	.15
124	Sandy Koufax (1964 and 1966)	12.00	5.50	1.20
125	Ed Kranepool (1966)	25.00	11.00	2.50
126A	Tony Kubek (dark background)	3.00	1.40	.30
126B	Tony Kubek (light background)	2.00	.90	.20
127A	Harvey Kuenn (1960) (Detroit)	5.00	2.35	.50
127B	Harvey Kuenn (1961) (plain uniform)	7.50	3.50	.75
127C	Harvey Kuenn (San Francisco) (1964 and 1966)	2.50	1.15	.25
128	Kurowski (1950)	3.00	1.40	.30
129	Eddie Lake (1947)	7.50	3.50	.75
130	Jim Landis (1964 and 1966)	2.00	.90	.20
131	Don Larsen	1.50	.70	.15
132A	Bob Lemon (left arm not shown)	5.00	2.35	.50
132B	Bob Lemon (left arm extended)	20.00	9.00	2.00
133	Buddy Lewis (1947)	7.50	3.50	.75
134	Johnny Lindell (1950)	7.50	3.50	.75
135	Phil Linz (1966)	10.00	4.75	1.00
136	Don Lock (1966)	10.00	4.75	1.00
137	Whitey Lockman	1.50	.70	.15
138	Johnny Logan	.75	.35	.07
139A	Dale Long (Pirates)	.75	.35	.07
139B	Dale Long (Cubs) (1961)	3.00	1.40	.30
140	Ed Lopat	3.00	1.40	.30
141A	Harry Lowery (sic, Lowrey)	1.50	.70	.15
141B	Harry Lowrey	1.50	.70	.15
142	Sal Maglie	1.50	.70	.15
143	Art Mahaffey (1964 and 1966)	2.00	.90	.20
144	Hank Majeski	.75	.35	.07
145	Frank Malzone	.75	.35	.07
146A	Mickey Mantle (batting to waist)	12.00	5.50	1.20
146B	Mickey Mantle (batting full) (1964 and 1966)	25.00	11.00	2.50
146C	Mickey Mantle POR (1966)	125.00	57.00	12.50
147	Marty Marion	3.00	1.40	.30
148	Roger Maris (1964 and 1966)	10.00	4.75	1.00
149	Willard Marshall	1.50	.70	.15
150A	Ed Matthews SCR (sic, Mathews)	6.00	2.80	.60
150B	Eddie Mathews SIG	7.50	3.50	.75
151	Ed Mayo	1.50	.70	.15
152A	Willie Mays (New York)	10.00	4.75	1.00
152B	Willie Mays (San Francisco)	10.00	4.75	1.00
153A	Bill Mazeroski POR (1960 and 1961)	3.00	1.40	.30
153B	Bill Mazeroski BAT (1964 and 1966)	3.00	1.40	.30
154	Ken McBride (1964 and 1966)	2.00	.90	.20
155A	Barney McCaskey (1950) (sic, McCoskey)	7.50	3.50	.75
155B	Barney McCoskey (1950)	75.00	35.00	7.50
156	Lindy McDaniel (1960 and 1961)	2.00	.90	.20
157	Gil McDougald	1.50	.70	.15
158	Albert Mele (1950)	7.50	3.50	.75
159	Sam Mele	1.50	.70	.15
160A	Orestes Minoso (White Sox)	1.50	.70	.15
160B	Orestes Minoso (Cleveland)	3.00	1.40	.30
161	Dale Mitchell	.75	.35	.07
162	Wally Moon (1964 and 1966)	3.00	1.40	.30
163	Don Mueller	1.50	.70	.15
164A	Stan Musial (three bats, kneeling)	7.50	3.50	.75
164B	Stan Musial BAT (1964)	25.00	11.00	2.50
165	Charles Neal (1964)	7.50	3.50	.75
166A	Don Newcombe (hands folded)	3.00	1.40	.30
166B	Don Newcombe (Brooklyn cap)	1.50	.70	.15
166C	Don Newcombe (plain cap)	1.50	.70	.15
167	Hal Newhouser	2.00	.90	.20
168	Ron Northey (1947)	7.50	3.50	.75
169	Bill O'Dell (1964 and 1966)	2.00	.90	.20
170	Andy Pafko (Yours Truly)	7.50	3.50	.75
171	Joe Page (1950)	5.00	2.35	.50
172	Satchel Paige	20.00	9.00	2.00
173	Milt Pappas	2.00	.90	.20

(1964 and 1966)

□ 174 Camilo Pascual	2.00	.90	.20

(1964 and 1966)

□ 175 Albie Pearson (1966)	10.00	4.75	1.00
□ 176 Johnny Pesky	.75	.35	.07
□ 177 Gary Peters (1966)	10.00	4.75	1.00
□ 178 Dave Philley	1.50	.70	.15
□ 179 Billy Pierce	1.50	.70	.15

(1960 and 1961)

□ 180 Jimmy Piersall (1964)	15.00	7.00	1.50
□ 181 Vada Pinson (1966)	3.00	1.40	.30

(1964 and 1966)

□ 182 Bob Porterfield	1.50	.70	.15
□ 183 John "Boog" Powell	20.00	9.00	2.00

(1966)

□ 184 Vic Raschi	3.00	1.40	.30
□ 185 Harold "Peewee" Reese ..	5.00	2.35	.50
□ 186 Del Rice	.75	.35	.07
□ 187 Bobby Richardson 1966.	30.00	14.00	3.00
□ 188 Phil Rizzuto	5.00	2.35	.50
□ 189A Robin Roberts SIG	4.00	1.85	.40
□ 189B Robin Roberts SCR	6.00	2.80	.60
□ 190 Brooks Robinson	10.00	4.75	1.00
□ 191 Eddie Robinson POR	1.50	.70	.15
□ 192 Floyd Robinson (1966) ...	10.00	4.75	1.00
□ 193 Frankie Robinson	10.00	4.75	1.00

(1964 and 1966)

□ 194 Jackie Robinson	9.00	4.25	.90
□ 195 Preacher Roe	3.00	1.40	.30
□ 196 Bob Rogers (1966)	10.00	4.75	1.00

(sic, Rodgers)

□ 197 Richard Rollins (1966)	10.00	4.75	1.00
□ 198 Pete Runnels (1964)	7.50	3.50	.75
□ 199 John Sain	3.00	1.40	.30
□ 200 Ron Santo	3.00	1.40	.30

(1964 and 1966)

□ 201 Henry Sauer	1.50	.70	.15
□ 202A Carl Sawatski	.75	.35	.07

(Milwaukee cap)

□ 202B Carl Sawatski	.75	.35	.07

(Philadelphia cap)

□ 202C Carl Sawatski (1961)	5.00	2.35	.50

(plain cap)

□ 203 Johnny Schmitz	1.50	.70	.15
□ 204A Red Schoendeinst	1.50	.70	.15

(one foot shown,
catching)

□ 204B Red Schoendeinst	3.00	1.40	.30

(both feet shown,
catching)

□ 204C Red Schoendinst BAT ...	1.50	.70	.15

(sic, schoendienst)

□ 205A Herb Score	1.50	.70	.15

(Cleveland cap)

□ 205B Herb Score (1961)	4.00	1.85	.40

(plain cap)

□ 206 Andy Seminick	1.50	.70	.15
□ 207 Rip Sewell (1947)	7.50	3.50	.75
□ 208 Norm Siebern	2.00	.90	.20

(1964 and 1966)

□ 209A Roy Sievers (1951)			

(Browns)

	3.00	1.40	.30
□ 209B Roy Sievers	1.50	.70	.15

(Senators)

□ 209C Roy Sievers (1961)	3.00	1.40	.30

(plain uniform)

□ 210 Curt Simmons	1.50	.70	.15
□ 211 Dick Sisler	1.50	.70	.15
□ 212A Bill Skowron			

(New York)

	1.50	.70	.15
□ 212B Bill "Moose" Skowron (1966)	25.00	11.00	2.50
□ 213 Enos Slaughter	4.00	1.85	.40
□ 214A Duke Snider			

(Brooklyn)

	7.00	3.25	.70
□ 214B Duke Snider			

(Los Angeles)

	9.00	4.25	.90
□ 215A Warren Spahn	5.00	2.35	.50

(Boston)

□ 215B Warren Spahn			

(Milwaukee) ....

	5.00	2.35	.50
□ 216 Stanley Spence (1950) ...	6.00	2.80	.60
□ 217A Ed Stanky			

(plain uniform) ....

	1.50	.70	.15
□ 217B Ed Stanky (Giants)	1.50	.70	.15
□ 218A Vern Stephens			

(Browns)

	1.50	.70	.15
□ 218B Vern Stephens			

(Red Sox)

	1.50	.70	.15
□ 219 Ed Stewart	1.50	.70	.15
□ 220 Snuffy Stirnweiss	6.00	2.80	.60

(1949)

□ 221 George"Birdie"Tebbets ...	3.00	1.40	.30

(1949)

□ 222A Frankie Thomas BAT	15.00	7.00	1.50

(Bob Skinner picture)
(1959)

□ 222B Frank Thomas (Cubs) ...	3.00	1.40	.30

(1960 and 1961)

□ 223 Lee Thomas	2.00	.90	.20

(1964 and 1966)

□ 224 Bobby Thomson	2.00	.90	.20
□ 225A Earl Torgeson			

(Braves) ....

	.75	.35	.07
□ 225B Earl Torgeson	1.50	.70	.15

(plain uniform)
(1960 and 1961)

□ 226 Gus Triandos	3.00	1.40	.30

(1960 and 1961)

□ 227 Virgil Trucks	1.50	.70	.15
□ 228 Johnny Vandermeer	9.00	4.25	.90

(1947)

□ 229 Emil Verban (1950)	5.00	2.35	.50

(1950 only)

□ 230A Mickey Vernon	1.50	.70	.15

(throwing)

□ 230B Mickey Vernon BAT	1.50	.70	.15
□ 231 Bill Voiselle (1947)	7.50	3.50	.75
□ 232 Leon Wagner	2.00	.90	.20

(1964 and 1966)

□ 233A Eddie Waitkus	5.00	2.35	.50

(Cub uniform)

□ 233B Eddie Waitkus	1.50	.70	.15

(plain uniform)

□ 233C Eddie Waitkus	6.00	2.80	.60

(Phillie uniform)

□ 234 Dick Wakefield	3.00	1.40	.30
□ 235 Harry Walker (1950)	4.00	1.85	.40
□ 236 Bucky Walters (1949)	3.00	1.40	.30
□ 237 Pete Ward (1966)	10.00	4.75	1.00
□ 238 Skeeter Webb	.00	.00	.00

(does not exist)

□ 239 Herman Wehmeier	1.50	.70	.15
□ 240A Vic Wertz (Tigers)	1.50	.70	.15
□ 240B Vic Wertz (Red Sox)	1.50	.70	.15
□ 241 Wally Westlake	1.50	.70	.15
□ 242 Wes Westrum	4.00	1.85	.40
□ 243 Billy Williams	6.00	2.80	.60

(1964 and 1966)

□ 244 Maurice Wills	5.00	2.35	.50

(1964 and 1966)

□ 245A Gene Woodling SCR	1.50	.70	.15
□ 245B Gene Woodling SIG	3.00	1.40	.30

(1961)

□ 246 Taffy Wright (1947)	7.50	3.50	.75
□ 247 Carl Yastrzemski	100.00	45.00	10.00

(1966)

□ 248 Al Zarilla (1951)	3.00	1.40	.30
□ 249A Gus Zernial SCR	1.50	.70	.15
□ 249B Gus Zernial SIG	3.00	1.40	.30

1948 Exhibit Hall of Fame

This exhibit set, entitled "Baseball's Great Hall of Fame", consists of black and white photos on gray background. The pictures are framed on the sides by Greek columns and a short biography is printed at the bottom. The cards are blank backed. Twenty four of the cards were reissued in 1974 on extremely white stock. Each card measures 3 3/8" by 5 3/8".

	MINT	VG-E	F-G
COMPLETE SET	180.00	80.00	15.00
COMMON PLAYER	2.00	.90	.20

□	1 G.C. Alexander	4.00	1.85	.40
□	2 Roger Bresnahan	2.00	.90	.20
□	3 Frank Chance	2.50	1.15	.25
□	4 Jack Chesbro	2.00	.90	.20
□	5 Fred Clarke	2.00	.90	.20
□	6 Ty Cobb	15.00	7.00	1.50
□	7 Mickey Cochrane	4.00	1.85	.40
□	8 Eddie Collins	2.00	.90	.20
□	9 Hugh Duffy	2.00	.90	.20
□	10 Johnny Evers	2.00	.90	.20
□	11 Frankie Frisch	2.50	1.15	.25
□	12 Lou Gehrig	15.00	7.00	1.50
□	13 Clark Griffith	2.00	.90	.20

□ 14 Robert "Lefty" Grove	4.00	1.85	.40
□ 15 Rogers Hornsby	6.00	2.80	.60
□ 16 Carl Hubbell	3.00	1.40	.30
□ 17 Hughie Jennings	2.00	.90	.20
□ 18 Walter Johnson	6.00	2.80	.60
□ 19 Willie Keeler	2.50	1.15	.25
□ 20 Nap Lajoie	4.00	1.85	.40
□ 21 Connie Mack	4.00	1.85	.40
□ 22 Christy Mathewson	6.00	2.80	.60
□ 23 John McGraw	4.00	1.85	.40
□ 24 Eddie Plank	2.50	1.15	.25
□ 25A Babe Ruth (swinging)	20.00	9.00	2.00
□ 25B Babe Ruth (bats in front) "ten bats" pose	80.00	35.00	7.00
□ 26 George Sisler	3.00	1.40	.30
□ 27 Tris Speaker	5.00	2.35	.50
□ 28 Joe Tinker	2.00	.90	.20
□ 29 Rube Waddell	2.00	.90	.20
□ 30 Honus Wagner	6.00	2.80	.60
□ 31 Ed Walsh	2.00	.90	.20
□ 32 Cy Young	4.00	1.85	.40

□ 5 1950 Philadelphia Phillies NL	7.50	3.50	.75
□ 6 1950 New York Yankees AL	15.00	7.00	1.50
□ 7 1951 New York Giants NL	10.00	4.75	1.00
□ 8 1951 New York Yankees AL	15.00	7.00	1.50
□ 9 1952 Brooklyn Dodgers NL	15.00	7.00	1.50
□ 10 1952 New York Yankees AL	15.00	7.00	1.50
□ 11 1954 New York Giants NL	10.00	4.75	1.00
□ 12 1954 Cleveland Indians AL	7.50	3.50	.75
□ 13 1955 Brooklyn Dodgers NL	15.00	7.00	1.50
□ 14 1955 New York Yankees AL	15.00	7.00	1.50
□ 15 1956 Brooklyn Dodgers NL	15.00	7.00	1.50
□ 16 1956 New York Yankees AL	15.00	7.00	1.50

1948-1956 Team Exhibits

The cards found listed in this classification were not a separate issue from the individual player cards of the same period but have been assembled together in the Price Guide for emphasis. Each of these 1948-1956 Exhibit team cards was issued to honor the champions of the National and American Leagues, except for 1953, when none were printed. Reprints of these popular cards are known to exist. Each card measures 3 3/8" by 5 3/8".

	MINT	VG-E	F-G
COMPLETE SET	150.00	70.00	15.00
COMMON PLAYER	7.50	3.50	.75
□ 1 1948 Boston Braves NL	7.50	3.50	.75
□ 2 1948 Cleveland Indians AL	7.50	3.50	.75
□ 3 1949 Brooklyn Dodgers NL	15.00	7.00	1.50
□ 4 1949 New York Yankees AL	15.00	7.00	1.50

1953 Canadian Exhibits

This numbered, blank-backed set depicts both major league players (reprinted from American Exhibit sets) and International League Montreal Royals. The cards (3 1/4" by 5 1/4") are slightly smaller than regular Exhibit issues and are printed on gray stock. Numbers 1-32 are found in green or wine- red color, while 33-64 are blue or reddish-brown. Cards 1-32 are numbered in a small, diamond-shaped white box at lower right; cards 33-64 have a large, hand-lettered number at upper right.

	MINT	VG-E	F-G
COMPLETE SET	275.00	120.00	25.00
COMMON PLAYER (1-32)	3.00	1.40	.30
COMMON PLAYER (33-64)	1.50	.70	.15
□ 1 Roe Preacher	4.50	2.10	.45
□ 2 Luke Easter	3.00	1.40	.30
□ 3 Gene Bearden	3.00	1.40	.30
□ 4 Chico Carrasquel	3.00	1.40	.30

<table>
<tr><td>☐ 63</td><td>Billy Goodman</td><td>2.50</td><td>1.15</td><td>.25</td></tr>
<tr><td>☐ 64</td><td>Alex Kellner</td><td>1.50</td><td>.70</td><td>.15</td></tr>
</table>

1960-61 Wrigley HOF Exhibits

WALTER PERRY JOHNSON

This Exhibit issue was distributed at Wrigley Field in Chicago in the early sixties. The set consists entirely of Hall of Famers, many of whom are depicted in their younger days. The set is complete at 24 cards and is interesting in that the full name of each respective Hall of famer is given on the front of the card. Card backs feature a postcard back on gray card stock. Each card measures 3 3/8" by 5 3/8".

		MINT	VG-E	F-G
COMPLETE SET		65.00	30.00	6.00
COMMON PLAYER (1-24)		2.00	.90	.20
☐ 1	Grover Cleveland Alexander	4.00	1.85	.40
☐ 2	Adrian Constantine Anson	4.00	1.85	.40
☐ 3	John Franklin Baker	2.00	.90	.20
☐ 4	Roger Phillip Bresnahan	2.00	.90	.20
☐ 5	Mordecai Peter Brown	2.00	.90	.20
☐ 6	Frank Leroy Chance	2.50	1.15	.25
☐ 7	Tyrus Raymond Cobb	15.00	7.00	1.50
☐ 8	Edward Trowbridge Collins	2.00	.90	.20
☐ 9	James J. Collins	2.00	.90	.20
☐ 10	John Joseph Evers	2.00	.90	.20
☐ 11	Henry Louis Gehrig	15.00	7.00	1.50
☐ 12	Clark C. Griffith	2.00	.90	.20
☐ 13	Walter Perry Johnson	7.50	3.50	.75
☐ 14	Anthony Michael Lazzeri	2.00	.90	.20
☐ 15	James Walter Vincent Maranville	2.00	.90	.20
☐ 16	Christopher Mathewson	6.00	2.80	.60
☐ 17	John Joseph McGraw	4.00	1.85	.40
☐ 18	Melvin Thomass Ott	4.00	1.85	.40
☐ 19	Herbert Jeffries Pennock	2.00	.90	.20
☐ 20	George Herman Ruth	25.00	11.00	2.50
☐ 21	Alloysius Harry Simmons	2.00	.90	.20
☐ 22	Tristram Speaker	5.00	2.35	.50
☐ 23	Joseph B. Tinker	2.00	.90	.20
☐ 24	John Peter Wagner	6.00	2.80	.60

☐ 5	Vic Raschi	4.00	1.85	.40
☐ 6	Monte Irvin	6.00	2.80	.60
☐ 7	Henry Sauer	3.00	1.40	.30
☐ 8	Ralph Branca	3.00	1.40	.30
☐ 9	Eddie Stanky	3.00	1.40	.30
☐ 10	Sam Jethroe	3.00	1.40	.30
☐ 11	Larry Doby	4.00	1.85	.40
☐ 12	Hal Newhouser	4.00	1.85	.40
☐ 13	Gil Hodges	10.00	4.75	1.00
☐ 14	Harry Brecheen	3.00	1.40	.30
☐ 15	Ed Lopat	4.00	1.85	.40
☐ 16	Don Newcombe	4.00	1.85	.40
☐ 17	Bob Feller	20.00	9.00	2.00
☐ 18	Tommy Holmes	3.00	1.40	.30
☐ 19	Jackie Robinson	30.00	14.00	3.00
☐ 20	Roy Campanella	30.00	14.00	3.00
☐ 21	Pee Wee Reese	10.00	4.75	1.00
☐ 22	Ralph Kiner	8.00	3.75	.80
☐ 23	Dom DiMaggio	4.00	1.85	.40
☐ 24	Bobby Doerr	6.00	2.80	.60
☐ 25	Phil Rizzuto	8.00	3.75	.80
☐ 26	Bob Elliott	3.00	1.40	.30
☐ 27	Tom Henrich	4.00	1.85	.40
☐ 28	Joe DiMaggio	100.00	45.00	10.00
☐ 29	Harry Lowery	3.00	1.40	.30
☐ 30	Ted Williams	40.00	18.00	4.00
☐ 31	Bob Lemon	6.00	2.80	.60
☐ 32	Warren Spahn	8.00	3.75	.80
☐ 33	Don Hoak	2.50	1.15	.25
☐ 34	Bob Alexander	1.50	.70	.15
☐ 35	Simmons	1.50	.70	.15
☐ 36	Steve Lembo	1.50	.70	.15
☐ 37	Norman Larker	2.50	1.15	.25
☐ 38	Bob Ludwick	1.50	.70	.15
☐ 39	Walter Moryn	1.50	.70	.15
☐ 40	Charlie Thompson	1.50	.70	.15
☐ 41	Ed Roebuck	2.50	1.15	.25
☐ 42	Rose	1.50	.70	.15
☐ 43	Edmundo Amoros	2.50	1.15	.25
☐ 44	Bob Milliken	1.50	.70	.15
☐ 45	Art Fabbro	1.50	.70	.15
☐ 46	Forrest Jacobs	1.50	.70	.15
☐ 47	Carmen Mauro	1.50	.70	.15
☐ 48	Walter Fiala	1.50	.70	.15
☐ 49	Rocky Nelson	1.50	.70	.15
☐ 50	Tom Lasorda	10.00	4.75	1.00
☐ 51	Ronnie Lee	1.50	.70	.15
☐ 52	Hampton Coleman	1.50	.70	.15
☐ 53	Frank Marchio	1.50	.70	.15
☐ 54	Samson	1.50	.70	.15
☐ 55	Gil Mills	1.50	.70	.15
☐ 56	Al Ronning	1.50	.70	.15
☐ 57	Stan Musial	15.00	7.00	1.50
☐ 58	Walker Cooper	1.50	.70	.15
☐ 59	Mickey Vernon	2.50	1.15	.25
☐ 60	Del Ennis	2.50	1.15	.25
☐ 61	Walter Alston	10.00	4.75	1.00
☐ 62	Dick Sisler	1.50	.70	.15

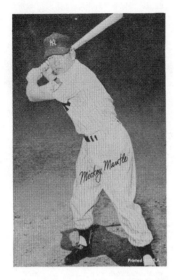

YEAR	CLUB	LEA.	POS.	G	AB	R	H	2B	3B	HR	RBI	SB	AVG
1949	Independence	K-om	SS	89	323	54	101	15	7	7	63	20	.313
1950	Joplin	W.A.	SS	137	519	141	199	30	12	26	136	22	.383
1951	Kansas City	A.A.	OF	40	166	32	60	9	3	11	50	5	.361
1951	New York	A.A.	OF	96	341	61	91	11	5	13	65	8	.267
1952	New York	A.L.	OF-3B	142	549	94	171	37	7	23	87	4	.311
1953	New York	A.L.	OF-SS	127	461	105	136	24	3	21	92	8	.295
1954	New York	A.L.	OF-2B	146	543	129	163	17	12	27	102	5	.300
1955	New York	A.L.	OF-SS	147	517	121	158	25	11	37	99	8	.306
1956	New York	A.L.	OF	150	533	132	188	22	5	52	130	10	.353
1957	New York	A.L.	OF	144	474	121	173	28	6	34	94	16	.365
1958	New York	A.L.	OF	150	519	127	158	21	1	42	97	18	.304
1959	New York	A.L.	OF	144	541	104	154	23	4	31	75	21	.285
1960	New York	A.L.	OF	153	527	119	145	17	6	40	94	14	.275
1961	New York	A.L.	OF	153	514	132	163	16	6	54	128	12	.317
MAJOR LEAGUE TOTALS				1552	5519	1245	1700	241	66	374	1063	124	.308

1962 Stat Back Exhibits

YEAR	CLUB	LEA.	POS.	G	AB	R	H	2B	3B	HR	RBI	SB	AVG
1950	Trenton	Int. St.	O.F.	81	306	50	108	20	8	4	55	7	.353
1951	Minneapolis	A.A.	O.F.	35	149	38	71	18	3	8	30	5	.477
1951	New York	N.L.	O.F.	121	464	59	127	22	5	20	68	7	.274
1952	New York	N.L.	O.F.	34	127	17	30	2	4	4	23	4	.236
1952-3	(IN MILITARY SERVICE)												
1954	New York	N.L.	O.F.	151	565	119	195	33	13	41	110	8	.345
1955	New York	N.L.	O.F.	152	580	123	185	18	13	51	127	24	.319
1956	New York	N.L.	O.F.	152	578	101	171	27	8	36	84	40	.296
1957	New York	N.L.	O.F.	152	585	112	195	26	20	35	97	38	.333
1958	San Francisco	N.L.	O.F.	152	600	121	208	33	11	29	96	31	.347
1959	San Francisco	N.L.	O.F.	151	575	125	180	43	5	34	104	27	.313
1960	San Francisco	N.L.	O.F.	153	595	107	190	29	12	29	103	25	.319
1961	San Francisco	N.L.	O.F.	154	572	129	176	32	3	40	123	18	.308
1962	San Francisco	N.L.	OF	162	621	130	189	36	8	49	141	18	.304
MAJOR LEAGUE TOTALS				1534	5862	1143	1846	301	102	368	1076	240	.314

1963 Stat Back Exhibits

1962 Exhibit Stat Back

The 32-card sheet was a standard production feature of the Exhibit Card Company, although generally more than one sheet comprised a set. The 32-card set issued in 1962 thus amounted to one-half a normal printing, and it is differentiated from other concurrent Exhibit issues by the inclusion of records, printed in black, on the reverse of each card. Each card measures 3 3/8" by 5 3/8".

	MINT	VG-E	F-G
COMPLETE SET	75.00	35.00	7.50
COMMON PLAYER (1-32)	1.00	.45	.10
☐ 1 Hank Aaron	10.00	4.75	1.00
☐ 2 Luis Aparicio	4.00	1.85	.40
☐ 3 Ernie Banks	5.00	2.35	.50
☐ 4 Larry "Yogi" Berra	5.00	2.35	.50
☐ 5 Ken Boyer	1.50	.70	.15
☐ 6 Lew Burdette	1.50	.70	.15
☐ 7 Norm Cash	1.50	.70	.15
☐ 8 Orlando Cepeda	1.50	.70	.15
☐ 9 Roberto Clemente	7.50	3.50	.75
☐10 Rocky Colavito	1.50	.70	.15
☐11 Ed "Whitey" Ford	5.00	2.35	.50
☐12 Nelson Fox	1.50	.70	.15
☐13 Tito Francona	1.00	.45	.10
☐14 Jim Gentile	1.00	.45	.10
☐15 Dick Groat	1.50	.70	.15
☐16 Don Hoak	1.00	.45	.10
☐17 Al Kaline	5.00	2.35	.50
☐18 Harmon Killebrew	4.00	1.85	.40
☐19 Sandy Koufax	7.50	3.50	.75
☐20 Jim Landis	1.00	.45	.10
☐21 Art Mahaffey	1.00	.45	.10
☐22 Frank Malzone	1.00	.45	.10
☐23 Mickey Mantle	25.00	11.00	2.50
☐24 Roger Maris	6.00	2.80	.60
☐25 Eddie Mathews	4.00	1.85	.40
☐26 Willie Mays	10.00	4.75	1.00
☐27 Wally Moon	1.00	.45	.10
☐28 Stan Musial	7.50	3.50	.75
☐29 Milt Pappas	1.00	.45	.10
☐30 Vada Pinson	1.50	.70	.15
☐31 Norm Siebern	1.00	.45	.10
☐32 Warren Spahn	4.00	1.85	.40

1963 Exhibit Stat Back

This 1963 Exhibit issue features 64 cards with statistics printed in red on the backs. Each card measures 3 3/8" X 5 3/8". The set is quite similar to the set of the previous year -- but this set can be distinguished by the red print on the backs.

	MINT	VG-E	F-G
COMPLETE SET	150.00	70.00	15.00
COMMON PLAYER (1-64)	1.00	.45	.10
☐ 1 Hank Aaron	10.00	4.75	1.00
☐ 2 Luis Aparicio	4.00	1.85	.40
☐ 3 Bob Aspromonte	1.00	.45	.10
☐ 4 Ernie Banks	5.00	2.35	.50
☐ 5 Steve Barber	1.00	.45	.10
☐ 6 Earl Battey	1.00	.45	.10
☐ 7 Larry "Yogi" Berra	6.00	2.80	.60
☐ 8 Ken Boyer	1.50	.70	.15
☐ 9 Lew Burdette	1.50	.70	.15
☐10 Johnny Callison	1.00	.45	.10
☐11 Norm Cash	1.50	.70	.15
☐12 Orlando Cepeda	1.50	.70	.15
☐13 Dean Chance	1.00	.45	.10
☐14 Tom Cheney	1.00	.45	.10
☐15 Roberto Clemente	8.00	3.75	.80
☐16 Rocky Colavito	1.50	.70	.15
☐17 "Choo Choo" Coleman	1.00	.45	.10
☐18 Roger Craig	1.00	.45	.10
☐19 Joe Cunningham	1.00	.45	.10
☐20 Don Drysdale	4.00	1.85	.40
☐21 Dick Farrell	1.00	.45	.10

☐22 Ed "Whitey" Ford	4.00	1.85	.40
☐23 Nelson Fox	1.50	.70	.15
☐24 Tito Francona	1.00	.45	.10
☐25 Jim Gentile	1.00	.45	.10
☐26 Tony Gonzales	1.00	.45	.10
☐27 Dick Groat	1.50	.70	.15
☐28 Ray Herbert	1.00	.45	.10
☐29 Chuck Hinton	1.00	.45	.10
☐30 Don Hoak	1.00	.45	.10
☐31 Frank Howard	1.50	.70	.15
☐32 Ken Hubbs	1.50	.70	.15
☐33 Joey Jay	1.00	.45	.10
☐34 Al Kaline	5.00	2.35	.50
☐35 Harmon Killebrew	4.00	1.85	.40
☐36 Sandy Koufax	8.00	3.75	.80
☐37 Harvey Kuenn	1.50	.70	.15
☐38 Jim Landis	1.00	.45	.10
☐39 Art Mahaffey	1.00	.45	.10
☐40 Frank Malzone	1.00	.45	.10
☐41 Mickey Mantle	25.00	11.00	2.50
☐42 Roger Maris	5.00	2.35	.50
☐43 Eddie Mathews	4.00	1.85	.40
☐44 Willie Mays	10.00	4.75	1.00
☐45 Bill Mazeroski	1.50	.70	.15
☐46 Ken McBride	1.00	.45	.10
☐47 Wally Moon	1.00	.45	.10
☐48 Stan Musial	8.00	3.75	.80
☐49 Charlie Neal	1.00	.45	.10
☐50 Bill O'Dell	1.00	.45	.10
☐51 Milt Pappas	1.00	.45	.10
☐52 Camilo Pascual	1.00	.45	.10
☐53 Jim Piersall	1.50	.70	.15
☐54 Vada Pinson	1.50	.70	.15
☐55 Brooks Robinson	6.00	2.80	.60
☐56 Frankie Robinson	5.00	2.35	.50
☐57 Pete Runnels	1.00	.45	.10
☐58 Ron Santo	1.50	.70	.15
☐59 Norm Siebern	1.00	.45	.10
☐60 Warren Spahn	4.00	1.85	.40
☐61 Lee Thomas	1.00	.45	.10
☐62 Leon Wagner	1.00	.45	.10
☐63 Billy Williams	3.00	1.40	.30
☐64 Maurice Wills	1.50	.70	.15

B18 Blankets

This set of felt-type cloth squares was issed in 1914 with several brands of cigarettes. Each blanket is a 5 1/4" square. Each player exists with two different color combinations based on his team; however, only those variations reflecting price differentials are listed in the checklist below. Cleveland players have either yellow or purple bases; New York Yankees players have either blue or green infields; St. Louis Browns players have either red or purple paths; Washington players have either brown or green bases; Brooklyn players have either blue or green infields; New York Giants players have either brown or green paths; Pittsburgh players have either red or purple bases; and St. Louis Cardinals players have either purple or yellow paths. Some blankets are known to exist in a (third) different color scheme -- those with red infields. These blankets are quite scarce and are listed in the checklist below. The complete set price below reflects a set with one blanket of each player, i.e., not including variations.

	MINT	VG-E	F-G
COMPLETE SET	1000.00	450.00	100.00
COMMON PLAYER	7.50	3.50	.75
CLEVELAND INDIANS			
☐ 1A Bassler yellow bases	25.00	11.00	2.50
☐ 1B Bassler purple bases	15.00	7.00	1.50
☐ 2A Chapman yellow bases	25.00	11.00	2.50
☐ 2B Chapman	15.00	7.00	1.50

purple bases
☐ 3A Graney 25.00 11.00 2.50
yellow bases
☐ 3B Graney 15.00 7.00 1.50
purple bases
☐ 4A Joe Jackson 60.00 27.00 6.00
yellow bases
☐ 4B Joe Jackson 45.00 20.00 4.50
purple bases
☐ 5A Leibold 25.00 11.00 2.50
yellow bases
☐ 5B Leibold 15.00 7.00 1.50
purple bases
☐ 6A Mitchell 25.00 11.00 2.50
yellow bases
☐ 6B Mitchell 15.00 7.00 1.50
purple bases
☐ 7A Olson 25.00 11.00 2.50
yellow bases
☐ 7B Olson 15.00 7.00 1.50
purple bases
☐ 8A O'Neil 25.00 11.00 2.50
yellow bases
☐ 8B O'Neil 15.00 7.00 1.50
purple bases
☐ 9A Turner 25.00 11.00 2.50
yellow bases
☐ 9B Turner 15.00 7.00 1.50
purple bases

DETROIT TIGERS
☐ 10A Baker 12.50 5.75 1.25
white infield
☐ 10B Baker 35.00 16.50 3.50
brown infield
☐ 10C Baker 150.00 70.00 15.00
red infield
☐ 11A Bauman (sic, Baumann) . 7.50 3.50 .75
white infield
☐ 11B Bauman (sic, Baumann) . 25.00 11.00 2.50
brown infield
☐ 11C Bauman (sic, Baumann) . 150.00 70.00 15.00
red infield
☐ 12A Burns .... 7.50 3.50 .75
white infield
☐ 12B Burns 25.00 11.00 2.50
brown infield
☐ 13A Cavanaugh (Kavanagh) ... 7.50 3.50 .75
white infield
☐ 13B Cavanaugh (Kavanagh) ... 25.00 11.00 2.50
brown infield
☐ 13C Cavanaugh (Kavanagh) ... 150.00 70.00 15.00
red infield
☐ 14A Cobb 125.00 57.00 12.50
white infield
☐ 14B Cobb 250.00 110.00 25.00
brown infield
☐ 14C Cobb 375.00 160.00 37.00
red infield
☐ 15A H. Coveleski .... 7.50 3.50 .75
white infield
☐ 15B H. Coveleski 25.00 11.00 2.50
brown infield
☐ 15C H. Coveleski 150.00 70.00 15.00
red infield
☐ 16A Demmitt .... 7.50 3.50 .75
white infield
☐ 16B Demmitt 25.00 11.00 2.50
brown infield
☐ 16C Demmitt 150.00 70.00 15.00
red infield
☐ 17A Gainor .... 7.50 3.50 .75
white infield
☐ 17B Gainor 25.00 11.00 2.50
brown infield
☐ 18 Kavanaugh (Kavanagh) ..... 7.50 3.50 .75
white infield
☐ 19A Moriarty .... 7.50 3.50 .75
white infield
☐ 19B Moriarty 25.00 11.00 2.50
brown infield
☐ 19C Moriarty 150.00 70.00 15.00
red infield

NEW YORK YANKEES
☐ 20 Boone .... 7.50 3.50 .75
☐ 21 Chance (3) 20.00 9.00 2.00
☐ 22 Cole .... 7.50 3.50 .75
☐ 23 Hartzell .... 7.50 3.50 .75
☐ 24 Keating .... 7.50 3.50 .75
☐ 25 Maisel .... 7.50 3.50 .75
☐ 26 Roger Peckinpaugh .... 7.50 3.50 .75
☐ 27 Sweeney .... 7.50 3.50 .75
☐ 28 Walsh .... 7.50 3.50 .75
ST. LOUIS BROWNS

☐ 29A Agnew 10.00 4.75 1.00
red paths
☐ 29B Agnew 15.00 7.00 1.50
purple paths
☐ 30A Austin 10.00 4.75 1.00
red paths
☐ 30B Austin 15.00 7.00 1.50
purple paths
☐ 31A Hamilton 10.00 4.75 1.00
red paths
☐ 31B Hamilton 15.00 7.00 1.50
purple paths
☐ 32A McAllister
(McAllester) 10.00 4.75 1.00
red paths
☐ 32B McAllister
(McAllester) 15.00 7.00 1.50
purple paths
☐ 33A Pratt 10.00 4.75 1.00
red paths
☐ 33B Pratt 15.00 7.00 1.50
purple paths
☐ 34A Shotton 10.00 4.75 1.00
red paths
☐ 34B Shotton 15.00 7.00 1.50
purple paths
☐ 35A Bobby Wallace 20.00 9.00 2.00
red paths
☐ 35B Bobby Wallace 35.00 16.50 3.50
purple paths
☐ 36A Walsh 10.00 4.75 1.00
red paths
☐ 36B Walsh 15.00 7.00 1.50
purple paths
☐ 37A Williams 10.00 4.75 1.00
red paths
☐ 37B Williams 15.00 7.00 1.50
purple paths

WASHINGTON SENATORS
☐ 38 Ainsmith .... 7.50 3.50 .75
☐ 39 Foster .... 7.50 3.50 .75
☐ 40 Gandil .... 7.50 3.50 .75
☐ 41 Walter Johnson 50.00 22.00 5.00
☐ 42 McBride .... 7.50 3.50 .75
☐ 43 Milan .... 7.50 3.50 .75
☐ 44 Moeller .... 7.50 3.50 .75
☐ 45 Morgan .... 7.50 3.50 .75
☐ 46 Shanks .... 7.50 3.50 .75

BOSTON BEES
☐ 47A Connolly .... 7.50 3.50 .75
white infield
☐ 47B Connolly 25.00 11.00 2.50
brown infield
☐ 48A Gowdy .... 7.50 3.50 .75
white infield
☐ 48B Gowdy 25.00 11.00 2.50
brown infield
☐ 48C Gowdy 150.00 70.00 15.00
red infield
☐ 49A Griffith .... 7.50 3.50 .75
white infield
☐ 49B Griffith 25.00 11.00 2.50
brown infield
☐ 49C Griffith 150.00 70.00 15.00
red infield
☐ 50A James .... 7.50 3.50 .75
white infield
☐ 50B James 25.00 11.00 2.50
brown infield
☐ 51A Mann .... 7.50 3.50 .75
white infield
☐ 51B Mann 25.00 11.00 2.50
brown infield
☐ 51C Mann 150.00 70.00 15.00
red infield
☐ 52A Maranville 15.00 7.00 1.50
white infield
☐ 52B Maranville 35.00 16.50 3.50
brown infield
☐ 52C Maranville 200.00 90.00 20.00
red infield
☐ 53A Perdue .... 7.50 3.50 .75
white infield
☐ 53B Perdue 25.00 11.00 2.50
brown infield
☐ 54A Tyler .... 7.50 3.50 .75
white infield
☐ 54B Tyler 25.00 11.00 2.50
brown infield
☐ 54C Tyler 150.00 70.00 15.00
red infield
☐ 55A Whaling .... 7.50 3.50 .75
white infield

□ 55B Whaling brown infield	25.00	11.00	2.50
□ 55C Whaling red infield	150.00	70.00	15.00

BROOKLYN DODGERS

□ 56 George Cutshaw	7.50	3.50	.75
□ 57 Jake Daubert	7.50	3.50	.75
□ 58 Hummel	7.50	3.50	.75
□ 59 Miller	7.50	3.50	.75
□ 60 Rucker	7.50	3.50	.75
□ 61 Smith	7.50	3.50	.75
□ 62 Casey Stengel	35.00	16.50	3.50
□ 63 Wagner	7.50	3.50	.75
□ 64 Zach Wheat	15.00	7.00	1.50

NEW YORK GIANTS

□ 65 Burns	7.50	3.50	.75
□ 66 Doyle	7.50	3.50	.75
□ 67 Fletcher	7.50	3.50	.75
□ 68 Grant	7.50	3.50	.75
□ 69 Meyers	7.50	3.50	.75
□ 70 Murray	7.50	3.50	.75
□ 71 Fred Snodgrass	7.50	3.50	.75
□ 72 Tesreau	7.50	3.50	.75
□ 73 Wiltse	7.50	3.50	.75

PITTSBURGH PIRATES

□ 74A Adams red bases	10.00	4.75	1.00
□ 74B Adams purple bases	15.00	7.00	1.50
□ 75A Max Carey red bases	20.00	9.00	1.75
□ 75B Max Carey purple bases	30.00	14.00	3.00
□ 76A Gibson red bases	10.00	4.75	1.00
□ 76B Gibson purple bases	15.00	7.00	1.50
□ 77A Hyatt red bases	10.00	4.75	1.00
□ 77B Hyatt purple bases	15.00	7.00	1.50
□ 78A Joe Kelley (Kelly) red bases	10.00	4.75	1.00
□ 78B Joe Kelley (Kelly) purple bases	15.00	7.00	1.50
□ 79A Konetchy red bases	10.00	4.75	1.00
□ 79B Konetchy purple bases	15.00	7.00	1.50
□ 80A Mowrey red bases	10.00	4.75	1.00
□ 80B Mowrey purple bases	15.00	7.00	1.50
□ 81A O'Toole red bases	10.00	4.75	1.00
□ 81B O'Toole purple bases	15.00	7.00	1.50
□ 82A Viox red bases	10.00	4.75	1.00
□ 82B Viox purple bases	15.00	7.00	1.50

ST. LOUIS CARDINALS

□ 83A Doak purple paths	15.00	7.00	1.50
□ 83B Doak yellow paths	25.00	11.00	2.50
□ 84A Dolan purple paths	15.00	7.00	1.50
□ 84B Dolan yellow paths	25.00	11.00	2.50
□ 85A Miller Huggins purple paths	30.00	14.00	3.00
□ 85B Miller Huggins yellow paths	40.00	18.00	4.00
□ 86A Miller purple paths	15.00	7.00	1.50
□ 86B Miller yellow paths	25.00	11.00	2.50
□ 87A Robinson purple paths	15.00	7.00	1.50
□ 87B Robinson yellow paths	25.00	11.00	2.50
□ 88A Sallee purple paths	15.00	7.00	1.50
□ 88B Sallee yellow paths	25.00	11.00	2.50
□ 89A Steele purple paths	15.00	7.00	1.50
□ 89B Steele yellow paths	25.00	11.00	2.50
□ 90A Whitted purple paths	15.00	7.00	1.50
□ 90B Whitted yellow paths	25.00	11.00	2.50

□ 91A Wilson purple paths	15.00	7.00	1.50
□ 91B Wilson yellow paths	25.00	11.00	2.50

BF2 Felt Pennants

These small triangular felt pennants were issued around 1916. The pennants themselves are 8 1/4" in length, whereas the unnumbered paper photos (glued on to the felt pennant) are 1 3/4" by 1 1/4". The photos are black and white and appear to have been taken from Sporting News issues of the same era.

	MINT	VG-E	F-G
COMPLETE SET	1500.00	700.00	140.00
COMMON PLAYER	10.00	4.75	1.00

BOSTON RED SOX

□ 1 Barry	10.00	4.75	1.00
□ 2 Cady	10.00	4.75	1.00
□ 3 Gainer	10.00	4.75	1.00
□ 4 Harry Hooper	20.00	9.00	2.00
□ 5 Leonard	10.00	4.75	1.00
□ 6 Lewis	10.00	4.75	1.00
□ 7 Joe Wood	12.00	5.50	1.20

CHICAGO WHITE SOX

□ 8 Benz	10.00	4.75	1.00
□ 9 Eddie Collins	20.00	9.00	2.00
□ 10 "Shauno" Collins	10.00	4.75	1.00
□ 11 E. Comiskey	20.00	9.00	2.00
□ 12 Red Faber	20.00	9.00	2.00
□ 13 Lapp	10.00	4.75	1.00
□ 14 Murphy	10.00	4.75	1.00
□ 15 Rowland	10.00	4.75	1.00
□ 16 Russell	10.00	4.75	1.00
□ 17 Ray Schalk	20.00	9.00	2.00
□ 18 Scott	10.00	4.75	1.00
□ 19 Ed Walsh	20.00	9.00	2.00
□ 20 Weaver	10.00	4.75	1.00

CLEVELAND INDIANS

□ 21 Ray Chapman	10.00	4.75	1.00
□ 22 Chick Gandil	10.00	4.75	1.00
□ 23 Morton	10.00	4.75	1.00

DETROIT TIGERS

□ 24 Bush	10.00	4.75	1.00
□ 25 Ty Cobb	150.00	70.00	15.00
□ 26 Coveleski	10.00	4.75	1.00
□ 27 Sam Crawford	20.00	9.00	2.00

B18 Blankets

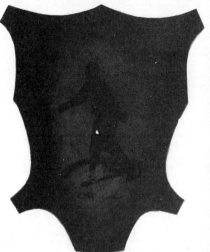

L1 Leathers

S81 Silks

☐ 28 Jean Dubuc	10.00	4.75	1.00
☐ 29 Oscar Stanage	10.00	4.75	1.00
☐ 30 Bobby Veach	10.00	4.75	1.00
☐ 31 Young	10.00	4.75	1.00
NEW YORK YANKEES			
☐ 32 Frank Baker	20.00	9.00	2.00
☐ 33 Gideon	10.00	4.75	1.00
☐ 34 Wally Pipp	12.00	5.50	1.20
PHILADELPHIA A'S			
☐ 35 Napoleon Lajoie	50.00	22.00	5.00
☐ 36 Connie Mack	40.00	18.00	4.00
☐ 37 Stuffy McInnis	10.00	4.75	1.00
☐ 38 Oldring	10.00	4.75	1.00
☐ 39 Wally Schang	10.00	4.75	1.00
ST. LOUIS BROWNS			
☐ 40 Hamilton	10.00	4.75	1.00
☐ 41 F. Jones	10.00	4.75	1.00
☐ 42 Lavan	10.00	4.75	1.00
☐ 43 George Sisler	30.00	14.00	3.00
WASHINGTON SENATORS			
☐ 44 Foster	10.00	4.75	1.00
☐ 45 Walter Johnson	75.00	35.00	7.50
☐ 46 Judge	10.00	4.75	1.00
☐ 47 McBride	10.00	4.75	1.00
☐ 48 Milan	10.00	4.75	1.00
☐ 49 Morgan	10.00	4.75	1.00
BOSTON BRAVES			
☐ 50 Johnny Evers	20.00	9.00	2.00
☐ 51 Hank Gowdy	10.00	4.75	1.00
☐ 52 James	10.00	4.75	1.00
☐ 53 Magee	10.00	4.75	1.00
☐ 54 Rabbit Maranville	20.00	9.00	2.00
☐ 55 Rudolph	10.00	4.75	1.00
☐ 56 Tyler	10.00	4.75	1.00
BROOKLYN DODGERS			
☐ 57 Jake Daubert	10.00	4.75	1.00
☐ 58 Rube Marquard	20.00	9.00	2.00
☐ 59 Meyers	10.00	4.75	1.00
☐ 60 O. Miller	10.00	4.75	1.00
☐ 61 Nap Rucker	10.00	4.75	1.00
CHICAGO CUBS			
☐ 62 Jimmy Archer	10.00	4.75	1.00
☐ 63 Mordecai Brown	20.00	9.00	2.00
☐ 64 Hendrix	10.00	4.75	1.00
☐ 65 Lavender	10.00	4.75	1.00
☐ 66 Saier	10.00	4.75	1.00
☐ 67 Schulte	10.00	4.75	1.00
☐ 68 Joe Tinker	20.00	9.00	2.00
☐ 69 Vaughn	10.00	4.75	1.00
☐ 70 Heine Zimmerman	10.00	4.75	1.00
CINCINNATI REDS			
☐ 71 Buck Herzog	10.00	4.75	1.00
☐ 72 Ivy Wingo	10.00	4.75	1.00
NEW YORK GIANTS			
☐ 73 George Burns	10.00	4.75	1.00
☐ 74 Dooin	10.00	4.75	1.00
☐ 75 Doyle	10.00	4.75	1.00
☐ 76 Kauff	10.00	4.75	1.00
☐ 77 Hans Lobert	10.00	4.75	1.00
☐ 78 John McGraw	30.00	14.00	3.00
☐ 79 Fred Merkle	10.00	4.75	1.00
☐ 80 Tesreau	10.00	4.75	1.00
PHILADELPHIA PHILLIES			
☐ 81 Grover C. Alexander	30.00	14.00	3.00
☐ 82 Dave Bancroft	20.00	9.00	2.00
☐ 83 Chief Bender	20.00	9.00	2.00
☐ 84 Gavvy Cravath	10.00	4.75	1.00
☐ 85 Josh Devore	10.00	4.75	1.00
☐ 86 Killeer	10.00	4.75	1.00
☐ 87 Fred Luderus	10.00	4.75	1.00
☐ 88 Moran	10.00	4.75	1.00
☐ 89 Dode Paskert	10.00	4.75	1.00
PITTSBURGH PIRATES			
☐ 90 Max Carey	20.00	9.00	2.00
☐ 91 Mamaux	10.00	4.75	1.00
☐ 92 Honus Wagner	50.00	22.00	5.00
ST. LOUIS CARDINALS			
☐ 93 Miller Huggins	25.00	11.00	2.50
☐ 94 Slim Sallee	10.00	4.75	1.00

Most collectors subscribe to at least one hobby magazine or newspaper. Check the advertisements in this book -- pick out one or more that you think are suitable.

L1 Leathers

This highly prized set of baseball player pictures on a piece of leather shaped to resemble the hide of a small animal was issued during the 1911 time period. Each "leather" measures 10" by 12". While the pictures are those of the T3 Turkey Red card premium set, only the most popular players of the time are depicted. The cards are numbered at the bottom part of the leather away from the central image.

		MINT	VG-E	F-G
COMPLETE SET		10000.00	4000.00	900.00
COMMON PLAYER		300.00	130.00	30.00
☐ 111 Rube Marquard				
New York NL		400.00	180.00	40.00
☐ 112 O'Toole				
Pittsburgh		300.00	130.00	30.00
☐ 113 Rube Benton				
Cincinnati		300.00	130.00	30.00
☐ 114 Grover C. Alexander				
Philadelphia NL		500.00	225.00	50.00
☐ 115 Russ Ford				
New York AL		300.00	130.00	30.00
☐ 116 John McGraw				
New York NL		500.00	225.00	50.00
☐ 117 Nap Rucker				
Brooklyn		300.00	130.00	30.00
☐ 118 Mitchell				
Cincinnati		300.00	130.00	30.00
☐ 119 Chief Bender				
Philadelphia AL		400.00	180.00	40.00
☐ 120 Frank Baker				
Philadelphia AL		400.00	180.00	40.00
☐ 121 Napoleon Lajoie				
Cleveland		500.00	225.00	50.00
☐ 122 Joe Tinker				
Chicago NL		400.00	180.00	40.00
☐ 123 Sherry Magee				
Philadelphia NL		300.00	130.00	30.00
☐ 124 Camnitz				
Pittsburgh		300.00	130.00	30.00
☐ 125 Eddie Collins				
Philadelphia AL		400.00	180.00	40.00
☐ 126 Dooin				
Philadelphia NL		300.00	130.00	30.00
☐ 127 Ty Cobb				
Detroit		1200.00	500.00	100.00
☐ 128 Hugh Jennings				
Detroit		400.00	180.00	40.00
☐ 129 Roger Bresnahan				
St. Louis NL		400.00	180.00	40.00
☐ 130 Jake Stahl				
Boston AL		300.00	130.00	30.00
☐ 131 Tris Speaker				
Boston AL		500.00	225.00	50.00
☐ 132 Welch				
Chicago AL		300.00	130.00	30.00
☐ 133 Christy Mathewson				
New York NL		750.00	350.00	75.00
☐ 134 Johnny Evers				
Chicago NL		400.00	180.00	40.00
☐ 135 Walter Johnson				
Washington		750.00	350.00	75.00

S74 Silks

Issued around 1911, these silk fabric collectibles have designs similar to the designs in the T205 Cigarette card set. The silk itself is 2" by 3" and the image is 1 1/4" by 2 3/8". The line work on the silks is in one color only, with colors of blue, red, brown, and several variations between red and brown known to exist. The field or stock color is known in white and several pastel tints. The cards are unnumbered but have been numbered and listed by

team in alphabetical order in the checklist below. Turkey Red and Old Mill Cigarettes are among the issuers of these silks.

	MINT	VG-E	F-G
COMPLETE SET	1800.00	800.00	150.00
COMMON PLAYER	12.00	5.50	1.20

BOSTON RED SOX

		MINT	VG-E	F-G
☐	1 Carrigan	12.00	5.50	1.20
☐	2 Ed Cicotte	12.00	5.50	1.20
☐	3 Tris Speaker	40.00	18.00	4.00
☐	4 Jake Stahl	12.00	5.50	1.20

CHICAGO WHITE SOX

☐	5 Hugh Duffy	30.00	14.00	3.00
☐	6 Amby McConnell	12.00	5.50	1.20
☐	7 Parent	12.00	5.50	1.20
☐	8 Payne	12.00	5.50	1.20
☐	9 Tannehill	12.00	5.50	1.20
☐	10 White	12.00	5.50	1.20

CLEVELAND INDIANS

☐	11 Turner	12.00	5.50	1.20
☐	12 Cy Young	40.00	18.00	4.00

DETROIT TIGERS

☐	13 Ty Cobb	175.00	80.00	18.00
☐	14 Delahanty	15.00	7.00	1.50
☐	15 Jones	12.00	5.50	1.20
☐	16 Moriarity	12.00	5.50	1.20
☐	17 Mullin	12.00	5.50	1.20
☐	18 Summers	12.00	5.50	1.20
☐	19 Willett	12.00	5.50	1.20

NEW YORK YANKEES

☐	20 Hal Chase	15.00	7.00	1.50
☐	21 Ford	12.00	5.50	1.20
☐	22 Hemphill	12.00	5.50	1.20
☐	23 Knight	12.00	5.50	1.20
☐	24 Quinn	12.00	5.50	1.20
☐	25 Wolter	12.00	5.50	1.20

PHILADELPHIA A'S

☐	26 Frank Baker	20.00	9.00	2.00
☐	27 Barry	12.00	5.50	1.20
☐	28 Chief Bender	20.00	9.00	2.00
☐	29 Eddie Collins	25.00	11.00	2.50
☐	30 Dygert	12.00	5.50	1.20
☐	31 Hartsel	12.00	5.50	1.20
☐	32 Krause	12.00	5.50	1.20
☐	33 Murphy	12.00	5.50	1.20
☐	34 Oldring	12.00	5.50	1.20

ST. LOUIS BROWNS

☐	35 Pelty	12.00	5.50	1.20
☐	36 Stone	12.00	5.50	1.20

☐	37 Bobby Wallace	20.00	9.00	2.00

WASHINGTON SENATORS

☐	38 Elberfeld	12.00	5.50	1.20
☐	39 Walter Johnson	75.00	35.00	7.50
☐	40 Germany Schaefer	12.00	5.50	1.20
☐	41 Gabby Street	12.00	5.50	1.20

BOSTON RUSTLERS

☐	42 Beck	12.00	5.50	1.20
☐	43 Graham	12.00	5.50	1.20
☐	44 Buck Herzog	12.00	5.50	1.20
☐	45 Mattern	12.00	5.50	1.20
☐	46 Shean	12.00	5.50	1.20

BROOKLYN DODGERS

☐	47 Barger (2)	12.00	5.50	1.20
☐	48 Bell	12.00	5.50	1.20
☐	49 Bergen	12.00	5.50	1.20
☐	50 Bill Dahlen	12.00	5.50	1.20
☐	51 Jake Daubert	12.00	5.50	1.20
☐	52 Hummel	12.00	5.50	1.20
☐	53 Scanlon	12.00	5.50	1.20
☐	54 Smith	12.00	5.50	1.20
☐	55 Zach Wheat	20.00	9.00	2.00

CHICAGO CUBS

☐	56 Mordecai Brown	20.00	9.00	2.00
☐	57 Frank Chance	25.00	11.00	2.50
☐	58 Johnny Evers	20.00	9.00	2.00
☐	59 Foxen	12.00	5.50	1.20
☐	60 Graham	12.00	5.50	1.20
☐	61 Kling	12.00	5.50	1.20
☐	62 McIntire	12.00	5.50	1.20
☐	63 Needham	12.00	5.50	1.20
☐	64 Overall	12.00	5.50	1.20
☐	65 Ed Reulbach	12.00	5.50	1.20
☐	66 Schulte	12.00	5.50	1.20
☐	67 Jimmy Sheckard	12.00	5.50	1.20
☐	68 Harry Steinfeldt	12.00	5.50	1.20
☐	69 Joe Tinker	20.00	9.00	2.00

CINCINNATI REDS

☐	70 Bescher	12.00	5.50	1.20
☐	71 Downey	12.00	5.50	1.20
☐	72 Fromme	12.00	5.50	1.20
☐	73 Grant	12.00	5.50	1.20
☐	74 Griffith	12.00	5.50	1.20
☐	75 Hoblitzell	12.00	5.50	1.20

NEW YORK GIANTS

☐	76 Ames	12.00	5.50	1.20
☐	77 Becker	12.00	5.50	1.20
☐	78 Bridwell	12.00	5.50	1.20
☐	79 Crandall	12.00	5.50	1.20
☐	80 Devlin	12.00	5.50	1.20
☐	81 Josh Devore	12.00	5.50	1.20
☐	82 Doyle	12.00	5.50	1.20
☐	83 Fletcher	12.00	5.50	1.20
☐	84 Rube Marquard	20.00	9.00	2.00
☐	85 Christy Mathewson	65.00	30.00	6.50
☐	86 John McGraw	35.00	16.50	3.50
☐	87 Fred Merkle	12.00	5.50	1.20
☐	88 Meyers	12.00	5.50	1.20
☐	89 Murray	12.00	5.50	1.20
☐	90 Raymond	12.00	5.50	1.20
☐	91 Schlei	12.00	5.50	1.20
☐	92 Fred Snodgrass	12.00	5.50	1.20
☐	93 Wiltse (2)	12.00	5.50	1.20

PHILADELPHIA PHILLIES

☐	94 Bates	12.00	5.50	1.20
☐	95 Dooin	12.00	5.50	1.20
☐	96 Doolan	12.00	5.50	1.20
☐	97 Ewing	12.00	5.50	1.20
☐	98 Hans Lobert	12.00	5.50	1.20
☐	99 Moran	12.00	5.50	1.20
☐	100 Dode Paskert	12.00	5.50	1.20
☐	101 Rowan	12.00	5.50	1.20
☐	102 Titus	12.00	5.50	1.20

PITTSBURGH PIRATES

☐	103 Byrne	12.00	5.50	1.20
☐	104 Camnitz	12.00	5.50	1.20
☐	105 Fred Clarke	20.00	9.00	2.00
☐	106 Flynn	12.00	5.50	1.20
☐	107 Gibson	12.00	5.50	1.20
☐	108 Leach	12.00	5.50	1.20
☐	109 Leifield	12.00	5.50	1.20
☐	110 Miller	12.00	5.50	1.20
☐	111 Deacon Phillippe	12.00	5.50	1.20
☐	112 White	12.00	5.50	1.20
☐	113 Wilson	12.00	5.50	1.20

ST. LOUIS CARDINALS

☐	114 Roger Bresnahan (2)	20.00	9.00	2.00
☐	115 Evans	12.00	5.50	1.20
☐	116 Hauser	12.00	5.50	1.20
☐	117 Miller Huggins	25.00	11.00	2.50
☐	118 Konetchy	12.00	5.50	1.20
☐	119 Oakes	12.00	5.50	1.20

S81 Large Silks

These large and attractive silks are found in two sizes -- approximately 5" by 7" or 7" by 9". Unlike the smaller S74 Baseball Silks, these silks are numbered, beginning with number 86 and ending at number 110. The pose of the picture is the same as that of the T3 Turkey Red baseball cards. The silks were issued in 1911 and are frequently found grouped on pillow covers. For some reason the silk of Mathewson appears to be the most plentiful member of this admittedly scarce issue.

		MINT	VG-E	F-G
COMPLETE SET		8000.00	3500.00	750.00
COMMON PLAYER		250.00	110.00	25.00

			MINT	VG-E	F-G
☐	86	Rube Marquard New York NL	350.00	150.00	35.00
☐	87	O'Toole Pittsburgh	250.00	110.00	25.00
☐	88	Rube Benton Cincinnati	250.00	110.00	25.00
☐	89	Grover C. Alexander Philadelphia NL	450.00	200.00	45.00
☐	90	Ford New York AL	250.00	110.00	25.00
☐	91	John McGraw New York NL	450.00	200.00	45.00
☐	92	Rucker Brooklyn	250.00	110.00	25.00
☐	93	Mitchell Cincinnati	250.00	110.00	25.00
☐	94	Chief Bender Philadelphia AL	350.00	150.00	35.00
☐	95	Frank Baker Philadelphia AL	350.00	150.00	35.00
☐	96	Napoleon Lajoie Cleveland	450.00	200.00	45.00
☐	97	Joe Tinker Chicago NL	350.00	150.00	35.00
☐	98	Sherry Magee Philadelphia NL	250.00	110.00	25.00
☐	99	Camnitz Pittsburgh	250.00	110.00	25.00
☐	100	Eddie Collins Philadelphia AL	350.00	150.00	35.00
☐	101	Dooin Philadelphia NL	250.00	110.00	25.00
☐	102	Ty Cobb Detroit	1200.00	500.00	100.00
☐	103	Hugh Jennings Detroit	350.00	150.00	35.00
☐	104	Roger Bresnahan St. Louis NL	350.00	150.00	35.00
☐	105	Jake Stahl Boston AL	250.00	110.00	25.00
☐	106	Tris Speaker Boston AL	450.00	200.00	45.00
☐	107	Ed Walsh Chicago AL	350.00	150.00	35.00
☐	108	Christy Mathewson New York NL	300.00	130.00	30.00
☐	109	Johnny Evers Chicago NL	350.00	150.00	35.00
☐	110	Walter Johnson Washington	750.00	350.00	75.00

1982 Burger King Lids

The cards in this 27 card set measure 3 11/16" diameter. During the summer of 1982, the Atlanta-area chain of Burger King restaurants issued a series of 27 "Collector Lids" in honor of the Atlanta Braves baseball team. A special cup listing the scores of the Braves 13-game season-opening win streak and crowned by a baseball player lid was given with the purchase of a large Coca-Cola. The black and white

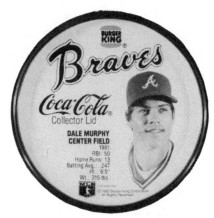

player photos are printed on a sturdy, glazed cardboard disc, the edges of which are attached to a red plastic rim. The lid is blank backed. The individual's name, height, weight, and 1981 record are listed, but the lids are not numbered. The MLB and Burger King logos, as well as the Coca-Cola TM line also appear on the disc.

		MINT	VG-E	F-G
COMPLETE SET		20.00	9.00	2.00
COMMON PLAYER		.50	.22	.05

		MINT	VG-E	F-G
☐ 1	Bruce Benedict	.50	.22	.05
☐ 2	Steve Bedrosian	1.00	.45	.10
☐ 3	Tommy Boggs	.50	.22	.05
☐ 4	Brett Butler	1.00	.45	.10
☐ 5	Rick Camp	.50	.22	.05
☐ 6	Chris Chambliss	.75	.35	.07
☐ 7	Ken Dayley	.75	.35	.07
☐ 8	Gene Garber	.75	.35	.07
☐ 9	Preston Hanna	.50	.22	.05
☐ 10	Terry Harper	.50	.22	.05
☐ 11	Bob Horner	2.50	1.15	.25
☐ 12	Al Hrabosky	.75	.35	.07
☐ 13	Glenn Hubbard	.75	.35	.07
☐ 14	Randy Johnson	.50	.22	.05
☐ 15	Rufino Linares	.50	.22	.05
☐ 16	Rick Mahler	.75	.35	.07
☐ 17	Larry McWilliams	.75	.35	.07
☐ 18	Dale Murphy	7.50	3.50	.75
☐ 19	Phil Niekro	2.50	1.15	.25
☐ 20	Biff Pocoroba	.50	.22	.05
☐ 21	Rafael Ramirez	.75	.35	.07
☐ 22	Jerry Royster	.50	.22	.05
☐ 23	Ken Smith	.50	.22	.05
☐ 24	Bob Walk	.50	.22	.05
☐ 25	Claudell Washington	1.00	.45	.10
☐ 26	Bob Watson	.75	.35	.07
☐ 27	Larry Whisenton	.50	.22	.05

1937 Dixie Lids

This unnumbered set of lids is actually a combined sport and non-sport set with 24 different lids. The lids are found in more than one size, approximately 2 11/16" in diameter as well as 2 5/16" in diameter. The 1937 lids are distinguished from the 1938 Dixie Lids by the fact that the 1937 lids are printed in black or wine-colored ink whereas the 1938 lids are printed in blue ink. In the checklist below only the sports subjects are checklisted; non-sport subjects (celebrities) included in this 24 card set are Gene

Dixies of **Meadow Gold Ice Cream**

Autry, Freddie Bartholomew, Bill Boyd, Johnny Mack Brown, Madeleine Carroll, Nelson Eddy, Clark Gable, Jean Harlow, Carole Lombard, Myrna Loy, Fred MacMurray, Ken Maynard, Merle Oberon, Eleanor Powell, William Powell, Luisa Rainer, Charles Starrett, and Robert Taylor. The catalog designation is F7-1.

	MINT	VG-E	F-G
COMPLETE SPORT (6)	225.00	100.00	20.00
COMMON BASEBALL	40.00	18.00	4.00
COMMON OTHER SPORTS	10.00	4.75	1.00
☐ 1 Georgia Coleman	10.00	4.75	1.00
(Olympic diving star)			
☐ 2 Charles Gehringer	60.00	27.00	6.00
(Detroit Tigers)			
☐ 3 Charles Hartnett	50.00	22.00	5.00
(Chicago Cubs)			
☐ 4 Carl Hubbell	75.00	35.00	7.50
(New York Giants)			
(mouth closed)			
☐ 5 Joe Medwick	60.00	27.00	6.00
(St. Louis Cardinals)			
☐ 6 Bill Tilden	15.00	7.00	1.50
(tennis star)			

1937 Dixie Premiums

This is a parallel issue to the lids -- an attractive "premium" large picture of each of the subjects in the Dixie Lid set. As with the lid set only the sports oriented subjects are listed below. They are printed on thick paper stock and feature a large color drawing on the front; each unnumbered premium measures approximately 8" by 10". The 1937 Premiums are distinguished from the 1938 Dixie Lid Premiums by the fact that the 1937 premiums contain a dark green border down the left margin whereas the 1938 premiums have a lighter green border completely around the photo. Also on the reverse, the 1937 Premiums have a large gray star and three light gray lines at the top.

	MINT	VG-E	F-G
COMPLETE SPORT SET (6)	200.00	90.00	20.00
COMMON BASEBALL	30.00	14.00	3.00
COMMON OTHER SPORTS	10.00	4.75	1.00
☐ 1 Georgia Coleman	10.00	4.75	1.00
(Olympic diving star)			
☐ 2 Charles Gehringer	50.00	22.00	5.00
(Detroit Tigers)			
☐ 3 Charles Hartnett	40.00	18.00	4.00
(Chicago Cubs)			
☐ 4 Carl Hubbell	60.00	27.00	6.00
(New York Giants)			
☐ 5 Joe Medwick	40.00	18.00	4.00
(St. Louis Cardinals)			
☐ 6 Bill Tilden	15.00	7.00	1.50
(tennis star)			

1938 Dixie Lids

This unnumbered set of lids is actually a combined sport and non-sport set with 24 different lids. The lids are found in more than one size, approximately 2 11/16" in diameter as well as 2 5/16" in diameter. The catalog designation is F7- 1.The 1938 lids are distinguished from the 1937 Dixie Lids by the fact that the 1938 lids are printed in blue ink whereas the 1938 lids are printed in black or wine-colored ink. In the checklist below only the sports subjects are checklisted; non-sport subjects (celebrities) included in this 24 card set are Don Ameche, Annabella, Gene Autry, Warner Baxter, William Boyd, Bobby Breen, Gary Cooper, Alice Fay, Sonja Henie, Tommy Kelly, June Lang, Colonel Tim McCoy, Tyrone Power, Tex Ritter, Simone Simon, Bob Steele, The Three Mesquiteers, and Jane Withers.

	MINT	VG-E	F-G
COMPLETE SPORT SET (6)	250.00	110.00	25.00
COMMON BASEBALL	30.00	14.00	3.00
COMMON OTHER SPORTS	10.00	4.75	1.00
☐ 1 Sam Baugh	30.00	14.00	3.00
(Washington Redskins)			
☐ 2 Bob Feller	80.00	37.00	8.00
(Cleveland Indians)			
☐ 3 Jimmie Foxx	70.00	32.00	7.00
(Boston Red Sox)			
☐ 4 Carl Hubbell	60.00	27.00	6.00
(New York Giants)			
(mouth open)			
☐ 5 Wally Moses	30.00	14.00	3.00
(Philadelphia A's)			
☐ 6 Bronco Nagurski	30.00	14.00	3.00
(football/wrestling)			

1938 Dixie Lids Premiums

This is a parallel issue to the lids -- an attractive "premium" large picture of each of the subjects in the Dixie Lid set. As with the lid set only the sports oriented subjects are listed below. They are printed on thick paper stock and feature a large color drawing on the front; each unnumbered premium measures approximately 8" by 10". The 1938 Premiums are distinguished from the 1937 Dixie Lid Premiums by the fact that the 1938 premiums contain a light green border completely around the photo on the front. Also on the reverse, the 1938 Premiums have a single gray line at the top leading to the player's name in script.

	MINT	VG-E	F-G
COMPLETE SET	250.00	110.00	25.00
COMMON BASEBALL	30.00	14.00	3.00
COMMON OTHER SPORTS	10.00	4.75	1.00
☐ 1 Sam Baugh	30.00	14.00	3.00

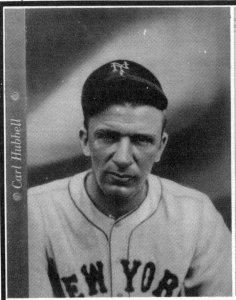

1937 Dixie Premium

1938 Dixie Premium

	(Washington Redskins)			
☐ 2	Bob Feller	80.00	37.00	8.00
	(Cleveland Indians)			
☐ 3	Jimmie Foxx	70.00	32.00	7.00
	(Boston Red Sox)			
☐ 4	Carl Hubbell	60.00	27.00	6.00
	(New York Giants)			
☐ 5	Wally Moses	30.00	14.00	3.00
	(Philadelphia A's)			
☐ 6	Bronco Nagurski	30.00	14.00	3.00
	(football/wrestling)			

☐ 18	Hank Sauer	60.00	27.00	6.00
	Chicago Cubs			
☐ 19	Al Schoendienst	75.00	35.00	7.50
	St. Louis Cardinals			
☐ 20	Andy Seminick *	75.00	35.00	7.50
	Ciccinnati Reds			
☐ 21	Bobby Shantz	75.00	35.00	7.50
	Philadelphia Athletics			
☐ 22	Enos Slaughter	100.00	45.00	10.00
	St. Louis Cardinals			
☐ 23	Virgil Trucks	60.00	27.00	6.00
	Detroit Tigers			
☐ 24	Gene Woodling	60.00	27.00	6.00
	New York Yankees			

1952 Dixie Lids

This scarce 24 lid set features all baseball subjects each measuring 2 11/16". The 1952 set was released very late in the year and in only one size; it is undoubtedly the toughest Dixie baseball set. The lids are found with a blue tint. The catalog designation for this set is F7-2A. Lids found without the tab attached are considered good condition at best. The asterisked lids below are those that were only available in 1952. The 50s Dixie Lids are distinguished from the 30's lids also by the fact that the 50s lids have the circular picture portion abruptly squared off near the bottom end of the lid where the player's name appears.

		MINT	VG-E	F-G
COMPLETE SET	....	1700.00	750.00	150.00
COMMON PLAYER	....	60.00	27.00	6.00
COMMON PLAYER *	....	75.00	35.00	7.50
☐ 1	Richie Ashburn	75.00	35.00	7.50
	Philadelphia Phillies			
☐ 2	Tommy Byrne *	75.00	35.00	7.50
	St. Louis Browns			
☐ 3	Chico Carrasquel	60.00	27.00	6.00
	Chicago White Sox			
☐ 4	Pete Castiglione *	75.00	35.00	7.50
	Pittsburgh Pirates			
☐ 5	Walker Cooper *	75.00	35.00	7.50
	Boston Braves			
☐ 6	Billy Cox	60.00	27.00	6.00
	Brooklyn Dodgers			
☐ 7	Ferris Fain	60.00	27.00	6.00
	Philadelphia Athletics			
☐ 8	Bobby Feller *	125.00	57.00	12.50
	Cleveland Indians			
☐ 9	Nelson Fox	75.00	35.00	7.50
	Chicago White Sox			
☐ 10	Monte Irvin	100.00	45.00	10.00
	New York Giants			
☐ 11	Ralph Kiner	100.00	45.00	10.00
	Pittsburgh Pirates			
☐ 12	Cass Michaels *	75.00	35.00	7.50
	St. Louis Browns			
☐ 13	Don Mueller	60.00	27.00	6.00
	New York Giants			
☐ 14	Mel Parnell	60.00	27.00	6.00
	Boston Red Sox			
☐ 15	Allie Reynolds	75.00	35.00	7.50
	New York Yankees			
☐ 16	Preacher Roe	75.00	35.00	7.50
	Brooklyn Dodgers			
☐ 17	Connie Ryan *	75.00	35.00	7.50
	Philadelphia Phillies			

1952 Dixie Premiums

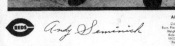

ANDY SEMINICK

The catalog designation is F7-2A. The 1952 Dixie Cup Baseball Premiums contain 1951 statistics. There are 24 (sepia-tinted) black and white photos each measuring approximately 8" by 10". Each photo has a facsimile autograph at the bottom. These large premium photos are blank backed and were printed on thick paper stock.

		MINT	VG-E	F-G
COMPLETE SET	....	300.00	130.00	30.00
COMMON PLAYER	....	10.00	4.75	1.00
☐ 1	Richie Ashburn	15.00	7.00	1.50
☐ 2	Tommy Byrne	10.00	4.75	1.00
☐ 3	Chico Carrasquel	10.00	4.75	1.00
☐ 4	Pete Castiglione	10.00	4.75	1.00
☐ 5	Walker Cooper	10.00	4.75	1.00
☐ 6	Billy Cox	10.00	4.75	1.00
☐ 7	Ferris Fain	10.00	4.75	1.00
☐ 8	Bob Feller	40.00	18.00	4.00
☐ 9	Nelson Fox	15.00	7.00	1.50
☐ 10	Monte Irvin	20.00	9.00	2.00
☐ 11	Ralph Kiner	25.00	11.00	2.50
☐ 12	Cass Michaels	10.00	4.75	1.00
☐ 13	Don Mueller	10.00	4.75	1.00
☐ 14	Mel Parnell	10.00	4.75	1.00
☐ 15	Allie Reynolds	15.00	7.00	1.50
☐ 16	Preacher Roe	15.00	7.00	1.50
☐ 17	Connie Ryan	10.00	4.75	1.00

		MINT	VG-E	F-G
☐ 18	Hank Sauer	10.00	4.75	1.00
☐ 19	Al Schoendienst	15.00	7.00	1.50
☐ 20	Andy Seminick	10.00	4.75	1.00
☐ 21	Bobby Shantz	12.00	5.50	1.20
☐ 22	Enos Slaughter	20.00	9.00	2.00
☐ 23	Virgil Trucks	10.00	4.75	1.00
☐ 24	Gene Woodling	10.00	4.75	1.00

1953 Dixie Lids

This 24 lid set features all baseball subjects each measuring 2 11/16". There are many different back types in existence. The lids are found with a wine tint. The catalog designation for this set is F7-2. Lids found without the tab attached are considered good condition at best.

		MINT	VG-E	F-G
COMPLETE SET		600.00	300.00	60.00
COMMON PLAYER		20.00	9.00	2.00
☐ 1	Richie Ashburn	25.00	11.00	2.50
☐ 2	Chico Carrasquel	20.00	9.00	2.00
☐ 3	Billy Cox	20.00	9.00	2.00
☐ 4	Ferris Fain	20.00	9.00	2.00
☐ 5	Nelson Fox	25.00	11.00	2.50
☐ 6A	Sid Gordon	40.00	18.00	4.00
	Boston Braves			
☐ 6B	Sid Gordon	20.00	9.00	2.00
	Milwaukee Braves			
☐ 7	Warren Hacker	20.00	9.00	2.00
☐ 8	Monte Irvin	30.00	14.00	3.00
☐ 9	Jack Jensen	25.00	11.00	2.50
☐ 10	Ralph Kiner	40.00	18.00	4.00
	Chicago Cubs			
☐ 11	Ted Kluszewski	25.00	11.00	2.50
☐ 12	Bob Lemon	30.00	14.00	3.00
☐ 13	Don Mueller	20.00	9.00	2.00
☐ 14	Mel Parnell	20.00	9.00	2.00
☐ 15	Jerry Priddy	20.00	9.00	2.00
☐ 16	Allie Reynolds	25.00	11.00	2.50
☐ 17	Preacher Roe	25.00	11.00	2.50
☐ 18	Hank Sauer	20.00	9.00	2.00
☐ 19	Al Schoendienst	25.00	11.00	2.50
☐ 20	Bobby Shantz	20.00	9.00	2.00
☐ 21	Enos Slaughter	40.00	18.00	4.00
☐ 22A	Warren Spahn	60.00	27.00	6.00
	Boston Braves			
☐ 22B	Warren Spahn	40.00	18.00	4.00
	Milwaukee Braves			
☐ 23A	Virgil Trucks	20.00	9.00	2.00
	Chicago White Sox			
☐ 23B	Virgil Trucks	20.00	9.00	2.00
	St. Louis Browns			
☐ 24	Gene Woodling	20.00	9.00	2.00

1953 Dixie Premiums

The catalog designation is F7-2A. The 1953 Dixie Cup Baseball Premiums contain 1952 statistics. There are 24 (sepia-tinted) black and white photos

VIRGIL TRUCKS
Pitcher—St. Louis Browns
Born: Birmingham, Ala., Apr. 26, 1919
Height: 5'11" Weight: 198
Bats: Right Throws: Right
1952 Record: Won, 5; Lost, 19

each measuring approximately 8" by 10". Each photo has a facsimile autograph at the bottom. These large premium photos are blank backed and were printed on thick paper stock.

		MINT	VG-E	F-G
COMPLETE SET		300.00	130.00	30.00
COMMON PLAYER		10.00	4.75	1.00
☐ 1	Richie Ashburn	15.00	7.00	1.50
☐ 2	Chico Carrasquel	10.00	4.75	1.00
☐ 3	Billy Cox	10.00	4.75	1.00
☐ 4	Ferris Fain	10.00	4.75	1.00
☐ 5	Nelson Fox	15.00	7.00	1.00
☐ 6	Sid Gordon	10.00	4.75	1.00
☐ 7	Warren Hacker	10.00	4.75	1.00
☐ 8	Monte Irvin	20.00	9.00	2.00
☐ 9	Jack Jensen	15.00	7.00	1.50
☐ 10	Ralph Kiner	25.00	11.00	2.50
☐ 11	Ted Kluszewski	15.00	7.00	1.50
☐ 12	Bob Lemon	20.00	9.00	2.00
☐ 13	Don Mueller	10.00	4.75	1.00
☐ 14	Mel Parnell	10.00	4.75	1.00
☐ 15	Jerry Priddy	10.00	4.75	1.00
☐ 16	Allie Reynolds	15.00	7.00	1.50
☐ 17	Preacher Roe	15.00	7.00	1.50
☐ 18	Hank Sauer	10.00	4.75	1.00
☐ 19	Al Schoendienst	15.00	7.00	1.50
☐ 20	Bobby Shantz	12.00	5.50	1.20
☐ 21	Enos Slaughter	25.00	11.00	2.50
☐ 22	Warren Spahn	35.00	16.50	3.50
☐ 23	Virgil Trucks	10.00	4.75	1.00
☐ 24	Gene Woodling	10.00	4.75	1.00

1954 Dixie Lids

This 18 lid set features all baseball subjects each measuring 2 11/16". There are many different back types in existence. The lids are typically found with a gray tint. The catalog designation for this set is F7-4. Lids found without the tab attached are considered good condition at best. This year is distinguishable by the fact that the lids say "Get

Dixie Lid 3-D Starviewer. Send 25 cents, this lid, name, address, to DIXIE, Box 630, New York 17, N.Y." around the border on the front. The lids have an "A" or "B" on the tab, which distinguished which side of the 3-D viewer was to be used for that particular card. The lids are also seen in a small (2 1/4") and large (3 3/16") size; these variations carry approximately double the prices below.

	MINT	VG-E	F-G
COMPLETE SET	300.00	130.00	30.00
COMMON PLAYER	12.00	5.50	1.20
☐ 1 Richie Ashburn	18.00	8.50	1.80
☐ 2 Clint Courtney	12.00	5.50	1.20
☐ 3 Sid Gordon	12.00	5.50	1.20
☐ 4 Billy Hoeft	12.00	5.50	1.20
☐ 5 Monte Irvin	25.00	11.00	2.50
☐ 6 Jackie Jensen	16.00	7.50	1.60
☐ 7 Ralph Kiner	25.00	11.00	2.50
☐ 8 Ted Kluszewski	18.00	8.50	1.80
☐ 9 Gil McDougald	16.00	7.50	1.60
☐ 10 Minnie Minoso	16.00	7.50	1.60
☐ 11 Danny O'Connell	12.00	5.50	1.20
☐ 12 Mel Parnell	12.00	5.50	1.20
☐ 13 Preacher Roe	16.00	7.50	1.60
☐ 14 Al Rosen	18.00	8.50	1.80
☐ 15 Al Schoendienst	16.00	7.50	1.60
☐ 16 Enos Slaughter	25.00	11.00	2.50
☐ 17 Gene Woodling	12.00	5.50	1.20
☐ 18 Gus Zernial	12.00	5.50	1.20

1963 French Bauer Caps

These are a 25 "card" set of (cardboard) milk bottle caps featuring personnel of the Cincinnati Reds. These unattractive cardboard caps are blank-backed and unnumbered; they are numbered below for convenience in alphabetical order. The caps are approximately 1 1/4" in diameter.

	MINT	VG-E	F-G
COMPLETE SET	200.00	90.00	20.00
COMMON PLAYER CAP	3.00	1.40	.30
☐ 1 Leo Cardenas	4.00	1.85	.40
☐ 2 Gordon Coleman	4.00	1.85	.40
☐ 3 Wm. O. DeWitt	3.00	1.40	.30
☐ 4 John Edwards	3.00	1.40	.30

☐ 5 Jesse Gonder	3.00	1.40	.30
☐ 6 Tommy Harper	4.00	1.85	.40
☐ 7 Bill Henry	3.00	1.40	.30
☐ 8 Eddie Kasko	3.00	1.40	.30
☐ 9 Marty Keough	3.00	1.40	.30
☐ 10 Jim Maloney	4.00	1.85	.40
☐ 11 Joe Nuxhall	4.00	1.85	.40
☐ 12 Reggie Otero	3.00	1.40	.30
☐ 13 Jim O'Toole	3.00	1.40	.30
☐ 14 Jim Owens	3.00	1.40	.30
☐ 15 Vada Pinson	6.00	2.80	.60
☐ 16 Bob Purkey	3.00	1.40	.30
☐ 17 Dr. Richard Rhode	3.00	1.40	.30
☐ 18 Frank Robinson	25.00	11.00	2.50
☐ 19 Pete Rose	100.00	45.00	10.00
☐ 20 Dick Sisler	3.00	1.40	.30
☐ 21 Bob Skinner	4.00	1.85	.40
☐ 22 John Tsitorius	3.00	1.40	.30
☐ 23 Jim Turner	3.00	1.40	.30
☐ 24 Al Worthington	3.00	1.40	.30
☐ 25 Dom Zanni	3.00	1.40	.30

1976 Icee Cincinnati

This unnumbered and blank-backed set of "lids" is complete at 12. Cards are listed below in alphabetical order. They are circular cards with the bottom squared off. The circle is approximately 2" in diameter. The fronts contain the MLB logo as well as the player's name, position, and team. The player photo is in black and white with the cap logo removed.

	MINT	VG-E	F-G
COMPLETE SET	20.00	9.00	1.50
COMMON PLAYER	.25	.10	.02
☐ 1 Johnny Bench	5.00	2.00	.45
☐ 2 Dave Concepcion	.50	.22	.05
☐ 3 Rawley Eastwick	.25	.10	.02
☐ 4 George Foster	.75	.35	.07
☐ 5 Cesar Geronimo	.25	.10	.02
☐ 6 Ken Griffey	.50	.22	.05
☐ 7 Don Gullett	.25	.10	.02
☐ 8 Will McEnaney	.25	.10	.02
☐ 9 Joe Morgan	2.00	.90	.15
☐ 10 Gary Nolan	.25	.10	.02
☐ 11 Tony Perez	.75	.35	.07
☐ 12 Pete Rose	12.00	5.00	.80

1973 Topps Candy Lids

One of Topps' most unusual test sets is this series of 55 color portraits of baseball players printed on the bottom of candy lids. These lids measure 1 7/8" in diameter. The product was called "Baseball Stars Bubble Gum" and consisted of a small tub of candy-coated gum kernels. Issued in 1973, the lids are unnumbered and each has a small tab. Underneath the picture is a small ribbon design which contains the player's name, team, and position.

		MINT	VG-E	F-G
	COMPLETE SET	175.00	75.00	15.00
	COMMON PLAYER	1.50	.70	.15
☐ 1	Hank Aaron	15.00	7.00	1.50
☐ 2	Dick Allen	2.00	.90	.20
☐ 3	Dusty Baker	2.00	.90	.20
☐ 4	Sal Bando	2.00	.90	.20
☐ 5	Johnny Bench	10.00	4.75	1.00
☐ 6	Bobby Bonds	2.00	.90	.20
☐ 7	Dick Bosman	1.50	.70	.15
☐ 8	Lou Brock	7.50	3.50	.75
☐ 9	Rod Carew	7.50	3.50	.75
☐ 10	Steve Carlton	7.50	3.50	.75
☐ 11	Nate Colbert	1.50	.70	.15
☐ 12	Willie Davis	1.50	.70	.15
☐ 13	Larry Dierker	1.50	.70	.15
☐ 14	Mike Epstein	1.50	.70	.15
☐ 15	Carlton Fisk	3.00	1.40	.30
☐ 16	Tim Foli	1.50	.70	.15
☐ 17	Ray Fosse	1.50	.70	.15
☐ 18	Bill Freehan	2.00	.90	.20
☐ 19	Bob Gibson	6.00	2.80	.60
☐ 20	Bud Harrelson	1.50	.70	.15
☐ 21	Jim Hunter	3.00	1.40	.30
☐ 22	Reggie Jackson	15.00	7.00	1.50
☐ 23	Fergie Jenkins	2.00	.90	.20
☐ 24	Al Kaline	10.00	4.75	1.00
☐ 25	Harmon Killebrew	7.50	3.50	.75
☐ 26	Clay Kirby	1.50	.70	.15
☐ 27	Mickey Lolich	2.00	.90	.20
☐ 28	Greg Luzinski	2.00	.90	.20
☐ 29	Willie McCovey	7.50	3.50	.75
☐ 30	Mike Marshall	1.50	.70	.15
☐ 31	Lee May	1.50	.70	.15
☐ 32	John Mayberry	1.50	.70	.15
☐ 33	Willie Mays	15.00	7.00	1.50
☐ 34	Thurman Munson	10.00	4.75	1.00
☐ 35	Bobby Murcer	2.00	.90	.20
☐ 36	Gary Nolan	1.50	.70	.15
☐ 37	Amos Otis	2.00	.90	.20
☐ 38	Jim Palmer	7.50	3.50	.75
☐ 39	Gaylord Perry	6.00	2.80	.60
☐ 40	Lou Piniella	2.00	.90	.20
☐ 41	Brooks Robinson	7.50	3.50	.75
☐ 42	Frank Robinson	6.00	2.80	.60
☐ 43	Ellie Rodriguez	1.50	.70	.15
☐ 44	Pete Rose	25.00	11.00	2.50
☐ 45	Nolan Ryan	10.00	4.75	1.00
☐ 46	Manny Sanguillen	1.50	.70	.15
☐ 47	George Scott	1.50	.70	.15
☐ 48	Tom Seaver	10.00	4.75	1.00
☐ 49	Chris Speier	1.50	.70	.15
☐ 50	Willie Stargell	5.00	2.35	.50
☐ 51	Don Sutton	4.00	1.85	.40
☐ 52	Joe Torre	2.00	.90	.20
☐ 53	Billy Williams	4.00	1.85	.40
☐ 54	Wilbur Wood	1.50	.70	.15
☐ 55	Carl Yastrzemski	15.00	7.00	1.50

Cracker Jack Pins

This 25 pin set is also known as the "PR4 Baseball Drawing Set" as the player portraits are actually line drawings. The pins measure approximately 13/16" in diameter. The pins are printed in gray and blue on a yellow background. The set was probably issued some time in the early thirties. Be careful not to get these pins wet as the inks are water soluble.

		MINT	VG-E	F-G
	COMPLETE SET	250.00	110.00	25.00
	COMMON PLAYER	8.00	3.75	.80
☐ 1	Charles Berry	8.00	3.75	.80
☐ 2	Bill Cissell	8.00	3.75	.80
☐ 3	KiKi Cuyler	12.00	5.50	1.20
☐ 4	Dizzy Dean	30.00	14.00	3.00
☐ 5	Wesley Ferrell	8.00	3.75	.80
☐ 6	Frank Frisch	15.00	7.00	1.50
☐ 7	Lou Gehrig	50.00	22.00	5.00
☐ 8	Vernon Gomez	15.00	7.00	1.50
☐ 9	Goose Goslin	12.00	5.50	1.20
☐ 10	George Grantham	8.00	3.75	.80
☐ 11	Charley Grimm	9.00	4.25	.90
☐ 12	Lefty Grove	18.00	8.50	1.80
☐ 13	Gabby Hartnett	12.00	5.50	1.20
☐ 14	Travis Jackson	12.00	5.50	1.20
☐ 15	Tony Lazzeri	10.00	4.75	1.00
☐ 16	Ted Lyons	12.00	5.50	1.20
☐ 17	Rabbit Maranville	12.00	5.50	1.20
☐ 18	Carl Reynolds	8.00	3.75	.80
☐ 19	Charles Ruffing	12.00	5.50	1.20
☐ 20	Al Simmons	12.00	5.50	1.20
☐ 21	Gus Suhr	8.00	3.75	.80
☐ 22	Bill Terry	15.00	7.00	1.50
☐ 23	Dazzy Vance	12.00	5.50	1.20
☐ 24	Paul Waner	12.00	5.50	1.20
☐ 25	Lon Warneke	8.00	3.75	.80

1984 Fun Foods Pins

These pins were mass marketed in early 1985 (the copyright notice on the pin backs indicate 1984) and feature 133 pins of the current stars of baseball. Each pin measures approximately 1 1/8" in diameter. There are other related "proof" type items available for this issue. The color border around the photo is coded for the player's team. On the back each pins is numbered; the player's position and a statistic are given.

	MINT	VG-E	F-G
COMPLETE SET	10.00	4.75	1.00
COMMON PLAYER	.03	.01	.00

		MINT	VG-E	F-G
☐ 1	Dave Winfield	.20	.09	.02
☐ 2	Lance Parrish	.15	.06	.01
☐ 3	Gary Carter	.20	.09	.02
☐ 4	Pete Rose	.50	.22	.05
☐ 5	Jim Rice	.15	.06	.01
☐ 6	George Brett	.30	.12	.03
☐ 7	Fernando Valenzuela	.15	.06	.01
☐ 8	Darryl Strawberry	.30	.12	.03
☐ 9	Steve Garvey	.25	.10	.02
☐ 10	Rollie Fingers	.07	.03	.01
☐ 11	Mike Schmidt	.25	.10	.02
☐ 12	Kent Tekulve	.03	.01	.00
☐ 13	Ryne Sandberg	.20	.09	.02
☐ 14	Bruce Sutter	.07	.03	.01
☐ 15	Tom Seaver	.20	.09	.02
☐ 16	Reggie Jackson	.30	.12	.03
☐ 17	Rickey Henderson	.30	.12	.03
☐ 18	Mark Langston	.05	.02	.00
☐ 19	Jack Clark	.05	.02	.00
☐ 20	Willie Randolph	.03	.01	.00
☐ 21	Kirk Gibson	.20	.09	.02
☐ 22	Andre Dawson	.10	.04	.01
☐ 23	Dave Concepcion	.05	.02	.00
☐ 24	Tony Armas	.05	.02	.00
☐ 25	Dan Quisenberry	.07	.03	.01
☐ 26	Pedro Guerrero	.15	.06	.01
☐ 27	Dwight Gooden	1.00	.45	.10
☐ 28	Tony Gwynn	.25	.10	.02
☐ 29	Robin Yount	.20	.09	.02
☐ 30	Steve Carlton	.20	.09	.02
☐ 31	Bill Madlock	.07	.03	.01
☐ 32	Rick Sutcliffe	.05	.02	.00
☐ 33	Willie McGee	.15	.06	.01
☐ 34	Greg Luzinski	.05	.02	.00
☐ 35	Rod Carew	.20	.09	.02
☐ 36	Dave Kingman	.07	.03	.01
☐ 37	Alvin Davis	.10	.04	.01
☐ 38	Chili Davis	.07	.03	.01
☐ 39	Don Baylor	.07	.03	.01
☐ 40	Alan Trammell	.10	.04	.01
☐ 41	Tim Raines	.20	.09	.02
☐ 42	Cesar Cedeno	.05	.02	.00
☐ 43	Wade Boggs	.50	.22	.05
☐ 44	Frank White	.03	.01	.00
☐ 45	Steve Sax	.07	.03	.01
☐ 46	George Foster	.07	.03	.01
☐ 47	Terry Kennedy	.05	.02	.00
☐ 48	Cecil Cooper	.07	.03	.01
☐ 49	John Denny	.03	.01	.00
☐ 50	John Candelaria	.03	.01	.00
☐ 51	Jody Davis	.05	.02	.00
☐ 52	George Hendrick	.03	.01	.00
☐ 53	Ron Kittle	.07	.03	.01
☐ 54	Fred Lynn	.10	.04	.01
☐ 55	Carney Lansford	.05	.02	.00
☐ 56	Gorman Thomas	.05	.02	.00
☐ 57	Manny Trillo	.03	.01	.00
☐ 58	Steve Kemp	.05	.02	.00
☐ 59	Jack Morris	.10	.04	.01
☐ 60	Dan Petry	.07	.03	.01
☐ 61	Mario Soto	.05	.02	.00
☐ 62	Dwight Evans	.07	.03	.01
☐ 63	Hal McRae	.05	.02	.00
☐ 64	Mike Marshall	.10	.04	.01
☐ 65	Mookie Wilson	.05	.02	.00
☐ 66	Graig Nettles	.10	.04	.01
☐ 67	Ben Oglivie	.05	.02	.00
☐ 68	Juan Samuel	.10	.04	.01
☐ 69	Johnny Ray	.07	.03	.01
☐ 70	Gary Matthews	.05	.02	.00
☐ 71	Ozzie Smith	.10	.04	.01
☐ 72	Carlton Fisk	.10	.04	.01
☐ 73	Doug DeCinces	.05	.02	.00
☐ 74	Joe Morgan	.15	.06	.01
☐ 75	Dave Stieb	.10	.04	.01
☐ 76	Buddy Bell	.07	.03	.01
☐ 77	Don Mattingly	.75	.35	.07
☐ 78	Lou Whitaker	.10	.04	.01
☐ 79	Willie Hernandez	.07	.03	.01
☐ 80	Dave Parker	.15	.06	.01
☐ 81	Bob Stanley	.05	.02	.00
☐ 82	Willie Wilson	.10	.04	.01
☐ 83	Orel Hershiser	.15	.06	.01
☐ 84	Rusty Staub	.05	.02	.00
☐ 85	Goose Gossage	.10	.04	.01
☐ 86	Don Sutton	.10	.04	.01
☐ 87	Al Holland	.03	.01	.00
☐ 88	Tony Pena	.07	.03	.01
☐ 89	Ron Cey	.07	.03	.01
☐ 90	Joaquin Andujar	.07	.03	.01
☐ 91	LaMarr Hoyt	.05	.02	.00
☐ 92	Tommy John	.10	.04	.01
☐ 93	Dwayne Murphy	.05	.02	.00
☐ 94	Willie Upshaw	.05	.02	.00
☐ 95	Gary Ward	.05	.02	.00
☐ 96	Ron Guidry	.10	.04	.01
☐ 97	Chet Lemon	.03	.01	.00
☐ 98	Aurelio Lopez	.03	.01	.00
☐ 99	Tony Perez	.07	.03	.01
☐ 100	Bill Buckner	.05	.02	.00
☐ 101	Mike Hargrove	.03	.01	.00
☐ 102	Scott McGregor	.05	.02	.00
☐ 103	Dale Murphy	.40	.18	.04
☐ 104	Keith Hernandez	.20	.09	.02
☐ 105	Paul Molitor	.07	.03	.01
☐ 106	Bert Blyleven	.07	.03	.01
☐ 107	Leon Durham	.07	.03	.01
☐ 108	Lee Smith	.05	.02	.00
☐ 109	Nolan Ryan	.20	.09	.02
☐ 110	Harold Baines	.15	.06	.01
☐ 111	Kent Hrbek	.15	.06	.01
☐ 112	Ron Davis	.03	.01	.00
☐ 113	George Bell	.10	.04	.01
☐ 114	Charlie Hough	.05	.02	.00
☐ 115	Phil Niekro	.15	.06	.01
☐ 116	Dave Righetti	.10	.04	.01
☐ 117	Darrell Evans	.05	.02	.00
☐ 118	Cal Ripken Jr.	.30	.12	.03
☐ 119	Eddie Murray	.30	.12	.03
☐ 120	Storm Davis	.07	.03	.01
☐ 121	Mike Boddicker	.07	.03	.01
☐ 122	Bob Horner	.15	.06	.01
☐ 123	Chris Chambliss	.05	.02	.00
☐ 124	Ted Simmons	.07	.03	.01
☐ 125	Andre Thornton	.05	.02	.00
☐ 126	Larry Bowa	.05	.02	.00
☐ 127	Bob Dernier	.03	.01	.00
☐ 128	Joe Niekro	.05	.02	.00
☐ 129	Jose Cruz	.07	.03	.01
☐ 130	Tom Brunansky	.10	.04	.01
☐ 131	Gary Gaetti	.10	.04	.01
☐ 132	Lloyd Moseby	.10	.04	.01
☐ 133	Frank Tanana	.05	.02	.00

1969 Kelly's Pins

This set of 20 red, white, and blue pins has a very heavy emphasis on the National League and especially the midwestern city teams. The pins are unnumbered and hence are listed below in alphabetical order. The sponsor was Kelly's Potato Chips. Each pin measures approximately 1 3/16" in diameter. A black and white player photo is encircled by a blue (NL) or red (AL) band containing the player and team name as well as "Kelly's" and "ZIP" The set was produced in 1969 with the approval of the MLBPA.

	MINT	VG-E	F-G
COMPLETE SET	100.00	45.00	10.00

COMMON PLAYER	2.00	.90	.20
☐ 1 Luis Aparicio			
Chicago White Sox	6.00	2.80	.60
☐ 2 Ernie Banks			
Chicago Cubs	7.50	3.50	.75
☐ 3 Glenn Beckert			
Chicago Cubs	2.00	.90	.20
☐ 4 Lou Brock			
St. Louis Cardinals	7.50	3.50	.75
☐ 5 Curt Flood			
St. Louis Cardinals	2.50	1.15	.25
☐ 6 Bob Gibson			
St. Louis Cardinals	7.50	3.50	.75
☐ 7 Joel Horlen			
Chicago White Sox	2.00	.90	.20
☐ 8 Al Kaline			
Detroit Tigers	7.50	3.50	.75
☐ 9 Don Kessinger			
Chicago Cubs	2.00	.90	.20
☐10 Mickey Lolich			
Detroit Tigers	2.50	1.15	.25
☐11 Juan Marichal			
San Francisco Giants	6.00	2.80	.60
☐12 Willie Mays			
San Francisco Giants	15.00	7.00	1.50
☐13 Tim McCarver			
St. Louis Cardinals	2.50	1.15	.25
☐14 Denny McLain			
Detroit Tigers	2.50	1.15	.25
☐15 Pete Rose			
Cincinnati Reds	25.00	11.00	2.50
☐16 Ron Santo			
Chicago Cubs	2.50	1.15	.25
☐17 Joe Torre			
St. Louis Cardinals	2.50	1.15	.25
☐18 Pete Ward			
Chicago White Sox	2.00	.90	.20
☐19 Billy Williams			
Chicago Cubs	5.00	2.35	.50
☐20 Carl Yastremski			
Boston Red Sox	15.00	7.00	1.50

1969 MLBPA Pins

This 1969 pin set of 60 was issued by the Major League Baseball Player's Association. Each pin is 7/8" in diameter. The pins are unnumbered and hence they are listed below in alphabetical order within each league. This 60 pin set contains 30 pins each of National League players and American League players. The outer bands of the pins are red for American League players and blue for National League players. The pictures on the pins are black and white, head only photos. The line "c 1969 MLBPA MFG. R.R. Winona, Minn." appears at the bottom of each pin. The asterisked players were also reprinted in 1983 and hence have a somewhat reduced value.

	MINT	VG-E	F-G
COMPLETE SET	75.00	35.00	7.50
COMMON PLAYER	.50	.22	.05

AMERICAN LEAGUE

☐ 1 Max Alvis			
Cleveland Indians	.50	.22	.05
☐ 2 Luis Aparicio			

Chicago White Sox	3.00	1.40	.30
☐ 3 George Brunet			
California Angels	.50	.22	.05
☐ 4 Rod Carew			
Minnesota Twins	5.00	2.35	.50
☐ 5 Dean Chance			
Minnesota Twins	.50	.22	.05
☐ 6 Bill Freehan			
Detroit Tigers	.75	.35	.07
☐ 7 Jim Fregosi			
California Angels	.75	.35	.07
☐ 8 Ken Harrelson			
Boston Red Sox	.75	.35	.07
☐ 9 Joel Horlen			
Chicago White Sox	.50	.22	.05
☐10 Tony Horton			
Cleveland Indians	.50	.22	.05
☐11 Willie Horton			
Detroit Tigers	.75	.35	.07
☐12 Frank Howard *			
Washington Senators	.50	.22	.05
☐13 Al Kaline *			
Detroit Tigers	3.00	1.40	.30
☐14 Harmon Killebrew			
Minnesota Twins	4.00	1.85	.40
☐15 Mickey Lolich			
Detroit Tigers	.75	.35	.07
☐16 Jim Lonborg			
Boston Red Sox	.50	.22	.05
☐17 Sam McDowell			
Cleveland Indians	.50	.22	.05
☐18 Denny McLain			
Detroit Tigers	.75	.35	.07
☐19 Rick Monday			
Oakland Athletics	.50	.22	.05
☐20 Tony Oliva *			
Minnesota Twins	.50	.22	.05
☐21 Joe Pepitone			
New York Yankees	.75	.35	.07
☐22 Boog Powell			
Baltimore Orioles	.75	.35	.07
☐23 Rick Reichardt			
California Angels	.50	.22	.05
☐24 Pete Richert			
Washington Senators	.50	.22	.05
☐25 Brooks Robinson *			
Baltimore Orioles	3.00	1.40	.30
☐26 Frank Robinson			
Baltimore Orioles	5.00	2.35	.50
☐27 Mel Stottlemyre			
New York Yankees	.75	.35	.07
☐28 Luis Tiant			
Cleveland Indians	.75	.35	.07
☐29 Pete Ward			
Chicago White Sox	.50	.22	.05
☐30 Carl Yastrzemski			
Boston Red Sox	12.00	5.50	1.20
NATIONAL LEAGUE			
☐31 Hank Aaron *			
Atlanta Braves	5.00	2.35	.50
☐32 Felipe Alou			
Atlanta Braves	.75	.35	.07
☐33 Richie Allen			
Philadelphia Phillies	.75	.35	.07
☐34 Ernie Banks			
Chicago Cubs	5.00	2.35	.50
☐35 Johnny Bench			
Cincinnati Reds	6.00	2.80	.60
☐36 Lou Brock			
St. Louis Cardinals	5.00	2.35	.50
☐37 Johnny Callison			
Philadelphia Phillies	.50	.22	.05
☐38 Orlando Cepeda *			
Atlanta Braves	.50	.22	.05
☐39 Roberto Clemente *			
Pittsburgh Pirates	5.00	2.35	.50
☐40 Willie Davis			
Los Angeles Dodgers	.50	.22	.05
☐41 Don Drysdale *			
Los Angeles Dodgers	2.00	.90	.20
☐42 Ron Fairly			
Los Angeles Dodgers	.50	.22	.05
☐43 Curt Flood			
St. Louis Cardinals	.75	.35	.07
☐44 Bob Gibson			
St. Louis Cardinals	4.00	1.85	.40
☐45 Bud Harrelson			
New York Mets	.50	.22	.05
☐46 Jim Ray Hart			
San Francisco Giants	.50	.22	.05
☐47 Tommy Helms			
Cincinnati Reds	.50	.22	.05
☐48 Don Kessinger			

		MINT	VG-E	F-G
	Chicago Cubs	.75	.35	.07
□ 49	Jerry Koosman			
	New York Mets	.75	.35	.07
□ 50	Jim Maloney			
	Cincinnati Reds	.75	.35	.07
□ 51	Juan Marichal *			
	San Francisco Giants	2.00	.90	.20
□ 52	Willie Mays *			
	San Francisco Giants	5.00	2.35	.50
□ 53	Tim McCarver			
	St. Louis Cardinals	.75	.35	.07
□ 54	Willie McCovey *			
	San Francisco Giants	3.00	1.40	.30
□ 55	Pete Rose			
	Cincinnati Reds	25.00	11.00	2.50
□ 56	Ron Santo *			
	Chicago Cubs	.50	.22	.05
□ 57	Ron Swoboda			
	New York Mets	.50	.22	.05
□ 58	Joe Torre			
	St. Louis Cardinals	.75	.35	.07
□ 59	Billy Williams *			
	Chicago Cubs	.75	.35	.07
□ 60	Jim Wynn			
	Houston Astros	.50	.22	.05

1983 MLBPA Pins

This pin set of 36 is apparently a reprinted set and is checklisted here in order to help collectors put a fair value on the pins that they are buying, selling, and trading. These are frequently mistaken for the 1969 issue after which they are patterned. There is no indication that this set was authorized by the Major League Baseball Player's Association. Each pin is 7/8" in diameter. This 36 pin set contains 18 pins each of National League players and American League players. The outer bands of the pins are red for American League players and blue for National League players. The pictures on the pins are black and white, head only photos. All of the players in the set had retired before 1984 and many had retired well before 1969. The line ''c 1969 MLBPA MFG. in U.S.A.'' appears at the bottom of each pin, i.e., no reference to Winona as with the 1969 set.

		MINT	VG-E	F-G
	COMPLETE SET	15.00	7.00	1.50
	COMMON PLAYER	.25	.10	.02
	AMERICAN LEAGUE			
□ 1	Bob Allison	.25	.10	.02
	Minnesota Twins			
□ 2	Yogi Berra	1.00	.45	.10
	New York Yankees			
□ 3	Norm Cash	.35	.15	.03
	Detroit Tigers			
□ 4	Joe DiMaggio	2.50	1.15	.25
	New York Yankees			
□ 5	Bobby Doerr	.50	.22	.05
	Boston Red Sox			
□ 6	Bob Feller	1.50	.70	.15
	Cleveland Indians			
□ 7	Whitey Ford	1.00	.45	.10
	New York Yankees			
□ 8	Nelson Fox	.35	.15	.03
	Chicago White Sox			
□ 9	Frank Howard	.25	.10	.02

		MINT	VG-E	F-G
	Washington Senators			
□ 10	Jim (Catfish) Hunter	.50	.22	.05
	Oakland A's			
□ 11	Al Kaline	1.00	.45	.10
	Detroit Tigers			
□ 12	Mickey Mantle	3.00	1.40	.30
	New York Yankees			
□ 13	Tony Oliva	.35	.15	.03
	Minnesota Twins			
□ 14	Satchel Paige	1.00	.45	.10
	St. Louis Browns			
□ 15	Phil Rizzuto	1.00	.45	.10
	New York Yankees			
□ 16	Brooks Robinson	1.00	.45	.10
	Baltimore Orioles			
□ 17	Bill Skowron	.35	.15	.03
	New York Yankees			
□ 18	Ted Williams	1.50	.70	.15
	Boston Red Sox			
	NATIONAL LEAGUE			
□ 19	Hank Aaron	1.50	.70	.15
	Atlanta Braves			
□ 20	Roy Campanella	1.50	.70	.15
	Brooklyn Dodgers			
□ 21	Orlando Cepeda	.35	.15	.03
	Atlanta Braves			
□ 22	Roberto Clemente	1.00	.45	.10
	Pittsburgh Pirates			
□ 23	Don Drysdale	.75	.35	.07
	Los Angeles Dodgers			
□ 24	Sandy Koufax	1.00	.45	.10
	Los Angeles Dodgers			
□ 25	Juan Marichal	.50	.22	.05
	San Francisco Giants			
□ 26	Eddie Mathews	.75	.35	.07
	Milwaukee Braves			
□ 27	Willie Mays	1.50	.70	.15
	San Francisco Giants			
□ 28	Willie McCovey	1.00	.45	.10
	San Francisco Giants			
□ 29	Stan Musial	1.00	.45	.10
	St. Louis Cardinals			
□ 30	Robin Roberts	.75	.35	.07
	Philadelphia Phillies			
□ 31	Jackie Robinson	1.50	.70	.15
	Brooklyn Dodgers			
□ 32	Ron Santo	.35	.15	.03
	Chicago Cubs			
□ 33	Duke Snider	1.00	.45	.10
	Brooklyn Dodgers			
□ 34	Warren Spahn	1.00	.45	.10
	Milwaukee Braves			
□ 35	Billy Williams	.50	.22	.05
	Chicago Cubs			
□ 36	Maury Wills	.50	.22	.05
	Los Angeles Dodgers			

Orbit Pins Numbered

These pins were thought to have been issued some time between 1932 and 1934. The catalog designation for these pins is PR2. These pins are skip-numbered which distinguishes them from the following set designated as PR3 which is unnumbered. Each pin is approximately 13/16" in diameter. On the front of the pin the team nickname is featured in all caps inside quotation marks. Player pictures are set against a green background with the player's name and team in a yellow strip.

	MINT	VG-E	F-G
COMPLETE SET	900.00	400.00	80.00
COMMON PLAYER	10.00	4.75	1.00

		MINT	VG-E	F-G
☐	1 Andrews			
	Boston Red Sox	10.00	4.75	1.00
☐	2 Reynolds			
	St. Louis Browns	10.00	4.75	1.00
☐	3 Riggs Stephenson			
	Chicago Cubs	12.00	5.50	1.20
☐	4 (Lon) Warneke			
	Chicago Cubs	10.00	4.75	1.00
☐	5 (Frank) Grube			
	Chicago White Sox	10.00	4.75	1.00
☐	6 "Kiki" Cuyler			
	Chicago Cubs	18.00	8.50	1.80
☐	7 (Marty) McManus			
	Boston Red Sox	10.00	4.75	1.00
☐	8A "Lefty" Clark			
	New York Giants	12.00	5.50	1.20
☐	8B "Lefty" Clark			
	Brooklyn Dodgers	50.00	22.00	5.00
☐	9 (George) Blaeholder			
	St. Louis Browns	10.00	4.75	1.00
☐	10 (Willie) Kamm			
	Cleveland Indians	10.00	4.75	1.00
☐	11 (Jimmy) "Dykes"			
	Chicago White Sox	12.00	5.50	1.20
☐	12 (Earl) Averill			
	Cleveland Indians	18.00	8.50	1.80
☐	13 Pat Malone			
	Chicago Cubs	10.00	4.75	1.00
☐	14 "Dizzy" Dean			
	St. Louis Cardinals	50.00	22.00	5.00
☐	15 (Dick) Bartell			
	Phila. Phillies	10.00	4.75	1.00
☐	16 Guy Bush			
	Chicago Cubs	10.00	4.75	1.00
☐	17 Tinning			
	Chicago Cubs	10.00	4.75	1.00
☐	18 Jimmy Foxx			
	Phila. Athletics	35.00	16.50	3.50
☐	19 "Mule" Haas			
	Chicago White Sox	10.00	4.75	1.00
☐	20 (Lew) Fonseca			
	Chicago White Sox	10.00	4.75	1.00
☐	21 "Pepper" Martin			
	St. Louis Cardinals	12.00	5.50	1.20
☐	22 Phil Collins			
	Phila. Phillies	10.00	4.75	1.00
☐	23 Cissell			
	Cleveland Indians	10.00	4.75	1.00
☐	24 Hadley			
	St. Louis Browns	10.00	4.75	1.00
☐	25 Smead Jolley			
	Boston Red Sox	10.00	4.75	1.00
☐	26 (Burleigh) Grimes			
	Chicago Cubs	18.00	8.50	1.80
☐	27 (Dale) Alexander			
	Boston Red Sox	10.00	4.75	1.00
☐	28 (Mickey) Cochrane			
	Phila. Athletics	25.00	11.00	2.50
☐	29 (Mel) Harder			
	Cleveland Indians	12.00	5.50	1.20
☐	30 Mark Koenig			
	Chicago Cubs	10.00	4.75	1.00
☐	31A "Lefty" O'Doul			
	New York Giants	12.00	5.50	1.20
☐	31B "Lefty" O'Doul			
	Brooklyn Dodgers	30.00	14.00	3.00
☐	32A (Woody) English			
	Chicago Cubs	10.00	4.75	1.00
☐	32B (Woody) English			
	Chicago Cubs			
	(without bat)	25.00	11.00	2.50
☐	33A (Billy) Jurges			
	Chicago Cubs	10.00	4.75	1.00
☐	33B (Billy) Jurges			
	Chicago Cubs			
	(without bat)	25.00	11.00	2.50
☐	34 Campbell			
	St. Louis Browns	10.00	4.75	1.00
☐	35 (Joe) Vosmik			
	Cleveland Indians	10.00	4.75	1.00
☐	36 Porter			
	Cleveland Indians	10.00	4.75	1.00
☐	37 Charlie Grimm			
	Chicago Cubs	12.00	5.50	1.20
☐	38 Geo. Earnshaw			
	Phila. Athletics	10.00	4.75	1.00
☐	39 Al Simmons			
	Chicago White Sox	18.00	8.50	1.80
☐	40 "Red" Lucas			

		MINT	VG-E	F-G
	Cincinnati Reds	10.00	4.75	1.00
☐	51 (Wally) Berger			
	Boston Braves	10.00	4.75	1.00
☐	52 Levey			
	St. Louis Browns	10.00	4.75	1.00
☐	58 (Ernie) Lombardi			
	Cincinnati Reds	18.00	8.50	1.80
☐	64 Burns			
	St. Louis Browns	10.00	4.75	1.00
☐	67 Billy Herman			
	Chicago Cubs	18.00	8.50	1.80
☐	72 Bill Hallahan			
	St. Louis Cardinals	10.00	4.75	1.00
☐	92 Brennan			
	New York Yankees	10.00	4.75	1.00
☐	96 Sam Byrd			
	New York Yankees	10.00	4.75	1.00
☐	99 Ben Chapman			
	New York Yankees	10.00	4.75	1.00
☐	103 John Allen			
	New York Yankees	10.00	4.75	1.00
☐	107 Tony Lazzeri			
	New York Yankees	15.00	7.00	1.50
☐	111 Earl Combs			
	New York Yankees	18.00	8.50	1.80
☐	116 Joe Sewell			
	New York Yankees	18.00	8.50	1.80
☐	120 Vernon Gomez			
	New York Yankees	25.00	11.00	2.50

Orbit Pins Unnumbered

These pins were thought to have been issued some time between 1932 and 1934. The catalog designation for these pins is PR3. These pins are unnumbered which distinguishes them from the set designated as PR2 which is skip-numbered. Each pin is approximately 13/16" in diameter. On the front of the pin the team nickname is featured in all caps inside quotation marks. Player pictures are set against a green background with the player's name and team in a yellow strip.

	MINT	VG-E	F-G
COMPLETE SET	1500.00	700.00	140.00
COMMON PLAYER	20.00	9.00	2.00

		MINT	VG-E	F-G
☐	1 (Dale) Alexander			
	Boston Red Sox	20.00	9.00	2.00
☐	2 Andrews			
	Boston Red Sox	20.00	9.00	2.00
☐	3 (Earl) Averill			
	Cleveland Indians	30.00	14.00	3.00
☐	4 (Dick) Bartell			
	Phila. Phillies	20.00	9.00	2.00
☐	5 (Wally) Berger			
	Boston Braves	20.00	9.00	2.00
☐	6 (George) Blaeholder			
	St. Louis Browns	20.00	9.00	2.00
☐	7 Burns			
	St. Louis Browns	20.00	9.00	2.00
☐	8 Guy Bush			
	Chicago Cubs	20.00	9.00	2.00
☐	9 Campbell			
	St. Louis Browns	20.00	9.00	2.00
☐	10 Cissell			
	Cleveland Indians	20.00	9.00	2.00
☐	11 "Lefty" Clark			
	Brooklyn Dodgers	20.00	9.00	2.00
☐	12 (Mickey) Cochrane			

	Phila. Athletics	40.00	18.00	4.00
□ 13	(Phil) Collins			
	Phila. Phillies	20.00	9.00	2.00
□ 14	(Kiki) Cuyler			
	Chicago Cubs	30.00	14.00	3.00
□ 15	Dizzy Dean			
	St. Louis Cardinals	60.00	27.00	6.00
□ 16	(Jimmy) "Dykes"			
	Chicago White Sox	22.00	10.00	2.20
□ 17	Geo. Earnshaw			
	Phila. Athletics	20.00	9.00	2.00
□ 18	(Woody) English			
	Chicago Cubs	20.00	9.00	2.00
□ 19	(Lew) Fonseca			
	Chicago White Sox	20.00	9.00	2.00
□ 20	Jimmie Foxx			
	Phila. Athletics	50.00	22.00	5.00
□ 21	(Burleigh) Grimes			
	Chicago Cubs	30.00	14.00	3.00
□ 22	Charlie Grimm			
	Chicago Cubs	22.00	10.00	2.20
□ 23	"Lefty" Grove			
	Phila. Athletics	40.00	18.00	4.00
□ 24	(Frank) Grube			
	Chicago White Sox	20.00	9.00	2.00
□ 25	(Mule) Haas			
	Chicago White Sox	20.00	9.00	2.00
□ 26	Hadley			
	St. Louis Browns	20.00	9.00	2.00
□ 27	"Chick" Hafey			
	Cincinnati Reds	30.00	14.00	3.00
□ 28	(Jesse) Haines			
	St. Louis Cardinals	30.00	14.00	3.00
□ 29	(Bill) Hallahan			
	St. Louis Cardinals	20.00	9.00	2.00
□ 30	(Mel) Harder			
	Cleveland Indians	22.00	10.00	2.20
□ 31	"Gabby" Hartnett			
	Chicago Cubs	30.00	14.00	3.00
□ 32	"Babe" Herman			
	Chicago Cubs	24.00	11.00	2.40
□ 33	Billy Herman			
	Chicago Cubs	30.00	14.00	3.00
□ 34	(Rogers) Hornsby			
	St. Louis Cardinals	60.00	27.00	6.00
□ 35	Johnson			
	Boston Red Sox	20.00	9.00	2.00
□ 36	Smead Jolley			
	Boston Red Sox	20.00	9.00	2.00
□ 37	(Billy) Jurges			
	Chicago Cubs	20.00	9.00	2.00
□ 38	(Willie) Kamm			
	Cleveland Indians	20.00	9.00	2.00
□ 39	(Mark) Koenig			
	Chicago Cubs	20.00	9.00	2.00
□ 40	Levey			
	St. Louis Browns	20.00	9.00	2.00
□ 41	(Ernie) Lombardi			
	Cincinnati Reds	30.00	14.00	3.00
□ 42	(Red) Lucas			
	Cincinnati Reds	20.00	9.00	2.00
□ 43	(Ted) Lyons			
	Chicago White Sox	30.00	14.00	3.00
□ 44	Connie Mack			
	Mgr. of Athletics	40.00	18.00	4.00
□ 45	Pat Malone			
	Chicago Cubs	20.00	9.00	2.00
□ 46	(Pepper) Martin			
	St. Louis Cardinals	24.00	11.00	2.40
□ 47	(Marty) McManus			
	Boston Red Sox	20.00	9.00	2.00
□ 48	Lefty O'Doul			
	Brooklyn Dodgers	24.00	11.00	2.40
□ 49	Porter			
	Cleveland Indians	20.00	9.00	2.00
□ 50	Reynolds			
	St. Louis Browns	20.00	9.00	2.00
□ 51	(Charlie) Root			
	Chicago Cubs	20.00	9.00	2.00
□ 52	Seeds			
	Boston Red Sox	20.00	9.00	2.00
□ 53	Al Simmons			
	Chicago White Sox	30.00	14.00	3.00
□ 54	(Riggs) Stephenson			
	Chicago Cubs	24.00	11.00	2.40
□ 55	Tinning			
	Chicago Cubs	20.00	9.00	2.00
□ 56	(Joe) Vosmik			
	Cleveland Indians	20.00	9.00	2.00
□ 57	(Rube) Walberg			
	Phila. Athletics	20.00	9.00	2.00
□ 58	Paul Waner			
	Pittsburgh Pirates	30.00	14.00	3.00
□ 59	(Lon) Warneke			
	Chicago Cubs	20.00	9.00	2.00
□ 60	Whitney			
	Phila. Phillies	20.00	9.00	2.00

Our National Game Pins

This set of 30 "buttons" (each measuring 7/8" in diameter) do not have a pin back but rather a tab or spike. They are frequently found with paper back "holder". The catalog designation for these "pins" is PM8. The photo is in black and white but printed in blue tones. Since these buttons are unnumbered, they are listed below in alphabetical order.

			MINT	VG-E	F-G
	COMPLETE SET		200.00	90.00	20.00
	COMMON PLAYER		3.00	1.40	.30
□	1	Wally Berger	3.00	1.40	.30
□	2	Lou Chiozza	3.00	1.40	.30
□	3	Joe Cronin	7.50	3.50	.75
□	4	Frank Crosetti	4.00	1.85	.40
□	5	Jerome (Dizzy) Dean	20.00	9.00	2.00
□	6	Frank DeMaree	3.00	1.40	.30
□	7	Joe DiMaggio	50.00	22.00	5.00
□	8	Bob Feller	15.00	7.00	1.50
□	9	Jimmie Foxx	15.00	7.00	1.50
□	10	Charles Gehringer	7.50	3.50	.75
□	11	Lou Gehrig	50.00	22.00	5.00
□	12	Lefty Gomez	7.50	3.50	.75
□	13	Hank Greenberg	7.50	3.50	.75
□	14	Irving (Bump) Hadley	3.00	1.40	.30
□	15	Leo Hartnett	6.00	2.80	.60
□	16	Carl Hubbell	7.50	3.50	.75
□	17	John (Buddy) Lewis	3.00	1.40	.30
□	18	Gus Mancuso	3.00	1.40	.30
□	19	Joe McCarthy	5.00	2.35	.50
□	20	Joe Medwick	6.00	2.80	.60
□	21	Joe Moore	3.00	1.40	.30
□	22	Mel Ott	7.50	3.50	.75
□	23	Jake Powell	3.00	1.40	.30
□	24	Jimmy Ripple	3.00	1.40	.30
□	25	Red Ruffing	6.00	2.80	.60
□	26	Hal Schumacher	3.00	1.40	.30
□	27	George Selkirk	3.00	1.40	.30
□	28	"Al" Simmons	6.00	2.80	.60
□	29	Bill Terry	7.50	3.50	.75
□	30	Harold Trosky	3.00	1.40	.30

Sweet Caporal Pins

This unnumbered set is numbered here for convenience in alphabetical order by team. Pins with larger letters are worth more. Large letter variations are indicated below by LL. The catalog designation is PT-3. These pins were produced and distributed roughly between 1910 and 1912. Each pin measures approximately 7/8" in diameter. The pins are essentially brown and white.

		MINT	VG-E	F-G
COMPLETE SET		2400.00	180.00	40.00
COMMON PLAYER		6.00	2.80	.60

COMMON LARGE LETTERS	10.00	4.75	1.00

BOSTON RED SOX

☐ 1A Carrigan	6.00	2.80	.60
☐ 1B Carrigan LL	10.00	4.75	1.00
☐ 2 Ed Cicotte	6.00	2.80	.60
☐ 3A Engle	6.00	2.80	.60
☐ 3B Engle LL	10.00	4.75	1.00
☐ 4 Harry Hooper	15.00	7.00	1.50
☐ 5 Ed Karger	6.00	2.80	.60
☐ 6A Tris Speaker	25.00	11.00	2.50
☐ 6B Tris Speaker LL	35.00	16.50	3.50
☐ 7 Heine Wagner	6.00	2.80	.60

CHICAGO WHITE SOX

☐ 8 Callahan	6.00	2.80	.60
☐ 9 Dougherty	6.00	2.80	.60
☐ 10A Hugh Duffy	15.00	7.00	1.50
☐ 10B Hugh Duffy LL	25.00	11.00	2.50
☐ 11A Bris Lord	6.00	2.80	.60
☐ 11B Bris Lord LL	10.00	4.75	1.00
☐ 12A McIntyre	6.00	2.80	.60
☐ 12B McIntyre LL	10.00	4.75	1.00
☐ 13 Parent	6.00	2.80	.60
☐ 14 Ed Walsh	15.00	7.00	1.50
☐ 15 White	6.00	2.80	.60

CLEVELAND NAPS

☐ 16 Ball	6.00	2.80	.60
☐ 17 Birmingham	6.00	2.80	.60
☐ 18 Napoleon Lajoie	30.00	14.00	3.00
☐ 19A Stovall	6.00	2.80	.60
☐ 19B Stovall LL	10.00	4.75	1.00
(different picture)			
☐ 20 Turner	20.00	9.00	2.00
☐ 21A "Cy" Young	30.00	14.00	3.00
☐ 21B Old Cy Young	40.00	18.00	4.00

DETROIT TIGERS

☐ 22A "Ty" Cobb	150.00	70.00	15.00
☐ 22B Cobb LL	225.00	100.00	22.00
☐ 23 Delahanty	6.00	2.80	.60
☐ 24 Donovan	20.00	9.00	2.00
☐ 25A Hugh Jennings	15.00	7.00	1.50
☐ 25B Hugh Jennings LL	25.00	11.00	2.50
☐ 26 Tom Jones	20.00	9.00	2.00
☐ 27 Killian	20.00	9.00	2.00
☐ 28A Mullen	6.00	2.80	.60
☐ 28B Mullin	6.00	2.80	.60
☐ 29 O'Leary	6.00	2.80	.60
☐ 30A Schmidt	6.00	2.80	.60
☐ 30B Schmidt LL	10.00	4.75	1.00
☐ 31 Oscar Stanage	6.00	2.80	.60

NEW YORK YANKEES

☐ 32A Hal Chase	8.00	3.75	.80
☐ 32B Hal Chase LL	12.00	5.50	1.20
☐ 33 Cree	20.00	9.00	2.00
☐ 34A Russ Ford	6.00	2.80	.60
☐ 34B Russ Ford LL	10.00	4.75	1.00
☐ 35 Hemphill	6.00	2.80	.60
☐ 36A Knight	6.00	2.80	.60
☐ 36B Knight LL	10.00	4.75	1.00
☐ 37 Quinn	6.00	2.80	.60
☐ 38 Warhop	20.00	9.00	2.00
☐ 39 Wolter	6.00	2.80	.60

PHILADELPHIA A'S

☐ 40 Frank Baker	15.00	7.00	1.50
☐ 41 Jack Barry	6.00	2.80	.60
☐ 42A "Chief" Bender	15.00	7.00	1.50
☐ 42B Bender LL	25.00	11.00	2.50
☐ 43A Eddie Collins	20.00	9.00	2.00
☐ 43B Collins LL	40.00	18.00	4.00
☐ 44 Dygert	6.00	2.80	.60
☐ 45 Hartsel	6.00	2.80	.60
☐ 46 Krause	6.00	2.80	.60
☐ 47 Livingston	6.00	2.80	.60
☐ 48 Murphy	6.00	2.80	.60
☐ 49 Oldring	6.00	2.80	.60
☐ 50A Ira Thomas	6.00	2.80	.60
☐ 50B Thomas LL	10.00	4.75	1.00

ST. LOUIS BROWNS

☐ 51A Austin	6.00	2.80	.60
☐ 51B Austin LL	10.00	4.75	1.00
☐ 52 Hoffman	6.00	2.80	.60
☐ 53A LaPorte	6.00	2.80	.60
☐ 53B LaPorte LL	10.00	4.75	1.00
☐ 54 Pelty	6.00	2.80	.60
☐ 55 Stone	6.00	2.80	.60
☐ 56A Bobby Wallace	15.00	7.00	1.50
☐ 56B Bobby Wallace	25.00	11.00	2.50
(no cap)			

WASHINGTON SENATORS

☐ 57A Elberfeld	6.00	2.80	.60
☐ 57B Elberfeld LL	10.00	4.75	1.00
☐ 58 Gray	6.00	2.80	.60
☐ 59 Groom	6.00	2.80	.60
☐ 60A Walter Johnson	45.00	20.00	4.50
☐ 60B Walter Johnson LL	75.00	35.00	7.50
☐ 61 McBride	6.00	2.80	.60
☐ 62 Milan	6.00	2.80	.60
☐ 63 Germany Schaefer	6.00	2.80	.60
☐ 64A Gabby Street	6.00	2.80	.60
☐ 64B Gabby Street LL	10.00	4.75	1.00

BOSTON RUSTLERS

☐ 65 Abbaticchio	6.00	2.80	.60
☐ 66 Ferguson	6.00	2.80	.60
☐ 67 Buck Herzog	6.00	2.80	.60
☐ 68A Mattern	6.00	2.80	.60
☐ 68B Mattern LL	10.00	4.75	1.00

BROOKLYN SUPERBAS

☐ 69 Barger	6.00	2.80	.60
☐ 70A Bell	6.00	2.80	.60
☐ 70B Bell LL	10.00	4.75	1.00
☐ 71 Bergen	6.00	2.80	.60
☐ 72 Dahlen	6.00	2.80	.60
☐ 73 Erwin	6.00	2.80	.60
☐ 74 Hummel	6.00	2.80	.60
☐ 75A Nap Rucker	6.00	2.80	.60
☐ 75B Nap Rucker LL	10.00	4.75	1.00
☐ 76 Scanlon	20.00	9.00	2.00
☐ 77 Smith	6.00	2.80	.60
☐ 78A Zach Wheat	15.00	7.00	1.50
☐ 78B Zach Wheat LL	25.00	11.00	2.50

CHICAGO CUBS

☐ 79A Jimmy Archer	6.00	2.80	.60
☐ 79B Jimmy Archer LL	10.00	4.75	1.00
☐ 80A Mordecai Brown	15.00	7.00	1.50
☐ 80B Mordecai Brown LL	25.00	11.00	2.50
☐ 81A Frank Chance	15.00	7.00	1.50
☐ 81B Frank Chance LL	25.00	11.00	2.50
☐ 82 Johnny Evers	15.00	7.00	1.50
☐ 83 Kroh	6.00	2.80	.60
☐ 84 McIntire	6.00	2.80	.60
☐ 85 Needham	20.00	9.00	2.00
☐ 86 Overall	20.00	9.00	2.00
☐ 87 Pfiester	6.00	2.80	.60
☐ 88 Ed Reulbach	6.00	2.80	.60
☐ 89 Richie	6.00	2.80	.60
☐ 90 Schulte	6.00	2.80	.60
☐ 91 Jimmy Sheckard	6.00	2.80	.60
☐ 92 Harry Steinfeldt	6.00	2.80	.60
☐ 93A Joe Tinker	15.00	7.00	1.50
☐ 93B Joe Tinker LL	25.00	11.00	2.50

CINCINNATI REDS

☐ 94 Bates	6.00	2.80	.60
☐ 95 Beebe	6.00	2.80	.60
☐ 96 Bescher	6.00	2.80	.60
☐ 97A Downey	6.00	2.80	.60
☐ 97B Downey LL	10.00	4.75	1.00
☐ 98 Fromme	6.00	2.80	.60
☐ 99 Gaspar	6.00	2.80	.60
☐ 100 Grant	20.00	9.00	2.00
☐ 101A Clark Griffith	15.00	7.00	1.50
☐ 101B Griffith LL	25.00	11.00	2.50
☐ 102 Hoblitzell	6.00	2.80	.60
☐ 103A McLean	6.00	2.80	.60
☐ 103B McLean LL	10.00	4.75	1.00
☐ 104 Mitchell	6.00	2.80	.60
☐ 105 Suggs	6.00	2.80	.60

NEW YORK GIANTS

☐ 106 Ames	6.00	2.80	.60
☐ 107 Becker	6.00	2.80	.60
☐ 108 Bridwell	6.00	2.80	.60
☐ 109 Doc Crandall	6.00	2.80	.60
☐ 110 Devlin	6.00	2.80	.60
☐ 111 Josh Devore	6.00	2.80	.60
☐ 112A Doyle	6.00	2.80	.60
☐ 112B Doyle LL	10.00	4.75	1.00
☐ 113 Drucke	6.00	2.80	.60
☐ 114 Buck Herzog	6.00	2.80	.60
☐ 115 Latham	6.00	2.80	.60
☐ 116 Rube Marquard	15.00	7.00	1.50
☐ 117A Christy Mathewson	40.00	18.00	4.00
☐ 117B Christy Mathewson LL	65.00	30.00	6.50
☐ 118A John McGraw	20.00	9.00	2.00
☐ 118B John McGraw LL	30.00	14.00	3.00

	MINT	VG-E	F-G
☐ 119 Fred Merkle	6.00	2.80	.60
☐ 120 "Chief" Meyers	6.00	2.80	.60
☐ 121 Murray	6.00	2.80	.60
☐ 122A Wilson	20.00	9.00	2.00
☐ 122B Wilson LL	10.00	4.75	1.00
☐ 123 Wiltse	6.00	2.80	.60
PHILADELPHIA PHILLIES			
☐ 124 Bransfield	20.00	9.00	2.00
☐ 125A Dooin	6.00	2.80	.60
☐ 125B Dooin LL	10.00	4.75	1.00
☐ 126A Doolan	6.00	2.80	.60
☐ 126B Doolan LL	10.00	4.75	1.00
☐ 127 Hans Lobert	6.00	2.80	.60
☐ 128 Sherry Magee	6.00	2.80	.60
☐ 129 Moran	6.00	2.80	.60
☐ 130A Dode Paskert	6.00	2.80	.60
☐ 130B Dode Paskert LL	10.00	4.75	1.00
☐ 131 Rowan	20.00	9.00	2.00
☐ 132A Titus	6.00	2.80	.60
☐ 132B Titus LL	10.00	4.75	1.00
PITTSBURGH PIRATES			
☐ 133 Byrne	6.00	2.80	.60
☐ 134A Camnitz	6.00	2.80	.60
☐ 134B Camnitz LL	10.00	4.75	1.00
☐ 135A Fred Clarke	15.00	7.00	1.50
☐ 135B Clarke LL	25.00	11.00	2.50
☐ 136 Flynn	6.00	2.80	.60
☐ 137 Gibson	6.00	2.80	.60
☐ 138 Tommy Leach	6.00	2.80	.60
☐ 138 Leach LL	10.00	4.75	1.00
☐ 139 Leever	6.00	2.80	.60
☐ 140 Leifield	6.00	2.80	.60
☐ 141 Maddox	6.00	2.80	.60
☐ 142 Miller	6.00	2.80	.60
☐ 143 Deacon Phillippe	6.00	2.80	.60
☐ 144 Wilson	6.00	2.80	.60
ST. LOUIS CARDINALS			
☐ 145A Roger Bresnahan	15.00	7.00	1.50
☐ 145B Roger Bresnahan LL	45.00	20.00	4.50
(different picture)			
☐ 146 Evans	6.00	2.80	.60
☐ 147 Harmon	6.00	2.80	.60
☐ 148 Hauser	20.00	9.00	2.00
☐ 149A Miller Huggins	15.00	7.00	1.50
☐ 149B Miller Huggins LL	25.00	11.00	2.50
☐ 150 Konetchy	6.00	2.80	.60
☐ 151A Oakes	6.00	2.80	.60
☐ 151B Oakes LL	10.00	4.75	1.00
☐ 152 Phelps	6.00	2.80	.60

1956 Topps Pins

This set of 60 full-color pins was Topps first and only baseball player pin set. Each pin measures 1 3/16" in diameter. Although the set was advertised to contain 90 pins, only 60 were issued. The checklist below lists the players in alphabetical order. Diering and Stobbs (asterisked below) are more difficult to obtain than other pins in the set.

	MINT	VG-E	F-G
COMPLETE SET	750.00	350.00	75.00
COMMON PLAYER	7.50	3.50	.75
BALTIMORE ORIOLES			
☐ 1 Chuck Diering OF *	100.00	45.00	10.00
☐ 2 Willie Miranda SS	7.50	3.50	.75
☐ 3 Hal Smith C	7.50	3.50	.75
☐ 4 Gus Triandos 1B	7.50	3.50	.75
CHICAGO CUBS			
☐ 5 Ernie Banks SS	20.00	9.00	2.00

	MINT	VG-E	F-G
☐ 6 Hank Sauer OF	5.50	2.60	.55
☐ 7 Bill Tremel P	7.50	3.50	.75
CLEVELAND INDIANS			
☐ 8 Jim Hegan C	7.50	3.50	.75
☐ 9 Don Mossi P	7.50	3.50	.75
☐ 10 Al Rosen 3B	9.00	4.25	.90
☐ 11 Al Smith OF	7.50	3.50	.75
KANSAS CITY A'S			
☐ 12 Jim Finigan 2B	7.50	3.50	.75
☐ 13 Hector Lopez 3B	7.50	3.50	.75
☐ 14 Vic Power 1B	7.50	3.50	.75
☐ 15 Gus Zernial OF	7.50	3.50	.75
MILWAUKEE BRAVES			
☐ 16 Hank Aaron OF	50.00	22.00	5.00
☐ 17 Gene Conley P	7.50	3.50	.75
☐ 18 Ed Mathews 3B	20.00	9.00	2.00
☐ 19 Warren Spahn P	20.00	9.00	2.00
PHILADELPHIA PHILLIES			
☐ 20 Ron Negray P	7.50	3.50	.75
☐ 21 Mayo Smith MGR	7.50	3.50	.75
☐ 22 Herman Wehmeier P	7.50	3.50	.75
BOSTON RED SOX			
☐ 23 Grady Hatton 3B	7.50	3.50	.75
☐ 24 Jackie Jensen OF	9.00	4.25	.90
☐ 25 Frank Sullivan P	7.50	3.50	.75
☐ 26 Ted Williams OF	50.00	22.00	5.00
NEW YORK YANKEES			
☐ 27 Yogi Berra C	35.00	16.50	3.50
☐ 28 Joe Collins 1B	7.50	3.50	.75
☐ 29 Phil Rizzuto SS	20.00	9.00	2.00
☐ 30 Bill Skowron 1B	9.00	4.25	.90
☐ 31 Bob Turley P	7.50	3.50	.75
CHICAGO WHITE SOX			
☐ 32 Dick Donovan P	7.50	3.50	.75
☐ 33 Jack Harshman P	7.50	3.50	.75
☐ 34 Bob Kennedy 3B	7.50	3.50	.75
☐ 35 Jim Rivera OF	7.50	3.50	.75
DETROIT TIGERS			
☐ 36 Ray Boone 3B	7.50	3.50	.75
☐ 37 Frank House C	7.50	3.50	.75
☐ 38 Al Kaline OF	25.00	11.00	2.50
NEW YORK GIANTS			
☐ 39 Ruben Gomez P	7.50	3.50	.75
☐ 40 Bobby Hofman 1F	7.50	3.50	.75
☐ 41 Willie Mays OF	50.00	22.00	5.00
PITTSBURGH PIRATES			
☐ 42 Dick Groat SS	9.00	4.25	.90
☐ 43 Dale Long 1B	7.50	3.50	.75
☐ 44 Johnny O'Brien 2B	7.50	3.50	.75
ST. LOUIS CARDINALS			
☐ 45 Luis Arroyo P	7.50	3.50	.75
☐ 46 Ken Boyer 3B	9.00	4.25	.90
☐ 47 Harvey Haddix P	7.50	3.50	.75
☐ 48 Wally Moon OF	7.50	3.50	.75
BROOKLYN DODGERS			
☐ 49 Sandy Amoros OF	7.50	3.50	.75
☐ 50 Gil Hodges 1B	20.00	9.00	2.00
☐ 51 Jackie Robinson 3B	40.00	18.00	4.00
☐ 52 Duke Snider OF	35.00	16.50	3.50
☐ 53 Karl Spooner P	7.50	3.50	.75
CINCINNATI REDLEGS			
☐ 54 Joe Black P	7.50	3.50	.75
☐ 55 Art Fowler P	7.50	3.50	.75
☐ 56 Ted Kluszewski 1B	9.00	4.25	.90
☐ 57 Roy McMillan SS	7.50	3.50	.75
WASHINGTON SENATORS			
☐ 58 Carlos Paula OF	7.50	3.50	.75
☐ 59 Roy Sievers OF	7.50	3.50	.75
☐ 60 Chuck Stobbs P *	50.00	22.00	5.00

Ward's Sporties

This pin set was put out by Ward Baking Co. around 1934. Each pin measures approximately 1 1/4" in diameter. The color scheme is red, white, and blue. The catalog designation for this eight pin set is PB6.

	MINT	VG-E	F-G
COMPLETE SET	350.00	150.00	30.00
COMMON PLAYER	35.00	16.50	3.50
☐ 1 Dizzy Dean	100.00	45.00	10.00
☐ 2 Jimmie Dykes	35.00	16.50	3.50
☐ 3 Jimmie Foxx	80.00	37.00	8.00
☐ 4 Frank Frisch	60.00	27.00	6.00

☐ 5 Charlie Gehringer	60.00	27.00	6.00
☐ 6 Charlie Grimm	35.00	16.50	3.50
☐ 7 Schoolboy Rowe	35.00	16.50	3.50
☐ 8 Jimmie Wilson	35.00	16.50	3.50

Yellow Basepath Pins

The catalog designation for this 32 pin set is PM-15. This relatively scarce set was probably issued around 1956 judging by the players included. Each pin measures approximately 7/8" in diameter. The front of the pin also contains a green "infield" background with a black and white photo of the player in the center.

	MINT	VG-E	F-G
COMPLETE SET	1000.00	450.00	100.00
COMMON PLAYER	20.00	9.00	2.00
☐ 1 Hank Aaron	100.00	45.00	10.00
☐ 2 Joe Adcock	25.00	11.00	2.50
☐ 3 Luis Aparicio	50.00	22.00	5.00
☐ 4 Richie Ashburn	35.00	16.50	3.50
☐ 5 Gene Baker	20.00	9.00	2.00
☐ 6 Ernie Banks	50.00	22.00	5.00
☐ 7 Yogi Berra	60.00	27.00	6.00
☐ 8 Bill Bruton	20.00	9.00	2.00
☐ 9 Larry Doby	30.00	14.00	3.00
☐ 10 Bob Friend	20.00	9.00	2.00
☐ 11 Nellie Fox	35.00	16.50	3.50
☐ 12 Jim Greengrass	20.00	9.00	2.00
☐ 13 Steve Gromek	20.00	9.00	2.00
☐ 14 Johnny Groth	20.00	9.00	2.00
☐ 15 Gil Hodges	40.00	18.00	4.00
☐ 16 Al Kaline	60.00	27.00	6.00
☐ 17 Ted Kluzewski	30.00	14.00	3.00
(sic, Kluszewski)			
☐ 18 Johnny Logan	20.00	9.00	2.00
☐ 19 Dale Long	20.00	9.00	2.00
☐ 20 Mickey Mantle	200.00	90.00	20.00
☐ 21 Ed Mathews	40.00	18.00	4.00
☐ 22 Orestes Minoso	30.00	14.00	3.00
☐ 23 Stan Musial	100.00	45.00	10.00
☐ 24 Don Newcombe	25.00	11.00	2.50
☐ 25 Bob Porterfield	20.00	9.00	2.00
☐ 26 Pee Wee Reese	50.00	22.00	5.00
☐ 27 Robin Roberts	40.00	18.00	4.00
☐ 28 Red Schoendienst	30.00	14.00	3.00
☐ 29 Duke Snider	80.00	37.00	8.00
☐ 30 Vern Stephens	20.00	9.00	2.00
☐ 31 Gene Woodling	20.00	9.00	2.00
☐ 32 Gus Zernial	20.00	9.00	2.00

The 1943 MP and Co. baseball card set consists of 24 player drawings each measuring 2 11/16" by 2 1/4". This company specialized in producing strips of cards to be sold in candy stores and provided a low quality but persistent challenge to other current sets. These unnumbered cards have been alphabetized and numbered in the checklist below. The ACC designation is R302-1.

	MINT	VG-E	F-G
COMPLETE SET	125.00	55.00	12.50
COMMON PLAYER (1-24)	2.50	1.15	.25
☐ 1 Ernie Bonham	2.50	1.15	.25
☐ 2 Lou Boudreau	6.00	2.80	.60
☐ 3 Dolph Camilli	2.50	1.15	.25
☐ 4 Mort Cooper	2.50	1.15	.25
☐ 5 Walker Cooper	2.50	1.15	.25
☐ 6 Joe Cronin	6.00	2.80	.60
☐ 7 Hank Danning	2.50	1.15	.25
☐ 8 Bill Dickey	8.00	3.75	.80
☐ 9 Joe DiMaggio	30.00	14.00	3.00
☐ 10 Bob Feller	12.00	5.50	1.20
☐ 11 Jimmy Foxx	12.00	5.50	1.20
☐ 12 Hank Greenberg	8.00	3.75	.80
☐ 13 Stan Hack	2.50	1.15	.25
☐ 14 Tom Henrich	3.00	1.40	.30
☐ 15 Carl Hubbell	8.00	3.75	.80
☐ 16 Joe Medwick	6.00	2.80	.60
☐ 17 John Mize	8.00	3.75	.80
☐ 18 Lou Novikoff	2.50	1.15	.25
☐ 19 Mel Ott	8.00	3.75	.80
☐ 20 Pee Wee Reese	12.00	5.50	1.20
☐ 21 Pete Reiser	3.00	1.40	.30
☐ 22 Charlie Ruffing	6.00	2.80	.60
☐ 23 Johnny Vander Meer	3.00	1.40	.30
☐ 24 Ted Williams	20.00	9.00	2.00

R302-2 MP

The 1949 rendition of MP and Co. was basically a re-issue of the 1943 set with different players and numbers on the back. The card fronts are even more washed out than the previous set. Card numbers 104, 118, and 120 are unknown and may be related to the two unnumbered cards found in the set. The ACC also lists this set as W523.

	MINT	VG-E	F-G
COMPLETE SET	125.00	55.00	12.50
COMMON PLAYER (100-126)	2.50	1.15	.25
☐ 100 Lou Boudreau	6.00	2.80	.60
☐ 101 Ted Williams	20.00	9.00	2.00
☐ 102 Buddy Kerr	2.50	1.15	.25
☐ 103 Bob Feller	12.00	5.50	1.20

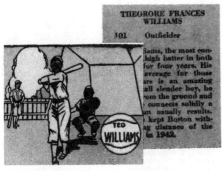

		MINT	VG-E	F-G
☐ 104	Unknown	.00	.00	.00
☐ 105	Joe DiMaggio	30.00	14.00	3.00
☐ 106	Pee Wee Reese	12.00	5.50	1.20
☐ 107	Ferris Fain	2.50	1.15	.25
☐ 108	Andy Pafko	2.50	1.15	.25
☐ 109	Del Ennis	2.50	1.15	.25
☐ 110	Ralph Kiner	8.00	3.75	.80
☐ 111	Nippy Jones	2.50	1.15	.25
☐ 112	Del Rice	2.50	1.15	.25
☐ 113	Hank Sauer	2.50	1.15	.25
☐ 114	Gil Coan	2.50	1.15	.25
☐ 115	Eddie Joost	2.50	1.15	.25
☐ 116	Alvin Dark	3.00	1.40	.30
☐ 117	Larry Berra	12.00	5.50	1.20
☐ 118	Unknown	.00	.00	.00
☐ 119	Bob Lemon	6.00	2.80	.60
☐ 120	Unknown	.00	.00	.00
☐ 121	Johnny Pesky	2.50	1.15	.25
☐ 122	Johnny Sain	3.50	1.65	.35
☐ 123	Hoot Evers	2.50	1.15	.25
☐ 124	Larry Doby	4.00	1.85	.40
UNNUMBERED CARDS				
☐ xxx	Tom Henrich	3.00	1.40	.30
☐ xxx	Al Kozar	2.50	1.15	.25

R303-A Premiums

This series of 48 paper premiums were issued in 1939 by the Goudey Company. Each premium photo measures 4" by 6 3/16". This set carries the name Diamond Stars Gum on the reverse, although the National Chicle Company who produced the Diamond Stars baseball cards is in no way connected with this set. The backs contain instructions on various baseball disciplines. The color of the set is brown, not the more reddish color

of sepia normally listed for this set.

		MINT	VG-E	F-G
COMPLETE SET		800.00	360.00	80.00
COMMON PLAYER		12.00	5.50	1.20
☐ 1	Luke Appling	18.00	8.50	1.80
☐ 2	Earl Averill	18.00	8.50	1.80
☐ 3	Wally Berger	12.00	5.50	1.20
☐ 4	Darrell Blanton	12.00	5.50	1.20
☐ 5	Zeke Bonura	12.00	5.50	1.20
☐ 6	Mace Brown	12.00	5.50	1.20
☐ 7	George Case	12.00	5.50	1.20
☐ 8	Ben Chapman	12.00	5.50	1.20
☐ 9	Joe Cronin	24.00	11.00	2.40
☐ 10	Frank Crosetti	14.00	6.50	1.40
☐ 11	Paul Derringer	14.00	6.50	1.40
☐ 12	Bill Dickey	24.00	11.00	2.40
☐ 13	Joe DiMaggio	125.00	57.00	12.50
☐ 14	Bob Feller	40.00	18.00	4.00
☐ 15	Jimmy Foxx	40.00	18.00	4.00
☐ 16	Charlie Gehringer	24.00	11.00	2.40
☐ 17	Lefty Gomez	24.00	11.00	2.40
☐ 18	Ival Goodman	12.00	5.50	1.20
☐ 19	Joe Gordon	14.00	6.50	1.40
☐ 20	Hank Greenberg	24.00	11.00	2.40
☐ 21	Buddy Hassett	12.00	5.50	1.20
☐ 22	Jeff Heath	12.00	5.50	1.20
☐ 23	Tom Henrich	14.00	6.50	1.40
☐ 24	Billy Herman	18.00	8.50	1.80
☐ 25	Frank Higgins	12.00	5.50	1.20
☐ 26	Fred Hutchinson	14.00	6.50	1.40
☐ 27	Bob Johnson	12.00	5.50	1.20
☐ 28	Ken Keltner	12.00	5.50	1.20
☐ 29	Mike Kreevich	12.00	5.50	1.20
☐ 30	Ernie Lombardi	18.00	8.50	1.80
☐ 31	Gus Mancuso	12.00	5.50	1.20
☐ 32	Eric McNair	12.00	5.50	1.20
☐ 33	Van Mungo	12.00	5.50	1.20
☐ 34	Buck Newsom	12.00	5.50	1.20
☐ 35	Mel Ott	24.00	11.00	2.40
☐ 36	Marvin Owen	12.00	5.50	1.20
☐ 37	Frankie Pytlak	12.00	5.50	1.20
☐ 38	Woody Rich	12.00	5.50	1.20
☐ 39	Charlie Root	12.00	5.50	1.20
☐ 40	Al Simmons	18.00	8.50	1.80
☐ 41	Jim Tabor	12.00	5.50	1.20
☐ 42	Cecil Travis	12.00	5.50	1.20
☐ 43	Hal Trosky	12.00	5.50	1.20
☐ 44	Arky Vaughn	18.00	8.50	1.80
☐ 45	Joe Vosmik	12.00	5.50	1.20
☐ 46	Lon Warneke	12.00	5.50	1.20
☐ 47	Ted Williams	60.00	27.00	6.00
☐ 48	Rudy York	12.00	5.50	1.20

R303-B Premiums

This set of 24 paper photos is slightly larger than its counterpart R303-A and was also issued in 1939. Each premium photo measures 4 3/4" by 7 5/16". The photos of R303-A series are the same ones depicted on these cards, and the reverses contain "How to" instructions and the Diamond Stars Gum name. The photos are the same as R303-A. This set comes in two distinct colors, black and sepia.

		MINT	VG-E	F-G
COMPLETE SET		400.00	180.00	40.00
COMMON PLAYER		10.00	4.75	1.00
☐ 1	Luke Appling	16.00	7.50	1.60
☐ 2	George Case	10.00	4.75	1.00
☐ 3	Ben Chapman	10.00	4.75	1.00
☐ 4	Joe Cronin	20.00	9.00	2.00
☐ 5	Bill Dickey	25.00	11.00	2.50
☐ 6	Joe DiMaggio	90.00	42.00	9.00
☐ 7	Bob Feller	35.00	16.50	3.50
☐ 8	Jimmy Foxx	35.00	16.50	3.50
☐ 9	Lefty Gomez	25.00	11.00	2.50
☐ 10	Ival Goodman	10.00	4.75	1.00
☐ 11	Joe Gordon	12.00	5.50	1.20
☐ 12	Hank Greenberg	20.00	9.00	2.00
☐ 13	Jeff Heath	10.00	4.75	1.00

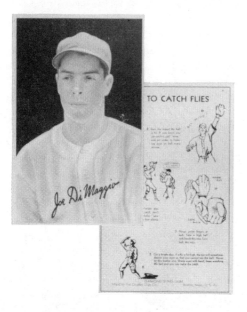

TO CATCH FLIES

☐ 14	Billy Herman	16.00	7.50	1.60
☐ 15	Frank Higgins	10.00	4.75	1.00
☐ 16	Ken Keltner	10.00	4.75	1.00
☐ 17	Mike Kreevich	10.00	4.75	1.00
☐ 18	Ernie Lombardi	16.00	7.50	1.60
☐ 19	Gus Mancuso	10.00	4.75	1.00
☐ 20	Mel Ott	25.00	11.00	2.50
☐ 21	Al Simmons	16.00	7.50	1.60
☐ 22	Arky Vaughn	16.00	7.50	1.60
☐ 23	Joe Vosmik	10.00	4.75	1.00
☐ 24	Rudy York	10.00	4.75	1.00

☐ 154	Al Simmons	60.00	27.00	6.00
☐ 155	Gordon Cochrane	75.00	35.00	7.50
☐ 156	Woody English	40.00	18.00	4.00
☐ 157	"Chuck" Klein	50.00	22.00	5.00
☐ 158	Dick Bartell	40.00	18.00	4.00
☐ 159	Pepper Martin	50.00	22.00	5.00
☐ 160	Earl Averill	60.00	27.00	6.00
☐ 161	William Dickey	75.00	35.00	7.50
☐ 162	Wesley Ferrell	40.00	18.00	4.00
☐ 163	Oral Hildebrand	40.00	18.00	4.00
☐ 164	William Kamm	40.00	18.00	4.00
☐ 165	Earl Whitehill	40.00	18.00	4.00
☐ 166	Charles Fullis	40.00	18.00	4.00
☐ 167	Jimmy Dykes	40.00	18.00	4.00
☐ 168	Ben Cantwell	40.00	18.00	4.00
☐ 169	George Earnshaw	40.00	18.00	4.00
☐ 170	Jackson Stephenson	40.00	18.00	4.00
☐ 171	Randolph Moore	40.00	18.00	4.00
☐ 172	Ted Lyons	60.00	27.00	6.00
☐ 173	Goose Goslin	60.00	27.00	6.00
☐ 174	Evar Swanson	40.00	18.00	4.00
☐ 175	Leroy Mahaffey	40.00	18.00	4.00
☐ 176	Joe Cronin	60.00	27.00	6.00
☐ 177	Tom Bridges	40.00	18.00	4.00
☐ 178	Henry Manush	60.00	27.00	6.00
☐ 179	Walter Stewart	40.00	18.00	4.00
☐ 180	Frank Pytlak	40.00	18.00	4.00
☐ 181	Dale Alexander	40.00	18.00	4.00
☐ 182	Robert Grove	75.00	35.00	7.50
☐ 183	Charles Gehringer	75.00	35.00	7.50
☐ 184	Lewis Fonseca	40.00	18.00	4.00
☐ 185	Alvin Crowder	40.00	18.00	4.00
☐ 186	Mickey Cochrane	75.00	35.00	7.50
☐ 187	Max Bishop	40.00	18.00	4.00
☐ 188	Connie Mack	75.00	35.00	7.50
☐ 189	Guy Bush	40.00	18.00	4.00
☐ 190	Charlie Root	40.00	18.00	4.00
☐ 191	Burleigh Grimes	60.00	27.00	6.00
☐ 192	Pat Malone	40.00	18.00	4.00
☐ 193	Woody English	40.00	18.00	4.00
☐ 194	Lonnie Warneke	40.00	18.00	4.00
☐ 195	Babe Herman	50.00	22.00	5.00
☐ 200	Gabby Hartnett	60.00	27.00	6.00
☐ 201	Paul Waner	60.00	27.00	6.00
☐ 202	Dizzy Dean	100.00	45.00	10.00
☐ 205	Jim Bottomley	60.00	27.00	6.00
☐ 207	Charles Hafey	60.00	27.00	6.00

R308 Self Develop

These very small (1 1/4" by 1 7/8") and unattractive cards are very scarce. They were produced by Tattoo Orbit around 1933. The set is presumed to include the numbers between 151 and 210; a few of the numbers are still unknown at this time. Badly over exposed cards are very difficult to identify and are considered (graded) fair at best.

	MINT	VG-E	F-G
COMPLETE SET	2500.00	1100.00	200.00
COMMON PLAYER	40.00	18.00	4.00
☐ 151 Vernon Gomez	75.00	35.00	7.50
☐ 152 Kiki Cuyler	60.00	27.00	6.00
☐ 153 Jimmy Foxx	100.00	45.00	10.00

R309-1 Goudey Premiums

The most ambitious premium issue of the Goudey Gum Company was the R309-1 set of 1934. Printed on heavy cardboard, the black , white picture was embellished with a gold, frame-like border and a back stand. Each of these thick cards measures 5 1/2" by 8 15/16".

	MINT	VG-E	F-G
COMPLETE SET	750.00	350.00	75.00
COMMON PLAYER (1-4)	150.00	70.00	15.00
☐ 1 American League All-Stars of 1933	150.00	70.00	15.00
☐ 2 National League All-Stars of 1933	150.00	70.00	15.00
☐ 3 World's Champions	200.00	90.00	20.00

of 1933
☐ 4 George Herman 300.00 130.00 30.00
      (Babe) Ruth

R309-2 Goudey Premiums

The cards in the R309-2 Goudey Premium set are unnumbered, glossy black and white photos on thin paper stock. Teams (1-3) and individual players (4-18) are featured in this relatively scarce premium set from 1935. The ballplayer is identified by his name rendered in longhand in the "wide pen" style of later Goudey issues. This written name is not a facsimile autograph. Each card measures 5 1/2" by 9".

	MINT	VG-E	F-G
COMPLETE SET	1000.00	450.00	100.00
COMMON PLAYER (1-18)	50.00	22.00	5.00
☐ 1 Boston Red Sox	50.00	22.00	5.00
☐ 2 Cleveland Indians	50.00	22.00	5.00
☐ 3 Washington Senators	50.00	22.00	5.00
☐ 4 Elden Auker	50.00	22.00	5.00
☐ 5 Johnny Babich	50.00	22.00	5.00
☐ 6 Dick Bartell	50.00	22.00	5.00
☐ 7 Lester R. Bell	50.00	22.00	5.00
☐ 8 Wally Berger	50.00	22.00	5.00
☐ 9 Mickey Cochrane	100.00	45.00	10.00
☐ 10 Ervin Fox	50.00	22.00	5.00
☐ 11 Vernon Gomez	100.00	45.00	10.00
☐ 12 Leon "Goose" Goslin	75.00	35.00	7.50
☐ 13 Hank Greenberg	100.00	45.00	10.00
☐ 14 Oscar Melillo	50.00	22.00	5.00
☐ 15 Mel Ott	100.00	45.00	10.00
☐ 16 Schoolboy Rowe	50.00	22.00	5.00
☐ 17 Vito Tamulis	50.00	22.00	5.00
☐ 18 Gerald Walker	50.00	22.00	5.00

R310 Butterfinger

This large-size premium set comes either in paper or on heavy cardboard stock with advertising for Butterfinger or other candy at the top. The heavy cardboard Butterfinger display advertising cards are

valued at double the prices in the list below. The cards are unnumbered and Foxx exists as Fox or Foxx. The ACC designation is R310. The cards measure 7 3/4" by 9 3/4" and have a thick off-white border around the player photo.

	MINT	VG-E	F-G
COMPLETE SET	750.00	350.00	75.00
COMMON PLAYER (1-65)	9.00	4.25	.90
☐ 1 Earl Averill	16.00	7.50	1.60
☐ 2 Richard Bartell	9.00	4.25	.90
☐ 3 Lawrence Benton	9.00	4.25	.90
☐ 4 Walter Berger	9.00	4.25	.90
☐ 5 Jim Bottomley	16.00	7.50	1.60
☐ 6 Ralph Boyle	9.00	4.25	.90
☐ 7 Tex Carleton	9.00	4.25	.90
☐ 8 Owen T. Carroll	9.00	4.25	.90
☐ 9 Ben Chapman	9.00	4.25	.90
☐ 10 Mickey Cochrane	20.00	9.00	2.00
☐ 11 James Collins	9.00	4.25	.90
☐ 12 Joe Cronin	20.00	9.00	2.00
☐ 13 Alvin Crowder	9.00	4.25	.90
☐ 14 "Dizzy" Dean	40.00	18.00	4.00
☐ 15 Paul Derringer	9.00	4.25	.90
☐ 16 William Dickey	20.00	9.00	2.00
☐ 17 Leo Durocher	16.00	7.50	1.60
☐ 18 George Earnshaw	9.00	4.25	.90
☐ 19 Richard Ferrell	16.00	7.50	1.60
☐ 20 Lew Fonseca	9.00	4.25	.90
☐ 21A Jimmy Fox (sic, Foxx)	40.00	18.00	4.00
☐ 21B Jimmy Foxx	40.00	18.00	4.00
☐ 22 Benny Frey	9.00	4.25	.90
☐ 23 Frankie Frisch	20.00	9.00	2.00
☐ 24 Lou Gehrig	60.00	27.00	6.00
☐ 25 Chas. Gehringer	20.00	9.00	2.00
☐ 26 Vernon Gomez	20.00	9.00	2.00
☐ 27 Ray Grabowski	9.00	4.25	.90
☐ 28 Robert Grove	25.00	11.00	2.50
☐ 29 George (Mule) Haas	9.00	4.25	.90
☐ 30 "Chick" Hafey	16.00	7.50	1.60
☐ 31 Stanley Harris	16.00	7.50	1.60
☐ 32 Francis J. Hogan	9.00	4.25	.90
☐ 33 Ed Holley	9.00	4.25	.90
☐ 34 Rogers Hornsby	35.00	16.50	3.50
☐ 35 Waite Hoyt	16.00	7.50	1.60
☐ 36 Walter Johnson	40.00	18.00	4.00
☐ 37 Jim Jordan	9.00	4.25	.90
☐ 38 Joe Kuhel	9.00	4.25	.90
☐ 39 Hal Lee	9.00	4.25	.90
☐ 40 Gus Mancuso	9.00	4.25	.90
☐ 41 Henry Manush	16.00	7.50	1.60
☐ 42 Fred Marberry	9.00	4.25	.90
☐ 43 Pepper Martin	12.00	5.50	1.20
☐ 44 Oscar Melillo	9.00	4.25	.90
☐ 45 Johnny Moore	9.00	4.25	.90
☐ 46 Joe Morrisey	9.00	4.25	.90
☐ 47 Joe Mowrey	9.00	4.25	.90
☐ 48 Bob O'Farrell	9.00	4.25	.90
☐ 49 Melvin Ott	25.00	11.00	2.50

☐ 50 Monte Pearson	9.00	4.25	.90
☐ 51 Carl Reynolds	9.00	4.25	.90
☐ 52 Chas. Ruffing	16.00	7.50	1.60
☐ 53 "Babe" Ruth	90.00	42.00	9.00
☐ 54 John "Blondy" Ryan	9.00	4.25	.90
☐ 55 Al Simmons	16.00	7.50	1.60
☐ 56 Al Spohrer	9.00	4.25	.90
☐ 57 Gus Suhr	9.00	4.25	.90
☐ 58 Steve Swetonic	9.00	4.25	.90
☐ 59 Dazzy Vance	16.00	7.50	1.60
☐ 60 Joe Vosmik	9.00	4.25	.90
☐ 61 Lloyd Waner	16.00	7.50	1.60
☐ 62 Paul Waner	16.00	7.50	1.60
☐ 63 Sam West	9.00	4.25	.90
☐ 64 Earl Whitehill	9.00	4.25	.90
☐ 65 Jimmy Wilson	9.00	4.25	.90

R311 Premiums

Gordon S. "Mickey" Cochrane

The 1936 R311 set of Portraits and Team Baseball Photos exist in two different forms, each measuring 6" by 8". Fifteen leather-like or uneven surface cards comprise the first type. Twenty eight glossy surface, sepia or black and white cards comprise the second type. The Boston Red Sox team exists with or without a sky above the building at the right of the card. Scarcities within the glossy subset include Pepper Martin, Mel Harder, Schoolboy Rowe, and the Dodgers, Pirates, Braves, and Columbus team cards; these are asterisked in the checklist below.

	MINT	VG-E	F-G
COMPLETE SET	1100.00	500.00	100.00
COMMON PLAYER (LEATHER)	20.00	9.00	2.00
COMMON PLAYER (GLOSSY)	10.00	4.75	1.00

LEATHERY

☐ L1 Paul Derringer	20.00	9.00	2.00
☐ L2 West Ferrell	20.00	9.00	2.00
☐ L3 Jimmy Foxx	50.00	22.00	5.00
☐ L4 Charlie Gehringer	40.00	18.00	4.00
☐ L5 Mel Harder	20.00	9.00	2.00
☐ L6 Gabby Hartnett	30.00	14.00	3.00
☐ L7 Rogers Hornsby	50.00	22.00	5.00

☐ L8 Connie Mack	40.00	18.00	4.00
☐ L9 Van Mungo	20.00	9.00	2.00
☐ L10 Steve O'Neill	20.00	9.00	2.00
☐ L11 Charles Ruffing	30.00	14.00	3.00
☐ L12 Joe DiMaggio Frank Crosetti Tony Lazzeri	100.00	45.00	10.00
☐ L13 Arky Vaughn and Honus Wagner	50.00	22.00	5.00
☐ L14 American League Pennant Winners 1935	20.00	9.00	2.00
☐ L15 National League Pennant Winners 1935	20.00	9.00	2.00

GLOSSY PHOTOS

☐ G1 Earl Averill	18.00	8.50	1.80
☐ G2 James L. "Jim" Bottomley	18.00	8.50	1.80
☐ G3 Gordon S. "Mickey" Cochrane	25.00	11.00	2.50
☐ G4 Joe Cronin	21.00	9.50	2.10
☐ G5 Jerome "Dizzy" Dean	40.00	18.00	4.00
☐ G6 Jimmy Dykes	10.00	4.75	1.00
☐ G7 Jimmy Foxx	40.00	18.00	4.00
☐ G8 Frankie Frisch	21.00	9.50	2.10
☐ G9 Henry "Hank" Greenberg	21.00	9.50	2.10
☐ G10 Mel Harder *	20.00	9.00	2.00
☐ G11 Ken Keltner	10.00	4.75	1.00
☐ G12 Pepper Martin *	40.00	18.00	4.00
☐ G13 Lynwood "Schoolboy" Rowe *	20.00	9.00	2.00
☐ G14 William "Bill" Terry	21.00	9.50	2.10
☐ G15 Harold "Pie" Traynor	18.00	8.50	1.80
☐ G16 American League All Stars - 1935	12.00	5.50	1.20
☐ G17 American League Pennant Winners 1934 (Detroit Tigers)	12.00	5.50	1.20
☐ G18 Boston Braves 1935 *	50.00	22.00	5.00
☐ G19A Boston Red Sox (with sky above building at right of the card)	12.00	5.50	1.20
☐ G19B Boston Red Sox (without sky)	12.00	5.50	1.20
☐ G20 Brooklyn Dodgers 1935 *	50.00	22.00	5.00
☐ G21 Chicago White Sox 1935	12.00	5.50	1.20
☐ G22 Columbus Red Birds 1934 Pennant Winners of Amer. Assoc. *	20.00	9.00	2.00
☐ G23 National League All Stars 1934	12.00	5.50	1.20
☐ G24 National League Champions 1935 (Chicago Cubs)	12.00	5.50	1.20
☐ G25 New York Yankees	12.00	5.50	1.20
☐ G26 Pittsburgh Pirates 1935 *	20.00	9.00	2.00
☐ G27 St. Louis Browns 1935	12.00	5.50	1.20
☐ G28 World Champions 1934 (St. Louis Cardinals)	12.00	5.50	1.20

R312 Photos

The 1936 R312 Baseball Photos set contains 25 color tinted, single player cards, listed with the letter A in the checklist; 14 multiple player cards, listed with the letter B in the checklist; 6 action cards with handwritten signatures, listed with the letter C in the checklist; and 5 action cards with printed titles, listed with the letter D in the checklist. The pictures are reminiscent of a water-color type painting in soft pastels. The Allen card is reportedly more difficult to obtain than other cards in the set.

	MINT	VG-E	F-G
COMPLETE SET	800.00	360.00	80.00
COMMON CARDS	12.00	5.50	1.20

☐ A1 John Thomas Allen	18.00	8.50	1.80
☐ A2 Cy Blanton	12.00	5.50	1.20
☐ A3 Mace Brown	12.00	5.50	1.20
☐ A4 Dolph Camilli	12.00	5.50	1.20

	"Big Jim" Weaver	18.00	8.50	1.80
☐ C1	Nick Altrock and	12.00	5.50	1.20
	Al Schacht: Clowning on the Diamond			
☐ C2	Bell (St. Louis)	12.00	5.50	1.20
	"Out At First" "Zeke" Bonura (first baseman)			
☐ C3	Jim Collins (Safe) and Stan Hack	12.00	5.50	1.20
☐ C4	Jimmie Foxx (batting with Luke Sewell catching)	18.00	8.50	1.80
☐ C5	(Al) Lopez Traps Two Cubs on Third Base	18.00	8.50	1.80
☐ C6	"Pie" Traynor and Augie Galan	18.00	8.50	1.80
☐ D1	Alvin Crowder after victory in the World Series	12.00	5.50	1.20
☐ D2	Floyd Vaughn present Pirate Shortstop and Coach Hans Wagner	18.00	8.50	1.80
☐ D3	Gabby Hartnett (crossing home plate after hitting homer...	18.00	8.50	1.80
☐ D4	Kids flock around Schoolboy Rowe as he leaves Cubs park...	12.00	5.50	1.20
☐ D5	Van Atta, St. Louis pitcher out at plate (Rick Ferrell, Boston, catching)	12.00	5.50	1.20

R313 Fine Pens

☐ A5	Gordon Cochrane	21.00	9.50	2.10
☐ A6	"Rip" Collins	12.00	5.50	1.20
☐ A7	Ki Ki Cuyler	18.00	8.50	1.80
☐ A8	Bill Dickey	25.00	11.00	2.50
☐ A9	Joe DiMaggio	125.00	57.00	12.50
☐ A10	"Chas." Dressen	12.00	5.50	1.20
☐ A11	Benny Frey	12.00	5.50	1.20
☐ A12	Hank Greenberg	21.00	9.50	2.10
☐ A13	Mel Harder	12.00	5.50	1.20
☐ A14	Rogers Hornsby	40.00	18.00	4.00
☐ A15	Ernie Lombardi	18.00	8.50	1.80
☐ A16	Pepper Martin	14.00	6.50	1.40
☐ A17	"Johnny" Mize	21.00	9.50	2.10
☐ A18	Van L. Mungo	12.00	5.50	1.20
☐ A19	Bud Parmalee	12.00	5.50	1.20
☐ A20	Chas. Ruffing	18.00	8.50	1.80
☐ A21	Eugene Schott	12.00	5.50	1.20
☐ A22	Casey Stengel	40.00	18.00	4.00
☐ A23	Bill Sullivan	12.00	5.50	1.20
☐ A24	Bill Swift	12.00	5.50	1.20
☐ A25	Ralph Winegarner	12.00	5.50	1.20
☐ B1	Ollie Bejma and Rollie Hemsley	12.00	5.50	1.20
☐ B2	Cliff Bolton and Earl Whitehill	12.00	5.50	1.20
☐ B3	Stan Bordagaray and George Earnshaw	12.00	5.50	1.20
☐ B4	Billy Herman, Phil Cavarretta, Stan Hack, and Bill Jurges	12.00	5.50	1.20
☐ B5	Pete "JoJo" Fox, Goose Goslin, and Jo Jo White	12.00	5.50	1.20
☐ B6	Billy Herman, Augie Galan, Fred Lindstrom, Gabby Hartnett, and five others	12.00	5.50	1.20
☐ B7	Bucky Harris and Joe Cronin	18.00	8.50	1.80
☐ B8	Gabby Hartnett and Lon Warneke (sic, Warneke)	12.00	5.50	1.20
☐ B9	Myril Hoag and Lefty Gomez	18.00	8.50	1.80
☐ B10	Allen Lothoron- Rogers Hornsby	18.00	8.50	1.80
☐ B11	Connie Mack and Lefty Grove	35.00	16.50	3.50
☐ B12	Taylor, Tris Speaker, and Kiki Cuyler	18.00	8.50	1.80
☐ B13	Walker, Mule Haas, and Mike Kreevich	12.00	5.50	1.20
☐ B14	Paul Waner, Lloyd Waner, and			

The 1936 Fine Pen Premiums were issued anonymously by the National Chicle Company. The set is complete at 120 cards. Each card measures 3 1/4" by 5 3/8". The cards are blank backed, unnumbered and among the those premiums that could be obtained directly from a retail outlet rather than through the mail only. Four types of cards exist. Cards portraying but one player are listed with the letter A in the checklist; cards which portray several players are listed with a B in the checklist; cards which feature action poses are listed with a C in the checklist. The ACC designation is R313.

	MINT	VG-E	F-G
COMPLETE SET (120)	650.00	300.00	65.00
COMMON CARDS (A)	3.00	1.40	.30
COMMON CARDS (B)	4.00	1.85	.40
COMMON CARDS (C)	4.00	1.85	.40

		MINT	VG-E	F-G
☐ A1	Melo Almada	3.00	1.40	.30
☐ A2	Paul Andrews	3.00	1.40	.30
☐ A3	Elden Auker	3.00	1.40	.30
☐ A4	Earl Averill	6.00	2.80	.60
☐ A5	Jim Becher	3.00	1.40	.30
☐ A6	Moe Berg	3.00	1.40	.30
☐ A7	Walter Berger	3.00	1.40	.30
☐ A8	Charles Berry	3.00	1.40	.30
☐ A9	Ralph Birkhofer	3.00	1.40	.30
☐ A10	"Cy" Blanton	3.00	1.40	.30
☐ A11	O. Bluege	3.00	1.40	.30
☐ A12	Cliff Bolton	3.00	1.40	.30
☐ A13	Zeke Bonura	3.00	1.40	.30
☐ A14	Thos. Bridges	3.00	1.40	.30
☐ A15	Sam Byrd	3.00	1.40	.30
☐ A16	Dolph Camilli	3.00	1.40	.30
☐ A17	Bruce Campbell	3.00	1.40	.30
☐ A18	Walter "Kit" Carson	3.00	1.40	.30
☐ A19	Ben Chapman	3.00	1.40	.30
☐ A20	"Rip" Collins	3.00	1.40	.30
☐ A21	Joe Cronin	8.00	3.75	.80
☐ A22	Frank Crosetti	4.00	1.85	.40
☐ A23	Paul Derringer	3.00	1.40	.30
☐ A24	Bill Dietrich	3.00	1.40	.30
☐ A25	Carl Doyle	3.00	1.40	.30
☐ A26	Pete Fox	3.00	1.40	.30
☐ A27	Frankie Frisch	8.00	3.75	.80
☐ A28	Milton Galatzer	3.00	1.40	.30
☐ A29	Chas. Gehringer	8.00	3.75	.80
☐ A30	Charley Gelbert	3.00	1.40	.30
☐ A31	Jose Gomez	3.00	1.40	.30
☐ A32	Vernon Gomez	8.00	3.75	.80
☐ A33	Leon Goslin	6.00	2.80	.60
☐ A34	Hank Gowdy	3.00	1.40	.30
☐ A35	"Hank" Greenberg	8.00	3.75	.80
☐ A36	"Lefty" Grove	10.00	4.75	1.00
☐ A37	Stan Hack	3.00	1.40	.30
☐ A38	Odell Hale	3.00	1.40	.30
☐ A39	Wild Bill Hallahan	3.00	1.40	.30
☐ A40	Mel Harder	3.00	1.40	.30
☐ A41	Stanley Bucky Harris	5.00	2.35	.50
☐ A42	Frank Higgins	3.00	1.40	.30
☐ A43	Oral C. Hildebrand	3.00	1.40	.30
☐ A44	Myril Hoag	3.00	1.40	.30
☐ A45	Rogers Hornsby	15.00	7.00	1.50
☐ A46	Waite Hoyt	6.00	2.80	.60
☐ A47	Willis G. Hudlin (2)	3.00	1.40	.30
☐ A48	"Woody" Jensen (2)	3.00	1.40	.30
☐ A49	Wm. Knickerbocker	3.00	1.40	.30
☐ A50	Joseph Kuhel	3.00	1.40	.30
☐ A51	Cookie Lavagetto	3.00	1.40	.30
☐ A52	Thornton Lee	3.00	1.40	.30
☐ A53	Red Lucas	3.00	1.40	.30
☐ A54	Pepper Martin	4.00	1.85	.40
☐ A55	Joe Medwick	7.00	3.25	.70
☐ A56	Oscar Melillo	3.00	1.40	.30
☐ A57	"Buddy" Meyer	3.00	1.40	.30
☐ A58	Wallace Moses	3.00	1.40	.30
☐ A59	V. Mungo	3.00	1.40	.30
☐ A60	Lamar Newsom	3.00	1.40	.30
☐ A61	Lewis "Buck" Newsom	3.00	1.40	.30
☐ A62	Steve O'Neill	3.00	1.40	.30
☐ A63	Tommie Padden	3.00	1.40	.30
☐ A64	E. Babe Phillips	3.00	1.40	.30
☐ A65	Bill Rogel (sic, Rogell)	3.00	1.40	.30
☐ A66	Lynn "Schoolboy" Rowe	4.00	1.85	.40
☐ A67	Al Simmons	7.00	3.25	.70
☐ A68	Leon "Moose" Solters	3.00	1.40	.30
☐ A69	Casey Stengel	15.00	7.00	1.50
☐ A70	Bill Swift	3.00	1.40	.30
☐ A71	Cecil Travis	3.00	1.40	.30
☐ A72	"Pie" Traynor	7.00	3.25	.70
☐ A73	Wm. Urbansky	3.00	1.40	.30
☐ A74	Arky Vaughn	6.00	2.80	.60
☐ A75	Joe Vosmik	3.00	1.40	.30
☐ A76	Honus Wagner	15.00	7.00	1.50
☐ A77	Rube Walberg	3.00	1.40	.30
☐ A78	Bill Walker	3.00	1.40	.30
☐ A79	Gerald Walker	3.00	1.40	.30
☐ A80	Bill Werber	3.00	1.40	.30

		MINT	VG-E	F-G
☐ A81	Sam West	3.00	1.40	.30
☐ A82	Pinkey Whitney	3.00	1.40	.30
☐ A83	Vernon Whitshire	3.00	1.40	.30
☐ A84	"Pep" Young	3.00	1.40	.30
☐ B1	Babe and his babes	4.00	1.85	.40
☐ B2	Stan Bordagaray and Geo. Earnshaw	4.00	1.85	.40
☐ B3	James Bucher and John Babich	4.00	1.85	.40
☐ B4	Ben Chapman and Bill Werber	4.00	1.85	.40
☐ B5	Chicago White Sox 1936	4.00	1.85	.40
☐ B6	Fence Busters	4.00	1.85	.40
☐ B7	Pete Fox, Al Simmons, and Mickey Cochrane	12.00	5.50	1.20
☐ B8	"Gabby" (Hartnett) and "KiKi" (Cuyler)	12.00	5.50	1.20
☐ B9	Lefty Gomez and Red Ruffing	12.00	5.50	1.20
☐ B10	Gabby Hartnett and Lon Warneke	6.00	2.80	.60
☐ B11	Diamond Daddies: Connie Mack and John McGraw	20.00	9.00	2.00
☐ B12	Capt. Bill Myer and Mgr. Chas. Dressen	4.00	1.85	.40
☐ B13	Paul and Lloyd Waner and Big Jim Weaver	8.00	3.75	.80
☐ B14	Wes and Rick (Ferrell)	8.00	3.75	.80
☐ C1	Nick Altrock and Al Schacht	4.00	1.85	.40
☐ C2	Big Bosses Clash - Dykes safe	4.00	1.85	.40
☐ C3	Bottomley tagging Gelbert	4.00	1.85	.40
☐ C4	Camilli catches Jurges off first	4.00	1.85	.40
☐ C5	CCS: Radcliffe safe Harnett catching	4.00	1.85	.40
☐ C6	CCS: L.Sewell blocks runner at plate	4.00	1.85	.40
☐ C7	CCS: Washington safe	4.00	1.85	.40
☐ C8	Joe DiMaggio slams it, Erickson catching	50.00	22.00	5.00
☐ C9	Double Play-McQuinn to Stine	4.00	1.85	.40
☐ C10	Dykes catches Crossetti between 2nd and 3rd	4.00	1.85	.40
☐ C11	Glenn uses football play at plate	4.00	1.85	.40
☐ C12	Greenberg doubles Dickey catching	10.00	4.75	1.00
☐ C13	Hassett makes the out	4.00	1.85	.40
☐ C14	Lombardi says "Ugh"	8.00	3.75	.80
☐ C15	McQuinn gets his man	4.00	1.85	.40
☐ C16	Randy Moore hurt stealing second	4.00	1.85	.40
☐ C17	T. Moore out at plate Wilson catching	4.00	1.85	.40
☐ C18	Sewell waits for ball while Clift scores	4.00	1.85	.40
☐ C19	Talking it over	4.00	1.85	.40
☐ C20	There she goes CCS	4.00	1.85	.40
☐ C21	Ump says "No" Cleveland vs. Detroit	4.00	1.85	.40
☐ C22	Lloyd Waner at bat, Gabby Hartnett behind plate	8.00	3.75	.80
☐ C23	World Series 1935, Goslin out at first	8.00	3.75	.80

R313A Gold Medal

The 1935 Gold Medal Flour series is complete at 12 cards. They were issued to commemorate the World Series of 1934 which featured the Detroit Tigers and the St. Louis Cardinals. Each card measures 3 1/4" by 5 3/8". The cards are blank backed and unnumbered. The catalog designation is R313A.

	MINT	VG-E	F-G
COMPLETE SET (12)	200.00	90.00	20.00
COMMON CARDS	12.00	5.50	1.20

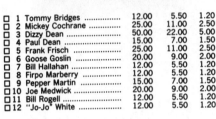

☐	1	Tommy Bridges	12.00	5.50	1.20
☐	2	Mickey Cochrane	25.00	11.00	2.50
☐	3	Dizzy Dean	50.00	22.00	5.00
☐	4	Paul Dean	15.00	7.00	1.50
☐	5	Frank Frisch	25.00	11.00	2.50
☐	6	Goose Goslin	20.00	9.00	2.00
☐	7	Bill Hallahan	12.00	5.50	1.20
☐	8	Firpo Marberry	12.00	5.50	1.20
☐	9	Pepper Martin	15.00	7.00	1.50
☐	10	Joe Medwick	20.00	9.00	2.00
☐	11	Bill Rogell	12.00	5.50	1.20
☐	12	"Jo-Jo" White	12.00	5.50	1.20

R314 Wide Pens

The 1936 Wide Pen Premiums were issued by the Goudey Gum Company. Each card measures 3 1/4" by 5 1/2". These black and white, unnumbered cards could be obtained directly from a retail outlet rather than through the mail only. Some of the cards are horizontally (HOR) oriented and are so indicated. Four types of this card exist. Type A contains cards, mainly individual players, with "Litho USA" in the bottom border. Type B does not have the "Litho USA" marking and comes both with and without a border. Type C cards are American players on creamy paper stock with medium thickness signatures and no "Litho USA" markings. Type D consists of Canadian players from Montreal (M) or Toronto (T) on creamy stock paper with non-glossy photos. The ACC designation is R314.

	MINT	VG-E	F-G
COMPLETE SET	1100.00	45.00	10.00
COMMON CARD (A)	3.00	1.40	.30
COMMON CARD (B)	4.50	2.10	.45
COMMON CARD (C)	4.50	2.10	.45
COMMON CARD (D)	10.00	4.75	1.00

☐ A1	Ethan Allen	3.00	1.40	.30
☐ A2	Earl Averill	6.00	2.80	.60
☐ A3	Dick Bartell HOR	3.00	1.40	.30
☐ A4	Dick Bartell (portrait)	6.00	2.80	.60
☐ A5	Walter Berger	3.00	1.40	.30
☐ A6	Geo. Blaeholder	3.00	1.40	.30

☐ A7	"Cy" Blanton (portrait)	3.00	1.40	.30
☐ A8	"Cliff" Bolton	3.00	1.40	.30
☐ A9	Stan Bordagaray	3.00	1.40	.30
☐ A10	Tommy Bridges (portrait)	3.00	1.40	.30
☐ A11	Bill Brubaker	3.00	1.40	.30
☐ A12	Sam Byrd	3.00	1.40	.30
☐ A13	Dolph Camilli	3.00	1.40	.30
☐ A14	Clydell Castleman (throwing)	3.00	1.40	.30
☐ A15	Clydell Castleman (portrait)	3.00	1.40	.30
☐ A16	Phil Cavaretta HOR	3.00	1.40	.30
☐ A17	"Mickey" Cochrane	12.00	5.50	1.20
☐ A18	Earl Coombs HOR	8.00	3.75	.80
☐ A19	Joe Coscarart	3.00	1.40	.30
☐ A20	Joe Cronin	8.00	3.75	.80
☐ A21	Frank Crosetti	4.00	1.85	.40
☐ A22	Tony Cuccinello	3.00	1.40	.30
☐ A23	"KiKi" Cuyler	6.00	2.80	.60
☐ A24	Curt Davis	3.00	1.40	.30
☐ A25	Virgil Davis HOR	3.00	1.40	.30
☐ A26	Paul Derringer	3.00	1.40	.30
☐ A27	"Bill" Dickey	12.00	5.50	1.20
☐ A28	Jimmy Dykes (kneeling)	3.00	1.40	.30
☐ A29	"Rick" Ferrell HOR	6.00	2.80	.60
☐ A30	Wes Ferrell	4.00	1.85	.40
☐ A31	Lou Finney	3.00	1.40	.30
☐ A32	Ervin "Pete" Fox (portrait)	3.00	1.40	.30
☐ A33	Tony Freitas	3.00	1.40	.30
☐ A34	Lonnie Frey	3.00	1.40	.30
☐ A35	Frankie Frisch	8.00	3.75	.80
☐ A36	"Augie" Galan (portrait)	3.00	1.40	.30
☐ A37	Charles Gehringer	8.00	3.75	.80
☐ A38	Charlie Gelbert	3.00	1.40	.30
☐ A39	"Lefty" Gomez	10.00	4.75	1.00
☐ A40	"Goose" Goslin	6.00	2.80	.60
☐ A41	Earl Grace	3.00	1.40	.30
☐ A42	Hank Greenberg (portrait)	8.00	3.75	.80
☐ A43	"Mule" Haas	3.00	1.40	.30
☐ A44	Odell Hale	3.00	1.40	.30
☐ A45	Bill Hallahan	3.00	1.40	.30
☐ A46	"Mel" Harder	3.00	1.40	.30
☐ A47	"Bucky" Harris	5.00	2.35	.50
☐ A48	"Gabby" Hartnett	20.00	9.00	2.00
☐ A49	Ray Hayworth	3.00	1.40	.30
☐ A50	Rolly Hemsley	3.00	1.40	.30
☐ A51	Babe Herman	4.00	1.85	.40
☐ A52	Frank Higgins (portrait)	3.00	1.40	.30
☐ A53	Oral Hildebrand	3.00	1.40	.30
☐ A54	Myril Hoag	3.00	1.40	.30

A55	Waite Hoyt	6.00	2.80	.60
A56	Woody Jensen	3.00	1.40	.30
A57	Bob Johnson	3.00	1.40	.30
A58	"Buck" Jordan	3.00	1.40	.30
A59	Alex Kampouris	3.00	1.40	.30
A60	"Chuck" Klein	8.00	3.75	.80
A61	Joe Kuhel	3.00	1.40	.30
A62	Lyn Lary	3.00	1.40	.30
A63	Harry Lavagetto	3.00	1.40	.30
A64	Sam Leslie	3.00	1.40	.30
A64	Freddie Lindstrom	6.00	2.80	.60
A66	Lombardi HOR	6.00	2.80	.60
A67	"Al" Lopez HOR	6.00	2.80	.60
A68	Dan MacFayden	3.00	1.40	.30
A69	John Marcum	3.00	1.40	.30
A70	"Pepper" Martin	4.00	1.85	.40
A71	Eric McNair	3.00	1.40	.30
A72	"Ducky" Medwick	7.00	3.25	.70
A73	Gene Moore	3.00	1.40	.30
A74	Randy Moore	3.00	1.40	.30
A75	Terry Moore	4.00	1.85	.40
A76	Edward Moriarty	3.00	1.40	.30
A77	"Wally" Moses (portrait)	3.00	1.40	.30
A78	"Buddy" Myer	3.00	1.40	.30
A79	"Buck" Newsom	3.00	1.40	.30
A80	Fred Ostermueller	3.00	1.40	.30
A81	Marvin Owen	3.00	1.40	.30
A82	Tommy Padden	3.00	1.40	.30
A83	Ray Pepper	3.00	1.40	.30
A84	Tony Piet	3.00	1.40	.30
A85	"Rabbit" Pytlak HOR	3.00	1.40	.30
A86	"Rip" Radcliff	3.00	1.40	.30
A87	Bobby Reis	3.00	1.40	.30
A88	"Lew" Riggs	3.00	1.40	.30
A89	Bill Rogell	3.00	1.40	.30
A90	"Red" Rolfe	3.00	1.40	.30
A91	"Schoolboy" Rowe (portrait)	4.00	1.85	.40
A92	Al Schacht	3.00	1.40	.30
A93	"Luke" Sewell	3.00	1.40	.30
A94	Al Simmons (portrait)	7.00	3.25	.70
A95	John Stone	3.00	1.40	.30
A96	Gus Suhr	3.00	1.40	.30
A97	Joe Sullivan	3.00	1.40	.30
A98	Bill Swift	3.00	1.40	.30
A99	Vito Tamulis	3.00	1.40	.30
A100	Dan Taylor	3.00	1.40	.30
A101	Cecil Travis	3.00	1.40	.30
A102	Hal Trosky (portrait)	3.00	1.40	.30
A103	"Bill" Urbanski	3.00	1.40	.30
A104	Russ Van Atta	3.00	1.40	.30
A105	"Arky" Vaughn	6.00	2.80	.60
A106	Gerald Walker	3.00	1.40	.30
A107	"Buck" Walters	4.00	1.85	.40
A108	Lloyd Waner	6.00	2.80	.60
A109	Paul Waner	6.00	2.80	.60
A110	"Lon" Warneke	3.00	1.40	.30
A111	Warstler	3.00	1.40	.30
A112	Bill Werber	3.00	1.40	.30
A113	"Jo-Jo" White	3.00	1.40	.30
A114	Burgess Whitehead	3.00	1.40	.30
A115	John Whitehead (portrait)	3.00	1.40	.30
A116	Whitlow Wyatt	3.00	1.40	.30
A117	Ben Chapman and Bill Werber	4.50	2.10	.45
A118	Joe DiMaggio and Joe McCarthy	50.00	22.00	5.00
A119	Wes and Rick Ferrell	8.00	3.75	.80
A120	Frank Pytlak and Steve O'Neill	3.00	1.40	.30
B1	Mel Almada	4.50	2.10	.45
B2	Lucius Appling (portrait)	8.00	3.75	.80
B3	Henry Bonura (portrait)	4.50	2.10	.45
B4	Herman Clifton	4.50	2.10	.45
B5	Roger "Doc" Cramer	4.50	2.10	.45
B6	Joe Cronin	10.00	4.75	1.00
B7	Jimmy Dykes	4.50	2.10	.45
B8	Ervin "Pete" Fox	4.50	2.10	.45
B9	Jimmy Foxx	20.00	9.00	2.00
B10	Hank Greenberg	12.00	5.50	1.20
B11	Oral Hildebrand	4.50	2.10	.45
B12	Alex Hooks HOR	4.50	2.10	.45
B13	Willis Hudlin	4.50	2.10	.45
B14	Bill Knickerbocker	4.50	2.10	.45
B15	Heinie Manush	8.00	3.75	.80
B16	Steve O'Neill	4.50	2.10	.45
B17	Marvin Owen	4.50	2.10	.45
B18	Al Simmons	9.00	4.25	.90
B19	Lem "Moose" Solters	4.50	2.10	.45
B20	Hal Trosky (batting)	4.50	2.10	.45
B21	Joe Vosmik (portrait)	4.50	2.10	.45
B22	Joe Vosmik (batting)	4.50	2.10	.45
B23	Earl Whitehill	4.50	2.10	.45
C1	"Luke" Appling (batting)	8.00	3.75	.80
C2	Earl Averill (portrait)	8.00	3.75	.80
C3	"Cy" Blanton	4.50	2.10	.45
C4	"Zeke" Bonura (batting)	4.50	2.10	.45
C5	Tom Bridges (portrait)	4.50	2.10	.45
C6	"Joe" DiMaggio	90.00	42.00	9.00
C7	"Bobby" Doerr	8.00	3.75	.80
C8	Jimmy Dykes HOR	4.50	2.10	.45
C9	"Bob" Feller	20.00	9.00	2.00
C10	"Elbie" Fletcher	4.50	2.10	.45
C11	Pete Fox (batting)	4.50	2.10	.45
C12	"Gus" Galan (batting)	4.50	2.10	.45
C13	Charles Gehringer	10.00	4.75	1.00
C14	Hank Greenberg	12.00	5.50	1.20
C15	Mel Harder	4.50	2.10	.45
C16	"Gabby" Hartnett	8.00	3.75	.80
C17	"Pinky" Higgins	4.50	2.10	.45
C18	Carl Hubbell	10.00	4.75	1.00
C19	"Wally" Moses (batting)	4.50	2.10	.45
C20	Lou Newsom	4.50	2.10	.45
C21	"Schoolboy" Rowe (throwing)	4.50	2.10	.45
C22	Julius Solters	4.50	2.10	.45
C23	"Hal" Trosky	4.50	2.10	.45
C24	Joe Vosmik (kneeling)	4.50	2.10	.45
C25	Johnnie Whitehead (throwing)	4.50	2.10	.45
D1	Buddy Bates (M)	10.00	4.75	1.00
D2	Del Bissonette (M)	10.00	4.75	1.00
D3	Lincoln Blakely (T)	10.00	4.75	1.00
D4	Isaac J. Boone (T)	10.00	4.75	1.00
D5	John H. Burnett (T)	10.00	4.75	1.00
D6	Leon Chagnon (M)	10.00	4.75	1.00
D7	Gus Dugas (M)	10.00	4.75	1.00
D8	Henry N. Erickson	10.00	4.75	1.00
D9	Art Funk (T)	10.00	4.75	1.00
D10	George Granger (M)	10.00	4.75	1.00
D11	Thomas G. Heath	10.00	4.75	1.00
D12	Phil Hensick (M)	10.00	4.75	1.00
D13	LeRoy Herrmann (T)	10.00	4.75	1.00
D14	Henry Johnson (M)	10.00	4.75	1.00
D15	Hal King (M)	10.00	4.75	1.00
D16	Charles S. Lucas (T)	10.00	4.75	1.00
D17	Edward S. Miller (T)	10.00	4.75	1.00
D18	Jake F. Mooty (T)	10.00	4.75	1.00
D19	Guy Moreau (T)	10.00	4.75	1.00
D20	George Murray (T)	10.00	4.75	1.00
D21	Glen Myatt (M)	10.00	4.75	1.00
D22	Lauri Myllykargos (M)	10.00	4.75	1.00
D23	Franci J. Nicholas (T)	10.00	4.75	1.00
D24	Bill O'Brien	10.00	4.75	1.00
D25	Thomas Oliver (T)	10.00	4.75	1.00
D26	James Pattison (T)	10.00	4.75	1.00
D27	Crip Polli (T)	10.00	4.75	1.00
D28	Harlin Pool (T)	10.00	4.75	1.00
D29	Walter Purcey (T)	10.00	4.75	1.00
D30	Bill Rhiel (M)	10.00	4.75	1.00
D31	Ben Sankey (M)	10.00	4.75	1.00
D32	Leslie Scarsella (M)	10.00	4.75	1.00
D33	Bob Seeds (M)	10.00	4.75	1.00
D34	Frank Shaughnessy (M)	12.00	5.50	1.20
D35	Harry Smythe (M)	10.00	4.75	1.00
D36	Ben Tate (M)	10.00	4.75	1.00
D37	Fresco Thompson (M)	12.00	5.50	1.20
D38	Charles Wilson (M)	10.00	4.75	1.00
D39	Francis Wistert HOR (T)	12.00	5.50	1.20

R315 Portraits and Action

"Babe" Ruth
"YANKEES"
FIELDER, YANKEES A. L.

This 1928 issue contains 58 black and white or yellow and black cards. The cards are blank backed and measure approximately 3 1/4" by 5 1/4". The cards are organized below alphabetically within each type. Type A features the player's name and team inside a white box. Type B features the player's position and team name printed below the frame line on the border. Type C shows the player's name hand lettered at the bottom of the card or near the player's legs. Type D has the position and team printed on the white border.

		MINT	VG-E	F-G
COMPLETE SET		325.00	150.00	30.00
COMMON PLAYER		4.00	1.85	.40
☐ A1	Earl Averill	8.00	3.75	.80
☐ A2	"Benny" Bengough	4.00	1.85	.40
☐ A3	Laurence Benton	4.00	1.85	.40
☐ A4	"Max" Bishop	4.00	1.85	.40
☐ A5	"Sunny Jim" Bottomley	8.00	3.75	.80
☐ A6	"Freddy" Fitzsimmons	4.00	1.85	.40
☐ A7	"Jimmy" Foxx	20.00	9.00	2.00
☐ A8	"Johnny" Fredericks	4.00	1.85	.40
☐ A9	Frank Frisch	10.00	4.50	.90
☐ A10	"Lou" Gehrig	40.00	18.00	4.00
☐ A11	"Goose" Goslin	8.00	3.75	.80
☐ A12	Burleigh Grimes	8.00	3.75	.80
☐ A13	"Lefty" Grove	12.00	5.50	1.20
☐ A14	"Mule" Haas	4.00	1.85	.40
☐ A15	"Babe" Herman	5.00	2.35	.50
☐ A16	"Roger" Hornsby	20.00	9.00	2.00
☐ A17	Karl Hubbell	10.00	4.75	1.00
☐ A18	"Stonewall" Jackson	8.00	3.75	.80
☐ A19	"Chuck" Klein	10.00	4.75	1.00
☐ A20	Mark Koenig	4.00	1.85	.40
☐ A21	"Tony" Lazzeri	6.00	2.80	.60
☐ A22	Fred Leach	4.00	1.85	.40
☐ A23	"Freddy" Lindstrom	8.00	3.75	.80
☐ A24	Fred Marberry	4.00	1.85	.40
☐ A25	"Bing" Miller	4.00	1.85	.40
☐ A26	Frank O'Doul	5.00	2.35	.50
☐ A27	"Bob" O'Farrell	4.00	1.85	.40
☐ A28	"Herbie" Pennock	8.00	3.75	.80
☐ A29	George Pipgras	4.00	1.85	.40
☐ A30	Andrew Reese	4.00	1.85	.40
☐ A31	"Babe" Ruth	60.00	27.00	6.00
☐ A32	"Bob" Shawkey	4.00	1.85	.40
☐ A33	"Al" Simmons	8.00	3.75	.80
☐ A34	"Riggs" Stephenson	5.00	2.35	.50
☐ A35	"Bill" Terry	10.00	4.75	1.00
☐ A36	"Pie" Traynor	10.00	4.75	1.00
☐ A37	"Dazzy" Vance	8.00	3.75	.80
☐ A38	Paul Waner	8.00	3.75	.80
☐ A39	"Hack" Wilson	10.00	4.75	1.00
☐ A40	"Tom" Zachary	4.00	1.85	.40
☐ B1	"Max" Bishop	4.00	1.85	.40
☐ B2	"Sunny Jim" Bottomley	8.00	3.75	.80
☐ B3	"Freddy" Fitzsimmons	4.00	1.85	.40
☐ B4	"Jimmy" Foxx	20.00	9.00	1.75
☐ B5	"Mule" Haas	4.00	1.85	.40
☐ B6	"Babe" Herman	5.00	2.35	.50
☐ B7	Karl Hubbell	10.00	4.75	1.00
☐ B8	"Stonewall" Jackson	8.00	3.75	.80
☐ B9	"Bing" Miller	4.00	1.85	.40
☐ B10	Andrew Reese	4.00	1.85	.40
☐ B11	Riggs Stephenson	5.00	2.35	.50
☐ B12	"Pie" Traynor	8.00	3.75	.80
☐ B13	"Dazzy" Vance	8.00	3.75	.80
☐ C1	Bill Cissell	4.00	1.85	.40
☐ C2	Harvey Hendricks	4.00	1.85	.40
☐ C3	Carl Reynolds	4.00	1.85	.40
☐ C4	Art Shires	4.00	1.85	.40
☐ D1	Bud Clancy	4.00	1.85	.40

R316 Portraits and Action

The 1929 R316 Portraits and Action Baseball set features 101 unnumbered, blank backed, black and white cards each measuring 3 1/2" by 4 1/2". The name of the player is written in script at the bottom of the card. The Hadley, Haines, Siebold, and Todt cards are considered scarce. On the other hand, the Babe Ruth card seems to be one of the more plentiful cards in the set.

		MINT	VG-E	F-G
COMPLETE SET		1300.00	600.00	125.00
COMMON PLAYER (1-101)		9.00	4.25	.90
☐	1 Ethan N. Allen	9.00	4.25	.90
☐	2 Dale Alexander	9.00	4.25	.90
☐	3 Larry Benton	9.00	4.25	.90
☐	4 Moe Berg	9.00	4.25	.90
☐	5 Max Bishop	9.00	4.25	.90
☐	6 Del Bissonette	9.00	4.25	.90
☐	7 Lucerne A. Blue	9.00	4.25	.90
☐	8 James Bottomley	18.00	8.50	1.80
☐	9 Guy T. Bush	9.00	4.25	.90
☐	10 Harold G. Carlson	9.00	4.25	.90
☐	11 Owen Carroll	9.00	4.25	.90
☐	12 Chalmers W. Cissell	9.00	4.25	.90
☐	13 Earl Combs	18.00	8.50	1.80
☐	14 Hugh M. Critz	9.00	4.25	.90
☐	15 H.J. DeBerry	9.00	4.25	.90
☐	16 Pete Donohue	9.00	4.25	.90
☐	17 Taylor Douthit	9.00	4.25	.90
☐	18 Chas W. Dressen	10.00	4.75	1.00
☐	19 Jimmy Dykes	10.00	4.75	1.00

☐	20	Howard Ehmke	9.00	4.25	.90
☐	21	Woody English	9.00	4.25	.90
☐	22	Urban Faber	18.00	8.50	1.80
☐	23	Fred Fitzsimmons	9.00	4.25	.90
☐	24	Lewis A. Fonseca	9.00	4.25	.90
☐	25	Horace H. Ford	9.00	4.25	.90
☐	26	Jimmy Foxx	30.00	14.00	3.00
☐	27	Frank Frisch	21.00	9.50	2.10
☐	28	Lou Gehrig	75.00	35.00	7.50
☐	29	Charles Gehringer	21.00	9.50	2.10
☐	30	Leon Goslin	18.00	8.50	1.80
☐	31	George Grantham	9.00	4.25	.90
☐	32	Grimes Burleigh	18.00	8.50	1.80
☐	33	Robert Grove	25.00	11.00	2.50
☐	34	Bump Hadley	90.00	42.00	9.00
☐	35	Charlie Hafey	18.00	8.50	1.80
☐	36	Jesse J. Haines	100.00	45.00	10.00
☐	37	Harvey Hendrick	9.00	4.25	.90
☐	38	Floyd C. Herman	10.00	4.75	1.00
☐	39	Andy High	9.00	4.25	.90
☐	40	Urban J. Hodapp	9.00	4.25	.90
☐	41	Frank Hogan	9.00	4.25	.90
☐	42	Rogers Hornsby	30.00	14.00	3.00
☐	43	Waite Hoyt	18.00	8.50	1.80
☐	44	Willis Hudlin	9.00	4.25	.90
☐	45	Frank O. Hurst	9.00	4.25	.90
☐	46	Charlie Jamieson	9.00	4.25	.90
☐	47	Roy C. Johnson	9.00	4.25	.90
☐	48	Percy Jones	9.00	4.25	.90
☐	49	Sam Jones	9.00	4.25	.90
☐	50	Joseph Judge	9.00	4.25	.90
☐	51	Willie Kamm	9.00	4.25	.90
☐	52	Charles Klein	18.00	8.50	1.80
☐	53	Mark Koenig	9.00	4.25	.90
☐	54	Ralph Kress	9.00	4.25	.90
☐	55	Fred M. Leach	9.00	4.25	.90
☐	56	Fred Lindstrom	18.00	8.50	1.80
☐	57	Ad Liska	9.00	4.25	.90
☐	58	Fred Lucas	9.00	4.25	.90
☐	59	Fred Maguire	9.00	4.25	.90
☐	60	Perce L. Malone	9.00	4.25	.90
☐	61	Harry Manush	18.00	8.50	1.80
☐	62	Walter Maranville	18.00	8.50	1.80
☐	63	Douglas McWeeney	9.00	4.25	.90
☐	64	Oscar Melillo	9.00	4.25	.90
☐	65	Ed "Bing" Miller	9.00	4.25	.90
☐	66	Frank O'Doul	10.00	4.75	1.00
☐	67	Melvin Ott	25.00	11.00	2.50
☐	68	Herbert Pennock	18.00	8.50	1.80
☐	69	William W. Regan	9.00	4.25	.90
☐	70	Harry F. Rice	9.00	4.25	.90
☐	71	Sam Rice	18.00	8.50	1.80
☐	72	Lance Richbourg	9.00	4.25	.90
☐	73	Eddie Rommel	9.00	4.25	.90
☐	74	Chas. H. Root	9.00	4.25	.90
☐	75	Ed Roush	18.00	8.50	1.80
☐	76	Harold Ruel	9.00	4.25	.90
☐	77	Charlie Ruffing	18.00	8.50	1.80
☐	78	Jack Russell	9.00	4.25	.90
☐	79	Babe Ruth	75.00	35.00	7.50
☐	80	Fred Schulte	9.00	4.25	.90
☐	81	Joe Sewell	18.00	8.50	1.80
☐	82	Luke Sewell	10.00	4.75	1.00
☐	83	Art Shires	9.00	4.25	.90
☐	84	Henry Seibold	90.00	42.00	9.00
☐	85	Al Simmons	18.00	8.50	1.80
☐	86	Bob Smith	9.00	4.25	.90
☐	87	Riggs Stephenson	10.00	4.75	1.00
☐	88	Wm. H. Terry	21.00	9.50	2.10
☐	89	Alphonse Thomas	9.00	4.25	.90
☐	90	Lafayette Thompson	9.00	4.25	.90
☐	91	Phil Todt	90.00	42.00	9.00
☐	92	Harold J. Traynor	18.00	8.50	1.80
☐	93	Dazzy Vance	18.00	8.50	1.80
☐	94	Lloyd Waner	18.00	8.50	1.80
☐	95	Paul Waner	18.00	8.50	1.80
☐	96	Jimmy Welsh	9.00	4.25	.90
☐	97	Earl Whitehill	9.00	4.25	.90
☐	98	A.C. Whitney	9.00	4.25	.90
☐	99	Claude Willoughby	9.00	4.25	.90
☐	100	Hack Wilson	21.00	9.50	2.10
☐	101	Tom Zachary	9.00	4.25	.90

Not sure about an abbreviation?
Just check our glossary and legend
found in the introductory section in
the front of the book.

R325 Goudey Knot Hole

The 1937 "Knot Hole League Game" was another
of the many innovative marketing ideas of the
Goudey Gum Company. Advertised as a series of
100 game cards promising "exciting" baseball
action, the set actually was limited to the 24 cards
listed below.

		MINT	VG-E	F-G
COMPLETE SET		120.00	55.00	12.00
COMMON PLAYER (1-24)		5.00	2.35	.50
☐ 1	Double/Foul	5.00	2.35	.50
☐ 2	Steals Home/Strike	5.00	2.35	.50
☐ 3	Ball/Out	5.00	2.35	.50
☐ 4	Strike/Ball	5.00	2.35	.50
☐ 5	Strike/Wild Pitch	5.00	2.35	.50
☐ 6	Ball/Out	5.00	2.35	.50
☐ 7	Bunt Scratch Hit/ Stolen Base	5.00	2.35	.50
☐ 8	Hit By Pitched Ball/Out	5.00	2.35	.50
☐ 9	Foul/Ball	5.00	2.35	.50
☐ 10	Foul/Double	5.00	2.35	.50
☐ 11	Out/Ball	5.00	2.35	.50
☐ 12	Foul/Force Out	5.00	2.35	.50
☐ 13	Out/Single	5.00	2.35	.50
☐ 14	Strike/Ball	5.00	2.35	.50
☐ 15	Foul Tip/Strike	5.00	2.35	.50
☐ 16	Unknown	6.00	2.80	.60
☐ 17	Ball/Out	5.00	2.35	.50
☐ 18	Out/Error	5.00	2.35	.50
☐ 19	Strike/Foul	5.00	2.35	.50
☐ 20	Double Play/Out	5.00	2.35	.50
☐ 21	Home Run/Ball	6.00	2.80	.60
☐ 22	Out/Strike	5.00	2.35	.50
☐ 23	Ball/Out	5.00	2.35	.50
☐ 24	Strike/Ball	5.00	2.35	.50

R326 Flip Movies

The 26 "Flip Movies" which comprise this set are a
miniature version (2" by 3") of the popular penny
arcade features of the period. Each movie comes in
two parts, clearly labeled, and there are several
cover colors as well as incorrect photos known to
exist.

		MINT	VG-E	F-G
COMPLETE SET		700.00	320.00	70.00
COMMON PLAYER (1-13)		20.00	9.00	2.00
☐ 1A	John Irving Burns (Poles Two Bagger)	20.00	9.00	2.00
☐ 1B	John Irving Burns (Poles Two Bagger)	20.00	9.00	2.00
☐ 2A	Joe Vosmik (Triples)	20.00	9.00	2.00

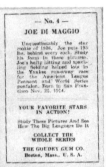

☐ 13A	Wally Berger (Puts One In The Bleachers)	20.00	9.00	2.00
☐ 13B	Wally Berger (Puts One In The Bleachers)	20.00	9.00	2.00

R332 Schutter-Johnson

This set of 50 cards was issued by the Schutter-Johnson Candy Corporation around 1930. Each card measures 2 1/4" by 2 7/8". While each card in the series is numbered, the ones in the checklist below are the only ones known at the present time. These black line-drawing cards on a red field are entitled "Major League Secrets" and feature tips from major league players on the reverse.

	MINT	VG-E	F-G
COMPLETE SET	1900.00	900.00	175.00
COMMON PLAYER	25.00	11.00	2.50

☐ 1	Al Simmons (Swings 2 or 3 bats)	35.00	16.50	3.50
☐ 2	Lloyd Waner's Batting Stance	35.00	16.50	3.50
☐ 3	(Kiki) Cuyler's Baserunning Tips	35.00	16.50	3.50
☐ 4	Frank Frisch (Chop Bunt)	50.00	22.00	5.00
☐ 5	Chick Hafey (Get Jump On Fly Balls)	40.00	18.00	4.00
☐ 6	(Umpire Bill Klem (Balk)	35.00	16.50	3.50
☐ 7	How to Practice Control (Rogers Hornsby Pitching Tips)	75.00	35.00	7.50
☐ 8	Carl Mays' "Under-hand Ball"	25.00	11.00	2.50
☐ 9	Umpire Charles Wrigley (Pitcher's feet with no base runners)	25.00	11.00	2.50
☐ 10	(Christy) Mathewson's Fade-Away Pitch	75.00	35.00	7.50
☐ 11	Bill Dickey (Waste Ball)	60.00	27.00	6.00
☐ 12	Walter Berger (don't step in the bucket	25.00	11.00	2.50
☐ 13	George Earnshaw's Curve	25.00	11.00	2.50
☐ 14	"Hack" Wilson (grip bat at extreme end)	40.00	18.00	4.00
☐ 15	Charley Grimm (testing pitcher at first)	25.00	11.00	2.50
☐ 16	Waner Brothers (word signs in outfield)	35.00	16.50	3.50
☐ 17	Chuck Klein (keep eye on ball)	40.00	18.00	4.00
☐ 18	Woody English (bunt flat-footed)	25.00	11.00	2.50

☐ 2B	Joe Vosmik (Triples)	20.00	9.00	2.00
☐ 3A	Mel Ott	50.00	22.00	5.00
☐ 3B	Mel Ott	50.00	22.00	5.00
☐ 4A	Joe DiMaggio (Socks A Sizzling Long Drive)	100.00	45.00	10.00
☐ 4B	Joe DiMaggio (Socks A Sizzling Line Drive)	100.00	45.00	10.00
☐ 5A	Wally Moses (Leans Against A Fast Ball)	20.00	9.00	2.00
☐ 5B	Wally Moses (Leans Against A Fast Ball)	20.00	9.00	2.00
☐ 6A	Van Lingle Mungo (Tosses Fire-Ball)	20.00	9.00	2.00
☐ 6B	Van Lingle Mungo (Tosses Fire-Ball)	20.00	9.00	2.00
☐ 7A	Luke Appling (Gets Set For Double Play	30.00	14.00	3.00
☐ 7B	Luke Appling (Gets Set For Double Play	30.00	14.00	3.00
☐ 8A	Bob Feller	50.00	22.00	5.00
☐ 8B	Bob Feller	50.00	22.00	5.00
☐ 9A	Paul Derringer (Demonstrates a Sharp Curve)	20.00	9.00	2.00
☐ 9B	Paul Derringer (Demonstrates a Sharp Curve)	20.00	9.00	2.00
☐ 10A	Paul Waner (Big Poison Smacks A Triple)	25.00	11.00	2.50
☐ 10B	Paul Waner (Big Poison Smacks A Triple)	25.00	11.00	2.50
☐ 11A	Joe Medwick (Bats Hard Grounder)	25.00	11.00	2.50
☐ 11B	Joe Medwick (Bats Hard Grounder)	25.00	11.00	2.50
☐ 12A	James Emory Foxx (Smacks A Homer)	50.00	22.00	5.00
☐ 12B	James Emory Foxx (Smacks A Homer)	50.00	22.00	5.00

☐ 19	Alexander's side arm Fastball	45.00	20.00	4.50
☐ 20	Lou Gehrig (hit ball where pitched)	150.00	70.00	15.00
☐ 21	Wes Ferrell's Wind-up	25.00	11.00	2.50
☐ 22	Carl Hubbell (Wind-up Pitching Tips)	45.00	20.00	4.50
☐ 23	Pie Traynor's Bunting Tips	40.00	18.00	4.00
☐ 24	Gus Mancuso (getting under foul ball)	25.00	11.00	2.50
☐ 25	Ben Cantwell (curve ball grip)	25.00	11.00	2.50
☐ 26	Babe Ruth's Advice	300.00	130.00	30.00
☐ 27	"Goose" Goslin (throw from outfield)	35.00	16.50	3.50
☐ 28	Earle Combs' Hands Apart Grip	35.00	16.50	3.50
☐ 29	Kiki Cuyler (halfslide)	35.00	16.50	3.50
☐ 30	Jimmy Wilson (delayed steal)	25.00	11.00	2.50
☐ 31	Dizzy Dean (curve ball)	80.00	37.00	8.00
☐ 32	Mickey Cochrane's signs	55.00	25.00	5.50
☐ 34	Si Johnson's Slow Ball	25.00	11.00	2.50
☐ 35	(Dizzy Dean) Fork Ball	80.00	37.00	8.00
☐ 36	Pepper Martin (bunting)	25.00	11.00	2.50
☐ 37	Joe Cronin (Battery Tips)	40.00	18.00	4.00
☐ 38	(Gabby Hartnett) Simple Batting Signs	35.00	16.50	3.50
☐ 39	Oscar Melillo (play ball, don't let ball play you)	25.00	11.00	2.50
☐ 40	Ben Chapman (hook slide)	25.00	11.00	2.50
☐ 41	John McGraw's Coaching Signs	60.00	27.00	6.00
☐ 42	Babe Ruth (choke grip)	300.00	130.00	30.00
☐ 43	"Red" Lucas (illegal action)	25.00	11.00	2.50
☐ 44	Charley Root (Holding Runners on First)	25.00	11.00	2.50
☐ 45	Dazzy Vance (drop pitch)	35.00	16.50	3.50
☐ 46	Hugh Critz (second baseman's throw)	25.00	11.00	2.50
☐ 47	Firpo Marberry (Raise Ball)	25.00	11.00	2.50
☐ 48	Grover Alexander (Full Windup)	50.00	22.00	5.00
☐ 49	Lefty Grove (fast ball grip)	60.00	27.00	6.00
☐ 50	Heine Meine (three types of curves)	25.00	11.00	2.50

☐ 407	Wilson Clark Brooklyn	30.00	14.00	3.00
☐ 408	"Lefty" Grove Athletics	75.00	35.00	7.50
☐ 409	Henry Johnson Red Sox	30.00	14.00	3.00
☐ 410	Jimmy Dykes White Sox	30.00	14.00	3.00
☐ 411	Henry Hine Schuble Detroit	30.00	14.00	3.00
☐ 412	Washington, Harris Makes Home Run	35.00	16.50	3.50
☐ 415	Safe At Third Base (Al Simmons)	45.00	20.00	4.50
☐ 416	A Safe Leap to 2nd Base (Henry Manush)	45.00	20.00	4.50
☐ 417	Glen Myatt Cleveland	30.00	14.00	3.00
☐ 418	Babe Herman Chicago Cubs	35.00	16.50	3.50
☐ 419	Frank Frisch St. L. Cardinals	60.00	27.00	6.00
☐ 420	A Safe Slide to the Home Plate	30.00	14.00	3.00
☐ 421	Pirates Paul Waner	45.00	20.00	4.50
☐ 422	Jimmy Wilson Cardinals	30.00	14.00	3.00
☐ 423	Charles Grimm Chicago Natl.	35.00	16.50	3.50
☐ 424	Phila Dick Bartell Natl. at bat	30.00	14.00	3.00
UNNUMBERED CARDS				
☐ xxx	Jimmy Fox (sic, Jimmie Foxx) Athletics	90.00	42.00	9.00
☐ xxx	Roy Johnson Red Sox	30.00	14.00	3.00
☐ xxx	Traynor Pitss (sic, Pittsburgh) is out	60.00	27.00	6.00

R337 Series Of 24

The cards in this 24 card set measure 2 5/16" by 2 13/16". The "Series of 24" is similar to the MP and Co. issues in terms of style and quality. Produced about 1932, this set is numbered 401-424, with the three missing numbers -- 403, 413 and 414 -- probably corresponding to the three known unnumbered players.

		MINT	VG-E	F-G
COMPLETE SET (24)		1000.00	450.00	100.00
COMMON PLAYER (401-427)		30.00	14.00	3.00
☐ 401	Johnny Vergez Giants	30.00	14.00	3.00
☐ 402	Babe Ruth New York Yankees	300.00	130.00	30.00
☐ 404	Red Sox/ Pipgras Out at First Base	30.00	14.00	3.00
☐ 405	Giants Bill Terry	60.00	27.00	6.00
☐ 406	George Connally Cleveland	30.00	14.00	3.00

R342 Thum Movies

These numbered booklets are the same dimensions (2" by 3") as the R326 Flip Movies except that these are twice the thickness as they comprise both parts within a single cover. They were produced by Goudey Gum.

		MINT	VG-E	F-G
COMPLETE SET		650.00	300.00	50.00
COMMON PLAYER		40.00	18.00	4.00
☐ 1	John Irving Burns	40.00	18.00	4.00
☐ 2	Joe Vosmik	40.00	18.00	4.00
☐ 3	Mel Ott	80.00	37.00	8.00
☐ 4	Joe DiMaggio	150.00	70.00	15.00
☐ 5	Wally Moses	40.00	18.00	4.00
☐ 6	Van Lingle Mungo	40.00	18.00	4.00
☐ 7	Luke Appling	60.00	27.00	6.00
☐ 8	Bob Feller	90.00	42.00	9.00
☐ 9	Paul Derringer	40.00	18.00	4.00

			MINT	VG-E	F-G
☐	10	Paul Waner	60.00	27.00	6.00
☐	11	Joe Medwick	60.00	27.00	6.00
☐	12	James Emory Foxx	90.00	42.00	9.00
☐	13	Wally Berger	40.00	18.00	4.00

			MINT	VG-E	F-G
		Floater)	20.00	9.00	2.00
☐	5	How to Run Bases	20.00	9.00	2.00
☐	6	How to Slide	20.00	9.00	2.00
☐	7	How to Catch Flies	20.00	9.00	2.00
☐	8	How to Field Grounders	20.00	9.00	2.00
☐	9	How to Tag A Man Out	20.00	9.00	2.00
☐	10	How to Cover A Base	20.00	9.00	2.00
☐	11	How to Bat	20.00	9.00	2.00
☐	12	How to Steal Bases	20.00	9.00	2.00
☐	13	How to Bunt	20.00	9.00	2.00
☐	14	How to Coach Base Runners	20.00	9.00	2.00
☐	15	How to Catch Behind the Bat	20.00	9.00	2.00
☐	16	How to Throw to Bases	20.00	9.00	2.00
☐	17	How to Signal	20.00	9.00	2.00
☐	18	How to Umpire Balls and Strikes	20.00	9.00	2.00
☐	19	How to Umpire Bases	20.00	9.00	2.00
☐	20	How to Lay Out a Ball Field	20.00	9.00	2.00

R344 Maranville Secrets

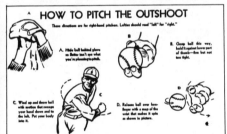

This paper set of 20 was issued in 1936 by the National Chicle Company. Each "card" measures 3 5/8" by 6". It carries the printing "Given only With Batter-Up Gum" on the back page. While the illustration shows the issue to be elongated, the papers were meant to be folded to create a four-page booklet. As the title implies, the set features instructional tips by Rabbit Maranville.

			MINT	VG-E	F-G
		COMPLETE SET	400.00	180.00	40.00
		COMMON CARD	20.00	9.00	2.00
☐	1	How to Pitch (the Out Shoot)	20.00	9.00	2.00
☐	2	How to Throw (the In Shoot)	20.00	9.00	2.00
☐	3	How to Pitch (the Drop)	20.00	9.00	2.00
☐	4	How to Pitch (the			

R346 Blue Tint

The cards in this 48 card set measure 2" by 2 5/8". The "Blue Tint" set derives its name from its distinctive coloration. Collector Ralph Triplette has pointed out in his research that the set was issued during 1948 and 1949, not in 1947 as had been previously commonly thought. The cards are blank-backed and unnumbered, and were issued in strips of six or eight. The set has a heavy emphasis on New York teams, especially the Yankees. Known variations are No. 2, Durocher, listed with Brooklyn or New York Giants, and No. 18, Ott, listed with Giants or no team designation. The set was initially listed in the ACC as R346 as well as being listed as W518. Although the W categorization is undoubtedly the more correct, nevertheless the R listing has become the popularly referenced designation for the set.

			MINT	VG-E	F-G
		COMPLETE SET	650.00	300.00	50.00
		COMMON PLAYER (1-48)	8.00	3.75	.80
☐	1	Bill Johnson	8.00	3.75	.80
☐	2A	Leo Durocher (Brooklyn Dodgers)	15.00	7.00	1.50
☐	2B	Leo Durocher (New York Giants)	15.00	7.00	1.50
☐	3	Marty Marion	10.00	4.75	1.00
☐	4	Ewell Blackwell	9.00	4.25	.90
☐	5	John Lindell	8.00	3.75	.80
☐	6	Larry Jansen	8.00	3.75	.80
☐	7	Ralph Kiner	15.00	7.00	1.50
☐	8	Chuck Dressen	9.00	4.25	.90
☐	9	Bobby Brown	12.00	5.50	1.20
☐	10	Luke Appling	15.00	7.00	1.50
☐	11	Bill Nicholson	8.00	3.75	.80
☐	12	Phil Masi	8.00	3.75	.80

		MINT	VG-E	F-G
☐13	Frank Shea	8.00	3.75	.80
☐14	Bob Dillinger	8.00	3.75	.80
☐15	Pete Suder	8.00	3.75	.80
☐16	Joe DiMaggio	100.00	45.00	10.00
☐17	John Corriden	8.00	3.75	.80
☐18A	Mel Ott (New York Giants)	35.00	16.50	3.50
☐18B	Mel Ott (no team designation)	35.00	16.50	3.50
☐19	Warren Rosar	8.00	3.75	.80
☐20	Warren Spahn	18.00	8.50	1.80
☐21	Allie Reynolds	12.00	5.50	1.20
☐22	Lou Boudreau	15.00	7.00	1.50
☐23	Hank Majeski (photo actually Randy Gumpert)	8.00	3.75	.80
☐24	Frank Crosetti	10.00	4.75	1.00
☐25	Gus Niarhos	8.00	3.75	.80
☐26	Bruce Edwards	8.00	3.75	.80
☐27	Rudy York	8.00	3.75	.80
☐28	Don Black	8.00	3.75	.80
☐29	Lou Gehrig	100.00	45.00	10.00
☐30	Johnny Mize	15.00	7.00	1.50
☐31	Ed Stanky	9.00	4.25	.90
☐32	Vic Raschi	10.00	4.75	1.00
☐33	Cliff Mapes	8.00	3.75	.80
☐34	Enos Slaughter	15.00	7.00	1.50
☐35	Hank Greenberg	15.00	7.00	1.50
☐36	Jackie Robinson	50.00	22.00	5.00
☐37	Frank Hiller	8.00	3.75	.80
☐38	Bob Elliott	9.00	4.25	.90
☐39	Harry Walker	8.00	3.75	.80
☐40	Ed Lopat	12.00	5.50	1.20
☐41	Bobby Thomson	10.00	4.75	1.00
☐42	Tommy Henrich	10.00	4.75	1.00
☐43	Bobby Feller	40.00	18.00	4.00
☐44	Ted Williams	60.00	27.00	6.00
☐45	Dixie Walker	8.00	3.75	.80
☐46	Johnny Vander Meer	9.00	4.25	.90
☐47	Clint Hartung	8.00	3.75	.80
☐48	Charlie Keller	9.00	4.25	.90

☐ 28	Bob Elliott	.35	.15	.03
☐ 31	Bob Feller	2.00	.90	.20
☐ 32	Frank Frisch	.75	.35	.07
☐ 35	Lou Gehrig	5.00	2.35	.50
☐ 36	Joe Gordon	.35	.15	.03
☐ 38	Hank Greenberg	.75	.35	.07
☐ 39	Lefty Grove	.75	.35	.07
☐ 42	Ken Heintzelman	.25	.10	.02
☐ 44	Jim Hearn	.25	.10	.02
☐ 46	Harry Heilman	.50	.22	.05
☐ 47	Tommy Henrich	.35	.15	.03
☐ 48	Roger Hornsby	1.50	.70	.15
☐ 50	Eddie Joost	.25	.10	.02
☐ 51	Nippy Jones	.25	.10	.02
☐ 54	Walter Johnson	2.00	.90	.20
☐ 55	Ellis Kinder	.25	.10	.02
☐ 56	Jim Konstanty	.35	.15	.03
☐ 58	Ralph Kiner	.75	.35	.07
☐ 59	Bob Lemon	.75	.35	.07
☐ 67	Connie Mack	.75	.35	.07
☐ 68	Christy Mathewson	2.00	.90	.20
☐ 69	Joe Medwick	.75	.35	.07
☐ 70	Johnny Mize	.75	.35	.07
☐ 71	Terry Moore	.35	.15	.03
☐ 72	Stan Musial	2.50	1.15	.25
☐ 73	Hal Newhouser	.35	.15	.03
☐ 74	Don Newcombe	.35	.15	.03
☐ 75	Lefty O'Doul	.35	.15	.03
☐ 77	Mel Parnell	.25	.10	.02
☐ 79	Gerald Priddy	.25	.10	.02
☐ 80	Dave Philley	.25	.10	.02
☐ 81	Bob Porterfield	.25	.10	.02
☐ 82	Andy Pafko	.25	.10	.02
☐ 83	Howie Pollet	.25	.10	.02
☐ 84	Herb Pennock	.50	.22	.05
☐ 85	Al Rosen	.50	.22	.05
☐ 86	Pee Wee Reese	.75	.35	.07
☐ 87	Del Rice	.25	.10	.02
☐ 92	Babe Ruth	10.00	4.75	1.00
☐ 93	Casey Stengel	1.50	.70	.15
☐ 94	Vern Stephens	.35	.15	.03
☐ 95	Duke Snider	1.50	.70	.15
☐ 96	Enos Slaughter	.75	.35	.07
☐ 97	Al Schoendienst	.35	.15	.03
☐ 98	Gerald Staley	.25	.10	.02
☐ 99	Clyde Shoun	.25	.10	.02
☐102	Al Simmons	.50	.22	.05
☐103	George Sisler	.75	.35	.07
☐104	Tris Speaker	1.00	.45	.10
☐105	Ed Stanky	.35	.15	.03
☐106	Virgil Trucks	.25	.10	.02
☐107	Henry Thompson	.25	.10	.02
☐109	Dazzy Vance	.50	.22	.05
☐110	Lloyd Waner	.50	.22	.05
☐111	Paul Waner	.50	.22	.05
☐112	Gene Woodling	.35	.15	.03
☐113	Ted Williams	3.00	1.40	.30
☐115	Wes Westrum	.25	.10	.02
☐117	Eddie Yost	.25	.10	.02
☐118	Al Zarilla	.25	.10	.02
☐119	Gus Zernial	.25	.10	.02
☐120	Sam Zoldack	.25	.10	.02

R423 Small Strip

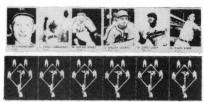

Many numbers of these small and unattractive cards are either unknown or do not exist for this issue of the early 1950s. The cards are printed on thin stock and measure 5/8" by 3/4"; sometimes they are found as a long horizontal strip of cards connected by a perforation. Cards are so small they are sometimes lost.

		MINT	VG-E	F-G
	COMPLETE SET	75.00	35.00	7.00
	COMMON PLAYER	.25	.10	.02
☐ 1	Richie Ashburn	.50	.22	.05
☐ 3	Frank Baumholtz	.25	.10	.02
☐ 4	Ralph Branca	.35	.15	.03
☐ 8	Harry Brecheen	.25	.10	.02
☐ 9	Chico Carrasquel	.25	.10	.02
☐ 10	Jerry Coleman	.25	.10	.02
☐ 11	Walker Cooper	.25	.10	.02
☐ 13	Phil Cavaretta	.35	.15	.03
☐ 14	Ty Cobb	5.00	2.35	.50
☐ 17	Frank Crosetti	.35	.15	.03
☐ 18	Larry Doby	.35	.15	.03
☐ 19	Walter Dropo	.25	.10	.02
☐ 21	Dizzy Dean	2.50	1.15	.25
☐ 22	Bill Dickey	.75	.35	.07
☐ 23	Murray Dickson	.25	.10	.02
☐ 24	Dom DiMaggio	.50	.22	.05
☐ 25	Joe DiMaggio	5.00	2.35	.50

1949 Eureka Stamps

This set features National League players -- apparently the promotion was not successful enough to warrant continuing on to do the American League, even though it is pre- announced in the back of the stamp album. Album is avalable to house the stamps. The album measures 7 1/2" by 9 1/4" whereas the individual stamps measure approximately 1 1/2" by 2". The stamps are numbered and are in full color. At the bottom of the stamp the player's name is given in a narrow yellow strip.

		MINT	VG-E	F-G
	COMPLETE SET	90.00	40.00	8.00
	COMMON PLAYER	.25	.10	.02
☐ 1	A.B. Happy Chandler	.35	.15	.03

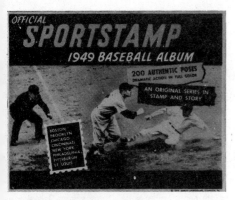

☐ 42	Eddie Miksis	.25	.10	.02
☐ 43	Paul Minner	.25	.10	.02
☐ 44	Sam Narron	.25	.10	.02
☐ 45	Don Newcombe	.50	.22	.05
☐ 46	Jake Pitler	.25	.10	.02
☐ 47	Pee Wee Reese	3.50	1.65	.35
☐ 48	Jackie Robinson	7.50	3.50	.75
☐ 49	Burt Shotton	.25	.10	.02
☐ 50	Duke Snider	7.50	3.50	.75
☐ 51	Dick Whitman	.25	.10	.02
CHICAGO CUBS				
☐ 52	Forrest Burgess	.25	.10	.02
☐ 53	Phil Cavaretta	.35	.15	.03
☐ 54	Bob Chipman	.25	.10	.02
☐ 55	Walter Dubiel	.25	.10	.02
☐ 56	Hank Edwards	.25	.10	.02
☐ 57	Frankie Gustine	.25	.10	.02
☐ 58	Hal Jeffcoat	.25	.10	.02
☐ 59	Emil Kush	.25	.10	.02
☐ 60	Doyle Lade	.25	.10	.02
☐ 61	Dutch Leonard	.25	.10	.02
☐ 62	Peanuts Lowery	.25	.10	.02
☐ 63	Gene Mauch	.35	.15	.03
☐ 64	Cal McLish	.25	.10	.02
☐ 65	Rube Novotney	.25	.10	.02
☐ 66	Andy Pafko	.25	.10	.02
☐ 67	Bob Ramazzotti	.25	.10	.02
☐ 68	Herman Reich	.25	.10	.02
☐ 69	Bob Rush	.25	.10	.02
☐ 70	Johnny Schmitz	.25	.10	.02
☐ 71	Bob Scheffing	.25	.10	.02
☐ 72	Roy Smalley	.25	.10	.02
☐ 73	Emil Verban	.25	.10	.02
☐ 74	Al Walker	.25	.10	.02
☐ 75	Harry Walker	.25	.10	.02
CINCINNATI REDS				
☐ 76	Bobby Adams	.25	.10	.02
☐ 77	Ewell Blackwell	.35	.15	.03
☐ 78	Jimmy Bloodworth	.25	.10	.02
☐ 79	Walker Cooper	.25	.10	.02
☐ 80	Tony Cuccinello	.25	.10	.02
☐ 81	Jess Dobernick	.25	.10	.02
☐ 82	Eddie Erautt	.25	.10	.02
☐ 83	Frank Fanovich	.25	.10	.02
☐ 84	Howie Fox	.25	.10	.02
☐ 85	Grady Hatton	.25	.10	.02
☐ 86	Homer Howell	.25	.10	.02
☐ 87	Ted Kluszewski	.75	.35	.07
☐ 88	Danny Litwhiler	.25	.10	.02
☐ 89	Everett Lively	.25	.10	.02
☐ 90	Lloyd Merriman	.25	.10	.02
☐ 91	Phil Page	.25	.10	.02
☐ 92	Kent Peterson	.25	.10	.02
☐ 93	Ken Raffensberger	.25	.10	.02
☐ 94	Luke Sewell	.25	.10	.02
☐ 95	Virgil Stallcup	.25	.10	.02
☐ 96	John Vander Meer	.35	.15	.03
☐ 97	Bucky Walters	.35	.15	.03
☐ 98	Herman Wehmeier	.25	.10	.02
☐ 99	Johnny Wyrostek	.25	.10	.02
☐ 100	Benny Zientara	.25	.10	.02
NEW YORK GIANTS				
☐ 101	Hank Behrman	.25	.10	.02
☐ 102	Leo Durocher	.75	.35	.07
☐ 103	Augie Galan	.25	.10	.02
☐ 104	Sid Gordon	.25	.10	.02
☐ 105	Bert Haas	.25	.10	.02
☐ 106	Andy Hansen	.25	.10	.02
☐ 107	Clint Hartung	.25	.10	.02
☐ 108	Kirby Higbe	.25	.10	.02
☐ 109	George Hausman	.25	.10	.02
☐ 110	Larry Jansen	.25	.10	.02
☐ 111	Sheldon Jones	.25	.10	.02
☐ 112	Monte Kennedy	.25	.10	.02
☐ 113	Buddy Kerr	.25	.10	.02
☐ 114	Dave Koslo	.25	.10	.02
☐ 115	Joe Lafata	.25	.10	.02
☐ 116	Whitey Lockman	.35	.15	.03
☐ 117	Jack Lohrke	.25	.10	.02
☐ 118	Willard Marshall	.25	.10	.02
☐ 119	Bill Milne	.25	.10	.02
☐ 120	Johnny Mize	1.50	.70	.15
☐ 121	Don Mueller	.35	.15	.03
☐ 122	Ray Mueller	.25	.10	.02
☐ 123	Bill Rigney	.25	.10	.02
☐ 124	Bobby Thomson	.50	.22	.05
☐ 125	Sam Webb	.25	.10	.02
☐ 126	Wes Westrum	.25	.10	.02
PHILADELPHIA PHILLIES				
☐ 127	Richie Ashburn	.75	.35	.07
☐ 128	Bennie Bengough	.25	.10	.02
☐ 129	Charlie Bicknell	.25	.10	.02
☐ 130	Buddy Blattner	.25	.10	.02

☐ 2	(Commissioner) Ford Frick	.50	.22	.05
BOSTON BRAVES	(N.L. President)			
☐ 3	Johnny Antonelli	.35	.15	.03
☐ 4	Red Barrett	.25	.10	.02
☐ 5	Clint Conatser	.25	.10	.02
☐ 6	Alvin Dark	.35	.15	.03
☐ 7	Bob Elliott	.35	.15	.03
☐ 8	Glenn Elliott	.25	.10	.02
☐ 9	Elbie Fletcher	.25	.10	.02
☐ 10	Bob Hall	.25	.10	.02
☐ 11	Jeff Heath	.25	.10	.02
☐ 12	Bobby Hogue	.25	.10	.02
☐ 13	Tommy Holmes	.35	.15	.03
☐ 14	Al Lakeman	.25	.10	.02
☐ 15	Phil Masi	.25	.10	.02
☐ 16	Nelson Potter	.25	.10	.02
☐ 17	Pete Reiser	.35	.15	.03
☐ 18	Rick Rickert	.25	.10	.02
☐ 19	Connie Ryan	.25	.10	.02
☐ 20	Jim Russell	.25	.10	.02
☐ 21	Johnny Sain	.35	.15	.03
☐ 22	Bill Salkeld	.25	.10	.02
☐ 23	Sibby Sisti	.25	.10	.02
☐ 24	Billy Southworth	.25	.10	.02
☐ 25	Warren Spahn	3.50	1.65	.35
☐ 26	Eddie Stanky	.35	.15	.03
☐ 27	Bill Voiselle	.25	.10	.02
BROOKLYN DODGERS				
☐ 28	Jack Banta	.25	.10	.02
☐ 29	Rex Barney	.25	.10	.02
☐ 30	Ralph Branca	.35	.15	.03
☐ 31	Tommy Brown	.25	.10	.02
☐ 32	Roy Campanella	7.50	3.50	.75
☐ 33	Billy Cox	.35	.15	.03
☐ 34	Bruce Edwards	.25	.10	.02
☐ 35	Carl Furillo	.75	.35	.07
☐ 36	Joe Hatten	.25	.10	.02
☐ 37	Gene Hermanski	.25	.10	.02
☐ 38	Gil Hodges	2.50	1.15	.25
☐ 39	Johnny Jorgensen	.25	.10	.02
☐ 40	Lefty Martin	.25	.10	.02
☐ 41	Mike McCormick	.25	.10	.02

☐ 131	Hank Borowy	.25	.10	.02
☐ 132	Ralph Caballero	.25	.10	.02
☐ 133	Blix Donnelly	.25	.10	.02
☐ 134	Del Ennis	.35	.15	.03
☐ 135	Granville Hamner	.25	.10	.02
☐ 136	Ken Heintzelman	.25	.10	.02
☐ 137	Stan Hollmig	.25	.10	.02
☐ 138	Willie Jones	.25	.10	.02
☐ 139	Jim Konstanty	.35	.15	.03
☐ 140	Stan Lopata	.25	.10	.02
☐ 141	Jackie Mayo	.25	.10	.02
☐ 142	Bill Nicholson	.25	.10	.02
☐ 143	Robin Roberts	2.50	1.15	.25
☐ 144	Schoolboy Rowe	.35	.15	.03
☐ 145	Eddie Sawyer	.25	.10	.02
☐ 146	Andy Seminick	.25	.10	.02
☐ 147	Ken Silvestri	.25	.10	.02
☐ 148	Curt Simmons	.35	.15	.03
☐ 149	Dick Sisler	.25	.10	.02
☐ 150	Ken Trinkle	.25	.10	.02
☐ 151	Eddie Waitkus	.25	.10	.02

PITTSBURGH PIRATES

☐ 152	Romanus Basgall	.25	.10	.02
☐ 153	Eddie Bockman	.25	.10	.02
☐ 154	Ernie Bonham	.25	.10	.02
☐ 155	Hugh Casey	.35	.15	.03
☐ 156	Pete Castiglione	.25	.10	.02
☐ 157	Cliff Chambers	.25	.10	.02
☐ 158	Murry Dickson	.25	.10	.02
☐ 159	Ed Fitzgerald	.25	.10	.02
☐ 160	Les Fleming	.25	.10	.02
☐ 161	Hal Gregg	.25	.10	.02
☐ 162	Goldie Holt	.25	.10	.02
☐ 163	Johnny Hopp	.25	.10	.02
☐ 164	Ralph Kiner	1.50	.70	.15
☐ 165	Vic Lombardi	.25	.10	.02
☐ 166	Clyde McCullough	.25	.10	.02
☐ 167	Bill Meyer	.25	.10	.02
☐ 168	Danny Murtaugh	.35	.15	.03
☐ 169	Barnacle Bill Posedel	.25	.10	.02
☐ 170	Elmer Riddle	.25	.10	.02
☐ 171	Stan Rojek	.25	.10	.02
☐ 172	Rip Sewell	.35	.15	.03
☐ 173	Eddie Stevens	.25	.10	.02
☐ 174	Dixie Walker	.25	.10	.02
☐ 175	Bill Werle	.25	.10	.02
☐ 176	Waldon Westlake	.25	.10	.02

ST. LOUIS CARDINALS

☐ 177	Bill Baker	.25	.10	.02
☐ 178	Al Brazle	.25	.10	.02
☐ 179	Harry Brecheen	.35	.15	.03
☐ 180	Chuck Diering	.25	.10	.02
☐ 181	Eddie Dyer	.35	.15	.03
☐ 182	Joe Garagiola	2.50	1.15	.25
☐ 183	Tom Glaviano	.25	.10	.02
☐ 184	Jim Hearn	.25	.10	.02
☐ 185	Ken Johnson	.25	.10	.02
☐ 186	Nippy Jones	.25	.10	.02
☐ 187	Ed Kazak	.25	.10	.02
☐ 188	Lou Klein	.25	.10	.02
☐ 189	Marty "Slats" Marion	.35	.15	.03
☐ 190	George Munger	.25	.10	.02
☐ 191	Stan Musial	6.00	2.80	.60
☐ 192	Spike Nelson	.25	.10	.02
☐ 193	Howie Pollett	.25	.10	.02
☐ 194	Bill Reeder	.25	.10	.02
☐ 195	Del Rice	.25	.10	.02
☐ 196	Ed Sauer	.25	.10	.02
☐ 197	Red Schoendienst	.35	.15	.03
☐ 198	Enos Slaughter	1.50	.70	.15
☐ 199	Ted Wilks	.25	.10	.02
☐ 200	Ray Yochim	.25	.10	.02

1982 Fleer Stamps

The stamps in this 242 stamp set measure 1 13/16" by 2 1/2". The 1982 Fleer stamp set consists of different individual stamps issued in strips of 10 stamps each. The stamps were issued in packages with the Fleer team logo stickers. The backs are blank, and an inexpensive album is available in which to place the stamps. A checklist is provided in the back of the album which lists 25 strips of 10 stamps.

The checklist below lists the individual stamps plus the strip to which the stamps are supposed to belong based on the album strip checklist. Complete strips have equal value to the sum of the individual stamps on the strip. Eight stamps have been doubly printed and are noted by two different strip numbers below.

	MINT	VG-E	F-G
COMPLETE SET	9.00	4.25	.90
COMMON PLAYER	.02	.01	.00
COMMON SHEET	.30	.12	.03

LOS ANGELES DODGERS

☐ 1	Fern. Valenzuela (G20)	.12	.05	.01
☐ 2	Rick Monday (G16)	.03	.01	.00
☐ 3	Ron Cey (G9)	.05	.02	.00
☐ 4	Dusty Baker (G20)	.03	.01	.00
☐ 5	Burt Hooton (G10)	.02	.01	.00
☐ 6	Pedro Guerrero (G23)	.10	.04	.01
☐ 7	Jerry Reuss (G12)	.03	.01	.00
☐ 8	Bill Russell (G7)	.02	.01	.00
☐ 9	Steve Garvey (G21)	.12	.05	.01
☐ 10	Davey Lopes (G19)	.03	.01	.00

CINCINNATI REDS

☐ 11	Tom Seaver (G7)	.10	.04	.01
☐ 12	George Foster (G17)	.05	.02	.00
☐ 13	Frank Pastore (G12)	.02	.01	.00
☐ 14	Dave Collins (G5)	.03	.01	.00
☐ 15	Dave Concepcion (G21)	.04	.01	.00
☐ 16	Ken Griffey (G6)	.04	.02	.00
☐ 17	Johnny Bench (G20)	.10	.04	.01
☐ 18	Ray Knight (G16)	.04	.02	.00
☐ 19	Mario Soto (G9)	.04	.02	.00
☐ 20	Ron Oester (G19)	.02	.01	.00

ST. LOUIS CARDINALS

☐ 21	Ken Oberkfell (G21)	.02	.01	.00
☐ 22	Bob Forsch (G4)	.02	.01	.00
☐ 23	Keith Hernandez (G19)	.08	.03	.01
☐ 24	Dane Iorg (G9)	.02	.01	.00
☐ 25	George Hendrick (G2)	.03	.01	.00
☐ 26	Gene Tenace (G24)	.02	.01	.00
☐ 27	Garry Templeton (G12)	.04	.02	.00
☐ 28	Bruce Sutter (G18)	.06	.02	.00
☐ 29	Darrell Porter (G14)	.03	.01	.00
☐ 30	Tom Herr (G3)	.03	.01	.00

MONTREAL EXPOS

☐ 31	Tim Raines (G11)	.10	.04	.01
☐ 32	Chris Speier (G13)	.02	.01	.00
☐ 33	Warren Cromartie (G22)	.02	.01	.00
☐ 34	Larry Parrish (G15)	.03	.01	.00
☐ 35	Andre Dawson (G10)	.09	.04	.01
☐ 36	Steve Rogers (G1,25)	.04	.02	.00
☐ 37	Jeff Reardon (G23)	.05	.02	.00
☐ 38	Rodney Scott (G12)	.02	.01	.00
☐ 39	Gary Carter (G14)	.12	.05	.01
☐ 40	Scott Sanderson (G6)	.02	.01	.00

HOUSTON ASTROS

☐ 41	Cesar Cedeno (G7)	.03	.01	.00
☐ 42	Nolan Ryan (G10)	.10	.04	.01
☐ 43	Don Sutton (G24)	.06	.02	.00
☐ 44	Terry Puhl (G15)	.03	.01	.00
☐ 45	Joe Niekro (G13)	.04	.02	.00
☐ 46	Tony Scott (G16)	.02	.01	.00
☐ 47	Joe Sambito (G1)	.03	.01	.00
☐ 48	Art Howe (G9)	.02	.01	.00
☐ 49	Bob Knepper (G18)	.05	.02	.00
☐ 50	Jose Cruz (G22)	.05	.02	.00

PHILADELPHIA PHILLIES

☐ 51	Pete Rose (G16)	.30	.12	.03
☐ 52	Dick Ruthven (G12)	.02	.01	.00

53	Mike Schmidt (G14)	.20	.09	.02
54	Steve Carlton (G17)	.12	.05	.01
55	Tug McGraw (G4)	.04	.02	.00
56	Larry Bowa (G4)	.04	.02	.00
57	Garry Maddox (G18)	.03	.01	.00
58	Gary Matthews (G4)	.04	.02	.00
59	Manny Trillo (G15)	.03	.01	.00
60	Lonnie Smith (G20)	.04	.02	.00
SAN FRANCISCO GIANTS				
61	Vida Blue (G11)	.04	.02	.00
62	Milt May (G12)	.02	.01	.00
63	Joe Morgan (G16)	.07	.03	.01
64	Enos Cabell (G8)	.02	.01	.00
65	Jack Clark (G18)	.06	.02	.00
ATLANTA BRAVES				
66	Claud.Washington (G19)	.03	.01	.00
67	Gaylord Perry (G16)	.08	.03	.01
68	Phil Niekro (G22)	.08	.03	.01
69	Bob Horner (G7)	.07	.03	.01
70	Chris Chambliss (G11)	.03	.01	.00
PITTSBURGH PIRATES				
71	Dave Parker (G15)	.08	.03	.01
72	Tony Pena (G11)	.05	.02	.00
73	Kent Tekulve (G23)	.03	.01	.00
74	Mike Easler (G18)	.04	.02	.00
75	Tim Foli (G13)	.02	.01	.00
76	Willie Stargell (G21)	.08	.03	.01
77	Bill Madlock (G5)	.07	.03	.01
78	Jim Bibby (G14)	.03	.01	.00
79	Omar Moreno (G17)	.03	.01	.00
80	Lee Lacy (G2)	.03	.01	.00
NEW YORK METS				
81	Hubie Brooks (G24)	.08	.03	.01
82	Rusty Staub (G4)	.05	.02	.00
83	Ellis Valentine (G13)	.03	.01	.00
84	Neil Allen (G1)	.03	.01	.00
85	Dave Kingman (G9)	.06	.02	.00
86	Mookie Wilson (G3)	.04	.02	.00
87	Doug Flynn (G11)	.02	.01	.00
88	Pat Zachry (G8)	.02	.01	.00
89	John Stearns (G6)	.02	.01	.00
90	Lee Mazzilli (G2)	.02	.01	.00
CHICAGO CUBS				
91	Ken Reitz (G23)	.02	.01	.00
92	Mike Krukow (G11)	.03	.01	.00
93	Jerry Morales (G10)	.02	.01	.00
94	Leon Durham (G22)	.06	.02	.00
95	Ivan DeJesus (G2)	.02	.01	.00
96	Bill Buckner (G17)	.05	.02	.00
97	Jim Tracy (G12)	.02	.01	.00
98	Steve Henderson (G14)	.02	.01	.00
99	Dick Tidrow (G14)	.02	.01	.00
100	Mike Tyson (G5)	.02	.01	.00
SAN DIEGO PADRES				
101	Ozzie Smith (G12)	.07	.03	.01
102	Ruppert Jones (G24)	.02	.01	.00
103	Brod Perkins (G10)	.02	.01	.00
104	Gene Richards (G15)	.02	.01	.00
105	Terry Kennedy (G22)	.05	.02	.00
COMBINATION STAMPS				
106	Jim Bibby and Willie Stargell (G4)	.07	.02	.00
107	Pete Rose and Larry Bowa (G21)	.12	.05	.01
108	Fernando Valenzuela and Warren Spahn(G1,G25)		.03	.01
109	Pete Rose and Dave Concepcion (G8)	.12	.05	.01
110	Reggie Jackson and Dave Winfield (G3)	.12	.05	.01
111	Fernando Valenzuela and Tom Lasorda (G4)	.07	.03	.01
NEW YORK YANKEES				
112	Reggie Jackson (G6)	.15	.06	.01
113	Dave Winfield (G3)	.12	.05	.01
114	Lou Piniella (G2)	.05	.02	.00
115	Tommy John (G9)	.05	.02	.00
116	Rich Gossage (G1,25)	.06	.02	.00
117	Ron Davis (G10)	.02	.01	.00
118	Rick Cerone (G5)	.02	.01	.00
119	Graig Nettles (G8)	.05	.02	.00
120	Ron Guidry (G24)	.07	.03	.01
121	Willie Randolph (G24)	.03	.01	.00
OAKLAND A'S				
122	Dwayne Murphy (G15)	.03	.01	.00
123	Rickey Henderson (G16)		.06	.01
124	Wayne Gross (G6)	.02	.01	.00
125	Mike Norris (G8)	.02	.01	.00
126	Rick Langford (G20)	.02	.01	.00
127	Jim Spencer (G17)	.02	.01	.00
128	Tony Armas (G12)	.05	.02	.00
129	Matt Keough (G7)	.02	.01	.00
130	Jeff Jones (G19)	.02	.01	.00
131	Steve McCatty (G3)	.02	.01	.00
MILWAUKEE BREWERS				
132	Rollie Fingers (G7)	.07	.03	.01
133	Jim Gantner (G15)	.02	.01	.00
134	Gorman Thomas (G6)	.06	.02	.00
135	Robin Yount (G13)	.12	.05	.01
136	Paul Molitor (G22)	.06	.02	.00
137	Ted Simmons (G10)	.06	.02	.00
138	Ben Oglivie (G23)	.04	.02	.00
139	Moose Haas (G21)	.03	.01	.00
140	Cecil Cooper (G24)	.07	.03	.01
141	Pete Vuckovich (G10)	.03	.01	.00
BALTIMORE ORIOLES				
142	Doug DeCinces (G21)	.05	.02	.00
143	Jim Palmer (G9)	.10	.04	.01
144	Steve Stone (G16)	.04	.02	.00
145	Mike Flanagan (G19)	.04	.02	.00
146	Rick Dempsey (G9)	.03	.01	.00
147	Al Bumbry (G14)	.02	.01	.00
148	Mark Belanger (G8)	.03	.01	.00
149	Scott McGregor(G23)	.03	.01	.00
150	Ken Singleton (G10)	.05	.02	.00
151	Eddie Murray (G5)	.15	.06	.01
DETROIT TIGERS				
152	Lance Parrish (G20)	.10	.04	.01
153	Dave Rozema (G15)	.02	.01	.00
154	Champ Summers (G13)	.02	.01	.00
155	Alan Trammell (G2)	.08	.03	.01
156	Lou Whitaker (G1,25)	.07	.03	.01
157	Milt Wilcox (G9)	.02	.01	.00
158	Kevin Saucier (G24)	.02	.01	.00
159	Jack Morris (G14)	.08	.03	.01
160	Steve Kemp (G7)	.04	.02	.00
161	Kirk Gibson (G3)	.10	.04	.01
BOSTON RED SOX				
162	Carl Yastrzemski (G3)	.20	.09	.02
163	Jim Rice (G21)	.12	.05	.01
164	Carney Lansford (G15)	.06	.02	.00
165	Dennis Eckersley (G6)	.04	.02	.00
166	Mike Torrez (G5)	.03	.01	.00
167	Dwight Evans (G19)	.06	.02	.00
168	Glenn Hoffman (G18)	.03	.01	.00
169	Bob Stanley (G20)	.03	.01	.00
170	Tony Perez (G16)	.07	.03	.01
171	Jerry Remy (G13)	.02	.01	.00
TEXAS RANGERS				
172	Buddy Bell (G5)	.07	.03	.01
173	Fergie Jenkins (G17)	.05	.02	.00
174	Mickey Rivers (G9)	.03	.01	.00
175	Bump Wills (G2)	.02	.01	.00
176	Jon Matlack (G20)	.03	.01	.00
177	Steve Comer (G23)	.02	.01	.00
178	Al Oliver (G1,25)	.07	.03	.01
179	Bill Stein (G3)	.02	.01	.00
180	Pat Putnam (G14)	.02	.01	.00
181	Jim Sundberg (G4)	.03	.01	.00
CHICAGO WHITE SOX				
182	Ron LeFlore (G4)	.04	.02	.00
183	Carlton Fisk (G11)	.08	.03	.01
184	Harold Baines (G18)	.08	.03	.01
185	Bill Almon (G2)	.02	.01	.00
186	Richard Dotson (G9)	.04	.02	.00
187	Greg Luzinski (G14)	.06	.02	.00
188	Mike Squires (G13)	.02	.01	.00
189	Britt Burns (G19)	.05	.02	.00
190	LaMarr Hoyt (G6)	.06	.02	.00
191	Chet Lemon (G22)	.04	.02	.00
CLEVELAND INDIANS				
192	Joe Charboneau (G20)	.03	.01	.00
193	Toby Harrah (G16)	.04	.02	.00
194	John Denny (G22)	.04	.02	.00
195	Rick Manning (G8)	.02	.01	.00
196	Miguel Dilone (G15)	.02	.01	.00
197	Bo Diaz (G13)	.03	.01	.00
198	Mike Hargrove (G17)	.03	.01	.00
199	Bert Blyleven (G11)	.06	.02	.00
200	Len Barker (G7)	.03	.01	.00
201	Andre Thornton (G18)	.05	.02	.00
KANSAS CITY ROYALS				
202	George Brett (G24)	.20	.09	.02
203	U.L. Washington (G25)	.02	.01	.00
204	Dan Quisenberry (G17)	.07	.03	.01
205	Larry Gura (G17)	.02	.01	.00
206	Willie Aikens (G22)	.03	.01	.00
207	Willie Wilson (G21)	.07	.03	.01
208	Dennis Leonard (G8)	.04	.02	.00
209	Frank White (G8)	.03	.01	.00
210	Hal McRae (G23)	.04	.02	.00
211	Amos Otis (G18)	.04	.02	.00
CALIFORNIA ANGELS				
212	Don Aase (G23)	.03	.01	.00
213	Butch Hobson (G6)	.02	.01	.00
214	Fred Lynn (G18)	.08	.03	.01

□ 215	Brian Downing (G10)	.03	.01	.00	
□ 216	Dan Ford (G5)	.03	.01	.00	
□ 217	Rod Carew (G5)	.12	.05	.01	
□ 218	Bobby Grich (G19)	.05	.02	.00	
□ 219	Rick Burleson (G11)	.04	.02	.00	
□ 220	Don Baylor (G3)	.07	.03	.01	
□ 221	Ken Forsch (G17)	.02	.01	.00	

SEATTLE MARINERS

□ 222	Bruce Bochte (G20)	.02	.01	.00
□ 223	Richie Zisk (G21)	.02	.01	.00
□ 224	Tom Paciorek (G19)	.02	.01	.00
□ 225	Julio Cruz (G8)	.02	.01	.00
□ 226	Jeff Burroughs (G23)	.02	.01	.00

MINNESOTA TWINS

□ 227	Doug Corbett (G8)	.02	.01	.00
□ 228	Roy Smalley (G24)	.03	.01	.00
□ 229	Gary Ward (G4)	.03	.01	.00
□ 230	John Castino (G7)	.02	.01	.00
□ 231	Rob Wilfong (G12)	.02	.01	.00

TORONTO BLUE JAYS

□ 232	Dave Stieb (G22)	.06	.02	.00
□ 233	Otto Velez (G13)	.02	.01	.00
□ 234	Damaso Garcia (G7)	.04	.02	.00
□ 235	J.Mayberry (G1,25)	.03	.01	.00
□ 236	Alfredo Griffin (G11)	.03	.01	.00

COMBINATION STAMPS

□ 237	Ted Williams and Carl Yastrzemski(G3)	.20	.09	.02
□ 238	Graig Nettles and Rick Cerone (G25)	.04	.02	.00
□ 239	Buddy Bell and George Brett (G25)	.12	.05	.01
□ 240	Jim Kaat and Steve Carlton (G2)	.08	.03	.01
□ 241	Dave Parker and Steve Carlton (G25)	.10	.04	.01
□ 242	Nolan Ryan and Ron Davis (G2)	.06	.02	.00

1983 Fleer Stamps

The stamps in this 288 stamp set measure 1 1/4" by 17/16". The 1983 Fleer stamp set features players and team logos. In all, 224 player stamps and 64 logos exist. Some of the stamps include baseball trivia quiz questions. The stamps were distributed on four different sheets of 72 stamps or in Vend-a- Stamp dispensers of 18 stamps each. Sixteen different dispenser strips were needed to complete the set. The prices listed below are for vertical strips which are found in the dispensers. In actuality, Sheet 1 consists of vertical strips 1-4; Sheet 2, vertical strips 5-8; Sheet 3, vertical strips 9-12; and Sheet 4, vertical strips 13-16.

	MINT	VG-E	F-G
COMPLETE SET	3.00	1.40	.30
COMMON STRIP	.25	.10	.02

□ 1 Vertical Strip 1	.30	.12	.03	

Pat Zachry/Chris Speier
Mike Schmidt/George Brett
Gaylord Perry/Montefusco
Toby Harrah/Bump Wills
Dodgers Logo/A's Logo
Davey Lopes/Ruppert Jones
Dale Berra/Angels Logo
Cardinals Logo/Jack Clark
Craig Swan

□ 2 Vertical Strip 2	.30	.12	.03

Tug McGraw/Roy Smalley
K.Tekulve/Dan Quisenberry
Reggie Smith/Wade Boggs
Rick Sutcliffe/Steve Howe
B.Downing/Phillies Logo
Cubs Logo/Dick Tidrow
Mario Soto/Ray Knight
Expos Logo/Astros Logo
Neil Allen/Mike Flanagan

□ 3 Vertical Strip 3	.30	.12	.03

W.Cromartie/F.Valenzuela
K.Hernandez/Bob McClure
J.Royster/Bill Buckner
Reggie Jackson/W.Stargell
Rick Monday/Giants Logo
Indians Logo/Ron Leflore
Lee Mazzilli/Buddy Bell
Pirates Logo/Mets Logo
D.Driessen/U.L.Washington

□ 4 Vertical Strip 4	.30	.12	.03

Don Sutton/Willie Upshaw
Robin Yount/Paul Molitor
D.DeCinces/Dave Winfield
Ken Forsch/Bob Forsch
R.Rhoden/White Sox Logo
Red Sox Logo/Gary Lavelle
Harold Baines/Ron Reed
Twins Logo/Orioles Logo
Luis DeLeon/D.Concepcion

□ 5 Vertical Strip 5	.40	.18	.04

C.Chambliss/Andre Dawson
Dwayne Murphy/G.Thomas
Ben Oglivie/Len Barker
C.Yastrzemski/Pete Rose
Mookie Wilson/Braves Logo
Yankees Logo/Greg Minton
Willie Aikens/D.Eckersley
Reds Logo/Tigers Logo
Sixto Lezcano/Ron Guidry

□ 6 Vertical Strip 6	.25	.10	.02

Rafael Ramirez/S.McGregor
G.Gossage/Bruce Sutter
Ken Oberkfell/Bo Diaz
Jim Rice/Fred Lynn
Jerry Reuss/Angels Logo
Cardinals Logo/Bob Bailor
Eric Show/Dusty Baker
Royals Logo/Mariners Logo
Steve Mura/Tom Underwood

□ 7 Vertical Strip 7	.30	.12	.03

Larry Parrish/J.Matlack
F.Bannister/Bob Horner
Garth Iorg/LaMarr Hoyt
Tim Raines/R.Henderson
Mark Clear/Expos Logo
Astros Logo/Ken Griffey
Eddie Milner/Hubie Brooks
Indians Logo/Dodgers Logo
Tommy John/Jeff Reardon

□ 8 Vertical Strip 8	.30	.12	.03

Tom Brunansky/Tom Hume
Tom Seaver/Jim Palmer
Lance Parrish/G.Foster
Al Oliver/Willie Wilson
Jim Sundberg/Pirates Logo
Mets Logo/Jason Thompson
Joe Morgan/Rollie Fingers
Ranger Logo/Phillies Logo
Lou Piniella/J.Wockenfuss

□ 9 Vertical Strip 9	.25	.10	.02

Jim Beattie/Manny Trillo
Johnny Bench/Ted Simmons
K.Moreland/Milt Wilcox
Hal McRae/Andre Thornton
Bill Caudill/Twins Logo
Orioles Logo/B.Castillo

M.Sarmiento/Gene Garber
Blue Jay Logo/Giants Logo
John Tudor/Dave Beard
☐ 10 Vertical Strip 10 30   .12   .03
Duane Kuiper/Eddie Murray
Art Howe/Dickie Thon
Dave Stieb/Ken Singleton
Cal Ripken/Steve Sax
Bob Watson/Reds Logo
Tigers Logo/Steve Rogers
Bob Stanley/J.Mumphrey
Brewers Logo/Chisox Logo
R.Manning/Darrell Porter
☐ 11 Vertical Strip 11 30   .12   .03
C.Fisk/Mike Richardt
Alan Ashby/Nolan Ryan
Cecil Cooper/Frank White
Kent Hrbek/Johnny Ray
Burt Hooton/Royals Logo
Mariners Logo/L.Biittner
Damaso Garcia/Mike Easler
Padres Logo/Braves Logo
Larry Herndon/Al Holland
☐ 12 Vertical Strip 12 30   .12   .03
Gary Carter/Garry Maddox
Joe Niekro/Phil Niekro
Bill Laskey/Bob Boone
Rod Carew/Bill Madlock
J.Koosman/Indians Logo
Dodgers Logo/Ed VandeBerg
Amos Otis/Dennis Leonard
A's Logo/Angels Logo
Rusty Staub/Dwight Evans
☐ 13 Vertical Strip 13 30   .12   .03
Dale Murphy/L.Christenson
Leon Durham/Greg Luzinski
G.Matthews/Lou Whitaker
Bruce Kison/Milt May
Randy Martz/Rangers Logo
Phillies Logo/Phil Garner
John Lowenstein/R.Cerone
Cubs Logo/Pirates Logo
C.Washington/Dave Parker
☐ 14 Vertical Strip 14 25   .10   .02
Danny Darwin/Tony Pena
Tom Paciorek/Steve Garvey
Charlie Lea/Mike Hargrove
Steve Kemp/Rich Dauer
Al Williams/Blue Jay Logo
Giants Logo/Jim Clancy
Hosken Powell/John Grubb
Expos Logo/Twins Logo
Al Bumbry/Ron Davis
☐ 15 Vertical Strip 15 25   .10   .02
Dan Spillner/F.Jenkins
Enos Cabell/Ken Landreaux
J.Andujar/Don Baylor
Lonnie Smith/Ozzie Smith
Ron Cey/Brewers Logo
White Sox Logo/W.Randolph
Cesar Cedeno/Richie Zisk
Red Sox Logo/Reds Logo
E.Valentine/A.Hammaker
☐ 16 Vertical Strip 16 25   .10   .02
Jose Cruz/Larry Bowa
Steve Carlton/P.Vuckovich
Graig Nettles/B.Bochte
Tippy Martinez/D.Martinez
Ivan DeJesus/Padres Logo
Braves Logo/Gary Ward
Jeff Burroughs/Vida Blue
Yankees Logo/Royals Logo
Carney Lansford/Tom Herr

1911 Helmar Stamps

Each stamp measures 1 1/8" by 1 3/8". The stamps are very thin and have an ornate, bright colorful border surrounding the black and white photo of the player. There are many different border color combinations. There is no identification of issuer to be found anywhere on the stamp. Since the stamps are unnumbered they are listed below alphabetically within team.

		MINT	VG-E	F-G
COMPLETE SET		1800.00	800.00	160.00
COMMON PLAYER		9.00	4.25	.90
BOSTON RED SOX				
☐ 1	Carrigan	9.00	4.25	.90
☐ 2	Ed Cicotte	10.00	4.75	1.00
☐ 3	Engle	9.00	4.25	.90
☐ 4	Tris Speaker	35.00	16.50	3.50
☐ 5	Heine Wagner	10.00	4.75	1.00
CHICAGO WHITE SOX				
☐ 6	Block	9.00	4.25	.90
☐ 7	Ping Bodie	9.00	4.25	.90
☐ 8	Callahan	9.00	4.25	.90
☐ 9	Shano Collins	9.00	4.25	.90
☐ 10	Dougherty	9.00	4.25	.90
☐ 11	Lord	9.00	4.25	.90
☐ 12	McConnell	9.00	4.25	.90
☐ 13	McIntyre	9.00	4.25	.90
☐ 14	Parent	9.00	4.25	.90
☐ 15	Scott	9.00	4.25	.90
☐ 16	Sullivan	9.00	4.25	.90
☐ 17	Tannehill	9.00	4.25	.90
☐ 18	Ed Walsh	18.00	8.50	1.80
☐ 19	White	9.00	4.25	.90
☐ 20	Young	9.00	4.25	.90
CLEVELAND INDIANS				
☐ 21	Ball	9.00	4.25	.90
☐ 22	Birmingham	9.00	4.25	.90
☐ 23	Davis	9.00	4.25	.90
☐ 24	Napoleon Lajoie	25.00	11.00	2.50
☐ 25	Livingston	9.00	4.25	.90
☐ 26	Turner	9.00	4.25	.90
DETROIT TIGERS				
☐ 27	Bush	9.00	4.25	.90
☐ 28	Ty Cobb	125.00	57.00	12.50
☐ 29	Sam Crawford	18.00	8.50	1.80
☐ 30	Delahanty	10.00	4.75	1.00
☐ 31	Donovan	9.00	4.25	.90
☐ 32	Hughie Jennings	18.00	8.50	1.80
☐ 33	Jones	9.00	4.25	.90
☐ 34	Moriarity	9.00	4.25	.90
☐ 35	Mullin	9.00	4.25	.90
☐ 36	Boss Schmidt	9.00	4.25	.90
☐ 37	Oscar Stanage	9.00	4.25	.90
☐ 38	Willett	9.00	4.25	.90
NEW YORK YANKEES				
☐ 39	Brockett	9.00	4.25	.90
☐ 40	Chase	12.00	5.50	1.20
☐ 41	Cree	9.00	4.25	.90
☐ 42	Fisher	9.00	4.25	.90
☐ 43	Ford	9.00	4.25	.90
☐ 44	Gardner	9.00	4.25	.90
☐ 45	Quinn	9.00	4.25	.90
☐ 46	Street	9.00	4.25	.90
☐ 47	Sweeney	9.00	4.25	.90
☐ 48	Vaughan	9.00	4.25	.90
☐ 49	Warhop	9.00	4.25	.90
☐ 50	Wolter	9.00	4.25	.90
☐ 51	Wolverton	9.00	4.25	.90
PHILADELPHIA A'S				
☐ 52	Frank Baker	18.00	8.50	1.80
☐ 53	Jack Barry	9.00	4.25	.90
☐ 54	Chief Bender	18.00	8.50	1.80
☐ 55	Eddie Collins	21.00	9.50	2.10
☐ 56	Krause	9.00	4.25	.90
☐ 57	Murphy	9.00	4.25	.90
☐ 58	Oldring	9.00	4.25	.90
☐ 59	Thomas	9.00	4.25	.90
ST. LOUIS BROWNS				
☐ 60	Jimmy Austin	9.00	4.25	.90

☐ 61	Lake	9.00	4.25	.90
☐ 62	LaPorte	9.00	4.25	.90
☐ 63	Pelty	9.00	4.25	.90
☐ 64	Powell	9.00	4.25	.90
☐ 65	Stovall	9.00	4.25	.90
☐ 66	Bobby Wallace	18.00	8.50	1.80

WASHINGTON SENATORS

☐ 67	Wid Conroy	9.00	4.25	.90
☐ 68	Gray	9.00	4.25	.90
☐ 69	Clark Griffith	18.00	8.50	1.80
☐ 70	Groom	9.00	4.25	.90
☐ 71	Hughes	9.00	4.25	.90
☐ 72	Walter Johnson	60.00	27.00	6.00
☐ 73	Knight	9.00	4.25	.90
☐ 74	McBride	9.00	4.25	.90
☐ 75	Milan	9.00	4.25	.90
☐ 76	Germany Schaefer	9.00	4.25	.90

BOSTON BEES

☐ 77	Bridwell	9.00	4.25	.90
☐ 78	Hank Gowdy	10.00	4.75	1.00
☐ 79	Kling	9.00	4.25	.90
☐ 80	Mattern	9.00	4.25	.90
☐ 81	Sweeney	9.00	4.25	.90

BROOKLYN DODGERS

☐ 82	Barger	9.00	4.25	.90
☐ 83	Bell	9.00	4.25	.90
☐ 84	Bill Dahlen	10.00	4.75	1.00
☐ 85	Jake Daubert	10.00	4.75	1.00
☐ 86	Erwin	9.00	4.25	.90
☐ 87	Hummel	9.00	4.25	.90
☐ 88	Nap Rucker	9.00	4.25	.90
☐ 89	Zach Wheat	18.00	8.50	1.80

CHICAGO CUBS

☐ 90	Jimmy Archer	9.00	4.25	.90
☐ 91	Mordecai Brown	18.00	8.50	1.80
☐ 92	Frank Chance	21.00	9.50	2.10
☐ 93	Cole	9.00	4.25	.90
☐ 94	Johnny Evers	18.00	8.50	1.80
☐ 95	Graham	9.00	4.25	.90
☐ 96	Hoffman	9.00	4.25	.90
☐ 97	Lennox	9.00	4.25	.90
☐ 98	McIntire	9.00	4.25	.90
☐ 99	Needham	9.00	4.25	.90
☐ 100	Ed Reulbach	10.00	4.75	1.00
☐ 101	Richie	9.00	4.25	.90
☐ 102	Richter	9.00	4.25	.90
☐ 103	Rowan	9.00	4.25	.90
☐ 104	Schulte	9.00	4.25	.90
☐ 105	Dave Shean	9.00	4.25	.90
☐ 106	Jimmy Sheckard	9.00	4.25	.90
☐ 107	Joe Tinker	18.00	8.50	1.80
☐ 108	Toney	9.00	4.25	.90

CINCINNATI REDS

☐ 109	Bates	9.00	4.25	.90
☐ 110	Bescher	9.00	4.25	.90
☐ 111	Burns	9.00	4.25	.90
☐ 112	Clarke	9.00	4.25	.90
☐ 113	Fromme	9.00	4.25	.90
☐ 114	Gaspar	9.00	4.25	.90
☐ 115	Grant	9.00	4.25	.90
☐ 116	Hoblitzell	9.00	4.25	.90
☐ 117	McLean	9.00	4.25	.90
☐ 118	Mitchell (2)	9.00	4.25	.90
☐ 119	Suggs	9.00	4.25	.90

NEW YORK GIANTS

☐ 120	Ames	9.00	4.25	.90
☐ 121	Becker	9.00	4.25	.90
☐ 122	Doc Crandall	9.00	4.25	.90
☐ 123	Devlin	9.00	4.25	.90
☐ 124	Josh Devore	9.00	4.25	.90
☐ 125	Doyle	10.00	4.75	1.00
☐ 126	Drucke	9.00	4.25	.90
☐ 127	Fletcher	9.00	4.25	.90
☐ 128	Hartley	9.00	4.25	.90
☐ 129	Buck Herzog	9.00	4.25	.90
☐ 130	Rube Marquard	18.00	8.50	1.80
☐ 131	Christy Mathewson	50.00	22.00	5.00
☐ 132	John McGraw	25.00	11.00	2.50
☐ 133	Fred Merkle	10.00	4.75	1.00
☐ 134	Meyers	9.00	4.25	.90
☐ 135	Murray	9.00	4.25	.90
☐ 136	Shafer	9.00	4.25	.90
☐ 137	Fred Snodgrass	10.00	4.75	1.00
☐ 138	Wilson	9.00	4.25	.90
☐ 139	Wiltse	9.00	4.25	.90

PHILADELPHIA PHILLIES

☐ 140	Beck	9.00	4.25	.90
☐ 141	Dooin	9.00	4.25	.90
☐ 142	Doolan	9.00	4.25	.90
☐ 143	Downey	9.00	4.25	.90
☐ 144	Otto Knabe	9.00	4.25	.90
☐ 145	Hans Lobert	9.00	4.25	.90
☐ 146	Fred Luderus	9.00	4.25	.90

☐ 147	Sherry Magee	9.00	4.25	.90
☐ 148	Moore	9.00	4.25	.90
☐ 149	Moran	9.00	4.25	.90
☐ 150	Dode Paskert	9.00	4.25	.90
☐ 151	Scanlan	9.00	4.25	.90
☐ 152	Titus	9.00	4.25	.90

PITTSBURGH PIRATES

☐ 153	Adams	9.00	4.25	.90
☐ 154	Byrne	9.00	4.25	.90
☐ 155	Camnitz	9.00	4.25	.90
☐ 156	Max Carey	18.00	8.50	1.80
☐ 157	Fred Clarke	18.00	8.50	1.80
☐ 158	Donlin	9.00	4.25	.90
☐ 159	Ferry	9.00	4.25	.90
☐ 160	Gibson	9.00	4.25	.90
☐ 161	Leach	9.50	4.50	.95
☐ 162	Leifield	9.00	4.25	.90
☐ 163	Miller	9.00	4.25	.90
☐ 164	O'Toole	9.00	4.25	.90
☐ 165	Simon	9.00	4.25	.90
☐ 166	Wilson	9.00	4.25	.90

ST. LOUIS CARDINALS

☐ 166	Bliss	9.00	4.25	.90
☐ 167	Roger Bresnahan	18.00	8.50	1.80
☐ 168	Evans	9.00	4.25	.90
☐ 169	Harmon	9.00	4.25	.90
☐ 170	Hauser	9.00	4.25	.90
☐ 171	Miller Huggins	18.00	8.50	1.80
☐ 172	Konetchy	9.00	4.25	.90
☐ 173	Mowrey	9.00	4.25	.90
☐ 174	Oakes	9.00	4.25	.90
☐ 175	Phelps	9.00	4.25	.90
☐ 176	Slim Sallee	9.00	4.25	.90
☐ 177	Steele	9.00	4.25	.90

1969 MLB Official Stamps

Each team is represented by nine players; hence the set consists of 216 player stamps each measuring approximately 1 3/4" by 2 7/8". There are two large albums available, one for each league. Also there are four smaller divisional albums each measuring approximately 4" by 7" and holding all the player stamps for a particular division. Stamps are unnumbered but are presented here in alphabetical order by team.

			MINT	VG-E	F-G
COMPLETE SET			10.00	4.75	1.00
COMMON PLAYER			.03	.01	.00

BALTIMORE ORIOLES

☐	1	Paul Blair	.05	.02	.00
☐	2	Don Buford	.03	.01	.00
☐	3	Andy Etchebarren	.03	.01	.00
☐	4	Dave Johnson	.10	.04	.01
☐	5	Dave McNally	.05	.02	.00
☐	6	Tom Phoebus	.03	.01	.00
☐	7	John "Boog" Powell	.10	.04	.01
☐	8	Brooks Robinson	.50	.22	.05
☐	9	Frank Robinson	.50	.22	.05

BOSTON RED SOX

☐	10	Mike Andrews	.03	.01	.00
☐	11	Ray Culp	.03	.01	.00
☐	12	Dick Ellsworth	.03	.01	.00
☐	13	Ken Harrelson	.10	.04	.01
☐	14	Jim Lonborg	.05	.02	.00
☐	15	Rico Petrocelli	.05	.02	.00
☐	16	Jose Santiago	.03	.01	.00
☐	17	George Scott	.05	.02	.00
☐	18	Reggie Smith	.10	.04	.01

CALIFORNIA ANGELS

☐	19	George Brunet	.03	.01	.00
☐	20	Vic Davalillo	.03	.01	.00
☐	21	Jim Fregosi	.07	.03	.01
☐	22	Chuck Hinton	.03	.01	.00
☐	23	Bobby Knoop	.03	.01	.00
☐	24	Jim McGlothlin	.03	.01	.00
☐	25	Rick Reichardt	.03	.01	.00
☐	26	Roger Repoz	.03	.01	.00
☐	27	Bob Rodgers	.05	.02	.00

CHICAGO WHITE SOX			
☐ 28 Luis Aparicio	.25	.10	.02
☐ 29 Ken Berry	.03	.01	.00
☐ 30 Joe Horlen	.03	.01	.00
☐ 31 Tommy John	.15	.06	.01
☐ 32 Duane Josephson	.03	.01	.00
☐ 33 Tom McCraw	.03	.01	.00
☐ 34 Gary Peters	.05	.02	.00
☐ 35 Pete Ward	.03	.01	.00
☐ 36 Wilbur Wood	.05	.02	.00
CLEVELAND INDIANS			
☐ 37 Max Alvis	.03	.01	.00
☐ 38 Joe Azcue	.03	.01	.00
☐ 39 Larry Brown	.03	.01	.00
☐ 40 Jose Cardenal	.03	.01	.00
☐ 41 Tony Horton	.03	.01	.00
☐ 42 Sam McDowell	.05	.02	.00
☐ 43 Sonny Siebert	.03	.01	.00
☐ 44 Luis Tiant	.05	.02	.00
☐ 45 Zoilo Versalles	.03	.01	.00
DETROIT TIGERS			
☐ 46 Norm Cash	.07	.03	.01
☐ 47 Bill Freehan	.07	.03	.01
☐ 48 Willie Horton	.07	.03	.01
☐ 49 Al Kaline	.50	.22	.05
☐ 50 Mickey Lolich	.07	.03	.01
☐ 51 Dick McAuliffe	.03	.01	.00
☐ 52 Denny McLain	.07	.03	.01
☐ 53 Jim Northrup	.03	.01	.00
☐ 54 Mickey Stanley	.03	.01	.00
KANSAS CITY ROYALS			
☐ 55 Jerry Adair	.03	.01	.00
☐ 56 Wally Bunker	.03	.01	.00
☐ 57 Moe Drabowsky	.03	.01	.00
☐ 58 Joe Foy	.03	.01	.00
☐ 59 Ed Kirkpatrick	.03	.01	.00
☐ 60 Dave Morehead	.03	.01	.00
☐ 61 Roger Nelson	.03	.01	.00
☐ 62 Paul Schaal	.03	.01	.00
☐ 63 Steve Whitaker	.03	.01	.00
MINNESOTA TWINS			
☐ 64 Bob Allison	.05	.02	.00
☐ 65 Rod Carew	.50	.22	.05
☐ 66 Dean Chance	.05	.02	.00
☐ 67 Jim Kaat	.10	.04	.01
☐ 68 Harmon Killebrew	.30	.12	.03
☐ 69 Tony Oliva	.10	.04	.01
☐ 70 John Roseboro	.03	.01	.00
☐ 71 Cesar Tovar	.03	.01	.00
☐ 72 Ted Uhlaender	.03	.01	.00
NEW YORK YANKEES			
☐ 73 Horace Clarke	.03	.01	.00
☐ 74 Jake Gibbs	.03	.01	.00
☐ 75 Steve Hamilton	.03	.01	.00
☐ 76 Joe Pepitone	.05	.02	.00
☐ 77 Fritz Peterson	.03	.01	.00
☐ 78 Bill Robinson	.03	.01	.00
☐ 79 Mel Stottlemyre	.05	.02	.00
☐ 80 Tom Tresh	.05	.02	.00
☐ 81 Roy White	.05	.02	.00

OAKLAND A'S			
☐ 82 Sal Bando	.05	.02	.00
☐ 83 Bert Campaneris	.07	.03	.01
☐ 84 Danny Cater	.03	.01	.00
☐ 85 John Donaldson	.03	.01	.00
☐ 86 Mike Hershberger	.03	.01	.00
☐ 87 Jim Hunter	.20	.09	.02
☐ 88 Rick Monday	.05	.02	.00
☐ 89 Jim Nash	.03	.01	.00
☐ 90 John Odom	.03	.01	.00
SEATTLE PILOTS			
☐ 91 Jack Aker	.03	.01	.00
☐ 92 Steve Barber	.03	.01	.00
☐ 93 Gary Bell	.03	.01	.00
☐ 94 Tommy Davis	.05	.02	.00
☐ 95 Tommy Harper	.03	.01	.00
☐ 96 Don Mincher	.03	.01	.00
☐ 97 Ray Oyler	.03	.01	.00
☐ 98 Rich Rollins	.03	.01	.00
☐ 99 Chico Salmon	.03	.01	.00
WASHINGTON SENATORS			
☐ 100 Bernie Allen	.03	.01	.00
☐ 101 Ed Brinkman	.03	.01	.00
☐ 102 Paul Casanova	.03	.01	.00
☐ 103 Joe Coleman Jr.	.03	.01	.00
☐ 104 Mike Epstein	.03	.01	.00
☐ 105 Frank Howard	.07	.03	.01
☐ 106 Ken McMullen	.03	.01	.00
☐ 107 Camilo Pascual	.03	.01	.00
☐ 108 Ed Stroud	.03	.01	.00
ATLANTA BRAVES			
☐ 109 Henry Aaron	.75	.35	.07
☐ 110 Felipe Alou	.05	.02	.00
☐ 111 Bob Aspromonte	.03	.01	.00
☐ 112 Rico Carty	.06	.02	.00
☐ 113 Orlando Cepeda	.10	.04	.01
☐ 114 Pat Jarvis	.03	.01	.00
☐ 115 Felix Millan	.03	.01	.00
☐ 116 Phil Niekro	.20	.09	.02
☐ 117 Milt Pappas	.05	.02	.00
CHICAGO CUBS			
☐ 118 Ernie Banks	.50	.22	.05
☐ 119 Glen Beckert	.03	.01	.00
☐ 120 Bill Hands	.03	.01	.00
☐ 121 Randy Hundley	.03	.01	.00
☐ 122 Fergie Jenkins	.07	.03	.01
☐ 123 Don Kessinger	.05	.02	.00
☐ 124 Phil Regan	.03	.01	.00
☐ 125 Ron Santo	.07	.03	.01
☐ 126 Billy Williams	.12	.05	.01
CINCINNATI REDS			
☐ 127 Johnny Bench	.50	.22	.05
☐ 128 Tony Cloninger	.03	.01	.00
☐ 129 Tommy Helms	.03	.01	.00
☐ 130 Jim Maloney	.05	.02	.00
☐ 131 Lee May	.05	.02	.00
☐ 132 Jim Merritt	.03	.01	.00
☐ 133 Gary Nolan	.03	.01	.00
☐ 134 Tony Perez	.10	.04	.01
☐ 135 Pete Rose	1.50	.70	.15
HOUSTON ASTROS			
☐ 136 Jesus Alou	.03	.01	.00
☐ 137 Curt Blefary	.03	.01	.00
☐ 138 Larry Dierker	.03	.01	.00
☐ 139 Johnny Edwards	.03	.01	.00
☐ 140 Dennis Menke	.03	.01	.00
☐ 141 Joe Morgan	.15	.06	.01
☐ 142 Doug Rader	.05	.02	.00
☐ 143 Don Wilson	.03	.01	.00
☐ 144 Jim Wynn	.05	.02	.00
LOS ANGELES DODGERS			
☐ 145 Willie Davis	.05	.02	.00
☐ 146 Ron Fairly	.03	.01	.00
☐ 147 Len Gabrielson	.03	.01	.00
☐ 148 Tom Haller	.03	.01	.00
☐ 149 Jim LeFebvre	.03	.01	.00
☐ 150 Claude Osteen	.05	.02	.00
☐ 151 Wes Parker	.05	.02	.00
☐ 152 Bill Singer	.03	.01	.00
☐ 153 Don Sutton	.15	.06	.01
MONTREAL EXPOS			
☐ 154 Bob Bailey	.03	.01	.00
☐ 155 John Bateman	.03	.01	.00
☐ 156 Ty Cline	.03	.01	.00
☐ 157 Jim Fairey	.03	.01	.00
☐ 158 Jim Grant	.03	.01	.00
☐ 159 Mack Jones	.03	.01	.00
☐ 160 Manny Mota	.05	.02	.00
☐ 161 Rusty Staub	.08	.03	.01
☐ 162 Maury Wills	.08	.03	.01
NEW YORK METS			
☐ 163 Tommy Agee	.03	.01	.00
☐ 164 Ed Charles	.03	.01	.00

☐ 165	Jerry Grote	.03	.01	.00
☐ 166	Bud Harrelson	.03	.01	.00
☐ 167	Cleon Jones	.03	.01	.00
☐ 168	Jerry Koosman	.06	.02	.00
☐ 169	Ed Kranepool	.03	.01	.00
☐ 170	Tom Seaver	.60	.28	.06
☐ 171	Ron Swoboda	.03	.01	.00
PHILADELPHIA PHILLIES				
☐ 172	Richie Allen	.07	.03	.01
☐ 173	Johnny Briggs	.03	.01	.00
☐ 174	Johnny Callison	.05	.02	.00
☐ 175	Woody Fryman	.03	.01	.00
☐ 176	Cookie Rojas	.03	.01	.00
☐ 177	Mike Ryan	.03	.01	.00
☐ 178	Chris Short	.03	.01	.00
☐ 179	Tony Taylor	.03	.01	.00
☐ 180	Rick Wise	.05	.02	.00
PITTSBURGH PIRATES				
☐ 181	Gene Alley	.03	.01	.00
☐ 182	Matty Alou	.05	.02	.00
☐ 183	Jim Bunning	.10	.04	.01
☐ 184	Roberto Clemente	.75	.35	.07
☐ 185	Ron Davis	.03	.01	.00
☐ 186	Jerry May	.03	.01	.00
☐ 187	Bill Mazeroski	.07	.03	.01
☐ 188	Willie Stargell	.35	.15	.03
☐ 189	Bob Veale	.03	.01	.00
SAN DIEGO PADRES				
☐ 190	Ollie Brown	.03	.01	.00
☐ 191	Al Ferrara	.03	.01	.00
☐ 192	Tony Gonzales	.03	.01	.00
☐ 193	Dick Kelley	.03	.01	.00
☐ 194	Bill McCool	.03	.01	.00
☐ 195	Dick Selma	.03	.01	.00
☐ 196	Tommy Sisk	.03	.01	.00
☐ 197	Ed Spiezio	.03	.01	.00
☐ 198	Larry Stahl	.03	.01	.00
SAN FRANCISCO GIANTS				
☐ 199	Jim Ray Hart	.05	.02	.00
☐ 200	Ron Hunt	.03	.01	.00
☐ 201	Hal Lanier	.07	.03	.01
☐ 202	Frank Linzy	.03	.01	.00
☐ 203	Juan Marichal	.25	.10	.02
☐ 204	Willie Mays	.75	.35	.07
☐ 205	Mike McCormick	.05	.02	.00
☐ 206	Willie McCovey	.35	.15	.03
☐ 207	Gaylord Perry	.20	.09	.02
ST. LOUIS CARDINALS				
☐ 208	Nelson Briles	.03	.01	.00
☐ 209	Lou Brock	.40	.18	.04
☐ 210	Curt Flood	.07	.03	.01
☐ 211	Bob Gibson	.40	.18	.04
☐ 212	Julian Javier	.05	.02	.00
☐ 213	Dal Maxvill	.03	.01	.00
☐ 214	Tim McCarver	.06	.02	.00
☐ 215	Mike Shannon	.05	.02	.00
☐ 216	Joe Torre	.08	.03	.01

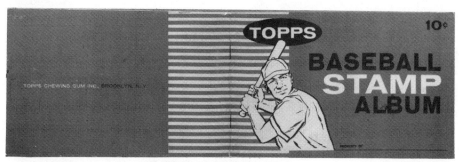

1961 Topps Stamp Album

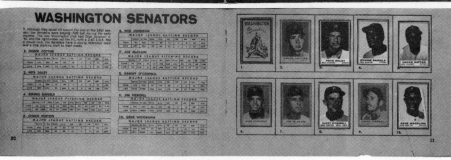

1962 Topps Stamp Album

1961 Topps Stamps

There are 207 different baseball players depicted in this stamp series, which was issued as an insert in packages of the regular Topps cards of 1961. The set is actually comprised of 208 stamps: 104 players are pictured on brown stamps and 104 players appear on green stamps, with Kaline found in both colors. The stamps were issued in attached pairs and an album was sold separately (10 cents) at retail outlets. Each stamp measures 1 3/8" by 1 3/16".

		MINT	VG-E	F-G
COMPLETE SET		100.00	45.00	10.00
COMMON PLAYER		.25	.10	.02

CHICAGO CUBS

☐ 1	George Altman	.25	.10	.02
☐ 2	Bob Anderson (brown)	.25	.10	.02
☐ 3	Richie Ashburn	.50	.22	.05
☐ 4	Ernie Banks	1.50	.70	.15
☐ 5	Ed Bouchee	.25	.10	.02
☐ 6	Jim Brewer	.25	.10	.02
☐ 7	Dick Ellsworth	.25	.10	.02
☐ 8	Don Elston	.25	.10	.02
☐ 9	Ron Santo	.35	.15	.03
☐ 10	Sammy Taylor	.25	.10	.02
☐ 11	Bob Will	.25	.10	.02
☐ 12	Billy Williams	.75	.35	.07

CINCINNATI REDS

☐ 13	Ed Bailey	.25	.10	.02
☐ 14	Gus Bell	.35	.15	.03
☐ 15	Jim Brosnan (brown)	.25	.10	.02
☐ 16	Chico Cardenas	.25	.10	.02
☐ 17	Gene Freese	.25	.10	.02
☐ 18	Eddie Kasko	.25	.10	.02
☐ 19	Jerry Lynch	.25	.10	.02
☐ 20	Billy Martin	.75	.35	.07
☐ 21	Jim O'Toole	.25	.10	.02
☐ 22	Vada Pinson	.35	.15	.03
☐ 23	Wally Post	.25	.10	.02
☐ 24	Frank Robinson	1.50	.70	.15

LOS ANGELES DODGERS

☐ 25	Tommy Davis	.35	.15	.03
☐ 26	Don Drysdale	1.50	.70	.15
☐ 27	Frank Howard (brown)	.35	.15	.03
☐ 28	Norm Larker	.25	.10	.02
☐ 29	Wally Moon	.35	.15	.03
☐ 30	Charlie Neal	.25	.10	.02
☐ 31	Johnny Podres	.35	.15	.03
☐ 32	Ed Roebuck	.25	.10	.02
☐ 33	Johnny Roseboro	.25	.10	.02
☐ 34	Larry Sherry	.25	.10	.02
☐ 35	Duke Snider	2.50	1.15	.25
☐ 36	Stan Williams	.25	.10	.02

MILWAUKEE BRAVES

☐ 37	Hank Aaron	4.00	1.85	.40
☐ 38	Joe Adcock	.35	.15	.03
☐ 39	Bill Bruton	.25	.10	.02
☐ 40	Bob Buhl	.25	.10	.02
☐ 41	Wes Covington (brown)	.25	.10	.02
☐ 42	Del Crandall	.35	.15	.03
☐ 43	Joey Jay	.25	.10	.02
☐ 44	Felix Mantilla	.25	.10	.02
☐ 45	Eddie Mathews	1.50	.70	.15
☐ 46	Roy McMillan	.25	.10	.02
☐ 47	Warren Spahn	1.50	.70	.15
☐ 48	Carlton Willey	.25	.10	.02

PHILADELPHIA PHILLIES

☐ 49	John Buzhardt	.25	.10	.02
☐ 50	Johnny Callison	.35	.15	.03
☐ 51	Tony Curry	.25	.10	.02
☐ 52	Clay Dalrymple (brown)	.25	.10	.02
☐ 53	Bobby Del Greco	.25	.10	.02
☐ 54	Dick Farrell	.25	.10	.02
☐ 55	Tony Gonzales	.25	.10	.02
☐ 56	Pancho Herrera	.25	.10	.02
☐ 57	Art Mahaffey	.25	.10	.02
☐ 58	Robin Roberts	1.50	.70	.15
☐ 59	Tony Taylor	.25	.10	.02
☐ 60	Lee Walls	.25	.10	.02

PITTSBURGH PIRATES

☐ 61	Smokey Burgess	.35	.15	.03
☐ 62	Elroy Face (brown)	.35	.15	.03
☐ 63	Bob Friend	.35	.15	.03
☐ 64	Dick Groat	.35	.15	.03
☐ 65	Don Hoak	.25	.10	.02
☐ 66	Vernon Law	.35	.15	.03
☐ 67	Bill Mazeroski	.50	.22	.05
☐ 68	Rocky Nelson	.25	.10	.02
☐ 69	Bob Skinner	.25	.10	.02
☐ 70	Hal Smith	.25	.10	.02
☐ 71	Dick Stuart	.35	.15	.03
☐ 72	Bill Virdon	.35	.15	.03

SAN FRANCISCO GIANTS

☐ 73	Don Blasingame	.25	.10	.02
☐ 74	Eddie Bressoud (brown)	.25	.10	.02
☐ 75	Orlando Cepeda	.75	.35	.07
☐ 76	Jim Davenport	.35	.15	.03
☐ 77	Harvey Kuenn	.35	.15	.03
☐ 78	Hobie Landrith	.25	.10	.02
☐ 79	Juan Marichal	1.50	.70	.15
☐ 80	Willie Mays	4.00	1.85	.40
☐ 81	Mike McCormick	.35	.15	.03
☐ 82	Willie McCovey	1.50	.70	.15
☐ 83	Billy O'Dell	.25	.10	.02
☐ 84	Jack Sanford	.25	.10	.02

ST. LOUIS CARDINALS

☐ 85	Ken Boyer	.50	.22	.05
☐ 86	Curt Flood	.50	.22	.05
☐ 87	Alex Grammas (brown)	.25	.10	.02
☐ 88	Larry Jackson	.25	.10	.02
☐ 89	Julian Javier	.25	.10	.02
☐ 90	Ron Kline	.25	.10	.02
☐ 91	Lindy McDaniel	.25	.10	.02
☐ 92	Stan Musial	3.50	1.65	.35
☐ 93	Curt Simmons	.35	.15	.03
☐ 94	Hal Smith	.25	.10	.02
☐ 95	Daryl Spencer	.25	.10	.02
☐ 96	Bill White	.35	.15	.03

BALTIMORE ORIOLES

☐ 97	Steve Barber	.25	.10	.02
☐ 98	Jackie Brandt (brown)	.25	.10	.02
☐ 99	Marv Breeding	.25	.10	.02
☐ 100	Chuck Estrada	.25	.10	.02
☐ 101	Jim Gentile	.35	.15	.03
☐ 102	Ron Hansen	.25	.10	.02
☐ 103	Milt Pappas	.35	.15	.03
☐ 104	Brooks Robinson	1.50	.70	.15
☐ 105	Gene Stephens	.25	.10	.02
☐ 106	Gus Triandos	.35	.15	.03
☐ 107	Hoyt Wilhelm	1.00	.45	.10

BOSTON RED SOX

☐ 108	Tom Brewer	.25	.10	.02
☐ 119	Gene Conley (brown)	.25	.10	.02
☐ 110	Ike Delock	.25	.10	.02
☐ 111	Gary Geiger	.25	.10	.02
☐ 112	Jackie Jensen	.35	.15	.03
☐ 113	Frank Malzone	.35	.15	.03
☐ 114	Bill Monbouquette	.25	.10	.02
☐ 115	Russ Nixon	.25	.10	.02
☐ 116	Pete Runnels	.35	.15	.03
☐ 117	Willie Tasby	.25	.10	.02
☐ 118	Vic Wertz	.25	.10	.02
☐ 119	Carl Yastrzemski	4.00	1.85	.40

CHICAGO WHITE SOX

☐ 120	Luis Aparicio	1.00	.45	.10
☐ 121	Russ Kemmerer (brown)	.25	.10	.02
☐ 122	Jim Landis	.25	.10	.02
☐ 123	Sherm Lollar	.25	.10	.02
☐ 124	J.C. Martin	.25	.10	.02
☐ 125	Minnie Minoso	.35	.15	.03
☐ 126	Billy Pierce	.35	.15	.03
☐ 127	Bob Shaw	.25	.10	.02
☐ 128	Al Smith	.25	.10	.02
☐ 129	Gerry Staley	.25	.10	.02
☐ 130	Early Wynn	1.00	.45	.10

CLEVELAND INDIANS

☐ 131	John Antonelli (brown)	.35	.15	.03
☐ 132	Ken Aspromonte	.25	.10	.02
☐ 133	Tito Francona	.35	.15	.03
☐ 134	Jim Grant	.25	.10	.02
☐ 135	Woody Held	.25	.10	.02
☐ 136	Barry Latman	.25	.10	.02
☐ 137	Jim Perry	.35	.15	.03
☐ 138	Jimmy Piersall	.35	.15	.03

☐ 139	Bubba Phillips	.25	.10	.02
☐ 140	Vic Power	.25	.10	.02
☐ 141	John Romano	.25	.10	.02
☐ 142	Johnny Temple	.25	.10	.02

DETROIT TIGERS

☐ 143	Hank Aguirre (brown)	.25	.10	.02
☐ 144	Frank Bolling	.25	.10	.02
☐ 145	Steve Boros	.35	.15	.03
☐ 146	Jim Bunning	.75	.35	.07
☐ 147	Norm Cash	.35	.15	.03
☐ 148	Harry Chiti	.25	.10	.02
☐ 149	Chico Fernandez	.25	.10	.02
☐ 150	Dick Gernert	.25	.10	.02
☐ 151	Al Kaline (green)	2.00	.90	.20
☐ 152	Al Kaline (brown)	2.00	.90	.20
☐ 153	Frank Lary	.35	.15	.03
☐ 154	Charlie Maxwell	.25	.10	.02
☐ 155	Dave Sisler	.25	.10	.02

KANSAS CITY A'S

☐ 156	Hank Bauer	.35	.15	.03
☐ 157	Bob Boyd (brown)	.25	.10	.02
☐ 158	Andy Carey	.25	.10	.02
☐ 159	Bud Daley	.25	.10	.02
☐ 160	Dick Hall	.25	.10	.02
☐ 161	J.C. Hartman	.25	.10	.02
☐ 162	Ray Herbert	.25	.10	.02
☐ 163	Whitey Herzog	.35	.15	.03
☐ 164	Jerry Lumpe	.25	.10	.02
☐ 165	Norm Siebern	.25	.10	.02
☐ 166	Marv Throneberry	.35	.15	.03
☐ 167	Bill Tuttle	.25	.10	.02
☐ 168	Dick Williams	.35	.15	.03

LOS ANGELES ANGELS

☐ 169	Jerry Casale (brown)	.25	.10	.02
☐ 170	Bob Cerv	.25	.10	.02
☐ 171	Ned Garver	.25	.10	.02
☐ 172	Ron Hunt	.25	.10	.02
☐ 173	Ted Kluszewski	.50	.22	.05
☐ 174	Bob Sadowski	.25	.10	.02
☐ 175	Eddie Yost	.25	.10	.02

MINNESOTA TWINS

☐ 176	Bob Allison	.35	.15	.03
☐ 177	Earl Battey (brown)	.25	.10	.02
☐ 178	Reno Bertoia	.25	.10	.02
☐ 179	Billy Gardner	.35	.15	.03
☐ 180	Jim Kaat	.50	.22	.05
☐ 181	Harmon Killebrew	1.50	.70	.15
☐ 182	Jim Lemon	.35	.15	.03
☐ 183	Camilo Pascual	.35	.15	.03
☐ 184	Pedro Ramos	.25	.10	.02
☐ 185	Chuck Stobbs	.25	.10	.02
☐ 186	Zoilo Versalles	.25	.10	.02
☐ 187	Pete Whisenant	.25	.10	.02

NEW YORK YANKEES

☐ 188	Luis Arroyo (brown)	.25	.10	.02
☐ 189	Yogi Berra	2.50	1.15	.25
☐ 190	John Blanchard	.25	.10	.02
☐ 191	Clete Boyer	.35	.15	.03
☐ 192	Art Ditmar	.25	.10	.02
☐ 193	Whitey Ford	2.00	.90	.20
☐ 194	Elston Howard	.50	.22	.05
☐ 195	Tony Kubek	.50	.22	.05
☐ 196	Mickey Mantle	10.00	4.75	1.00
☐ 197	Roger Maris	2.50	1.15	.25
☐ 198	Bobby Shantz	.35	.15	.03
☐ 199	Bill Stafford	.25	.10	.02
☐ 200	Bob Turley	.35	.15	.03

WASHINGTON SENATORS

☐ 201	Bud Daley (brown)	.25	.10	.02
☐ 202	Dick Donovan	.25	.10	.02
☐ 203	Bobby Klaus	.25	.10	.02
☐ 204	Johnny Klippstein	.25	.10	.02
☐ 205	Dale Long	.25	.10	.02
☐ 206	Ray Semproch	.25	.10	.02
☐ 207	Gene Woodling	.35	.15	.03

1962 Topps Stamps

The 200 baseball player stamps inserted into the Topps regular issue of 1962 are color photos set upon red or yellow backgrounds (100 players for each color). They came in two-stamp panels with a small additional strip which contained advertising for an album. The illustration at left shows the

Callison stamp, which is misspelled "Callizon". Roy Sievers appears with Kansas City or Philadelphia. Each stamp measures 1 3/8" by 1 7/8".

	MINT	VG-E	F-G
COMPLETE SET	100.00	45.00	10.00
COMMON PLAYER	.25	.10	.02

BALTIMORE ORIOLES

☐ 1	Baltimore Emblem	.25	.10	.02
☐ 2	Jerry Adair	.25	.10	.02
☐ 3	Jackie Brandt	.25	.10	.02
☐ 4	Chuck Estrada	.25	.10	.02
☐ 5	Jim Gentile	.35	.15	.03
☐ 6	Ron Hansen	.25	.10	.02
☐ 7	Milt Pappas	.35	.15	.03
☐ 8	Brooks Robinson	1.50	.70	.15
☐ 9	Gus Triandos	.35	.15	.03
☐ 10	Hoyt Wilhelm	1.00	.45	

BOSTON RED SOX

☐ 11	Boston Emblem	.25	.10	.02
☐ 12	Mike Fornieles	.25	.10	.02
☐ 13	Gary Geiger	.25	.10	.02
☐ 14	Frank Malzone	.35	.15	.03
☐ 15	Bill Monbouquette	.25	.10	.02
☐ 16	Russ Nixon	.25	.10	.02
☐ 17	Pete Runnels	.35	.15	.03
☐ 18	Chuck Schilling	.25	.10	.02
☐ 19	Don Schwall	.25	.10	.02
☐ 20	Carl Yastrzemski	5.00	2.35	.50

CHICAGO WHITE SOX

☐ 21	Chicago Emblem	.25	.10	.02
☐ 22	Luis Aparicio	1.00	.45	.10
☐ 23	Camilo Carreon	.25	.10	.02
☐ 24	Nellie Fox	.75	.35	.07
☐ 25	Ray Herbert	.25	.10	.02
☐ 26	Jim Landis	.25	.10	.02
☐ 27	J.C. Martin	.25	.10	.02
☐ 28	Juan Pizzaro	.25	.10	.02
☐ 29	Floyd Robinson	.25	.10	.02
☐ 30	Early Wynn	1.00	.45	.10

CLEVELAND INDIANS

☐ 31	Cleveland Emblem	.25	.10	.02
☐ 32	Ty Cline	.25	.10	.02
☐ 33	Dick Donovan	.25	.10	.02
☐ 34	Tito Francona	.35	.15	.03
☐ 35	Woddy Held	.25	.10	.02
☐ 36	Barry Latman	.25	.10	.02
☐ 37	Jim Perry	.35	.15	.03
☐ 38	Bubba Phillips	.25	.10	.02
☐ 39	Vic Power	.25	.10	.02
☐ 40	Johnny Romano	.25	.10	.02

DETROIT TIGERS

☐ 41	Detroit Emblem	.25	.10	.02
☐ 42	Steve Boros	.35	.15	.03
☐ 43	Bill Bruton	.25	.10	.02
☐ 44	Jim Bunning	.75	.35	.07
☐ 45	Norm Cash	.35	.15	.03
☐ 46	Rocky Colavito	.50	.22	.05
☐ 47	Al Kaline	2.00	.90	.20
☐ 48	Frank Lary	.35	.15	.03
☐ 49	Don Mossi	.35	.15	.03
☐ 50	Jake Wood	.25	.10	.02

KANSAS CITY A'S

☐ 51	Kansas City Emblem	.25	.10	.02
☐ 52	Jim Archer	.25	.10	.02
☐ 53	Dick Howser	.35	.15	.03
☐ 54	Jerry Lumpe	.25	.10	.02
☐ 55	Leo Posada	.25	.10	.02
☐ 56	Bob Shaw	.25	.10	.02
☐ 57	Norm Siebern	.25	.10	.02
☐ 58	Roy Sievers	.50	.22	.05
	(see also 169)			
☐ 59	Gene Stephens	.25	.10	.02
☐ 60	Haywood Sullivan	.35	.15	.03
☐ 61	Jerry Walker	.25	.10	.02

LOS ANGELES ANGELS
□	62	Los Angeles Emblem	.25	.10	.02
□	63	Steve Bilko	.25	.10	.02
□	64	Ted Bowsfield	.25	.10	.02
□	65	Ken Hunt	.25	.10	.02
□	66	Ken McBride	.25	.10	.02
□	67	Albie Pearson	.25	.10	.02
□	68	Bob Rodgers	.25	.10	.02
□	69	George Thomas	.25	.10	.02
□	70	Lee Thomas	.25	.10	.02
□	71	Leon Wagner	.25	.10	.02

MINNESOTA TWINS
□	72	Minnesota Emblem	.25	.10	.02
□	73	Bob Allison	.35	.15	.03
□	74	Earl Battey	.25	.10	.02
□	75	Lenny Green	.25	.10	.02
□	76	Harmon Killebrew	1.50	.70	.15
□	77	Jack Kralick	.25	.10	.02
□	78	Camilo Pascual	.35	.15	.03
□	79	Pedro Ramos	.25	.10	.02
□	80	Bill Tuttle	.25	.10	.02
□	81	Zoilo Versailles	.25	.10	.02

NEW YORK YANKEES
□	82	New York Emblem	.25	.10	.02
□	83	Yogi Berra	2.50	1.15	.25
□	84	Clete Boyer	.35	.15	.03
□	85	Whitey Ford	2.00	.90	.20
□	86	Elston Howard	.50	.22	.05
□	87	Tony Kubek	.50	.22	.05
□	88	Mickey Mantle	10.00	4.75	1.00
□	89	Roger Maris	2.50	1.15	.25
□	90	Bobby Richardson	.50	.22	.05
□	91	Bill Skowron	.35	.15	.03

WASHINGTON SENATORS
□	92	Washington Emblem	.25	.10	.02
□	93	Chuck Cottier	.35	.15	.03
□	94	Pete Daley	.25	.10	.02
□	95	Bennie Daniels	.25	.10	.02
□	96	Chuck Hinton	.25	.10	.02
□	97	Bob Johnson	.25	.10	.02
□	98	Joe McClain	.25	.10	.02
□	99	Danny O'Connell	.25	.10	.02
□	100	Jimmy Piersall	.35	.15	.03
□	101	Gene Woodling	.25	.10	.02

CHICAGO CUBS
□	102	Chicago Emblem	.25	.10	.02
□	103	George Altman	.25	.10	.02
□	104	Ernie Banks	1.50	.70	.15
□	105	Dick Bertell	.25	.10	.02
□	106	Don Cardwell	.25	.10	.02
□	107	Dick Ellsworth	.25	.10	.02
□	108	Glen Hobbie	.25	.10	.02
□	109	Ron Santo	.50	.22	.05
□	110	Barney Schultz	.25	.10	.02
□	111	Billy Williams	.75	.35	.07

CINCINNATI REDS
□	112	Cincinnati Emblem	.25	.10	.02
□	113	Gordon Coleman	.25	.10	.02
□	114	John Edwards	.25	.10	.02
□	115	Gene Freese	.25	.10	.02
□	116	Joe Jay	.25	.10	.02
□	117	Eddie Kasko	.25	.10	.02
□	118	Jim O'Toole	.25	.10	.02
□	119	Vada Pinson	.35	.15	.03
□	120	Bob Purkey	.25	.10	.02
□	121	Frank Robinson	1.50	.70	.15

HOUSTON COLT .45'S
□	122	Houston Emblem	.25	.10	.02
□	123	Joe Amalfitano	.25	.10	.02
□	124	Bob Aspromonte	.25	.10	.02
□	125	Dick Farrell	.25	.10	.02
□	126	Al Heist	.25	.10	.02
□	127	Sam Jones	.25	.10	.02
□	128	Bobby Shantz	.35	.15	.03
□	129	Hal W. Smith	.25	.10	.02
□	130	Al Spangler	.25	.10	.02
□	131	Bob Tiefenauer	.25	.10	.02

LOS ANGELES DODGERS
□	132	Los Angeles Emblem	.25	.10	.02
□	133	Don Drysdale	1.50	.70	.15
□	134	Ron Fairly	.25	.10	.02
□	135	Frank Howard	.35	.15	.03
□	136	Sandy Koufax	3.00	1.40	.30
□	137	Wally Moon	.35	.15	.03
□	138	Johnny Podres	.35	.15	.03
□	139	John Roseboro	.25	.10	.02
□	140	Duke Snider	2.50	1.15	.25
□	141	Daryl Spencer	.25	.10	.02

MILWAUKEE BRAVES
□	142	Milwaukee Emblem	.25	.10	.02
□	143	Hank Aaron	4.00	1.85	.40
□	144	Joe Adcock	.35	.15	.03
□	145	Frank Bolling	.25	.10	.02

□	146	Lou Burdette	.35	.15	.03
□	147	Del Crandall	.35	.15	.03
□	148	Ed Mathews	1.50	.70	.15
□	149	Roy McMillan	.25	.10	.02
□	150	Warren Spahn	2.00	.90	.20
□	151	Joe Torre	.50	.22	.05

NEW YORK METS
□	152	New York Emblem	.25	.10	.02
□	153	Gus Bell	.35	.15	.03
□	154	Roger Craig	.35	.15	.03
□	155	Gil Hodges	1.50	.70	.15
□	156	Jay Hook	.25	.10	.02
□	157	Hobie Landrith	.25	.10	.02
□	158	Felix Mantilla	.25	.10	.02
□	159	Bob L. Miller	.25	.10	.02
□	160	Lee Walls	.25	.10	.02
□	161	Don Zimmer	.35	.15	.03

PHILADELPHIA PHILLIES
□	162	Philadelphia Emblem	.25	.10	.02
□	163	Ruben Amaro	.25	.10	.02
□	164	Jack Baldschun	.25	.10	.02
□	165	Johnny Callison	.35	.15	.03
□	166	Clay Dalrymple	.25	.10	.02
□	167	Don Demeter	.25	.10	.02
□	168	Tony Gonzalez	.25	.10	.02
□	169	Roy Sievers	.50	.22	.05
		(see also 58)			
□	170	Tony Taylor	.25	.10	.02
□	171	Art Mahaffey	.25	.10	.02

PITTSBURGH PIRATES
□	172	Pittsburgh Emblem	.25	.10	.02
□	173	Smoky Burgess	.35	.15	.03
□	174	Bob Clemente	3.50	1.65	.35
□	175	Roy Face	.35	.15	.03
□	176	Bob Friend	.35	.15	.03
□	177	Dick Groat	.35	.15	.03
□	178	Don Hoak	.25	.10	.02
□	179	Bill Mazeroski	.50	.22	.05
□	180	Dick Stuart	.35	.15	.03
□	181	Bill Virdon	.35	.15	.03

ST. LOUIS CARDINALS
□	182	St. Louis Emblem	.25	.10	.02
□	183	Ken Boyer	.50	.22	.05
□	184	Larry Jackson	.25	.10	.02
□	185	Julian Javier	.25	.10	.02
□	186	Tim McCarver	.35	.15	.03
□	187	Lindy McDaniel	.25	.10	.02
□	188	Minnie Minoso	.35	.15	.03
□	189	Stan Musial	3.50	1.65	.35
□	190	Ray Sadecki	.25	.10	.02
□	191	Bill White	.35	.15	.03

SAN FRANCISCO GIANTS
□	192	San Francisco Emblem	.25	.10	.02
□	193	Felipe Alou	.35	.15	.03
□	194	Ed Bailey	.25	.10	.02
□	195	Orlando Cepeda	.75	.35	.07
□	196	Jim Davenport	.35	.15	.03
□	197	Harvey Kuenn	.35	.15	.03
□	198	Juan Marichal	1.50	.70	.15
□	199	Willie Mays	4.00	1.85	.40
□	200	Mike McCormick	.35	.15	.03
□	201	Stu Miller	.25	.10	.02

1964 Topps Stamps

Many of the 100 color portraits of baseball players featured in this 1964 Topps stamp series show players without caps. Each small stamp is 1" by 1 1/2". The subject's name, team and position are found in a colored rectangle beneath the picture area. Each sheet is numbered in the upper left hand corner outside the picture area. The stamps were issued in sheets of 10 but an album to hold this particular set has not yet been seen.

			MINT	VG-E	F-G
COMPLETE SET			100.00	45.00	10.00
COMMON PLAYER			.50	.22	.05

SHEET ONE
□	1	Ed Charles	.50	.22	.05
□	2	Vada Pinson	.75	.35	.07
□	3	Jimmy Hall	.50	.22	.05

☐	31	Juan Pizarro	.50	.22	.05
☐	32	Jim Maloney	.60	.28	.06
☐	33	Ron Santo	.75	.35	.07
☐	34	Harmon Killebrew	2.50	1.15	.25
☐	35	Ed Roebuck	.50	.22	.05
☐	36	Boog Powell	.75	.35	.07
☐	37	Jim Grant	.50	.22	.05
☐	38	Hank Aguirre	.50	.22	.05
☐	39	Juan Marichal	2.00	.90	.20
☐	40	Bill Mazeroski	.75	.35	.07

SHEET FIVE

☐	41	Dick Radatz	.60	.28	.06
☐	42	Albie Pearson	.50	.22	.05
☐	43	Tommy Harper	.60	.28	.06
☐	44	Carl Willey	.50	.22	.05
☐	45	Jim Bouton	.75	.35	.07
☐	46	Ron Perranoski	.50	.22	.05
☐	47	Chuck Hinton	.50	.22	.05
☐	48	John Romano	.50	.22	.05
☐	49	Norm Cash	.75	.35	.07
☐	50	Orlando Cepeda	1.00	.45	.10

SHEET SIX

☐	51	Dick Stuart	.60	.28	.06
☐	52	Rich Rollins	.50	.22	.05
☐	53	Mickey Mantle	10.00	4.75	1.00
☐	54	Steve Barber	.50	.22	.05
☐	55	Jim O'Toole	.50	.22	.05
☐	56	Gary Peters	.50	.22	.05
☐	57	Warren Spahn	2.50	1.15	.25
☐	58	Tony Gonzalez	.50	.22	.05
☐	59	Joe Torre	.75	.35	.07
☐	60	Jim Fregosi	.60	.28	.06

SHEET SEVEN

☐	61	Ken Boyer	.75	.35	.07
☐	62	Felipe Alou	.75	.35	.07
☐	63	Jim Davenport	.60	.28	.06
☐	64	Tommy Davis	.75	.35	.07
☐	65	Rocky Colavito	.75	.35	.07
☐	66	Bob Friend	.50	.22	.05
☐	67	Billy Moran	.50	.22	.05
☐	68	Bill Freehan	.60	.28	.06
☐	69	George Altman	.50	.22	.05
☐	70	Ken Johnson	.50	.22	.05

SHEET EIGHT

☐	71	Earl Battey	.50	.22	.05
☐	72	Elston Howard	.75	.35	.07
☐	73	Billy Williams	1.00	.45	.10
☐	74	Claude Osteen	.60	.28	.06
☐	75	Jim Gentile	.60	.28	.06
☐	76	Donn Clendenon	.50	.22	.05
☐	77	Ernie Broglio	.50	.22	.05
☐	78	Hal Woodeshick	.50	.22	.05
☐	79	Don Drysdale	2.50	1.15	.25
☐	80	John Callison	.60	.28	.06

SHEET NINE

☐	81	Dick Groat	.60	.28	.06
☐	82	Moe Drabowsky	.50	.22	.05
☐	83	Frank Howard	.75	.35	.07
☐	84	Hank Aaron	6.00	2.80	.60
☐	85	Al Jackson	.50	.22	.05
☐	86	Jerry Lumpe	.50	.22	.05
☐	87	Wayne Causey	.50	.22	.05
☐	88	Rusty Staub	.75	.35	.07
☐	89	Ken McBride	.50	.22	.05
☐	90	Jack Baldschun	.50	.22	.05

SHEET TEN

☐	91	Sandy Koufax	4.00	1.85	.40
☐	92	Camilo Pascual	.60	.28	.06
☐	93	Ron Hunt	.50	.22	.05
☐	94	Willie McCovey	2.50	1.15	.25
☐	95	Al Kaline	3.00	1.40	.30
☐	96	Ray Culp	.50	.22	.05
☐	97	Ed Mathews	2.50	1.15	.25
☐	98	Dick Farrell	.50	.22	.05
☐	99	Lee Thomas	.50	.22	.05
☐	100	Vic Davalillo	.50	.22	.05

☐	4	Milt Pappas	.60	.28	.06
☐	5	Dick Ellsworth	.50	.22	.05
☐	6	Frank Malzone	.60	.28	.06
☐	7	Max Alvis	.50	.22	.05
☐	8	Pete Ward	.50	.22	.05
☐	9	Tony Taylor	.50	.22	.05
☐	10	Bill White	.60	.28	.06

SHEET TWO

☐	11	Don Zimmer	.60	.28	.06
☐	12	Bobby Richardson	.75	.35	.07
☐	13	Larry Jackson	.50	.22	.05
☐	14	Norm Siebern	.50	.22	.05
☐	15	Frank Robinson	2.50	1.15	.25
☐	16	Bob Aspromonte	.50	.22	.05
☐	17	Al McBean	.50	.22	.05
☐	18	Floyd Robinson	.50	.22	.05
☐	19	Bill Monbouquette	.50	.22	.05
☐	20	Willie Mays	6.00	2.80	.60

SHEET THREE

☐	21	Brooks Robinson	3.00	1.40	.30
☐	22	Joe Pepitone	.60	.28	.06
☐	23	Carl Yastrzemski	6.00	2.80	.60
☐	24	Don Lock	.50	.22	.05
☐	25	Ernie Banks	2.50	1.15	.25
☐	26	Dave Nicholson	.50	.22	.05
☐	27	Bob Clemente	6.00	2.80	.60
☐	28	Curt Flood	.75	.35	.07
☐	29	Woody Held	.50	.22	.05
☐	30	Jesse Gonder	.50	.22	.05

SHEET FOUR

1969 Topps Stamps

The 1969 Topps set of baseball player stamps contains 240 individual stamps and 24 separate albums — 10 stamps and one album per major league team. The stamps were issued in strips of 12 and have gummed backs. Each stamp measures 1" by

1 7/16". The eight-page albums are bright orange and have an autograph feature on the back cover. The stamps are numbered here alphabetically within each team and the teams are listed in alphabetical order within league.

	MINT	VG-E	F-G
COMPLETE SET	50.00	22.00	5.00
COMMON PLAYER	.15	.06	.01

ATLANTA BRAVES

☐	1 Hank Aaron	2.50	1.15	.25
☐	2 Felipe Alou	.25	.10	.02
☐	3 Clete Boyer	.25	.10	.02
☐	4 Tito Francona	.15	.06	.01
☐	5 Sonny Jackson	.15	.06	.01
☐	6 Pat Jarvis	.15	.06	.01
☐	7 Felix Millan	.15	.06	.01
☐	8 Milt Pappas	.25	.10	.02
☐	9 Ron Reed	.15	.06	.01
☐	10 Joe Torre	.40	.18	.04

CINCINNATI REDS

☐	11 Ted Abernathy	.15	.06	.01
☐	12 Gerry Arrigo	.15	.06	.01
☐	13 Johnny Bench	1.50	.70	.15
☐	14 Tommy Helms	.15	.06	.01
☐	15 Alex Johnson	.15	.06	.01
☐	16 Jim Maloney	.25	.10	.02
☐	17 Lee May	.25	.10	.02
☐	18 Tony Perez	.50	.22	.05
☐	19 Pete Rose	6.00	2.80	.60
☐	20 Bobby Tolan	.15	.06	.01

CHICAGO CUBS

☐	21 Ernie Banks	1.50	.70	.15
☐	22 Glenn Beckert	.15	.06	.01
☐	23 Bill Hands	.15	.06	.01
☐	24 Randy Hundley	.15	.06	.01
☐	25 Ferguson Jenkins	.50	.22	.05
☐	26 Don Kessinger	.25	.10	.02
☐	27 Adolpho Phillips	.15	.06	.01
☐	28 Phil Regan	.15	.06	.01
☐	29 Ron Santo	.40	.18	.04
☐	30 Billy Williams	.75	.35	.07

HOUSTON ASTROS

☐	31 Bob Aspromonte	.15	.06	.01
☐	32 Larry Dierker	.15	.06	.01
☐	33 Johnny Edwards	.15	.06	.01
☐	34 Denver Lemaster	.15	.06	.01
☐	35 Denis Menke	.15	.06	.01
☐	36 Joe Morgan	1.00	.45	.10
☐	37 Doug Rader	.25	.10	.02
☐	38 Rusty Staub	.40	.18	.04
☐	39 Don Wilson	.15	.06	.01
☐	40 Jim Wynn	.25	.10	.02

LOS ANGELES DODGERS

☐	41 Willie Davis	.25	.10	.02
☐	42 Don Drysdale	1.50	.70	.15
☐	43 Ron Fairly	.15	.06	.01
☐	44 Len Gabrielson	.15	.06	.01
☐	45 Tom Haller	.15	.06	.01
☐	46 Ron Lefebvre	.15	.06	.01
☐	47 Claude Osteen	.25	.10	.02
☐	48 Paul Popovich	.15	.06	.01
☐	49 Bill Singer	.15	.06	.01
☐	50 Don Sutton	.75	.35	.07

MONTREAL EXPOS

☐	51 Jesus Alou	.15	.06	.01
☐	52 Bob Bailey	.15	.06	.01
☐	53 John Bateman	.15	.06	.01
☐	54 Donn Clendenon	.15	.06	.01
☐	55 Jim Grant	.15	.06	.01
☐	56 Larry Jaster	.15	.06	.01
☐	57 Mack Jones	.15	.06	.01
☐	58 Manny Mota	.25	.10	.02
☐	59 Sutherland	.15	.06	.01
☐	60 Maury Wills	.50	.22	.05

NEW YORK METS

☐	61 Tommy Agee	.15	.06	.01
☐	62 Ed Charles	.15	.06	.01
☐	63 Jerry Grote	.15	.06	.01
☐	64 Bud Harrelson	.15	.06	.01
☐	65 Cleon Jones	.15	.06	.01
☐	66 Jerry Koosman	.25	.10	.02
☐	67 Ed Kranepool	.15	.06	.01
☐	68 Tom Seaver	2.00	.90	.20
☐	69 Art Shamsky	.15	.06	.01
☐	70 Ron Swoboda	.15	.06	.01

PHILADELPHIA PHILLIES

☐	71 Richie Allen	.40	.18	.04
☐	72 John Briggs	.15	.06	.01
☐	73 John Callison	.25	.10	.02
☐	74 Clay Dalrymple	.15	.06	.01
☐	75 Woody Fryman	.15	.06	.01
☐	76 Don Lock	.15	.06	.01
☐	77 Cookie Rojas	.15	.06	.01
☐	78 Chris Short	.15	.06	.01
☐	79 Ron Taylor	.15	.06	.01
☐	80 Rick Wise	.15	.06	.01

PITTSBURGH PIRATES

☐	81 Gene Alley	.15	.06	.01
☐	82 Matty Alou	.25	.10	.02
☐	83 Steve Blass	.25	.10	.02
☐	84 Jim Bunning	.60	.28	.06
☐	85 Roberto Clemente	2.50	1.15	.25
☐	86 Ron Kline	.15	.06	.01
☐	87 Jerry May	.15	.06	.01
☐	88 Bill Mazeroski	.40	.18	.04
☐	89 Willie Stargell	1.50	.70	.15
☐	90 Bob Veale	.15	.06	.01

SAN DIEGO PADRES

☐	91 Jose Arcia	.15	.06	.01
☐	92 Ollie Brown	.15	.06	.01
☐	93 Al Ferrara	.15	.06	.01
☐	94 Tony Gonzalez	.15	.06	.01
☐	95 Dave Giusti	.15	.06	.01
☐	96 Alvin McBean	.15	.06	.01
☐	97 Orlando Pena	.15	.06	.01
☐	98 Dick Selma	.15	.06	.01
☐	99 Larry Stahl	.15	.06	.01
☐	100 Zoilo Versalles	.15	.06	.01

SAN FRANCISCO GIANTS

☐ 101	Bobby Bolin	.15	.06	.01
☐ 102	Jim Davenport	.25	.10	.02
☐ 103	Dick Dietz	.15	.06	.01
☐ 104	Jim Ray Hart	.15	.06	.01
☐ 105	Ron Hunt	.15	.06	.01
☐ 106	Hal Lanier	.25	.10	.02
☐ 107	Juan Marichal	1.00	.45	.10
☐ 108	Willie Mays	2.50	1.15	.25
☐ 109	Willie McCovey	1.50	.70	.15
☐ 110	Gaylord Perry	1.00	.45	.10

ST. LOUIS CARDINALS

☐ 111	Nelson Briles	.15	.06	.01
☐ 112	Lou Brock	1.50	.70	.15
☐ 113	Orlando Cepeda	.75	.35	.07
☐ 114	Curt Flood	.40	.18	.04
☐ 115	Bob Gibson	1.25	.60	.12
☐ 116	Julian Javier	.15	.06	.01
☐ 117	Dal Maxvill	.15	.06	.01
☐ 118	Tim McCarver	.25	.10	.02
☐ 119	Vada Pinson	.25	.10	.02
☐ 120	Mike Shannon	.25	.10	.02

BALTIMORE ORIOLES

☐ 121	Mark Belanger	.25	.10	.02
☐ 122	Curt Blefary	.15	.06	.01
☐ 123	Don Buford	.15	.06	.01
☐ 124	Jim Hardin	.15	.06	.01
☐ 125	Dave Johnson	.25	.10	.02
☐ 126	Dave McNally	.25	.10	.02
☐ 127	Tom Phoebus	.15	.06	.01
☐ 128	Boog Powell	.40	.18	.04
☐ 129	Brooks Robinson	2.00	.90	.20
☐ 130	Frank Robinson	1.50	.70	.15

BOSTON RED SOX

☐ 131	Mike Andrews	.15	.06	.01
☐ 132	Ray Culp	.15	.06	.01
☐ 133	Russ Gibson	.15	.06	.01
☐ 134	Ken Harrelson	.40	.18	.04
☐ 135	Jim Lonborg	.25	.10	.02
☐ 136	Rico Petrocelli	.25	.10	.02
☐ 137	Jose Santiago	.15	.06	.01
☐ 138	George Scott	.25	.10	.02
☐ 139	Reggie Smith	.40	.18	.04
☐ 140	Carl Yastrzemski	3.00	1.40	.30

CALIFORNIA ANGELS

☐ 141	George Brunet	.15	.06	.01
☐ 142	Vic Davalillo	.15	.06	.01
☐ 143	Eddie Fisher	.15	.06	.01
☐ 144	Jim Fregosi	.25	.10	.02
☐ 145	Bobby Knoop	.15	.06	.01
☐ 146	Jim McGlothlin	.15	.06	.01
☐ 147	Rick Reichardt	.15	.06	.01
☐ 148	Roger Repoz	.15	.06	.01
☐ 149	Bob Rodgers	.15	.06	.01
☐ 150	Tom Satriano	.15	.06	.01

CHICAGO WHITE SOX

☐ 151	Sandy Alomar	.15	.06	.01
☐ 152	Luis Aparicio	1.00	.45	.10
☐ 153	Ken Berry	.15	.06	.01
☐ 154	Joel Horlen	.15	.06	.01
☐ 155	Tommy John	.75	.35	.07
☐ 156	Duane Josephson	.15	.06	.01
☐ 157	Gary Peters	.15	.06	.01
☐ 158	Gary Wagner	.15	.06	.01
☐ 159	Pete Ward	.15	.06	.01
☐ 160	Wilbur Wood	.15	.06	.01

CLEVELAND INDIANS

☐ 161	Max Alvis	.15	.06	.01
☐ 162	Joe Azcue	.15	.06	.01
☐ 163	Larry Brown	.15	.06	.01
☐ 164	Jose Cardenal	.15	.06	.01
☐ 165	Lee Maye	.15	.06	.01
☐ 166	Sam McDowell	.25	.10	.02
☐ 167	Sonny Siebert	.15	.06	.01
☐ 168	Duke Sims	.15	.06	.01
☐ 169	Luis Tiant	.25	.10	.02
☐ 170	Stan Williams	.15	.06	.01

DETROIT TIGERS

☐ 171	Norm Cash	.40	.18	.04
☐ 172	Bill Freehan	.25	.10	.02
☐ 173	Willie Horton	.25	.10	.02
☐ 174	Al Kaline	1.50	.70	.15
☐ 175	Mickey Lolich	.40	.18	.04
☐ 176	Dick McAuliffe	.15	.06	.01
☐ 177	Denny McLain	.40	.18	.04
☐ 178	Bill Northrup	.15	.06	.01
☐ 179	Mickey Stanley	.15	.06	.01
☐ 180	Don Wert	.15	.06	.01

KANSAS CITY ROYALS

☐ 181	Jerry Adair	.15	.06	.01
☐ 182	Wally Bunker	.15	.06	.01
☐ 183	Moe Drabowsky	.15	.06	.01
☐ 184	Joe Foy	.15	.06	.01
☐ 185	Jackie Hernandez	.15	.06	.01

☐ 186	Roger Nelson	.15	.06	.01
☐ 187	Bob Oliver	.15	.06	.01
☐ 188	Paul Schaal	.15	.06	.01
☐ 189	Steve Whitaker	.15	.06	.01
☐ 190	Hoyt Wilhelm	1.00	.45	.10

MINNESOTA TWINS

☐ 191	Bob Allison	.25	.10	.02
☐ 192	Rod Carew	2.00	.90	.20
☐ 193	Dean Chance	.25	.10	.02
☐ 194	Jim Kaat	.50	.22	.05
☐ 195	Harmon Killebrew	1.25	.60	.12
☐ 196	Tony Oliva	.50	.22	.05
☐ 197	Ron Perranoski	.15	.06	.01
☐ 198	John Roseboro	.15	.06	.01
☐ 199	Cesar Tovar	.15	.06	.01
☐ 200	Ted Uhlaender	.15	.06	.01

NEW YORK YANKEES

☐ 201	Stan Bahnsen	.15	.06	.01
☐ 202	Horace Clarke	.15	.06	.01
☐ 203	Jake Gibbs	.15	.06	.01
☐ 204	Andy Kosko	.15	.06	.01
☐ 205	Mickey Mantle	6.00	2.80	.60
☐ 206	Joe Pepitone	.25	.10	.02
☐ 207	Bill Robinson	.15	.06	.01
☐ 208	Mel Stottlemyre	.25	.10	.02
☐ 209	Tom Tresh	.25	.10	.02
☐ 210	Roy White	.25	.10	.02

OAKLAND A'S

☐ 211	Sal Bando	.25	.10	.02
☐ 212	Bert Campaneris	.25	.10	.02
☐ 213	Danny Cater	.15	.06	.01
☐ 214	Dave Duncan	.15	.06	.01
☐ 215	Dick Green	.15	.06	.01
☐ 216	Jim Hunter	.75	.35	.07
☐ 217	Lew Krausse	.15	.06	.01
☐ 218	Rick Monday	.25	.10	.02
☐ 219	Jim Nash	.15	.06	.01
☐ 220	John Odom	.15	.06	.01

SEATTLE PILOTS

☐ 221	Jack Aker	.15	.06	.01
☐ 222	Steve Barber	.15	.06	.01
☐ 223	Gary Bell	.15	.06	.01
☐ 224	Tommy Davis	.25	.10	.02
☐ 225	Tommy Harper	.15	.06	.01
☐ 226	Jerry McNertney	.15	.06	.01
☐ 227	Mike Mincher	.15	.06	.01
☐ 228	Ray Oyler	.15	.06	.01
☐ 229	Rich Rollins	.15	.06	.01
☐ 230	Chico Salmon	.15	.06	.01

WASHINGTON SENATORS

☐ 231	Bernie Allen	.15	.06	.01
☐ 232	Ed Brinkman	.15	.06	.01
☐ 233	Paul Casanova	.15	.06	.01
☐ 234	Joe Coleman	.15	.06	.01
☐ 235	Mike Epstein	.15	.06	.01
☐ 236	Jim Hannan	.15	.06	.01
☐ 237	Dennis Higgins	.15	.06	.01
☐ 238	Frank Howard	.25	.10	.02
☐ 239	Ken McMullen	.15	.06	.01
☐ 240	Camilo Pascual	.25	.10	.02

1974 Topps Stamps

The 240 color portraits depicted on stamps in this 1974 Topps series have the player's name, team and position inside an oval below the picture area. Each stamp measures 1" by 1 1/2". The stamps were marketed in strips of six, along with an album, in their own wrapper. The booklets have eight pages and measure 2 1/2" X 3 7/8". There are 24 albums, one for each team, designed to hold 10 stamps apiece.

		MINT	VG-E	F-G
COMPLETE SET		70.00	32.00	7.00
COMMON PLAYER		.20	.09	.02

ATLANTA BRAVES

☐	1 Hank Aaron	2.50	1.15	.25
☐	2 Dusty Baker	.30	.12	.03
☐	3 Darrell Evans	.40	.18	.04
☐	4 Ralph Garr	.30	.12	.03
☐	5 Roric Harrison	.20	.09	.02

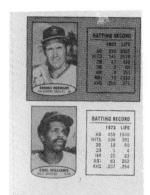

☐	45	Joe Ferguson	.20	.09	.02
☐	46	Davey Lopes	.40	.18	.04
☐	47	Andy Messersmith	.30	.12	.03
☐	48	Claude Osteen	.30	.12	.03
☐	49	Bill Russell	.30	.12	.03
☐	50	Don Sutton	.75	.35	.07

MONTREAL EXPOS

☐	51	Bob Bailey	.20	.09	.02
☐	52	John Boccabella	.20	.09	.02
☐	53	Ron Fairly	.20	.09	.02
☐	54	Tim Foli	.20	.09	.02
☐	55	Ron Hunt	.20	.09	.02
☐	56	Mike Jorgensen	.20	.09	.02
☐	57	Mike Marshall	.30	.12	.03
☐	58	Steve Renko	.20	.09	.02
☐	59	Steve Rogers	.40	.18	.04
☐	60	Ken Singleton	.40	.18	.04

NEW YORK METS

☐	61	Wayne Garrett	.20	.09	.02
☐	62	Jerry Grote	.20	.09	.02
☐	63	Bud Harrelson	.20	.09	.02
☐	64	Cleon Jones	.20	.09	.02
☐	65	Jerry Koosman	.30	.12	.03
☐	66	Jon Matlack	.30	.12	.03
☐	67	Tug McGraw	.40	.18	.04
☐	68	Felix Millan	.20	.09	.02
☐	69	John Milner	.20	.09	.02
☐	70	Tom Seaver	2.00	.90	.20

PHILADELPHIA PHILLIES

☐	71	Bob Boone	.30	.12	.03
☐	72	Larry Bowa	.40	.18	.04
☐	73	Steve Carlton	1.50	.70	.15
☐	74	Bill Grabarkewitz	.20	.09	.02
☐	75	Jim Lonborg	.30	.12	.03
☐	76	Greg Luzinski	.40	.18	.04
☐	77	Willie Montanez	.20	.09	.02
☐	78	Bill Robinson	.20	.09	.02
☐	79	Wayne Twitchell	.20	.09	.02
☐	80	Del Unser	.20	.09	.02

PITTSBURGH PIRATES

☐	81	Nelson Briles	.20	.09	.02
☐	82	Dock Ellis	.20	.09	.02
☐	83	Dave Giusti	.20	.09	.02
☐	84	Richie Hebner	.20	.09	.02
☐	85	Al Oliver	.40	.18	.04
☐	86	Dave Parker	1.50	.70	.15
☐	87	Manny Sanguillen	.30	.12	.03
☐	88	Willie Stargell	1.00	.45	.10
☐	89	Rennie Stennett	.20	.09	.02
☐	90	Richie Zisk	.30	.12	.03

SAN DIEGO PADRES

☐	91	Nate Colbert	.20	.09	.02
☐	92	Bill Grief	.20	.09	.02
☐	93	Johnny Grubb	.20	.09	.02
☐	94	Randy Jones	.30	.12	.03
☐	95	Fred Kendall	.20	.09	.02
☐	96	Clay Kirby	.20	.09	.02
☐	97	Willie McCovey	1.00	.45	.10
☐	98	Jerry Morales	.20	.09	.02
☐	99	Dave Roberts	.20	.09	.02
☐	100	Dave Winfield	2.50	1.15	.25

SAN FRANCISCO GIANTS

☐	101	Bobby Bonds	.40	.18	.04
☐	102	Tom Bradley	.20	.09	.02
☐	103	Ron Bryant	.20	.09	.02
☐	104	Tito Fuentes	.20	.09	.02
☐	105	Ed Goodson	.20	.09	.02
☐	106	Dave Kingman	.75	.35	.07
☐	107	Garry Maddox	.30	.12	.03
☐	108	Dave Rader	.20	.09	.02
☐	109	Elias Sosa	.20	.09	.02
☐	110	Chris Speier	.20	.09	.02

ST. LOUIS CARDINALS

☐	111	Lou Brock	1.50	.70	.15
☐	112	Reggie Cleveland	.20	.09	.02
☐	113	Jose Cruz	.30	.12	.03
☐	114	Bob Gibson	1.00	.45	.10
☐	115	Tim McCarver	.30	.12	.03
☐	116	Ted Simmons	.40	.18	.04
☐	117	Ted Sizemore	.20	.09	.02
☐	118	Reggie Smith	.40	.18	.04
☐	119	Joe Torre	.50	.22	.05
☐	120	Mike Tyson	.20	.09	.02

BALTIMORE ORIOLES

☐	121	Don Baylor	.50	.22	.05
☐	122	Mark Belanger	.30	.12	.03
☐	123	Paul Blair	.30	.12	.03
☐	124	Tommy Davis	.30	.12	.03
☐	125	Bobby Grich	.40	.18	.04
☐	126	Grant Jackson	.20	.09	.02
☐	127	Dave McNally	.30	.12	.03
☐	128	Jim Palmer	1.50	.70	.15
☐	129	Brooks Robinson	1.50	.70	.15

6	Dave Johnson	.40	.18	.04
7	Mike Lum	.20	.09	.02
8	Carl Morton	.20	.09	.02
9	Phil Niekro	.75	.35	.07
10	Johnny Oates	.20	.09	.02

CHICAGO CUBS

11	Glen Beckert	.20	.09	.02
12	Jose Cardenal	.20	.09	.02
13	Vic Harris	.20	.09	.02
14	Burt Hooton	.20	.09	.02
15	Randy Hundley	.20	.09	.02
16	Don Kessinger	.30	.12	.03
17	Rick Monday	.30	.12	.03
18	Rick Reuschel	.30	.12	.03
19	Ron Santo	.40	.18	.04
20	Billy Williams	.75	.35	.07

CINCINNATI REDS

21	Johnny Bench	2.00	.90	.20
22	Jack Billingham	.20	.09	.02
23	Pedro Borbon	.20	.09	.02
24	Dave Concepcion	.50	.22	.05
25	Dan Driessen	.30	.12	.03
26	Ceasar Geronimo	.20	.09	.02
27	Don Gullett	.30	.12	.03
28	Joe Morgan	.75	.35	.07
29	Tony Perez	.50	.22	.05
30	Pete Rose	4.00	1.85	.40

HOUSTON ASTROS

31	Cesar Cedeno	.40	.18	.04
32	Tommy Helms	.20	.09	.02
33	Lee May	.30	.12	.03
34	Roger Metzger	.20	.09	.02
35	Doug Rader	.30	.12	.03
36	J.R. Richard	.40	.18	.04
37	Dave Roberts	.20	.09	.02
38	Jerry Reuss	.30	.12	.03
39	Bob Watson	.30	.12	.03
40	Jim Wynn	.30	.12	.03

LOS ANGELES DODGERS

41	Bill Buckner	.40	.18	.04
42	Ron Cey	.40	.18	.04
43	Willie Crawford	.20	.09	.02
44	Willie Davis	.30	.12	.03

☐ 130 Earl Williams	.20	.09	.02

BOSTON RED SOX

☐ 131 Luis Aparicio	1.00	.45	.10
☐ 132 Orlando Cepeda	.75	.35	.07
☐ 133 Carlton Fisk	.75	.35	.07
☐ 134 Tommy Harper	.30	.12	.03
☐ 135 Bill Lee	.30	.12	.03
☐ 136 Rick Miller	.20	.09	.02
☐ 137 Roger Moret	.20	.09	.02
☐ 138 Luis Tiant	.40	.18	.04
☐ 139 Rick Wise	.20	.09	.02
☐ 140 Carl Yastrzemski	2.50	1.15	.25

CALIFORNIA ANGELS

☐ 141 Sandy Alomar	.20	.09	.02
☐ 142 Mike Epstein	.20	.09	.02
☐ 143 Bob Oliver	.20	.09	.02
☐ 144 Vada Pinson	.30	.12	.03
☐ 145 Frank Robinson	1.50	.70	.15
☐ 146 Ellie Rodriguez	.20	.09	.02
☐ 147 Nolan Ryan	1.50	.70	.15
☐ 148 Richie Scheinblum	.20	.09	.02
☐ 149 Bill Singer	.20	.09	.02
☐ 150 Bobby Valentine	.40	.18	.04

CHICAGO WHITE SOX

☐ 151 Dick Allen	.40	.18	.04
☐ 152 Stan Bahnsen	.20	.09	.02
☐ 153 Terry Forster	.30	.12	.03
☐ 154 Ken Henderson	.20	.09	.02
☐ 155 Ed Herrmann	.20	.09	.02
☐ 156 Pat Kelly	.20	.09	.02
☐ 157 Carlos May	.20	.09	.02
☐ 158 Bill Melton	.20	.09	.02
☐ 159 Jorge Orta	.20	.09	.02
☐ 160 Wilbur Wood	.20	.09	.02

CLEVELAND INDIANS

☐ 161 Buddy Bell	.40	.18	.04
☐ 162 Chris Chambliss	.30	.12	.03
☐ 163 Frank Duffy	.20	.09	.02
☐ 164 Dave Duncan	.20	.09	.02
☐ 165 John Ellis	.20	.09	.02
☐ 166 Oscar Gamble	.30	.12	.03
☐ 167 George Hendrick	.30	.12	.03
☐ 168 Gaylord Perry	.75	.35	.07
☐ 169 Charlie Spikes	.20	.09	.02
☐ 170 Dick Tidrow	.20	.09	.02

DETROIT TIGERS

☐ 171 Ed Brinkman	.20	.09	.02
☐ 172 Norm Cash	.40	.18	.04
☐ 173 Joe Coleman	.20	.09	.02
☐ 174 Bill Freehan	.30	.12	.03
☐ 175 John Hiller	.30	.12	.03
☐ 176 Willie Horton	.30	.12	.03
☐ 177 Al Kaline	1.50	.70	.15
☐ 178 Mickey Lolich	.40	.18	.04
☐ 179 Aurelio Rodriguez	.20	.09	.02
☐ 180 Mickey Stanley	.20	.09	.02

KANSAS CITY ROYALS

☐ 181 Steve Busby	.30	.12	.03
☐ 182 Fran Healy	.20	.09	.02
☐ 183 Ed Kirkpatrick	.20	.09	.02
☐ 184 John Mayberry	.30	.12	.03
☐ 185 Amos Otis	.40	.18	.04
☐ 186 Fred Patek	.20	.09	.02
☐ 187 Marty Pattin	.20	.09	.02
☐ 188 Lou Piniella	.40	.18	.04
☐ 189 Cookie Rojas	.20	.09	.02
☐ 190 Paul Splittorff	.20	.09	.02

MILWAUKEE BREWERS

☐ 191 Jerry Bell	.20	.09	.02
☐ 192 Johnny Briggs	.20	.09	.02
☐ 193 Jim Colborn	.20	.09	.02
☐ 194 Bob Collucio	.20	.09	.02
☐ 195 Pedro Garcia	.20	.09	.02
☐ 196 Dave May	.20	.09	.02
☐ 197 Don Money	.30	.12	.03
☐ 198 Darrell Porter	.30	.12	.03
☐ 199 George Scott	.30	.12	.03
☐ 200 Jim Slaton	.20	.09	.02

MINNESOTA TWINS

☐ 201 Bert Blyleven	.40	.18	.04
☐ 202 Steve Braun	.20	.09	.02
☐ 203 Rod Carew	2.00	.90	.20
☐ 204 Ray Corbin	.20	.09	.02
☐ 205 Bobby Darwin	.20	.09	.02
☐ 206 Joe Decker	.20	.09	.02
☐ 207 Jim Holt	.20	.09	.02
☐ 208 Harmon Killebrew	1.25	.60	.12
☐ 209 George Mitterwald	.20	.09	.02
☐ 210 Tony Oliva	.50	.22	.05

NEW YORK YANKEES

☐ 211 Ron Blomberg	.20	.09	.02
☐ 212 Sparky Lyle	.40	.18	.04
☐ 213 George Medich	.30	.12	.03
☐ 214 Gene Michaels	.30	.12	.03
☐ 215 Thurman Munson	2.00	.90	.20
☐ 216 Bobby Murcer	.40	.18	.04
☐ 217 Graig Nettles	.60	.28	.06
☐ 218 Mel Stottlemyre	.30	.12	.03
☐ 219 Otto Velez	.20	.09	.02
☐ 220 Roy White	.30	.12	.03

OAKLAND A'S

☐ 221 Sal Bando	.30	.12	.03
☐ 222 Vida Blue	.60	.28	.06
☐ 223 Bert Campaneris	.30	.12	.03
☐ 224 Ken Holtzman	.30	.12	.03
☐ 225 Jim Hunter	.75	.35	.07
☐ 226 Reggie Jackson	2.00	.90	.20
☐ 227 Deron Johnson	.20	.09	.02
☐ 228 Bill North	.20	.09	.02
☐ 229 Joe Rudi	.30	.12	.03
☐ 230 Gene Tenace	.30	.12	.03

TEXAS RANGERS

☐ 231 Jim Bibby	.30	.12	.03
☐ 232 Jeff Burroughs	.30	.12	.03
☐ 233 David Clyde	.20	.09	.02
☐ 234 Jim Fregosi	.30	.12	.03
☐ 235 Toby Harrah	.30	.12	.03
☐ 236 Ferguson Jenkins	.40	.18	.04
☐ 237 Alex Johnson	.20	.09	.02
☐ 238 Dave Nelson	.20	.09	.02
☐ 239 Jim Spencer	.20	.09	.02
☐ 240 Bill Sudakis	.20	.09	.02

1984 Borden's Reds

This set of eight stickers featuring Eric Davis' first Cincinnati card, was produced as two sheets of four by Borden's Dairy. The sheets are perforated so that the individual stickers may be separated. The sheet of four stickers measures approximately 5 1/2" by 8" whereas the individual stickers measure 2 1/2" by 3 7/8". The backs of the stickers feature discount "cents off" coupons applicable to Borden's products. The fronts feature a full color photo of the player in a bold red border. The stickers are not numbered except that each player's uniform number is given prominently on the front. The sheets are arbitrarily numbered one and two and designated in the checklist below.

	MINT	VG-E	F-G
COMPLETE SET	4.00	1.85	.40
COMMON PLAYER	.25	.10	.02
☐ 2 Gary Redus (sheet 2)	.35	.15	.03
☐ 16 Ron Oester (sheet 1)	.25	.10	.02
☐ 20 Eddie Milner (sheet 2)	.35	.15	.03
☐ 24 Tony Perez (sheet 2)	.50	.22	.05
☐ 36 Mario Soto (sheet 1)	.35	.15	.03
☐ 39 Dave Parker (sheet 1)	1.00	.45	.10
☐ 44 Eric Davis (sheet 1)	2.00	.90	.20
☐ 46 Jeff Russell (sheet 2)	.25	.10	.02

1970 Dunkin Donuts Cubs

This set of six (bumper) stickers (apparently commemorating the Cubs near-miss in 1969) was produced and distributed by Dunkin Donuts. The stickers are approximately 4 1/16" by 8 1/16" and are in color. Each sticker features a facsimile

1983 Bordens Stickers

1970 Dunkin Donuts Stickers

autograph in the upper left hand corner.

	MINT	VG-E	F-G
COMPLETE SET	12.00	5.50	1.20
COMMON PLAYER	1.00	.45	.10
☐1 Ernie Banks	5.00	2.35	.50
☐2 Glenn Beckert	1.00	.45	.10
☐3 Randy Hundley	1.00	.45	.10
☐4 Don Kessinger	1.50	.70	.15
☐5 Ron Santo	2.00	.90	.20
☐6 Billy Williams	3.00	1.40	.30

1981 Fleer Star Stickers

The stickers in this 128 sticker set measure 2 1/2"
by 3 1/2". The 1981 Fleer Baseball Star Stickers
consist of numbered cards with peelable, full
color sticker fronts and three unnumbered checklist. The
backs of the numbered player cards are the same
as the 1981 Fleer regular issue cards except for the
numbers, while the checklist cards have sticker
fronts of Jackson (1-42), Brett (43-83) and Schmidt
(84-125).

	MINT	VG-E	F-G
COMPLETE SET	36.00	17.00	3.60
COMMON PLAYER (1-128)	.18	.08	.01
☐ 1 Steve Garvey	2.00	.90	.20
☐ 2 Ron LeFlore	.18	.08	.01
☐ 3 Ron Cey	.40	.18	.04
☐ 4 Dave Revering	.18	.08	.01
☐ 5 Tony Armas	.40	.18	.04
☐ 6 Mike Norris	.18	.08	.01
☐ 7 Steve Kemp	.30	.12	.03
☐ 8 Bruce Bochte	.18	.08	.01
☐ 9 Mike Schmidt	2.50	1.15	.25
☐ 10 Scott McGregor	.25	.10	.02
☐ 11 Buddy Bell	.40	.18	.04
☐ 12 Carney Lansford	.40	.18	.04
☐ 13 Carl Yastrzemski	2.50	1.15	.25
☐ 14 Ben Oglivie	.25	.10	.02
☐ 15 Willie Stargell	.80	.40	.08
☐ 16 Cecil Cooper	.60	.28	.06
☐ 17 Gene Richards	.18	.08	.01
☐ 18 Jim Kern	.18	.08	.01
☐ 19 Jerry Koosman	.25	.10	.02
☐ 20 Larry Bowa	.25	.10	.02
☐ 21 Kent Tekulve	.18	.08	.01
☐ 22 Dan Driessen	.18	.08	.01
☐ 23 Phil Niekro	.80	.40	.08
☐ 24 Dan Quisenberry	.60	.28	.06
☐ 25 Dave Winfield	1.75	.85	.17
☐ 26 Dave Parker	.80	.40	.08
☐ 27 Rick Langford	.18	.08	.01
☐ 28 Amos Otis	.25	.10	.02
☐ 29 Bill Buckner	.30	.12	.03
☐ 30 Al Bumbry	.18	.08	.01
☐ 31 Bake McBride	.18	.08	.01
☐ 32 Mickey Rivers	.18	.08	.01
☐ 33 Rick Burleson	.25	.10	.02

	MINT	VG-E	F-G
☐ 34 Dennis Eckersley	.25	.10	.02
☐ 35 Cesar Cedeno	.25	.10	.02
☐ 36 Enos Cabell	.18	.08	.01
☐ 37 Johnny Bench	1.75	.85	.17
☐ 38 Robin Yount	1.75	.85	.17
☐ 39 Mark Belanger	.18	.08	.01
☐ 40 Rod Carew	1.75	.85	.17
☐ 41 George Foster	.80	.40	.08
☐ 42 Lee Mazzilli	.18	.08	.01
☐ 43 Triple Threat:	1.75	.85	.17
Pete Rose			
Larry Bowa			
Mike Schmidt			
☐ 44 J.R. Richard	.25	.10	.02
☐ 45 Lou Piniella	.30	.12	.03
☐ 46 Ken Landreaux	.18	.08	.01
☐ 47 Rollie Fingers	.60	.28	.06
☐ 48 Joaquin Andujar	.25	.10	.02
☐ 49 Tom Seaver	1.75	.85	.17
☐ 50 Bobby Grich	.30	.12	.03
☐ 51 Jon Matlack	.18	.08	.01
☐ 52 Jack Clark	.40	.18	.04
☐ 53 Jim Rice	1.75	.85	.17
☐ 54 Rickey Henderson	2.00	.90	.20
☐ 55 Roy Smalley	.18	.08	.01
☐ 56 Mike Flanagan	.25	.10	.02
☐ 57 Steve Rogers	.25	.10	.02
☐ 58 Carlton Fisk	.50	.22	.05
☐ 59 Don Sutton	.60	.28	.06
☐ 60 Ken Griffey	.25	.10	.02
☐ 61 Burt Hooton	.18	.08	.01
☐ 62 Dusty Baker	.25	.10	.02
☐ 63 Vida Blue	.25	.10	.02
☐ 64 Al Oliver	.50	.22	.05
☐ 65 Jim Bibby	.18	.08	.01
☐ 66 Tony Perez	.60	.28	.06
☐ 67 Davy Lopes	.25	.10	.02
☐ 68 Bill Russell	.25	.10	.02
☐ 69 Larry Parrish	.18	.08	.01
☐ 70 Garry Maddox	.18	.08	.01
☐ 71 Phil Garner	.18	.08	.01
☐ 72 Graig Nettles	.50	.22	.05
☐ 73 Gary Carter	1.75	.85	.17
☐ 74 Pete Rose	4.00	1.85	.40
☐ 75 Greg Luzinski	.30	.12	.03
☐ 76 Ron Guidry	.50	.22	.05
☐ 77 Gorman Thomas	.30	.12	.03
☐ 78 Jose Cruz	.30	.12	.03
☐ 79 Bob Boone	.18	.08	.01
☐ 80 Bruce Sutter	.50	.22	.05
☐ 81 Chris Chambliss	.25	.10	.02
☐ 82 Paul Molitor	.30	.12	.03
☐ 83 Tug McGraw	.25	.10	.02
☐ 84 Ferguson Jenkins	.35	.15	.03
☐ 85 Steve Carlton	1.75	.85	.17
☐ 86 Miguel Dilone	.18	.08	.01
☐ 87 Reggie Smith	.25	.10	.02
☐ 88 Rick Cerone	.18	.08	.01
☐ 89 Alan Trammell	.60	.28	.06
☐ 90 Doug DeCinces	.35	.15	.03
☐ 91 Sparky Lyle	.25	.10	.02
☐ 92 Warren Cromartie	.18	.08	.01
☐ 93 Rick Reuschel	.18	.08	.01
☐ 94 Larry Hisle	.18	.08	.01
☐ 95 Paul Splittorff	.18	.08	.01
☐ 96 Manny Trillo	.18	.08	.01
☐ 97 Frank White	.25	.10	.02
☐ 98 Fred Lynn	.60	.28	.06
☐ 99 Bob Horner	.60	.28	.06
☐100 Omar Moreno	.18	.08	.01
☐101 Dave Concepcion	.25	.10	.02
☐102 Larry Gura	.18	.08	.01
☐103 Ken Singleton	.25	.10	.02
☐104 Steve Stone	.18	.08	.01
☐105 Richie Zisk	.18	.08	.01
☐106 Willie Wilson	.50	.22	.05
☐107 Willie Randolph	.25	.10	.02
☐108 Nolan Ryan	1.50	.70	.15
☐109 Joe Morgan	.80	.40	.08
☐110 Bucky Dent	.18	.08	.01
☐111 Dave Kingman	.30	.12	.03
☐112 John Castino	.18	.08	.01
☐113 Joe Rudi	.18	.08	.01
☐114 Ed Farmer	.18	.08	.01
☐115 Reggie Jackson	2.50	1.15	.25
☐116 George Brett	2.50	1.15	.25
☐117 Eddie Murray	2.50	1.15	.25
☐118 Rich Gossage	.60	.28	.06
☐119 Dale Murphy	3.00	1.40	.30
☐120 Ted Simmons	.30	.12	.03
☐121 Tommy John	.50	.22	.05
☐122 Don Baylor	.50	.22	.05
☐123 Andre Dawson	1.00	.45	.10

☐ 124	Jim Palmer	1.00	.45	.10
☐ 125	Garry Templeton	.40	.18	.04
☐ 126	Checklist 1 -	1.25	.25	.05
	Reggie Jackson			
☐ 127	Checklist 2 -	1.25	.25	.05
	George Brett			
☐ 128	Checklist 3 -	1.25	.25	.05
	Mike Schmidt			

1983 Fleer Stickers

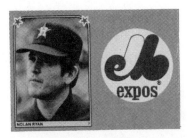

The stickers in this 270 sticker set measure 1 13/16" by 2 1/2". The 1983 Fleer stickers set was issued in strips of 10 stickers plus two team logos per strip. No album was issued for the stickers. The fronts contain player photos surrounded by a blue border with two red stars on the upper portion of a yellow frameline. While all of the players could be attained on 27 different strips, it was necessary to have 30 different strips to obtain all of the team logos. The three variation strips are listed with an A and B in the checklist below. All strips are numbered below in alphabetical order according to the leftmost player on the strip. There are a few instances where the logo pictured on the front of the card relates to a different team checklisted on the back of the card. The backs of the logo stamps feature either a team checklist (CL) or poster offer (PO).

	MINT	VG-E	F-G
COMPLETE SET	10.00	4.75	1.00
COMMON STRIP	.40	.18	.04

	MINT	VG-E	F-G
☐ Strip 1A	.40	.18	.04
182 Floyd Bannister			
143 Al Oliver/Pete Rose			
249 Whitaker/Angels Logo CL			
192 R.Henderson/91 P.Niekro			
223 Kennedy/125 K.Moreland			
207 N.Ryan/Red Sox Logo PO			
112 Valenzuela/74 T.Pena			
☐ Strip 1B	.40	.18	.04
182 Floyd Bannister			
143 Al Oliver/Pete Rose			
249 Whitaker/Braves Logo CL			
192 R.Henderson/91 P.Niekro			
223 Kennedy/125 K.Moreland			
207 N.Ryan/Expos Logo PO			
112 F.Valenzuela/74 T.Pena			
☐ Strip 2	.40	.18	.04
51 F.Breining/158 Luzinski			
248 M.Wilcox/Reds Logo PO			
239 G.Foster/216 Mario Soto			
202 E.Murray/121 D.Baker			
110 G.Iorg/Blue Jay Logo CL			
78 Lee Lacy/46 Ken Griffey			
☐ Strip 3	.60	.28	.06
250 Tom Brookens/29 G.Zahn			
204 D.Thon/Phillies Logo PO			
198 C.Ripken/174 Pete Rose			
140 D.Baker/Dale Murphy			
139 B.Castillo/115 B.Hooten			

		MINT	VG-E	F-G
xx Royals Logo CL				
80 M.Easler/49 R.Smith				
☐ Strip 4		.40	.18	.04
59 Burgmeier/53 C.Davis				
230 Bailor/Brewers Logo PO				
258 Fryman/185 B.Bochte				
220 Krenchicki/166 B.Sample				
114 R.Monday/Mets Logo CL				
75 Sarmiento/Robin Yount				
☐ Strip 5		.40	.18	.04
21 M.Caldwell/133 R.Davis				
246 R.Manning/Jays Logo PO				
155 H.Baines/82 Rick Camp				
167 J.Grubb/89 S.Bedrosian				
222 R.Jones/Tigers Logo CL				
113 S.Garvey/34 Bob Boone				
☐ Strip 6		.40	.18	.04
70 John Candelaria				
263 Bill Gullickson				
231 Craig Swan/A's Logo CL				
196 Rich Dauer/177 Bo Diaz				
132 Buckner/10 Ozzie Smith				
69 Dw.Evans/Astros Logo PO				
134 O'Connor/191 Underwood				
☐ Strip 7		.40	.18	.04
26 Rod Carew/38 G.Nettles				
152 J.Koosman/Astro Logo PO				
228 T.Lollar/212 Alan Ashby				
261 Cromartie/189 Dw.Murphy				
108 Clancy/Orioles Logo CL				
15 Ben Oglivie/52 Lavelle				
☐ Strip 8		.40	.18	.04
179 Caudill/226 T.Flannery				
241 Thornton/Yankee Logo PO				
257 Speier/205 Phil Garner				
129 Martz/43 Rick Cerone				
25 T.John/A's Logo CL				
103 L.Gura/73 Kent Tekulve				
☐ Strip 9		.40	.18	.04
221 Cedeno/271 Art Howe				
168 Larry Parrish				
xx Cardinals Logo PO				
42 D.Collins/81 Stargell				
107 J.McLaughlin/251 Lemon				
227 Garry Templeton				
xx Phillies Logo CL				
105 D.Garcia/186 Burroughs				
☐ Strip 10		.40	.18	.04
86 Chambliss/99 Amos Otis				
xx Twins Logo PO				
242 Mike Hargrove				
178 Gary Matthews/149 Kemp				
218 Seaver/254 Wockenfuss				
xx Rangers Logo CL				
20 G.Thomas/24 Steve Renko				
☐ Strip 11		.40	.18	.04
48 J.Clark/83 Bob Watson				
44 Randolph/Pirate Logo CL				
23 C.Cooper/201 T.Martinez				
234 John Stearns/163 Hough				
126 Tidrow/Indians Logo PO				
93 Bob Walk/122 Ron Cey				
☐ Strip 12		.40	.18	.04
264 A.Dawson/244 Sorensen				
xx Royals Logo PO/209 Puhl				
169 DeJesus/106 H.Powell				
141 Nolan Ryan/Alan Ashby				
31 Fred Lynn/Reds Logo CL				
61 Clear/161 Danny Darwin				
☐ Strip 13		.40	.18	.04
63 Eckersley/57 B.Laskey				
47 Ron Guidry/Cubs Logo CL				
96 Vida Blue/138 Brunansky				
245 Len Barker/217 Driessen				
180 Ed VandeBerg				
xx Dodgers Logo PO				
124 Bump Wills/153 C.Fisk				
☐ Strip 14		.40	.18	.04
87 Gene Garber/45 Piniella				
100 Dan Quisenberry				
xx Padres Logo PO				
14 P.Vuckovich/173 Maddox				
130 F.Jenkins/131 Durham				
22 T.Simmons/Reds Logo CL				
270 Montefusco/269 Hendrick				
☐ Strip 15		.40	.18	.04
159 L.Hoyt/266 Charlie Lea				
238 R.Staub/Rangers Logo CL				
206 Jose Cruz/162 L.Johnson				
183 Richie Zisk/36 Gossage				
68 J.Remy/Orioles Logo PO				
119 Steve Howe				
97 U.L. Washington				

☐ Strip 16 .... .40 .18 .04
58 D.Kuiper/11 Bob Forsch
85 R.Ramirez/Mets Logo CL
142 Moreno/L.Lacey (sic)
160 G.Wright/187 Dave Beard
247 Harrah/268 Al Oliver
xx Expos Logo PO
102 Hal McRae/64 Wade Boggs
☐ Strip 17 .... .40 .18 .04
190 R.Langford/128 L.Bowa
5 D.Iorg/Expos Logo CL
252 J.Morris/193 M.Flanagan
184 Al Cowens/156 B.Burns
12 Gantner/Royals Logo PO
60 Yastrzemski/28 K.Forsch
☐ Strip 18 .... .40 .18 .04
150 R.Law/235 E.Valentine
181 G.Perry/Red Sox Logo CL
147 Ray Knight/Tom Hume
135 Kent Hrbek/101 W.Aikens
13 R.Fingers/71 B.Madlock
xx Giants Logo PO
67 C.Lansford/41 J.Mumphrey
☐ Strip 19A .... .50 .22 .05
90 Dale Murphy/260 S.Rogers
214 J.Bench/Mariner Logo PO
262 G.Carter/164 Buddy Bell
19 Molitor/3 Darrell Porter
55 J.Morgan/Yankees Logo CL
65 B.Stanley/33 Don Baylor
☐ Strip 19B .... .50 .22 .05
90 Dale Murphy/260 S.Rogers
214 J.Bench/Angels Logo PO
262 G.Carter/164 Buddy Bell
19 Molitor/3 Darrell Porter
55 J.Morgan/Pirates Logo CL
65 B.Stanley/33 Don Baylor
☐ Strip 20 .... .40 .18 .04
210 Joe Niekro/50 Hammaker
127 Campbell/Giants Logo PO
6 K.Hernandez/267 J.Reardon
256 Larry Herndon
146 Ben Oglivie/Hal McRae
172 R.Reed/Brewers Logo CL
30 D.DeCinces/92 J.Royster
☐ Strip 21 .... .40 .18 .04
8 Oberkfell/56 Al Holland
120 Ken Landreaux
xx White Sox Logo PO
151 Ron LeFlore/175 Trillo
197 John Lowenstein
219 Dave Concepcion
232 D.Kingman/Cubs Logo CL
253 Trammell/259 Sanderson
☐ Strip 22 .... .40 .18 .04
116 B.Russell/84 Bob Horner
35 B.Downing/Tigers Logo PO
2 W.McGee/136 Gary Ward
171 T.McGraw/236 Neil Allen
255 Lance Parrish
xx Twins Logo CL
88 C.Washington/77 D.Berra
☐ Strip 23 .... .40 .18 .04
4 Lonnie Smith/188 Lopes
215 Biittner/Braves Logo PO
265 Raines/200 Jim Palmer
148 Buddy Bell/C.Fisk
95 D.Leonard/17 Bob McClure
xx Cards Logo CL/54 Minton
27 Bruce Kison
☐ Strip 24 .... .50 .22 .05
240 Sutcliffe/237 P.Zachry
213 T.Hume/Dodgers Logo CL
194 McGregor/176 S.Carlton
157 Tom Paciorek
145 Rose/Schmidt/Knight
104 W.Wilson/Tigers Logo PO
9 John Stuper/37 R.Smalley
☐ Strip 25A .... .60 .28 .06
1 B.Sutter/40 Lee Mazzilli
72 D.Parker/Padres Logo CL
118 S.Sax/144 R.Henderson
170 M.Schmidt/195 Singleton
233 Mookie Wilson
xx White Sox Logo PO
98 G.Brett/243 Spillner
☐ Strip 25B .... .60 .28 .06
1 B.Sutter/40 Lee Mazzilli
72 D.Parker/Mariner Logo CL
118 S.Sax/144 R.Henderson
170 M.Schmidt/195 Singleton
233 M.Wilson/Twins Logo CL
98 G.Brett/243 Dan Spillner

☐ Strip 26 .... .40 .18 .04
94 Frank White/62 Torrez
66 Jim Rice/Indians Logo CL
123 Reuss/137 Al Williams
165 Matlack/76 Johnny Ray
208 Ray Knight/Mets Logo PO
203 Al Bumbry/225 Eric Show
☐ Strip 27 .... .50 .22 .05
39 Winfield/32 R.Jackson
16 D.Sutton/Orioles Logo CL
7 Andujar/117 P.Guerrero
154 Barojas/199 D.Martinez
111 D.Stieb/Pirates Logo PO
109 B.Bonnell/229 S.Lezcano

1984 Fleer Stickers

The stickers in this 126 sticker set measure 1 15/16" by 2 1/2". The 1984 Fleer sticker set is a very attractive set with a beige border. Many players are featured more than once in the set due to the fact that the album issued to house the set contains league leader categories in which to place the stickers. The checklist below lists the categories. These stickers were originally issued in packs of six for 25 cents plus a team logo.

		MINT	VG-E	F-G
COMPLETE SET		7.00	3.25	.70
COMMON PLAYER		.03	.01	.00
GAME WINNING RBI'S				
☐ 1	Dickie Thon	.05	.02	.00
☐ 2	Ken Landreaux	.03	.01	.00
☐ 3	Darrell Evans	.05	.02	.00
☐ 4	Harold Baines	.10	.04	.01
☐ 5	Dave Winfield	.20	.09	.02
BATTING AVERAGE				
☐ 6	Bill Madlock	.07	.03	.01
☐ 7	Lonnie Smith	.05	.02	.00
☐ 8	Jose Cruz	.05	.02	.00
☐ 9	George Hendrick	.05	.02	.00
☐ 10	Ray Knight	.03	.01	.00
☐ 11	Wade Boggs	.35	.15	.03
☐ 12	Rod Carew	.20	.09	.02
☐ 13	Lou Whitaker	.10	.04	.01
☐ 14	Alan Trammell	.12	.05	.01
☐ 15	Cal Ripken	.25	.10	.02
HOME RUNS LEADERS				
☐ 16	Mike Schmidt	.25	.10	.02
☐ 17	Dale Murphy	.30	.12	.03
☐ 18	Andre Dawson	.12	.05	.01
☐ 19	Pedro Guerrero	.12	.05	.01
☐ 20	Jim Rice	.20	.09	.02
☐ 21	Tony Armas	.05	.02	.00
☐ 22	Ron Kittle	.10	.04	.01
☐ 23	Eddie Murray	.25	.10	.02
HITS LEADERS				
☐ 24	Jose Cruz	.05	.02	.00
☐ 25	Andre Dawson	.12	.05	.01
☐ 26	Rafael Ramirez	.03	.01	.00
☐ 27	Al Oliver	.07	.03	.01
☐ 28	Wade Boggs	.35	.15	.03
☐ 29	Cal Ripken	.25	.10	.02
☐ 30	Lou Whitaker	.10	.04	.01
☐ 31	Cecil Cooper	.07	.03	.01

SLUGGING PERCENTAGE

☐ 32 Dale Murphy	.30	.12	.03
☐ 33 Andre Dawson	.12	.05	.01
☐ 34 Pedro Guerrero	.12	.05	.01
☐ 35 Mike Schmidt	.25	.10	.02
☐ 36 George Brett	.25	.10	.02
☐ 37 Jim Rice	.20	.09	.02
☐ 38 Eddie Murray	.25	.10	.02
☐ 39 Carlton Fisk	.10	.04	.01

PINCH HITS

☐ 40 Rusty Staub	.05	.02	.00
☐ 41 Duane Walker	.03	.01	.00
☐ 42 Steve Braun	.03	.01	.00
☐ 43 Kurt Bevacqua	.03	.01	.00

DESIGNATED HITTERS HITS

☐ 44 Hal McRae	.05	.02	.00
☐ 45 Don Baylor	.07	.03	.01
☐ 46 Ken Singleton	.05	.02	.00
☐ 47 Greg Luzinski	.05	.02	.00

ON BASE PERCENTAGE

☐ 48 Mike Schmidt	.25	.10	.02
☐ 49 Keith Hernandez	.15	.06	.01
☐ 50 Dale Murphy	.30	.12	.03
☐ 51 Tim Raines	.20	.09	.02
☐ 52 Wade Boggs	.35	.15	.03
☐ 53 Rickey Henderson	.30	.12	.03
☐ 54 Rod Carew	.20	.09	.02
☐ 55 Ken Singleton	.05	.02	.00

WON LOST PERCENTAGE

☐ 56 John Denny	.05	.02	.00
☐ 57 John Candelaria	.03	.01	.00
☐ 58 Larry McWilliams	.03	.01	.00
☐ 59 Pascual Perez	.03	.01	.00
☐ 60 Jesse Orosco	.05	.02	.00
☐ 61 Moose Haas	.03	.01	.00
☐ 62 Richard Dotson	.05	.02	.00
☐ 63 Mike Flanagan	.05	.02	.00
☐ 64 Scott McGregor	.05	.02	.00

EARNED RUN AVERAGE

☐ 65 Atlee Hammaker	.03	.01	.00
☐ 66 Rick Honeycutt	.03	.01	.00

SAVES LEADERS

☐ 67 Lee Smith	.07	.03	.01
☐ 68 Al Holland	.05	.02	.00
☐ 69 Greg Minton	.03	.01	.00
☐ 70 Bruce Sutter	.08	.03	.01
☐ 71 Jeff Reardon	.05	.02	.00
☐ 72 Frank DiPino	.03	.01	.00
☐ 73 Dan Quisenberry	.08	.03	.01
☐ 74 Bob Stanley	.03	.01	.00
☐ 75 Ron Davis	.03	.01	.00
☐ 76 Bill Caudill	.03	.01	.00
☐ 77 Peter Ladd	.03	.01	.00

STRIKEOUTS

☐ 78 Steve Carlton	.20	.09	.02
☐ 79 Mario Soto	.05	.02	.00
☐ 80 Larry McWilliams	.03	.01	.00
☐ 81 Fernando Valenzuela	.20	.09	.02
☐ 82 Nolan Ryan	.20	.09	.02
☐ 83 Jack Morris	.15	.06	.01
☐ 84 Floyd Bannister	.05	.02	.00
☐ 85 Dave Stieb	.10	.04	.01
☐ 86 Dave Righetti	.10	.04	.01
☐ 87 Rick Sutcliffe	.10	.04	.01

STEALS LEADERS

☐ 88 Tim Raines	.20	.09	.02
☐ 89 Alan Wiggins	.05	.02	.00
☐ 90 Steve Sax	.08	.03	.01
☐ 91 Mookie Wilson	.03	.01	.00
☐ 92 Rickey Henderson	.30	.12	.03
☐ 93 Rudy Law	.03	.01	.00
☐ 94 Willie Wilson	.08	.03	.01
☐ 95 Julio Cruz	.03	.01	.00

FUTURE HALL OF FAMERS

☐ 96 Johnny Bench	.20	.09	.02
☐ 97 Carl Yastrzemski	.25	.10	.02
☐ 98 Gaylord Perry	.15	.06	.01
☐ 99 Pete Rose	.30	.12	.03
☐ 100 Joe Morgan	.10	.04	.01
☐ 101 Steve Carlton	.20	.09	.02
☐ 102 Jim Palmer	.15	.06	.01
☐ 103 Rod Carew	.20	.09	.02

ROOKIE STARS

☐ 104 Darryl Strawberry	.35	.15	.03
☐ 105 Craig McMurtry	.05	.02	.00
☐ 106 Mel Hall	.10	.04	.01
☐ 107 Lee Tunnell	.05	.02	.00
☐ 108 Bill Dawley	.03	.01	.00
☐ 109 Ron Kittle	.10	.04	.01
☐ 110 Mike Boddicker	.10	.04	.01
☐ 111 Julio Franco	.12	.05	.01
☐ 112 Daryl Sconiers	.03	.01	.00
☐ 113 Neal Heaton	.03	.01	.00

WORLD SERIES BATTING

☐ 114 John Shelby	.03	.01	.00
☐ 115 Rick Dempsey	.03	.01	.00
☐ 116 John Lowenstein	.03	.01	.00
☐ 117 Jim Dwyer	.03	.01	.00
☐ 118 Bo Diaz	.03	.01	.00
☐ 119 Pete Rose	.30	.12	.03
☐ 120 Joe Morgan	.10	.04	.01
☐ 121 Garry Matthews	.05	.02	.00
☐ 122 Garry Maddox	.05	.02	.00

PLAYOFF MANAGERS

☐ 123 Paul Owens	.03	.01	.00
☐ 124 Tom Lasorda	.05	.02	.00
☐ 125 Joe Altobelli	.03	.01	.00
☐ 126 Tony LaRussa	.03	.01	.00

1985 Fleer Star Stickers

The stickers in this 126 sticker set measure 1 15/16" by 2 1/2". The 1985 Fleer stickers set can be housed in a Fleer sticker album. As usual, the stickers are numbered on the fronts. A distinctive feature of the set is the inclusion of stop-action photos on cards 62 through 79. These photos are actually a series of six consecutive stickers which depict a player in action through the course of an activity; e.g., Eddie Murray's swing, Tom Seaver's wind up, and Mike Schmidt fielding. The backs of these stickers are blue and similar in design to past years.

	MINT	VG-E	F-G
COMPLETE SET	7.00	3.25	.70
COMMON PLAYER	.03	.01	.00

☐	1 Pete Rose	.35	.15	.03
☐	2 Pete Rose	.25	.10	.02
☐	3 Pete Rose	.25	.10	.02
☐	4 Don Mattingly	.40	.18	.04
☐	5 Dave Winfield	.20	.09	.02
☐	6 Wade Boggs	.35	.15	.03
☐	7 Buddy Bell	.07	.03	.01
☐	8 Tony Gwynn	.20	.09	.02
☐	9 Lee Lacy	.05	.02	.00
☐	10 Chili Davis	.07	.03	.01
☐	11 Ryne Sandberg	.25	.10	.02
☐	12 Tony Armas	.05	.02	.00
☐	13 Jim Rice	.20	.09	.02
☐	14 Dave Kingman	.07	.03	.01
☐	15 Alvin Davis	.20	.09	.02
☐	16 Gary Carter	.20	.09	.02
☐	17 Mike Schmidt	.20	.09	.02
☐	18 Dale Murphy	.25	.10	.02
☐	19 Ron Cey	.05	.02	.00
☐	20 Eddie Murray	.20	.09	.02
☐	21 Harold Baines	.10	.04	.01
☐	22 Kirk Gibson	.10	.04	.01
☐	23 Jim Rice	.20	.09	.02
☐	24 Gary Matthews	.05	.02	.00
☐	25 Keith Hernandez	.15	.06	.01
☐	26 Gary Carter	.20	.09	.02
☐	27 George Hendrick	.05	.02	.00
☐	28 Tony Armas	.05	.02	.00
☐	29 Dave Kingman	.07	.03	.01
☐	30 Dwayne Murphy	.03	.01	.00

☐	31	Lance Parrish	.15	.06	.01
☐	32	Andre Thornton	.05	.02	.00
☐	33	Dale Murphy	.25	.10	.02
☐	34	Mike Schmidt	.20	.09	.02
☐	35	Gary Carter	.20	.09	.02
☐	36	Darryl Strawberry	.30	.12	.03
☐	37	Don Mattingly	.35	.15	.03
☐	38	Larry Parrish	.05	.02	.00
☐	39	George Bell	.08	.03	.01
☐	40	Dwight Evans	.07	.03	.01
☐	41	Cal Ripken	.25	.10	.02
☐	42	Tim Raines	.20	.09	.02
☐	43	Johnny Ray	.07	.03	.01
☐	44	Juan Samuel	.15	.06	.01
☐	45	Ryne Sandberg	.25	.10	.02
☐	46	Mike Easler	.03	.01	.00
☐	47	Andre Thornton	.05	.02	.00
☐	48	Dave Kingman	.07	.03	.01
☐	49	Don Baylor	.07	.03	.01
☐	50	Rusty Staub	.03	.01	.00
☐	51	Steve Braun	.03	.01	.00
☐	52	Kevin Bass	.05	.02	.00
☐	53	Greg Gross	.03	.01	.00
☐	54	Rickey Henderson	.25	.10	.02
☐	55	Dave Collins	.05	.02	.00
☐	56	Brett Butler	.07	.03	.01
☐	57	Gary Pettis	.05	.02	.00
☐	58	Tim Raines	.20	.09	.02
☐	59	Juan Samuel	.15	.06	.01
☐	60	Alan Wiggins	.05	.02	.00
☐	61	Lonnie Smith	.05	.02	.00

STOP ACTION (62-79)

☐	62	Eddie Murray SA	.15	.06	.01
☐	63	Eddie Murray SA	.15	.06	.01
☐	64	Eddie Murray SA	.15	.06	.01
☐	65	Eddie Murray SA	.15	.06	.01
☐	66	Eddie Murray SA	.15	.06	.01
☐	67	Eddie Murray SA	.15	.06	.01
☐	68	Tom Seaver SA	.10	.04	.01
☐	69	Tom Seaver SA	.10	.04	.01
☐	70	Tom Seaver SA	.10	.04	.01
☐	71	Tom Seaver SA	.10	.04	.01
☐	72	Tom Seaver SA	.10	.04	.01
☐	73	Tom Seaver SA	.10	.04	.01
☐	74	Mike Schmidt SA	.15	.06	.01
☐	75	Mike Schmidt SA	.15	.06	.01
☐	76	Mike Schmidt SA	.15	.06	.01
☐	77	Mike Schmidt SA	.15	.06	.01
☐	78	Mike Schmidt SA	.15	.06	.01
☐	79	Mike Schmidt SA	.15	.06	.01
☐	80	Mike Boddicker	.05	.02	.00
☐	81	Bert Blyleven	.05	.02	.00
☐	82	Jack Morris	.10	.04	.01
☐	83	Dan Petry	.07	.03	.01
☐	84	Frank Viola	.05	.02	.00
☐	85	Joaquin Andujar	.05	.02	.00
☐	86	Mario Soto	.05	.02	.00
☐	87	Dwight Gooden	.50	.22	.05
☐	88	Joe Niekro	.05	.02	.00
☐	89	Rick Sutcliffe	.10	.04	.01
☐	90	Mike Boddicker	.05	.02	.00
☐	91	Dave Stieb	.10	.04	.01
☐	92	Bert Blyleven	.05	.02	.00
☐	93	Phil Niekro	.12	.05	.01
☐	94	Alejandro Pena	.05	.02	.00
☐	95	Dwight Gooden	.50	.22	.05
☐	96	Orel Hershiser	.12	.05	.01
☐	97	Rick Rhoden	.05	.02	.00
☐	98	John Candelaria	.05	.02	.00
☐	99	Dan Quisenberry	.08	.03	.01
☐	100	Bil Caudill	.03	.01	.00
☐	101	Willie Hernandez	.08	.03	.01
☐	102	Dave Righetti	.08	.03	.01
☐	103	Ron Davis	.03	.01	.00
☐	104	Bruce Sutter	.08	.03	.01
☐	105	Lee Smith	.05	.02	.00
☐	106	Jesse Orosco	.05	.02	.00
☐	107	Al Holland	.03	.01	.00
☐	108	Goose Gossage	.08	.03	.01
☐	109	Mark Langston	.05	.02	.00
☐	110	Dave Stieb	.08	.03	.01
☐	111	Mike Witt	.08	.03	.01
☐	112	Bert Blyleven	.05	.02	.00
☐	113	Dwight Gooden	.50	.22	.05
☐	114	Fernando Valenzuela	.15	.06	.01
☐	115	Nolan Ryan	.15	.06	.01
☐	116	Mario Soto	.05	.02	.00
☐	117	Ron Darling	.12	.05	.01
☐	118	Dan Gladden	.08	.03	.01
☐	119	Jeff Stone	.08	.03	.01
☐	120	John Franco	.05	.02	.00
☐	121	Barbaro Garbey	.03	.01	.00
☐	122	Kirby Puckett	.25	.10	.02

☐	123	Roger Clemens	.35	.15	.03
☐	124	Bret Saberhagen	.15	.06	.01
☐	125	Sparky Anderson	.05	.02	.00
☐	126	Dick Williams	.03	.01	.00

1986 Fleer Stickers

The stickers in this 132 sticker set are standard card size, 2 1/2" by 3 1/2". The card photo on the front is surrounded by a yellow border and a cranberry frame. The backs are printed in blue and black on white card stock. The backs contain year by year statistical information. They are numbered on the back in the upper left hand corner.

		MINT	VG-E	F-G
COMPLETE SET (1-132)		18.00	8.50	1.80
COMMON PLAYER		.05	.02	.00

☐	1	Harold Baines	.25	.10	.02
☐	2	Jesse Barfield	.25	.10	.02
☐	3	Don Baylor	.15	.06	.01
☐	4	Juan Beniquez	.05	.02	.00
☐	5	Tim Birtsas	.10	.04	.01
☐	6	Bert Blyleven	.15	.06	.01
☐	7	Bruce Bochte	.05	.02	.00
☐	8	Wade Boggs	1.25	.60	.12
☐	9	Dennis Boyd	.15	.06	.01
☐	10	Phil Bradley	.25	.10	.02
☐	11	George Brett	.75	.35	.07
☐	12	Hubie Brooks	.15	.06	.01
☐	13	Chris Brown	.75	.35	.07
☐	14	Tom Browning	.25	.10	.02
☐	15	Tom Brunansky	.10	.04	.01
☐	16	Bill Buckner	.10	.04	.01
☐	17	Britt Burns	.05	.02	.00
☐	18	Brett Butler	.10	.04	.01
☐	19	Jose Canseco	3.50	1.65	.35
☐	20	Rod Carew	.35	.15	.03
☐	21	Steve Carlton	.35	.15	.03
☐	22	Don Carman	.20	.09	.02
☐	23	Gary Carter	.50	.22	.05
☐	24	Jack Clark	.20	.09	.02
☐	25	Vince Coleman	2.00	.90	.20
☐	26	Cecil Cooper	.20	.09	.02
☐	27	Jose Cruz	.10	.04	.01
☐	28	Ron Darling	.25	.10	.02
☐	29	Alvin Davis	.25	.10	.02
☐	30	Jody Davis	.10	.04	.01
☐	31	Mike Davis	.10	.04	.01
☐	32	Andre Dawson	.20	.09	.02
☐	33	Mariano Duncan	.35	.15	.03
☐	34	Shawon Dunston	.15	.06	.01
☐	35	Leon Durham	.10	.04	.01
☐	36	Darrell Evans	.10	.04	.01
☐	37	Tony Fernandez	.15	.06	.01
☐	38	Carlton Fisk	.15	.06	.01
☐	39	John Franco	.10	.04	.01
☐	40	Julio Franco	.10	.04	.01
☐	41	Damaso Garcia	.10	.04	.01
☐	42	Scott Garrelts	.10	.04	.01
☐	43	Steve Garvey	.50	.22	.05
☐	44	Rich Gedman	.10	.04	.01

☐	45	Kirk Gibson	.25	.10	.02
☐	46	Dwight Gooden	2.50	1.15	.25
☐	47	Pedro Guerrero	.25	.10	.02
☐	48	Ron Guidry	.20	.09	.02
☐	49	Ozzie Guillen	.35	.15	.03
☐	50	Tony Gwynn	.35	.15	.03
☐	51	Andy Hawkins	.05	.02	.00
☐	52	Von Hayes	.10	.04	.01
☐	53	Rickey Henderson	.75	.35	.07
☐	54	Tom Henke	.10	.04	.01
☐	55	Keith Hernandez	.25	.10	.02
☐	56	Willie Hernandez	.10	.04	.01
☐	57	Tommy Herr	.10	.04	.01
☐	58	Orel Hershiser	.35	.15	.03
☐	59	Teddy Higuera	.50	.22	.05
☐	60	Bob Horner	.25	.10	.02
☐	61	Charlie Hough	.05	.02	.00
☐	62	Jay Howell	.05	.02	.00
☐	63	LaMarr Hoyt	.10	.04	.01
☐	64	Kent Hrbek	.25	.10	.02
☐	65	Reggie Jackson	.50	.22	.05
☐	66	Bob James	.05	.02	.00
☐	67	Dave Kingman	.10	.04	.01
☐	68	Ron Kittle	.10	.04	.01
☐	69	Charlie Leibrandt	.10	.04	.01
☐	70	Fred Lynn	.20	.09	.02
☐	71	Mike Marshall	.20	.09	.02
☐	72	Don Mattingly	1.50	.70	.15
☐	73	Oddibe McDowell	.50	.22	.05
☐	74	Willie McGee	.25	.10	.02
☐	75	Scott McGregor	.10	.04	.01
☐	76	Paul Molitor	.10	.04	.01
☐	77	Charlie Moore	.05	.02	.00
☐	78	Keith Moreland	.10	.04	.01
☐	79	Jack Morris	.15	.06	.01
☐	80	Dale Murphy	1.00	.45	.10
☐	81	Eddie Murray	.75	.35	.07
☐	82	Phil Niekro	.25	.10	.02
☐	83	Joe Orsulak	.15	.06	.01
☐	84	Dave Parker	.25	.10	.02
☐	85	Lance Parrish	.25	.10	.02
☐	86	Larry Parrish	.10	.04	.01
☐	87	Tony Pena	.20	.09	.02
☐	88	Gary Pettis	.10	.04	.01
☐	89	Jim Presley	.35	.15	.03
☐	90	Kirby Puckett	.75	.35	.07
☐	91	Dan Quisenberry	.20	.09	.02
☐	92	Tim Raines	.25	.10	.02
☐	93	Johnny Ray	.10	.04	.01
☐	94	Jeff Reardon	.10	.04	.01
☐	95	Rick Reuschel	.05	.02	.00
☐	96	Jim Rice	.25	.10	.02
☐	97	Dave Righetti	.20	.09	.02
☐	98	Earnie Riles	.25	.10	.02
☐	99	Cal Ripken	.50	.22	.05
☐	100	Ron Romanick	.10	.04	.01
☐	101	Pete Rose	1.25	.60	.12
☐	102	Nolan Ryan	.50	.22	.05
☐	103	Bret Saberhagen	.50	.22	.05
☐	104	Mark Salas	.10	.04	.01
☐	105	Juan Samuel	.20	.09	.02
☐	106	Ryne Sandberg	.50	.22	.05
☐	107	Mike Schmidt	.50	.22	.05
☐	108	Mike Scott	.15	.06	.01
☐	109	Tom Seaver	.35	.15	.03
☐	110	Bryn Smith	.10	.04	.01
☐	111	Dave Smith	.10	.04	.01
☐	112	Lonnie Smith	.10	.04	.01
☐	113	Ozzie Smith	.25	.10	.02
☐	114	Mario Soto	.10	.04	.01
☐	115	Dave Stieb	.20	.09	.02
☐	116	Darryl Strawberry	.75	.35	.07
☐	117	Bruce Sutter	.20	.09	.02
☐	118	Garry Templeton	.10	.04	.01
☐	119	Gorman Thomas	.15	.06	.01
☐	120	Andre Thornton	.10	.04	.01
☐	121	Alan Trammell	.25	.10	.02
☐	122	John Tudor	.15	.06	.01
☐	123	Fernando Valenzuela	.25	.10	.02
☐	124	Frank Viola	.10	.04	.01
☐	125	Gary Ward	.05	.02	.00
☐	126	Lou Whitaker	.25	.10	.02
☐	127	Frank White	.10	.04	.01
☐	128	Glenn Wilson	.10	.04	.01
☐	129	Willie Wilson	.20	.09	.02
☐	130	Dave Winfield	.35	.15	.03
☐	131	Robin Yount	.35	.15	.03
☐	132	Checklist:	1.50	.40	.10
		Dwight Gooden			
		Dale Murphy			

1949 Lummis Peanut Butter

The cards in this 12 card set measure 3 1/4" by 4 1/4". The 1949 Lummis set of black and white, unnumbered action poses depicts Philadelphia Phillies only. These "cards" are actually stickers and were distributed locally by Lummis Peanut Butter and Sealtest Dairy Products. The prices listed below are for the harder-to-find Lummis variety; Sealtest "cards" are worth 10% less. The ACC designation is F343.

			MINT	VG-E	F-G
	COMPLETE SET		600.00	275.00	60.00
	COMMON PLAYER (1-12)		40.00	18.00	4.00
☐	1	Rich Ashburn	90.00	42.00	9.00
☐	2	Hank Borowy	40.00	18.00	4.00
☐	3	Del Ennis	50.00	22.00	5.00
☐	4	Granny Hamner	40.00	18.00	4.00
☐	5	Puddinhead Jones	40.00	18.00	4.00
☐	6	Russ Meyer	40.00	18.00	4.00
☐	7	Bill Nicholson	40.00	18.00	4.00
☐	8	Robin Roberts	120.00	55.00	12.00
☐	9	Schoolboy Rowe	50.00	22.00	5.00
☐	10	Andy Seminick	40.00	18.00	4.00
☐	11	Curt Simmons	50.00	22.00	5.00
☐	12	Ed Waitkus	40.00	18.00	4.00

1981 Topps Stickers

The stickers in this 262 sticker set measure 1 15/16" by 2 9/16". The 1981 Topps Stickers set was produced for Topps by Panini (an Italian company). Each sticker is numbered on both front and back. The backs contain the player's name and position, but team affiliations are not listed. An album is available to house the set. The first 32 stickers depict players of various sports; stickers 33-240 are players arranged by teams. Stickers 241-262 have color photos of "all star" players printed on silver (A.L.) or gold (N.L.) foil.

	MINT	VG-E	F-G
COMPLETE SET	12.00	5.50	1.20
COMMON PLAYER (1-240)	.03	.01	.00
COMMON FOIL (241-262)	.20	.09	.02

25

STEVE CARLTON
Pitcher

NEED STICKERS
TO COMPLETE YOUR COLLECTION?
See inside back cover of the
TOPPS BASEBALL STICKER ALBUM

©1981 TOPPS Chewing Gum, Inc.

☐ 1 Steve Stone	.04	.02	.00
☐ 2 Tommy John and Mike Norris	.04	.02	.00
☐ 3 Rudy May	.03	.01	.00
☐ 4 Mike Norris	.03	.01	.00
☐ 5 Len Barker	.03	.01	.00
☐ 6 Mike Norris	.03	.01	.00
☐ 7 Dan Quisenberry	.07	.03	.01
☐ 8 Rich Gossage	.07	.03	.01
☐ 9 George Brett	.30	.12	.03
☐ 10 Cecil Cooper	.10	.04	.01
☐ 11 Reggie Jackson and Ben Oglivie	.12	.05	.01
☐ 12 Gorman Thomas	.07	.03	.01
☐ 13 Cecil Cooper	.10	.04	.01
☐ 14 George Brett and Ben Oglivie	.10	.04	.01
☐ 15 Rickey Henderson	.30	.12	.03
☐ 16 Willie Wilson	.10	.04	.01
☐ 17 Bill Buckner	.07	.03	.01
☐ 18 Keith Hernandez	.12	.05	.01
☐ 19 Mike Schmidt	.25	.10	.02
☐ 20 Bob Horner	.15	.06	.01
☐ 21 Mike Schmidt	.25	.10	.02
☐ 22 George Hendrick	.05	.02	.00
☐ 23 Ron LeFlore	.03	.01	.00
☐ 24 Omar Moreno	.03	.01	.00
☐ 25 Steve Carlton	.20	.09	.02
☐ 26 Joe Niekro	.05	.02	.00
☐ 27 Don Sutton	.07	.03	.01
☐ 28 Steve Carlton	.20	.09	.02
☐ 29 Steve Carlton	.20	.09	.02
☐ 30 Nolan Ryan	.20	.09	.02
☐ 31 Rollie Fingers and Tom Hume	.05	.02	.00
☐ 32 Bruce Sutter	.08	.03	.01

BALTIMORE ORIOLES

☐ 33 Ken Singleton	.05	.02	.00
☐ 34 Eddie Murray	.25	.10	.02
☐ 35 Al Bumbry	.03	.01	.00
☐ 36 Rich Dauer	.03	.01	.00
☐ 37 Scott McGregor	.05	.02	.00
☐ 38 Rick Dempsey	.05	.02	.00
☐ 39 Jim Palmer	.15	.06	.01
☐ 40 Steve Stone	.04	.02	.00

BOSTON RED SOX

☐ 41 Jim Rice	.18	.08	.01
☐ 42 Fred Lynn	.12	.05	.01
☐ 43 Carney Lansford	.07	.03	.01
☐ 44 Tony Perez	.07	.03	.01
☐ 45 Carl Yastrzemski	.30	.12	.03
☐ 46 Carlton Fisk	.10	.04	.01
☐ 47 Dave Stapleton	.03	.01	.00
☐ 48 Dennis Eckersley	.04	.02	.00

CALIFORNIA ANGELS

☐ 49 Rod Carew	.20	.09	.02
☐ 50 Brian Downing	.03	.01	.00
☐ 51 Don Baylor	.08	.03	.01
☐ 52 Rick Burleson	.05	.02	.00
☐ 53 Bobby Grich	.05	.02	.00
☐ 54 Butch Hobson	.03	.01	.00
☐ 55 Andy Hassler	.03	.01	.00
☐ 56 Frank Tanana	.04	.02	.00

CHICAGO WHITE SOX

☐ 57 Chet Lemon	.05	.02	.00
☐ 58 Lamar Johnson	.03	.01	.00
☐ 59 Wayne Nordhagen	.03	.01	.00
☐ 60 Jim Morrison	.03	.01	.00
☐ 61 Bob Molinaro	.03	.01	.00
☐ 62 Rich Dotson	.05	.02	.00
☐ 63 Britt Burns	.05	.02	.00
☐ 64 Ed Farmer	.03	.01	.00

CLEVELAND INDIANS

☐ 65 Toby Harrah	.05	.02	.00
☐ 66 Joe Charboneau	.05	.02	.00
☐ 67 Miguel Dilone	.03	.01	.00
☐ 68 Mike Hargrove	.04	.02	.00
☐ 69 Rick Manning	.03	.01	.00
☐ 70 Andre Thornton	.07	.03	.01
☐ 71 Ron Hassey	.03	.01	.00
☐ 72 Len Barker	.04	.02	.00

DETROIT TIGERS

☐ 73 Lance Parrish	.15	.06	.01
☐ 74 Steve Kemp	.06	.02	.00
☐ 75 Alan Trammell	.12	.05	.01
☐ 76 Champ Summers	.03	.01	.00
☐ 77 Rick Peters	.03	.01	.00
☐ 78 Kirk Gibson	.20	.09	.02
☐ 79 Johnny Wockenfus	.03	.01	.00
☐ 80 Jack Morris	.12	.05	.01

KANSAS CITY ROYALS

☐ 81 Willie Wilson	.08	.03	.01
☐ 82 George Brett	.30	.12	.03
☐ 83 Frank White	.05	.02	.00
☐ 84 Willie Aikens	.05	.02	.00
☐ 85 Clint Hurdle	.03	.01	.00
☐ 86 Hal McRae	.05	.02	.00
☐ 87 Dennis Leonard	.05	.02	.00
☐ 88 Larry Gura	.04	.02	.00
☐ 89 American League Pennant Winner	.04	.02	.00
☐ 90 American League Pennant Winner	.04	.02	.00

MILWAUKEE BREWERS

☐ 91 Paul Molitor	.08	.03	.01
☐ 92 Ben Oglivie	.06	.02	.00
☐ 93 Cecil Cooper	.10	.04	.01
☐ 94 Ted Simmons	.10	.04	.01
☐ 95 Robin Yount	.20	.09	.02
☐ 96 Gorman Thomas	.06	.02	.00
☐ 97 Mike Caldwell	.04	.02	.00
☐ 98 Moose Haas	.03	.01	.00

MINNESOTA TWINS

☐ 99 John Castino	.04	.02	.00
☐ 100 Roy Smalley	.04	.02	.00
☐ 101 Ken Landreaux	.04	.02	.00
☐ 102 Butch Wynegar	.03	.01	.00
☐ 103 Ron Jackson	.03	.01	.00
☐ 104 Jerry Koosman	.05	.02	.00
☐ 105 Roger Erickson	.03	.01	.00
☐ 106 Doug Corbett	.04	.02	.00

NEW YORK YANKEES

☐ 107 Reggie Jackson	.25	.10	.02
☐ 108 Willie Randolph	.06	.02	.00
☐ 109 Rick Cerone	.04	.02	.00
☐ 110 Bucky Dent	.05	.02	.00
☐ 111 Dave Winfield	.20	.09	.02
☐ 112 Ron Guidry	.10	.04	.01
☐ 113 Rich Gossage	.10	.04	.01
☐ 114 Tommy John	.08	.03	.01

OAKLAND A'S

☐ 115 Rickey Henderson	.30	.12	.03
☐ 116 Tony Armas	.07	.03	.01
☐ 117 Dave Revering	.03	.01	.00
☐ 118 Wayne Gross	.03	.01	.00
☐ 119 Dwayne Murphy	.05	.02	.00
☐ 120 Jeff Newman	.03	.01	.00
☐ 121 Rick Langford	.03	.01	.00
☐ 122 Mike Norris	.03	.01	.00

SEATTLE MARINERS

☐ 123 Bruce Bochte	.03	.01	.00
☐ 124 Tom Paciorek	.03	.01	.00
☐ 125 Dan Meyer	.03	.01	.00
☐ 126 Julio Cruz	.03	.01	.00
☐ 127 Richie Zisk	.04	.02	.00
☐ 128 Floyd Bannister	.05	.02	.00
☐ 129 Shane Rawley	.05	.02	.00

TEXAS RANGERS

☐ 130 Buddy Bell	.08	.03	.01
☐ 131 Al Oliver	.10	.04	.01
☐ 132 Mickey Rivers	.05	.02	.00
☐ 133 Jim Sundberg	.05	.02	.00
☐ 134 Bump Wills	.03	.01	.00
☐ 135 Jon Matlack	.04	.02	.00
☐ 136 Danny Darwin	.04	.02	.00

TORONTO BLUE JAYS

☐ 137 Damaso Garcia	.06	.02	.00
☐ 138 Otto Velez	.03	.01	.00
☐ 139 John Mayberry	.05	.02	.00
☐ 140 Alfredo Griffin	.03	.01	.00
☐ 141 Alvis Woods	.03	.01	.00
☐ 142 Dave Stieb	.08	.03	.01
☐ 143 Jim Clancy	.04	.02	.00

ATLANTA BRAVES

☐ 144 Gary Matthews	.06	.02	.00
☐ 145 Bob Horner	.15	.06	.01

☐ 146	Dale Murphy	.30	.12	.03
☐ 147	Chris Chambliss	.05	.02	.00
☐ 148	Phil Niekro	.12	.05	.01
☐ 149	Glenn Hubbard	.03	.01	.00
☐ 150	Rick Camp	.03	.01	.00

CHICAGO CUBS

☐ 151	Dave Kingman	.07	.03	.01
☐ 152	Bill Caudill	.04	.02	.00
☐ 153	Bill Buckner	.07	.03	.01
☐ 154	Barry Foote	.03	.01	.00
☐ 155	Mike Tyson	.03	.01	.00
☐ 156	Ivan DeJesus	.03	.01	.00
☐ 157	Rick Reuschel	.05	.02	.00
☐ 158	Ken Reitz	.03	.01	.00

CINCINNATI REDS

☐ 159	George Foster	.10	.04	.01
☐ 160	Johnny Bench	.20	.09	.02
☐ 161	Dave Concepcion	.07	.03	.01
☐ 162	Dave Collins	.05	.02	.00
☐ 163	Ken Griffey	.06	.02	.00
☐ 164	Dan Driessen	.04	.02	.00
☐ 165	Tom Seaver	.20	.09	.02
☐ 166	Tom Hume	.03	.01	.00

HOUSTON ASTROS

☐ 167	Cesar Cedeno	.05	.02	.00
☐ 168	Rafael Landestoy	.03	.01	.00
☐ 169	Jose Cruz	.07	.03	.01
☐ 170	Art Howe	.03	.01	.00
☐ 171	Terry Puhl	.04	.02	.00
☐ 172	Joe Sambito	.04	.02	.00
☐ 173	Nolan Ryan	.20	.09	.02
☐ 174	Joe Niekro	.05	.02	.00

LOS ANGELES DODGERS

☐ 175	Dave Lopes	.05	.02	.00
☐ 176	Steve Garvey	.25	.10	.02
☐ 177	Ron Cey	.08	.03	.01
☐ 178	Reggie Smith	.05	.02	.00
☐ 179	Bill Russell	.03	.01	.00
☐ 180	Burt Hooton	.03	.01	.00
☐ 181	Jerry Reuss	.05	.02	.00
☐ 182	Dusty Baker	.06	.02	.00

MONTREAL EXPOS

☐ 183	Larry Parrish	.06	.02	.00
☐ 184	Gary Carter	.25	.10	.02
☐ 185	Rodney Scott	.03	.01	.00
☐ 186	Ellis Valentine	.03	.01	.00
☐ 187	Andre Dawson	.12	.05	.01
☐ 188	Warren Cromartie	.03	.01	.00
☐ 189	Chris Speier	.03	.01	.00
☐ 190	Steve Rogers	.05	.02	.00

NEW YORK METS

☐ 191	Lee Mazzilli	.03	.01	.00
☐ 192	Doug Flynn	.03	.01	.00
☐ 193	Steve Henderson	.04	.02	.00
☐ 194	John Stearns	.03	.01	.00
☐ 195	Joel Youngblood	.03	.01	.00
☐ 196	Frank Taveras	.03	.01	.00
☐ 197	Pat Zachry	.03	.01	.00
☐ 198	Neil Allen	.04	.02	.00

PHILADELPHIA PHILLIES

☐ 199	Mike Schmidt	.25	.10	.02
☐ 200	Pete Rose	.40	.18	.04
☐ 201	Larry Bowa	.06	.02	.00
☐ 202	Bake McBride	.03	.01	.00
☐ 203	Bob Boone	.04	.02	.00
☐ 204	Garry Maddox	.04	.02	.00
☐ 205	Tug McGraw	.06	.02	.00
☐ 206	Steve Carlton	.20	.09	.02
☐ 207	N.L. Pennant Winner (World Champions)	.04	.02	.00
☐ 208	N.L. Pennant Winner (World Champions)	.04	.02	.00

PITTSBURGH PIRATES

☐ 209	Phil Garner	.04	.02	.00
☐ 210	Dave Parker	.12	.05	.01
☐ 211	Omar Moreno	.03	.01	.00
☐ 212	Mike Easler	.05	.02	.00
☐ 213	Bill Madlock	.10	.04	.01
☐ 214	Ed Ott	.03	.01	.00
☐ 215	Willie Stargell	.15	.06	.01
☐ 216	Jim Bibby	.03	.01	.00

ST. LOUIS CARDINALS

☐ 217	Garry Templeton	.08	.03	.01
☐ 218	Sixto Lezcano	.03	.01	.00
☐ 219	Keith Hernandez	.15	.06	.01
☐ 220	George Hendrick	.05	.02	.00
☐ 221	Bruce Sutter	.10	.04	.01
☐ 222	Ken Oberkfell	.03	.01	.00
☐ 223	Tony Scott	.03	.01	.00
☐ 224	Darrell Porter	.04	.02	.00

SAN DIEGO PADRES

☐ 225	Gene Richards	.03	.01	.00
☐ 226	Broderick Perkins	.03	.01	.00
☐ 227	Jerry Mumphrey	.03	.01	.00
☐ 228	Luis Salazar	.03	.01	.00
☐ 229	Jerry Turner	.03	.01	.00
☐ 230	Ozzie Smith	.10	.04	.01
☐ 231	John Curtis	.03	.01	.00
☐ 232	Rick Wise	.03	.01	.00

SAN FRANCISCO GIANTS

☐ 233	Terry Whitfield	.03	.01	.00
☐ 234	Jack Clark	.10	.04	.01
☐ 235	Darrell Evans	.08	.03	.01
☐ 236	Larry Herndon	.04	.02	.00
☐ 237	Milt May	.03	.01	.00
☐ 238	Greg Minton	.04	.02	.00
☐ 239	Vida Blue	.07	.03	.01
☐ 240	Eddie Whitson	.05	.02	.00

FOILS (ALL STARS)

☐ 241	Cecil Cooper	.25	.10	.02
☐ 242	Willie Randolph	.20	.09	.02
☐ 243	George Brett	.60	.28	.06
☐ 244	Robin Yount	.50	.22	.05
☐ 245	Reggie Jackson	.60	.28	.06
☐ 246	Al Oliver	.25	.10	.02
☐ 247	Willie Wilson	.25	.10	.02
☐ 248	Rick Cerone	.20	.09	.02
☐ 249	Steve Stone	.20	.09	.02
☐ 250	Tommy John	.25	.10	.02
☐ 251	Rich Gossage	.25	.10	.02
☐ 252	Steve Garvey	.50	.22	.05
☐ 253	Phil Garner	.20	.09	.02
☐ 254	Mike Schmidt	.60	.28	.06
☐ 255	Garry Templeton	.20	.09	.02
☐ 256	George Hendrick	.20	.09	.02
☐ 257	Dave Parker	.30	.12	.03
☐ 258	Cesar Cedeno	.20	.09	.02
☐ 259	Gary Carter	.50	.22	.05
☐ 260	Jim Bibby	.20	.09	.02
☐ 261	Steve Carlton	.50	.22	.05
☐ 262	Tug McGraw	.20	.09	.02

1982 Topps Stickers

The stickers in this 260 sticker series measure 1 15/16" by 2 9/16". The 1982 edition of Topps stickers contains peelable stickers of the same general design of those issued in 1981. Color borders were introduced this year, blue for the N.L. and red for the A.L. The stickers are numbered on both front and back, with no printed team affiliation on the sticker itself. Stickers 121-140 are "foil cards" of All Stars from both leagues. The stickers were issued both as inserts in the regular 1982 issue and in individual, gumless packs. An album for the set was available in retail stores.

	MINT	VG-E	F-G
COMPLETE SET (260)	12.00	5.50	1.20
COMMON PLAYER (1-120)	.03	.01	.00
COMMON PLAYER (121-140)	.20	.09	.02
COMMON PLAYER (141-260)	.03	.01	.00

☐ 1	NL BA: Bill Madlock	.10	.04	.01
☐ 2	AL BA: Carney Lansford	.04	.02	.00
☐ 3	NL HR: Mike Schmidt	.20	.09	.02

☐ 4	AL HR: Tony Armas	.10	.04	.01
	Bobby Grich			
	Dwight Evans			
	Eddie Murray			
☐ 5	NL RBI: Mike Schmidt	.20	.09	.02
☐ 6	AL RBI: Eddie Murray	.20	.09	.02
☐ 7	NL SB: Tim Raines	.15	.06	.01
☐ 8	AL SB: Henderson	.20	.09	.02
☐ 9	NL Victory: Tom Seaver	.12	.05	.01
☐ 10	AL Victory:	.04	.02	.00
	Steve McCatty			
	Dennis Martinez			
	Pete Vuckovich			
	Jack Morris			
☐ 11	NL Strikeouts:			
	Fernando Valenzuela	.15	.06	.01
☐ 12	AL Strikeouts:			
	Len Barker	.04	.02	.00
☐ 13	NL ERA: Nolan Ryan	.15	.06	.01
☐ 14	AL ERA: Steve McCatty	.04	.02	.00
☐ 15	NL Fireman:			
	Bruce Sutter	.08	.03	.01
☐ 16	AL Fireman:	.08	.03	.01
	Rollie Fingers			
ATLANTA BRAVES				
☐ 17	Chris Chambliss	.04	.02	.00
☐ 18	Bob Horner	.12	.05	.01
☐ 19	Dale Murphy	.30	.12	.03
☐ 20	Phil Niekro	.12	.05	.01
☐ 21	Bruce Benedict	.03	.01	.00
☐ 22	Claudell Washington	.06	.02	.00
☐ 23	Glenn Hubbard	.04	.02	.00
☐ 24	Rick Camp	.03	.01	.00
CHICAGO CUBS				
☐ 25	Leon Durham	.10	.04	.01
☐ 26	Ken Reitz	.03	.01	.00
☐ 27	Dick Tidrow	.03	.01	.00
☐ 28	Tim Blackwell	.03	.01	.00
☐ 29	Bill Buckner	.08	.03	.01
☐ 30	Steve Henderson	.03	.01	.00
☐ 31	Mike Krukow	.04	.02	.00
☐ 32	Ivan DeJesus	.03	.01	.00
CINCINNATI REDS				
☐ 33	Dave Collins	.05	.02	.00
☐ 34	Ron Oester	.03	.01	.00
☐ 35	Johnny Bench	.20	.09	.02
☐ 36	Tom Seaver	.20	.09	.02
☐ 37	Dave Concepcion	.07	.03	.01
☐ 38	Ken Griffey	.06	.02	.00
☐ 39	Ray Knight	.05	.02	.00
☐ 40	George Foster	.10	.04	.01
HOUSTON ASTROS				
☐ 41	Nolan Ryan	.20	.09	.02
☐ 42	Terry Puhl	.04	.02	.00
☐ 43	Art Howe	.03	.01	.00
☐ 44	Jose Cruz	.08	.03	.01
☐ 45	Bob Knepper	.06	.02	.00
☐ 46	Craig Reynolds	.03	.01	.00
☐ 47	Cesar Cedeno	.05	.02	.00
☐ 48	Alan Ashby	.03	.01	.00
LOS ANGELES DODGERS				
☐ 49	Ken Landreaux	.05	.02	.00
☐ 50	Fernando Valenzuela	.20	.09	.02
☐ 51	Ron Cey	.08	.03	.01
☐ 52	Dusty Baker	.05	.02	.00
☐ 53	Burt Hooton	.03	.01	.00
☐ 54	Steve Garvey	.25	.10	.02
☐ 55	Pedro Guerrero	.15	.06	.01
☐ 56	Jerry Reuss	.05	.02	.00
MONTREAL EXPOS				
☐ 57	Andre Dawson	.12	.05	.01
☐ 58	Chris Speier	.03	.01	.00
☐ 59	Steve Rogers	.05	.02	.00
☐ 60	Warren Cromartie	.03	.01	.00
☐ 61	Gary Carter	.25	.10	.02
☐ 62	Tim Raines	.15	.06	.01
☐ 63	Scott Sanderson	.04	.02	.00
☐ 64	Larry Parrish	.04	.02	.00
☐ 65	Joel Youngblood	.03	.01	.00
NEW YORK METS				
☐ 66	Neil Allen	.04	.02	.00
☐ 67	Lee Mazzilli	.04	.02	.00
☐ 68	Hubie Brooks	.10	.04	.01
☐ 69	Ellis Valentine	.04	.02	.00
☐ 70	Doug Flynn	.03	.01	.00
☐ 71	Pat Zachry	.03	.01	.00
☐ 72	Dave Kingman	.08	.03	.01
PHILADELPHIA PHILLIES				
☐ 73	Garry Maddox	.04	.02	.00
☐ 74	Mike Schmidt	.30	.12	.03
☐ 75	Steve Carlton	.20	.09	.02
☐ 76	Manny Trillo	.04	.02	.00
☐ 77	Bob Boone	.04	.02	.00
☐ 78	Pete Rose	.45	.20	.04
☐ 79	Gary Matthews	.06	.02	.00
☐ 80	Larry Bowa	.06	.02	.00
PITTSBURGH PIRATES				
☐ 81	Omar Moreno	.04	.02	.00
☐ 82	Rick Rhoden	.04	.02	.00
☐ 83	Bill Madlock	.09	.04	.01
☐ 84	Mike Easler	.05	.02	.00
☐ 85	Willie Stargell	.15	.06	.01
☐ 86	Jim Bibby	.04	.02	.00
☐ 87	Dave Parker	.15	.06	.01
☐ 88	Tim Foli	.03	.01	.00
ST. LOUIS CARDINALS				
☐ 89	Ken Oberkfell	.03	.01	.00
☐ 90	Bob Forsch	.03	.01	.00
☐ 91	George Hendrick	.05	.02	.00
☐ 92	Keith Hernandez	.15	.06	.01
☐ 93	Darrell Porter	.04	.02	.00
☐ 94	Bruce Sutter	.10	.04	.01
☐ 95	Sixto Lezcano	.03	.01	.00
☐ 96	Garry Templeton	.06	.02	.00
SAN DIEGO PADRES				
☐ 97	Juan Eichelberger	.03	.01	.00
☐ 98	Broderick Perkins	.03	.01	.00
☐ 99	Ruppert Jones	.04	.02	.00
☐ 100	Terry Kennedy	.07	.03	.01
☐ 101	Luis Salazar	.03	.01	.00
☐ 102	Gary Lucas	.03	.01	.00
☐ 103	Gene Richards	.03	.01	.00
☐ 104	Ozzie Smith	.10	.04	.01
SAN FRANCISCO GIANTS				
☐ 105	Enos Cabell	.03	.01	.00
☐ 106	Jack Clark	.10	.04	.01
☐ 107	Greg Minton	.04	.02	.00
☐ 108	Johnnie LeMaster	.03	.01	.00
☐ 109	Larry Herndon	.05	.02	.00
☐ 110	Milt May	.03	.01	.00
☐ 111	Vida Blue	.07	.03	.01
☐ 112	Darrell Evans	.05	.02	.00
HIGHLIGHTS (113-120)				
☐ 113	HL: Len Barker	.04	.02	.00
☐ 114	HL: Julio Cruz	.04	.02	.00
☐ 115	HL: Billy Martin	.07	.03	.01
☐ 116	HL: Tim Raines	.15	.06	.01
☐ 117	HL: Pete Rose	.30	.12	.03
☐ 118	HL: Bill Stein	.04	.02	.00
☐ 119	HL: F.Valenzuela	.20	.09	.02
☐ 120	HL: Carl Yastrzemski	.25	.10	.02
NL ALL STARS (121-130)				
☐ 121	Pete Rose AS	.75	.35	.07
☐ 122	Manny Trillo AS	.20	.09	.02
☐ 123	Mike Schmidt AS	.60	.28	.06
☐ 124	Dave Concepcion AS	.25	.10	.02
☐ 125	Andre Dawson AS	.35	.15	.03
☐ 126	George Foster AS	.25	.10	.02
☐ 127	Dave Parker AS	.30	.12	.03
☐ 128	Gary Carter AS	.50	.22	.05
☐ 129	Steve Carlton AS	.50	.22	.05
☐ 130	Bruce Sutter AS	.25	.10	.02
AL ALL STARS (131-140)				
☐ 131	Rod Carew AS	.50	.22	.05
☐ 132	Jerry Remy AS	.20	.09	.02
☐ 133	George Brett AS	.60	.28	.06
☐ 134	Rick Burleson AS	.20	.09	.02
☐ 135	Dwight Evans AS	.25	.10	.02
☐ 136	Ken Singleton AS	.20	.09	.02
☐ 137	Dave Winfield AS	.50	.22	.05
☐ 138	Carlton Fisk AS	.25	.10	.02
☐ 139	Jack Morris AS	.30	.12	.03
☐ 140	Rich Gossage AS	.30	.12	.03
BALTIMORE ORIOLES				
☐ 141	Al Bumbry	.03	.01	.00
☐ 142	Doug DeCinces	.07	.03	.01
☐ 143	Scott McGregor	.04	.02	.00
☐ 144	Ken Singleton	.06	.02	.00
☐ 145	Eddie Murray	.25	.10	.02
☐ 146	Jim Palmer	.15	.06	.01
☐ 147	Rich Dauer	.03	.01	.00
☐ 148	Mike Flanagan	.05	.02	.00
BOSTON RED SOX				
☐ 149	Jerry Remy	.03	.01	.00
☐ 150	Jim Rice	.20	.09	.02
☐ 151	Mike Torrez	.04	.02	.00
☐ 152	Tony Perez	.07	.03	.01
☐ 153	Dwight Evans	.09	.04	.01
☐ 154	Mark Clear	.03	.01	.00
☐ 155	Carl Yastrzemski	.30	.12	.03
☐ 156	Carney Lansford	.08	.03	.01
CALIFORNIA ANGELS				
☐ 157	Rick Burleson	.05	.02	.00
☐ 158	Don Baylor	.08	.03	.01
☐ 159	Ken Forsch	.03	.01	.00
☐ 160	Rod Carew	.20	.09	.02

☐ 161	Fred Lynn	.12	.05	.01
☐ 162	Bob Grich	.07	.03	.01
☐ 163	Dan Ford	.04	.02	.00
☐ 164	Butch Hobson	.03	.01	.00

CHICAGO WHITE SOX

☐ 165	Greg Luzinski	.06	.02	.00
☐ 166	Rich Dotson	.06	.02	.00
☐ 167	Billy Almon	.03	.01	.00
☐ 168	Chet Lemon	.06	.02	.00
☐ 169	Steve Trout	.03	.01	.00
☐ 170	Carlton Fisk	.10	.04	.01
☐ 171	Tony Bernazard	.03	.01	.00
☐ 172	Ron LeFlore	.04	.02	.00

CLEVELAND INDIANS

☐ 173	Bert Blyleven	.09	.04	.01
☐ 174	Andre Thornton	.07	.03	.01
☐ 175	Jorge Orta	.03	.01	.00
☐ 176	Bo Diaz	.04	.02	.00
☐ 177	Toby Harrah	.04	.02	.00
☐ 178	Len Barker	.04	.02	.00
☐ 179	Rick Manning	.03	.01	.00
☐ 180	Mike Hargrove	.04	.02	.00

DETROIT TIGERS

☐ 181	Alan Trammell	.15	.06	.01
☐ 182	Al Cowens	.03	.01	.00
☐ 183	Jack Morris	.15	.06	.01
☐ 184	Kirk Gibson	.15	.06	.01
☐ 185	Steve Kemp	.06	.02	.00
☐ 186	Milt Wilcox	.03	.01	.00
☐ 187	Lou Whitaker	.10	.04	.01
☐ 188	Lance Parrish	.15	.06	.01

KANSAS CITY ROYALS

☐ 189	Willie Wilson	.10	.04	.01
☐ 190	George Brett	.30	.12	.03
☐ 191	Dennis Leonard	.04	.02	.00
☐ 192	John Wathan	.03	.01	.00
☐ 193	Frank White	.05	.02	.00
☐ 194	Amos Otis	.05	.02	.00
☐ 195	Larry Gura	.04	.02	.00
☐ 196	Willie Aikens	.04	.02	.00

MILWAUKEE BREWERS

☐ 197	Ben Oglivie	.05	.02	.00
☐ 198	Rollie Fingers	.10	.04	.01
☐ 199	Cecil Cooper	.10	.04	.01
☐ 200	Paul Molitor	.08	.03	.01
☐ 201	Ted Simmons	.10	.04	.01
☐ 202	Pete Vuckovich	.04	.02	.00
☐ 203	Robin Yount	.20	.09	.02
☐ 204	Gorman Thomas	.07	.03	.01

MINNESOTA TWINS

☐ 205	Rob Wilfong	.03	.01	.00
☐ 206	Hosken Powell	.03	.01	.00
☐ 207	Roy Smalley	.04	.02	.00
☐ 208	Butch Wynegar	.04	.02	.00
☐ 209	John Castino	.04	.02	.00
☐ 210	Doug Corbett	.03	.01	.00
☐ 211	Roger Erickson	.03	.01	.00
☐ 212	Mickey Hatcher	.03	.01	.00

NEW YORK YANKEES

☐ 213	Dave Winfield	.20	.09	.02
☐ 214	Tommy John	.10	.04	.01
☐ 215	Graig Nettles	.08	.03	.01
☐ 216	Reggie Jackson	.30	.12	.03
☐ 217	Rich Gossage	.10	.04	.01
☐ 218	Rick Cerone	.04	.02	.00
☐ 219	Willie Randolph	.05	.02	.00
☐ 220	Jerry Mumphrey	.04	.02	.00
☐ 221	Rickey Henderson	.30	.12	.03

OAKLAND A'S

☐ 222	Mike Norris	.04	.02	.00
☐ 223	Jim Spencer	.03	.01	.00
☐ 224	Tony Armas	.08	.03	.01
☐ 225	Matt Keough	.03	.01	.00
☐ 226	Cliff Johnson	.03	.01	.00
☐ 227	Dwayne Murphy	.05	.02	.00
☐ 228	Steve McCatty	.03	.01	.00

SEATTLE MARINERS

☐ 229	Richie Zisk	.05	.02	.00
☐ 230	Lenny Randle	.03	.01	.00
☐ 231	Jeff Burroughs	.03	.01	.00
☐ 232	Bruce Bochte	.04	.02	.00
☐ 233	Gary Gray	.03	.01	.00
☐ 234	Floyd Bannister	.04	.02	.00
☐ 235	Julio Cruz	.03	.01	.00
☐ 236	Tom Paciorek	.03	.01	.00

TEXAS RANGERS

☐ 237	Danny Darwin	.04	.02	.00
☐ 238	Buddy Bell	.08	.03	.01
☐ 239	Al Oliver	.10	.04	.01
☐ 240	Jim Sundberg	.05	.02	.00
☐ 241	Pat Putnam	.03	.01	.00
☐ 242	Steve Comer	.03	.01	.00
☐ 243	Mickey Rivers	.05	.02	.00

☐ 244	Bump Wills	.03	.01	.00

TORONTO BLUE JAYS

☐ 245	Damaso Garcia	.07	.03	.01
☐ 246	Lloyd Moseby	.10	.04	.01
☐ 247	Ernie Whitt	.03	.01	.00
☐ 248	John Mayberry	.04	.02	.00
☐ 249	Otto Velez	.03	.01	.00
☐ 250	Dave Stieb	.10	.04	.01
☐ 251	Barry Bonnell	.03	.01	.00
☐ 252	Alfredo Griffin	.03	.01	.00
☐ 253	1981 NL Playoffs (Carter looking)	.07	.03	.01
☐ 254	1981 AL Playoffs (action at plate)	.05	.02	.00
☐ 255	Dodgers Team World Champions (left half photo)	.05	.02	.00
☐ 256	Dodgers Team World Champions (right half photo)	.05	.02	.00
☐ 257	World Series (Fernando Valenzuela)	.10	.04	.01
☐ 258	World Series (Garvey swinging)	.10	.04	.01
☐ 259	World Series Jerry Reuss and Steve Yeager	.05	.02	.00
☐ 260	World Series P.Guerrero swings	.10	.04	.01

1982 Topps Sticker Variations

181

ALAN TRAMMELL
Shortstop

TO COLLECT ALL YOUR STICKERS...
ask your store for the new 1982
Topps Sticker Album.
COMING SOON!

IT'S **Topps** FOR SPORTS
© 1982 TOPPS CHEWING GUM, INC.

This 48 card (skip numbered) set is actually a slightly different version of the 1982 Topps stickers. They are the same size (1 15/16" by 2 9/16") and are easily confused. They were mass produced for insertion into the regular packs of cards that year. They are distinguishable from the "other" sticker set by the fact that these refer to "Coming Soon" on the back. There are no foils in this set. All of the stickers in this set depict a single player. Choice of players for this small set appears to have been systematic, i.e., taking every fourth player between #17 and #109 and every fifth player between #151 and #251. Supposedly this set was given to salesman to promote the regular issue.

			MINT	VG-E	F-G
COMPLETE SET			2.00	.90	.20
COMMON PLAYER			.03	.01	.00
☐	17	Chris Chambliss	.04	.02	.00
☐	21	Bruce Benedict	.03	.01	.00
☐	25	Leon Durham	.07	.03	.01
☐	29	Bill Buckner	.05	.02	.00
☐	33	Dave Collins	.04	.02	.00
☐	37	Dave Concepcion	.06	.02	.00
☐	41	Nolan Ryan	.12	.05	.01
☐	45	Bob Knepper	.05	.02	.00
☐	49	Ken Landreaux	.04	.02	.00
☐	53	Burt Hooton	.03	.01	.00
☐	57	Andre Dawson	.08	.03	.01
☐	61	Gary Carter	.15	.06	.01
☐	65	Joel Youngblood	.03	.01	.00
☐	69	Ellis Valentine	.03	.01	.00
☐	73	Garry Maddox	.04	.02	.00
☐	77	Bob Boone	.04	.02	.00

☐	81	Omar Moreno	.03	.01	.00
☐	85	Willie Stargell	.08	.03	.01
☐	89	Ken Oberkfell	.03	.01	.00
☐	93	Darrell Porter	.03	.01	.00
☐	97	Juan Eichelberger	.03	.01	.00
☐	101	Luis Salazar	.03	.01	.00
☐	105	Enos Cabell	.03	.01	.00
☐	109	Larry Herndon	.03	.01	.00
☐	143	Scott McGregor	.04	.02	.00
☐	148	Mike Flanagan	.04	.02	.00
☐	151	Mike Torrez	.03	.01	.00
☐	156	Carney Lansford	.05	.02	.00
☐	161	Fred Lynn	.07	.03	.01
☐	166	Rich Dotson	.04	.02	.00
☐	171	Tony Bernazard	.03	.01	.00
☐	176	Bo Diaz	.03	.01	.00
☐	181	Alan Trammell	.07	.03	.01
☐	186	Milt Wilcox	.03	.01	.00
☐	191	Dennis Leonard	.04	.02	.00
☐	196	Willie Aikens	.04	.02	.00
☐	201	Ted Simmons	.06	.02	.00
☐	206	Hosken Powell	.03	.01	.00
☐	211	Roger Erickson	.03	.01	.00
☐	215	Graig Nettles	.07	.03	.01
☐	216	Reggie Jackson	.15	.06	.01
☐	221	Rickey Henderson	.20	.09	.02
☐	226	Cliff Johnson	.03	.01	.00
☐	231	Jeff Burroughs	.03	.01	.00
☐	236	Tom Paciorek	.03	.01	.00
☐	241	Pat Putnam	.03	.01	.00
☐	246	Lloyd Moseby	.07	.03	.01
☐	251	Barry Bonnell	.03	.01	.00

1983 Topps Stickers

The stickers in this 330 sticker set measure 1 15/16" by 2 9/16". The 1983 Topps Sticker set has been expanded compared to last year's total of 260. There are 28 foil cards (each of which is asterisked in the checklist below), including four of former superstars, and there are also two combination cards (17 and 206). In addition, there are mini-series for 1982 Records (135-146 and 191-202), 1982 Playoffs (147-158) and 1982 World Series (179-190). An album to house the set was sold separately at retail outlets.

		MINT	VG-E	F-G
COMPLETE SET		12.00	5.50	1.20
COMMON PLAYER		.03	.01	.00
COMMON FOILS (ASTERISK)		.20	.09	.02

☐	1	Hank Aaron *	.50	.22	.05
☐	2	Babe Ruth *	.60	.28	.06
☐	3	Willie Mays *	.50	.22	.05
☐	4	Frank Robinson *	.35	.15	.03
☐	5	Reggie Jackson	.25	.10	.02
☐	6	Carl Yastrzemski	.25	.10	.02
☐	7	Johnny Bench	.20	.09	.02
☐	8	Tony Perez	.07	.03	.01
☐	9	Lee May	.04	.02	.00
☐	10	Mike Schmidt	.25	.10	.02
☐	11	Dave Kingman	.09	.04	.01
☐	12	Reggie Smith	.04	.02	.00
☐	13	Graig Nettles	.08	.03	.01

☐	14	Rusty Staub	.04	.02	.00
☐	15	Willie Wilson	.09	.04	.01
☐	16	LaMarr Hoyt	.06	.02	.00
☐	17	Reggie Jackson and Gorman Thomas	.10	.04	.01
☐	18	Floyd Bannister	.05	.02	.00
☐	19	Hal McRae	.05	.02	.00
☐	20	Rick Sutcliffe	.10	.04	.01
☐	21	Rickey Henderson	.30	.12	.03
☐	22	Dan Quisenberry	.10	.04	.01
BALTIMORE ORIOLES					
☐	23	Jim Palmer *	.35	.15	.03
☐	24	John Lowenstein	.03	.01	.00
☐	25	Mike Flanagan	.04	.02	.00
☐	26	Cal Ripken	.25	.10	.02
☐	27	Rich Dauer	.03	.01	.00
☐	28	Ken Singleton	.06	.02	.00
☐	29	Eddie Murray	.25	.10	.02
☐	30	Rick Dempsey	.04	.02	.00
BOSTON RED SOX					
☐	31	Carl Yastrzemski *	.50	.22	.05
☐	32	Carney Lansford	.07	.03	.01
☐	33	Jerry Remy	.03	.01	.00
☐	34	Dennis Eckersley	.05	.02	.00
☐	35	Dave Stapleton	.03	.01	.00
☐	36	Mark Clear	.03	.01	.00
☐	37	Jim Rice	.20	.09	.02
☐	38	Dwight Evans	.09	.04	.01
CALIFORNIA ANGELS					
☐	39	Rod Carew	.20	.09	.02
☐	40	Don Baylor	.07	.03	.01
☐	41	Reggie Jackson *	.50	.22	.05
☐	42	Geoff Zahn	.03	.01	.00
☐	43	Bobby Grich	.05	.02	.00
☐	44	Fred Lynn	.10	.04	.01
☐	45	Bob Boone	.03	.01	.00
☐	46	Doug DeCinces	.06	.02	.00
CHICAGO WHITE SOX					
☐	47	Tom Paciorek	.03	.01	.00
☐	48	Britt Burns	.04	.02	.00
☐	49	Tony Bernazard	.04	.02	.00
☐	50	Steve Kemp	.06	.02	.00
☐	51	Greg Luzinski *	.20	.09	.02
☐	52	Harold Baines	.15	.06	.01
☐	53	LaMarr Hoyt	.06	.02	.00
☐	54	Carlton Fisk	.10	.04	.01
CLEVELAND INDIANS					
☐	55	Andre Thornton *	.20	.09	.02
☐	56	Mike Hargrove	.04	.02	.00
☐	57	Len Barker	.04	.02	.00
☐	58	Toby Harrah	.04	.02	.00
☐	59	Dan Spillner	.03	.01	.00
☐	60	Rick Manning	.03	.01	.00
☐	61	Rick Sutcliffe	.10	.04	.01
☐	62	Ron Hassey	.03	.01	.00
DETROIT TIGERS					
☐	63	Lance Parrish *	.30	.12	.03
☐	64	John Wockenfuss	.03	.01	.00
☐	65	Lou Whitaker	.10	.04	.01
☐	66	Alan Trammell	.15	.06	.01
☐	67	Kirk Gibson	.15	.06	.01
☐	68	Larry Herndon	.05	.02	.00
☐	69	Jack Morris	.15	.06	.01
☐	70	Dan Petry	.08	.03	.01
KANSAS CITY ROYALS					
☐	71	Frank White	.05	.02	.00
☐	72	Amos Otis	.05	.02	.00
☐	73	Willie Wilson *	.25	.10	.02
☐	74	Dan Quisenberry	.10	.04	.01
☐	75	Hal McRae	.05	.02	.00
☐	76	George Brett	.30	.12	.03
☐	77	Larry Gura	.05	.02	.00
☐	78	John Wathan	.03	.01	.00
MILWAUKEE BREWERS					
☐	79	Rollie Fingers	.09	.04	.01
☐	80	Cecil Cooper	.09	.04	.01
☐	81	Robin Yount *	.40	.18	.04
☐	82	Ben Oglivie	.05	.02	.00
☐	83	Paul Molitor	.08	.03	.01
☐	84	Gorman Thomas	.06	.02	.00
☐	85	Ted Simmons	.07	.03	.01
☐	86	Pete Vuckovich	.04	.02	.00
MINNESOTA TWINS					
☐	87	Gary Gaetti	.08	.03	.01
☐	88	Kent Hrbek *	.50	.22	.05
☐	89	John Castino	.03	.01	.00
☐	90	Tom Brunansky	.10	.04	.01
☐	91	Bobby Mitchell	.03	.01	.00
☐	92	Gary Ward	.04	.02	.00
☐	93	Tim Laudner	.03	.01	.00
☐	94	Ron Davis	.03	.01	.00
NEW YORK YANKEES					
☐	95	Willie Randolph	.05	.02	.00

☐ 96	Roy Smalley	.04	.02	.00
☐ 97	Jerry Mumphrey	.04	.02	.00
☐ 98	Ken Griffey	.06	.02	.00
☐ 99	Dave Winfield *	.50	.22	.05
☐ 100	Rich Gossage	.10	.04	.01
☐ 101	Butch Wynegar	.03	.01	.00
☐ 102	Ron Guidry	.12	.05	.01
OAKLAND A'S				
☐ 103	Rickey Henderson *	.50	.22	.05
☐ 104	Mike Heath	.03	.01	.00
☐ 105	Dave Lopes	.04	.02	.00
☐ 106	Rick Langford	.03	.01	.00
☐ 107	Dwayne Murphy	.05	.02	.00
☐ 108	Tony Armas	.08	.03	.01
☐ 109	Matt Keough	.03	.01	.00
☐ 110	Danny Meyer	.03	.01	.00
SEATTLE MARINERS				
☐ 111	Bruce Bochte	.03	.01	.00
☐ 112	Julio Cruz	.03	.01	.00
☐ 113	Floyd Bannister	.05	.02	.00
☐ 114	Gaylord Perry *	.30	.12	.03
☐ 115	Al Cowens	.03	.01	.00
☐ 116	Richie Zisk	.04	.02	.00
☐ 117	Jim Essian	.03	.01	.00
☐ 118	Bill Caudill	.05	.02	.00
TEXAS RANGERS				
☐ 119	Buddy Bell *	.25	.10	.02
☐ 120	Larry Parrish	.05	.02	.00
☐ 121	Danny Darwin	.03	.01	.00
☐ 122	Bucky Dent	.05	.02	.00
☐ 123	Johnny Grubb	.03	.01	.00
☐ 124	George Wright	.05	.02	.00
☐ 125	Charlie Hough	.04	.02	.00
☐ 126	Jim Sundberg	.05	.02	.00
TORONTO BLUE JAYS				
☐ 127	Dave Stieb *	.30	.12	.03
☐ 128	Willie Upshaw	.05	.02	.00
☐ 129	Alfredo Griffin	.04	.02	.00
☐ 130	Lloyd Moseby	.10	.04	.01
☐ 131	Ernie Whitt	.03	.01	.00
☐ 132	Jim Clancy	.04	.02	.00
☐ 133	Barry Bonnell	.03	.01	.00
☐ 134	Damaso Garcia	.06	.02	.00
RECORD BREAKERS				
☐ 135	RB: Jim Kaat	.05	.02	.00
☐ 136	RB: Jim Kaat	.05	.02	.00
☐ 137	RB: Greg Minton	.03	.01	.00
☐ 138	RB: Greg Minton	.03	.01	.00
☐ 139	RB: Paul Molitor	.07	.03	.01
☐ 140	RB: Paul Molitor	.07	.03	.01
☐ 141	RB: Manny Trillo	.03	.01	.00
☐ 142	RB: Manny Trillo	.03	.01	.00
☐ 143	RB: Joel Youngblood	.03	.01	.00
☐ 144	RB: Joel Youngblood	.03	.01	.00
☐ 145	RB: Robin Yount	.15	.06	.01
☐ 146	RB: Robin Yount	.15	.06	.01
PLAYOFF ACTION				
☐ 147	Playoffs: Willie McGee	.09	.04	.01
☐ 148	Playoffs: Darrell Porter	.04	.02	.00
☐ 149	Playoffs: Darrell Porter	.04	.02	.00
☐ 150	Playoffs: Robin Yount	.15	.06	.01
☐ 151	Playoffs: Bruce Benedict	.03	.01	.00
☐ 152	Playoffs: Bruce Benedict	.03	.01	.00
☐ 153	Playoffs: George Hendrick	.04	.02	.00
☐ 154	Playoffs: Bruce Benedict	.03	.01	.00
☐ 155	Playoffs: Doug DeCinces	.05	.02	.00
☐ 156	Playoffs: Paul Molitor	.06	.02	.00
☐ 157	Playoffs: Charlie Moore	.03	.01	.00
☐ 158	Playoffs: Fred Lynn	.10	.04	.01
☐ 159	Rickey Henderson	.30	.12	.03
☐ 160	Dale Murphy	.30	.12	.03
☐ 161	Willie Wilson	.09	.04	.01
☐ 162	Jack Clark	.09	.04	.01
☐ 163	Reggie Jackson	.25	.10	.02
☐ 164	Andre Dawson	.12	.05	.01
☐ 165	Dan Quisenberry	.09	.04	.01
☐ 166	Bruce Sutter	.09	.04	.01
☐ 167	Robin Yount	.20	.09	.02
☐ 168	Ozzie Smith	.09	.04	.01
☐ 169	Frank White	.05	.02	.00
☐ 170	Phil Garner	.04	.02	.00
☐ 171	Doug DeCinces	.06	.02	.00
☐ 172	Mike Schmidt	.25	.10	.02
☐ 173	Cecil Cooper	.10	.04	.01
☐ 174	Al Oliver	.10	.04	.01
☐ 175	Jim Palmer	.15	.06	.01
☐ 176	Steve Carlton	.20	.09	.02
☐ 177	Carlton Fisk	.10	.04	.01
☐ 178	Gary Carter	.25	.10	.02
WORLD SERIES ACTION				
☐ 179	WS: Joaquin Andujar	.05	.02	.00
☐ 180	WS: Ozzie Smith	.08	.03	.01
☐ 181	WS: Cecil Cooper	.07	.03	.01
☐ 182	WS: Darrell Porter	.04	.02	.00
☐ 183	WS: Darrell Porter	.04	.02	.00
☐ 184	WS: Mike Caldwell	.04	.02	.00
☐ 185	WS: Mike Caldwell	.04	.02	.00
☐ 186	WS: Ozzie Smith	.08	.03	.01
☐ 187	WS: Bruce Sutter	.08	.03	.01
☐ 188	WS: Keith Hernandez	.10	.04	.01
☐ 189	WS: Dane Iorg	.03	.01	.00
☐ 190	WS: Dane Iorg	.03	.01	.00
RECORD BREAKERS				
☐ 191	RB: Tony Armas	.05	.02	.00
☐ 192	RB: Tony Armas	.05	.02	.00
☐ 193	RB: Lance Parrish	.10	.04	.01
☐ 194	RB: Lance Parrish	.10	.04	.01
☐ 195	RB: John Wathan	.03	.01	.00
☐ 196	RB: John Wathan	.03	.01	.00
☐ 197	RB: Rickey Henderson	.15	.06	.01
☐ 198	RB: Rickey Henderson	.15	.06	.01
☐ 199	RB: Rickey Henderson	.15	.06	.01
☐ 200	RB: Rickey Henderson	.15	.06	.01
☐ 201	RB: Rickey Henderson	.15	.06	.01
☐ 202	RB: Rickey Henderson	.15	.06	.01
☐ 203	Steve Carlton	.15	.06	.01
☐ 204	Steve Carlton	.15	.06	.01
☐ 205	Al Oliver	.10	.04	.01
☐ 206	Dale Murphy and Al Oliver	.12	.05	.01
☐ 207	Dave Kingman	.10	.04	.01
☐ 208	Steve Rogers	.05	.02	.00
☐ 209	Bruce Sutter	.09	.04	.01
☐ 210	Tim Raines	.15	.06	.01
ATLANTA BRAVES				
☐ 211	Dale Murphy *	.60	.28	.06
☐ 212	Chris Chambliss	.05	.02	.00
☐ 213	Gene Garber	.03	.01	.00
☐ 214	Bob Horner	.12	.05	.01
☐ 215	Glenn Hubbard	.03	.01	.00
☐ 216	Claudell Washington	.05	.02	.00
☐ 217	Bruce Benedict	.03	.01	.00
☐ 218	Phil Niekro	.12	.05	.01
CHICAGO CUBS				
☐ 219	Leon Durham *	.25	.10	.02
☐ 220	Jay Johnstone	.04	.02	.00
☐ 221	Larry Bowa	.05	.02	.00
☐ 222	Keith Moreland	.05	.02	.00
☐ 223	Bill Buckner	.07	.03	.01
☐ 224	Fergie Jenkins	.07	.03	.01
☐ 225	Dick Tidrow	.03	.01	.00
☐ 226	Jody Davis	.08	.03	.01
CINCINNATI REDS				
☐ 227	Dave Concepcion	.06	.02	.00
☐ 228	Dan Driessen	.04	.02	.00
☐ 229	Johnny Bench	.20	.09	.02
☐ 230	Ron Oester	.03	.01	.00
☐ 231	Cesar Cedeno	.05	.02	.00
☐ 232	Alex Trevino	.03	.01	.00
☐ 233	Tom Seaver	.20	.09	.02
☐ 234	Mario Soto	.06	.02	.00
HOUSTON ASTROS				
☐ 235	Nolan Ryan *	.50	.22	.05
☐ 236	Art Howe	.03	.01	.00
☐ 237	Phil Garner	.05	.02	.00
☐ 238	Ray Knight	.06	.02	.00
☐ 239	Terry Puhl	.03	.01	.00
☐ 240	Joe Niekro	.06	.02	.00
☐ 241	Alan Ashby	.03	.01	.00
☐ 242	Jose Cruz	.07	.03	.01
LOS ANGELES DODGERS				
☐ 243	Steve Garvey	.25	.10	.02
☐ 244	Ron Cey	.08	.03	.01
☐ 245	Dusty Baker	.06	.02	.00
☐ 246	Ken Landreaux	.04	.02	.00
☐ 247	Jerry Reuss	.06	.02	.00
☐ 248	Pedro Guerrero	.15	.06	.01
☐ 249	Bill Russell	.04	.02	.00
☐ 250	Fernando Valenzuela *	.45	.20	.04
MONTREAL EXPOS				
☐ 251	Al Oliver *	.25	.10	.02
☐ 252	Andre Dawson	.12	.05	.01
☐ 253	Tim Raines	.15	.06	.01
☐ 254	Jeff Reardon	.07	.03	.01

☐ 255	Gary Carter	.25	.10	.02
☐ 256	Steve Rogers	.05	.02	.00
☐ 257	Tim Wallach	.08	.03	.01
☐ 258	Chris Speier	.03	.01	.00

NEW YORK METS

☐ 259	Dave Kingman	.09	.04	.01
☐ 260	Bob Bailor	.03	.01	.00
☐ 261	Hubie Brooks	.10	.04	.01
☐ 262	Craig Swan	.03	.01	.00
☐ 263	George Foster	.10	.04	.01
☐ 264	John Stearns	.03	.01	.00
☐ 265	Neil Allen	.05	.02	.00
☐ 266	Mookie Wilson *	.20	.09	.02

PHILADELPHIA PHILLIES

☐ 267	Steve Carlton *	.40	.18	.04
☐ 268	Manny Trillo	.03	.01	.00
☐ 269	Gary Matthews	.05	.02	.00
☐ 270	Mike Schmidt	.25	.10	.02
☐ 271	Ivan DeJesus	.03	.01	.00
☐ 272	Pete Rose	.40	.18	.04
☐ 273	Bo Diaz	.04	.02	.00
☐ 274	Sid Monge	.03	.01	.00

PITTSBURGH PIRATES

☐ 275	Bill Madlock *	.25	.10	.02
☐ 276	Jason Thompson	.04	.02	.00
☐ 277	Don Robinson	.03	.01	.00
☐ 278	Omar Moreno	.04	.02	.00
☐ 279	Dale Berra	.04	.02	.00
☐ 280	Dave Parker	.15	.06	.01
☐ 281	Tony Pena	.09	.04	.01
☐ 282	John Candelaria	.06	.02	.00

ST. LOUIS CARDINALS

☐ 283	Lonnie Smith	.05	.02	.00
☐ 284	Bruce Sutter *	.25	.10	.02
☐ 285	George Hendrick	.05	.02	.00
☐ 286	Tom Herr	.05	.02	.00
☐ 287	Ken Oberkfell	.03	.01	.00
☐ 288	Ozzie Smith	.09	.04	.01
☐ 289	Bob Forsch	.03	.01	.00
☐ 290	Keith Hernandez	.15	.06	.01

SAN DIEGO PADRES

☐ 291	Garry Templeton	.07	.03	.01
☐ 292	Broderick Perkins	.03	.01	.00
☐ 293	Terry Kennedy *	.20	.09	.02
☐ 294	Gene Richards	.03	.01	.00
☐ 295	Ruppert Jones	.04	.02	.00
☐ 296	Tim Lollar	.04	.02	.00
☐ 297	John Montefusco	.04	.02	.00
☐ 298	Sixto Lezcano	.03	.01	.00

SAN FRANCISCO GIANTS

☐ 299	Greg Minton	.04	.02	.00
☐ 300	Jack Clark *	.25	.10	.02
☐ 301	Milt May	.03	.01	.00
☐ 302	Reggie Smith	.06	.02	.00
☐ 303	Joe Morgan	.12	.05	.01
☐ 304	John LeMaster	.03	.01	.00
☐ 305	Darrell Evans	.07	.03	.01
☐ 306	Al Holland	.05	.02	.00

YOUNG STARS

☐ 307	Jesse Barfield	.12	.05	.01
☐ 308	Wade Boggs	.50	.22	.05
☐ 309	Tom Brunansky	.10	.04	.01
☐ 310	Storm Davis	.08	.03	.01
☐ 311	Von Hayes	.12	.05	.01
☐ 312	Dave Hostetler	.05	.02	.00
☐ 313	Kent Hrbek	.20	.09	.02
☐ 314	Tim Laudner	.03	.01	.00
☐ 315	Cal Ripken	.25	.10	.02
☐ 316	Andre Robertson	.05	.02	.00
☐ 317	Ed VandeBerg	.05	.02	.00
☐ 318	Glenn Wilson	.07	.03	.01
☐ 319	Chili Davis	.12	.05	.01
☐ 320	Bob Dernier	.08	.03	.01
☐ 321	Terry Francona	.07	.03	.01
☐ 322	Brian Giles	.04	.02	.00
☐ 323	David Green	.06	.02	.00
☐ 324	Atlee Hammaker	.05	.02	.00
☐ 325	Bill Laskey	.05	.02	.00
☐ 326	Willie McGee	.15	.06	.01
☐ 327	Johnny Ray	.15	.06	.01
☐ 328	Ryne Sandberg	.35	.15	.03
☐ 329	Steve Sax	.15	.06	.01
☐ 330	Eric Show	.06	.02	.00

Not sure about an abbreviation?
Just check our glossary and legend found in the introductory section in the front of the book.

1983 Topps Sticker Boxes

The cards in this eight (box) card set measure 2 1/2" by 3 1/2". The 1983 Topps baseball stickers were distributed in boxes which themselves contained a baseball card. In all there were eight different boxes each originally containing 30 stickers but no foils; hence, eight blank-backed cards comprise the box set. The box itself contained an offer for the sticker album and featured a Reggie Jackson photo. Stickers in the boxes came in six strips of five. The prices below reflect the value of the cards on the outside of the box only.

	MINT	VG-E	F-G
COMPLETE SET	6.00	2.80	.60
COMMON PLAYER	.50	.22	.05
☐ 1 Fernando Valenzuela	.60	.28	.06
☐ 2 Gary Carter	.80	.40	.08
☐ 3 Mike Schmidt	.80	.40	.08
☐ 4 Reggie Jackson	.80	.40	.08
☐ 5 Jim Palmer	.60	.28	.06
☐ 6 Rollie Fingers	.50	.22	.05
☐ 7 Pete Rose	1.25	.60	.12
☐ 8 Rickey Henderson	.90	.40	.09

1984 Topps Stickers

**385
DARRYL STRAWBERRY**

The stickers in this 386 sticker set measure 1 15/16" by 2 9/16". This set of stickers is the largest sticker set issued by Topps. The stickers are numbered on both the fronts and backs and contain an offer on the back to obtain 10 additional stickers of your choice. The stickers were also issued in strips of five stickers in a box of seven strips.

	MINT	VG-E	F-G
COMPLETE SET	12.00	5.50	1.20
COMMON PLAYER (1-178)	.03	.01	.00
COMMON PLAYER (179-198)	.20	.09	.02
COMMON PLAYER (199-386)	.03	.01	.00
☐ 1 Steve Carlton (top half)	.20	.09	.02
☐ 2 Steve Carlton (bottom half)	.15	.06	.01
☐ 3 Rickey Henderson (top half)	.15	.06	.01
☐ 4 Rickey Henderson (bottom half)	.15	.06	.01
☐ 5 Fred Lynn (top half)	.09	.04	.01
☐ 6 Fred Lynn (bottom half)	.06	.02	.00
☐ 7 Greg Luzinski (top half)	.05	.02	.00
☐ 8 Greg Luzinski (bottom half)	.04	.02	.00
☐ 9 Dan Quisenberry (top half)	.07	.03	.01

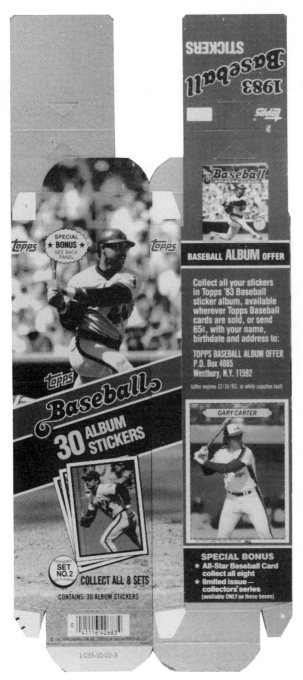

1983 Topps Sticker Boxes

1984 Topps Sticker Boxes

☐ 10 Dan Quisenberry	.05	.02	.00
(bottom half)			

CHAMPIONSHIP SERIES

☐ 11 Champ. Series	.05	.02	.00
LaMarr Hoyt			
☐ 12 Champ. Series	.04	.02	.00
Mike Flanagan			
☐ 13 Champ. Series	.05	.02	.00
Mike Boddicker			
☐ 14 Champ. Series	.04	.02	.00
Tito Landrum			
☐ 15 Champ. Series	.10	.04	.01
Steve Carlton			
☐ 16 Champ. Series	.10	.04	.01
Fernando Valenzuela			
☐ 17 Champ. Series	.04	.02	.00
Charlie Hudson			
☐ 18 Champ. Series	.04	.02	.00
Gary Matthews			

WORLD SERIES (19-26)

☐ 19 World Series	.04	.02	.00
John Denny			
☐ 20 World Series	.03	.01	.00
John Lowenstein			
☐ 21 World Series	.10	.04	.01
Jim Palmer			
☐ 22 World Series	.03	.01	.00
Benny Ayala			
☐ 23 World Series	.04	.02	.00
Rick Dempsey			
☐ 24 World Series	.08	.03	.01
Cal Ripken swings			
☐ 25 World Series	.03	.01	.00
Sammy Stewart			
☐ 26 World Series	.07	.03	.01
Eddie Murray			
at dugout			

ATLANTA BRAVES

☐ 27 Dale Murphy	.25	.10	.02
☐ 28 Chris Chambliss	.04	.02	.00
☐ 29 Glenn Hubbard	.03	.01	.00
☐ 30 Bob Horner	.12	.05	.01
☐ 31 Phil Niekro	.12	.05	.01
☐ 32 Claudell Washington	.06	.02	.00
☐ 33 Rafael Ramirez	.03	.01	.00
☐ 34 Bruce Benedict	.03	.01	.00
☐ 35 Gene Garber	.03	.01	.00
☐ 36 Pascual Perez	.03	.01	.00
☐ 37 Jerry Royster	.03	.01	.00
☐ 38 Steve Bedrosian	.05	.02	.00

CHICAGO CUBS

☐ 39 Keith Moreland	.04	.02	.00
☐ 40 Leon Durham	.10	.04	.01
☐ 41 Ron Cey	.08	.03	.01
☐ 42 Bill Buckner	.07	.03	.01
☐ 43 Jody Davis	.07	.03	.01
☐ 44 Lee Smith	.05	.02	.00
☐ 45 Ryne Sandberg	.35	.15	.03
☐ 46 Larry Bowa	.06	.02	.00
☐ 47 Chuck Rainey	.03	.01	.00
☐ 48 Ferguson Jenkins	.07	.03	.01
☐ 49 Dick Ruthven	.03	.01	.00
☐ 50 Jay Johnstone	.04	.02	.00

CINCINNATI REDS

☐ 51 Mario Soto	.06	.02	.00
☐ 52 Gary Redus	.07	.03	.01
☐ 53 Ron Oester	.03	.01	.00
☐ 54 Cesar Cedeno	.05	.02	.00
☐ 55 Dan Driessen	.03	.01	.00
☐ 56 Dave Concepcion	.06	.02	.00
☐ 57 Dann Bilardello	.03	.01	.00
☐ 58 Joe Price	.03	.01	.00
☐ 59 Tom Hume	.03	.01	.00
☐ 60 Eddie Milner	.05	.02	.00
☐ 61 Paul Householder	.03	.01	.00
☐ 62 Bill Scherrer	.03	.01	.00

HOUSTON ASTROS

☐ 63 Phil Garner	.05	.02	.00
☐ 64 Dickie Thon	.06	.02	.00
☐ 65 Jose Cruz	.07	.03	.01
☐ 66 Nolan Ryan	.18	.08	.01
☐ 67 Terry Puhl	.04	.02	.00
☐ 68 Ray Knight	.06	.02	.00
☐ 69 Joe Niekro	.06	.02	.00
☐ 70 Jerry Mumphrey	.04	.02	.00
☐ 71 Bill Dawley	.03	.01	.00
☐ 72 Alan Ashby	.03	.01	.00
☐ 73 Denny Walling	.03	.01	.00
☐ 74 Frank DiPino	.04	.02	.00

LOS ANGELES DODGERS

☐ 75 Pedro Guerrero	.15	.06	.01
☐ 76 Ken Landreaux	.04	.02	.00
☐ 77 Bill Russell	.05	.02	.00
☐ 78 Steve Sax	.10	.04	.01
☐ 79 Fernando Valenzuela	.15	.06	.01
☐ 80 Dusty Baker	.06	.02	.00
☐ 81 Jerry Reuss	.05	.02	.00
☐ 82 Alejandro Pena	.06	.02	.00
☐ 83 Rick Monday	.04	.02	.00
☐ 84 Rick Honeycutt	.04	.02	.00
☐ 85 Mike Marshall	.10	.04	.01
☐ 86 Steve Yeager	.04	.02	.00

MONTREAL EXPOS

☐ 87 Al Oliver	.10	.04	.01
☐ 88 Steve Rogers	.05	.02	.00
☐ 89 Jeff Reardon	.07	.03	.01
☐ 90 Gary Carter	.25	.10	.02
☐ 91 Tim Raines	.18	.08	.01
☐ 92 Andre Dawson	.12	.05	.01
☐ 93 Manny Trillo	.04	.02	.00
☐ 94 Tim Wallach	.08	.03	.01
☐ 95 Chris Speier	.03	.01	.00
☐ 96 Bill Gullickson	.04	.02	.00
☐ 97 Doug Flynn	.03	.01	.00
☐ 98 Charlie Lea	.04	.02	.00
☐ 99 Bill Madlock	.12	.05	.01
☐ 100 Wade Boggs	.35	.15	.03
☐ 101 Mike Schmidt	.25	.10	.02
☐ 102A Jim Rice	.25	.10	.02
☐ 102B Reggie Jackson	.20	.09	.02

NEW YORK METS

☐ 103 Hubie Brooks	.10	.04	.01
☐ 104 Jesse Orosco	.05	.02	.00
☐ 105 George Foster	.10	.04	.01
☐ 106 Tom Seaver	.20	.09	.02
☐ 107 Keith Hernandez	.15	.06	.01
☐ 108 Mookie Wilson	.06	.02	.00
☐ 109 Bob Bailor	.03	.01	.00
☐ 110 Walt Terrell	.06	.02	.00
☐ 111 Brian Giles	.03	.01	.00
☐ 112 Jose Oquendo	.03	.01	.00
☐ 113 Mike Torrez	.03	.01	.00
☐ 114 Junior Ortiz	.03	.01	.00

PHILADELPHIA PHILLIES

☐ 115 Pete Rose	.35	.15	.03
☐ 116 Joe Morgan	.15	.06	.01
☐ 117 Mike Schmidt	.25	.10	.02
☐ 118 Gary Matthews	.05	.02	.00
☐ 119 Steve Carlton	.18	.08	.01
☐ 120 Bo Diaz	.04	.02	.00
☐ 121 Ivan DeJesus	.03	.01	.00
☐ 122 John Denny	.05	.02	.00
☐ 123 Garry Maddox	.04	.02	.00
☐ 124 Von Hayes	.12	.05	.01
☐ 125 Al Holland	.04	.02	.00
☐ 126 Tony Perez	.08	.03	.01

PITTSBURGH PIRATES

☐ 127 John Candelaria	.06	.02	.00
☐ 128 Jason Thompson	.04	.02	.00
☐ 129 Tony Pena	.09	.04	.01
☐ 130 Dave Parker	.15	.06	.01
☐ 131 Bill Madlock	.10	.04	.01
☐ 132 Kent Tekulve	.05	.02	.00
☐ 133 Larry McWilliams	.03	.01	.00
☐ 134 Johnny Ray	.10	.04	.01
☐ 135 Marvell Wynne	.04	.02	.00
☐ 136 Dale Berra	.04	.02	.00
☐ 137 Mike Easler	.05	.02	.00
☐ 138 Lee Lacy	.05	.02	.00

ST. LOUIS CARDINALS

☐ 139 George Hendrick	.05	.02	.00
☐ 140 Lonnie Smith	.05	.02	.00
☐ 141 Willie McGee	.10	.04	.00
☐ 142 Tom Herr	.05	.02	.00
☐ 143 Darrell Porter	.04	.02	.00
☐ 144 Ozzie Smith	.09	.04	.01
☐ 145 Bruce Sutter	.09	.04	.01
☐ 146 Dave LaPoint	.03	.01	.00
☐ 147 Neil Allen	.04	.02	.00
☐ 148 Ken Oberkfell	.03	.01	.00
☐ 149 David Green	.04	.02	.00
☐ 150 Andy Van Slyke	.10	.04	.01

SAN DIEGO PADRES

☐ 151 Garry Templeton	.06	.02	.00
☐ 152 Juan Bonilla	.03	.01	.00
☐ 153 Alan Wiggins	.05	.02	.00
☐ 154 Terry Kennedy	.07	.03	.01
☐ 155 Dave Dravecky	.07	.03	.01
☐ 156 Steve Garvey	.25	.10	.02
☐ 157 Bobby Brown	.03	.01	.00
☐ 158 Ruppert Jones	.04	.02	.00
☐ 159 Luis Salazar	.03	.01	.00
☐ 160 Tony Gwynn	.35	.15	.03
☐ 161 Gary Lucas	.04	.02	.00
☐ 162 Eric Show	.04	.02	.00

SAN FRANCISCO GIANTS

☐ 163	Darrell Evans	.07	.03	.01
☐ 164	Gary Lavelle	.04	.02	.00
☐ 165	Atlee Hammaker	.05	.02	.00
☐ 166	Jeff Leonard	.07	.03	.01
☐ 167	Jack Clark	.10	.04	.01
☐ 168	Johnny LeMaster	.03	.01	.00
☐ 169	Duane Kuiper	.03	.01	.00
☐ 170	Tom O'Malley	.04	.02	.00
☐ 171	Chili Davis	.10	.04	.01
☐ 172	Bill Laskey	.04	.02	.00
☐ 173	Joel Youngblood	.03	.01	.00
☐ 174	Bob Brenly	.07	.03	.01
☐ 175	Atlee Hammaker	.04	.02	.00
☐ 176	Rick Honeycutt	.04	.02	.00
☐ 177	John Denny	.06	.02	.00
☐ 178	LaMarr Hoyt	.06	.02	.00

FOILS (179-198)

☐ 179	Tim Raines	.35	.15	.03
☐ 180	Dale Murphy	.50	.22	.05
☐ 181	Andre Dawson	.30	.12	.03
☐ 182	Steve Rogers	.20	.09	.02
☐ 183	Gary Carter	.45	.20	.04
☐ 184	Steve Carlton	.35	.15	.03
☐ 185	George Hendrick	.20	.09	.02
☐ 186	Johnny Ray	.25	.10	.02
☐ 187	Ozzie Smith	.25	.10	.02
☐ 188	Mike Schmidt	.50	.22	.05
☐ 189	Jim Rice	.35	.15	.03
☐ 190	Dave Winfield	.35	.15	.03
☐ 191	Lloyd Moseby	.25	.10	.02
☐ 192	LaMarr Hoyt	.20	.09	.02
☐ 193	Ted Simmons	.20	.09	.02
☐ 194	Ron Guidry	.25	.10	.02
☐ 195	Eddie Murray	.50	.22	.05
☐ 196	Lou Whitaker	.25	.10	.02
☐ 197	Cal Ripken	.50	.22	.05
☐ 198	George Brett	.60	.28	.06
☐ 199	Dale Murphy	.30	.12	.03
☐ 200A	Cecil Cooper	.08	.03	.01
☐ 200B	Jim Rice	.12	.05	.01
☐ 201	Tim Raines	.15	.06	.01
☐ 202	Rickey Henderson	.25	.10	.02

BALTIMORE ORIOLES

☐ 203	Eddie Murray	.25	.10	.02
☐ 204	Cal Ripken	.25	.10	.02
☐ 205	Gary Roenicke	.04	.02	.00
☐ 206	Ken Singleton	.05	.02	.00
☐ 207	Scott McGregor	.04	.02	.00
☐ 208	Tippy Martinez	.04	.02	.00
☐ 209	John Lowenstein	.03	.01	.00
☐ 210	Mike Flanagan	.05	.02	.00
☐ 211	Jim Palmer	.15	.06	.01
☐ 212	Dan Ford	.04	.02	.00
☐ 213	Rick Dempsey	.05	.02	.00
☐ 214	Rich Dauer	.03	.01	.00

BOSTON RED SOX

☐ 215	Jerry Remy	.03	.01	.00
☐ 216	Wade Boggs	.35	.15	.03
☐ 217	Jim Rice	.20	.09	.02
☐ 218	Tony Armas	.07	.03	.01
☐ 219	Dwight Evans	.08	.03	.01
☐ 220	Bob Stanley	.05	.02	.00
☐ 221	Dave Stapleton	.03	.01	.00
☐ 222	Rich Gedman	.07	.03	.01
☐ 223	Glenn Hoffman	.03	.01	.00
☐ 224	Dennis Eckersley	.05	.02	.00
☐ 225	John Tudor	.07	.03	.01
☐ 226	Bruce Hurst	.05	.02	.00

CALIFORNIA ANGELS

☐ 227	Rod Carew	.20	.09	.02
☐ 228	Bobby Grich	.06	.02	.00
☐ 229	Doug DeCinces	.06	.02	.00
☐ 230	Fred Lynn	.12	.05	.01
☐ 231	Reggie Jackson	.25	.10	.02
☐ 232	Tommy John	.10	.04	.01
☐ 233	Luis Sanchez	.03	.01	.00
☐ 234	Bob Boone	.04	.02	.00
☐ 235	Bruce Kison	.03	.01	.00
☐ 236	Brian Downing	.04	.02	.00
☐ 237	Ken Forsch	.03	.01	.00
☐ 238	Rick Burleson	.05	.02	.00

CHICAGO WHITE SOX

☐ 239	Dennis Lamp	.03	.01	.00
☐ 240	LaMarr Hoyt	.06	.02	.00
☐ 241	Richard Dotson	.05	.02	.00
☐ 242	Harold Baines	.15	.06	.01
☐ 243	Carlton Fisk	.10	.04	.01
☐ 244	Greg Luzinski	.06	.02	.00
☐ 245	Rudy Law	.03	.01	.00
☐ 246	Tom Paciorek	.03	.01	.00
☐ 247	Floyd Bannister	.05	.02	.00
☐ 248	Julio Cruz	.03	.01	.00
☐ 249	Vance Law	.03	.01	.00

☐ 250	Scott Fletcher	.05	.02	.00

CLEVELAND INDIANS

☐ 251	Toby Harrah	.04	.02	.00
☐ 252	Pat Tabler	.06	.02	.00
☐ 253	Gorman Thomas	.06	.02	.00
☐ 254	Rick Sutcliffe	.10	.04	.01
☐ 255	Andre Thornton	.06	.02	.00
☐ 256	Bake McBride	.04	.02	.00
☐ 257	Alan Bannister	.03	.01	.00
☐ 258	Jamie Easterly	.03	.01	.00
☐ 259	Lary Sorenson	.03	.01	.00
☐ 260	Mike Hargrove	.04	.02	.00
☐ 261	Bert Blyleven	.08	.03	.01
☐ 262	Ron Hassey	.03	.01	.00

DETROIT TIGERS

☐ 263	Jack Morris	.15	.06	.01
☐ 264	Larry Herndon	.04	.02	.00
☐ 265	Lance Parrish	.15	.06	.01
☐ 266	Alan Trammell	.15	.06	.01
☐ 267	Lou Whitaker	.10	.04	.01
☐ 268	Aurelio Lopez	.03	.01	.00
☐ 269	Dan Petry	.08	.03	.01
☐ 270	Glenn Wilson	.08	.03	.01
☐ 271	Chet Lemon	.05	.02	.00
☐ 272	Kirk Gibson	.15	.06	.01
☐ 273	Enos Cabell	.03	.01	.00
☐ 274	Johnny Wockenfuss	.03	.01	.00

KANSAS CITY ROYALS

☐ 275	George Brett	.30	.12	.03
☐ 276	Willie Aikens	.05	.02	.00
☐ 277	Frank White	.05	.02	.00
☐ 278	Hal McRae	.05	.02	.00
☐ 279	Dan Quisenberry	.09	.04	.01
☐ 280	Willie Wilson	.09	.04	.01
☐ 281	Paul Splittorff	.03	.01	.00
☐ 282	U.L. Washington	.03	.01	.00
☐ 283	Bud Black	.05	.02	.00
☐ 284	John Wathan	.03	.01	.00
☐ 285	Larry Gura	.05	.02	.00
☐ 286	Pat Sheridan	.05	.02	.00
☐ 287A	Rusty Staub	.05	.02	.00
☐ 287B	Dave Righetti	.07	.03	.01
☐ 288A	Bob Forsch	.05	.02	.00
☐ 288B	Mike Warren	.05	.02	.00
☐ 289	Al Holland	.05	.02	.00
☐ 290	Dan Quisenberry	.09	.04	.01

MILWAUKEE BREWERS

☐ 291	Cecil Cooper	.09	.04	.01
☐ 292	Moose Haas	.04	.02	.00
☐ 293	Ted Simmons	.09	.04	.01
☐ 294	Paul Molitor	.08	.03	.01
☐ 295	Robin Yount	.18	.08	.01
☐ 296	Ben Oglivie	.05	.02	.00
☐ 297	Tom Tellman	.03	.01	.00
☐ 298	Jim Gantner	.04	.02	.00
☐ 299	Rick Manning	.03	.01	.00
☐ 300	Don Sutton	.12	.05	.01
☐ 301	Charlie Moore	.03	.01	.00
☐ 302	Jim Slaton	.03	.01	.00

MINNESOTA TWINS

☐ 303	Gary Ward	.05	.02	.00
☐ 304	Tom Brunansky	.10	.04	.01
☐ 305	Kent Hrbek	.20	.09	.02
☐ 306	Gary Gaetti	.08	.03	.01
☐ 307	John Castino	.03	.01	.00
☐ 308	Ken Schrom	.04	.02	.00
☐ 309	Ron Davis	.04	.02	.00
☐ 310	Lenny Faedo	.03	.01	.00
☐ 311	Darrell Brown	.03	.01	.00
☐ 312	Frank Viola	.07	.03	.01
☐ 313	Dave Engle	.05	.02	.00
☐ 314	Randy Bush	.03	.01	.00

NEW YORK YANKEES

☐ 315	Dave Righetti	.10	.04	.01
☐ 316	Rich Gossage	.10	.04	.01
☐ 317	Ken Griffey	.06	.02	.00
☐ 318	Ron Guidry	.12	.05	.01
☐ 319	Dave Winfield	.20	.09	.02
☐ 320	Don Baylor	.08	.03	.01
☐ 321	Butch Wynegar	.04	.02	.00
☐ 322	Omar Moreno	.03	.01	.00
☐ 323	Andre Robertson	.03	.01	.00
☐ 324	Willie Randolph	.04	.02	.00
☐ 325	Don Mattingly	.40	.18	.04
☐ 326	Graig Nettles	.10	.04	.01

OAKLAND A'S

☐ 327	Rickey Henderson	.25	.10	.02
☐ 328	Carney Lansford	.08	.03	.01
☐ 329	Jeff Burroughs	.04	.02	.00
☐ 330	Chris Codiroli	.04	.02	.00
☐ 331	Dave Lopes	.04	.02	.00
☐ 332	Dwayne Murphy	.05	.02	.00
☐ 333	Wayne Gross	.03	.01	.00

		MINT	VG-E	F-G
☐ 334	Bill Almon	.03	.01	.00
☐ 335	Tom Underwood	.03	.01	.00
☐ 336	Dave Beard	.03	.01	.00
☐ 337	Mike Heath	.03	.01	.00
☐ 338	Mike Davis	.05	.02	.00

SEATTLE MARINERS

☐ 339	Pat Putnam	.03	.01	.00
☐ 340	Tony Bernazard	.04	.02	.00
☐ 341	Steve Henderson	.03	.01	.00
☐ 342	Richie Zisk	.04	.02	.00
☐ 343	Dave Henderson	.04	.02	.00
☐ 344	Al Cowens	.03	.01	.00
☐ 345	Bill Caudill	.05	.02	.00
☐ 346	Jim Beattie	.03	.01	.00
☐ 347	Rick Nelson	.03	.01	.00
☐ 348	Roy Thomas	.03	.01	.00
☐ 349	Spike Owen	.07	.03	.01
☐ 350	Jamie Allen	.03	.01	.00

TEXAS RANGERS

☐ 351	Buddy Bell	.09	.04	.01
☐ 352	Billy Sample	.03	.01	.00
☐ 353	George Wright	.04	.02	.00
☐ 354	Larry Parrish	.05	.02	.00
☐ 355	Jim Sundberg	.05	.02	.00
☐ 356	Charlie Hough	.04	.02	.00
☐ 357	Pete O'Brien	.10	.04	.01
☐ 358	Wayne Tolleson	.03	.01	.00
☐ 359	Danny Darwin	.03	.01	.00
☐ 360	Dave Stewart	.05	.02	.00
☐ 361	Mickey Rivers	.05	.02	.00
☐ 362	Bucky Dent	.05	.02	.00

TORONTO BLUE JAYS

☐ 363	Willie Upshaw	.06	.02	.00
☐ 364	Damaso Garcia	.06	.02	.00
☐ 365	Lloyd Moseby	.10	.04	.01
☐ 366	Cliff Johnson	.03	.01	.00
☐ 367	Jim Clancy	.04	.02	.00
☐ 368	Dave Stieb	.10	.04	.01
☐ 369	Alfredo Griffin	.04	.02	.00
☐ 370	Barry Bonnell	.04	.02	.00
☐ 371	Luis Leal	.03	.01	.00
☐ 372	Jesse Barfield	.12	.05	.01
☐ 373	Ernie Whitt	.03	.01	.00
☐ 374	Rance Mulliniks	.03	.01	.00

YOUNG STARS

☐ 375	Mike Boddicker	.06	.02	.00
☐ 376	Greg Brock	.06	.02	.00
☐ 377	Bill Doran	.08	.03	.01
☐ 378	Nick Esasky	.06	.02	.00
☐ 379	Julio Franco	.08	.03	.01
☐ 380	Mel Hall	.08	.03	.01
☐ 381	Bob Kearney	.05	.02	.00
☐ 382	Ron Kittle	.09	.04	.01
☐ 383	Carmelo Martinez	.06	.02	.00
☐ 384	Craig McMurtry	.05	.02	.00
☐ 385	Darryl Strawberry	.50	.22	.05
☐ 386	Matt Young	.07	.03	.01

1984 Topps Sticker Boxes

The cards in this 24 card set measure 2 1/2" by 3 1/2". For the second straight year, Topps issued blank-backed baseball cards on the boxes containing its stickers. Two cards per box were issued featuring "24 Leaders in Batting Average in 1983 — Righties, Lefties and Switch Hitters." Officially called Super Bats Picture Cards, the player's name and 1983 batting average were featured within the dotted line cut-out around the card. The team name and batting side(s) of the player were on the outside of the dotted line. The price below includes only the cards on the box. Box 10 was not issued.

		MINT	VG-E	F-G
COMPLETE SET		7.00	3.25	.70
COMMON PAIR		.50	.22	.05
☐ 1	Al Oliver/ Lou Whitaker	.50	.22	.05
☐ 2	Ken Oberkfell/ Ted Simmons	.50	.22	.05
☐ 3	Alan Wiggins/	.50	.22	.05

		MINT	VG-E	F-G
	Hal McRae			
☐ 4	Tim Raines/ Lloyd Moseby	.75	.35	.07
☐ 5	Lonnie Smith/ Willie Wilson	.60	.28	.06
☐ 6	Keith Hernandez/ Robin Yount	.75	.35	.07
☐ 7	Johnny Ray/ Wade Boggs	1.50	.70	.15
☐ 8	Willie McGee/ Ken Singleton	.60	.28	.06
☐ 9	Ray Knight/ Alan Trammell	.50	.22	.05
☐ 11	George Hendrick/ Rod Carew	.75	.35	.07
☐ 12	Bill Madlock/ Eddie Murray	.90	.40	.09
☐ 13	Jose Cruz/ Cal Ripken	.90	.40	.09

1985 Topps Stickers

The stickers in this 376 sticker set measure 2 1/8" by 3". The stickers are numbered on both the fronts and backs and contain an offer on the back to obtain either a poster or an autographed ball of the team of your choice. An album for the stickers was available at retail outlets. For those stickers featuring more than one player, the other numbers on that sticker are given in parentheses.

		MINT	VG-E	F-G
COMPLETE SET		12.00	5.50	1.20
COMMON PLAYER		.03	.01	.00
COMMON FOIL PLAYER		.20	.09	.02
☐ 1	Steve Garvey FOIL (top half)	.30	.12	.03
☐ 2	Steve Garvey FOIL (bottom half)	.20	.09	.02
☐ 3	Dwight Gooden (top half)	.35	.15	.03
☐ 4	Dwight Gooden (bottom half)	.20	.09	.02
☐ 5	Joe Morgan (top half)	.12	.05	.01
☐ 6	Joe Morgan (bottom half)	.07	.03	.01
☐ 7	Don Sutton (top half)	.12	.05	.01
☐ 8	Don Sutton (bottom half)	.07	.03	.01
☐ 9	AL Championships (Jack Morris)	.12	.05	.01
☐ 10	AL Championships (Milt Wilcox)	.03	.01	.00
☐ 11	AL Championships (Kirk Gibson)	.15	.06	.01
☐ 12	NL Championships (Cubs at plate)	.03	.01	.00
☐ 13	NL Championships (Steve Garvey swings)	.15	.06	.01
☐ 14	NL Championships (Steve Garvey)	.15	.06	.01

15	World Series (Jack Morris)	.12	.05	.01
16	World Series (Kurt Bevacqua)	.03	.01	.00
17	World Series (Milt Wilcox)	.03	.01	.00
18	World Series (Alan Trammell ready to throw)	.08	.03	.01
19	World Series (Kirk Gibson)	.12	.05	.01
20	World Series (Alan Trammell)	.12	.05	.01
21	World Series (Chet Lemon back)	.04	.02	.00

ATLANTA BRAVES

22	Dale Murphy	.30	.12	.03
23	Steve Bedrosian	.04	.02	.00
24	Bob Horner	.12	.05	.01
25	Claudell Washington	.05	.02	.00
26	Rick Mahler (212)	.03	.01	.00
27	Rafael Ramirez (213)	.03	.01	.00
28	Craig McMurtry (214)	.03	.01	.00
29	Chris Chambliss (215)	.03	.01	.00
30	Alex Trevino (216)	.03	.01	.00
31	Bruce Benedict (217)	.03	.01	.00
32	Ken Oberkfell (218)	.03	.01	.00
33	Glenn Hubbard (219)	.03	.01	.00

CHICAGO CUBS

34	Ryne Sandberg	.25	.10	.02
35	Rick Sutcliffe	.10	.04	.01
36	Leon Durham	.08	.03	.01
37	Jody Davis	.07	.03	.01
38	Bob Dernier (224)	.03	.01	.00
39	Keith Moreland (225)	.03	.01	.00
40	Scott Sanderson (226)	.03	.01	.00
41	Lee Smith (227)	.03	.01	.00
42	Ron Cey (228)	.04	.02	.00
43	Steve Trout (229)	.03	.01	.00
44	Gary Matthews (230)	.04	.02	.00
45	Larry Bowa (231)	.04	.02	.00

CINCINATTI REDS

46	Mario Soto	.05	.02	.00
47	Dave Parker	.15	.06	.01
48	Dave Concepcion	.06	.02	.00
49	Gary Redus	.05	.02	.00
50	Ted Power (236)	.04	.02	.00
51	Nick Esasky (237)	.04	.02	.00
52	Duane Walker (238)	.03	.01	.00
53	Eddie Milner (239)	.03	.01	.00
54	Ron Oester (240)	.03	.01	.00
55	Cesar Cedeno (241)	.04	.02	.00
56	Joe Price (242)	.03	.01	.00
57	Pete Rose (243)	.15	.06	.01

HOUSTON ASTROS

58	Nolan Ryan	.20	.09	.02
59	Jose Cruz	.07	.03	.01
60	Jerry Mumphrey	.03	.01	.00
61	Enos Cabell	.03	.01	.00
62	Bob Knepper (248)	.04	.02	.00
63	Dickie Thon (249)	.04	.02	.00
64	Phil Garner (250)	.03	.01	.00
65	Craig Reynolds (251)	.03	.01	.00
66	Frank DiPino (252)	.03	.01	.00
67	Terry Puhl (253)	.03	.01	.00
68	Bill Doran (254)	.04	.02	.00
69	Joe Niekro (255)	.04	.02	.00

LOS ANGELES DODGERS

70	Pedro Guerrero	.15	.06	.01
71	Fernando Valenzuela	.15	.06	.01
72	Mike Marshall	.09	.04	.01
73	Alejandro Pena	.05	.02	.00
74	Orel Hershiser (260)	.07	.03	.01
75	Ken Landreaux (261)	.04	.02	.00
76	Bill Russell (262)	.04	.02	.00
77	Steve Sax (263)	.05	.02	.00
78	Rick Honeycutt (264)	.03	.01	.00
79	Mike Scioscia (265)	.03	.01	.00
80	Tom Niedenfuer (266)	.03	.01	.00
81	Candy Maldonado (267)	.04	.02	.00

MONTREAL EXPOS

82	Tim Raines	.15	.06	.01
83	Gary Carter	.25	.10	.02
84	Charlie Lea	.04	.02	.00
85	Jeff Reardon	.06	.02	.00
86	Andre Dawson (272)	.06	.02	.00
87	Tim Wallach (273)	.05	.02	.00
88	Terry Francona (274)	.03	.01	.00
89	Steve Rogers (275)	.03	.01	.00
90	Bryn Smith (276)	.03	.01	.00
91	Bill Gullickson (277)	.03	.01	.00
92	Dan Driessen (278)	.03	.01	.00
93	Doug Flynn (279)	.03	.01	.00

QUADRUPLE STICKERS

94	Mike Schmidt (170/192/280)	.05	.02	.00
95	Tony Armas (171/193/281)	.03	.01	.00
96	Dale Murphy (172/194/282)	.07	.03	.01
97	Rick Sutcliffe (173/195/283)	.04	.02	.00

NEW YORK METS

98	Keith Hernandez	.15	.06	.01
99	George Foster	.09	.04	.01
100	Darryl Strawberry	.30	.12	.03
101	Jesse Orosco	.04	.02	.00
102	Mookie Wilson (288)	.03	.01	.00
103	Doug Sisk (289)	.03	.01	.00
104	Hubie Brooks (290)	.04	.02	.00
105	Ron Darling (291)	.06	.02	.00
106	Wally Backman (292)	.03	.01	.00
107	Dwight Gooden (293)	.15	.06	.01
108	Mike Fitzgerald (294)	.03	.01	.00
109	Walt Terrell (295)	.04	.02	.00

PHILADELPHIA PHILLIES

110	Ozzie Virgil	.03	.01	.00
111	Mike Schmidt	.25	.10	.02
112	Steve Carlton	.20	.09	.02
113	Al Holland	.03	.01	.00
114	Juan Samuel (300)	.05	.02	.00
115	Von Hayes (301)	.05	.02	.00
116	Jeff Stone (302)	.04	.02	.00
117	Jerry Koosman (303)	.04	.02	.00
118	Al Oliver (304)	.04	.02	.00
119	John Denny (305)	.03	.01	.00
120	Charles Hudson (306)	.03	.01	.00
121	Garry Maddox (307)	.03	.01	.00

PITTSBURGH PIRATES

122	Bill Madlock	.09	.04	.01
123	John Candelaria	.05	.02	.00
124	Tony Pena	.09	.04	.01
125	Jason Thompson	.04	.02	.00
126	Lee Lacy (312)	.03	.01	.00
127	Rick Rhoden (313)	.04	.02	.00
128	Doug Frobel (314)	.03	.01	.00
129	Kent Tekulve (315)	.03	.01	.00
130	Johnny Ray (316)	.05	.02	.00
131	Marvell Wynne (317)	.03	.01	.00
132	Larry McWilliams (318)	.03	.01	.00
133	Dale Berra (319)	.03	.01	.00

ST. LOUIS CARDINALS

134	George Hendrick	.05	.02	.00
135	Bruce Sutter	.08	.03	.01
136	Joaquin Andujar	.05	.02	.00
137	Ozzie Smith	.08	.03	.01
138	Andy Van Slyke (324)	.04	.02	.00
139	Lonnie Smith (325)	.04	.02	.00
140	Darrell Porter (326)	.03	.01	.00
141	Willie McGee (327)	.05	.02	.00
142	Tom Herr (328)	.04	.02	.00
143	Dave LaPoint (329)	.03	.01	.00
144	Neil Allen (330)	.03	.01	.00
145	David Green (331)	.03	.01	.00

SAN DIEGO PADRES

146	Tony Gwynn	.25	.10	.02
147	Rich Gossage	.09	.04	.01
148	Terry Kennedy	.06	.02	.00
149	Steve Garvey	.20	.09	.02
150	Alan Wiggins (336)	.03	.01	.00
151	Garry Templeton (337)	.03	.01	.00
152	Ed Whitson (338)	.03	.01	.00
153	Tim Lollar (339)	.03	.01	.00
154	Dave Dravecky (340)	.04	.02	.00
155	Graig Nettles (341)	.05	.02	.00
156	Eric Show (342)	.03	.01	.00
157	Carmelo Martinez (343)	.03	.01	.00

SAN FRANCISCO GIANTS

158	Bob Brenly	.05	.02	.00
159	Gary Lavelle	.03	.01	.00
161	Jeff Leonard	.05	.02	.00
160	Jack Clark	.09	.04	.01
162	Chili Davis (348)	.05	.02	.00
163	Mike Krukow (349)	.03	.01	.00
164	Johnnie LeMaster (350)	.03	.01	.00
165	Atlee Hammaker (351)	.03	.01	.00
166	Dan Gladden (352)	.04	.02	.00
167	Greg Minton (353)	.03	.01	.00
168	Joel Youngblood (354)	.03	.01	.00
169	Frank Williams (355)	.03	.01	.00

QUADRUPLE STICKERS

170	Tony Gwynn (94/192/280)	.10	.04	.01
171	Don Mattingly (95/193/281)	.15	.06	.01
172	Bruce Sutter	.04	.02	.00

(96/194/282)
□ 173 Dan Quisenberry .... .04 .02 .00
(97/195/283)

ALL STAR FOILS (174-191)

□ 174 Tony Gwynn FOIL .... .35 .15 .03
□ 175 Ryne Sandberg FOIL .... .35 .15 .03
□ 176 Steve Garvey FOIL .... .35 .15 .03
□ 177 Dale Murphy FOIL .... .50 .22 .05
□ 179 Darryl Strawberry FOIL ... .50 .22 .05
□ 180 Gary Carter FOIL .... .45 .20 .04
□ 181 Ozzie Smith FOIL .... .25 .10 .02
□ 182 Charlie Lea FOIL .... .20 .09 .02
□ 183 Lou Whitaker FOIL .... .25 .10 .02
□ 184 Rod Carew FOIL .... .35 .15 .03
□ 185 Cal Ripken FOIL .... .45 .20 .04
□ 186 Dave Winfield FOIL .... .40 .18 .04
□ 187 Reggie Jackson FOIL .... .50 .22 .05
□ 188 George Brett FOIL .... .50 .22 .05
□ 189 Lance Parrish FOIL .... .35 .15 .03
□ 190 Chet Lemon FOIL .... .20 .09 .02
□ 191 Dave Stieb FOIL .... .25 .10 .02

QUADRUPLE STICKERS

□ 192 Gary Carter .... .10 .04 .01
(94/170/280)
□ 193 Mike Schmidt .... .10 .04 .01
(95/171/281)
□ 194 Tony Armas .... .04 .02 .00
(96/172/282)
□ 195 Mike Witt .... .05 .02 .00
(97/173/283)

BALTIMORE ORIOLES

□ 196 Eddie Murray .... .25 .10 .02
□ 197 Cal Ripken .... .25 .10 .02
□ 198 Scott McGregor .... .04 .02 .00
□ 199 Rick Dempsey .... .04 .02 .00
□ 200 Tippy Martinez (360) .... .03 .01 .00
□ 201 Ken Singleton (361) .... .04 .02 .00
□ 202 Mike Boddicker (362) ..... .04 .02 .00
□ 203 Rich Dauer (363) .... .03 .01 .00
□ 204 John Shelby (364) .... .03 .01 .00
□ 205 Al Bumbry (365) .... .03 .01 .00
□ 206 John Lowenstein (366) ... .03 .01 .00
□ 207 Mike Flanagan (367) .... .04 .02 .00

BOSTON RED SOX

□ 208 Jim Rice .... .20 .09 .02
□ 209 Tony Armas .... .08 .03 .01
□ 210 Wade Boggs .... .35 .15 .03
□ 211 Bruce Hurst .... .04 .02 .00
□ 212 Dwight Evans (26) .... .04 .02 .00
□ 213 Mike Easler (27) .... .04 .02 .00
□ 214 Bill Buckner (28) .... .04 .02 .00
□ 215 Bob Stanley (29) .... .04 .02 .00
□ 216 Jackie Gutierrez (30) ...... .03 .01 .00
□ 217 Rich Gedman (31) .... .04 .02 .00
□ 218 Jerry Remy (32) .... .03 .01 .00
□ 219 Marty Barrett (33) .... .04 .02 .00

CALIFORNIA ANGELS

□ 220 Reggie Jackson .... .25 .10 .02
□ 221 Geoff Zahn .... .03 .01 .00
□ 222 Doug DeCinces .... .06 .02 .00
□ 223 Rod Carew .... .20 .09 .02
□ 224 Brian Downing (38) .... .03 .01 .00
□ 225 Fred Lynn (39) .... .05 .02 .00
□ 226 Gary Pettis (40) .... .05 .02 .00
□ 227 Mike Witt (41) .... .05 .02 .00
□ 228 Bob Boone (42) .... .04 .02 .00
□ 229 Tommy John (43) .... .05 .02 .00
□ 230 Bobby Grich (44) .... .04 .02 .00
□ 231 Ron Romanick (45) .... .03 .01 .00

CHICAGO WHITE SOX

□ 232 Ron Kittle .... .08 .03 .01
□ 233 Richard Dotson .... .05 .02 .00
□ 234 Harold Baines .... .15 .06 .01
□ 235 Tom Seaver .... .20 .09 .02
□ 236 Greg Walker (50) .... .07 .03 .01
□ 237 Roy Smalley (51) .... .03 .01 .00
□ 238 Greg Luzinski (52) .... .04 .02 .00
□ 239 Julio Cruz (53) .... .03 .01 .00
□ 240 Scott Fletcher (54) .... .03 .01 .00
□ 241 Rudy Law (55) .... .03 .01 .00
□ 242 Vance Law (56) .... .03 .01 .00
□ 243 Carlton Fisk (57) .... .05 .02 .00

CLEVELAND INDIANS

□ 244 Andre Thornton .... .06 .02 .00
□ 245 Julio Franco .... .08 .03 .01
□ 246 Brett Butler .... .07 .03 .01
□ 247 Bert Blyleven .... .07 .03 .01
□ 248 Mike Hargrove (62) .... .03 .01 .00
□ 249 George Vukovich (63) ...... .03 .01 .00
□ 250 Pat Tabler (64) .... .04 .02 .00
□ 251 Brook Jacoby (65) .... .06 .02 .00
□ 252 Tony Bernazard (66) .... .03 .01 .00
□ 253 Ernie Camacho (67) .... .03 .01 .00

□ 254 Mel Hall (68) .... .06 .02 .00
□ 255 Carmen Castillo (69) ...... .03 .01 .00

DETROIT TIGERS

□ 256 Jack Morris .... .12 .05 .01
□ 257 Willie Hernandez .... .09 .04 .01
□ 258 Alan Trammell .... .12 .05 .01
□ 259 Lance Parrish .... .15 .06 .01
□ 260 Chet Lemon (74) .... .04 .02 .00
□ 261 Lou Whitaker (75) .... .05 .02 .00
□ 262 Howard Johnson (76) ...... .03 .01 .00
□ 263 Barbaro Garbey (77) .... .03 .01 .00
□ 264 Dan Petry (78) .... .05 .02 .00
□ 265 Aurelio Lopez (79) .... .03 .01 .00
□ 266 Larry Herndon (80) .... .03 .01 .00
□ 267 Kirk Gibson (81) .... .08 .03 .01

KANSAS CITY ROYALS

□ 268 George Brett .... .30 .12 .03
□ 269 Dan Quisenberry .... .09 .04 .01
□ 270 Hal McRae .... .04 .02 .00
□ 271 Steve Balboni .... .05 .02 .00
□ 272 Pat Sheridan (86) .... .03 .01 .00
□ 273 Jorge Orta (87) .... .03 .01 .00
□ 274 Frank White (88) .... .04 .02 .00
□ 275 Bud Black (89) .... .03 .01 .00
□ 276 Darryl Motley (90) .... .03 .01 .00
□ 277 Willie Wilson (91) .... .05 .02 .00
□ 278 Larry Gura (92) .... .03 .01 .00
□ 279 Don Slaught (93) .... .04 .02 .00

QUADRUPLE STICKERS

□ 280 Dwight Gooden .... .20 .09 .02
(94/170/192)
□ 281 Mark Langston .... .05 .02 .00
(95/171/193)
□ 282 Tim Raines .... .07 .03 .01
(96/172/194)
□ 283 Rickey Henderson .... .12 .05 .01
(97/173/195/283)

MILWAUKEE BREWERS

□ 284 Robin Yount .... .20 .09 .02
□ 285 Rollie Fingers .... .09 .04 .01
□ 286 Jim Sundberg .... .04 .02 .00
□ 287 Cecil Cooper .... .08 .03 .01
□ 288 Jamie Cocanower (102) ... .03 .01 .00
□ 289 Mike Caldwell (103) .... .03 .01 .00
□ 290 Don Sutton (104) .... .05 .02 .00
□ 291 Rick Manning (105) .... .03 .01 .00
□ 292 Ben Oglivie (106) .... .04 .02 .00
□ 293 Moose Haas (107) .... .03 .01 .00
□ 294 Ted Simmons (108) .... .05 .02 .00
□ 295 Jim Gantner (109) .... .03 .01 .00

MINNESOTA TWINS

□ 296 Kent Hrbek .... .15 .06 .01
□ 297 Ron Davis .... .04 .02 .00
□ 298 Dave Engle .... .03 .01 .00
□ 299 Tom Brunansky .... .10 .04 .01
□ 300 Frank Viola (114) .... .04 .02 .00
□ 301 Mike Smithson (115) .... .03 .01 .00
□ 302 Gary Gaetti (116) .... .05 .02 .00
□ 303 Tim Teufel (117) .... .04 .02 .00
□ 304 Mickey Hatcher (118) ...... .03 .01 .00
□ 305 John Butcher (119) .... .03 .01 .00
□ 306 Darrell Brown (120) .... .03 .01 .00
□ 307 Kirby Puckett (121) .... .10 .04 .01

NEW YORK YANKEES

□ 308 Dave Winfield .... .20 .09 .02
□ 309 Phil Niekro .... .12 .05 .01
□ 310 Don Mattingly .... .35 .15 .03
□ 311 Don Baylor .... .08 .03 .01
□ 312 Willie Randolph (126) ...... .04 .02 .00
□ 313 Ron Guidry (127) .... .05 .02 .00
□ 314 Dave Righetti (128) .... .05 .02 .00
□ 315 Bobby Meacham (129) ..... .03 .01 .00
□ 316 Butch Wynegar (130) ...... .03 .01 .00
□ 317 Mike Pagliarulo (131) ..... .10 .04 .01
□ 318 Joe Cowley (132) .... .03 .01 .00
□ 319 John Montefusco (133) .. .03 .01 .00

OAKLAND A'S

□ 320 Dave Kingman .... .08 .03 .01
□ 321 Rickey Henderson .... .20 .09 .02
□ 322 Bill Caudill .... .04 .02 .00
□ 323 Dwayne Murphy .... .04 .02 .00
□ 324 Steve McCatty (138) .... .03 .01 .00
□ 325 Joe Morgan (139) .... .05 .02 .00
□ 326 Mike Heath (140) .... .03 .01 .00
□ 327 Chris Codiroli (141) .... .03 .01 .00
□ 328 Ray Burris (142) .... .03 .01 .00
□ 329 Tony Phillips (143) .... .03 .01 .00
□ 330 Carney Lansford (144) .... .04 .02 .00
□ 331 Bruce Bochte (145) .... .03 .01 .00

SEATTLE MARINERS

□ 332 Alvin Davis .... .20 .09 .02
□ 333 Al Cowens .... .04 .02 .00
□ 334 Jim Beattie .... .03 .01 .00

		MINT	VG-E	F-G
☐ 335	Bob Kearney	.03	.01	.00
☐ 336	Ed Vandeberg (150)	.04	.02	.00
☐ 337	Mark Langston (151)	.05	.02	.00
☐ 338	Dave Henderson (152) ...	.03	.01	.00
☐ 339	Spike Owen (153)	.04	.02	.00
☐ 340	Matt Young (154)	.03	.01	.00
☐ 341	Jack Perconte (155)	.03	.01	.00
☐ 342	Barry Bonnell (156)	.03	.01	.00
☐ 343	Mike Stanton (157)	.03	.01	.00

TEXAS RANGERS

☐ 344	Pete O'Brien	.08	.03	.01
☐ 345	Charlie Hough	.04	.02	.00
☐ 346	Larry Parrish	.04	.02	.00
☐ 347	Buddy Bell	.07	.03	.01
☐ 348	Frank Tanana (162)	.03	.01	.00
☐ 349	Curt Wilkerson (163)	.03	.01	.00
☐ 350	Jeff Kunkel (164)	.03	.01	.00
☐ 351	Billy Sample (165)	.03	.01	.00
☐ 352	Danny Darwin (166)	.03	.01	.00
☐ 353	Gary Ward (167)	.03	.01	.00
☐ 354	Mike Mason (168)	.03	.01	.00
☐ 355	Mickey Rivers (169)	.03	.01	.00

TORONTO BLUE JAYS

☐ 356	Dave Stieb	.10	.04	.01
☐ 357	Damaso Garcia	.06	.02	.00
☐ 358	Willie Upshaw	.05	.02	.00
☐ 359	Lloyd Moseby	.09	.04	.01
☐ 360	George Bell (200)	.06	.02	.00
☐ 361	Luis Leal (201)	.03	.01	.00
☐ 362	Jesse Barfield (202)	.06	.02	.00
☐ 363	Dave Collins (203)	.03	.01	.00
☐ 364	Roy Lee Jackson (204) ...	.03	.01	.00
☐ 365	Doyle Alexander (205)	.03	.01	.00
☐ 366	Alfredo Griffin (206)	.03	.01	.00
☐ 367	Cliff Johnson (207)	.03	.01	.00

YOUNG STARS

☐ 368	Alvin Davis	.20	.09	.02
☐ 369	Juan Samuel	.12	.05	.01
☐ 370	Brook Jacoby	.10	.04	.01
☐ 371	Mark Langston and .... Dwight Gooden	.20	.09	.02
☐ 372	Mike Fitzgerald	.06	.02	.00
☐ 373	Jackie Gutierrez	.04	.02	.00
☐ 374	Dan Gladden	.08	.03	.01
☐ 375	Carmelo Martinez	.05	.02	.00
☐ 376	Kirby Puckett	.30	.12	.03

1986 Topps Stickers

The stickers in this 315 sticker set measure 2 1/8" by 3". The stickers are numbered on both the fronts and backs and contain offers on the back to obtain either a trip for four to Spring Training of the team of your choice or a complete set of Topps baseball cards directly from Topps. An album for the stickers was available at retail outlets. For those stickers featuring more than one player, the other numbers on that sticker are given in parentheses.

	MINT	VG-E	F-G
COMPLETE SET	12.00	5.50	1.20
COMMON PLAYER	.03	.01	.00
COMMON FOIL PLAYER	.20	.09	.02

☐ 1	Pete Rose FOIL .... (top half)	.40	.18	.04
☐ 2	Pete Rose FOIL .... (bottom half)	.25	.10	.02
☐ 3	George Brett (175)	.10	.04	.01
☐ 4	Rod Carew (178)	.09	.04	.01
☐ 5	Vince Coleman (179)	.10	.04	.01
☐ 6	Dwight Gooden (180)	.15	.06	.01
☐ 7	Phil Niekro (181)	.06	.02	.00
☐ 8	Tony Perez (182)	.04	.02	.00
☐ 9	Nolan Ryan (183)	.07	.03	.01
☐ 10	Tom Seaver (184)	.07	.03	.01
☐ 11	NL Championship .... (Ozzie Smith batting)	.07	.03	.01
☐ 12	NL Championship .... (Bill Madlock)	.07	.03	.01
☐ 13	NL Championship .... (Cardinals celebrate)	.05	.02	.00
☐ 14	AL Championship .... (Al Oliver swings)	.04	.02	.00
☐ 15	AL Championship .... (Jim Sundberg)	.04	.02	.00
☐ 16	AL Championship .... (George Brett swings)	.12	.05	.01
☐ 17	World Series .... (Bret Saberhagen)	.10	.04	.01
☐ 18	World Series .... (Dane Iorg swings)	.03	.01	.00
☐ 19	World Series .... (Tito Landrum)	.03	.01	.00
☐ 20	World Series .... (John Tudor)	.05	.02	.00
☐ 21	World Series .... (Buddy Biancalana)	.04	.02	.00
☐ 22	World Series .... (Darryl Motley)	.03	.01	.00
☐ 23	World Series .... (George Brett and Frank White)	.07	.03	.01

HOUSTON ASTROS

☐ 24	Nolan Ryan	.20	.09	.02
☐ 25	Bill Doran	.07	.03	.01
☐ 26	Jose Cruz (185)	.04	.02	.00
☐ 27	Mike Scott (188)	.04	.02	.00
☐ 28	Kevin Bass (189)	.04	.02	.00
☐ 29	Glenn Davis (190)	.12	.05	.01
☐ 30	Mark Bailey (191)	.03	.01	.00
☐ 31	Dave Smith (192)	.04	.02	.00
☐ 32	Phil Garner (193)	.03	.01	.00
☐ 33	Dickie Thon (194)	.04	.02	.00

ATLANTA BRAVES

☐ 34	Bob Horner	.12	.05	.01
☐ 35	Dale Murphy	.25	.10	.02
☐ 36	Glenn Hubbard (195)	.03	.01	.00
☐ 37	Bruce Sutter (198)	.05	.02	.00
☐ 38	Ken Oberkfell (199)	.03	.01	.00
☐ 39	Claud.Washington (200) .	.04	.02	.00
☐ 40	Steve Bedrosian (201)	.03	.01	.00
☐ 41	Terry Harper (202)	.03	.01	.00
☐ 42	Rafael Ramirez (203)	.03	.01	.00
☐ 43	Rick Mahler (204)	.03	.01	.00

ST. LOUIS CARDINALS

☐ 44	Joaquin Andujar	.06	.02	.00
☐ 45	Willie McGee	.09	.04	.01
☐ 46	Ozzie Smith (205)	.05	.02	.00
☐ 47	Vince Coleman (208)	.09	.04	.01
☐ 48	Danny Cox (209)	.03	.01	.00
☐ 49	Tom Herr (210)	.04	.02	.00
☐ 50	Jack Clark (211)	.05	.02	.00
☐ 51	Andy Van Slyke (212)	.05	.02	.00
☐ 52	John Tudor (213)	.04	.02	.00
☐ 53	Terry Pendleton (214)	.04	.02	.00

CHICAGO CUBS

☐ 54	Keith Moreland	.05	.02	.00
☐ 55	Ryne Sandberg	.25	.10	.02
☐ 56	Lee Smith (215)	.05	.02	.00
☐ 57	Steve Trout (218)	.03	.01	.00
☐ 58	Jody Davis (219)	.05	.02	.00
☐ 59	Gary Matthews (220)	.03	.01	.00
☐ 60	Leon Durham (221)	.05	.02	.00
☐ 61	Rick Sutcliffe (222)	.05	.02	.00
☐ 62	Dennis Eckersley (223) ...	.03	.01	.00
☐ 63	Bob Dernier (224)	.03	.01	.00

LOS ANGELES DODGERS

☐ 64	Fernando Valenzuela	.15	.06	.01
☐ 65	Pedro Guerrero	.15	.06	.01
☐ 66	Jerry Reuss (225)	.04	.02	.00
☐ 67	Greg Brock (228)	.04	.02	.00
☐ 68	Mike Scioscia (229)	.03	.01	.00
☐ 69	Ken Howell (230)	.03	.01	.00
☐ 70	Bill Madlock (231)	.05	.02	.00
☐ 71	Mike Marshall (232)	.06	.02	.00

☐ 72 Steve Sax (233)	.06	.02	.00
☐ 73 Orel Hershiser (234)	.07	.03	.01
MONTREAL EXPOS			
☐ 74 Andre Dawson	.12	.05	.01
☐ 75 Tim Raines	.15	.06	.01
☐ 76 Jeff Reardon (235)	.05	.02	.00
☐ 77 Hubie Brooks (238)	.05	.02	.00
☐ 78 Bill Gullickson (239)	.03	.01	.00
☐ 79 Bryn Smith (240)	.03	.01	.00
☐ 80 Terry Francona (241)	.03	.01	.00
☐ 81 Vance Law (242)	.03	.01	.00
☐ 82 Tim Wallach (243)	.05	.02	.00
☐ 83 Herm Winningham (244)	.03	.01	.00
SAN FRANCISCO GIANTS			
☐ 84 Jeff Leonard	.06	.02	.00
☐ 85 Chris Brown	.25	.10	.02
☐ 86 Scott Garrelts (245)	.05	.02	.00
☐ 87 Jose Uribe (248)	.03	.01	.00
☐ 88 Manny Trillo (249)	.03	.01	.00
☐ 89 Dan Driessen (250)	.03	.01	.00
☐ 90 Dan Gladden (251)	.05	.02	.00
☐ 91 Mark Davis (252)	.03	.01	.00
☐ 92 Bob Brenly (253)	.05	.02	.00
☐ 93 Mike Krukow (254)	.04	.02	.00
NEW YORK METS			
☐ 94 Dwight Gooden	.45	.20	.04
☐ 95 Darryl Strawberry	.30	.12	.03
☐ 96 Gary Carter (255)	.15	.06	.01
☐ 97 Wally Backman (258)	.04	.02	.00
☐ 98 Ron Darling (259)	.07	.03	.01
☐ 99 Keith Hernandez (260)	.08	.03	.01
☐ 100 George Foster (261)	.06	.02	.00
☐ 101 Howard Johnson (262)	.03	.01	.00
☐ 102 Rafael Santana (263)	.03	.01	.00
☐ 103 Roger McDowell (264)	.06	.02	.00
SAN DIEGO PADRES			
☐ 104 Steve Garvey	.25	.10	.02
☐ 105 Tony Gwynn	.25	.10	.02
☐ 106 Craig Nettles (265)	.05	.02	.00
☐ 107 Rich Gossage (268)	.05	.02	.00
☐ 108 Andy Hawkins (269)	.04	.02	.00
☐ 109 Carmelo Martinez (270)	.04	.02	.00
☐ 110 Garry Templeton (271)	.04	.02	.00
☐ 111 Terry Kennedy (272)	.04	.02	.00
☐ 112 Tim Flannery (273)	.03	.01	.00
☐ 113 LaMarr Hoyt (274)	.04	.02	.00
PHILADELPHIA PHILLIES			
☐ 114 Mike Schmidt	.25	.10	.02
☐ 115 Ozzie Virgil	.05	.02	.00
☐ 116 Steve Carlton (275)	.10	.04	.01
☐ 117 Garry Maddox (278)	.03	.01	.00
☐ 118 Glenn Wilson (279)	.04	.02	.00
☐ 119 Kevin Gross (280)	.03	.01	.00
☐ 120 Von Hayes (281)	.05	.02	.00
☐ 121 Juan Samuel (282)	.05	.02	.00
☐ 122 Rick Schu (283)	.05	.02	.00
☐ 123 Shane Rawley (284)	.03	.01	.00
PITTSBURGH PIRATES			
☐ 124 Johnny Ray	.10	.04	.01
☐ 125 Tony Pena	.09	.04	.01
☐ 126 Rick Reuschel (285)	.04	.02	.00
☐ 127 Sammy Khalifa (288)	.04	.02	.00
☐ 128 Marvell Wynne (289)	.03	.01	.00
☐ 129 Jason Thompson (290)	.03	.01	.00
☐ 130 Rick Rhoden (291)	.03	.01	.00
☐ 131 Bill Almon (292)	.03	.01	.00
☐ 132 Joe Orsulak (293)	.04	.02	.00
☐ 133 Jim Morrison (294)	.03	.01	.00
CINCINNATI REDS			
☐ 134 Pete Rose	.35	.15	.03
☐ 135 Dave Parker	.15	.06	.01
☐ 136 Mario Soto (295)	.04	.02	.00
☐ 137 Dave Concepcion (298)	.05	.02	.00
☐ 138 Ron Oester (299)	.03	.01	.00
☐ 139 Buddy Bell (300)	.05	.02	.00
☐ 140 Ted Power (301)	.03	.01	.00
☐ 141 Tom Browning (302)	.06	.02	.00
☐ 142 John Franco (303)	.05	.02	.00
☐ 143 Tony Perez (304)	.06	.02	.00
☐ 144 Willie McGee (305)	.07	.03	.01
☐ 145 Dale Murphy (306)	.10	.04	.01
FOILS (146-163)			
☐ 146 Tony Gwynn FOIL	.35	.15	.03
☐ 147 Tom Herr FOIL	.20	.09	.02
☐ 148 Steve Garvey FOIL	.40	.18	.04
☐ 149 Dale Murphy FOIL	.50	.22	.05
☐ 150 Darryl Strawberry FOIL	.50	.22	.05
☐ 151 Graig Nettles FOIL	.25	.10	.02
☐ 152 Terry Kennedy FOIL	.20	.09	.02
☐ 153 Ozzie Smith FOIL	.25	.10	.02
☐ 154 LaMarr Hoyt FOIL	.20	.09	.02
☐ 155 Rickey Henderson FOIL	.50	.22	.05
☐ 156 Lou Whitaker FOIL	.25	.10	.02
☐ 157 George Brett FOIL	.50	.22	.05
☐ 158 Eddie Murray FOIL	.50	.22	.05
☐ 159 Cal Ripken FOIL	.50	.22	.05
☐ 160 Dave Winfield FOIL	.40	.18	.04
☐ 161 Jim Rice FOIL	.35	.15	.03
☐ 162 Carlton Fisk FOIL	.30	.12	.03
☐ 163 Jack Morris FOIL	.25	.10	.02
☐ 164 Wade Boggs (307)	.15	.06	.01
☐ 165 Darrell Evans (308)	.04	.02	.00
OAKLAND A'S			
☐ 166 Mike Davis	.05	.02	.00
☐ 167 Dave Kingman	.07	.03	.01
☐ 168 Alfredo Griffin (309)	.03	.01	.00
☐ 169 Carney Lansford (310)	.04	.02	.00
☐ 170 Bruce Bochte (311)	.03	.01	.00
☐ 171 Dwayne Murphy (312)	.04	.02	.00
☐ 172 Dave Collins (313)	.03	.01	.00
☐ 173 Chris Codiroli (314)	.03	.01	.00
☐ 174 Mike Heath (315)	.03	.01	.00
☐ 175 Jay Howell (3)	.04	.02	.00
CALIFORNIA ANGELS			
☐ 176 Rod Carew	.20	.09	.02
☐ 177 Reggie Jackson	.25	.10	.02
☐ 178 Doug DeCinces (4)	.04	.02	.00
☐ 179 Bob Boone (5)	.03	.01	.00
☐ 180 Ron Romanick (6)	.03	.01	.00
☐ 181 Bob Grich (7)	.04	.02	.00
☐ 182 Donnie Moore (8)	.03	.01	.00
☐ 183 Brian Downing (9)	.03	.01	.00
☐ 184 Ruppert Jones (10)	.03	.01	.00
☐ 185 Juan Beniquez (26)	.03	.01	.00
TORONTO BLUE JAYS			
☐ 186 Dave Stieb	.10	.04	.01
☐ 187 Jorge Bell	.10	.04	.01
☐ 188 Willie Upshaw (27)	.04	.02	.00
☐ 189 Tom Henke (28)	.05	.02	.00
☐ 190 Damaso Garcia (29)	.04	.02	.00
☐ 191 Jimmy Key (30)	.05	.02	.00
☐ 192 Jesse Barfield (31)	.06	.02	.00
☐ 193 Dennis Lamp (32)	.03	.01	.00
☐ 194 Tony Fernandez (33)	.07	.03	.01
☐ 195 Lloyd Moseby (36)	.06	.02	.00
MILWAUKEE BREWERS			
☐ 196 Cecil Cooper	.08	.03	.01
☐ 197 Robin Yount	.20	.09	.02
☐ 198 Rollie Fingers (37)	.06	.02	.00
☐ 199 Ted Simmons (38)	.06	.02	.00
☐ 200 Ben Oglivie (39)	.04	.02	.00
☐ 201 Moose Haas (40)	.03	.01	.00
☐ 202 Jim Gantner (41)	.03	.01	.00
☐ 203 Paul Molitor (42)	.05	.02	.00
☐ 204 Charlie Moore (43)	.03	.01	.00
☐ 205 Danny Darwin (46)	.03	.01	.00
CLEVELAND INDIANS			
☐ 206 Brett Butler	.07	.03	.01
☐ 207 Brook Jacoby	.09	.04	.01
☐ 208 Andre Thornton (47)	.04	.02	.00
☐ 209 Tom Waddell (48)	.03	.01	.00
☐ 210 Tony Bernazard (49)	.03	.01	.00
☐ 211 Julio Franco (50)	.05	.02	.00
☐ 212 Pat Tabler (51)	.04	.02	.00
☐ 213 Joe Carter (52)	.09	.04	.01
☐ 214 George Vukovich (53)	.03	.01	.00
☐ 215 Rich Thompson (56)	.03	.01	.00
SEATTLE MARINERS			
☐ 216 Gorman Thomas	.06	.02	.00
☐ 217 Phil Bradley	.12	.05	.01
☐ 218 Alvin Davis (57)	.07	.03	.01
☐ 219 Jim Presley (58)	.09	.04	.01
☐ 220 Matt Young (59)	.03	.01	.00
☐ 221 Mike Moore (60)	.04	.02	.00
☐ 222 Dave Henderson (61)	.04	.02	.00
☐ 223 Ed Nunez (62)	.04	.02	.00
☐ 224 Spike Owen (63)	.04	.02	.00
☐ 225 Mark Langston (66)	.05	.02	.00
BALTIMORE ORIOLES			
☐ 226 Cal Ripken	.25	.10	.02
☐ 227 Eddie Murray	.25	.10	.02
☐ 228 Fred Lynn (67)	.05	.02	.00
☐ 229 Lee Lacy (68)	.03	.01	.00
☐ 230 Scott McGregor (69)	.03	.01	.00
☐ 231 Storm Davis (70)	.04	.02	.00
☐ 232 Rick Dempsey (71)	.04	.02	.00
☐ 233 Mike Boddicker (72)	.04	.02	.00
☐ 234 Mike Young (73)	.05	.02	.00
☐ 235 Sammy Stewart (76)	.03	.01	.00
TEXAS RANGERS			
☐ 236 Pete O'Brien	.08	.03	.01
☐ 237 Oddibe McDowell	.20	.09	.02
☐ 238 Toby Harrah (77)	.03	.01	.00
☐ 239 Gary Ward (78)	.03	.01	.00
☐ 240 Larry Parrish (79)	.03	.01	.00
☐ 241 Charlie Hough (80)	.03	.01	.00

☐ 242 Burt Hooton (81) .... .03 .01 .00
☐ 243 Don Slaught (82) .... .03 .01 .00
☐ 244 Curt Wilkerson (83) .... .03 .01 .00
☐ 245 Greg Harris (86) .... .03 .01 .00
BOSTON RED SOX
☐ 246 Jim Rice .... .20 .09 .02
☐ 247 Wade Boggs .... .35 .15 .03
☐ 248 Rich Gedman (87) .... .05 .02 .00
☐ 249 Dennis Boyd (88) .... .05 .02 .00
☐ 250 Marty Barrett (89) .... .04 .02 .00
☐ 251 Dwight Evans (90) .... .05 .02 .00
☐ 252 Bill Buckner (91) .... .05 .02 .00
☐ 253 Bob Stanley (92) .... .04 .02 .00
☐ 254 Tony Armas (93) .... .05 .02 .00
☐ 255 Mike Easler (96) .... .04 .02 .00
KANSAS CITY ROYALS
☐ 256 George Brett .... .30 .12 .03
☐ 257 Dan Quisenberry .... .09 .04 .01
☐ 258 Willie Wilson (97) .... .05 .02 .00
☐ 259 Jim Sundberg (98) .... .04 .02 .00
☐ 260 Bret Saberhagen (99) ..... .07 .03 .01
☐ 261 Bud Black (100) .... .03 .01 .00
☐ 262 Charlie Leibrandt(101) ... .03 .01 .00
☐ 263 Frank White (102) .... .04 .02 .00
☐ 264 Lonnie Smith (103) .... .04 .02 .00
☐ 265 Steve Balboni (106) ...... .04 .02 .00
DETROIT TIGERS
☐ 266 Kirk Gibson .... .15 .06 .01
☐ 267 Alan Trammell .... .15 .06 .01
☐ 268 Jack Morris (107) .... .07 .03 .01
☐ 269 Darrell Evans (108) ...... .04 .02 .00
☐ 270 Dan Petry (109) .... .05 .02 .00
☐ 271 Larry Herndon (110) ...... .03 .01 .00
☐ 272 Lou Whitaker (111) ...... .07 .03 .01
☐ 273 Lance Parrish (112) ...... .08 .03 .01
☐ 274 Chet Lemon (113) .... .04 .02 .00
☐ 275 Willie Hernandez (116) ... .05 .02 .00
MINNESOTA TWINS
☐ 276 Tom Brunansky .... .10 .04 .01
☐ 277 Kent Hrbek .... .15 .06 .01
☐ 278 Mark Salas (117) .... .04 .02 .00
☐ 280 Tim Teufel (119) .... .04 .02 .00
☐ 279 Bert Blyleven (118) ...... .07 .03 .01
☐ 281 Ron Davis (120) .... .04 .02 .00
☐ 282 Mike Smithson (121) ..... .03 .01 .00
☐ 283 Gary Gaetti (122) .... .07 .03 .01
☐ 284 Frank Viola (123) .... .06 .02 .00
☐ 285 Kirby Puckett (126) ...... .25 .10 .02
CHICAGO WHITE SOX
☐ 286 Carlton Fisk .... .09 .04 .01
☐ 287 Tom Seaver .... .18 .08 .01
☐ 288 Harold Baines (127) ...... .08 .03 .01
☐ 289 Ron Kittle (128) .... .06 .02 .00
☐ 290 Bob James (129) .... .04 .02 .00
☐ 291 Rudy Law (130) .... .03 .01 .00
☐ 292 Britt Burns (131) .... .04 .02 .00
☐ 293 Greg Walker (132) .... .05 .02 .00
☐ 294 Ozzie Guillen (133) ...... .08 .03 .01
☐ 295 Tim Hulett (136) .... .04 .02 .00
NEW YORK YANKEES
☐ 296 Don Mattingly .... .35 .15 .03
☐ 297 Rickey Henderson .... .25 .10 .02
☐ 298 Dave Winfield (137) ...... .12 .05 .01
☐ 299 Butch Wynegar (138) ..... .03 .01 .00
☐ 300 Don Baylor (139) .... .05 .02 .00
☐ 301 Eddie Whitson (140) ...... .03 .01 .00
☐ 302 Ron Guidry (141) .... .05 .02 .00
☐ 303 Dave Righetti (142) ...... .05 .02 .00
☐ 304 Bobby Meacham (143) ... .03 .01 .00
☐ 305 Willie Randolph (144) ..... .04 .02 .00
YOUNG STARS
☐ 306 Vince Coleman (145) ...... .15 .06 .01
☐ 307 Oddibe McDowell (164) .. .09 .04 .01
☐ 308 Larry Sheets (165) .... .08 .03 .01
☐ 309 Ozzie Guillen (168) ...... .08 .03 .01
☐ 310 Ernie Riles (169) .... .06 .02 .00
☐ 311 Chris Brown (170) .... .15 .06 .01
☐ 312 Brian Fisher and .... .08 .03 .01
Roger McDowell (171)
☐ 313 Tom Browning (172) ...... .06 .02 .00
☐ 314 Glenn Davis (173) .... .15 .06 .01
☐ 315 Mark Salas (174) .... .04 .02 .00

Most collectors subscribe to at least
one hobby magazine or newspaper.
Check the advertisements in this
book -- pick out one or more that
you think are suitable.

1956 Topps Hocus Focus

This 1956 Topps issue is often confused with the
Magic Photos issue of 1950. The R714-26 (ACC
designation) set comes in two types, which we have
arbitrarily labeled A and B. Style A, the larger size
(1" by 1 5/8"), contains 18 baseball subjects -- the
ones known are checklisted below. Type B, the
smaller size (7/8" by 1 3/8"), is reported to contain
baseball subjects, those known are checklisted
below. Like the Magic Photo set, these cards were
"developed" by sunlight. The baseball players in
these sets are but a portion of the total cards in the
set. Dogs, personalities, and other subjects were
also featured.

		MINT	VG-E	F-G
COMPLETE SET		500.00	225.00	45.00
COMMON PLAYER		12.00	5.50	1.20
LARGE SIZE (A)				
☐ A1	Dick Groat (43)	12.00	5.50	1.20
☐ A2	Ed Lopat (44)	15.00	6.50	1.50
☐ A3	Hank Sauer (30)	12.00	5.50	1.20
☐ A4	Dusty Rhodes (86)	12.00	5.50	1.20
☐ A5	Ted Williams (5)	50.00	22.00	4.50
☐ A6	Harvey Haddix (5)	12.00	5.50	1.20
☐ A7	Ray Boone (31)	12.00	5.50	1.20
☐ A8	Al Rosen (69)	15.00	7.00	1.50
☐ A9	Mayo Smith (51)	12.00	5.50	1.20
☐ A10	Warren Spahn (87)	25.00	11.50	2.25
☐ A11	Jim Rivera (67)	12.00	5.50	1.20
☐ A12	Ted Kluszewski (79)	15.00	6.50	1.50
☐ A13	Gus Zernial (49)	12.00	5.50	1.20
☐ A14	Jackie Robinson (13)	40.00	18.00	4.00
☐ A15	Hal Smith (42)	12.00	5.50	1.20
☐ A16	Johnny Schmitz (84)	12.00	5.50	1.20
☐ A17	Spook Jacobs (60)	12.00	5.50	1.20
☐ A18	Mel Parnell (18)	15.00	6.50	1.40
SMALL SIZE (B)				
☐ B1	Babe Ruth (117)	100.00	45.00	10.00
☐ B3	Dick Groat (43)	12.00	5.50	1.20
☐ B8	Harvey Haddix (26)	12.00	5.50	1.20
☐ B9	Ray Boone (31)	12.00	5.50	1.20
☐ B12	Warren Spahn (87)	25.00	11.00	2.50
☐ B13	Jim Rivera (67)	12.00	5.50	1.20
☐ B14	Ted Kluszewski (79)	15.00	7.00	1.50
☐ B15	Gus Zernial (49)	12.00	5.50	1.20
☐ B18	Johnny Schmitz (84)	12.00	5.50	1.20
☐ B20	Karl Spooner (122)	12.00	5.50	1.20
☐ B21	Ed Mathews (109)	25.00	11.00	2.50

1960 Topps Tattoos

The 1960 Topps baseball tattoos are actually the
reverses of the wrappers in which the (one cent)
product "Tattoo Bubble Gum" was packaged. The
dimensions given (1 9/16" by 3 1/2") are for the
entire wrapper. The wrapper lists instructions on
how to apply the tattoo. The tattoos are
unnumbered and are colored. There are 96 tattoos

FIRST BASE
SPORTS NOSTALGIA SHOP

231 Webb Chapel Village
Dallas, Texas 75229
(214) 243-5271

N

I—35 (Stemmons)
Webb Chapel
Hwy 635 (LBJ)
Forest Lane
First Base
Hwy 75→
N. Central
Expwy

OPEN: TUESDAY THROUGH SATURDAY
11 A.M. to 7 P.M.

We are located on the Southeast corner of Webb Chapel and Forest just 15 minutes from the airport. Our large (1650 square foot showroom) store is convenient to all parts of Dallas being only one block south of the LBJ (635) Freeway at the Webb Chapel exit. Many collectors (and dealers) have told us that our store is the most complete they've ever seen. Just look on the opposite page for a few of our offers. We want you for a customer — please stop in and see for yourself.

FIRST
BASE

Sincerely,

Wayne Grove
Gervise Ford

P.S.   We are always interested in buying your cards — let us know what you have.

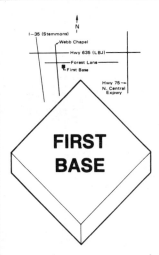

I-35 (Stemmons)
Webb Chapel
Hwy 635 (LBJ)
Forest Lane
First Base
Hwy 75 →
N. Central
Expwy
N

FIRST BASE

We have a large mail order catalog; just send us $1.00 for postage and handling for the catalog. Below is a partial list of items we have available for sale. Include an appropriate extra amount for postage on any of the sets or offers below which you select. All inquiries require a self-addressed stamped envelope. We have most Topps, Fleer, Donruss, etc. Sets and Singles for sale. These are listed in our catalog that we will send you. Better yet, why don't you stop in some time and see for yourself.

SPECIAL OFFERS

COMPLETE SETS

1985 Performance Rangers (28)	$4.95
1984 Jarvis Press Rangers (28)	$4.95
1983 Affil. Foods Rangers (28)	$4.95
1984 Ralston-Purina Baseball (33)	$4.95
1983 Seven-Eleven 3-D Coins (12)	$12.95
1981 Topps 5x7 Dodgers/Angels (18)	$4.95
1978 Tucson Toros Sample/Darwin 24	$3.50
1980 Tucson Toros Heep/Knicely 24	$3.00
1983 Dallas Cowboy Police (28)	$9.95
1981 Dallas Cowboy Police (14)	$7.95
1980 Dallas Cowboy Police (14)	$9.95
1979 Dallas Cowboy Police (15)	$13.95
1981 Shell Dallas Cowboys (6)	$6.95
1981 Shell National Set (6)	$6.95
includes Payton and Campbell	

BASEBALL CARD LOTS

1958 Topps 25 diff (f-vg)	$4.95
1959 Topps 25 diff (f-vg)	$3.95
1960 Topps 25 diff (f-vg)	$3.50
1961 Topps 25 diff (f-vg)	$3.50
1962 Topps 25 diff (f-vg)	$3.50
1963 Topps 25 diff (f-vg)	$3.25
1964 Topps 25 diff (f-vg)	$3.25
1965 Topps 25 diff (f-vg)	$3.25
1966 Topps 25 diff (f-vg)	$2.95
1967 Topps 25 diff (f-vg)	$2.95
1968 Topps 25 diff (f-vg)	$2.95
1969 Topps 25 diff (f-vg)	$2.75
1970 Topps 25 diff (f-vg)	$1.95
1971 Topps 25 diff (f-vg)	$1.75
1972 Topps 25 diff (f-vg)	$1.75

#1: Type set: One card from each year of Topps baseball 1952 through 1986, our choice of cards 35 cards for $9.95.

#2: Baseball cigarette card from 1910, our choice $5.95.

#3: 500 assorted (mostly different) baseball cards from 1978 to 1984 in excellent condition for $16.95

#4: Dallas Cowboy Weekly: 20 different back issues, our choice, for $14.95. We also have most single issues from 1977 to date available from $1.00 to $2.00 each. Send your want list. Some older issues also available.

#5: Poster: Robert Redford as "The Natural" plus a free Bucky Dent "Best Little Shortstop in Texas" poster for $6.95 postpaid.

#6: 1978 Topps baseball cards 50 different in excellent to mint condition $2.50.

#7: 1979 Topps baseball cards 50 different in excellent to mint condition includes some stars $2.95.

#8: 1980 Topps baseball cards 50 different in excellent to mint condition includes some stars $2.95.

#9: 1981 Topps baseball cards 50 different in excellent to mint condition includes some stars $2.95.

#10: 89 different 1984-85 Topps hockey cards in excellent to mint condition includes some stars $2.50.

#11: 66 different 1981-82 Topps basketball cards in excellent to mint condition includes stars (Bird, Magic, Kareem, Dr. J, etc.) $3.50.

#12: 115 different 1983 Topps football cards in excellent to mint condition includes many stars $2.95.

#13: Donruss puzzle sets: Complete set of all seven puzzle card sets (Ruth, Cobb, Mantle, Williams, Snider, Gehrig, Aaron) for $9.95.

#14: 1985 Dallas Cowboy Media Guide (not issued to the public) $4.95; Cowboy Bluebook $12.95.

#15: 1981 Topps Baseball Scratch-Offs 36 panels (108 players) for $3.50.

#16: 1983 Fleer Baseball Stamps set of 224 (stamps on 4 sheets) for $3.95.

#17: 1979 Scottsdale Dodge Arizona Convention postcard set of 9 including Jocko Conlan, Charlie Grimm, Tom and Dick Van Arsdale, etc. for $2.95.

FIRST BASE

231 Webb Chapel Village
Dallas, Texas 75229
(214) 243-5271

in the set: 55 players, 16 team logos, 15 action shots, and 10 autographed balls.

	MINT	VG-E	F-G
COMPLETE SET	500.00	225.00	50.00
COMMON PLAYER (1-55)	5.00	2.35	.50
COMMON TEAM (56-71)	2.50	1.15	.25
COMMON ACTION (72-86)	2.50	1.15	.25
COMMON BALL (87-96)	2.50	1.15	.25

PLAYERS (1-55)

		MINT	VG-E	F-G
☐	1 Hank Aaron	40.00	18.00	4.00
☐	2 Bob Allison	5.00	2.35	.50
☐	3 Johnny Antonelli	5.00	2.35	.50
☐	4 Richie Ashburn	7.50	3.50	.75
☐	5 Ernie Banks	20.00	9.00	2.00
☐	6 Yogi Berra	30.00	14.00	3.00
☐	7 Lew Burdette	6.00	2.80	.60
☐	8 Orlando Cepeda	9.00	4.25	.90
☐	9 Rocky Colavito	7.50	3.50	.75
☐	10 Joe Cunningham	5.00	2.35	.50
☐	11 Bud Daley	5.00	2.35	.50
☐	12 Don Drysdale	16.00	7.50	1.60
☐	13 Ryne Duren	6.00	2.80	.60
☐	14 Roy Face	6.00	2.80	.60
☐	15 Whitey Ford	20.00	9.00	2.00
☐	16 Nellie Fox	9.00	4.25	.90
☐	17 Tito Francona	5.00	2.35	.50
☐	18 Gene Freese	5.00	2.35	.50
☐	19 Jim Gilliam	7.50	3.50	.75
☐	20 Dick Groat	6.00	2.80	.60
☐	21 Ray Herbert	5.00	2.35	.50
☐	22 Glen Hobbie	5.00	2.35	.50
☐	23 Jackie Jensen	7.50	3.50	.75
☐	24 Sam Jones	5.00	2.35	.50
☐	25 Al Kaline	25.00	11.00	2.50
☐	26 Harmon Killebrew	16.00	7.50	1.60
☐	27 Harvey Kuenn	7.50	3.50	.75
☐	28 Frank Lary	5.00	2.35	.50
☐	29 Vern Law	6.00	2.80	.60
☐	30 Frank Malzone	5.00	2.35	.50
☐	31 Mickey Mantle	125.00	57.00	12.50
☐	32 Roger Maris	20.00	9.00	2.00
☐	33 Eddie Mathews	16.00	7.50	1.60
☐	34 Willie Mays	40.00	18.00	4.00
☐	35 Cal McLish	5.00	2.35	.50
☐	36 Wally Moon	5.00	2.35	.50
☐	37 Walt Moryn	5.00	2.35	.50
☐	38 Don Mossi	5.00	2.35	.50
☐	39 Stan Musial	35.00	16.50	3.50
☐	40 Charley Neal	5.00	2.35	.50
☐	41 Don Newcombe	6.00	2.80	.60
☐	42 Milt Pappas	6.00	2.80	.60

		MINT	VG-E	F-G
☐	43 Camilo Pascual	5.00	2.35	.50
☐	44 Billy Pierce	6.00	2.80	.60
☐	45 Robin Roberts	16.00	7.50	1.60
☐	46 Frank Robinson	20.00	9.00	2.00
☐	47 Pete Runnells	5.00	2.35	.50
☐	48 Herb Score	6.00	2.80	.60
☐	49 Warren Spahn	20.00	9.00	2.00
☐	50 Johnny Temple	5.00	2.35	.50
☐	51 Gus Triandos	5.00	2.35	.50
☐	52 Jerry Walker	5.00	2.35	.50
☐	53 Bill White	6.00	2.80	.60
☐	54 Gene Woodling	5.00	2.35	.50
☐	55 Early Wynn	15.00	7.00	1.50

TEAM TATOOS

		MINT	VG-E	F-G
☐	56 Chicago Cubs	2.50	1.15	.25
☐	57 Cincinnati Reds	2.50	1.15	.25
☐	58 Los Angeles Dodgers	2.50	1.15	.25
☐	59 Milwaukee Braves	2.50	1.15	.25
☐	60 Philadelphia Phillies	2.50	1.15	.25
☐	61 Pittsburgh Pirates	2.50	1.15	.25
☐	62 St. Louis Cardinals	2.50	1.15	.25
☐	63 San Francisco Giants	2.50	1.15	.25
☐	64 Baltimore Orioles	2.50	1.15	.25
☐	65 Boston Red Sox	2.50	1.15	.25
☐	66 Chicago White Sox	2.50	1.15	.25
☐	67 Cleveland Indians	2.50	1.15	.25
☐	68 Detroit Tigers	2.50	1.15	.25
☐	69 Kansas City Athletics	2.50	1.15	.25
☐	70 New York Yankees	5.00	2.35	.50
☐	71 Washington Senators	2.50	1.15	.25

ACTION SHOTS (72-86)

		MINT	VG-E	F-G
☐	72 Circus Catch	2.50	1.15	.25
☐	73 Double Play	2.50	1.15	.25
☐	74 Grand Slam Homer	2.50	1.15	.25
☐	75 Great Catch	2.50	1.15	.25
☐	76 Left Hand Batter	2.50	1.15	.25
☐	77 Left Hand Pitcher	2.50	1.15	.25
☐	78 Out at First	2.50	1.15	.25
☐	79 Out at Home	2.50	1.15	.25
☐	80 Right Hand Batter	2.50	1.15	.25
☐	81 Right Hand Pitcher	2.50	1.15	.25
☐	82 Right Hand Pitcher	2.50	1.15	.25
	(different pose)			
☐	83 Run Down	2.50	1.15	.25
☐	84 Stolen Base	2.50	1.15	.25
☐	85 The Final Word	2.50	1.15	.25
☐	86 Twisting Foul	2.50	1.15	.25

AUTOGRAPHED BALLS (87-96)

		MINT	VG-E	F-G
☐	87 Richie Ashburn	3.50	1.65	.35
	(autographed ball)			
☐	88 Rocky Colavito	3.50	1.65	.35
	(autographed ball)			
☐	89 Roy Face	2.50	1.15	.25
	(autographed ball)			
☐	90 Jackie Jensen	3.50	1.65	.35
	(autographed ball)			
☐	91 Harmon Killebrew	5.00	2.35	.50
	(autographed ball)			
☐	92 Mickey Mantle	15.00	7.00	1.50
	(autographed ball)			
☐	93 Willie Mays	7.50	3.50	.75
	(autographed ball)			
☐	94 Stan Musial	7.50	3.50	.75
	(autographed ball)			
☐	95 Billy Pierce	2.50	1.15	.25
	(autographed ball)			
☐	96 Jerry Walker	2.50	1.15	.25
	(autographed ball)			

1961 Topps Magic Rub Offs

There are 36 "Magic Rub-Offs" in this set of inserts also marketed in packages of 1961 Topps baseball cards. Each rub off measures 2 1/16" by 3 1/16". Of this number, 18 are team designs, while the remaining 18 depict players. The latter, one from each team, were apparently selected for their unusual nicknames. Note: The Duke Maas insert is misspelled "Mass".

	MINT	VG-E	F-G
COMPLETE SET	75.00	35.00	7.50
COMMON TEAM (1-18)	1.00	.45	.10
COMMON PLAYER (19-36)	2.00	.90	.20

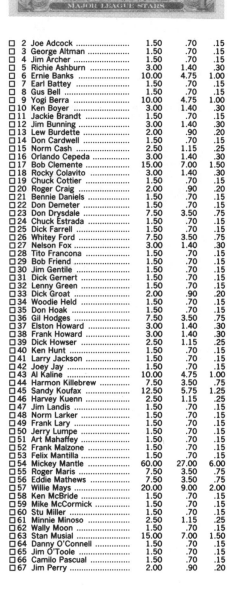

TEAM RUBOFFS

☐	1	Detroit Tigers	1.25	.60	.12
☐	2	New York Yankees	2.50	1.15	.25
☐	3	Minnesota Twins	1.00	.45	.10
☐	4	Washington Senators	1.00	.45	.10
☐	5	Boston Red Sox	1.25	.60	.12
☐	6	Los Angeles Angels	1.00	.45	.10
☐	7	Kansas City A's	1.00	.45	.10
☐	8	Baltimore Orioles	1.00	.45	.10
☐	9	Chicago White Sox	1.00	.45	.10
☐	10	Cleveland Indians	1.00	.45	.10
☐	11	Pittsburgh Pirates	1.00	.45	.10
☐	12	San Francisco Giants	1.00	.45	.10
☐	13	Los Angeles Dodgers	1.25	.60	.12
☐	14	Philadelphia Phillies	1.00	.45	.10
☐	15	Cincinnati Redlegs	1.00	.45	.10
☐	16	St. Louis Cardinals	1.00	.45	.10
☐	17	Chicago Cubs	1.00	.45	.10
☐	18	Milwaukee Braves	1.00	.45	.10

PLAYER RUB OFFS

☐	19	John Romano	2.00	.90	.20
☐	20	Ray Moore	2.00	.90	.20
☐	21	Ernie Banks	10.00	4.75	1.00
☐	22	Charlie Maxwell	2.00	.90	.20
☐	23	Yogi Berra	10.00	4.75	1.00
☐	24	Henry"Dutch" Dotterer	2.00	.90	.20
☐	25	Jim Brosnan	2.00	.90	.20
☐	26	Billy Martin	4.00	1.85	.40
☐	27	Jackie Brandt	2.00	.90	.20
☐	28	Duke Mass	2.00	.90	.20
		(sic, Maas)			
☐	29	Pete Runnels	2.00	.90	.20
☐	30	Joe Gordon	2.00	.90	.20
☐	31	Sad Sam Jones	2.00	.90	.20
☐	32	Walt Moryn	2.00	.90	.20
☐	33	Harvey Haddix	2.00	.90	.20
☐	34	Frank Howard	4.00	1.85	.40
☐	35	Turk Lown	2.00	.90	.20
☐	36	Frank Herrera	2.00	.90	.20

1962 Topps Bucks

There are 96 "Baseball Bucks" in this unusual set released in its own one-cent package in 1962. Each "buck" measures 1 3/4" by 4 1/8". Each depicts a player with accompanying biography and facsimile autograph to the left. To the right is found a drawing of the player's home stadium, and his team and position are listed under the ribbon design containing his name. The team affiliation and league are also indicated within circles on the reverse.

	MINT	VG-E	F-G
COMPLETE SET	300.00	130.00	30.00
COMMON PLAYER	1.50	.70	.15

☐	1	Henry Aaron	20.00	9.00	2.00

☐	2	Joe Adcock	1.50	.70	.15
☐	3	George Altman	1.50	.70	.15
☐	4	Jim Archer	1.50	.70	.15
☐	5	Richie Ashburn	3.00	1.40	.30
☐	6	Ernie Banks	10.00	4.75	1.00
☐	7	Earl Battey	1.50	.70	.15
☐	8	Gus Bell	1.50	.70	.15
☐	9	Yogi Berra	10.00	4.75	1.00
☐	10	Ken Boyer	3.00	1.40	.30
☐	11	Jackie Brandt	1.50	.70	.15
☐	12	Jim Bunning	3.00	1.40	.30
☐	13	Lew Burdette	2.00	.90	.20
☐	14	Don Cardwell	1.50	.70	.15
☐	15	Norm Cash	2.50	1.15	.25
☐	16	Orlando Cepeda	3.00	1.40	.30
☐	17	Bob Clemente	15.00	7.00	1.50
☐	18	Rocky Colavito	3.00	1.40	.30
☐	19	Chuck Cottier	1.50	.70	.15
☐	20	Roger Craig	2.00	.90	.20
☐	21	Bennie Daniels	1.50	.70	.15
☐	22	Don Demeter	1.50	.70	.15
☐	23	Don Drysdale	7.50	3.50	.75
☐	24	Chuck Estrada	1.50	.70	.15
☐	25	Dick Farrell	1.50	.70	.15
☐	26	Whitey Ford	7.50	3.50	.75
☐	27	Nelson Fox	3.00	1.40	.30
☐	28	Tito Francona	1.50	.70	.15
☐	29	Bob Friend	1.50	.70	.15
☐	30	Jim Gentile	1.50	.70	.15
☐	31	Dick Gernert	1.50	.70	.15
☐	32	Lenny Green	1.50	.70	.15
☐	33	Dick Groat	2.00	.90	.20
☐	34	Woodie Held	1.50	.70	.15
☐	35	Don Hoak	1.50	.70	.15
☐	36	Gil Hodges	7.50	3.50	.75
☐	37	Elston Howard	3.00	1.40	.30
☐	38	Frank Howard	3.00	1.40	.30
☐	39	Dick Howser	2.50	1.15	.25
☐	40	Ken Hunt	1.50	.70	.15
☐	41	Larry Jackson	1.50	.70	.15
☐	42	Joey Jay	1.50	.70	.15
☐	43	Al Kaline	10.00	4.75	1.00
☐	44	Harmon Killebrew	7.50	3.50	.75
☐	45	Sandy Koufax	12.50	5.75	1.25
☐	46	Harvey Kuenn	2.50	1.15	.25
☐	47	Jim Landis	1.50	.70	.15
☐	48	Norm Larker	1.50	.70	.15
☐	49	Frank Lary	1.50	.70	.15
☐	50	Jerry Lumpe	1.50	.70	.15
☐	51	Art Mahaffey	1.50	.70	.15
☐	52	Frank Malzone	1.50	.70	.15
☐	53	Felix Mantilla	1.50	.70	.15
☐	54	Mickey Mantle	60.00	27.00	6.00
☐	55	Roger Maris	7.50	3.50	.75
☐	56	Eddie Mathews	7.50	3.50	.75
☐	57	Willie Mays	20.00	9.00	2.00
☐	58	Ken McBride	1.50	.70	.15
☐	59	Mike McCormick	1.50	.70	.15
☐	60	Stu Miller	1.50	.70	.15
☐	61	Minnie Minoso	2.50	1.15	.25
☐	62	Wally Moon	1.50	.70	.15
☐	63	Stan Musial	15.00	7.00	1.50
☐	64	Danny O'Connell	1.50	.70	.15
☐	65	Jim O'Toole	1.50	.70	.15
☐	66	Camilo Pascual	1.50	.70	.15
☐	67	Jim Perry	2.00	.90	.20

		MINT	VG-E	F-G
☐ 68	Jimmy Piersall	2.00	.90	.20
☐ 69	Vada Pinson	2.50	1.15	.25
☐ 70	Juan Pizarro	1.50	.70	.15
☐ 71	Johnny Podres	2.00	.90	.20
☐ 72	Vic Power	1.50	.70	.15
☐ 73	Bob Purkey	1.50	.70	.15
☐ 74	Pedro Ramos	1.50	.70	.15
☐ 75	Brooks Robinson	10.00	4.75	1.00
☐ 76	Floyd Robinson	1.50	.70	.15
☐ 77	Frank Robinson	10.00	4.75	1.00
☐ 78	John Romano	1.50	.70	.15
☐ 79	Pete Runnels	1.50	.70	.15
☐ 80	Don Schwall	1.50	.70	.15
☐ 81	Bobby Shantz	2.00	.90	.20
☐ 82	Norm Siebern	1.50	.70	.15
☐ 83	Roy Sievers	1.50	.70	.15
☐ 84	Hal Smith	1.50	.70	.15
☐ 85	Warren Spahn	7.50	3.50	.75
☐ 86	Dick Stuart	2.00	.90	.20
☐ 87	Tony Taylor	1.50	.70	.15
☐ 88	Leroy Thomas	1.50	.70	.15
☐ 89	Gus Triandos	1.50	.70	.15
☐ 90	Leon Wagner	1.50	.70	.15
☐ 91	Jerry Walker	1.50	.70	.15
☐ 92	Billl White	2.00	.90	.20
☐ 93	Billy Williams	5.00	2.35	.50
☐ 94	Gene Woodling	1.50	.70	.15
☐ 95	Early Wynn	6.00	2.80	.60
☐ 96	Carl Yastrzemski	25.00	11.00	2.50

		MINT	VG-E	F-G
☐ 19	Ken Hubbs	1.00	.45	.10
☐ 20	Al Jackson	.75	.35	.07
☐ 21	Al Kaline	6.00	2.80	.60
☐ 22	Harmon Killebrew	4.00	1.85	.40
☐ 23	Sandy Koufax	7.50	3.50	.75
☐ 24	Jerry Lumpe	.75	.35	.07
☐ 25	Art Mahaffey	.75	.35	.07
☐ 26	Mickey Mantle	20.00	9.00	2.00
☐ 27	Willie Mays	9.00	4.25	.90
☐ 28	Bill Mazeroski	1.00	.45	.10
☐ 29	Bill Monbouquette	.75	.35	.07
☐ 30	Stan Musial	7.50	3.50	.75
☐ 31	Camilo Pascual	.75	.35	.07
☐ 32	Bob Purkey	.75	.35	.07
☐ 33	Bobby Richardson	1.00	.45	.10
☐ 34	Brooks Robinson	6.00	2.80	.60
☐ 35	Floyd Robinson	.75	.35	.07
☐ 36	Frank Robinson	5.00	2.35	.50
☐ 37	Bob Rodgers	.75	.35	.07
☐ 38	Johnny Romano	.75	.35	.07
☐ 39	Jack Sanford	.75	.35	.07
☐ 40	Norm Siebern	.75	.35	.07
☐ 41	Warren Spahn	5.00	2.35	.50
☐ 42	Dave Stenhouse	.75	.35	.07
☐ 43	Ralph Terry	.75	.35	.07
☐ 44	Lee Thomas	.75	.35	.07
☐ 45	Bill White	1.00	.45	.10
☐ 46	Carl Yastrzemski	10.00	4.75	1.00

1963 Topps Stick-On Inserts

Stick-on inserts were found in several series of the 1963 Topps cards. Each sticker measures 1 1/4" by 2 3/4". They are found either with blank backs or with instructions on the reverse. The player photo is in color inside an oval with name, team, and postion below. Since these inserts were unnumbered, they are ordered below alphabetically.

		MINT	VG-E	F-G
	COMPLETE SET	75.00	35.00	7.50
	COMMON PLAYER (1-46)	.75	.35	.07
☐ 1	Hank Aaron	9.00	4.25	.90
☐ 2	Luis Aparicio	3.00	1.40	.30
☐ 3	Richie Ashburn	1.50	.70	.15
☐ 4	Bob Aspromonte	.75	.35	.07
☐ 5	Ernie Banks	5.00	2.35	.50
☐ 6	Ken Boyer	1.50	.70	.15
☐ 7	Jim Bunning	1.50	.70	.15
☐ 8	Johnny Callison	.75	.35	.07
☐ 9	Bob Clemente	7.50	3.50	.75
☐ 10	Orlando Cepeda	1.50	.70	.15
☐ 11	Rocky Colavito	1.50	.70	.15
☐ 12	Tommy Davis	1.00	.45	.10
☐ 13	Dick Donovan	.75	.35	.07
☐ 14	Don Drysdale	4.00	1.85	.40
☐ 15	Dick Farrell	.75	.35	.07
☐ 16	Jim Gentile	.75	.35	.07
☐ 17	Ray Herbert	.75	.35	.07
☐ 18	Chuck Hinton	.75	.35	.07

1964 Topps Tattoos

These tattoos measure 1 9/16" by 3 1/2" and are printed in color on very thin paper. One side gives instructions for applying the tattoo, whereas the picture side gives the team logo and name (1-20) or the player's face, name, and team (21-75). The tattoos are unnumbered and are presented below in alphabetical order for convenience.

		MINT	VG-E	F-G
	COMPLETE SET	325.00	150.00	30.00
	COMMON TEAM (1-20)	2.00	.90	.20
	COMMON PLAYER (21-75)	3.00	1.40	.30
	TEAM TATTOOS			
☐ 1	Baltimore Orioles	2.00	.90	.20
☐ 2	Boston Red Sox	2.00	.90	.20
☐ 3	California Angels	2.00	.90	.20
☐ 4	Chicago Cubs	2.00	.90	.20
☐ 5	Chicago White Sox	2.00	.90	.20
☐ 6	Cincinnati Reds	2.00	.90	.20
☐ 7	Cleveland Indians	2.00	.90	.20
☐ 8	Detroit Tigers	2.00	.90	.20
☐ 9	Houston Astros	2.00	.90	.20
☐ 10	Kansas City Athletics	2.00	.90	.20
☐ 11	Los Angeles Dodgers	2.00	.90	.20
☐ 12	Milwaukee Braves	2.00	.90	.20
☐ 13	Minnesota Twins	2.00	.90	.20
☐ 14	New York Mets	2.00	.90	.20
☐ 15	New York Yankees	2.00	.90	.20
☐ 16	Philadelphia Phillies	2.00	.90	.20
☐ 17	Pittsburgh Pirates	2.00	.90	.20
☐ 18	St. Louis Cardinals	2.00	.90	.20
☐ 19	San Francisco Giants	2.00	.90	.20
☐ 20	Washington Senators	2.00	.90	.20

PLAYER TATTOOS

21	Hank Aaron	35.00	16.50	3.50
22	Max Alvis	3.00	1.40	.30
23	Hank Aguirre	3.00	1.40	.30
24	Ernie Banks	20.00	9.00	2.00
25	Steve Barber	3.00	1.40	.30
26	Ken Boyer	7.50	3.50	.75
27	John Callison	3.00	1.40	.30
28	Norm Cash	5.00	2.35	.50
29	Wayne Causey	3.00	1.40	.30
30	Orlando Cepeda	7.50	3.50	.75
31	Rocky Colavito	6.00	2.80	.60
32	Ray Culp	3.00	1.40	.30
33	Vic Davalillo	3.00	1.40	.30
34	Moe Drabowski	3.00	1.40	.30
35	Dick Ellsworth	3.00	1.40	.30
36	Curt Flood	5.00	2.35	.50
37	Bill Freehan	4.00	1.85	.40
38	Jim Fregosi	4.00	1.85	.40
39	Bob Friend	3.00	1.40	.30
40	Dick Groat	5.00	2.35	.50
41	Woody Held	3.00	1.40	.30
42	Frank Howard	6.00	2.80	.60
43	Al Jackson	3.00	1.40	.30
44	Larry Jackson	3.00	1.40	.30
45	Ken Johnson	3.00	1.40	.30
46	Al Kaline	20.00	9.00	2.00
47	Harmon Killebrew	12.50	5.75	1.25
48	Sandy Koufax	25.00	11.00	2.50
49	Don Lock	3.00	1.40	.30
50	Frank Malzone	3.00	1.40	.30
51	Mickey Mantle	75.00	35.00	7.50
52	Eddie Mathews	15.00	7.00	1.50
53	Willie Mays	35.00	16.50	3.50
54	Bill Mazeroski	5.00	2.35	.50
55	Ken McBride	3.00	1.40	.30
56	Bill Monbouquette	3.00	1.40	.30
57	Dave Nicholson	3.00	1.40	.30
58	Claude Osteen	3.00	1.40	.30
59	Milt Pappas	4.00	1.85	.40
60	Camilo Pascual	3.00	1.40	.30
61	Albie Pearson	3.00	1.40	.30
62	Ron Perranoski	3.00	1.40	.30
63	Gary Peters	3.00	1.40	.30
64	Boog Powell	6.00	2.80	.60
65	Frank Robinson	15.00	7.00	1.50
66	Johnny Romano	3.00	1.40	.30
67	Norm Siebern	3.00	1.40	.30
68	Warren Spahn	15.00	7.00	1.50
69	Dick Stuart	4.00	1.85	.40
70	Lee Thomas	3.00	1.40	.30
71	Joe Torre	7.50	3.50	.75
72	Pete Ward	3.00	1.40	.30
73	Carlton Willey	3.00	1.40	.30
74	Billy Williams	7.50	3.50	.75
75	Carl Yastrzemski	35.00	16.50	3.50

		MINT	VG-E	F-G
	COMPLETE SET	75.00	35.00	7.50
	COMMON PLAYER	.60	.28	.06
BLUE PANELS				
1	Bob Allison	.60	.28	.06
2	Max Alvis	.60	.28	.06
3	Luis Aparicio	2.00	.90	.20
4	Walt Bond	.60	.28	.06
5	Jim Bouton	1.00	.45	.10
6	Jim Bunning	1.00	.45	.10
7	Rico Carty	.75	.35	.07
8	Wayne Causey	.60	.28	.06
9	Orlando Cepeda	1.00	.45	.10
10	Dean Chance	.60	.28	.06
11	Tony Conigliaro	.75	.35	.07
12	Bill Freehan	.75	.35	.07
13	Jim Fregosi	.75	.35	.07
14	Bob Gibson	3.50	1.65	.35
15	Dick Groat	.75	.35	.07
16	Tom Haller	.60	.28	.06
17	Al Jackson	.60	.28	.06
18	Bobby Knoop	.60	.28	.06
19	Jim Maloney	.75	.35	.07
20	Juan Marichal	2.50	1.15	.25
21	Lee Maye	.60	.28	.06
22	Jim O'Toole	.60	.28	.06
23	Camilo Pascual	.60	.28	.06
24	Vada Pinson	1.00	.45	.10
25	Juan Pizzaro	.60	.28	.06
26	Bobby Richardson	1.00	.45	.10
27	Bob Rodgers	.60	.28	.06
28	John Roseboro	.60	.28	.06
29	Dick Stuart	.75	.35	.07
30	Luis Tiant	1.00	.45	.10
31	Joe Torre	1.00	.45	.10
32	Bob Veale	.60	.28	.06
33	Leon Wagner	.60	.28	.06
34	Dave Wickersham	.60	.28	.06
35	Billy Williams	1.50	.70	.15
36	Carl Yastrzemski	9.00	4.25	.90
RED PANELS				
37	Henry Aaron	7.50	3.50	.75
38	Richie Allen	1.00	.45	.10
39	Ken Aspromonte	.60	.28	.06
40	Ken Boyer	1.00	.45	.10
41	Johnny Callison	.75	.35	.07
42	Dean Chance	.60	.28	.06
43	Joe Christopher	.60	.28	.06
44	Bob Clemente	6.00	2.80	.60
45	Rocky Colavito	1.00	.45	.10
46	Tommy Davis	.75	.35	.07
47	Don Drysdale	2.50	1.15	.25
48	Chuck Hinton	.60	.28	.06
49	Frank Howard	1.00	.45	.10
50	Ron Hunt	.60	.28	.06
51	Al Kaline	4.00	1.85	.40
52	Harmon Killebrew	2.50	1.15	.25
53	Jim King	.60	.28	.06
54	Ron Kline	.60	.28	.06
55	Sandy Koufax	6.00	2.80	.60
56	Ed Kranepool	.60	.28	.06
57	Mickey Mantle	15.00	7.00	1.50
58	Willie Mays	7.50	3.50	.75
59	Bill Mazeroski	1.00	.45	.10
60	Tony Oliva	1.50	.70	.15
61	Milt Pappas	.75	.35	.07
62	Gary Peters	.60	.28	.06
63	Boog Powell	1.00	.45	.10
64	Dick Radatz	.60	.28	.06
65	Brooks Robinson	5.00	2.35	.50
66	Frank Robinson	4.00	1.85	.40
67	Ron Santo	1.00	.45	.10
68	Diego Segui	.60	.28	.06
69	Bill Skowron	.75	.35	.07
70	Al Spangler	.60	.28	.06
71	Pete Ward	.60	.28	.06
72	Bill White	.75	.35	.07

1965 Topps Transfers

The 1965 Topps transfers (2" by 3") were issued in series of 24 each as inserts in three of the regular 1965 Topps cards series. Thirty-six of the transfers feature blue bands at the top and bottom while 36 feature red bands at the top and bottom. The team name and position are listed in the top band while the player's name is listed in the bottom band. Transfers 1-36 have blue panels whereas 37-72 have Red panels.

1966 Topps Rub-Offs

There are 120 "rub-offs" in the Topps insert set of 1966, of which 100 depict players and the remaining 20 show team pennants. Each rub off measures 2 1/16" by 3". The color player photos are vertical while the team pennants are horizontal; both types of transfer have a large black printer's mark. These rub-offs were originally printed in rolls of 20 and are frequently still found this way.

		MINT	VG-E	F-G
	COMPLETE SET	75.00	35.00	7.50
	COMMON PLAYER	.40	.18	.04
	CHICAGO WHITE SOX			
☐ 1	Chicago White Sox	.40	.18	.04
☐ 2	Pete Ward	.40	.18	.04
☐ 3	Frank Robinson	.40	.18	.04
☐ 4	Bill Skowron	.50	.22	.05
☐ 5	Joel Horlen	.40	.18	.04
☐ 6	Eddie Fisher	.40	.18	.04
	HOUSTON ASTROS			
☐ 7	Houston Astros	.40	.18	.04

☐ 8	Bob Bruce	.40	.18	.04
☐ 9	Joe Morgan	1.50	.70	.15
☐ 10	Dick Farrell	.40	.18	.04
☐ 11	Jim Wynn	.50	.22	.05
☐ 12	Bob Aspromonte	.40	.18	.04
	LOS ANGELES DODGERS			
☐ 13	Los Angeles Dodgers	.50	.22	.05
☐ 14	Sandy Koufax	3.50	1.65	.35
☐ 15	John Roseboro	.40	.18	.04
☐ 16	Don Drysdale	2.00	.90	.20
☐ 17	Willie Davis	.50	.22	.05
☐ 18	Ron Fairly	.40	.18	.04
	NEW YORK METS			
☐ 19	New York Mets	.50	.22	.05
☐ 20	Ed Kranepool	.40	.18	.04
☐ 21	Gary Kroll	.40	.18	.04
☐ 22	Jack Fisher	.40	.18	.04
☐ 23	Ron Swoboda	.40	.18	.04
☐ 24	Johnny Lewis	.40	.18	.04
	SAN FRANCISCO GIANTS			
☐ 25	San Francisco Giants	.40	.18	.04
☐ 26	Willie McCovey	2.00	.90	.20
☐ 27	Willie Mays	5.00	2.35	.50
☐ 28	Jim Ray Hart	.40	.18	.04
☐ 29	Juan Marichal	2.00	.90	.20
☐ 30	Jesus Alou	.40	.18	.04
	WASHINGTON SENATORS			
☐ 31	Washington Senators	.40	.18	.04
☐ 32	Phil Ortega	.40	.18	.04
☐ 33	Frank Howard	.60	.28	.06
☐ 34	Don Lock	.40	.18	.04
☐ 35	Ken McMullen	.40	.18	.04
☐ 36	Pete Richert	.40	.18	.04
	ST. LOUIS CARDINALS			
☐ 37	St. Louis Cardinals	.40	.18	.04
☐ 38	Bill White	.50	.22	.05
☐ 39	Bob Gibson	2.00	.90	.20
☐ 40	Tim McCarver	.50	.22	.05
☐ 41	Ken Boyer	.75	.35	.07
☐ 42	Curt Flood	.60	.28	.06
	PITTSBURGH PIRATES			
☐ 43	Pittsburgh Pirates	.40	.18	.04
☐ 44	Willie Stargell	2.00	.90	.20
☐ 45	Bill Mazeroski	.60	.28	.06
☐ 46	Bob Veale	.40	.18	.04
☐ 47	Bob Clemente	5.00	2.35	.50
☐ 48	Vern Law	.50	.22	.05
	MINNESOTA TWINS			
☐ 49	Minnesota Twins	.40	.18	.04
☐ 50	Harmon Killebrew	2.00	.90	.20
☐ 51	Jimmie Hall	.40	.18	.04
☐ 52	Tony Oliva	.75	.35	.07
☐ 53	Jim Grant	.50	.22	.05
☐ 54	Earl Battey	.50	.22	.05
	NEW YORK YANKEES			
☐ 55	New York Yankees	.50	.22	.05
☐ 56	Bobby Richardson	.60	.28	.06
☐ 57	Mickey Mantle	12.00	5.50	1.20
☐ 58	Mel Stottlemyre	.50	.22	.05

☐ 59	Tom Tresh	.50	.22	.05
☐ 60	Whitey Ford	2.00	.90	.20
	DETROIT TIGERS			
☐ 61	Detroit Tigers	.40	.18	.04
☐ 62	Willie Horton	.50	.22	.05
☐ 63	Bill Freehan	.50	.22	.05
☐ 64	Dick McAuliffe	.40	.18	.04
☐ 65	Mickey Lolich	.60	.28	.06
☐ 66	Al Kaline	3.50	1.65	.35
	CLEVELAND INDIANS			
☐ 67	Cleveland Indians	.40	.18	.04
☐ 68	Max Alvis	.40	.18	.04
☐ 69	Ralph Terry	.40	.18	.04
☐ 70	Vic Davalillo	.40	.18	.04
☐ 71	Sam McDowell	.50	.22	.05
☐ 72	Rocky Colavito	.75	.35	.07
	PHILADELPHIA PHILLIES			
☐ 73	Philadelphia Phillies	.40	.18	.04
☐ 74	Richie Allen	.75	.35	.07
☐ 75	Dick Stuart	.50	.22	.05
☐ 76	Johnny Callison	.50	.22	.05
☐ 77	Cookie Rojas	.40	.18	.04
☐ 78	Jim Bunning	.75	.35	.07
	CALIFORNIA ANGELS			
☐ 79	California Angels	.40	.18	.04
☐ 80	Jose Cardenal	.40	.18	.04
☐ 81	Bobby Knoop	.40	.18	.04
☐ 82	Fred Newman	.40	.18	.04
☐ 83	Dean Chance	.50	.22	.05
☐ 84	Jim Fregosi	.60	.28	.06
	BALTIMORE ORIOLES			
☐ 85	Baltimore Orioles	.40	.18	.04
☐ 86	Jerry Adair	.40	.18	.04
☐ 87	Curt Blefary	.40	.18	.04
☐ 88	Milt Pappas	.50	.22	.05
☐ 89	Johnny Orsino	.40	.18	.04
☐ 90	Brooks Robinson	3.00	1.40	.30
	CINCINNATI REDS			
☐ 91	Cincinnati Reds	.40	.18	.04
☐ 92	Sammy Ellis	.40	.18	.04
☐ 93	Jim Maloney	.50	.22	.05
☐ 94	Frank Robinson	2.50	1.15	.25
☐ 95	Pete Rose	10.00	4.75	1.00
☐ 96	Deron Johnson	.40	.18	.04
	CHICAGO CUBS			
☐ 97	Chicago Cubs	.40	.18	.04
☐ 98	Ernie Banks	3.50	1.65	.35
☐ 99	Don Landrum	.40	.18	.04
☐ 100	Dick Ellsworth	.50	.22	.05
☐ 101	Billy Williams	1.00	.45	.10
☐ 102	Ron Santo	.60	.28	.06
	KANSAS CITY A'S			
☐ 103	Kansas City Athletics	.40	.18	.04
☐ 104	Fred Talbot	.40	.18	.04
☐ 105	John O'Donoghue	.40	.18	.04
☐ 106	Ed Charles	.40	.18	.04
☐ 107	Ken Harrelson	.60	.28	.06
☐ 108	Bert Campaneris	.50	.22	.05
	BOSTON RED SOX			
☐ 109	Boston Red Sox	.50	.22	.05
☐ 110	Carl Yastrzemski	6.00	2.80	.60
☐ 111	Dick Radatz	.40	.18	.04
☐ 112	Felix Mantilla	.40	.18	.04
☐ 113	Tony Conigliaro	.60	.28	.06
☐ 114	Bill Monbouquette	.40	.18	.04
	MILWAUKEE BRAVES			
☐ 115	Milwaukee Braves	.40	.18	.04
☐ 116	Tony Cloninger	.40	.18	.04
☐ 117	Henry Aaron	5.00	2.35	.50
☐ 118	Eddie Mathews	2.50	1.15	.25
☐ 119	Denis Menke	.40	.18	.04
☐ 120	Joe Torre	.75	.35	.07

1967 Topps Paper Inserts

The wrappers of the 1967 Topps cards have the set advertised as follows: "Extra -- All Star Pin-up inside." Printed on (5" by 7") paper in full color, the "All Star" inserts have fold lines which are generally not noticeable when stored carefully. They are numbered and carry a facsimile autograph.

		MINT	VG-E	F-G
	COMPLETE SET	16.00	7.50	1.60
	COMMON PLAYER (1-32)	.25	.10	.02
☐ 1	Boog Powell	.35	.15	.03
☐ 2	Bert Campaneris	.30	.12	.03
☐ 3	Brooks Robinson	1.50	.70	.15

			MINT	VG-E	F-G
☐	4	Tommie Agee	.25	.10	.02
☐	5	Carl Yastrzemski	2.50	1.15	.25
☐	6	Mickey Mantle	5.00	2.35	.50
☐	7	Frank Howard	.30	.12	.03
☐	8	Sam McDowell	.30	.12	.03
☐	9	Orlando Cepeda	.35	.15	.03
☐	10	Chico Cardenas	.25	.10	.02

☐	11	Bob Clemente	2.50	1.15	.25
☐	12	Willie Mays	2.50	1.15	.25
☐	13	Cleon Jones	.25	.10	.02
☐	14	John Callison	.30	.12	.03
☐	15	Hank Aaron	2.50	1.15	.25
☐	16	Don Drysdale	1.00	.45	.10
☐	17	Bobby Knoop	.25	.10	.02
☐	18	Tony Oliva	.45	.20	.04
☐	19	Frank Robinson	1.50	.70	.15
☐	20	Denny McLain	.45	.20	.04
☐	21	Al Kaline	1.50	.70	.15
☐	22	Joe Pepitone	.30	.12	.03
☐	23	Harmon Killebrew	1.00	.45	.10
☐	24	Leon Wagner	.25	.10	.02
☐	25	Joe Morgan	.75	.35	.07
☐	26	Ron Santo	.35	.15	.03
☐	27	Joe Torre	.45	.20	.04
☐	28	Juan Marichal	1.00	.45	.10
☐	29	Matty Alou	.30	.12	.03
☐	30	Felipe Alou	.30	.12	.03
☐	31	Ron Hunt	.25	.10	.02
☐	32	Willie McCovey	1.00	.45	.10

1967 Topps Pirate Stickers

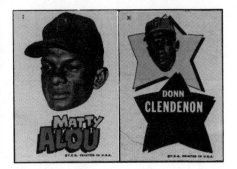

This was a limited production "test" issue for Topps. It is very similar to the Red Sox "test" issue following. The stickers are blank backed and measure 2 1/2" by 3 1/2". The stickers look like cards from the front and are somewhat attractive in spite of the "no neck" presentation of many of the players' photos. The cards are numbered on the front.

		MINT	VG-E	F-G
COMPLETE SET		175.00	80.00	18.00
COMMON PLAYER		3.00	1.40	.30
☐ 1	Gene Alley	4.00	1.85	.40
☐ 2	Matty Alou	4.00	1.85	.40

☐	3	Dennis Ribant	3.00	1.40	.30
☐	4	Steve Blass	4.00	1.85	.40
☐	5	Juan Pizarro	3.00	1.40	.30
☐	6	Roberto Clemente	60.00	25.00	6.00
☐	7	Donn Clendenon	4.00	1.85	.40
☐	8	Elroy Face	4.00	1.85	.40
☐	9	Woodie Fryman	3.00	1.40	.30
☐	10	Jesse Gonder	3.00	1.40	.30
☐	11	Vern Law	4.00	1.85	.40
☐	12	Al McBean	3.00	1.40	.30
☐	13	Jerry May	3.00	1.40	.30
☐	14	Bil Mazeroski	6.00	2.80	.60
☐	15	Pete Mikkelsen	3.00	1.40	.30
☐	16	Manny Mota	4.00	1.85	.40
☐	17	Bill O'Dell	3.00	1.40	.30
☐	18	Jose Pagan	3.00	1.40	.30
☐	19	Jim Pagliaroni	3.00	1.40	.30
☐	20	Johnny Pesky COACH	3.00	1.40	.30
☐	21	Tommie Sisk	3.00	1.40	.30
☐	22	Willie Stargell	25.00	11.00	2.50
☐	23	Bob Veale	4.00	1.85	.40
☐	24	Harry Walker MGR	3.00	1.40	.30
☐	25	"I Love the Pirates"	3.00	1.40	.30
☐	26	"Let's Go Pirates"	3.00	1.40	.30
☐	27	Bob Clemente for Mayor	30.00	14.00	3.00
☐	28	Matty Alou, NL Batting Champion	4.00	1.85	.40
☐	29	"Happiness is a Pirate Win"	3.00	1.40	.30
☐	30	"Donn Clendenon is my Hero"	4.00	1.85	.40
☐	31	Willie Stargell, Pirates HR Champion	15.00	7.00	1.50
☐	32	Pirates logo	3.00	1.40	.30
☐	33	Pirates pennant	3.00	1.40	.30

1967 Topps Red Sox Stickers

This was a limited production "test" issue for Topps. It is very similar to the Pirates "test" issue preceding. The stickers are blank backed and measure 2 1/2" by 3 1/2". The stickers look like cards from the front and are somewhat attractive in spite of the "no neck" presentation of many of the players' photos. The cards are numbered on the front.

		MINT	VG-E	F-G
COMPLETE SET		175.00	80.00	18.00
COMMON PLAYER		3.00	1.40	.30
☐ 1	Dennis Bennett	3.00	1.40	.30
☐ 2	Darrell Brandon	3.00	1.40	.30
☐ 3	Tony Conigliaro	6.00	2.80	.60
☐ 4	Don Demeter	3.00	1.40	.30
☐ 5	Hank Fischer	3.00	1.40	.30
☐ 6	Joe Foy	3.00	1.40	.30
☐ 7	Mike Andrews	3.00	1.40	.30
☐ 8	Dalton Jones	3.00	1.40	.30
☐ 9	Jim Lonborg	5.00	2.35	.50
☐ 10	Don McMahon	3.00	1.40	.30
☐ 11	Dave Morehead	3.00	1.40	.30
☐ 12	Reggie Smith	6.00	2.80	.60
☐ 13	Rico Petrocelli	5.00	2.35	.50
☐ 14	Mike Ryan	3.00	1.40	.30
☐ 15	Jose Santiago	3.00	1.40	.30
☐ 16	George Scott	4.00	1.85	.40
☐ 17	Sal Maglie COACH	4.00	1.85	.40

			MINT	VG-E	F-G
☐ 18	George Smith		3.00	1.40	.30
☐ 19	Lee Stange		3.00	1.40	.30
☐ 20	Jerry Stephenson		3.00	1.40	.30
☐ 21	Jose Tartabull		3.00	1.40	.30
☐ 22	George Thomas		3.00	1.40	.30
☐ 23	Bob Tillman		3.00	1.40	.30
☐ 24	John Wyatt		3.00	1.40	.30
☐ 25	Carl Yastrzemski		60.00	25.00	6.00
☐ 26	Dick Williams MGR		6.00	2.80	.60
☐ 27	"I Love the Red Sox"		3.00	1.40	.30
☐ 28	"Let's Go Red Sox"		3.00	1.40	.30
☐ 29	Carl Yastrzemski for Mayor		30.00	14.00	3.00
☐ 30	"Tony Conigliaro is my Hero"		5.00	2.35	.50
☐ 31	"Happiness is a Boston Win"		3.00	1.40	.30
☐ 32	Red Sox logo		3.00	1.40	.30
☐ 33	Red Sox pennant		3.00	1.40	.30

1967 Topps Giant Stand Ups

This test issue is quite scarce. The set features a color portrait photo of the player on a distinctive black background on heavy card stock. Each card measures 3 1/16" by 5 1/4" and is blank backed. The cards are numbered on the front in the lower left corner. Cards are found both with and without the stand up die cut.

		MINT	VG-E	F-G
COMPLETE SET		5000.00	2000.00	400.00
COMMON PLAYER		60.00	27.00	6.00
☐ 1	Pete Rose	900.00	400.00	90.00
☐ 2	Gary Peters	60.00	27.00	6.00
☐ 3	Frank Robinson	150.00	70.00	15.00
☐ 4	Jim Lonborg	60.00	27.00	6.00
☐ 5	Ron Swoboda	60.00	27.00	6.00
☐ 6	Harmon Killebrew	150.00	70.00	15.00
☐ 7	Bob Clemente	500.00	225.00	50.00
☐ 8	Mickey Mantle	900.00	400.00	90.00
☐ 9	Jim Fregosi	60.00	27.00	6.00
☐ 10	Al Kaline	250.00	110.00	25.00
☐ 11	Don Drysdale	150.00	70.00	15.00
☐ 12	Dean Chance	60.00	27.00	6.00
☐ 13	Orlando Cepeda	75.00	35.00	7.50
☐ 14	Tim McCarver	75.00	35.00	7.50
☐ 15	Frank Howard	75.00	35.00	7.50
☐ 16	Max Alvis	60.00	27.00	6.00
☐ 17	Rusty Staub	75.00	35.00	7.50
☐ 18	Richie Allen	75.00	35.00	7.50
☐ 19	Willie Mays	600.00	275.00	60.00
☐ 20	Hank Aaron	600.00	275.00	60.00
☐ 21	Carl Yastrzemski	750.00	350.00	75.00
☐ 22	Ron Santo	75.00	35.00	7.50
☐ 23	Jim Hunter	90.00	42.00	9.00
☐ 24	Jim Wynn	60.00	27.00	6.00

1968 Topps Posters

This 1968 color poster set is not an "insert" but was issued separately with a piece of gum and in its own wrapper. The posters are numbered at the lower left and the player's name and team appear in a large star. The poster was folded six times to fit into the package, so fold lines are a factor in grading. Each poster measures 9 3/4" by 18 1/8".

		MINT	VG-E	F-G
COMPLETE SET		150.00	70.00	15.00
COMMON PLAYER (1-24)		1.50	.70	.15
☐ 1	Dean Chance	1.50	.70	.15
☐ 2	Max Alvis	1.50	.70	.15
☐ 3	Frank Howard	2.00	.90	.20
☐ 4	Jim Fregosi	2.00	.90	.20
☐ 5	Jim Hunter	3.50	1.65	.35
☐ 6	Bob Clemente	12.00	5.50	1.20
☐ 7	Don Drysdale	5.00	2.35	.50
☐ 8	Jim Wynn	2.00	.90	.20
☐ 9	Al Kaline	7.50	3.50	.75
☐ 10	Harmon Killebrew	5.00	2.35	.50
☐ 11	Jim Lonborg	2.00	.90	.20
☐ 12	Orlando Cepeda	2.50	1.15	.25
☐ 13	Gary Peters	1.50	.70	.15
☐ 14	Hank Aaron	12.00	5.50	1.20
☐ 15	Richie Allen	2.00	.90	.20
☐ 16	Carl Yastrzemski	15.00	7.00	1.50
☐ 17	Ron Swoboda	1.50	.70	.15
☐ 18	Mickey Mantle	30.00	14.00	3.00
☐ 19	Tim McCarver	2.00	.90	.20
☐ 20	Willie Mays	12.00	5.50	1.20
☐ 21	Ron Santo	2.00	.90	.20
☐ 22	Rusty Staub	2.00	.90	.20
☐ 23	Pete Rose	30.00	14.00	3.00
☐ 24	Frank Robinson	6.00	2.80	.60

1968 Topps Action Stickers

This test issue is a set of 16 long stickers which is perforated and can be divided into three stickers. The middle sticker features a large sticker depicting only one player, whereas the top and bottom stickers feature three smaller stickers. These stickers are attractive and colorful.

	MINT	VG-E	F-G
COMPLETE SET	1000.00	450.00	100.00
COMMON INDIVIDUAL PANEL	5.00	2.35	.50
COMMON TRIPLE PANEL	25.00	11.00	2.50
☐ 1A Joel Horlen Orlando Cepeda Bill Mazeroski	5.00	2.35	.50
☐ 1B Carl Yastrzemski	100.00	45.00	10.00
☐ 1C Mel Stottlemyre Al Kaline Claude Osteen	10.00	4.75	1.00
☐ 2A Pete Ward Mike McCormick Ron Swoboda	5.00	2.35	.50
☐ 2B Harmon Killebrew	35.00	16.50	3.50
☐ 2C George Scott Tom Phoebus Don Drysdale	6.00	2.80	.60
☐ 3A Jim Maloney Joe Pepitone Henry Aaron	10.00	4.75	1.00
☐ 3B Frank Robinson	50.00	22.00	5.00
☐ 3C Paul Casanova Rick Reichardt Tom Seaver	10.00	4.75	1.00
☐ 4A Frank Robinson Jim Lefebvre Dean Chance	7.00	3.25	.70
☐ 4B Ron Santo	15.00	7.00	1.50
☐ 4C Johnny Callison Jim Lonborg Bob Aspromonte	5.00	2.35	.50
☐ 5A Bert Campaneris Ron Santo Al Downing	5.00	2.35	.50
☐ 5B Willie Mays	100.00	45.00	10.00
☐ 5C Pete Rose Ed Kranepool Willie Horton	20.00	9.00	2.00
☐ 6A Carl Yastrzemski Max Alvis Walt Williams	12.00	5.50	1.20
☐ 6B Al Kaline	60.00	27.00	6.00
☐ 6C Ernie Banks Tim McCarver Rusty Staub	10.00	4.75	1.00
☐ 7A Willie McCovey Rick Monday Steve Hargan	7.00	3.25	.70
☐ 7B Mickey Mantle	200.00	90.00	20.00
☐ 7C Rod Carew Tony Gonzalez Billy Williams	10.00	4.75	1.00
☐ 8A Ken Boyer Don Mincher Jim Bunning	6.00	2.80	.60
☐ 8B Joel Horlen	15.00	7.00	1.50
☐ 8C Tony Conigliaro Ken McMullen Mike Cuellar	5.00	2.35	.50
☐ 9A Harmon Killebrew Jim Fregosi Earl Wilson	6.00	2.80	.60
☐ 9B Orlando Cepeda	15.00	7.00	1.50
☐ 9C Roberto Clemente Willie Mays Chris Short	25.00	11.00	2.50
☐ 10A Mickey Mantle Jim Hunter Vada Pinson	30.00	14.00	3.00
☐ 10B Hank Aaron	100.00	45.00	10.00
☐ 10C Gary Peters Bob Gibson Ken Harrelson	6.00	2.80	.60
☐ 11A Tony Oliva Bob Veale Bill Freehan	5.00	2.35	.50
☐ 11B Don Drysdale	35.00	16.50	3.50
☐ 11C Frank Howard Fergie Jenkins Jim Wynn	6.00	2.80	.60
☐ 12A Joe Torre Dick Allen Jim McGlothlin	5.00	2.35	.50
☐ 12B Roberto Clemente	100.00	45.00	10.00
☐ 12C Brooks Robinson Tony Perez Sam McDowell	10.00	4.75	1.00
☐ 13A Frank Robinson Jim Lefebvre Dean Chance	7.00	3.25	.70
☐ 13B Carl Yastrzemski	100.00	45.00	10.00
☐ 13C Tom Phoebus George Scott Don Drysdale	6.00	2.80	.60
☐ 14A Joel Horlen Orlando Cepeda Bill Mazeroski	6.00	2.80	.60
☐ 14B Harmon Killebrew	35.00	16.50	3.50
☐ 14C Paul Casanova Rick Reichardt Tom Seaver	10.00	4.75	1.00
☐ 15A Pete Ward Mike McCormick Ron Swoboda	10.00	4.75	1.00
☐ 15B Frank Robinson	50.00	22.00	5.00
☐ 15C Johnny Callison Jim Lonborg Bob Aspromonte	5.00	2.35	.50
☐ 16A Jim Maloney Joe Pepitone Henry Aaron	10.00	4.75	1.00
☐ 16B Ron Santo	15.00	7.00	1.50
☐ 16C Mel Stottlemyre Al Kaline Claude Osteen	7.00	3.25	.70

1969 Topps Team Posters

This set was issued as a separate set by Topps, but was apparently not widely distributed. It was folded many times to fit the packaging and hence is typically found with relatively heavy fold creases. Each poster measures approximately 12" by 20". These posters are in full color with a blank back. Each team features nine or ten individual players; a few noteworthy players are listed in the checklist below. Each player photo is accompanied by a facsimile autograph. The posters are numbered in the bottom left corner.

	MINT	VG-E	F-G
COMPLETE SET	650.00	300.00	60.00
COMMON PLAYER	10.00	4.75	1.00

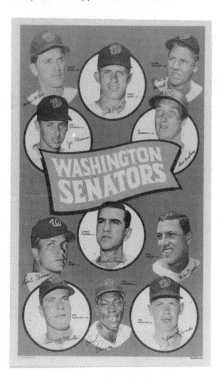

1969 Topps Four in One

This was a test issue consisting of 25 sticker cards (blank back). Each card measures 2 1/2" by 3 1/2" and features four mini-stickers. These unnumbered stickers are ordered in the checklist below alphabetically by the upper left player's name on each card. Each mini-card featured is from the 1969 Topps second series.

		MINT	VG-E	F-G
COMPLETE SET		850.00	400.00	80.00
COMMON PLAYER		10.00	4.75	1.00
☐ 1	Jerry Adair	100.00	45.00	10.00
	Don Wilson			
	Willie Mays			
	Johnny Morris			
☐ 2	Astros Rookies	10.00	4.75	1.00
	Wally Bunker			
	Joe Gibbon			
	Don Cardwell			
☐ 3	Donn Clendenon	10.00	4.75	1.00
	Woody Woodward			
	Tommie Aaron			
	Jim Britton			
☐ 4	Tommy Davis	15.00	7.00	1.50
	Don Pavletich			
	W.S. Game 4			
	Vada Pinson			
☐ 5	Ron Fairly	10.00	4.75	1.00
	Rick Wise			
	Max Alvis			
	Glenn Beckert			
☐ 6	Jim French	10.00	4.75	1.00
	Dick Selma			
	Johnny Callison			
	Lum Harris			
☐ 7	Bob Gibson	50.00	22.00	5.00
	W.S. Game 3			
	Rick Reichardt			
	Larry Haney			
☐ 8	Andy Kosco	15.00	7.00	1.50
	Ron Reed			
	Jim Bunning			
	Ollie Brown			
☐ 9	Jim Lefebvre	10.00	4.75	1.00
	John Purdin			
	Bill Dillman			
	John Roseboro			
☐ 10	Felix Millan	10.00	4.75	1.00
	Bill Hands			
	Lindy McDaniel			
	Chuck Harrison			
☐ 11	Mel Nelson	15.00	7.00	1.50
	Dave Johnson			
	Jack Hiatt			
	Tommie Sisk			
☐ 12	John Odom	15.00	7.00	1.50
	Leo Durocher			
	Wilbur Wood			
	Clay Dalrymple			
☐ 13	Ray Oyler	10.00	4.75	1.00
	Hank Bauer			
	Kevin Collins			
	Russ Snyder			
☐ 14	Jim Perry	15.00	7.00	1.50

☐ 1	Atlanta Braves	50.00	22.00	5.00
	Hank Aaron			
☐ 2	Baltimore Orioles	50.00	22.00	5.00
	Brooks Robinson			
	Frank Robinson			
☐ 3	Boston Red Sox	60.00	27.00	6.00
	Carl Yastrzemski			
☐ 4	California Angels	10.00	4.75	1.00
☐ 5	Chicago Cubs	25.00	11.00	2.50
	Ernie Banks			
☐ 6	Chicago White Sox	15.00	7.00	1.50
☐ 7	Cincinnati Reds	75.00	35.00	7.50
	Pete Rose			
☐ 8	Cleveland Indians	10.00	4.75	1.00
☐ 9	Detroit Tigers	25.00	11.00	2.50
	Al Kaline			
☐ 10	Houston Astros	10.00	4.75	1.00
☐ 11	Kansas City Royals	10.00	4.75	1.00
☐ 12	Los Angeles Dodgers	25.00	11.00	2.50
☐ 13	Minnesota Twins	25.00	11.00	2.50
	Rod Carew			
☐ 14	Montreal Expos	10.00	4.75	1.00
☐ 15	New York Mets	50.00	22.00	5.00
	Tom Seaver			
☐ 16	New York Yankees	75.00	35.00	7.50
	Mickey Mantle			
☐ 17	Oakland A's	50.00	22.00	5.00
	Reggie Jackson			
☐ 18	Philadelphia Phillies	10.00	4.75	1.00
☐ 19	Pittsburgh Pirates	50.00	22.00	5.00
	Roberto Clemente			
☐ 20	St. Louis Cardinals	35.00	16.50	3.50
	Lou Brock			
	Bob Gibson			
☐ 21	San Diego Padres	10.00	4.75	1.00
☐ 22	San Francisco Giants	50.00	22.00	5.00
	Willie Mays			
☐ 23	Seattle Pilots	20.00	9.00	2.00
☐ 24	Washington Senators	10.00	4.75	1.00

> **Not sure about an abbreviation? Just check our glossary and legend found in the introductory section in the front of the book.**

	W.S. Game 7			
	Gerry Arrigo			
	Red Sox Rookies			
☐ 15	Doug Rader	10.00	4.75	1.00
	Bill McCool			
	Roberto Pena			
	W.S. Game 2			
☐ 16	Bob Rodgers	10.00	4.75	1.00
	Willie Horton			
	Roy Face			
	Ed Brinkman			
☐ 17	Ray Sadecki	10.00	4.75	1.00
	Dave Baldwin			
	J.C. Martin			
	Dave May			
☐ 18	Mike Shannon	15.00	7.00	1.50
	W.S. Game 1			
	Jose Pagan			
	Tom Phoebus			
☐ 19	Lee Stange	300.00	130.00	30.00
	Don Sutton			
	Ted Uhlaender			
	Pete Rose			
☐ 20	Jim Weaver	10.00	4.75	1.00
	Dick Tracewski			
	Joe Grzenda			
	Frank Howard			
☐ 21	White Sox Rookies	15.00	7.00	1.50
	Denny McLain			
	Grant Jackson			
	Joe Azcue			
☐ 22	Stan Williams	10.00	4.75	1.00
	John Edwards			
	Jim Fairey			
	Phillies Rookies			
☐ 23	W.S. Celebration	10.00	4.75	1.00
	Leon Wagner			
	Johh Bateman			
	Willie Smith			
☐ 24	Yankees Rookies	15.00	7.00	1.50
	Chris Cannizzaro			
	W.S. Game 5			
	Bob Hendley			
☐ 25	Carl Yastrzemski	200.00	90.00	20.00
	Rico Petrocelli			
	Joe Nossek			
	Cards Rookies			

1970 Topps Paper Insert

In 1970 Topps raised its price per package of cards to ten cents, and a series of 24 color posters was included as a bonus to the collector. Each thin-paper poster is numbered and features a large portrait and a smaller, black, white action pose. It was folded five times to fit the packaging. Each poster measures 8 11/16" by 9 5/8".

		MINT	VG-E	F-G
COMPLETE SET		25.00	11.00	2.50
COMMON PLAYER (1-24)		.50	.22	.05
☐ 1	Joe Horlen	.50	.22	.05
☐ 2	Phil Niekro	1.50	.70	.15
☐ 3	Willie Davis	.60	.28	.06
☐ 4	Lou Brock	3.00	1.40	.30
☐ 5	Ron Santo	.75	.35	.07
☐ 6	Ken Harrelson	.75	.35	.07
☐ 7	Willie McCovey	2.50	1.15	.25
☐ 8	Rick Wise	.50	.22	.05
☐ 9	Andy Messersmith	.60	.28	.06
☐ 10	Ron Fairly	.60	.28	.06
☐ 11	Johnny Bench	4.00	1.85	.40
☐ 12	Frank Robinson	2.50	1.15	.25
☐ 13	Tommie Agee	.50	.22	.05
☐ 14	Roy White	.50	.22	.05
☐ 15	Larry Dierker	.50	.22	.05
☐ 16	Rod Carew	3.00	1.40	.30
☐ 17	Don Mincher	.50	.22	.05
☐ 18	Ollie Brown	.50	.22	.05
☐ 19	Ed Kirkpatrick	.50	.22	.05
☐ 20	Reggie Smith	.75	.35	.07
☐ 21	Bob Clemente	5.00	2.35	.50
☐ 22	Frank Howard	.75	.35	.07
☐ 23	Bert Campaneris	.60	.28	.06
☐ 24	Denny McLain	.75	.35	.07

1970 Topps Story Booklets

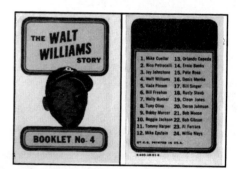

Inserted into packages of the 1970 Topps regular issue of cards, there are 24 miniature biographies of ballplayers in the set. Each numbered paper booklet contains six pages of comic book style story and a checklist of the booklet is available on the back page. These little booklets measure 2 1/2" by 3 7/16".

		MINT	VG-E	F-G
COMPLETE SET		15.00	7.00	1.50
COMMON PLAYER (1-24)		.30	.12	.03
☐ 1	Mike Cuellar	.35	.15	.03
☐ 2	Rico Petrocelli	.35	.15	.03
☐ 3	Jay Johnstone	.35	.15	.03
☐ 4	Walt Williams	.30	.12	.03
☐ 5	Vada Pinson	.45	.20	.04
☐ 6	Bill Freehan	.45	.20	.04
☐ 7	Wally Bunker	.30	.12	.03
☐ 8	Tony Oliva	.60	.28	.06
☐ 9	Bobby Murcer	.45	.20	.04
☐ 10	Reggie Jackson	3.00	1.40	.30
☐ 11	Tommy Harper	.30	.12	.03
☐ 12	Mike Epstein	.30	.12	.03
☐ 13	Orlando Cepeda	.60	.28	.06
☐ 14	Ernie Banks	2.00	.90	.20
☐ 15	Pete Rose	6.00	2.80	.60

☐ 16	Denis Menke	.30	.12	.03
☐ 17	Bill Singer	.30	.12	.03
☐ 18	Rusty Staub	.50	.22	.05
☐ 19	Cleon Jones	.30	.12	.03
☐ 20	Deron Johnson	.30	.12	.03
☐ 21	Bob Moose	.30	.12	.03
☐ 22	Bob Moose	1.50	.70	.15
☐ 23	Al Ferrara	.30	.12	.03
☐ 24	Willie Mays	3.00	1.40	.30

☐ 17	Lou Piniella	.50	.22	.05
☐ 18	Boog Powell	.50	.22	.05
☐ 19	Tom Seaver	2.50	1.15	.25
☐ 20	Jim Spencer	.30	.12	.03
☐ 21	Willie Stargell	1.50	.70	.15
☐ 22	Mel Stottlemyre	.40	.18	.04
☐ 23	Jim Wynn	.30	.12	.03
☐ 24	Carl Yastrzemski	4.00	1.85	.40

1970-71 Topps Scratchoffs

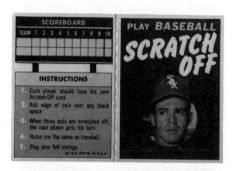

1971 Topps Tattoos

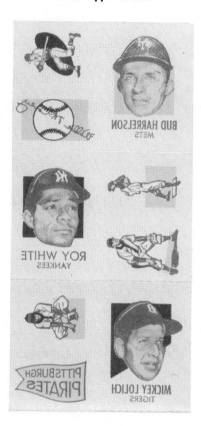

The 1970-71 Topps Scratch-off inserts are heavy cardboard, folded inserts issued with the regular card series of those years. Unfolded, they form a game board upon which a baseball game is played by means of rubbing off black ink from the playing squares to reveal moves. Inserts with white centers were issued in 1970 and inserts with red centers in 1971. Unfolded, these inserts measure 3 3/8" by 5".

	MINT	VG-E	F-G
COMPLETE SET	20.00	9.00	2.00
COMMON PLAYER (1-24)	.30	.12	.03
☐ 1 Hank Aaron	3.00	1.40	.30
☐ 2 Rich Allen	.60	.28	.06
☐ 3 Luis Aparicio	1.00	.45	.10
☐ 4 Sal Bando	.40	.18	.04
☐ 5 Glenn Beckert	.35	.15	.03
☐ 6 Dick Bosman	.30	.12	.03
☐ 7 Nate Colbert	.30	.12	.03
☐ 8 Mike Hegan	.30	.12	.03
☐ 9 Mack Jones	.30	.12	.03
☐ 10 Al Kaline	2.50	1.15	.25
☐ 11 Harmon Killebrew	1.50	.70	.15
☐ 12 Juan Marichal	1.50	.70	.15
☐ 13 Tim McCarver	.40	.18	.04
☐ 14 Sam McDowell	.40	.18	.04
☐ 15 Claude Osteen	.40	.18	.04
☐ 16 Tony Perez	.60	.28	.06

There are 16 different sheets (3 1/2" X 14 1/4") of baseball tattoos issued by Topps in 1971. Each contains two distinct sizes (1 3/4" by 2 3/8" and 1 3/16" by 1 3/4") of tattoos; those of players feature flesh-tone faces on red or yellow backgrounds; those of baseball figures, facsimile autographs (these are denoted by AU in the checklist), and team pennants are one-half the player tattoo size. The "Baseball Tattoos" logo panel at the top of each sheet contains the sheet number. The small baseball figures are not priced in the checklist. The complete tattoo panel prices can be figured as the sum of the individual (player, team, and autograph) tatoos.

	MINT	VG-E	F-G
COMPLETE SET	35.00	16.50	3.50
COMMON PLAYER	.15	.06	.01

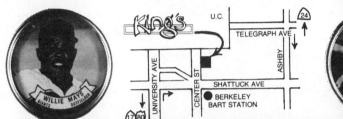

TATTOO SHEET ONE

☐ 1	Sal Bando	.20	.09	.02
☐ 2	Dick Bosman	.15	.06	.01
☐ 3	Nate Colbert	.15	.06	.01
☐ 4	Cleon Jones	.15	.06	.01
☐ 5	Juan Marichal	.60	.28	.06
☐ 6	Brooks Robinson	1.00	.45	.10
☐ 7	Brooks Robinson AU	.25	.10	.02
☐ 8	Montreal Expos	.15	.06	.01
☐ 9	San Francisco Giants	.15	.06	.01

TATTOO SHEET TWO

☐ 10	Glen Beckert	.15	.06	.01
☐ 11	Tommy Harper	.15	.06	.01
☐ 12	Ken Henderson	.15	.06	.01
☐ 13	Carl Yastrzemski	2.00	.90	.20
☐ 14	Carl Yastrzemski AU	.40	.18	.04
☐ 15	Boston Red Sox	.20	.09	.02
☐ 16	New York Mets	.20	.09	.02

TATTOO SHEET THREE

☐ 17	Orlando Cepeda	.30	.12	.03
☐ 18	Jim Fregosi	.20	.09	.02
☐ 19	Jim Fregosi AU	.15	.06	.01
☐ 20	Randy Hundley	.15	.06	.01
☐ 21	Reggie Jackson	1.50	.70	.15
☐ 22	Jerry Koosman	.25	.10	.02
☐ 23	Jim Palmer	.75	.35	.07
☐ 24	Philadelphia Phillies	.15	.06	.01
☐ 25	New York Yankees	.20	.09	.02

TATTOO SHEET FOUR

☐ 26	Dick Dietz	.15	.06	.01
☐ 27	Clarence Gaston	.15	.06	.01
☐ 28	Dave Johnson	.25	.10	.02
☐ 29	Sam McDowell	.20	.09	.02
☐ 30	Sam McDowell AU	.15	.06	.01
☐ 31	Gary Nolan	.15	.06	.01
☐ 32	Amos Otis	.25	.10	.02
☐ 33	Kansas City Royals	.15	.06	.01
☐ 34	Oakland A's	.15	.06	.01

TATTOO SHEET FIVE

☐ 35	Billy Grabarkewitz	.15	.06	.01
☐ 36	Al Kaline	1.00	.45	.10
☐ 37	Al Kaline AU	.25	.10	.02
☐ 38	Lee May	.20	.09	.02
☐ 39	Tom Murphy	.15	.06	.01
☐ 40	Vada Pinson	.25	.10	.02
☐ 41	Manny Sanguillen	.20	.09	.02
☐ 42	Atlanta Braves	.15	.06	.01
☐ 43	Los Angeles Dodgers	.20	.09	.02

TATTOO SHEET SIX

☐ 44	Luis Aparicio	.60	.28	.06
☐ 45	Paul Blair	.20	.09	.02
☐ 46	Chris Cannizzaro	.15	.06	.01
☐ 47	Donn Clendenon	.15	.06	.01
☐ 48	Larry Dierker	.15	.06	.01
☐ 49	Harmon Killebrew	.75	.35	.07
☐ 50	Harmon Killebrew AU	.20	.09	.02
☐ 51	Chicago Cubs	.15	.06	.01
☐ 52	Cincinnati Reds	.15	.06	.01

TATTOO SHEET SEVEN

☐ 53	Rich Allen	.30	.12	.03
☐ 54	Bert Campaneris	.20	.09	.02
☐ 55	Don Money	.20	.09	.02
☐ 56	Boog Powell	.30	.12	.03
☐ 57	Boog Powell AU	.15	.06	.01
☐ 58	Ted Savage	.15	.06	.01
☐ 59	Rusty Staub	.25	.10	.02
☐ 60	Cleveland Indians	.15	.06	.01
☐ 61	Milwaukee Brewers	.15	.06	.01

TATTOO SHEET EIGHT

☐ 62	Leo Cardenas	.15	.06	.01
☐ 63	Bill Hands	.15	.06	.01
☐ 64	Frank Howard	.25	.10	.02
☐ 65	Frank Howard AU	.15	.06	.01
☐ 66	Wes Parker	.20	.09	.02
☐ 67	Reggie Smith	.25	.10	.02
☐ 68	Willie Stargell	.75	.35	.07
☐ 69	Chicago White Sox	.15	.06	.01
☐ 70	San Diego Padres	.15	.06	.01

TATTOO SHEET NINE

☐ 71	Hank Aaron	1.50	.70	.15
☐ 72	Hank Aaron AU	.30	.12	.03
☐ 73	Tommy Agee	.15	.06	.01
☐ 74	Jim Hunter	.50	.22	.05
☐ 75	Dick McAuliffe	.15	.06	.01
☐ 76	Tony Perez	.35	.15	.03
☐ 77	Lou Pinella	.25	.10	.02
☐ 78	Detroit Tigers	.20	.09	.02

TATTOO SHEET TEN

☐ 79	Roberto Clemente	1.50	.70	.15
☐ 80	Tony Conigliaro	.25	.10	.02
☐ 81	Fergie Jenkins	.30	.12	.03
☐ 82	Fergie Jenkins AU	.15	.06	.01
☐ 83	Thurman Munson	1.00	.45	.10

☐ 84	Gary Peters	.15	.06	.01
☐ 85	Joe Torre	.30	.12	.03
☐ 86	Baltimore Orioles	.20	.09	.02

TATTOO SHEET ELEVEN

☐ 87	Johnny Bench	1.00	.45	.10
☐ 88	Johnny Bench AU	.30	.12	.03
☐ 89	Rico Carty	.20	.09	.02
☐ 90	Bill Mazeroski	.25	.10	.02
☐ 91	Bob Oliver	.15	.06	.01
☐ 92	Rico Petrocelli	.20	.09	.02
☐ 93	Floyd Robinson	.15	.06	.01
☐ 94	Washington Senators	.15	.06	.01

TATTOO SHEET TWELVE

☐ 95	Bill Freehan	.25	.10	.02
☐ 96	Dave McNally	.20	.09	.02
☐ 97	Felix Millan	.15	.06	.01
☐ 98	Mel Stottlemyre	.20	.09	.02
☐ 99	Bob Tolan	.15	.06	.01
☐ 100	Billy Williams	.50	.22	.05
☐ 101	Billy Williams AU	.20	.09	.02
☐ 102	Houston Astros	.15	.06	.01

TATTOO SHEET THIRTEEN

☐ 103	Ray Culp	.15	.06	.01
☐ 104	Bud Harrelson	.15	.06	.01
☐ 105	Mickey Lolich	.25	.10	.02
☐ 106	Willie McCovey	.75	.35	.07
☐ 107	Willie McCovey AU	.25	.10	.02
☐ 108	Ron Santo	.30	.12	.03
☐ 109	Roy White	.20	.09	.02
☐ 110	Pittsburgh Pirates	.15	.06	.01

TATTOO SHEET FOURTEEN

☐ 111	Bill Melton	.15	.06	.01
☐ 112	Jim Perry	.20	.09	.02
☐ 113	Pete Rose	3.00	1.40	.30
☐ 114	Tom Seaver	1.50	.70	.15
☐ 115	Tom Seaver AU	.30	.12	.03
☐ 116	Maury Wills	.35	.15	.03
☐ 117	Clyde Wright	.15	.06	.01
☐ 118	Minnesota Twins	.15	.06	.01

TATTOO SHEET FIFTEEN

☐ 119	Rod Carew	1.50	.70	.15
☐ 120	Bob Gibson	1.00	.45	.10
☐ 121	Bob Gibson AU	.25	.10	.02
☐ 122	Alex Johnson	.15	.06	.01
☐ 123	Don Kessinger	.20	.09	.02
☐ 124	Jim Merritt	.15	.06	.01
☐ 125	Rick Monday	.20	.09	.02
☐ 126	St. Louis Cardinals	.20	.09	.02

TATTOO SHEET SIXTEEN

☐ 127	Larry Bowa	.25	.10	.02
☐ 128	Mike Cuellar	.15	.06	.01
☐ 129	Ray Fosse	.15	.06	.01
☐ 130	Willie Mays	1.50	.70	.15
☐ 131	Willie Mays AU	.30	.12	.03
☐ 132	Carl Morton	.15	.06	.01
☐ 133	Tony Oliva	.30	.12	.03
☐ 134	California Angels	.15	.06	.01

1972 Topps Posters

This giant (9 7/16" by 18"), full-color series of 24 paper-thin posters was issued as a separate set in 1972. The posters are individually numbered and, unlike other Topps posters described in this book, are borderless. They are printed on thin paper and were folded five times to facilitate packaging.

	MINT	VG-E	F-G
COMPLETE SET	75.00	35.00	7.50
COMMON PLAYER (1-24)	.75	.35	.07

☐ 1	Dave McNally	.75	.35	.07
☐ 2	Carl Yastrzemski	10.00	4.75	1.00
☐ 3	Bill Melton	.75	.35	.07
☐ 4	Ray Fosse	.75	.35	.07
☐ 5	Mickey Lolich	1.00	.45	.10
☐ 6	Amos Otis	1.00	.45	.10
☐ 7	Tony Oliva	1.00	.45	.10
☐ 8	Vida Blue	1.25	.60	.12
☐ 9	Hank Aaron	9.00	4.25	.90
☐ 10	Fergie Jenkins	1.50	.70	.15
☐ 11	Pete Rose	25.00	11.00	2.50
☐ 12	Willie Davis	.75	.35	.07
☐ 13	Tom Seaver	9.00	4.25	.90
☐ 14	Rick Wise	.75	.35	.07

☐ 3 Johnny Mize			
(53 Topps 77)	75.00	35.00	7.50
☐ 4 Jackie Robinson			
(53 Topps 1)	125.00	57.00	12.50
☐ 5 Carl Furillo			
(53 Topps 272)			
(Bill Antonello)	40.00	18.00	4.00
☐ 6 Al Rosen			
(53 Topps 187)			
(Jim Fridley)	40.00	18.00	4.00
☐ 7 Hal Newhouser			
(53 Topps 228)	40.00	18.00	4.00
☐ 8 Clyde McCullough			
(53 Topps 222)			
(Vic Janowicz)	30.00	14.00	3.00

1972 Topps Cloth Test

These "test" issue cards look like 1972 Topps cards except that they are on a "cloth sticker". Each card measures 2 1/2" by 3 1/2". The "cards" in this set are all taken from the third series of the 1972 Topps regular issue. Cards are blank backed and unnumbered. They are listed below in alphabetical order.

		MINT	VG-E	F-G
COMPLETE SET		175.00	80.00	18.00
COMMON PLAYER		5.00	2.35	.50
☐	1 Hank Aaron	50.00	22.00	5.00
☐	2 Luis Aparicio IA	10.00	4.75	1.00
☐	3 Ike Brown	5.00	2.35	.50
☐	4 Johnny Callison	6.00	2.80	.60
☐	5 Checklist 264-319	5.00	2.35	.50
☐	6 Roberto Clemente	25.00	11.00	2.50
☐	7 Dave Concepcion	7.00	3.25	.70
☐	8 Ron Cook	5.00	2.35	.50
☐	9 Willie Davis	6.00	2.80	.60
☐	10 Al Fitzmorris	5.00	2.35	.50
☐	11 Bobby Floyd	5.00	2.35	.50
☐	12 Roy Foster	5.00	2.35	.50

☐ 15	Willie Stargell	4.00	1.85	.40
☐ 16	Joe Torre	1.50	.70	.15
☐ 17	Willie Mays	9.00	4.25	.90
☐ 18	Andy Messersmith	.75	.35	.07
☐ 19	Wilbur Wood	.75	.35	.07
☐ 20	Harmon Killebrew	5.00	2.35	.50
☐ 21	Billy Williams	4.00	1.85	.40
☐ 22	Bud Harrelson	.75	.35	.07
☐ 23	Roberto Clemente	9.00	4.25	.90
☐ 24	Willie McCovey	6.00	2.80	.60

1972 Topps Test

These "test" issue cards were made to look like 1953 Topps cards as the cards show drawings rather than photos. Each card measures 2 1/2" by 3 1/2". Printing on the back is in blue ink on gray card stock.

	MINT	VG-E	F-G
COMPLETE SET	400.00	180.00	40.00
COMMON PLAYER	30.00	14.00	3.00
☐1 Satchell Paige			
(53 Topps 220)	125.00	57.00	12.50
☐2 "Peanuts" Lowrey			
(53 Topps 16)	30.00	14.00	3.00

☐ 13	Jim Fregosi KP	6.00	2.80	.60
☐ 14	Danny Frisella IA	5.00	2.35	.50
☐ 15	Woody Fryman	5.00	2.35	.50
☐ 16	Terry Harmon	5.00	2.35	.50
☐ 17	Frank Howard	6.00	2.80	.60
☐ 18	Ron Klimkowski	5.00	2.35	.50
☐ 19	Joe Lahoud	5.00	2.35	.50
☐ 20	Jim Lefebvre	5.00	2.35	.50
☐ 21	Elliott Maddox	5.00	2.35	.50
☐ 22	Marty Martinez	5.00	2.35	.50
☐ 23	Willie McCovey	15.00	7.00	1.50
☐ 24	Hal McRae	6.00	2.80	.60
☐ 25	Syd O'Brien	5.00	2.35	.50
☐ 26	Red Sox Team	6.00	2.80	.60
☐ 27	Aurelio Rodriguez	5.00	2.35	.50
☐ 28	Al Severinsen	5.00	2.35	.50
☐ 29	Art Shamsky	5.00	2.35	.50
☐ 30	Steve Stone	6.00	2.80	.60
☐ 31	Stan Swanson	5.00	2.35	.50
☐ 32	Bob Watson	6.00	2.80	.60
☐ 33	Roy White	6.00	2.80	.60

1973 Topps Team Checklists

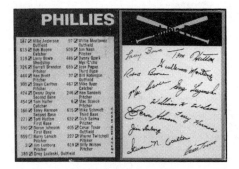

This 24 card set (measuring 2 1/2" by 3 1/2") is rather difficult to find. These blue bordered team checklist cards are very similar in design to the mass produced red trim team checklist cards issued by Topps the next year.

		MINT	VG-E	F-G
COMPLETE SET		60.00	27.00	6.00
COMMON TEAM		2.50	1.15	.25
☐ 1	Atlanta Braves	2.50	1.15	.25
☐ 2	Baltimore Orioles	2.50	1.15	.25
☐ 3	Boston Red Sox	2.50	1.15	.25
☐ 4	California Angels	2.50	1.15	.25
☐ 5	Chicago Cubs	2.50	1.15	.25
☐ 6	Chicago White Sox	2.50	1.15	.25
☐ 7	Cincinnati Reds	2.50	1.15	.25
☐ 8	Cleveland Indians	2.50	1.15	.25
☐ 9	Detroit Tigers	2.50	1.15	.25
☐ 10	Houston Astros	2.50	1.15	.25
☐ 11	Kansas City Royals	2.50	1.15	.25
☐ 12	Los Angeles Dodgers	2.50	1.15	.25
☐ 13	Milwaukee Brewers	2.50	1.15	.25
☐ 14	Minnesota Twins	2.50	1.15	.25
☐ 15	Montreal Expos	2.50	1.15	.25
☐ 16	New York Mets	2.50	1.15	.25
☐ 17	New York Yankees	2.50	1.15	.25
☐ 18	Oakland A's	2.50	1.15	.25
☐ 19	Philadelphia Phillies	2.50	1.15	.25
☐ 20	Pittsburgh Pirates	2.50	1.15	.25
☐ 21	San Diego Padres	2.50	1.15	.25
☐ 22	San Francisco Giants	2.50	1.15	.25
☐ 23	St. Louis Cardinals	2.50	1.15	.25
☐ 24	Texas Rangers	2.50	1.15	.25

1978 Topps Zest

This 5 card set (measuring 2 1/2" by 3 1/2") is very similar to the 1978 Topps regular issue. Although the cards were produced by Topps, they were used in a promotion for Zest Soap. The card numbers are different and the backs are written in English and Spanish. By the choice of players in this small set, Zest appears to have been targeting the Hispanic community. Each player's card number in the regular 1978 Topps set is also given.

		MINT	VG-E	F-G
COMPLETE SET		5.00	2.00	.40
COMMON PLAYER		1.00	.45	.10
☐ 1	Joaquin Andujar 78T-158	1.00	.45	.10
☐ 2	Bert Campaneris 78T-260	1.00	.45	.10
☐ 3	Ed Figueroa 78T-365	1.00	.45	.10
☐ 4	Willie Montanez 78T-38	1.00	.45	.10
☐ 5	Many Mota 78T-228	1.00	45	.10

1979 Topps Comics

This 33 card (comic) set, which measures approximately 3" by 3 1/4", is rather plentiful in spite of the fact that it was originally touted as a limited edition "test" issue. This flimsy set has never been very popular with collectors. These waxy comics are numbered and are blank backed. Each comic also features an "Inside Baseball" tip in the lower right corner.

	MINT	VG-E	F-G
COMPLETE SET	6.50	3.00	.50
COMMON PLAYER	.10	.04	.01
☐ 1 Eddie Murray	.35	.15	.03
☐ 2 Jim Rice	.25	.10	.02
☐ 3 Carl Yastrzemski	.40	.18	.04
☐ 4 Nolan Ryan	.25	.10	.02
☐ 5 Chet Lemon	.10	.04	.01
☐ 6 Andre Thornton	.10	.04	.01
☐ 7 Rusty Staub	.10	.04	.01
☐ 8 Ron LeFlore	.10	.04	.01
☐ 9 George Brett	.35	.15	.03
☐ 10 Larry Hisle	.10	.04	.01
☐ 11 Rod Carew	.25	.10	.02
☐ 12 Reggie Jackson	.35	.15	.03
☐ 13 Ron Guidry	.15	.06	.01
☐ 14 Mitchell Page	.10	.04	.01
☐ 15 Leon Roberts	.10	.04	.01
☐ 16 Al Oliver	.15	.06	.01
☐ 17 John Mayberry	.10	.04	.01
☐ 18 Bob Horner	.15	.06	.01
☐ 19 Phil Niekro	.15	.06	.01
☐ 20 Dave Kingman	.15	.06	.01
☐ 21 Johnny Bench	.25	.10	.02
☐ 22 Tom Seaver	.25	.10	.02
☐ 23 J.R. Richard	.10	.04	.01
☐ 24 Steve Garvey	.35	.15	.03
☐ 25 Reggie Smith	.10	.04	.01
☐ 26 Ross Grimsley	.10	.04	.01
☐ 27 Craig Swan	.10	.04	.01
☐ 28 Pete Rose	.75	.35	.07
☐ 29 Dave Parker	.20	.09	.02
☐ 30 Ted Simmons	.15	.06	.01
☐ 31 Dave Winfield	.25	.10	.02
☐ 32 Jack Clark	.15	.06	.01
☐ 33 Vida Blue	.10	.04	.01

1981 Topps Scratchoffs

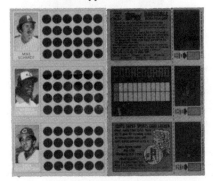

The cards in this 108 card set measure 1 13/16"
by 3 1/4" in a three-card panel measuring 3 1/4"
by 5 1/4". The 1981 Topps Scratch-Offs were
issued in their own wrapper with bubble gum. The
title "Scratch-Off" refers to the black dots of each
card which, when rubbed or scraped with a hard
edge, reveal a baseball game. While there are only
108 possible individual cards in the set, there are
144 possible panels combinations. The N.L. players
appear with green backgrounds and A.L. players
with red backgrounds. Some cards are found
without dots. An intact panel is worth 20% more
than the sum of its individual cards.

	MINT	VG-E	F-G
COMPLETE SET	3.25	1.50	.32
COMMON PLAYER	.02	.01	.00

AMERICAN LEAGUERS

☐ 1 George Brett	.15	.06	.01
☐ 2 Cecil Cooper	.06	.02	.00
☐ 3 Reggie Jackson	.15	.06	.01
☐ 4 Al Oliver	.06	.02	.00
☐ 5 Fred Lynn	.06	.02	.00
☐ 6 Tony Armas	.03	.01	.00
☐ 7 Ben Oglivie	.03	.01	.00
☐ 8 Tony Perez	.04	.02	.00
☐ 9 Eddie Murray	.15	.06	.01
☐ 10 Robin Yount	.12	.05	.01
☐ 11 Steve Kemp	.04	.02	.00
☐ 12 Joe Charboneau	.03	.01	.00
☐ 13 Jim Rice	.10	.04	.01
☐ 14 Lance Parrish	.08	.03	.01
☐ 15 John Mayberry	.02	.01	.00
☐ 16 Richie Zisk	.02	.01	.00
☐ 17 Ken Singleton	.03	.01	.00
☐ 18 Rod Carew	.10	.04	.01
☐ 19 Rick Manning	.02	.01	.00
☐ 20 Willie Wilson	.05	.02	.00
☐ 21 Buddy Bell	.04	.02	.00
☐ 22 Dave Revering	.02	.01	.00
☐ 23 Tom Paciorek	.02	.01	.00
☐ 24 Champ Summers	.02	.01	.00
☐ 25 Carney Lansford	.04	.02	.00
☐ 26 Lamar Johnson	.02	.01	.00
☐ 27 Willie Aikens	.02	.01	.00
☐ 28 Rick Cerone	.02	.01	.00
☐ 29 Al Bumbry	.02	.01	.00
☐ 30 Bruce Bochte	.02	.01	.00
☐ 31 Mickey Rivers	.03	.01	.00
☐ 32 Mike Hargrove	.02	.01	.00
☐ 33 John Castino	.02	.01	.00
☐ 34 Chet Lemon	.03	.01	.00
☐ 35 Paul Molitor	.04	.02	.00
☐ 36 Willie Randolph	.02	.01	.00
☐ 37 Rick Burleson	.02	.01	.00
☐ 38 Alan Trammell	.08	.03	.01
☐ 39 Rickey Henderson	.15	.06	.01
☐ 40 Dan Meyer	.02	.01	.00
☐ 41 Ken Landreaux	.02	.01	.00
☐ 42 Damaso Garcia	.03	.01	.00
☐ 43 Roy Smalley	.02	.01	.00
☐ 44 Otto Velez	.02	.01	.00
☐ 45 Sixto Lezcano	.02	.01	.00
☐ 46 Toby Harrah	.03	.01	.00
☐ 47 Frank White	.03	.01	.00
☐ 48 Dave Stapleton	.03	.01	.00
☐ 49 Steve Stone	.03	.01	.00
☐ 50 Jim Palmer	.10	.04	.01
☐ 51 Larry Gura	.02	.01	.00
☐ 52 Tommy John	.06	.02	.00
☐ 53 Mike Norris	.02	.01	.00
☐ 54 Ed Farmer	.02	.01	.00

NATIONAL LEAGUERS

☐ 55 Bill Buckner	.05	.02	.00
☐ 56 Steve Garvey	.15	.06	.01
☐ 57 Reggie Smith	.04	.02	.00
☐ 58 Bake McBride	.02	.01	.00
☐ 59 Dave Parker	.07	.03	.01
☐ 60 Mike Schmidt	.15	.06	.01
☐ 61 Bob Horner	.06	.02	.00
☐ 62 Pete Rose	.25	.10	.02
☐ 63 Ted Simmons	.05	.02	.00
☐ 64 Johnny Bench	.12	.05	.01
☐ 65 George Foster	.05	.02	.00
☐ 66 Gary Carter	.15	.06	.01
☐ 67 Keith Hernandez	.08	.03	.01
☐ 68 Ozzie Smith	.06	.02	.00
☐ 69 Dave Kingman	.06	.02	.00
☐ 70 Jack Clark	.05	.02	.00
☐ 71 Dusty Baker	.03	.01	.00
☐ 72 Dale Murphy	.15	.06	.01
☐ 73 Ron Cey	.05	.02	.00
☐ 74 Greg Luzinski	.05	.02	.00
☐ 75 Lee Mazzilli	.02	.01	.00
☐ 76 Gary Matthews	.03	.01	.00
☐ 77 Cesar Cedeno	.03	.01	.00
☐ 78 Warren Cromartie	.02	.01	.00
☐ 79 Steve Henderson	.02	.01	.00
☐ 80 Ellis Valentine	.02	.01	.00
☐ 81 Mike Easler	.03	.01	.00
☐ 82 Garry Templeton	.04	.02	.00
☐ 83 Jose Cruz	.05	.02	.00
☐ 84 Dave Collins	.03	.01	.00
☐ 85 George Hendrick	.04	.02	.00
☐ 86 Gene Richards	.02	.01	.00
☐ 87 Terry Whitfield	.02	.01	.00
☐ 88 Terry Puhl	.03	.01	.00
☐ 89 Larry Parrish	.04	.02	.00
☐ 90 Andre Dawson	.08	.03	.01
☐ 91 Ken Griffey	.05	.02	.00
☐ 92 Dave Lopes	.03	.01	.00

☐ 93	Doug Flynn	.02	.01	.00
☐ 94	Ivan DeJesus	.02	.01	.00
☐ 95	Dave Concepcion	.04	.02	.00
☐ 96	John Stearns	.02	.01	.00
☐ 97	Jerry Mumphrey	.02	.01	.00
☐ 98	Jerry Martin	.02	.01	.00
☐ 99	Art Howe	.02	.01	.00
☐100	Omar Moreno	.03	.01	.00
☐101	Ken Reitz	.02	.01	.00
☐102	Phil Garner	.02	.01	.00
☐103	Jerry Reuss	.03	.01	.00
☐104	Steve Carlton	.12	.05	.01
☐105	Jim Bibby	.02	.01	.00
☐106	Steve Rogers	.04	.02	.00
☐107	Tom Seaver	.12	.05	.01
☐108	Vida Blue	.03	.01	.00

1983 Topps Foldouts

The cards in this 85 card set measure 3 1/2" by 5 5/16". The 1983 Fold-Outs were an innovation by Topps featuring five sets of 17 postcard-size photos each. Each of the five sets had a theme of career leaders in a particular category. The five categories -- batting leaders, home run leaders, stolen base leaders, pitching leaders and relief aces -- featured the 17 top active players in their respective categories. If a player were a leader in more than one category, he is pictured in more than one of the five sets. These foldout booklets are typically sold intact and are priced below at one price per complete panel. Each picture contains a facsimile autograph as well. The quality of the photos is very good. In the checklist below the leaders are listed in order of their career standing as shown on each foldout.

	MINT	VG-E	F-G
COMPLETE SET (5)	5.00	2.35	.50
COMMON PANEL	1.00	.45	.10
☐ 1 Career Wins	1.25	.60	.12

Gaylord Perry, 307
Steve Carlton/Jim Kaat
Fergie Jenkins/Tom Seaver
Jim Palmer/Don Sutton
Phil Niekro/Tommy John
Nolan Ryan/Vida Blue
Jerry Koosman/Mike Torrez
Bert Blyleven/Joe Niekro
Jerry Reuss/P.Splittorff

	MINT	VG-E	F-G
☐ 2 Home Run Leaders	1.50	.70	.15

Reggie Jackson, 464
Carl Yastrzemski/J.Bench
Tony Perez/Mike Schmidt
Dave Kingman/Graig Nettles
Rusty Staub/Greg Luzinski
G.Foster/John Mayberry
Bobby Murcer/Joe Morgan

Jim Rice/Rick Monday
Darrell Evans/Ron Cey

	MINT	VG-E	F-G
☐ 3 Batting Leaders	1.50	.70	.15

Rod Carew, .331
George Brett/Bill Madlock
Lonnie Smith/Willie Wilson
Pete Rose/Dave Parker
Cecil Cooper/Jim Rice
Al Oliver/Pedro Guerrero
Ken Griffey/Fred Lynn
Steve Garvey/B.McBride
Keith Hernandez/D.lorg

	MINT	VG-E	F-G
☐ 4 Relief Aces	1.00	.45	.10

Rollie Fingers, 301
Bruce Sutter/R.Gossage
Tug McGraw/G.Garber
K.Tekulve/Bill Campbell
T.Forster/Tom Burgmeier
G.Lavelle/Dan Quisenberry
Jim Kern/Randy Moffitt
Ron Reed/Elias Sosa
Ed Farmer/Greg Minton

	MINT	VG-E	F-G
☐ 5 Steals Leaders	1.00	.45	.10

Joe Morgan, 663
Cesar Cedeno/Ron Leflore
Davey Lopes/Omar Moreno
Rod Carew/Amos Otis
Rickey Henderson/L.Bowa
Willie Wilson/Don Baylor
Julio Cruz/Mickey Rivers
Dave Concepcion/Jose Cruz
Garry Maddox/Al Bumbry

1984 Topps Rub Downs

The cards in this 112 player (32 different sheets) set measure 2 3/8" by 3 5/16". The Topps Rub Downs set was actually similar to earlier Topps tatoo or decal-type offerings. The full color photo could be transfered from the rub down to another surface by rubbing a coin over the paper backing. Distributed in packages of two rub down sheets, some contained two or three player action poses, others head shots and various pieces of player equipment. Players from all teams were included in the set. Although the sheets are unnumbered, they are numbered here in alphabetical order based on each card first being placed in alphabetical order.

	MINT	VG-E	F-G
COMPLETE SET	5.00	2.35	.50
COMMON PLAYER	.15	.06	.01
☐ 1 Tony Armas	.15	.06	.01

Harold Baines
Lonnie Smith

	MINT	VG-E	F-G
☐ 2 Don Baylor	.15	.06	.01

George Hendrick
Ron Kittle
Johnnie LeMaster

	MINT	VG-E	F-G
☐ 3 Buddy Bell	.15	.06	.01

	Ray Knight			
	Lloyd Moseby			
☐ 4	Bruce Benedict	.15	.06	.01
	Atlee Hammaker			
	Frank White			
☐ 5	Wade Boggs	.35	.15	.03
	Rick Dempsey			
	Keith Hernandez			
☐ 6	George Brett	.25	.10	.02
	Andre Dawson			
	Paul Molitor			
	Alan Wiggins			
☐ 7	Tom Brunansky	.35	.15	.03
	Pedro Guerrero			
	Darryl Strawberry			
☐ 8	Bill Buckner	.15	.06	.01
	Rich Gossage			
	Dave Stieb			
	Rick Sutcliffe			
☐ 9	Rod Carew	.20	.09	.02
	Carlton Fisk			
	Johnny Ray			
	Matt Young			
☐ 10	Steve Carlton	.20	.09	.02
	Bob Horner			
	Dan Quisenberry			
☐ 11	Gary Carter	.20	.09	.02
	Phil Garner			
	Ron Guidry			
☐ 12	Ron Cey	.15	.06	.01
	Steve Kemp			
	Greg Luzinski			
	Kent Tekulve			
☐ 13	Chris Chambliss	.15	.06	.01
	Dwight Evans			
	Julio Franco			
☐ 14	Jack Clark	.20	.09	.02
	Damaso Garcia			
	Hal McRae			
	Lance Parrish			
☐ 15	Dave Concepcion	.15	.06	.01
	Cecil Cooper			
	Fred Lynn			
	Jesse Orosco			
☐ 16	Jose Cruz	.20	.09	.02
	Gary Matthews			
	Jack Morris			
	Jim Rice			
☐ 17	Ron Davis	.20	.09	.02
	Kent Hrbek			
	Tom Seaver			
☐ 18	John Denny	.15	.06	.01
	Carney Lansford			
	Mario Soto			
	Lou Whitaker			
☐ 19	Leon Durham	.15	.06	.01
	Dave Lopes			
	Steve Sax			
☐ 20	George Foster	.15	.06	.01
	Gary Gaetti			
	Bobby Grich			
	Gary Redus			
☐ 21	Steve Garvey	.20	.09	.02
	Jerry Remy			
	Bill Russell			
	George Wright			
☐ 22	Moose Haas	.15	.06	.01
	Bruce Sutter			
	Dickie Thon			
	Andre Thornton			
☐ 23	Toby Harrah	.25	.10	.02
	Pat Putnam			
	Tim Raines			
	Mike Schmidt			
☐ 24	Rickey Henderson	.50	.22	.05
	Dave Righetti			
	Pete Rose			
☐ 25	Steve Henderson	.15	.06	.01
	Bill Madlock			
	Alan Trammell			
☐ 26	LaMarr Hoyt	.20	.09	.02
	Larry Parrish			
	Nolan Ryan			
☐ 27	Reggie Jackson	.20	.09	.02
	Eric Show			
	Jason Thompson			
☐ 28	Tommy John	.20	.09	.02
	Terry Kennedy			
	Eddie Murray			
	Ozzie Smith			
☐ 29	Jeff Leonard	.30	.12	.03
	Dale Murphy			
	Ken Singleton			

	Dave Winfield			
☐ 30	Craig McMurtry	.25	.10	.02
	Cal Ripken			
	Steve Rogers			
	Willie Upshaw			
☐ 31	Ben Oglivie	.20	.09	.02
	Jim Palmer			
	Darrell Porter			
☐ 32	Tony Pena	.25	.10	.02
	Fernando Valenzuela			
	Robin Yount			

1985 Topps Rub Downs

The cards in this 112 player (32 different sheets) set measure 2 3/8" by 3 5/16". The full color photo could be transferred from the rub down to another surface by rubbing a coin over the paper backing. Distributed in packages of two rub down sheets, some contained two or three player action poses, others head shots and various pieces of player equipment. Players from all teams were included in the set. Although the sheets are unnumbered, they are numbered here in alphabetical order based on each card first being placed in alphabetical order.

		MINT	VG-E	F-G
COMPLETE SET		5.00	2.35	.50
COMMON PLAYER		.15	.06	.01
☐ 1	Tony Armas	.15	.06	.01
	Harold Baines			
	Lonnie Smith			
☐ 2	Don Baylor	.15	.06	.01
	George Hendrick			
	Ron Kittle			
	Johnnie LeMaster			
☐ 3	Buddy Bell	.20	.09	.02
	Tony Gwynn			
	Lloyd Moseby			
☐ 4	Bruce Benedict	.15	.06	.01
	Atlee Hammaker			
	Frank White			
☐ 5	Mike Boddicker	.20	.09	.02
	Rod Carew			
	Carlton Fisk			
	Johnny Ray			
☐ 6	Wade Boggs	.30	.12	.03
	Rick Dempsey			
	Keith Hernandez			
☐ 7	George Brett	.25	.10	.02
	Andre Dawson			
	Paul Molitor			
	Alan Wiggins			
☐ 8	Tom Brunansky	.30	.12	.03
	Pedro Guerrero			
	Darryl Strawberry			
☐ 9	Bill Buckner	.25	.10	.02
	Tim Raines			
	Ryne Sandberg			
	Mike Schmidt			

☐ 10	Steve Carlton	.20	.09	.02
	Bob Horner			
	Dan Quisenberry			
☐ 11	Gary Carter	.20	.09	.02
	Phil Garner			
	Ron Guidry			
☐ 12	Jack Clark	.20	.09	.02
	Damaso Garcia			
	Hal McRae			
	Lance Parrish			
☐ 13	Dave Concepcion	.15	.06	.01
	Cecil Cooper			
	Fred Lynn			
	Jesse Orosco			
☐ 14	Jose Cruz	.20	.09	.02
	Jack Morris			
	Jim Rice			
	Rick Sutcliffe			
☐ 15	Alvin Davis	.15	.06	.01
	Steve Kemp			
	Greg Luzinski			
	Kent Tekulve			
☐ 16	Ron Davis	.15	.06	.01
	Kent Hrbek			
	Juan Samuel			
☐ 17	John Denny	.15	.06	.01
	Carney Lansford			
	Mario Soto			
	Lou Whitaker			
☐ 18	Leon Durham	.15	.06	.01
	Willie Hernandez			
	Steve Sax			
☐ 19	Dwight Evans	.35	.15	.03
	Julio Franco			
	Dwight Gooden			
☐ 20	George Foster	.15	.06	.01
	Gary Gaetti			
	Bobby Grich			
	Gary Redus			
☐ 21	Steve Garvey	.20	.09	.02
	Jerry Remy			
	Bill Russell			
	George Wright			
☐ 22	Kirk Gibson	.35	.15	.03
	Rich Gossage			
	Don Mattingly			
	Dave Stieb			
☐ 23	Moose Haas	.15	.06	.01
	Bruce Sutter			
	Dickie Thon			
	Andre Thornton			
☐ 24	Rickey Henderson	.40	.18	.04
	Dave Righetti			
	Pete Rose			
☐ 25	Steve Henderson	.15	.06	.01
	Bill Madlock			
	Alan Trammell			
☐ 26	LaMarr Hoyt	.20	.09	.02
	Larry Parrish			
	Nolan Ryan			
☐ 27	Reggie Jackson	.20	.09	.02
	Eric Show			
	Jason Thompson			
☐ 28	Terry Kennedy	.20	.09	.02
	Eddie Murray			
	Tom Seaver			
	Ozzie Smith			
☐ 29	Mark Langston	.15	.06	.01
	Ben Oglivie			
	Darrell Porter			
☐ 30	Jeff Leonard	.25	.10	.02
	Gary Matthews			
	Dale Murphy			
	Dave Winfield			
☐ 31	Craig McMurtry	.20	.09	.02
	Cal Ripken			
	Steve Rogers			
	Willie Upshaw			
☐ 32	Tony Pena	.25	.10	.02
	Fernando Valenzuela			
	Robin Yount			

1986 Topps Tattoos

This set of 24 different tattoo sheets was distributed one sheet (with gum) per pack as a separate issue by Topps. Each tattoo sheet measures approximately 3 7/16" by 14 1/4" whereas the individual player tattoos are 1 13/16" by 2 3/8". The wrapper advertises 18 tattoos in the pack, which includes eight small (half-size) generic action shots. The checklist below lists only the individual player tattoos; they are listed in order of appearance top to bottom on the sheet. Each tattoo sheet is numbered at the top.

	MINT	VG-E	F-G
COMPLETE SET	6.00	2.80	.60
COMMON PLAYER	.25	.10	.02
☐ 1 Sheet 1	.25	.10	.02
Dickie Thon/C.Leibrandt			
Dave Winfield/Lee Smith			
Julio Franco/K.Hernandez			
J.Perconte/Rich Gossage			
☐ 2 Sheet 2	.30	.12	.03
Dale Murphy/Brian Fisher			
Bret Saberhagen/S.Dunston			
Jesse Barfield/Moose Haas			
D.Eckersley/Mike Moore			
☐ 3 Sheet 3	.25	.10	.02
S.Carlton/Dan Quisenberry			
Bob James/Bob Brenly			
George Bell/Jose DeLeon			
Andre Thornton/Bob Horner			
☐ 4 Sheet 4	.25	.10	.02
Johnny Ray/Darrell Evans			
Mike Davis/Leon Durham			
Harold Baines/Cal Ripken			
Glenn Hubbard/Ted Simmons			
☐ 5 Sheet 5	.25	.10	.02
Jesse Orosco/Rick Dempsey			
John Candelaria/Tony Pena			
B.Jacoby/Gary Matthews			
O.Guillen/Steve Garvey			

☐ 6 Sheet 6	.35	.15	.03
Ron Kittle/Pete Rose			
Sammy Khalifa/B.Bochte			
S.McGregor/Mookie Wilson			
George Brett/Cecil Cooper			
☐ 7 Sheet 7	.30	.12	.03
Larry Sheets/John Franco			
G.Nettles/Don Mattingly			
C.Lansford/Rick Reuschel			
Don Sutton/Mike Schmidt			
☐ 8 Sheet 8	.25	.10	.02
Phil Niekro/Ryne Sandberg			
Mike Krukow/Fred Lynn			
Willie Hernandez/P.Tabler			
Ed Nunez/Cecilio Guante			
☐ 9 Sheet 9	.25	.10	.02
C.Codiroli/Glenn Wilson			
Rick Rhoden/Brett Butler			
Robin Yount/Dave Parker			
Jim Gantner/Charlie Hough			
☐ 10 Sheet 10	.30	.12	.03
Chet Lemon/Mike Smithson			
Ron Darling/Tom Seaver			
Von Hayes/Tom Browning			
B.Sutter/Alan Trammell			
☐ 11 Sheet 11	.25	.10	.02
Rick Mahler/Dave Righetti			
Jay Howell/Jose Cruz			
Jack Morris/Tony Armas			
Mike Young/Rafael Ramirez			
☐ 12 Sheet 12	.25	.10	.02
K.Moreland/Alvin Davis			
Doug DeCinces/John Tudor			
Jim Presley/Andy Hawkins			
Dennis Lamp/Mario Soto			
☐ 13 Sheet 13	.30	.12	.03
C.Hudson/Dwight Evans			
Kirby Puckett/Jody Davis			
Eddie Murray/Jose Uribe			
Ron Hassey/Hubie Brooks			
☐ 14 Sheet 14	.25	.10	.02
LaMarr Hoyt/Brian Downing			
Ron Guidry/Dan Driessen			
T.Bernazard/Garry Maddox			
Phil Bradley/Bill Buckner			
☐ 15 Sheet 15	.25	.10	.02
Tito Landrum/Hal McRae			
Joe Carter/Jeff Leonard			
Tony Fernandez/J.Samuel			
Buddy Bell/W.Randolph			
☐ 16 Sheet 16	.30	.12	.03
S.Garrelts/Dennis Boyd			
Donnie Moore/Tony Perez			
Vince Coleman/A.Griffin			
Frank White/Ozzie Smith			
☐ 17 Sheet 17	.30	.12	.03
C.Washington/Rich Gedman			
Reg.Jackson/T.Pendleton			
Mark Salas/Mike Marshall			
Kent Hrbek/Tim Raines			
☐ 18 Sheet 18	.35	.15	.03
Ron Davis/Glenn Davis			
Chris Brown/Burt Hooton			
D.Strawberry/T.Brunansky			
Tim Wallach/Frank Viola			
☐ 19 Sheet 19	.25	.10	.02
Jack Clark/Toby Harrah			
Larry Parrish/M.Scioscia			
Pete O'Brien/Bill Doran			
G.Templeton/Bill Madlock			
☐ 20 Sheet 20	.50	.20	.04
Dwight Gooden/A.Dawson			
Roger McDowell/O.McDowell			
Gary Carter/O.Hershiser			
Jim Rice/Dwayne Murphy			
☐ 21 Sheet 21	.25	.10	.02
Steve Balboni/R.Sutcliffe			
Charlie Lea/Mike Easler			
Steve Sax/Gary Ward			
L.Moseby/Willie Wilson			
☐ 22 Sheet 22	.35	.15	.03
Lance Parrish/Tom Herr			
Bryn Smith/Kirk Gibson			
Jeff Reardon/G.Thomas			
Wade Boggs/D.Concepcion			
☐ 23 Sheet 23	.25	.10	.02
Dave Stieb/Willie McGee			
Bob Grich/Paul Molitor			
Pedro Guerrero/C.Fisk			
Mike Scott/Lou Whitaker			
☐ 24 Sheet 24	.30	.12	.03
Tony Gwynn/R.Henderson			
Damaso Garcia/Nolan Ryan			

B.Blyleven/F.Valenzuela
Ben Oglivie/Phil Garner

1986 Topps Pete Rose

This set of 120 different cards is dedicated to Pete Rose; every card is a Pete Rose. The set was sold in a red and white box and distributed by Renata Galasso, Inc. The cards are standard size, 2 1/2" by 3 1/2". The checklist below gives the distinguishing features of each of the cards. Many of the backs feature a question and answer back. Since many of the pictures are very similar, the back question is frequently excerpted below. The first three cards feature traditional statistical backs and the last 30 cards (91-120) feature backs that form a puzzle, which, when completely assembled, shows in color all of Pete's Topps baseball cards up through 1985. In the set there are several cards which picture paintings of Pete by artist Ron Lewis. The cards are numbered on the back.

		MINT	VG-E	F-G
COMPLETE SET		12.00	5.50	1.20
COMMON PLAYER		.15	.06	.01
☐ 1	Statistics 60s	.15	.06	.01
	(Lewis painting)			
☐ 2	Statistics 70s	.15	.06	.01
	(crew cut photo)			
☐ 3	Statistics 80s	.15	.06	.01
☐ 4	Pete and kids with	.15	.06	.01
	Hickok Belt			
☐ 5	Pete and son	.15	.06	.01
	(hit number 3631)			
☐ 6	Pete polishing	.15	.06	.01
	old roadster			
☐ 7	Pete plays softball	.15	.06	.01
☐ 8	4000th hit as Expo	.15	.06	.01
☐ 9	Pete in Army	.15	.06	.01
☐ 10	Did Pete collect?	.15	.06	.01
	(Lewis painting)			
☐ 11	Pete's hobbies?	.15	.06	.01
☐ 12	Sibling relationships	.15	.06	.01
☐ 13	Pete's nationality	.15	.06	.01
☐ 14	Think of the Past?	.15	.06	.01
☐ 15	Being Drafted?	.15	.06	.01
☐ 16	Served in Armed Forces .	.15	.06	.01
☐ 17	Association with Dad	.15	.06	.01
☐ 18	No nickname	.15	.06	.01
☐ 19	Typical teenager?	.15	.06	.01
☐ 20	All-City Football	.15	.06	.01
	(Lewis painting)			
☐ 21	Dad's influence	.15	.06	.01
☐ 22	Pete's idol?	.15	.06	.01
☐ 23	Misses Dad	.15	.06	.01
☐ 24	Natural Ability	.15	.06	.01
☐ 25	What position?	.15	.06	.01
☐ 26	First Tryout?	.15	.06	.01
☐ 27	New Drafting System	.15	.06	.01
☐ 28	Natural Switcher	.15	.06	.01
☐ 29	Concentrating on Left	.15	.06	.01
☐ 30	Pete on phone	.15	.06	.01
	(Lewis painting)			
☐ 31	Might not make it?	.15	.06	.01

☐	32	First ML game	.15	.06	.01	☐	75	On deck before hit 4192	.15	.06	.01
☐	33	Nervous in first game	.15	.06	.01						
☐	34	Talked to old timers	.15	.06	.01	☐	76	Hit 4192 Swing	.15	.06	.01
☐	35	Enjoyed talking to the greats	.15	.06	.01	☐	77	Hit 4192 Follow thru	.15	.06	.01
						☐	78	Watching 4192	.15	.06	.01
☐	36	Favorite position	.15	.06	.01	☐	79	Keep in shape	.15	.06	.01
☐	37	Toughest position	.15	.06	.01	☐	80	Key to Hitting	.15	.06	.01
☐	38	Pete in batting cage	.15	.06	.01	☐	81	Batting Practice	.15	.06	.01
☐	39	Previous managers	.15	.06	.01	☐	82	How to Pitch to Pete	.15	.06	.01
☐	40	Big adjustment (Lewis painting)	.15	.06	.01	☐	83	Hugs Pete Jr.	.15	.06	.01
						☐	84	Knockdown pitches	.15	.06	.01
☐	41	30 Triples in 1961	.15	.06	.01	☐	85	Spitball	.15	.06	.01
☐	42	Winter ball	.15	.06	.01	☐	86	Illegal pitches	.15	.06	.01
☐	43	Rookie of the Year	.15	.06	.01	☐	87	Babe Ruth	.15	.06	.01
☐	44	Kennedy assasination	.15	.06	.01	☐	88	Talking to Reagan	.15	.06	.01
☐	45	Run to first on walks	.15	.06	.01	☐	89	Compared to Cobb	.15	.06	.01
☐	46	Showboating?	.15	.06	.01	☐	90	Goals Left?	.15	.06	.01
☐	47	Remembered for what?	.15	.06	.01	☐	91	Standing in dugout	.15	.06	.01
☐	48	Charlie Hustle	.15	.06	.01	☐	92	Expo batting left	.15	.06	.01
☐	49	Play with enthusiasm	.15	.06	.01	☐	93	Red batting left	.15	.06	.01
☐	50	Lose enthusiasm?	.15	.06	.01	☐	94	Red looking right	.15	.06	.01
☐	51	Enjoy traveling?	.15	.06	.01	☐	95	Phillies with fence	.15	.06	.01
☐	52	America	.15	.06	.01	☐	96	Pete's goatee	.15	.06	.01
☐	53	Favorite food	.15	.06	.01	☐	97	Reds smiling left	.15	.06	.01
☐	54	Goal setting?	.15	.06	.01	☐	98	Reds batting right	.15	.06	.01
☐	55	Guess hitter?	.15	.06	.01	☐	99	Pete as a boy	.15	.06	.01
☐	56	Pete and Tyler with horse	.15	.06	.01	☐	100	Reds holding bat	.15	.06	.01
						☐	101	Reds batting left (Lewis painting)	.15	.06	.01
☐	57	Artificial turf	.15	.06	.01						
☐	58	Day or Night?	.15	.06	.01	☐	102	Reds swinging left	.15	.06	.01
☐	59	Broken Concentration?	.15	.06	.01	☐	103	Phillies pensive	.15	.06	.01
☐	60	Favorite park (Lewis painting)	.15	.06	.01	☐	104	Reds first base	.15	.06	.01
						☐	105	Reds smiling 60s	.15	.06	.01
☐	61	Consecutive games	.15	.06	.01	☐	106	Collision at home	.15	.06	.01
☐	62	Toughest pitchers	.15	.06	.01	☐	107	Reds looking straight	.15	.06	.01
☐	63	Bear down	.15	.06	.01	☐	108	Reds batting left (looking serious)	.15	.06	.01
☐	64	Head first slide	.15	.06	.01						
☐	65	Sliding advice	.15	.06	.01	☐	109	Head First Slide	.15	.06	.01
☐	66	Proudest record	.15	.06	.01	☐	110	Swing follow through	.15	.06	.01
☐	67	Wanted to be Manager?	.15	.06	.01	☐	111	Pre-game warm up	.15	.06	.01
☐	68	Fosse collision	.15	.06	.01	☐	112	Reds batting left 80s	.15	.06	.01
☐	69	Pete got hurt in Fosse collision	.15	.06	.01	☐	113	Diving for pop up	.15	.06	.01
						☐	114	Expo at locker	.15	.06	.01
☐	70	Harrelson fight (Lewis painting)	.15	.06	.01	☐	115	Pete with son	.15	.06	.01
						☐	116	Collision at plate	.15	.06	.01
☐	71	Transition to outfield	.15	.06	.01	☐	117	In batting cage	.15	.06	.01
☐	72	Asked to outfield	.15	.06	.01	☐	118	Reds batting left 70s	.15	.06	.01
☐	73	World Champs	.15	.06	.01	☐	119	On one knee	.15	.06	.01
☐	74	Lineup card	.15	.06	.01	☐	120	Scoreboard	.15	.06	.01

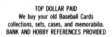

The Encyclopedia of Baseball Cards

The Old Judge

AUTHOR

Lew Lipset

P.O. BOX 137
CENTEREACH, N.Y. 11720
(516) 961-3286

Hours M-F 10-7 Sat 10-6
Sunday 12-6

J.J.'s Budget Baseball Cards
Bought, Sold and Appraised

20249 Saticoy
Canoga Pk, CA 91306
(Just West of Winnetka Near Batting Cage)

Tel. (818) 709-1003
JOEL HELLMANN

MIDWEST SPORTCARDS
Baseball Cards and Supplies

Box 109
Webberville, Mich. 48892
(517) 521-3854

Rosie Jones

P.O. Box 544
Cherry Hill, New Jersey 08003

609/428-6744

John E. Spalding
Advanced Collector
5551 Fern Drive
San Jose, CA 95124
(408) 264-5530

Jim Bordonaro
Salada Coins
Buy-Sell-Trade
7515 Colonial
Niagara Falls, NY 14304

Steve Leone
Dixie Lids
Sports and Non-Sports
Buy-Sell-Trade
94 Pond Street
Salem, NH 03079
(603) 898-4900

TOM REID's Baseball Store
526 Franklin Ave., Nutley, N.J. 07110

WE BUY AND SELL OLD
BASEBALL and FOOTBALL CARDS
PROGRAMS • YEARBOOKS
BASEBALL ADVERTISING ITEMS
BOXING ITEMS, ETC.

STORE HOURS:
Monday and Friday nights 6 to 8:30 P.M.
Saturdays - call for hours

Telephone: 201 - 748-4299

244

$2.50

July 1986

Volume 3, Number 6 - Issue #19

MICKEY MANTLE
NEW YORK YANKEES   OUTFIELD

Curren
Price Guid

Who's
& Who's

Subscribe Now.

$2.50

BECKETT
BASEBALL CARD
MONTHLY

September 1986

Volume 3, Number 8 - Issue #21

PETE ROSE

Current
Price Guide

Who's Hot
& Who's Not